Alan Rogers

Britain
& Ireland

Quality camping & caravanning parks

INSPECTED
CAMPSITES
& SELECTED

Compiled by: Alan Rogers Guides Ltd

Designed by: Paul Effenberg, Vine Design Ltd

Maps created by Customised Mapping (01769 540044)
contain background data provided by GisDATA Ltd
Maps are © Alan Rogers Guides and GisDATA Ltd 2007

© Alan Rogers Guides Ltd 2007

Published by: Alan Rogers Guides Ltd,
Spelmonden Old Oast, Goudhurst, Kent TN17 1HE
www.alanrogers.com Tel: 01580 214000

British Library Cataloguing-in-Publication Data:
A catalogue record for this book is available from the
British Library.

ISBN-13 978-0-9550486-9-2

Printed in Great Britain by J H Haynes & Co Ltd

Contents

the Alan Rogers
approach

Alan Rogers

Last year we celebrated the publication of the fortieth editions of the Alan Rogers Guides. Since Alan Rogers published the first campsite guide that bore his name, the range has expanded to six titles covering 27 countries. What's more, Alan Rogers Guides are now firmly established in the Netherlands too: all six titles are also published in Dutch and stocked by well over 90% of all Dutch bookshops.

There are over 5,000 camping and caravanning parks in Britain and Ireland of varying quality: this guide contains impartially written reports on over 550, including some of the very finest, each being individually inspected and selected. All the usual maps and indexes are also included, designed to help you find the choice of park that's right for you. We hope you enjoy some happy and safe travels – and some pleasurable 'armchair touring' in the meantime!

A question of quality

The criteria we use when inspecting and selecting parks are numerous, but the most important by far is the question of good quality. People want different things from their choice of campsite so we try to include a range of campsite 'styles' to cater for a wide variety of preferences: from those seeking a small peaceful campsite in the heart of the countryside, to visitors looking for an 'all singing, all dancing' park in a popular seaside resort. Those with more specific interests, such as sporting facilities, cultural events or historical attractions, are also catered for.

The size of the park, whether it's part of a chain or privately owned, makes no difference in terms of it being required to meet our exacting standards in respect of its quality and it being 'fit for purpose'. In other words, irrespective of the size of the park, or the number of facilities it offers, we consider and evaluate the welcome, the pitches, the sanitary facilities, the cleanliness, the general maintenance and even the location.

" ...the campsites included in this book have been chosen entirely on merit, and no payment of any sort is made by them for their inclusion."

Alan Rogers, 1968

INSPECTED & SELECTED SINCE 1968

Expert opinions

We rely on our dedicated team of Site Assessors, all of whom are experienced campers, caravanners or motorcaravanners, to visit and recommend parks. Each year they travel some 100,000 miles around Europe inspecting new campsites for the guide and re-inspecting the existing ones. Our thanks are due to them for their enthusiastic efforts, their diligence and integrity.

We also appreciate the feedback we receive from many of our readers and we always make a point of following up complaints, suggestions or recommendations for possible new parks. Of course we get a few grumbles too – but it really is a few, and those we do receive usually relate to overcrowding or to poor maintenance during the peak school holiday period. Please bear in mind that, although we are interested to hear about any complaints, we have no contractual relationship with the campsites featured in our guides and are therefore not in a position to intervene in any dispute between a reader and a campsite.

HIGHLY RESPECTED BY SITE OWNERS AND READERS ALIKE, THERE IS NO BETTER GUIDE WHEN IT COMES TO FORMING AN INDEPENDENT VIEW OF A CAMPSITE'S QUALITY. WHEN YOU NEED TO BE CONFIDENT IN YOUR CHOICE OF CAMPSITE, YOU NEED THE ALAN ROGERS GUIDE.

- ☑ Parks only included on merit
- ☑ Parks cannot pay to be included
- ☑ Independently inspected, rigorously assessed
- ☑ Impartial reviews
- ☑ Over 40 years of expertise

Independent and honest

Whilst the content and scope of the Alan Rogers guides have expanded considerably since the early editions, our selection of campsites still employs exactly the same philosophy and criteria as defined by Alan Rogers in 1968.

'telling it how it is'

Firstly, and most importantly, our selection is based entirely on our own rigorous and independent inspection and selection process. Campsites cannot buy their way into our guides – indeed the extensive Report which is written by us, not by the site owner, is provided free of charge so we are free to say what we think and to provide an honest, 'warts and all' description. This is written in plain English and without the use of confusing icons or symbols.

Written in plain English, our guides are exceptionally easy to use, although a few words of explanation regarding the layout and content may be helpful. For England we have used official tourist board regions and the counties within them. For Wales, Scotland and Ireland (north and south) we use the counties.

The Reports – *Example of an entry*

Site Number **Park name**
Postal Address (including county)
Telephone number. Email address

A description of the park in which we try to give an idea of its general features – its size, its situation, its strengths and its weaknesses. This section should provide a picture of the park itself with reference to the facilities that are provided and if they impact on its appearance or character. We include details on pitch numbers, electricity (with amperage), hardstandings etc. in this section as pitch design, planning and terracing affects the park's overall appearance. Similarly we include reference to pitches used for caravan holiday homes, chalets, and the like. Importantly at the end of this column we indicate if there are any restrictions, e.g. no tents, no children, naturist sites.

Facilities

Lists more specific information on the park's facilities and amenities and, where available, the dates when these facilities are open (if not for the whole season). Off site: here we give distances to various local amenities, for example, local shops, the nearest beach, plus our featured activities (bicycle hire, fishing, horse riding, boat launching). Where we have space we list suggestions for activities and local tourist attractions.

Open: Park opening dates.

Directions

Separated from the main text in order that they may be read and assimilated more easily by a navigator en-route. Bear in mind that road improvement schemes can result in road numbers being altered.

O.S.GR: Ordnance Survey grid references are included for those using OS maps.

GPS: references are provided as we obtain them for satellite navigation systems (in degrees and minutes).

Charges 2008

Indexes

Our three indexes allow you to find parks by their number and name, by region and park name, or by the town or village where the park is situated. See also the handy Quick Reference sections at the back.

Campsite Maps

The maps at the back relate to the geographical areas and will help you identify the approximate position of each campsite. The colour of the campsite name indicates whether it is open all year or not. You will certainly need more detailed maps, for example the Ordnance Survey road atlas.

Facilities

Toilet blocks

We assume that toilet blocks will be equipped with WCs, washbasins with hot and cold water and hot showers with dividers or curtains, and will have all necessary shelves, hooks, plugs and mirrors. We also assume that there will be an identified chemical toilet disposal point, and that the campsite will provide water and waste water drainage points and bin areas. If not the case, we comment. We do mention certain features that some readers find important: washbasins in cubicles, facilities for babies, facilities for those with disabilities and motorcaravan service points. Readers with disabilities are advised to contact the site of their choice to ensure that facilities are appropriate to their needs.

Shop

Basic or fully supplied, and opening dates.

Bars, restaurants, takeaway facilities and entertainment

We try hard to supply opening and closing dates (if other than the campsite opening dates) and to identify if there are discos or other entertainment.

Children's play areas

Fenced and with safety surface (e.g. sand, bark or pea-gravel).

Swimming pools

If particularly special, we cover in detail in our main campsite description but reference is always included under our Facilities listings. Opening dates, charges and levels of supervision are provided where we have been notified.

Leisure facilities

For example, playing fields, bicycle hire, organised activities and entertainment.

Dogs

If dogs are not accepted or restrictions apply, we state it here. Check the quick reference list at the back of the guide.

Off site

This briefly covers leisure facilities, tourist attractions, restaurants etc. nearby.

Charges

These are the latest provided to us by the parks. In those few cases where 2007 or 2008 prices are not given, we try to give a general guide.

Opening dates

These are advised to us during the early autumn of the previous year – parks can, and sometimes do, alter these dates before the start of the following season, often for good reasons. If you intend to visit shortly after a published opening date, or shortly before the closing date, it is wise to check that it will actually be open at the time required. Similarly some parks operate a restricted service during the low season, only opening some of their facilities (e.g. swimming pools) during the main season; where we know about this, and have the relevant dates, we indicate it – again if you are at all doubtful it is wise to check.

Special Pitches

We note an ever increasing number of 'special' pitches under a variety of fancy names (for example, Executive, Panorama, Super). These provide a range of extra facilities such as waste water disposal, TV and phone connections, hardstanding, patios, etc. and they are often booked up well in advance. Readers interested in such pitches should contact the park concerned to check exactly what is provided. People with disabilities are also advised to telephone before turning up to ensure that facilities are appropriate to their particular needs.

The Alan Rogers Guides have long been an authoritative voice when it comes to an independent assessment of a campsite's quality.

But now is the chance to hear your **voice** - your **opinions**, your **assessments**, your **tips**.....

Visit
www.mycamping.info

and be part of it.

WHETHER YOU'RE AN 'OLD HAND' IN TERMS OF CAMPING AND CARAVANNING OR ARE CONTEMPLATING YOUR FIRST TRIP, A REGULAR READER OF OUR GUIDES OR A NEW 'CONVERT', WE WISH YOU WELL IN YOUR TRAVELS AND HOPE WE HAVE BEEN ABLE TO HELP IN SOME WAY.

WE ARE, OF COURSE, ALSO OUT AND ABOUT OURSELVES, VISITING SITES, TALKING TO OWNERS AND READERS, AND GENERALLY CHECKING ON STANDARDS AND NEW DEVELOPMENTS.

We wish all our readers thoroughly enjoyable Camping and Caravanning in 2008 – favoured by good weather of course!

THE ALAN ROGERS TEAM

have you visited

www.alanrogers.com

yet?

INSPECTED CAMPSITES & SELECTED

Alan Rogers

Our website has fast become the first-stop for countless caravanners, motorhome owners and campers all wanting reliable, impartial and detailed information for their next trip.

It features a fully searchable database of the best campsites in the UK & Ireland, and the rest of Europe: over 2,000 campsites in 26 countries.

Regions

SCOTLAND

Northumbria

NORTHERN IRELAND

Cumbria

Yorkshire

North West England

Heart of England

REPUBLIC OF IRELAND

WALES

East of England

Southern England

London

South East England

South West England

Channel Islands

the Alan Rogers
awards

In 2004 we introduced the first ever Alan Rogers Campsite Awards.

Before making our awards, we carefully consider more than 2000 campsites featured in our guides, taking into account comments from our site assessors, our head office team and, of course, our readers.

Our award winners come from the four corners of Europe, from southern Portugal to the Czech Republic, and this year we are making awards to campsites in 14 different countries.

Needless to say, it's an extremely difficult task to choose our eventual winners, but we believe that we have identified a number of campsites with truly outstanding characteristics.

In each case, we have selected an outright winner, along with two highly commended runners-up.

Listed below are full details of each of our award categories and our winners for 2007.

Alan Rogers Progress Award 2007

This award reflects the hard work and commitment undertaken by particular site owners to improve and upgrade their site.

WINNER

AU0060 Natterersee, Austria

RUNNERS-UP

BE0712   Ile de Faigneul, Belgium

DE3672   Elbsee, Germany

Alan Rogers Welcome Award 2007

This award takes account of sites offering a particularly friendly welcome and maintaining a friendly ambience throughout reader's holidays.

WINNER

FR24090 Soleil Plage, France

RUNNERS-UP

IR9610   Mannix Point, Ireland

UK4640   Goosewood, England

Alan Rogers Active Holiday Award 2007

This award reflects sites in outstanding locations which are ideally suited for active holidays, notably walking or cycling, but which could extend to include such activities as winter sports or water sports

WINNER

DK2170 Klim Strand, Denmark

RUNNERS-UP

FR09060 Pre Lombard, France

DE3450   Munstertal, Germany

Alan Rogers Motorhome Award 2007

Motorhome sales are increasing and this award acknowledges sites which, in our opinion, have made outstanding efforts to welcome motorhome clients.

WINNER

PO8210 Campismo Albufeira, Portugal

RUNNERS-UP

IR9650   Woodlands Park, Ireland

FR29180 Les Embruns, France

Alan Rogers 4 Seasons Award 2007

This award is made to outstanding sites with extended opening dates and which welcome clients to a uniformly high standard throughout the year.

WINNER

CH9575	Eienwaldi, Switzerland

RUNNERS-UP

AU0440	Schluga, Austria
IT6814	Flaminio, Italy

Alan Rogers Seaside Award 2007

This award is made for sites which we feel are outstandingly suitable for a really excellent seaside holiday.

WINNER

ES8030	Nautic Almata, Spain

RUNNERS-UP

FR85210	Les Ecureuils, France
IT6036	Ca Pasquali, Italy

Alan Rogers Country Award 2007

This award contrasts with our former award and acknowledges sites which are attractively located in delightful, rural locations.

WINNER

UK1020	Oakdown, England

RUNNERS-UP

CZ4896	Camping Country, Czech Republic
NL5980	De Roos, Netherlands

Alan Rogers Rented Accommodation Award 2007

Given the increasing importance of rented accommodation on many campsites, we feel that it is important to acknowledge sites which have made a particular effort in creating a high quality 'rented accommodation' park.

WINNER

ES8480	Sanguli, Spain

RUNNERS-UP

NL5575	Scheldeoord, Netherlands
CR6736	Valdaliso, Croatia

Alan Rogers Unique Site Award 2007

This award acknowledges sites with unique, outstanding features – something which simply cannot be found elsewhere and which is an important attraction of the site.

WINNER

FR78040	Huttopia Rambouillet, France

RUNNERS-UP

FR80070	Ferme des Aulnes, France
UK1590	Exe Valley, England

Alan Rogers Family Site Award 2007

Many sites claim to be child friendly but this award acknowledges the sites we feel to be the very best in this respect.

WINNER

NL5985	Beerze Bulten, Netherlands

RUNNERS-UP

UK0170	Trevella, England
ES8540	Torre del Sol, Spain
IT6014	Villaggio Turistico Internazionale, Italy

Alan Rogers Readers' Award 2007

In 2005 we introduced a new award, which we believe to be the most important, our Readers' Award. We simply invited our readers (by means of an on-line poll at www.alanrogers.com) to nominate the site they enjoyed most. The outright winner for 2007 is:

WINNER

ES8530	Playa Montroig Resort, Spain

Alan Rogers Special Award 2007

A special award is made to acknowledge sites which we feel have overcome a very significant setback, and have, not only returned to their former condition, but has added extra amenities and can therefore be fairly considered to be even better than before. In 2007 we acknowledged two campsites, which have undergone major problems and have made highly impressive recoveries.

CH9510	Aareg, Switzerland
IT6845	San Nicola, Italy

NEW

Whether you have a caravan, a motorhome or a tent, the UnityPlus Card is for you. It's not a club but it offers great benefits and it's free! Quite simply, it offers unique discounts for campers and caravanners on a range of products including cheap ferry deals, discounted holidays, camping accessories, specialist insurance and more.

Full details at www.**unity-plus**.com

Request your UnityPlus Card today!

The West Country is a diverse region of beautiful sandy beaches, steep craggy cliffs, desolate moors and rolling green hills. Home of clotted cream teas, it also boasts a range of historical and modern attractions, including the celebrated Eden Project.

THE SOUTH WEST COMPRISES: CORNWALL, DEVON, SOMERSET, BATH, BRISTOL, SOUTH GLOUCESTERSHIRE, WILTSHIRE AND WEST DORSET.

With its dramatic cliffs, pounded by the Atlantic ocean, and beautiful coastline boasting warm waters, soft sandy beaches and small seaside towns, Cornwall is one of England's most popular holiday destinations. The coast is also a surfers' paradise, while inland the wild and rugged Bodmin Moors dominate the landscape. In Devon, the Dartmoor National Park has sweeping moorland and granite tors where wild ponies roam freely. Much of the countryside is gentle rolling green fields, dotted with pretty thatched cottages. The coastline around Torbay is known as the English Riviera which, due to its temperate climate, allows palm trees to grow. Stretching across East Devon and West Dorset is the fossil-ridden Jurassic Coast, a World Heritage Site. West Dorset is also home to Lyme Regis and Weymouth, which comes alive in summer when regular entertainment, including a carnival and fireworks, is held along the seafront. Famous for its cider and cheese, Somerset is good walking country, with the Exmoor National Park, which also straddles Devon. Wiltshire's natural attractions include the Marlborough Downs, Savernake Forest and the River Avon. It also boasts one of the most famous prehistoric sites in the world, the ancient stone circles of Stonehenge.

Places of interest

Bath: World Heritage Site full of Roman and Georgian architecture, elegant streets such as the Circle and Royal Crescent, Roman baths.

Bristol: steeped in maritime history with the world's first great Ocean Liner; Brunel's Clifton Suspension bridge; range of museums and art galleries.

Cornwall: seaside town of St Ives; Land's End; Eden Project; Penzance and St Michael's Mount.

Devon: popular seaside resorts of Torquay, Paignton and Brixham; cities of Exeter and Plymouth.

Somerset: Weston-Super-Mare; Wells Cathedral; Cheddar Gorge and Wookey Hole caves.

West Dorset: Dorchester, home of Thomas Hardy; Isle of Portland; Abbotsbury village, with swannery.

Wiltshire: Salisbury; Glastonbury; Longleat manor house and safari park.

Did you know?

Chesil Beach is an 18 mile stretch of fortress-like walls of pebbles, formed 12,000 years ago.

There are numerous white horses carved into the landscape across the South West.

The Jurassic Coast is a Natural World Heritage Site stretching for 95 miles.

The Black Death entered England through the port in Weymouth in 1348.

Britain's oldest complete skeleton, Cheddar Man, was buried in Gough's Cave 9,000 years ago.

At 404 feet Salisbury Cathedral has the tallest medieval spire in the world.

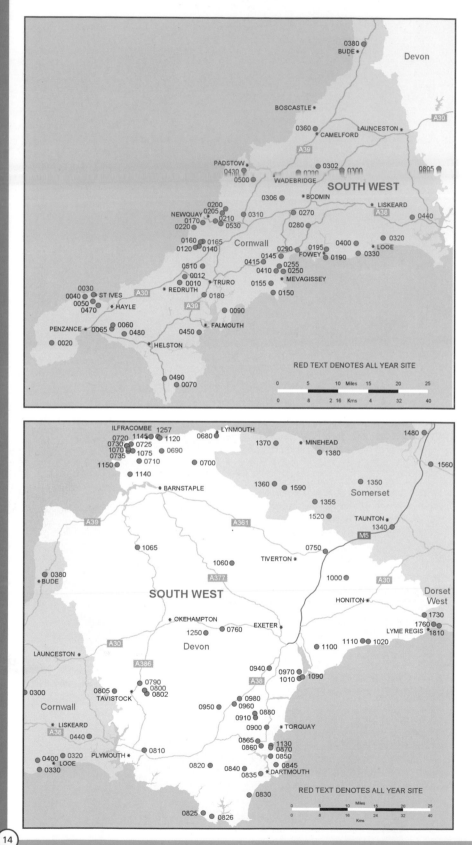

Map 1 (Cornwall)

Devon
0380 BUDE *
BOSCASTLE *
0360 CAMELFORD *
LAUNCESTON *
A30
A39
0302 0300 0805
PADSTOW *
0430 0500
WADEBRIDGE
SOUTH WEST
0306 * BODMIN
* LISKEARD
A38 0440
0200 0270
NEWQUAY 0205 0310
0170 0210 0280
0220 0530
0160 0165 0320
0120 0140 Cornwall 0400 * LOOE
0510 0290 0195 0330
0012 0145 FOWEY 0190
0010 * 0415 0255
0030 REDRUTH 0410 0250
0040 ST IVES A30 0155 * MEVAGISSEY
0050 0180
0470 HAYLE * 0150
0060 A39
PENZANCE * 0065 0090
0020 0480 0450 * FALMOUTH
HELSTON *
0490
0070

RED TEXT DENOTES ALL YEAR SITE

0 5 10 Miles 15 20 25
0 8 2 16 Kms 4 32 40

Map 2 (Devon/Somerset)

ILFRACOMBE 1257 LYNMOUTH
0720 1145 1120 0680 1480
0730 0725 1370 * MINEHEAD 1560
1070 1075 0690 1380
0735 0710 1350
1150 0700 Somerset
1140 1360 1590
* BARNSTAPLE 1355
1520 TAUNTON *
A39 A361 1340
M5
1065
1060 0750 A30
TIVERTON *
A377 1000 HONITON *
Dorset
West
SOUTH WEST 1730
OKEHAMPTON * 1760
1250 0760 EXETER * LYME REGIS 1810
A30 Devon 1110 1020
LAUNCESTON * A386 1100
0300 0790 0940 0970
Cornwall 0805 0800 1010 1090
0802 TAVISTOCK *
* LISKEARD 0950 0980
A38 0440 0960
0400 0320 0910 0880
0330 LOOE * 0900
PLYMOUTH * 0810 * TORQUAY
0865 1130
0860 0870
0820 0840 0850
0835 0845
DARTMOUTH *
0830
0825 0826

RED TEXT DENOTES ALL YEAR SITE

0 5 10 Miles 15 20 25
0 8 16 Kms 24 32 40

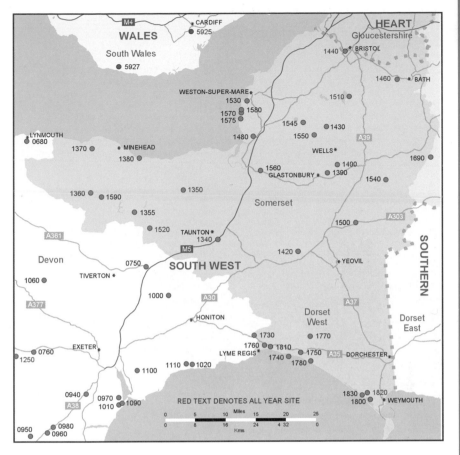

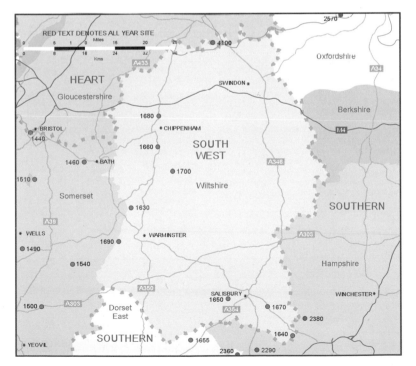

UK0010 Chacewater Park

Cox Hill, Chacewater, Truro TR4 8LY (Cornwall)
Tel: **01209 820762**. Email: **enquiries@chacewaterpark.co.uk**

For those who want to be away from the hectic coastal resorts and to take advantage of the peace and quiet of an 'adults only' park, this will be an excellent value-for-money choice. Chacewater has a pleasant rural situation and the site is run with care and attention by Richard Peterken and his daughters Debbie and Mandy. It provides 100 level touring pitches, all with electricity (10A) and 80 with hardstanding, in two large field areas (slight slope) edged with trees or in small bays formed by hedges. There are 29 serviced pitches (electricity, water, and drainage connections) and an area for dog owners. The modern reception is not at the entrance but through the park to one side in a pleasant courtyard area. Truro is only 5 miles and there is a good choice of beaches north or south within 5-10 miles.

Facilities

The main toilet block provides well equipped showers and two en-suite units, along with dishwashing sinks under cover and a laundry room. Second fully equipped block near reception providing roomy showers open direct to outside. Gas supplies. Icepack service. Library in reception. Only adults are accepted (over 30 yrs). One dog (certain breeds) only by arrangement. Off site: Golf, riding and bicycle hire, all within 3 miles. Cornish tramways/railway coast to coast trail to walk or cycle nearby.

Open: 1 May - 30 September.

Directions

From the A30 approx. 28 miles west of Bodmin take A3047 signed Scorrier and continue under bridge to roundabout and take left towards St Day. Continue for 500 yards turning right at the crossroads onto the B3298 signed St Day and continue for 1 mile. Turn left at the crossroads and continue for 3/4 of a mile, then turn left at the crossroad with blue camping sign (by Truro Tractors). Chacewater Park is the next right. O.S.GR: SW742439.

Charges 2007

Per unit incl. 2 adults	£ 12.00 - £ 15.00
dog (one only)	£ 1.00

Weekly rates for pre-booked pitches. Discounts for senior citizens. Weekly rates for pre-booked pitches.

UK0020 Cardinney Camping Park

Crows-an-Wra, St Buryan, Penzance TR19 6HX (Cornwall)
Tel: **01736 810880**. Email: **cardinney@btinternet.com**

A friendly Geordie welcome awaits from the owner, Kevin Lindley, when you visit Cardinney, which is perfectly situated for visiting the famous Lands End beauty spots and tourist attractions and also within easy driving distance of small Cornish beaches and coves. The level field is divided into three camping areas by Cornish stone walls and flowering shrubs, allowing for 105 individual, marked, level pitches, 70 with 10A electricity and some with hardstanding. The combined café and bar with an attractive outdoor terrace acts as reception and a social point providing breakfasts, takeaway food at most times and good cheer in the evenings. Somewhat behind the site a National Trust viewpoint gives panoramic views to the Isles of Scilly, Cape Cornwall and the Lizard point and the ancient Iron Age settlement of Carn Euny is 20 minutes walk.

Facilities

Fully equipped toilet block originally built over 30 years ago but adapted over the years. It includes a deep sink for babies and laundry facilities. Bar and café with TV. Games room with pool table. At times care and maintenance can be a little haphazard. Off site: Coastal, cliff top walks, surfing beaches and Minnack Open Air Theatre nearby. Fishing 3 miles, bicycle hire 5 miles, riding 4 miles.

Open: 1 February - 30 November.

Directions

Park is signed before Crows-an-Wra on the main Penzance - Lands End A30 road, 5 miles west of Penzance. O.S.GR: SW426285.

Charges 2007

Per unit incl. 2 persons	£ 8.00 - £ 11.50
incl. electricity	£ 10.50 - £ 14.50
extra person	£ 3.50
child (2-5 yrs)	£ 2.00

Less for stays over 2 weeks.

UK0012 Killiwerris Camping & Caravan Park

Penstraze, Chacewater, Truro TR4 8PF (Cornwall)

Tel: **01872 561356**. Email: **info@killiwerris.co.uk**

Tucked down a Cornish lane, Killiwerris is a rare find. It has been developed from a large garden and the field surrounding the house into a small and delightful touring park which provides 20 good-sized pitches for caravans and motorcaravans. Of these, 17 are semi-separated either by low fencing or hedging, 15 with hardstanding in the front field with flowering shrubs sheltered by Monteray pines and other indigenous trees. The birds love it, as do adult humans – the park is 'adult only' so it is very peaceful. Three further pitches are found in the back field. Electricity (10/16A) is available for all the pitches with water points between two. The park is now owned by the Ashurst family and being centrally situated five miles from the city of Truro and four from the coastal village of St Agnes, this is an ideal base to explore the Cornish countryside.

Facilities

A small heated toilet block provides for all needs with one shower each for men and women and ladies having one toilet/washbasin cubicle. Grab rails for disabled visitors. Dishwashing sink under cover and separate laundry room. Recycling bins. Off site: Bus stop 8 minutes level walk. Chacewater village (shop, pub, etc.) 1 mile. Beach 4.5 miles. Fishing 2 miles. Golf 2 miles. Riding 1.5 miles. Bicycle hire 2-3 miles

Open: Easter - end October.

Directions

Using the A30 in the direction of Penzance, exit at Chiverton Cross roundabout (this is large roundabout 28 miles west of Bodmin signed for Truro and St Agnes). Take third exit for Blackwater and in 500 yards turn left into Kea Down Road. park is 1 mile on right. O.S.GR: SW753455. GPS: N50:15.930 W05:09.300

Charges 2007

Per unit incl. 2 persons, electricity and awning	£ 12.00 - £ 14.50
extra person	£ 3.50
dog (max. 2)	£ 0.50
No credit cards.	

UK0030 Ayr Holiday Park

Higher Ayr, St Ives TR26 1EJ (Cornwall)

Tel: **01736 795855**. Email: **recept@ayrholidaypark.co.uk**

Ayr Holiday Park has an unparalleled position overlooking St Ives Bay and Porthmeor beach and is a popular well cared for site. On first arrival it may seem to be all caravan holiday homes, but behind them is a series of naturally sloping fields with marvellous views providing a total of 90 pitches, of which 40 are for touring caravans and motorcaravans. These pitches are on grass, all with 16A electricity and several fully serviced. An extra field for tents is open in July and August. A 'state of the art' toilet block provides excellent facilities in a colourful and modern design. St Ives centre with restaurants, bars and supermarkets is within easy walking distance, as is the new Tate Gallery. There is direct access to the coastal footpath.

Facilities

The excellent toilet block includes two family shower rooms and facilities for baby changing and disabled people. Wetsuit showers. Fully equipped laundry room. Motorcaravan point. Games room with pool table and TV, hot drinks and snack machines. Adventure play area and football field. Contact park if you wish to take a dog. Off site: Spa shop nearby. Tate Gallery and beaches within walking distance. Leisure centre with indoor pool nearby. Golf 1 mile. Riding 2 miles. Sea and coarse fishing 2-3 miles.

Open: All year.

Directions

Three hundred yards after leaving the A30 turn left at mini-roundabout following signs for St Ives for heavy vehicles and day visitors (not town centre direction). After approx. 2 miles this joins the B3311 and then the B3306 about 1 mile from St Ives (an octagonal building on your left). Still heading for St Ives turn left at a mini-roundabout following camping signs through residential areas. Park entrance is 600 yds at Ayr Terrace. O.S.GR: SW515388.

Charges 2007

Per person	£ 3.25 - £ 5.25
child (5-16 yrs)	£ 1.50 - £ 2.50
pitch	£ 5.50 - £ 16.00
with services, plus	£ 3.50

UK0040 Trevalgan Touring Park

Trevalgan Touring Park, St Ives TR26 3BJ (Cornwall)

Tel: **01736** 792048. Email: recept@trevalgantouringpark.co.uk

Trevalgan is owned by the same family that owns Ayr Holiday Park. It is a quiet, traditional style of park, located on the cliffs 1.5 miles west of bustling St Ives. It is a truly rural location where you can enjoy spectacular views and an abundance of flora and fauna. There are 120 clearly marked pitches (88 with 16A electricity and some with water as well) in two level fields edged by Cornish stone walls – it could be a little exposed on a windy day. The park is very popular with walkers with direct access to the coastal path. A member of the Countryside Discovery group.

Facilities

A fully equipped toilet block includes a baby room and facilities for disabled visitors. Motorcaravan service point. Campers' kitchen. Small shop (in reception). Mobile shop calls daily. Gas supplies. Games field, adventure play area and crazy golf. Giant draughts and chess. Purpose built games room with TV and coffee machine. Off site: Fishing 3 miles, bicycle hire 8 miles, riding and golf within 2 miles. Regular bus service to St Ives and back June - mid September. As well as the coastal path, a path leads to St Ives across the fields (30-40 minutes).

Open: 1 May - 30 September.

Directions

Approach site down a narrow Cornish lane from the B3306 St Ives - Lands End road, following sign. O.S.GR: SW490400.

Charges 2007

Per person	£ 3.25 - £ 4.25
child (5-16 yrs)	£ 1.50 - £ 2.25
pitch	£ 5.00 - £ 10.50
incl. electricity (16A)	£ 8.50 - £ 13.75
dog	£ 1.75

RAC AA

For a more rural experience

'A touring park just 2 miles from St.Ives town centre. Beautiful scenery, new facilities, serviced pitches, summer bus service to town. Ideal for families, walkers, cyclists - explore St.Ives and West Cornwall.'

www.trevalgantouringpark.co.uk   Telephone: 01736 796433

UK0050 Polmanter Tourist Park

Halsetown, St Ives TR26 3LX (Cornwall)

Tel: **01736** 795640. Email: reception@polmanter.com

A popular and attractively developed park, Polmanter is located high up at the back of St Ives, with wonderful sea and country views. The Osborne family have worked hard to develop Polmanter as a complete family base. Converted farm buildings provide a cosy bar lounge with conservatory overlooking the heated swimming pool. The 250 touring pitches (no caravan holiday homes) are well spaced in several fields divided by established, shrubs and hedges giving large, level, individual pitches with connecting tarmac roads. There are 87 serviced pitches with electricity, water, waste water and TV point, 10 with hardstanding. The remaining pitches all have 16A electricity. It is a busy park with a happy atmosphere within 1.5 miles of St Ives. A footpath leads from the park (20 minutes downhill) or there is a bus service from the park in high season (hourly, 10.00 - midnight). A member of the Best of British group.

Facilities

Three fully equipped toilet blocks can be heated and include en-suite family rooms, facilities for disabled visitors and a baby room beside the fully equipped laundry. Motorcaravan service point. Well stocked shop. Bar with food and family area (Whitsun - mid Sept). Takeaway. Heated swimming pool (Whitsun - mid Sept). Some entertainment (peak season). Tennis courts. Putting. Play area. Sports field. Games room with two pool tables, table tennis and games machines. Off site: Golf 1 mile. Fishing, riding, bicycle hire and boat launching facilities within 2 miles. New indoor pool and leisure centre at St Ives. Note: dogs are banned from the St Ives beaches in high season.

Open: Easter - 31 October (full facilities to 10 Sept).

Directions

Take A3074 to St Ives from the A30 and then first left at a mini-roundabout taking 'Holiday Route' (B3311) to St Ives (Halsetown). At T-junction turn right for Halsetown, right again at the Halsetown Inn then first left. O.S.GR: SW509392. GPS: N50:11.771 W05:29.461

Charges 2007

Per unit incl. 2 persons and awning	£ 11.00 - £ 21.00
incl. mains services	£ 14.00 - £ 27.00
extra person	£ 2.50 - £ 6.00
child (3-15 yrs)	£ 2.00 - £ 4.50
dog (max. 2)	free - £ 2.00
Camping Cheques accepted.	

UK0060 River Valley Country Park

Relubbus, Penzance TR20 9ER (Cornwall)

Tel: **01736 763398**. Email: **rivervalley@surfbay.dircon.co.uk**

River Valley is a quiet park set in the 18 acres of a partly wooded, peaceful river valley. It offers a mix of 75 timber lodges, caravan holiday homes and 50 touring pitches. The large, well spaced touring pitches are in small meadows or natural clearings. Most are clearly defined with shrubs, hedges or trees and 15A electrical connections are available. The caravan holiday homes and lodges, some privately owned, are in more or less separate areas, beside the river at the far end of the park or on the hillside at the back. A fence separates the park from the river and there is a pleasant walk for 2.5 miles alongside it, popular for walking dogs. Much of the valley is a protected nature reserve and the park encourages wildlife by not using weed killers and by leaving parts uncut – badgers, foxes, herons, kingfishers and glow-worms are regular visitors. St Michael's Mount is only 3 miles and can be reached by footpath. This is a very special park, very well run by Brian and Eileen Milsom. A member of the Surf Bay Leisure Group.

Facilities

Three well maintained toilet blocks include family shower rooms. Some private cabins for ladies and make-up room with hair dryers. Separate laundry facilities and baby bath. Covered dishwashing sinks. Motorcaravan service point. Shop/reception. Off site: Bicycle hire 5 miles. Riding, fishing and golf 3 miles. Beach 3 miles.

Open: 31 March - 27 October.

Directions

From A30 at St Michaels Mount roundabout, take A394 towards Helston. At next roundabout take B3280 to Relubbus. In approx. 3 miles in village turn left just over a small bridge. O.S.GR: SW566320.

Charges 2007

Per unit incl. 2 persons and electricity	£ 8.50 - £ 17.50
extra person	£ 1.50 - £ 3.25
dog	£ 1.00

Min. charge 2 adults per vehicle.

UK0065 Wayfarers Camping & Caravan Park

Relubbus Lane, St Hilary, Penzance TR20 9EF (Cornwall)

Tel: **01736 763326**. Email: **elaine@wayfarerspark.co.uk**

Wayfarers is a neat and tidy garden like park reserved for adults only in rural Cornwall. Sheltered by perimeter trees and consisting of two finely mown fields interspersed by shrubs and palm-like trees, 42 places are available for caravans (up to 23 ft, single axle), motorcaravans (up to 22 ft) and tents, plus 4 holiday caravans to rent. There are 36 pitches with 16A electricity with hardstanding available on 24. Should you enjoy walking you can follow the River Hayle down to St Erth. There are many more suggestions with maps and a display of leaflets in the information room, including a star chart.

Facilities

The modern toilet block is fully equipped. Ladies have a wash cubicle and there are two smart en-suite shower rooms (key system). Fully equipped laundry. Dishwashing sinks in own house. Shop stocks basics. No twin axle caravans. Only one dog per unit and none in the tent area. Off site: Two pubs with food in Goldsithney 1 mile. Fishing 1 mile. Golf 1.5 miles. Riding 1 mile. Bicycle hire 2 miles. Boat launching 5 miles. Beach 2 miles. Sailing 5 miles.

Open: April - September.

Directions

Following the A30 Penzance road take the A394 Helston road after the St Ives turning. Follow for approx 1 mile then turn left on the B3280 and pass through Goldsithney village and site is 1 mile further on left. O.S.GR: SW559314.
GPS: N50:07.990 W05:25.010

Charges 2007

Per unit incl. 2 persons and electricity	£ 10.50 - £ 17.00
extra person	£ 4.00

UK0070 Silver Sands Holiday Park

Gwendreath, Ruan Minor, Helston TR12 7LZ (Cornwall)

Tel: **01326 290631**. Email: **enquiries@silversandsholidaypark.co.uk**

Silver Sands is a small, peaceful 'away-from-it-all' park in a remote part of the Lizard peninsula, the most southerly part of mainland Britain and an 'area of outstanding natural beauty'. It is tucked away behind two other holiday home parks (possible noise in season). The park itself has 16 caravan holiday homes, along with 36 touring pitches of which 20 have 5A electrical hook-ups. The pitches are large, attractively situated and divided into individual bays by flowering shrubs and bushes. The adjoining tent field has similar pitches (4 with electricity) where the shrubs are growing (some pitches are slightly sloping). A member of the Countryside Discovery group. The park is only reached after passing Culdrose Naval Base and the Goonhilly Earth Station down a single track road. A half mile footpath leads down through a small valley to the twin beaches of Kennack Sands (one is dog-free) divided by a small headland. This is generally an unspoilt walking area with the coastal path passing through and under the care of English Nature.

Facilities

The fully equipped toilet block includes an en-suite room for disabled visitors, doubling as a family room. Some play equipment. An undeveloped three-acre field can be used for walking, kite flying, etc. Off site: Restaurant 20 yards on the next park, pub within walking distance. Fishing 1 mile. Bicycle hire 5 miles. Boat launching 2 or 7 miles. Riding 5 miles. Golf 6 miles.

Open: 31 March - mid September.

Directions

From Helston take A3038 Lizard road. After Culdrose turn left on B3293 passing Goonhilly after 4 miles. At next crossroads turn right (Kennack Sands), continue for 1.5 miles then left to Gwendreath on single track road - site is 1 mile. O.S.GR: SW732170.

Charges 2007

Per unit incl. 2 persons	£ 10.00 - £ 14.00
incl. electricity	£ 11.00 - £ 17.00
extra person	£ 2.50 - £ 3.90
child (under16 yrs)	£ 1.00 - £ 1.80
dog	£ 1.10 - £ 1.80

Reductions for some bookings.

Silver Sands
Holiday Park (Helston, Cornwall, TR12 7LZ)
HOLIDAY HOMES
TOURING CARAVANS &TENTS
tel:01326 290631
www.silversandsholidaypark.co.uk
enquiries@silversandsholidaypark.co.uk

UK0120 Silverbow Park

Goonhavern, Truro TR4 9NX (Cornwall)

Tel: **01872 572347**

Silverbow has been developed by the Taylor family over many years and they are justifiably proud of their efforts. They believe Silverbow is a way of life and staying is an experience – they have certainly created a relaxed and tranquil atmosphere seeking to encourage couples and young families (teenagers are not accepted). Hard work, planting and landscaping has provided a beautiful environment set in 21 acres. There are 90 tourist pitches which are all of good size and include 69 'super' pitches in a newly developed area, with electricity, water and drainaway, which are even larger. Many are on a slight slope with some attractive views. There are also 15 park-owned, high quality leisure homes. Much free space is not used for camping, including an excellent sports area, as well as wild meadow and wooded areas ideal for walks. A natural area with ponds has been created to encourage wildlife. The park is 2.5 miles from the long sandy beach at Perranporth.

Facilities

Two good toilet blocks include private cabins, four family shower/toilet rooms, two accessible for wheelchairs, and a bath on payment. Laundry room. Motorcaravan services. Free freezer service. Shop for basics (mid May - mid Sept). Covered, heated swimming pool and small paddling pool (mid May - mid Sept) gated and sheltered by high surrounding garden walls. Games room with pool table, table tennis and tourist information. Adventure playground. Play field. Tennis. Off site: Gliding, riding and fishing nearby. Concessionary green fees are available at Perranporth golf club. Pub within walking distance.

Open: Early May - end September.

Directions

Entrance is directly off the main A3075 road 0.5 miles south of Goonhavern. O.S.GR: SW781531. GPS: N50:20.194 W05:07.238

Charges 2007

Per unit incl. 2 persons	£ 10.00 - £ 20.00
extra person under 50 yrs	£ 3.00 - £ 6.00
extra child (2-12 yrs) or adult over 50 yrs	£ 2.50 - £ 4.50
full service pitch incl. electricity	£ 6.00
dog	free - £ 1.50

Children over 12 yrs with or without parents not accepted. Discounts available.

UK0090 Trethem Mill Touring Park

St Just-in-Roseland, St Mawes, Truro TR2 5JF (Cornwall)
Tel: **01872 580504**. Email: **reception@trethem.com**

The Akeroyd family are proud of their park and work hard to keep it really well maintained. They aim to attract couples and families who seek peace and tranquillity, and can manage without a bar and on-site entertainment. Trethem is a 'strictly touring' park with 84 pitches all with electricity, 15 with water and waste water. Over 60 are on hardstanding with TV connections. The pitches are large, most on slightly sloping ground, some terraced, with the lower field more level and sheltered. All are individual or in bays, divided by hedging (some still growing) giving your own area. Generally there is a good spacious feel, with a tarmac circular access road and careful landscaping (the park is a mass of colour in season). The area around reception is particularly pretty where a small watermill has been built amongst the flowers – the sound of gently flowing water is very relaxing. St Mawes is a very popular, pretty village on the Roseland peninsula, which is itself an 'area of outstanding natural beauty'. Only three miles away, Trethem Mill is well placed for either sailing, walking the coastal path around the peninsula, visiting the gardens of Trelissick or Heligan, or simply lazing on the nearby beaches.

Facilities

The well equipped central toilet block is kept spotlessly clean and is heated in cooler weather. En-suite facilities for disabled visitors. Baby room (under 4s). Laundry sinks. Reception/shop, only small but well stocked and licensed. Freezer for ice packs (free). Motorcaravan services. Well equipped adventure playground (closed at 21.00). Large field for ball games. Extra field for dog walking. WiFi access. Off site: Fishing 1.5 miles. Boat launching 2 miles. Bicycle hire 4 miles. Golf 6 miles. Riding 8 miles.

Open: 1 April - mid October.

Directions

From Tregony follow A3078 to St Mawes. About 2 miles after passing through Trewithian, watch for caravan and camping sign. O.S.GR: SW863264.

Charges 2007

Per unit incl. 2 persons	
and electricity	£ 14.00 - £ 20.00
incl. services	£ 18.00 - £ 24.00
extra person	£ 5.00
child (3-14 yrs)	£ 3.00
dog	£ 1.00

trethem mill
TOURING PARK
★★★★★

...step away from the ordinary...

St Just In Roseland Truro Cornwall TR2 5JF
Tel: **01872 580504**

www.trethem.com

UK0145 Trewhiddle Holiday Estate

Pentewan Road, St Austell PL26 7AD (Cornwall)
Tel: **01726 879420**. Email: **holidays@trewhiddle.com**

Trewhiddle Village is a traditional style holiday park, complete with a large number of caravan holiday homes and three camping fields, is now under the same ownership as Sea View International (UK0150). The touring fields cover six acres and provide about 112 pitches for all types of unit, with or without electricity. The fields are sloping and edged with tall, mature trees and stone walls. The pitches are numbered and there are some views across to other fields. A swimming pool with a slide is an added attraction and the nearest beach is only 1.5 miles. Plans are in hand to upgrade the park.

Facilities

The toilet blocks were in need of some care and attention when we visited, but this work is planned. Laundry room. Shop. Trewhiddle pub with restaurant and takeaway. Swimming pool. Play area. Games room. Bicycle hire. Off site: Beach and sailing 1.5 miles. Boat launching and fishing 5 miles. Golf 4 miles. Riding 6 miles. Eden Project 5 miles. Lost Gardens of Heligan 2/3 miles. Cycle trail.

Open: All year excl. February.

Directions

From the St Austell ring road take B3273 to Mevagissy. Site is just under a mile on the right. O.S.GR: SX006511. GPS: N50:19.473 W04:47.790

Charges 2007

Per unit incl. 2 persons	
and electricity	£ 8.00 - £ 24.00
extra person (over 5 yrs)	£ 3.00 - £ 5.00
dog	£ 3.00

UK0140 Penrose Farm Touring Park

Goonhavern, Truro TR4 9QF (Cornwall)

Tel: **01872 573185**. Email: **penroseholidays@hotmail.co.uk**

Penrose Farm, now in the hands of the Welch family, has a quiet and comfortable atmosphere on the edge of the village of Goonhavern. The park is level and sheltered, with the pitches spread over five fields with flower beds and bushes set amongst them. These colourful flowers and those at the entrance give the park a neat and well cared for feel. There are over 100 pitches with 16A electricity, many with hardstanding, water and drainage, plus a few seasonal places and 5 privately owned caravan holiday homes. An adventure playground and a pets area with rabbits and fish will amuse children and the family are now offering a simple café menu, including breakfast. It is only a short walk to the village and its popular pub, and buses to Newquay stop in the village. The superb beach at Perranporth is only 2.5 miles. To retain the quiet family image, there are no plans for bars or entertainment and only couples and families are welcome.

Facilities

The fully equipped toilet block is well maintained and includes four en-suite family rooms. Facilities for disabled visitors. Well equipped laundry. Dishwashing sinks. Small shop. Gas supplies. Takeaway incl. breakfast. Adventure playground. Table tennis. Caravan storage. Off site: Fishing or riding 0.5 miles, golf 1 mile.

Open: 1 April - 31 October.

Directions

Take A30 from Exeter past Bodmin and Indian Queens. Just after wind farm take B3285 to Perranporth. Park is on the left as you enter Goonhavern village. O.S.GR: SW790535. GPS: N50:20.408 W05:06.394

Charges 2007

Per unit incl. 2 persons and electricity	£ 10.00 - £ 21.00
incl. services	£ 11.00 - £ 25.00
extra person (5 yrs and over)	£ 3.00 - £ 3.50
dog free - £ 2.00	

Less 50p for over 60s if booked.

Penrose Farm

* Quiet family park - no club/bar
* Families & couples only
* Award winning private superloos
* Animal Centre
* Adventure play area
* Just over 2 miles from
* Perranporth beach
* Good spacing
* Level & sheltered

Goonhavern, Nr Truro, Cornwall, TR4 9QF
Tel: 01872 573 185
www.penrosefarm.co.uk

UK0155 Tregarton Park

Gorran, Mevagissey, St Austell PL26 6NF (Cornwall)

Tel: **01726 843666**. Email: **reception@tregarton.co.uk**

Run by the welcoming Hicks family, Tregarton Park itself dates back to the 16th century. Although the listed buildings have created some problems in providing modern facilities, the Hicks have done well with their conversions. The 12 acre caravan park is made up of four meadows, with wonderful rural views. The 125 pitches, all with electric hook ups (10A), are of generous size with most separated by either hedges or fencing. All have been terraced, although the park itself is quite hilly.

Facilities

The tiled toilet block is fully equipped. Facilities for disabled visitors. Laundry room and enclosed dishwashing area. Well stocked shop with groceries and camping supplies. Takeaway. Gas supplies. Heated swimming pool. Tourist information. Dog exercise meadow. Playground. Facilities are open Whitsun - mid Sept. Off site: Eden project 9 miles. Heligan Gardens 2 miles. Mevagissey 2 miles. Beaches 2 miles. Fishing trips available from Mevagissey and Gorran Haven.

Open: 20 March - 1 November.

Directions

Leave St Austell travelling south on the B3273 and pass through London Apprentice and Pentewen. Follow Tregarton Park signs by turning right at crossroads (top of hill) towards the Lost Gardens of Heligan and Gorran Haven. Don't go into Mevagissey. O.S.GR: SW989435. GPS: N50:15.528 W04:49.765

Charges 2007

Per unit incl. 2 persons, electricity and awning	£ 4.50 - £ 21.50
extra person (over 4 yrs)	£ 3.00 - £ 5.50

UK0150 Sea View International

Boswinger, Gorran Haven, St Austell PL26 6LL (Cornwall)

Tel: **01726 843425**. Email: **holidays@seaviewinternational.com**

Sea View is an impreesive, well cared for park, its quality reflected in the awards it has won. The enthusiastic owners Mr and Mrs Royden and their team are continually improving the park with the aim of providing quality camping. Although somewhat exposed, the park is colourful with flower beds and flowering shrubs and has well manicured grass of exceptional quality. The area around the swimming pool is particularly attractive, with sunbathing areas with free sun-beds on tiled terraces surrounded by flowers creating private little areas, all with magnificent views of the sea and the distant headland. A whole new area has been developed at the top of the park with uninterrupted views, 31 large, hedged, fully serviced grass pitches and a new toilet block providing excellent, en-suite family shower rooms. The remaining, established pitches (163, also with views) all have 16A electricity and 43 are fully serviced, including 12 hardstandings suitable for large motorhomes. There are 38 caravan holiday homes for hire in a separate area. A family barbecue area has been established in the large recreation field between the two areas. There is plenty to do and see in this area, from the gardens of Heligan and Trelissick, to Lanhydroc House and the seal sanctuary, not forgetting the safe beaches, one of which is only a half mile walk from the park.

Facilities

Excellent toilet facilities are well maintained and heated providing for all needs, including en-suite facilities, bathrooms (on payment), baby baths and facilities for disabled visitors. Campers' kitchen. Dishwashing area. Well equipped laundry. Motorcaravan service point with car washing facilities. Shop and off-licence with gas (June - end Sept). Takeaway (Whit - mid Sept). Swimming pool (all season, heated end May - mid Sept). Large playing field with room for leisure activities. Tennis, volleyball, badminton, football, putting green, table tennis, crazy golf, petanque. Fenced play area for under 7s. Adventure playground. Games room. Bicycle hire. Field for dog walks. Certain breeds of dog are not accepted. Off site: Fishing 0.5 miles. Boat launching 2 miles. Riding 1 mile. Golf 9 miles. Community bus picks up at the park.

Open: 1 April - 31 October.

Directions

From St Austell take B3273 towards Mevagissey; 1 mile before Mevagissey village turn right at Gorran and camp sign and continue towards Gorran for 5 miles. Fork right at camp sign and follow signs to park. O.S.GR: SW991412. GPS: N50:14.214 W04:49.202

Charges 2007

Per unit incl. 2 persons and electricity	£ 12.00 - £ 31.00
incl. water and drainage	£ 15.00 - £ 33.00
extra person (over 4 yrs)	£ 3.00 - £ 5.00
pup tent	£ 2.50
dog (limited breeds and numbers)	£ 3.00
Special off-peak offers.	

UK0160 Newperran Holiday Park

Rejerrah, Newquay TR8 5QJ (Cornwall)

Tel: **01872 572407**. Email: **holidays@newperran.co.uk**

see advertisement on page 28

Newperran is a large, level park in rural Cornish countryside. Being on high ground, it is quite open but this also gives excellent views of the coast and surrounding countryside. The owners, Keith and Christine Brewer, have rebuilt the reception, shop and pub to a very high standard. The traditional layout of the park provides a number of flat, well drained meadows divided into over 370 individual pitches with 10/16A electricity. Some fields have larger and reservable spaces with more free space in the centre. There are now 61 fully serviced pitches, some with hardstanding and a TV point. Newperran is only 2.5 miles from Perranporth beach, but there is a free heated swimming pool with sunbathing area and paddling pool on the park. A state of the art entrance barrier is now in place operating on recognition of your number plate. The Pub or Cottage Inn as it is called, is a very comfortable area with a log burner for low season warmth and family entertainment such as quiz nights in high season. A separate café operates on a franchise basis. This is a well run park with plenty of space and activities for families with a few caravan holiday homes to rent. There are plans to provide a specialist naturist area but advanced booking will be required.

Facilities

Toilet facilities comprise four clean blocks, two heated and three refurbished to a very high standard. Facilities include washbasins in cabins, family rooms, baby room, hairdressing room and a unit for disabled visitors. Laundry room. Well stocked self-service licensed shop. Licensed bar (mid May - Oct). Café (all seaosn). Outdoor heated swimming pool with paddling pool (Whitsun - Sept). Adventure playground and separate toddlers' play area. Games room with TV, pool tables and games machines. TV room. Crazy golf. Off site: Riding or golf 2 miles. Fishing 1 mile. Goonhavern village within walking distance with pubs and post office. Beach 2.5 miles.

Open: Easter - October.

Directions

Turn off A3075 to west at camping sign 7 miles south of Newquay and just north of Goonhavern village. O.S.GR: SW794546.
GPS: N50:21.026 W05:06.109

Charges 2007

Per person	£ 4.20 - £ 7.30
child (3-16 yrs)	£ 2.30 - £ 4.65
pitch incl. electricity	£ 4.00 - £ 12.00
car	£ 1.25

UK0180 Carnon Downs Caravan & Camping Park

Carnon Downs, Truro TR3 6JJ (Cornwall)

Tel: **01872 862283**. Email: **info@carnon-downs-caravanpark.co.uk**

Carnon Downs is an excellent all year park run personally and enthusiastically by Simon Vallance, a very forward thinking owner. It has been thoughtfully laid out so that all pitches back onto attractive hedging or areas of flowering shrubs and arranged to provide some pleasant bays or other, more open grass areas. Gravel roads connect the 146 pitches, most with electricity (10/16A) and over 70 with hardstanding. Of these 46 are fully serviced, with the new ones being exceptionally large and surrounded by young shrubs. On arrival you will receive a warm welcome, a neatly presented layout plan of the park and a touring information pack including comprehensive details on walks and cycle paths leading from the park. Some of the park's amenities are to be found in the round-house next to the TV and information room. The round-house used to house the donkeys that turned the mill which once operated on the site! Although one side of the park is next to the A39 road, it is well screened with a band of mature woodland so noise should be minimal. This quiet, quality family park is well situated to explore the tip of Cornwall. A member of the Best of British group.

Facilities

An excellent modern, light and airy, heated block provides 12 en-suite units and dishwashing. Two other well maintained toilet blocks, also heated, include some washbasins in cubicles and showers (unisex). Three good family bath/shower rooms, one suitable for use by disabled people or families. Mother and toddler room, two baby sinks and full sized bath. Two laundries with freezers. Motorcaravan service point (ask at reception). Gas, newspapers and caravan accessories. General room with TV, library, table tennis and tourist information. Recycling centre. Good dog walks. Caravan storage. Off site: Pub/restaurant 100 yds across the road. Fishing 5 miles. Riding or bicycle hire 2 miles. Golf 1 mile. Walks direct from site.

Open: All year.

Directions

From Truro take A39 Falmouth road. After 3 miles, park entrance is directly off the Carnon Downs roundabout. O.S.GR: SW805406.

Charges 2007

Per unit incl. 2 persons and electricity	£ 15.00 - £ 21.00
extra person	£ 3.00
child (5-14 yrs)	£ 2.50
all service hardstanding	£ 2.00

24

UK0165 Monkey Tree Holiday Park

Rejerrah, Newquay TR8 5QR (Cornwall)

Tel: **01872 572032**. Email: **enquiries@monkeytreeholidaypark.co.uk**

Monkey Tree now covers 56 acres and boasts an impressive entrance and smart reception. There are 500 pitches with 450 for touring units and 50 caravan holiday homes to rent in their own area. The pitches in the original part of the park benefit from mature hedging which offers a degree of privacy which the new ones lack, but all have been planted with individual hedges. The pitches are of a good size and most have electricity (13/16A). Serviced pitches are being developed with hardstanding and some extra large pitches which include the use of private fcilities in the toilet block. During the holiday season there is lots going on at Monkey Tree and all the family should find something to keep them amused. For the little ones there is a morning Kid's Club, for older children there are adventure playgrounds, well fenced for safety, trampolines, bouncy castles and an amusement arcade and pool tables. For everyone there is an outdoor heated pool, paddling pool and a sauna. The club and restaurant are popular with entertainment for children in the early part of the evening and bingo, karaoke, disco and cabaret acts to follow. Themed weekends are organised early and late in the season (Halloween is especially popular). Venturing off the park there are wonderful beaches, a range of watersports and places such as the Eden Project and Flambards a must to visit.

Facilities

The original block (refurbished) supplements two new modern timber blocks with heating, providing for all needs including facilities for babies and disabled visitors. Private en-suite facilities for use with the super pitches. Laundry. Motorcaravan services. Gas supplies. Shop (mornings only in low season). Club with entertainment, bar, and restaurant (main season and B.Hs). Takeaway (high season). Super new tent with bar, takeaway and plenty of seating. Outdoor pool and paddling pool (Whitsun - end Sept). Trampolines (supervised, with charge). Bouncy castles. Three adventure play areas. Amusement arcade. Pool tables. Fishing lakes. Caravan storage. Off site: Golf, riding, boat launching and sailing 5 miles.

Open: All year.

Directions

Follow the A30 ignoring all signs for Newquay. At Carland Cross with windmills on the right, carry straight over following signs for Perranporth. After 1 mile turn right at Boxheater Junction on B3285 signed Perranporth and Goonhavern. Follow for 0.5 miles then turn right into Scotland Road for 1 mile to park on the left. O.S.GR: SW801546.

Charges 2007

Per person	£ 3.75 - £ 6.20
child (3-14 yrs)	free - £ 3.75
pitch incl. electricity	£ 3.50
incl. services	£ 7.50 - £ 10.50

UK0190 Polruan Holidays Camping & Caravanning

Polruan-by-Fowey PL23 1QH (Cornwall)

Tel: **01726 870263**. Email: **polholiday@aol.com**

Polruan is a rural site in an elevated position not far from Fowey in an area of Outstanding Natural Beauty 200 metres from the Coastal path. With 47 touring pitches and 10 holiday homes to let, this is a very pleasant little site. The holiday homes are arranged in a neat circle, with a central area for some tourers, including 7 pitches with gravel hardstanding and electricity, one fully serviced. The remaining touring pitches are in an adjacent field with 8 electricity hook-ups, which is part level for motorcaravans and part on a gentle slope for tents. There are marvellous sea views.

Facilities

The fully equipped sanitary block of older design has modern, controllable showers, large enough for an adult and child. New laundry room and dishwashing sinks. Motorcaravan service facilities. Range of recycling bins. Reception (with a small terrace) doubles as a small shop for basics and gas and also an off-licence. Drinks machine and a freezer for ice packs, tourist information and bus timetables (for Looe, etc). Sloping field area with swings. Off site: Fishing 0.5 miles. Riding or bicycle hire 3 miles. Golf 10 miles. Coastal path 200 m.

Open: Easter - 29 September.

Directions

From main A390 at East Taphouse take B3359 towards Looe. After 5 miles fork right signed Bodinnick and ferry. Watch for signs for Polruan and site to left. Follow these carefully along narrow Cornish lanes to site on right just before village. O.S.GR: SX133509.

Charges 2007

Per unit incl. 1 or 2 persons and electricity	£ 7.75 - £ 15.50
extra person	£ 2.00

No credit cards.

25

UK0170 Trevella Caravan Park

Crantock, Newquay TR8 5EW (Cornwall)

Tel: **01637 830308**. Email: **holidays@trevella.co.uk**

One of the best known and respected of Cornish parks with its colourful flowerbeds (a regular winner of a 'Newquay in Bloom' award), Trevella is also one of the first to fill up and has a longer season than most. Well organised, the pitches are in a number of adjoining meadows, most of which are on a slight slope. Of the 250 pitches for touring units (any type), some 200 can be reserved and these are marked, individual ones. Over 200 pitches have electricity (10A), with 59 serviced pitches (with hardstanding, electricity and TV hook-ups, water, waste water), some extra large with sewage drain as well. Trevella is essentially a quiet family touring park with the accent on orderliness and cleanliness; on-site evening activities are limited. However, Andy's Kitchen offers good home-cooked food. Access is free to two fishing lakes, (permits from reception); with some fishing instruction and wildlife talks for youngsters in season. There is a pleasant walk around the lakes, which are a haven for wildlife and a protected nature reserve. It is also possible to walk to Crantock beach but check the tides first. A member of the Best of British group.

Facilities

Kept very clean, three blocks provide good coverage with individual washbasins in private cabins for ladies, hairdressing room and baby room. New Laundry. Well stocked supermarket and heated outdoor pool (both Easter - October). Freezer pack service. Café for hot dishes and snacks to take away or eat there, including breakfast. Games room. Separate TV room. Crazy golf, large adventure playground, separate play and sports area and pets corner. Fishing. Off site: Shuttle bus service to Newquay in high season. Nearest beach is 0.5 miles on foot, 1 mile by car and Newquay is 2 miles. Pubs and restaurants at Crantock, 1 mile. Riding 1 mile, golf 3 miles

Open: Easter - 31 October.

Directions

To avoid Newquay leave A30 or A392 at Indian Queens, straight over crossroads with A39 and A3058, left at A3075 junction and first right at camp sign. O.S.GR: SW802598.
GPS: N50:23.838 W05:05.768

Charges 2007

Per person	£ 4.20 - £ 7.30
child (3-16 yrs)	£ 2.30 - £ 5.20
pitch incl. electricity	£ 4.00
with services	£ 8.00 - £ 11.00

Families and couples only.

UK0220 Trevornick Holiday Park

Holywell Bay, Newquay TR8 5PW (Cornwall)

Tel: **01637 830531**. Email: **bookings@trevornick.co.uk**

Trevornick, once a working farm, is a modern, busy and well run family touring park providing a very wide range of amenities close to one of Cornwall's finest beaches. A modern reception with welcoming staff sets the tone for your holiday. The park is well managed with facilities and standards constantly monitored. It has grown to provide caravanners and campers (no holiday caravans but 68 very well equipped 'Eurotents') with 440 large grass pitches (350 with 10A electricity and 55 fully serviced with electricity, water, drain and TV connection with DVD channel) on five level fields and two terraced areas. There are few trees, but some good views. Providing 'all singing, all dancing' facilities for fun-packed family holidays, farm buildings now house the Farm Club. It provides much entertainment from bingo and quizzes to shows, discos and cabaret. The newly redesigned Stables restaurant also opens for breakfast and the Hungrey Horse provides takeaways. The rest of the development provides a pool complex, an 18 hole golf course, with a small, quiet club house offering bar meals and lovely views out to sea and three fishing lakes. Next door is the Holywell Bay 'fun' park (reduced rates) and the sandy beach is five minutes by car or a downhill walk from the park. An innovative idea is the 'Hire shop' where it is possible rent anything you might have forgotten from sheets, a fridge, travel cot, etc. to a camera or a wet suit to catch the famous Cornish surf!

Facilities

Five modern toilet blocks provide showers (20p), 2 family bathrooms, baby bath, laundry facilities, and provision for disabled visitors. Well stocked supermarket with bread made on site (both from late May). Hire shop. Bars (with TV), restaurant, cafe and takeaway. Entertainment (every night in season). Heated outdoor pool, paddling pool, sunbathing decks, solarium, sauna and massage chair. Health and beauty salon. Super Fort Knox style adventure playground, crazy golf, Kiddies Club and indoor play area (for 2-8 yr olds at a small charge). Amusement arcade. Bowling alley.18-hole pitch and putt with golf pro shop. Bicycle hire. Coarse fishing with three lakes. Only limited facilities open at Easter and from 8 Sept. Off site: Bicycle hire and boat launching 4 miles, riding within 1 mile.

Open: Easter - mid September.

Directions

From A3075 approach to Newquay - Perranporth road, turn towards Cubert and Holywell Bay. Continue through Cubert to park on the right. O.S.GR: SW776586. GPS: N50:23.099 W05:07.736

Charges 2007

Per person	£ 4.90 - £ 8.85
child (4-14 yrs)	£ 1.25 - £ 6.25
electricity	£ 4.50
'super' 'premium' or 'jumbo' pitch incl. electricity	£ 8.50 - £ 14.75
dog	£ 3.45 - £ 3.75

Families and couples only.
Many special discounts.

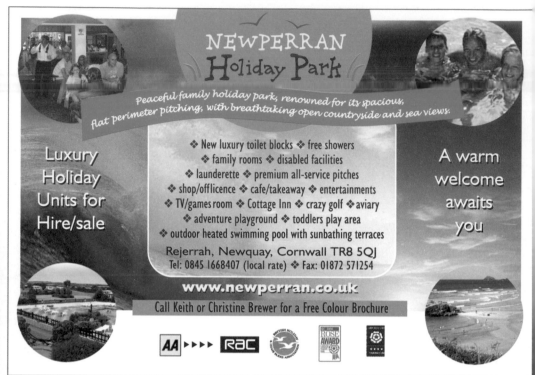

UK0210 Hendra Holiday Park

Newquay TR8 4NY (Cornwall)

Tel: **01637 875778**. Email: **jn@hendra.co.uk**

Hendra is a long-established holiday park for all the family with a wide range of facilities and a comprehensive entertainment programme. There are comedians, show bands, cabaret, dancing, bingo, discos, plus a super pool complex. The 420 touring pitches are on well mown, slightly sloping grass fields with country views and mature trees, some more sheltered than others. There are 280 caravan holiday homes in separate fields (some are to rent). With tarmac roads and lighting, 200 pitches have electricity (16A) and 28 pitches are fully serviced including water, electricity, light, sewer drainage, satellite TV connections and some innovative awning pads (dogs are not accepted on these pitches). The entrance and reception are very attractive with a mass of well tended flower beds which, along with the other facilities, form an attractive, village-like centre to the park. The 'star of the show' at Hendra is the Oasis complex consisting of an indoor fun pool with flumes, river rapids and beach. It is open to the public – really a mini water-park. The outdoor heated pool with grass sunbathing area is free to campers and activities are well catered for with a range of amenities. The park is only 1.5 miles from Newquay and its fabulous surfing beaches and a bus to the town passes the gate. Hendra welcomes families and couples.

Facilities

Three modern fully equipped toilet blocks including facilities for babies and disabled visitors. Large launderette. Motorcaravan services. Gas supplies. Well stocked shop. Various bars and restaurants, open all season (limited hours in early season). Pizzeria (main season only). Takeaway. Outdoor swimming pool. Indoor pool complex (cost £2.50 per family group, max. 4 persons, under 5s free; timed sessions are if very busy). Various play areas including one for soft play. Tennis. Minigolf. Bowling. Off site: Fishing or riding 1 mile. Bicycle hire or golf 2 miles. Beach 1.5 miles.

Open: 23 March - 31 October.

Directions

Park is on left side of A392 Indian Queens - Newquay road at Newquay side of Quintrell Downs. O.S.GR: SW833601. GPS: N50:24.146 W05:02.949

Charges 2007

Per person	£ 4.35 - £ 7.75
child (3-14 yrs)	£ 1.30 - £ 4.99
pitch incl. electricity	£ 4.75 - £ 18.00

Minimum charges at peak times.

29

UK0205 Treloy Touring Park

Newquay TR8 4JN (Cornwall)

Tel: **01637 872063**. Email: **treloy-tp@btconnect.com**

see advertisement on page 29

Just three miles from the wonderful beaches around Newquay, yet peacefully located away from the crowds, Treloy is a pretty park. Family owned and run, there are 197 pitches, many level, some slightly sloping, all with 16A electricity and 20 fully serviced. All are used for touring units and perhaps this contributes towards the relaxed family atmosphere. Treloy has an interesting history – it was leased by the present owner's father to the RAF during the war. Now the bases built then provide hardstanding for caravans. Attractively interspersed with shrubs, they now form a pleasant landscape feature. Elsewhere hydrangeas edge the roads around the more open pitches and more trees are being planted. St Mawgan, the RAF air sea rescue base and Newquay's airport are nearby but there is little disturbance. There is an hourly bus service to Newquay from the park entrance which means the coast and beaches can be enjoyed without taking the car. On return to Treloy there is the Park Chef and the Surfrider's Bar for meals and drinks. If you do not fancy the beach there is a pool on the park. This is a real family park providing for all ages.

Facilities

Two toilet blocks of similar design, one newer with toilets and washbasins only and one with showers as well. Baby room with two large sinks. En-suite facilities for disabled visitors (key). Laundry and dishwashing. Gas. Shop with all necessities. Bar (20/5-15/9). Pleasant café with a good reputation and including breakfast (20/5-1/9). Swimming pool (walled and gated). Play areas and field with goal posts. Nature trail. Family entertainment such as magic shows, bingo, folk and rock music. Off site: Fishing 1 mile. Golf 0.5 miles. Riding and boat launching 3 miles. Other beaches such as Watergate Bay, Mawgan Porth and Porth beach are a short car journey.

Open: 20 May - 15 September.

Directions

From A39 St Columb Major take the B3059 for Newquay. Park is signed after about 4 miles. O.S.GR: SW858625. GPS: N50:25.972 W05:00.750

Charges 2007

Per person	£ 5.00 - £ 7.10
child (3-14 yrs)	£ 3.00 - £ 4.25
pitch incl. electricity	£ 3.50
incl. services	£ 5.50
dog	£ 1.00 - £ 1.50

UK0195 Penmarlam Caravan & Camping Park

Bodinnick-by-Fowey, Fowey PL23 1LZ (Cornwall)

Tel: **01726 870088**. Email: **info@penmarlampark.co.uk**

Penmarlam is situated high above the estuary opposite Fowey, close to the village of Bodinnick which is famous for being the home of Daphne du Maurier. Marcus Wallace took over this park in 2003 and has been busy developing it by adding a new camping field, new toilet facilties and a new reception and shop which also acts as the village shop for Bodinnick (this means it is well stocked). The original field is level and sheltered with a circular concrete access road and 30 electric pitches on grass. The new field has a slight slope, is divided with wild banks and enjoys good countryside views. There are 35 pitches with electricity here (in total over the two fields there are 65 now including 6 with electric, water and waste water). The new building that houses reception, shop and the toilet facilities is well situated between the two fields. It is fitted with a loop system for deaf visitors, the owner can 'sign' as well as speaking French, Spanish and some German! Internet access is provided here, with wireless access possible from the pitches. Some of our readers will be attracted by easy access to a slipway (£8) and boat moorings near the park entrance, This also makes for a pleasant walk with picnic tables overlooking the river at the bottom.

Facilities

The modern, colourful and heated toilet block is fully equipped including a baby and toddler room in the ladies', a separate en-suite unit for disabled visitors which can double as a family room. Licensed shop with fresh fruit and vegetables, Video, DVD and book library open all year. Off site: Car or passenger ferry for Fowey. Annual Daphne du Maurier Festival of Arts and Literature is held in Fowey every May. Fowey Regatta held in August when some 2,500 visiting yachts boost the substantial resident yacht population.

Open: 21 March - 31 October.

Directions

From the main A390 road at East Taphouse take B3359 towards Looe. After 5 miles fork right, signed Bodinnick and ferry. Site is signed on the right 1 mile past village of Lanteglos Highway, just before Bodinnick village. O.S.GR: SK130527.

Charges 2007

Per unit incl. 2 persons	£ 6.00 - £ 8.00
incl. electricity	£ 8.00 - £ 10.50
extra person	£ 3.00 - £ 5.00
child (3-6 yrs)	£ 1.50 - £ 2.50

UK0230 **Glenmorris Park**

Longstone Road, St Mabyn PL30 3BY (Cornwall)
Tel: **01208 841677**. Email: **info@glenmorris.co.uk**

The beaches of north Cornwall and the wilds of Bodmin Moor are all an easy drive from Glenmorris Park. The park is being gradually improved and carefully maintained by the Hayman family and it provides a spacious and relaxed atmosphere. There are 80 level pitches, 60 with 16A electricity, on well drained and well mown grass with 20 hardstandings. There are some caravan holiday homes to let. A nice, sheltered outdoor pool is an added attraction. However, there is no bar although the local village inn has a good reputation for food. The Camel Trail is only two miles, providing a means to cycle or walk all the way to Bodmin, Wadebridge or Padstow. Bodmin and Wadebridge are only five or six miles for supermarket shopping. It is also possible to telephone 'Cor Link' and they will arrange to transport you to the nearest bus route.

Facilities

The fully equipped modern toilet block includes 1 en-suite unit per sex. Dishwashing sinks and laundry. Heated outdoor swimming pool and paddling pool (late May - early Sept), surrounded by a sheltered, paved and grass sunbathing areas. Good, fenced adventure play area with bark safety base. Tiny tots play area. Refurbished Games room for teenagers. Caravan storage. Off site: Fishing, riding or golf 3 miles, bicycle hire 5 miles.

Open: 1 April - mid October.

Directions

From Bodmin or Wadebridge on A389, take B3266 north signed Camelford. At village of Longstone turn left signed St Mabyn and brown camping sign. Site is 400 yds. on right. Ignore all other signs to St Mabyn. O.S.GR: SX053732. GPS: N50:31.668 W04:44.711

Charges 2007

Per person	£ 4.00 - £ 5.50
child (3-15 yrs)	£ 1.25 - £ 1.50
electricity (16A)	£ 3.30
dog	£ 1.00
Weekly rate available.	

Peaceful & Relaxing Holidays

Glenmorris Park

Enjoy a peaceful and relaxing holiday in the middle of the beautiful Cornish countryside and close by coastlines.
Heated Luxury Holiday Homes and Bungalows,
80 Touring Pitches, Electric hook-ups,
Heated Shower Block, Heated Outdoor Swimming Pool,
Children's Play area and Games room.

St Mabyn, Nr Wadebridge, Cornwall PL30 3BY

www.glenmorris.co.uk
01208 841677

UK0200 **Newquay Holiday Park**

Newquay TR8 4HS (Cornwall)
Tel: **01637 871111**. Email: **enquiries@parkdean.com**

Part of the Parkdean Group, Newquay Holiday Park lies peacefully on a terraced hillside only just outside the town, 2 miles from the beaches and town centre. Its main feature is an attractively laid out group of three heated swimming pools with a giant water slide (lifeguards in attendance) and 'green' sunbathing areas overlooked by a terrace for cool drinks. With a large proportion of caravan holiday homes (for let), there are still two fields used for touing units. These provide 187 marked pitches in hedged fields, some sloping, marked out by lines but with nothing between them. Electricity (16A) is available. Family entertainment is provided each night with live music, discos etc.

Facilities

Two good-sized, modern toilet blocks include a unit for disabled visitors and baby bath. An extra block is opened for the main season when facilities may be under pressure. Launderette. Well stocked self-service shop. Gas supplies. Bar/lounge with Sky TV. New café/restaurant (good value). Outdoor pool complex with slide (and lifeguards). Pitch and putt and crazy golf. Playground and adventure play area. Children's club. Recreation field. Amusement arcade. Pool tables.

Open: Easter - October.

Directions

Park is east of Newquay on A3059 road 1 mile east of junction with A3058. O.S.GR: SW853626. GPS: N50:25.350 W05:01.470

Charges 2007

Per unit incl. 4 persons	£ 7.00 - £ 27.00
with services	£ 10.00 - £ 30.00
extra person	
(over 3 yrs; up to 4 people)	£ 2.00 - £ 4.00
dog	£ 2.50

UK0250 Pentewan Sands Holiday Park

Pentewan, St Austell PL26 6BT (Cornwall)

Tel: **01726 843485**. Email: **info@pentewan.co.uk**

Pentewan Sands is a popular, well managed family park with an ideal position right beside a wide sandy private beach. A busy, 32 acre holiday park with lots going on, there are 501 touring pitches, 401 with electricity, and 120 caravan holiday homes for hire. The good-sized pitches are on level grass with nothing between them, and are marked and numbered by frontage stones, mostly in rows adjoining access roads. A good sized free heated pool with a paddling pool is beside the Beach Club. This contains a restaurant, two bars upstairs and a further one downstairs opening on to the pool area, open all day and serving good value food in season. A full entertainment programme, beach activities, scuba diving, windsurfing courses and a club for children are organised, and a small watersports centre is on the beach. Jet-skis are not permitted and 4WD vehicles are not allowed on the beach. The Pentewan Valley Trail, a six mile route for cycling or walking follows the old carriageway to Mevagissey with its throngs of tourists (two miles by the main road). The park and the beach have been owned by the Tremayne family for over 60 years.

Facilities

Four main toilet blocks receive heavy use in peak season but are maintained by individual cleaners. Two bathrooms, a baby room and facilities for disabled people. Well equipped laundry room and dishwashing sinks. Motorcaravan service point. Large, self-service shop with off-licence, bistro and fast food (Whitsun - mid Sept). Bars, bar meals (Easter - mid Sept, limited hours early and late season). Entertainment programme. Swimming pools (supervised and open Whitsun - mid Sept). Playground. Games room with arcade games. Tennis. Bicycle hire. Slipway and boat launching (Whitsun - mid Sept). Freezer service for ice packs. Battery charging service. Gas available. Security barrier at entrance. Caravan and boat storage. Dogs are not accepted. Off site: Bicycle hire in village 0.5 miles. Riding or golf 2 miles.

Open: 18 March - 30 October.

Directions

From St Austell ring road take B3273 for Mevagissey. Park is 3.5 miles, where the road meets the sea. O.S.GR: SX018468. GPS: N50:17.297 W04:47.145

Charges 2007

Per unit incl. 2 persons	
and electricity	£ 12.45 - £ 27.05
extra person	£ 1.80 - £ 4.60
child (3-15 yrs)	£ 1.10 - £ 3.45
extra small tent, boat or car	£ 1.70 - £ 2.40
Sea front pitch plus 10-20%.	

UK0255 Sun Valley Holiday Park

Pentewan Road, St Austell Bay, Mevagissey PL26 6DJ (Cornwall)

Tel: **01726 843266**. Email: **reception@sunvalleyholidays.co.uk**

This very neat, tidy holiday park has been developed in the grounds of a country house which is now split into holiday apartments. Set in a sheltered situation on the road from St Austell to Pentewan, Sun Valley has the appearance of a park, helped by the wonderful mature cedars which are over 250 years old. Over 75 caravan holiday homes have been carefully landscaped into the 20 acres, together with 25 level touring pitches. Hardstandings and 10A electricity hook ups are available. Excellent facilities include a restaurant, bar, indoor heated swimming pool and tennis courts. Children are not forgotten either with a paddling pool, soft ball play area for little ones, a games room, an adventure play area, plus equipment for under fives, not to mention resident donkeys. Bikes are also available to hire on the park. There is lots to do on here, never mind the wonderful sandy beach down the road, and plenty of places to visit in the area including the Eden Project, Charlestown, Mevagissey, Fowey and the Lost Gardens of Heligan. A member of the Best of British group.

Facilities

Heated en-suite family rooms offer home from home comfort with a baby changing station and ramped access for disabled people. Dishwashing undercover. Fully equipped laundry in the pool block. Washing lines provided. Shop (limited hours in low seasons). Clubhouse with bar, restaurant (also limited in low season). Indoor pool (all season). Off site: Beach 1 mile. Golf 1.5 miles. Riding 5 miles. Bus stop at park entrance (hourly service).

Open: Easter/1 April - October half term.

Directions

From the St Austell ring road take B3273 for Mevagissey. After village of London Apprentice watch for site entrance on right (about 1 mile). O.S.GR: SX006484. GPS: N50:18.030 W04:48.070

Charges 2007

Per unit incl. 2 persons,	
electricity	£ 15.00 - £ 32.50
extra person	£ 3.00
child (2-12 yrs)	£ 1.50
dog	free - £ 1.00

UK0290 Carlyon Bay Caravan & Camping Park

Bethesda, Carlyon Bay, St Austell PL25 3RE (Cornwall)

Tel: **01726 812735**. Email: **holidays@carlyonbay.net**

Tranquil open meadows edged by mature woodland, well cared for by the Taylor family, provide a beautiful holiday setting with the nearest beach five minutes walk from the top gate. The original farm buildings have been converted and added to, providing an attractive centre to the park, also home for the owners, with a certain individuality of design which is very pleasing, particularly in the impressively tiled toilet blocks which are of excellent quality and design. The 180 pitches in five areas are spacious and allow for a family meadow and a dog free meadow (high season only). All are on flat, terraced or gently sloping grass with flowers and flowering shrubs in some areas. The 115 pitches with electricity (10/16A) are marked and include 8 with full services, 6 with hardstanding. The attractive kidney shaped, heated swimming pool with a paddling pool, are walled and paved for sunbathing. This is part of the central, covered area used for entertainment in high season for families and children. There is also a pleasant family pub and Ben's Playworld for children within walking distance. The coastal footpath passes nearby. Buses to run from the park entrance.

Facilities

Three individually designed, modern toilet blocks (one heated) provide a full range of comfortable facilities for all your needs - almost home from home! Dishwashing sinks. Fully equipped laundry room (hot water metered). Modern reception with little shop (limited hours out of season). Takeaway (May - mid Sept). Swimming and paddling pools (Whitsun - Sept). TV lounge, crazy golf, table tennis and pool table. Two play areas, one adventure type. Eden Project tickets available. Off site: Golf course near the park entrance. Riding 3 miles. Bicycle hire 4 miles. Sailing 2 miles. Boat launching 5 miles. Eden Project 2 miles.

Open: Easter/1 April - end September.

Directions

From Plymouth direction on A390, pass Lostwithiel and 1 mile after village of St Blazey, turn left at roundabout beside Britannia Inn. After 400 yds turn right on a concrete road and right again at site sign. O.S.GR: SX053526. GPS: N50:20.451 W04:44.233

Charges 2007

Per unit incl. 2 persons	
and electricity	£ 10.00 - £ 25.00
serviced pitch	£ 14.00 - £ 27.00
extra person	£ 5.00
child (3-17 yrs)	£ 3.00 - £ 4.00
dog (max 2)	£ 2.50
Camping Cheques accepted.	

UK0280 Powderham Castle Holiday Park

Lanlivery, Lostwithiel PL30 5BU (Cornwall)

Tel: **01208 872277**. Email: **powderhamcastletp@tiscali.co.uk**

A pleasant, peaceful touring park, Powderham Castle has plenty of sheltered green space and a natural, uncommercialised atmosphere. This has been enhanced by careful planting of trees and shrubs to form a series of linked paddocks with an unfenced stream running through. The park has 38 private caravan holiday homes in a separate field and 59 numbered touring pitches spread round the perimeter of the paddocks, each with 10-15 pitches. All have electricity connections (5/10A) and 12 have hardstanding (awning groundsheets must be lifted alternate days).

Facilities

The single well equipped toilet block is quite a walk from some pitches. Family washroom and unit for disabled visitors. Laundry room. Motorcaravan service point. Gas supplies. Play area. TV room. Games room. Putting green. Off site: Fresh water fishing 1.5 miles. Beach 4 miles.

Open: Easter/1 April - 31 October.

Directions

Park approach road leads off A390 road 1.5 miles southwest of Lostwithiel. Follow camping signs. No other approach is advised. O.S.GR: SX083592.

Charges 2007

Per unit incl. 2 persons	£ 11.00 - £ 15.00
extra person	£ 1.00 - £ 2.00

33

UK0270 Mena Caravan & Camping Park

Lanivet, Bodmin PL30 5HW (Cornwall)

Tel: **01208 831845**. Email: **mena@campsitesincornwall.co.uk**

A peaceful, simple park, Mena is tucked away in the Cornish countryside, yet close to the main routes, and a warm welcome awaits. A few years ago it was a field for cows and with hard work and care it has been developed into a comfortable, yet natural site. Set in 15 acres of secluded countryside, it is spacious and never crowded offering only 25 level grass pitches on well drained, slightly sloping grass. There are 12 electricity connections (10A). A large comfortable area with a veranda provides facilities for making tea and coffee. Mena means 'hilltop' in the Cornish language and the site is actually situated at the geographical centre of Cornwall, overlooked by Helman's Tor, one of the highest points on Bodmin Moor. It is also close to the Saints' Way, the pilgrim route from Ireland where they crossed by land from Padstow to Fowey on their way to France. With its position, visitors can choose between beaches on the north or south coast. Lanivet village has a shop and a pub serving meals.

Facilities

Four toilet and washbasin cabins are in an older wooden building. Two new showers and two toilets are behind the veranda building. On the opposite side of the site is a new en-suite facility for disabled visitors, part of a building housing a large games room with three quarter size snooker table, TV and darts. Swings, etc. for children in the central grass area. Fishing lake (licence required). Two mobile homes for hire. Off site: Lanivet village with shop and pub 2 miles. Riding 1 mile. Golf 2 miles. Bicycle hire 3 or 5 miles. Nearest beach 8 miles. Eden Project 4 miles.

Open: Mid March - 1 October.

Directions

From Bodmin by-pass take A391 for St Austell. After 0.5 miles take first left (unsigned). In 0.75 miles turn right signed Lostwithiel. In 0.5 miles at top of hill turn right (keep Celtic Cross on left). Continue straight on for 0.5 miles (road narrows) and turn right into site lane. O.S.GR: SX041625. GPS: N50:25.816 W04:45.430

Charges 2007

Per unit incl. 2 persons	£ 8.50 - £ 18.50
incl. electricity	£ 11.00 - £ 21.00
extra person	£ 1.00 - £ 1.75
child (3-6 yrs)	£ 1.50 - £ 2.50

No credit or debit cards.

UK0300 The Colliford Tavern Campsite

Colliford Lake, St Neot, Liskeard PL14 6PZ (Cornwall)

Tel: **01208 821335**. Email: **info@colliford.com**

Colliford Tavern must be unique, quietly situated high on Bodmin Moor near Colliford Lake but hidden and protected by tall pines with a camping area and a tavern. The tavern is run as a free house with a bar, dining room, a family room with outside terrace, garden, water wheel and a good, fenced play area with a Wendy House. It is open to campers and caravanners and the general public. The camping area is quiet and simple and has been kept very natural with short grass (helped by the rabbits) and sheltered from the moor by tall pines. The main field provides 40 fairly level pitches with 19 electric hook-ups (16A) and 6 hardstandings. Reception is in the tavern building. The site gate is closed at night but there is a 24 hour bell. Ideally situated for Colliford Lake and the Moor be it for walking, fly fishing (permits available) or birdwatching, the park is also suitable for excursions to both the north or south coast.

Facilities

The pine-fitted, heated toilet block is fully equipped and includes a baby room and unit for disabled people (no shower), laundry sink and two washing-up sinks. Service wash and tumble dry (Monday to Friday). Restaurant and bar. Play area. Some occasional family entertainment. Tickets available for the Eden Project (20-30 minutes by car). Barbecues permitted with prior permission.

Open: Easter - end October.

Directions

Approaching on the A30 travelling south, pass the Jamaica Inn and site is signed a further 1-1.5 miles on the left. Follow for 0.5 miles and site is signed beside Colliford Lake Park. O.S.GR: SX168730. GPS: N50:32.216 W04:34.936

Charges 2007

Per unit incl. 2 persons	£ 13.00
extra person (over 12 yrs)	£ 4.00
electricity (16A)	£ 3.00
child (5-12 yrs)	£ 2.00
dog	£ 0.50

UK0302 South Penquite Farm

South Penquite, Blisland, Bodmin PL30 4LH (Cornwall)

Tel: **01208 850491**. Email: **thefarm@bodminmoor.co.uk**

South Penquite offers real camping with no frills, set on a 80 hectare hill farm high on Bodmin Moor between the villages of Blisland and St Breward. The farm achieved organic status in 2001 and runs a flock of 300 ewes and a herd of 40 cattle. You will also find horses, ponies, chickens, geese, ducks and, when we visited, a pair of turkeys which had escaped the Christmas cull and showed their approval or not by the skin around their necks changing colour! A farm walk of some two miles takes you over most of the farm and some of the moor taking in a Bronze Age hut settlement, the river and a standing stone. It is also possible to fish for brown trout on the farm's stretch of the De Lank river – a tributary of the Camel. The camping is small scale and intended to have a low impact on the surrounding environment. Tents or simple motorcaravans can pitch around the edge of three walled fields, roughly cut in the midst of the moor. You can find shelter or a view. Four Yurts – round Mongolian tents, are available to rent in one field, complete with wood burning stoves – quite original. Take a look at the farm's website which offers a fascinating insight into life and work at South Penquite.

Facilities

Simple but adequate, there are separate toilets and washbasins for men and women, plus 4 new large showers. Two outside Belfast sinks. Washing machine and dryer. LPG gas available. Facilities for field studies and opportunities for educational groups and schools to learn about the local environment. Fishing (requires an EA rod licence and tokens available from the Westcountry Rivers Trust). Dogs are not accepted. Off site: Walking, riding and cycling. Sustrans Route 3 passes close by. North and south coasts within easy reach.

Open: 14 May - mid October.

Directions

Travelling into Cornwall on A30 over Bodmin Moor pass Jamaica Inn and sign for Colliford Lake and watch for St Breward sign (to right) immediately at end of dual-carriageway. Follow this narrow road over the open moor for about 2 miles ignoring any turns to left or right. Also ignore right turn to St Breward just before you arrive at the South Penquite sign. Follow track over stone bridge beside ford through farm gate and then bear to left to camping fields. Walk back to book in at Farm House. O.S.GR: SX104752. GPS: N50:32.670 W04:40.310

Charges 2008

Per person	£ 5.00
child (5-16 yrs)	£ 3.00

Less 10% for stays of 5 nights or more.
No Credit Cards.

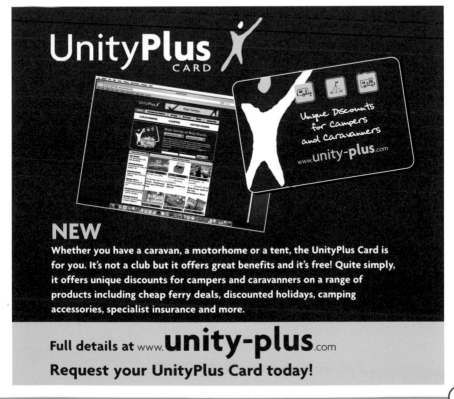

UK0306 Ruthern Valley Holidays

Ruthernbridge, Bodmin PL30 5LU (Cornwall)

Tel: 01208 831395. Email: camping@ruthernvalley.com

This is a little gem of a site set in 7.5 acres of woodland, tucked away in a peaceful little valley not far from Bodmin. The park was landscaped over 30 years ago with an amazing range of trees and shrubs. It is now owned by Andrew and Nicola Johnson who will bring their talents and expertise to this tranquil small park. The landscaping lends itself to the informal layout of the level touring pitches and the self catering accommodation. Twelve wooden chalet/bungalows and six caravan holiday homes blend into the natural wooded environment. There are 16 touring pitches informally spaced but numbered in the main, tree-lined field, six with electricity, and a further 13 in smaller fields and alcove areas amongst the woods with a small stream meandering through and alive with bluebells when we visited. A very good adventure type play area is set away from the pitches, and a small, basic toilet block and a little shop complete the provision. This is a site for relaxing with time to enjoy the simpler pastimes of walking or birdwatching. Over 40 different species of bird have been recorded.

Facilities

The small toilet block provides everything necessary including a shower each per sex plus washing machines, dryer, laundry sink and dishwashing sinks (H&C). There is a newly built shower and solar hot water heating system. The shop with basic provisions shares with reception (reduced hours in low season). Barbecue hire. Play area with excellent equipment including five-a-side goal posts. Dogs are not accepted in touring areas during July/Aug. Bicycle hire (delivered to site). Off site: Nearest pub 3-4 miles. Riding 4 miles.

Open: April - October.

Directions

Approaching Bodmin from A30 or A38 turn right at first mini roundabout and proceed anti-clockwise on the inner ring road. Go straight over double mini-roundabout, leaving Bodmin on A389/A391 towards St Austell. Ignore first Nanstallon - Ruthernbridge sign, after 1.5 miles, at top of hill, turn right. At Nanstallon village sign (0.75 miles), turn left then filter left. Continue for 1 mile dropping down into Ruthernbridge. Turn left immediately before bridge. Site is on left in 300 yards. O.S.GR: SX012668. GPS: N50:27.873 W04:48.114

Charges 2007

Per unit incl. 2 persons	£ 11.00 - £ 13.00
with electricity	£ 13.00 - £ 15.50
extra person over 4 yrs	£ 2.50

UK0310 Trekenning Tourist Park

St Columb Major, Newquay TR8 4JF (Cornwall)

Tel: 01637 880462. Email: holidays@trekenning.co.uk

Trekenning is a very useful park with easy access just off the A39 roundabout at St Columb Major. It comprises a large sloping field with neatly cut grass and all the facilities tucked into the top corner. There are 75 pitches, 68 with 10A electricity and semi-terraced. The star of the show is undoubtedly the kidney shaped pool and paddling pool which are in a garden-like setting with gazebos and sun loungers surrounded by lawn and overlooked by a patio bar at the top – lovely for summer evenings. The 'olde worlde' upstairs bar is a cosy feature serving food as well. Entertainment is provided most nights in the main season. The A39 runs parallel to one side of the site, so there may be road noise.

Facilities

Two toilet blocks, one with showers and washbasins, the other with two en-suite bathrooms (50p) and six large family showers, well refurbished. Laundry room. Covered dishwashing sinks. Shop for basics (July/Aug). Bar (all season) with food on demand. Free freezer service. Play area. Outdoor pool with poolside bar (Whitsun - end Aug). Games room with table tennis and pool and some amusement machines. Takeaway including breakfasts (B.Hs and July/Aug). Off site: Fishing 1 mile. Riding and golf 2 miles. Bicycle hire 6 miles.

Open: All year.

Directions

Take A3059 turning to Newquay from St Columb Major then turn immediately left; park is signed (this was the old road). O.S.GR: SW907625.

Charges 2007

Per unit incl. 2 persons	£ 11.00 - £ 15.00
incl. electricity	£ 14.00 - £ 18.00
extra person	£ 4.50 - £ 6.50
child (3-15 yrs)	£ 2.00 - £ 4.50
dog	£ 3.00

UK0320 Polborder House Caravan & Camping Park

Bucklawren Road, St Martins by Looe PL13 1NZ (Cornwall)

Tel: **01503 240265**. Email: **reception@peaceful-polborder.co.uk**

Under new ownership, Polborder House is a lovely site which may appeal to those who prefer a quiet, well kept little family site to the larger ones with many on-site activities. With good countryside views, up to 37 touring units can be accommodated on well tended grass. Pitches are marked with some hedging between pairs of pitches to give privacy and most have electrical connections (10A). There are also a number of hardstandings and 14 serviced pitches. The new owners, Amanda and Dale Byers, live on the park and are most helpful. The nearest beach a 20-25 minutes walk from a gate in the corner of the park. This is a good area for walking with links to the coastal path through Duchy woodland.

Facilities

The fully equipped sanitary block (key entry) includes a baby room, fully equipped laundry room, and three covered sinks outside for dishwashing. En-suite toilet unit for disabled visitors has a ramped approach. Rubbish is recycled. Shop (all season) for gas and basics, and some camping accessories. Toddler's play area. Hut with tourist information. Off site: Fishing, golf and boat launching within 2 miles. Riding 6 miles. Restaurant 500 m. Diving school at Seaton, scuba centre and fishing trips at Looe. Seaton 2 miles, Looe 2.5 miles.

Open: All year.

Directions

Park is less than half a mile south of the B3253. Turn off 2 miles east of Looe and follow signs to park and Monkey Sanctuary at junctions; care is needed with narrow road. O.S.GR: SX283555. GPS: N50:22.633 W04:25.110

Charges 2007

Per unit incl. 2 persons	£ 9.00 - £ 12.75
extra person	£ 4.00 - £ 4.80
child (5-16 yrs)	£ 2.00 - £ 2.40

Less 10% for senior citizens for booked stays over 7 nights.

UK0330 Killigarth Manor Caravan Park

Polperro, Looe PL13 2JQ (Cornwall)

Tel: **01271 866766**. Email: **holiday@johnfowlerholidays.com**

A substantial part of Killigarth Estate is occupied by caravan holiday homes but a separate part is allocated to touring units and it is a good choice for those that like a range of facilities and entertainment. It provides 202 marked, level or gently sloping grass pitches, of which 75 are taken by seasonal units, and a tenting paddock. There are 73 electric hook-ups (16A) for tourers. A range of bars (e.g. Smugglers' Bar, Sportsman's Lounge and Harbour Lights Club) and a large entertainment area with stage, mini-cinema, family room, amusements and games areas, a new restaurant, takeaway and bar snacks, a heated indoor pool, fitness centre with gym, sauna and sun bed, and a sun terrace with beautiful views. Early evening 'young entertainment' is followed later by live shows, discos or groups and a programme of competitions, quizzes or family films on a large TV. This park is popular with families with children of all ages and there is much to do in the area.

Facilities

One large, and fully equipped toilet block. Dishwashing facilities under cover. Facilities for disabled visitors are in the main block. Well equipped laundry with sinks. Well stocked mini-market (all season). Bars and restaurant. Takeaway. Indoor pool with children's pool. Fitness centre. New indoor play area for under-fives and other play areas. Amusement arcade. Tennis court (£3/hour). Crazy golf. Bus service in high season. Off site: Fishing and boat launching approx. 1 mile

Open: 1 March - 31 October.

Directions

From Looe take A387 towards Polperro. After 3.5 miles, fork left immediately past a bus shelter and phone box at sign to Killigarth. Site is 0.25 miles. O.S.GR: SX213519. GPS: N50:20.291 W04:30.608

Charges guide

Per person	£ 3.25 - £ 3.80
child (3-16 yrs)	£ 1.70 - £ 2.00
pitch	£ 2.75 - £ 6.00
electricity	£ 2.00

Pup tents not permitted to share a pitch with another unit. Special offers available.

CHOICE OF 15 SUPERB HOLIDAY PARKS
Ilfracombe, Bude, Torbay, Looe, Newquay & St Ives

★ FREE! Kids Club
★ FREE! Bedlinen
★ FREE! Colour Television
★ FREE! Electricity/Gas
★ FREE! Heated Swimming Pool
★ FREE! Nightly Entertainment

JOHN FOWLER HOLIDAY PARKS
Qoute Ref: AR
01271 866766
johnfowlerholidays.com

37

UK0360 Lakefield Caravan Park

Lower Pendavey Farm, Camelford PL32 9TX (Cornwall)

Tel: **01840 213279**. Email: **lakefield@pendavey.fsnet.co.uk**

Lakefield is a small, simple touring park on what was a working farm. Now the main focus is on the BHS approved equestrian centre. With only 30 pitches, it is no surprise that the owners, Maureen and Dennis Perring, know all the campers. The well-spaced pitches backing onto hedges and with 24 electric hook-ups (16A) are in view of the small, fenced lake watched over by one of Cornwall's first wind farms. The white-washed café/reception, converted from an old barn is open all day offering traditional Cornish fare. A dozen colourful picnic tables are dotted about the site. Children will love the animals and 'Wabbit World'. With over 30 horses, the riding school is very much part of the site, offering lessons and hacks with qualified supervision and instruction. You can even bring your own horse. Nearby, Tintagel, Boscastle, Bodmin Moor and many beaches wait to be explored.

Facilities

Simple but adequate toilet block. Washing machine and dryer in the ladies' and a dishwashing sink and a laundry sink outside but under cover. Toilet for disabled visitors at Riding Centre. Shop and tea room. Gas supplies. Torches may be useful. Off site: Fishing (sea 4 miles, coarse 5 miles). Golf 2 miles.

Open: 1 April - 31 October.

Directions

Follow B3266 north from Camelford. Park access is directly from this road on the left just before the turning for Tintagel, clearly signed. O.S.GR: SX097852.

Charges 2007

Per unit incl. 2 persons	£ 6.00 - £ 10.00
extra person (5 yrs and over)	£ 1.00
electricity	£ 2.50

UK0400 Trelay Farmpark

Pelynt, Looe PL13 2JX (Cornwall)

Tel: **01503 220900**. Email: **stay@trelay.co.uk**

Situated a little back from the coast, just over three miles from Looe and Polperro in a rural situation, this is a real gem of a park. Neat, tidy and quiet, despite the name, there is no farm. On your right as you drive in, and quite attractively arranged amongst herbaceous shrubs, are caravan holiday homes . The touring area is behind and slightly above, on level to gently sloping, neatly cut grass. An oval hardcore road connects the good sized, numbered pitches that border the site and back onto hedges, the majority with rural views. There are 43 pitches with electricity hook-ups, with a further 12 pitches for tents, etc. You will receive a good welcome from the enthusiastic owners.

Facilities

Excellent, spacious chalet-type toilet block, purpose built, heated, well equipped and maintained, with large cubicles. Some semi-private washbasins. En-suite unit with ramp for disabled visitors. Washing machine and dryer. Gas supplies. Free use of fridge/freezer and ice pack service. Off site: Village 0.5 mile. Looe and Polperro within 3 miles. Bus service from the village.

Open: 30 March - end October.

Directions

From A390 Lostwithiel road take B3359 south at Middle or East Taphouse towards Looe and Polperro. Site is signed 0.5 miles past Pelynt on the left. O.S.GR: SX210545. GPS: N50:21.735 W04:31.133

Charges guide

Per unit incl. 2 persons	£ 7.50 - £ 12.00
electricity	£ 2.00
No credit cards.	

UK0430 Padstow Touring Park

Trerethern, Padstow PL28 8LE (Cornwall)

Tel: **01841 532061**. Email: **mail@padstowtouringpark.co.uk**

Padstow Touring Park has wonderful views over looking the Camel Estuary and Padstow. Originally open fields, bushes and shrubs have now been grown to break up the gently sloping fields. There are 150 pitches, over half with 10A electricity and some with hardstanding. 'Kernow' pitches have access to private, en-suite facilities. The site can accommodate up to 32-34 ft. motorhomes. Padstow itself is a mile away, either by public footpath downhill through the fields (20-30 minutes) or by bicycles on the road. A bus service passes (the site is a request stop) and reception holds timetables.

Facilities

One standard toilet block and one new, include six en-suite shower rooms, one suitable for disabled visitors and one for families Exclusive washrooms for use with the 'Kernow' pitches. Laundry. Reception/shop for gas, camping equipment and provisions (peak season). Bread to order. Play area. WiFi access. Off site: Nearest beach is at Padstow, others are within 2 miles. Golf 5 miles.

Open: All year.

Directions

Park is on the main A389 road into Padstow, on the right about 1 mile before the town. If towing or in a motorhome avoid A389 between Wadebridge and St Issey; instead take B3274 which can take large units. O.S.GR: SW912739. GPS: N50:31.623 W04:56.951

Charges 2007

Per unit incl. 2 persons	£ 10.00 - £ 25.50
electricity	£ 3.00 - £ 3.50

UK0380 Wooda Farm Park

Poughill, Bude EX23 9HJ (Cornwall)

Tel: **01288 352069**. Email: **enquiries@wooda.co.uk**

Wooda Farm is spacious and well organised, with some nice touches. A quality, family run park, it is part of a working farm, under two miles from the sandy, surfing beaches of Bude. In peaceful farmland with plenty of open spaces (and some up and down walking), there are marvellous views of sea and countryside. The 200 large pitches are spread over four meadows on level or gently sloping grass. There are 142 with electricity connections (10A), 63 hardstanding hedged 'premier' pitches (electricity, water, waste water) and 5 premier pitches with Sky TV, linked by tarmac roads. A late arrivals area has electricity. Beside the shop and reception at the entrance are 55 caravan holiday homes for let. A few friendly farm animals welcome assistance at feeding time! Tractor and trailer rides, archery and clay pigeon shooting with tuition are provided according to season and demand, plus woodland (to find the pixies) and orchard walks and excellent coarse fishing. There is much to do in the area – sandy beaches with coastal walks, and Tintagel with King Arthur's Castle and Clovelly nearby. A member of the Best of British group.

Facilities

Three well maintained toilet blocks, one heated, include a unit suitable for disabled people, two baby rooms and five en-suite family bathrooms for hire (small charge). Two laundry rooms. Motorcravan service point. Self-service shop with off-licence (reduced hours out of season). Attractive courtyard bar with bar meals and pleasant restaurant with home cooking (reduced hours out of season). Play area in separate field. 9 hole 'fun' golf course (clubs provided). Games room with TV. Badminton. Tennis. Coarse fishing in 1.5 acre lake (permits from reception). Certain breeds of dogs not accepted. Caravan storage. Internet access. Off site: Local village Inn is five minutes walk. Leisure Centre and Splash Pool in Bude.

Open: 1 April - October.

Directions

Park is north of Bude at Poughill; turn off A39 on north side of Stratton on minor road for Coombe Valley, following camp signs at junctions. O.S.GR: SS225080.

Charges 2007

Per unit incl. 2 persons	£ 11.00 - £ 17.00
with electricity	£ 13.00 - £ 19.00
incl. water and drainage	£ 15.00 - £ 22.00
extra person	£ 3.00 - £ 4.50
child (3-15 yrs)	£ 2.00 - £ 3.50

Camping Cheques accepted.

In the Countryside - Beside the Sea

The Colwill family welcome you to Wooda Farm Park set in 27 acres of parkland with spectacular views of sea and countryside - an excellent base for touring the delights of Cornwall and Devon.

• Fishing • Fun Golf • Family Bathrooms
• Heated Facilities • All-weather Pitches

www.wooda.co.uk
Tel: 01288 352069

Wooda
Farm Park
In the Countryside - Beside the Sea

Wooda Farm Park, Bude, Cornwall EX23 9HJ

mycamping.info

It's all about **YOU** and **YOUR** experiences...

So get involved today!
Visit www.mycamping.info

UK0410 Heligan Woods Holiday Park

St Ewe, St Austell PL26 6EL (Cornwall)
Tel: **01726 843485**. Email: **info@heliganwoods.co.uk**

A peaceful park in a mature garden setting, Heligan Woods complements its sister site, Pentewan Sands with its busy beach life and many activities. Part of this park's boundary actually edges The Lost Gardens of Heligan (although nothing can be seen), and at some time the land must have been part of the Gardens. One can enjoy the mature trees and flowering shrubs here which have been further landscaped to provide an attractive situation for a number of holiday homes (some for rent, 5 privately owned). These face out over a part of the 'Lost Valley' of Heligan fame and are interspersed with touring pitches, with some below on sloping grass and others in a more level situation amongst trees and shrubs. In all, there are 100 good sized touring pitches, 80 with 16A electricity. The many facilities of Pentewan Sands are open to Heligan Woods visitors. There is access to the Pentewan Trail to ride or cycle into Mevagissey or Pentewan.

Facilities

Fully equipped and well kept, the modern, heated toilet block includes a unisex room with bath and small size bath. Dishwashing sinks under cover. Fully equipped laundry room. Small shop (peak season only). Adventure playground. Off site: Riding 4 miles, golf 5 miles. Lost Gardens of Heligan next door.

Open: 1 February - 30 November.

Directions

From St Austell ring road take B3273 for Mevagissey. After 3.5 miles, pass Pentewan Sands, continue up the hill and turn right following site signs. Park is on left just before reaching Heligan Gardens. O.S.GR: SW999464. GPS: N50:17.330 W04:48.725

Charges 2007

Per unit incl. 2 persons and electricity	£ 9.95 - £ 22.95
extra person	£ 1.75 - £ 3.85
child (3-15 yrs)	£ 1.00 - £ 2.80
extra tent, car or boat	£ 1.55 - £ 2.00

UK0415 Trencreek Farm Country Holiday Park

Hewas Water, St Austell PL26 7JG (Cornwall)
Tel: **01726 882540**. Email: **reception@trencreek.co.uk**   *see advertisement on page 19*

Trencreek Farm is a friendly, well equipped park set in 56 acres of rolling Cornish countryside of woodland and lakes and is a wonderful place for a family holiday. Although no longer a working farm, there are some animals to see, including pot bellied pigs and pigmy goats, carefully kept in pens. The grassy pitches are of a good size, most with electrical connections and arranged around the edges of sloping fields. The camping fields surround the former, central farm buildings which have been converted to house all the amenities, including a heated swimming pool. Also very popular are four small course fishing lakes, each of which is stocked with a different range of fish. The park managers, Bev and Gary Cox, have worked hard to bring the park up to standard and encourage a happy and friendly atmosphere. In peak season they organise a club for children (15.00-17.00, Monday to Friday), along with quiz nights in the bar. The animals are an obvious attraction for children and the fishing lakes for fathers, but there is always the pool for the rest of the family. Mobile homes and chalets are available for hire. A member of the Surf Bay Leisure group.

Facilities

Two traditional style toilet blocks are supplemented by a chalet block containing five en-suite units per sex (charged). Laundrette. Shop. Bar, restaurant. Takeaway food. Heated swimming pool. Tennis court. Sports field. Fishing (small charge). Adventure play area. TV and games room. Children's farm. Off site: Nearest beach 4 miles. Golf (18-hole) 3 miles. Riding and bicycle hire 4 miles. Shipwreck rescue and heritage centre 5 miles. The Lost Gardens of Heligan 3 miles. Eden Project 3 miles.

Open: 7 April - 29 October.

Directions

Site is four miles west of St Austell. Take the A390 and then fork left to join the B3287 and the site is 1 mile further on the left. O.S.GR: SW965484.

Charges 2007

Per pitch incl. 2 persons	£ 8.50 - £ 16.00
incl. electricity	£ 10.45 - £ 18.00
extra person (over 3 yrs)	£ 1.50
dog	£ 1.00

UK0440 Dolbeare Caravan & Camping Park

St Ive Road, Landrake, Saltash PL12 5AF (Cornwall)

Tel: **01752 851332**. Email: **reception@dolbeare.co.uk**

Ian and Chris are now the proud owners of this small, but well kept park. Dolbeare is in a rural setting (but very easily accessible from the main A38) and consists of a large rectangular field of neat grass edged with trees and sloping slightly at the top, connected by a gravel road, and a camping paddock. All 66 pitches are on hardsatnding and have 16A electricity connections. An extra field provides the camping paddock and can also be used for rallies. Part of it is set aside for a games field with a dog walk being developed at the top of the park. A new low level adventure play area has been added, along with giant chess and Connect 4 games. At reception, leaflets are provided on 'Where to Eat', 'Where to Walk' and 'Suggestions for what to do' with good tourist information and maps. Dog kennels nearby can provide day care from £3.50, but the drawback is that there could be some noise depending on season and wind direction. This is a very usefully situated park said to be 20 minutes from everywhere – Plymouth, beaches, National Trust properties, Dartmoor and Bodmin Moor, etc.

Facilities

The fully equipped heated toilet block to one side of the field. Indoor dishwashing sinks. Laundry next to reception. Fridge and freezer in camping field. Motorcaravan services. Reception doubles as a small shop for basics including gas (limited hours out of main season). Site barrier (card system with £5 deposit). Off site: Fishing and riding 3 miles. Golf 5.5 miles. Nearest beach 8 miles.

Open: All year.

Directions

After crossing the Tamar Bridge into Cornwall, continue on A38 for a further 4 miles. In Landrake village turn right following signs and site is 0.75 miles on the right. O.S.GR: SX366616.

Charges 2007

Per unit incl. 2 persons and electricity	£ 13.20 - £ 18.60
extra person	£ 3.50
child (5-16 yrs)	£ 2.25

UK0450 Pennance Mill Farm Chalet & Camping Park

Maenporth, Falmouth TR11 5HJ (Cornwall)

Tel: **01326 317431**

Pennance Mill Farm has been in the hands of the Jewell family for three generations and is listed as a typical Cornish farmstead in an Area of Outstanding Natural Beauty (AONB) and you can enjoy the woodland walk with 200 year old beech trees. In the high season skittles, country games and barbecue evenings are organised, all in keeping with the relaxed and friendly atmosphere generated by the owners. The camping area is situated in four sheltered south-facing and fairly level fields with views over the countryside and providing for 75 pitches, all of which have 16A electricity and 8 hardstanding. Caravans are accepted however this is not a site for those who like neat manicured lawns and flower beds. An old mill wheel reminds one of the site's origins and you book in at the farmhouse. Continuing on past the site for half a mile, you come to the sandy beach at Maenporth safe for bathing, windsurfing and diving. A bus service now runs to the beach and the town centre.

Facilities

The two toilet blocks are fully equipped. The first near the entrance is the original one but it is well kept with good hot water, washing machine, dryer, laundry and dishwashing sinks. The block in the top meadow is more modern, heated and includes dishwashing sinks. Small farm shop including some basic provisions (open 9.00-10.30 and 17.30-18.30). Gas supplies. Small play meadow with new play equipment. Table tennis. Off site: New Maritime Museum. Tennis courts, golf course and pitch and putt within walking distance. Coastal footpath to the Helford River.

Open: Easter - November.

Directions

From Truro, follow signs for Falmouth on A39. At first roundabout pass Asda then turn right at next roundabout signed Maenporth and industrial estates (on Bickland Water Road). Follow brown international camping sigps for 1.5 miles and continue down the hill to site on your left as the road bends to the right. O.S.GR: SW789307. GPS: N50:08.099 W05:05.560

Charges 2007

Per person	£ 4.50 - £ 5.50
child (over 3 yrs)	£ 1.75 - £ 2.00
pitch	£ 4.00 - £ 5.00
electricity	£ 2.00

UK0470 Little Trevarrack Holiday Park

Laity Lane, Carbis Bay, St Ives TR26 3HW (Cornwall)

Tel: 01736 797580. Email: info@littletrevarrack.co.uk

Little Trevarrack is a traditional Cornish park covering 20 acres, with wonderful views from the top of the site across St Ives bay towards Hayle and the surrounding countryside. It is owned by Neil, son of the owners of Polmanter Park and Annette Osborne and now has a smart, large, new reception and entrance. There are 234 pitches, in five open fields (the top ones with gentle slopes), 153 with 16A electricity and 15 with water and drain as well. Bushes and hedging have grown to provide individual pitches and give a continental appearance to the park. A smart new heated outdoor pool was added in 2007 with a paddling pool and sunbathing area. Landscaped and fenced, a new play area is alongside. Carbis Bay with its safe sandy beach is ideal for families with young children and is less than a mile away. In high season a bus runs hourly into St Ives. This is a developing park which will provide a quiet, peaceful base from which to explore St Ives and the southern tip of Cornwall.

Facilities

The large, central toilet block is modern and well equipped. Baby room and facilities for disabled visitors in the reception building. Laundry. Heated swimming and paddling pools. Games room. Information room with internet access. Play area and play field. Putting. Wild flower field with paths for dog walking. No kites allowed. Early and late arrivals area. Off site: Golf and riding 2 miles. Bicycle hire 4 miles. Beach and fishing 1 mile. Dogs are banned from the St Ives beaches in high season.

Open: Easter/1 April - end September.

Directions

Follow signs for St Ives and take A3074 to Carbis Bay. Site is signed on left opposite junction to Carbis Bay beach. Follow road for 150 yds, cross small crossroads and site is 250 m. on right. O.S.GR: SW52737. GPS: N50:11.234 W05:28.250

Charges 2007

Per unit incl. 2 persons	
and electricity	£ 13.50 - £ 23.00
with water and waste water	£ 14.50 - £ 25.00
extra person	£ 2.50 - £ 6.00
child (3-15 yrs)	£ 2.00 - £ 4.00
dog (max. 2)	£ 1.00 - £ 2.50

UK0490 Mullion Holiday Park

Helston TR12 7LJ (Cornwall)

Tel: 0870 4447774. Email: touring@weststarholidays.co.uk

see advertisement on page 109

For those who enjoy plenty of entertainment, both social and active in a holiday environment, Mullion would be a good choice. This holiday park is situated on the Lizard peninsula with its sandy beaches and coves. It has all the trimmings – indoor and outdoor pools, super play areas, clubs, bars and a wide range of nightly entertainment. Recent developments include a new look 'Stargate Club' and a 'village square' with a bandstand. These amenities form the core of the park and are well organised and managed. The touring area past the holiday homes has a more relaxed atmosphere and is set on natural heathland with clumps of bramble and gorse which provide breaks and recesses making for a more informal layout. Linked by a circular gravel road, all 160 pitches are numbered, 10 with hardstanding and 105 with electricity connections (16A). Land drainage could be a problem if there is heavy continuous rain. A resident warden is based at the touring section. Eurotents for hire.

Facilities

A central modern toilet block is fully equipped and includes a baby unit and bath. It is supplemented with additional 'portacabin' style facilities for high season. Washing machines. Large launderette in main complex. Freezer pack service. Large supermarket. Pub with family room, restaurant and takeaway (half board or breakfast options). Stargate Club with live shows and cabarets, big screen satellite TV. Excellent outdoor play areas (fenced). Toddlers' soft play area. Amusement arcade, bowling alley. Heated outdoor pool and paddling pool (26/5-8/9). Heated indoor fun pool with slide, both supervised. Sauna and solarium. Crazy golf, pitch and putt. Barbecue.

Open: 20 May - 9 September.

Directions

From Helston take A3083 for The Lizard and continue for 7 miles. Site on left immediately after the right turning for Mullion. O.S.GR: SW698185. GPS: N50:01.267 W05:12.883

Charges 2007

Per pitch	£ 12.75 - £ 27.50
with electricity	£ 15.75 - £ 30.50
super hook-up incl. electricity, TV point, fresh water	£ 17.25 - £ 32.00
dog (max 2)	£ 5.00

Half board or breakfast options available.

UK0480 Boscrege Caravan Park

Ashton, Helston TR13 9TG (Cornwall)

Tel: **01736 762231**. Email: **enquiries@caravanparkcornwall.com**

A pretty little site covering 12 acres and hidden deep in the countryside in an area of outstanding natural beauty (AONB), Boscrege will suit those who want a quiet peaceful base for their Cornish holiday. The main large touring field nestles at the foot of Tregonning Hill with its striking hill top cross, and has neatly cut grass with a gentle slope from the top. The pitches are generously spaced around the edge, backing on to hedging and leaving plenty of room in the centre for ball games. Three small, attractive paddock areas, two with caravan holiday homes (26 in total), the other for tourers, complete the total provision of 51 pitches, 28 with 10A electricity. A nature trail has been developed which will help you identify the birds which can be seen around the park. This park is a welcome retreat for couples and families with young children.

Facilities

The traditional style toilet block is showing its age somewhat but is fully equipped including a smaller basin for children (M/F). Dishwashing sinks, laundry sink, washing machine and dryer and microwave. Reception keeps emergency supplies. Two play areas for smaller children and central ball area. Amusement machines, pool table and TV room. New nature trail and dog-walking area. Off site: Godolphin House and garden. Whole of the tip of Cornwall easily accessible – the Lizard, Lands End. Nearest beach (Praa Sands) 2 miles. Fishing 1 mile. Golf and riding 2 miles. Bicycle hire and boat launching 5 miles.

Open: Easter/1 April - 31 October.

Directions

From Helston take A394 for Penzance. At top of Sithney Common Hill turn right just before Jet garage onto B3302 (Hayle) road. Pass Sithney General Stores on left and take next left for Carleen and Godolphin Cross. Continue on this road to Godolphin Cross village and turn left at side of Godolphin Arms signed Ashton. Proceed up hill bearing left at top until you see camp signs where road turns sharply left and go straight over into lane leading to Boscrege. O.S.GR: 593305.

Charges 2007

Per unit	£ 5.00 - £ 14.95
electricity	£ 2.95
extra small tent	£ 2.00
No charge for dogs (max. 3).	

UK0500 Trewince Farm Holiday Park

St Issey, Wadebridge PL27 7RL (Cornwall)

Tel: **01208 812830**

A well established and popular park, Trewince Farm is four miles from Padstow has been developed around a dairy farm with magnificent countryside views. Careful landscaping with flowering shrubs and bushes makes this an attractive setting. There are 35 caravan holiday homes discreetly terraced, some privately owned, some to let. Two touring areas on higher ground provide both hardstanding and level grass pitches with a sheltered tent area. Over half of the 120 touring pitches have electricity (10A) and 34 have water and drainage. The park's main feature is an excellent sheltered, walled and heated swimming pool with paddling pool, and paved sunbathing area. Farm rides and pasty suppers in the barn are organised in the high season.

Facilities

Two fully equipped, well maintained toilet blocks include washbasins in cabins, hair care rooms, dishwashing under cover and laundry rooms. Also children's room with bath (20p) and facilities for disabled visitors. Well stocked shop (all season) by reception. Fish and chip van calls twice weekly, a butcher once a week. Swimming pool. Play area. Games room. Crazy golf. New fishing lake. Off site: Riding 3 miles. Golf and bicycle hire 3.5 miles. Beach 4.5 miles. Pubs and restaurants in nearby village of St Issey. Camel Trail nearby for walking or cycling (goes to Padstow).

Open: 23 March - 31 October.

Directions

From Wadebridge follow A39 towards St Columb and pick up the A389 for Padstow. Site signed on left in 2 miles. Follow for short distance to park entrance on right. O.S. GR: SW937715.

Charges 2007

Per unit incl. 2 persons	£ 9.00 - £ 14.00
incl. electricity	£ 10.00 - £ 15.50
hardstanding, drainage and electricity	£ 11.00 - £ 16.00
extra person	£ 3.50
child (3-15 yrs)	£ 1.85 - £ 2.90

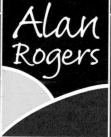

UK0530 Trethiggey Touring Park

Quintrell Downs, Newquay TR8 4LG (Cornwall)

Tel: **01637 877672**. Email: **enquiries@trethiggey.co.uk**

Trethiggey is a garden-like park with a ten month season, set some three miles back from the busy Newquay beaches and night life, with an enjoyable, informal style. With natural areas including a small wildlife pond and fishing lakes to enjoy, conservation is high on the agenda. There are 157 pitches, 110 with 16A electricity, some with hardstanding and a few also serviced with water and sewage connection. Some level pitches are formally arranged, with others more informal on gently sloping grass amidst 12 caravan holiday homes. A tent field is opened for the main season. A bistro and barbecue bar are very popular. Facilities maintain the informal touch with reception alongside the Trethiggey Trading Post which provides basic supplies, an off-licence and a small library. The attractive bistro-style café a terrace operates in school holidays for breakfasts and simple evening meals, with children catered for. At weekends in peak season the barbecue bar is an added attraction.

Facilities

Two fully equipped, heated shower blocks, one in traditional style. En-suite facilities for families and disabled visitors. Baby bathroom. Motorcaravan service point. Laundry facilities and wet suit wash. Games room at each toilet block with TV and amusement machines. Shop. Café and takeaway. Adventure play area and recreation field. Coarse fishing. WiFi access. Off site: Riding 2 miles. Golf and bicycle hire 3 miles. All the delights of Newquay within 3 miles with nightly minibus service (book in shop). Pub within walking distance.

Open: 2 March - 2 January.

Directions

Site is a few hundred yards south of roundabout where A393 crosses the A3058 at Quintrell Downs (beside the A3058). O.S. GR:SW846596. GPS: N50:23.810 W05:01.698

Charges 2007

Per person	£ 4.25 - £ 6.85
child (4-15 yrs)	£ 1.85 - £ 4.25
pitch incl. electricity	£ 3.20 - £ 6.00
dog	£ 1.80 - £ 2.50

UK0510 Summer Valley Touring Park

Shortlanesend, Truro TR4 9DW (Cornwall)

Tel: **01872 277878**. Email: **res@summervalley.co.uk**

Summer Valley is a quiet and mature, but very pleasant, small rural park suitable for visiting both the north and south coast of Cornwall. South facing, the park consists of a large well kept grass area with reception and facilities to one side. A tarmac road circles this and mature trees edge the whole site providing shelter but still allowing rural views. Caravans go on the central area which slopes gently and is divided down the centre with more mature trees and shrubs. The pitches around the perimeter area are semi-divided by shrubs and used more for tents. There is provision for 60 units of all types, but only 50 are used, 45 with electricity connections (10/16A). A pleasant little sitting room provides a small library and tourist information, useful for campers in inclement weather. A small, wooded area at the bottom of the park is ideal for dog walking. The owners live on site and provide a warm welcome. A Countryside Discovery site.

Facilities

A good quality, solid toilet block is well maintained with ladies to the left and men to the right, plus unisex showers. Washbasins in cabins and one shower/toilet en-suite per sex. Laundry facilities. Campers' rest room with library. Reception/licensed shop (basics) with freezer pack service (reduced hours out of main season). Gas supplies. Small play area hidden in a corner but part of the central area is left for ball games. Off site: Village of Shortlanesend within walking distance with post office and pub. Fishing 2.5 miles. Golf 3 miles. Riding 5 miles. Bicycle hire 2.5 miles. Perranporth beach 6 miles (dogs are allowed away from the village end).

Open: 31 March - 31 October.

Directions

From Truro take B3284 north, signed Perranporth. Follow for 2.5 miles and site is signed on left just through the village of Shortlanesend. O.S.GR: SW 800479.

Charges 2007

Per unit incl. 2 persons and electricity	£ 11.50 - £ 14.50
extra person	£ 1.50
child (3-16 yrs)	£ 1.00
dog	£ 0.25

45

UK1070 Woolacombe Bay Holiday Village

Sandy Lane, Woolacombe EX34 7AH (Devon)

Tel: **01271 870343**. Email: **goodtimes@woolacombe.com**

Woolacombe Bay Holiday Village, and its sister site Golden Coast Holiday Village nearby, are well known holiday parks providing a range of holiday accommodation from caravan holiday homes to luxury lodges, apartments and villas, with many on site amenities including pools, restaurants and bars, and providing a wide range of entertainment. A camping section at the Woolacombe Bay park caters for tents and trailer tents only, so touring visitors can enjoy all the activities and entertainment of both parks. Partly terraced out of the hillside and partly on the hill top with some existing pine trees but with many more trees planted for landscaping, the site has magnificent views out across the bay. Marked and numbered pitches have been provided on grass for 150 tents, 97 with electricity (10/16A). All should be level, having been terraced where necessary and they are connected by gravel roads. Some up and down walking is needed for the toilet block. A bus service (small charge) runs between the two parks, the third and fourth parks in the group (Twitchen Parc and Easewell Farm) and the beach during the main season, although there is a footpath to the beach from the site. The three larger parks have varied entertainment programmes and children's clubs and Woolacombe Bay also boasts a health spa and beauty suite.

Facilities

A smart central toilet block has excellent facilities, including en-suite shower and washrooms and separate toilets, baby facilities, and also a sauna and steam room. Separate dishwashing and laundry rooms. Two units for disabled visitors. Supermarket. Bars, restaurant and entertainment. Indoor (heated) and outdoor pools with flumes and slides. Sauna and gym. Beauty and holistic treatments. Wide range of sporting activities. Tennis. ATM. Dogs are welcome at Woolacombe Bay but not at Golden Coast. Off site: Fishing and riding 1 mile. Beach 1 mile.

Open: 11 May - 21 September (camping).

Directions

Take A361 Barnstaple - Ilfracombe road through Braunton. Turn left at Mullacott Cross roundabout towards Woolacombe then right towards Mortehoe. Now follow the camping signs by turning left and park is on the left. O.S.GR: SS469443.
GPS: N51:10.627 W04:11.479

Charges 2007

Per caravan or motorcaravan	
with all persons	£ 15.00 - £ 50.00
serviced pitch	£ 18.00 - £ 52.00
tent - person	£ 5.00 - £ 16.00
tent - child (5-15 yrs)	£ 2.50 - £ 8.00

UK1075 Golden Coast Holiday Village

Station Road, Woolacombe EX34 7HW (Devon)

Tel: **01271 870343**. Email: **goodtimes@woolacombe.com**

The Golden Coast Holiday Village is part of the Woolacombe Bay Holiday Parcs group that includes Woolacombe Bay, Twitchen Parc and the recently acquired Easewell Farm Holiday Parc. It predominantly comprises brick-built holiday accommodation, however, there are two small camping areas providing 91 pitches, 18 of which are fully serviced. The toilet block is adequate rather than good, and was quite clean at the time of our visit. Campers can enjoy an extensive program of entertainment for children and adults, and qualified nursery nurses run an OFSTED approved crèche. A shuttle bus runs between the four parks and to the beach several times a day (it costs £1 per person per holiday). A visit to the Old Mill Inn should not be missed; it serves bar meals, and has an excellent beer garden with adventure play area for the children. The range of amenities and facilities at this large park will suit families looking for a lively holiday filled with activities and entertainment.

Facilities

A fairly new building provides good facilities. Washing machine and dryer in the ladies' section. Large, well stocked supermarket, boutique and beauty salon. Indoor and outdoor swimming pools, outdoor flume, sauna and solarium. Bar, club, Old Mill Inn, restaurant and takeaway. Floodlit tennis court. Adventure playgrounds. Snooker. Games room. Soft play area and crèche. Ceramics studio. Learn to swim classes. 9-hole golf course. Indoor and outdoor bowls, ten-pin bowling complex. Fishing lake. Woodland walks. Shuttle bus. Off site: Woolacombe beach is about 2 miles, and for walkers there is the coastal path. Amenities at sister parks available to all visitors.

Open: 12 February - 2 January.

Directions

From Barnstaple, take A361 (signed Braunton and Ilfracombe). Turn left on B3343 (signed Woolacombe) and follow the road towards the town. The park is on the left near the top of the hill. O.S.GR: SS480435. GPS: N51:10.350 W04:10.366

Charges 2007

Per caravan or motorcaravan	£ 15.00 - £ 50.00
with services	£ 18.00 - £ 52.00
tent - per person	£ 5.00 - £ 16.00
tent - per child (5-15 yrs)	£ 2.50 - £ 8.00

UK0720 Easewell Farm Holiday Parc

Mortehoe, Woolacombe EX34 7EH (Devon)

Tel: **01271 870343**. Email: **goodtimes@woolacombe.com**

Near the sandy beaches of Woolacombe, Easewell Farm is now part of the Woolacombe Bay Holiday Parc group who own the Woolacombe Bay, Golden Coast and Twitchen parks. A shuttle bus runs between the four parks and to the beach (tickets £1 per person per holiday). This is a traditional style touring park which during the day is a hive of activity, but the nights are quiet and peaceful. The largest of the camping fields is sloping with superb views across the headland to the sea. Two smaller fields are terraced and one area has hardstandings. Together they provide 302 pitches, 124 with electricity connections (15A) and 20 also with TV and water connections. Also available are a lovely four bedroomed farmhouse (sleeping ten), a pretty two bedroomed cottage (five beds) and a caravan holiday home. The shop is well stocked (gas available), there is a takeaway and restaurant and an attractive bar with patio overlooking a small duck pond. The park has its own very well maintained 9-hole golf course which is popular and has reduced fees for campers. One of the huge redundant farm buildings has been put to excellent use: divided into three areas, it provides table tennis and pool, a skittle alley and two lanes of flat green bowling with changing rooms. Walks to the local village and along the coastal path are easy from the site and a bus to Ilfracombe and Barnstaple stops 100 yards from the entrance.

Facilities

The central toilet block has been regularly upgraded and can be heated. Two washbasins in the ladies have hoses for hair washing, controllable showers (no dividers). Small area with baby bath facilities. Dishwashing sinks under cover. Laundry. These facilities are arranged around the farmhouse area and include a very well equipped unit for disabled people with everything in one large room including a hairdryer. Motorcaravan service point. Shop. Bar. Golf. Small heated indoor swimming pool is well used, as are games and TV rooms. Fenced play area with bark base. Indoor skittle alley, bowls, and table tennis. In high season only one dog per pitch is allowed. Off site: Fishing or riding 1 mile, bicycle hire 3 miles. Tarka Trail for walking and riding. Boat trips to Lundy Island.

Open: Easter - end October.

Directions

From Barnstaple, take A361 Ilfracombe road through Braunton. Turn left at Mullacott Cross roundabout on B3343 to Woolacombe, turning right after 2-3 miles to Mortehoe. Park is on right before village. O.S.GR: SS465455. GPS: N51:11.118 W04:11.936

Charges 2007

Per caravan or motorcaravan	£ 15.00 - £ 50.00
with services	£ 18.00 - £ 52.00
tent - person	£ 5.00 - £ 16.00
tent - child (5-15 yrs)	£ 2.50 - £ 8.00

UK0730 Twitchen Parc

Mortehoe, Woolacombe EX34 7ES (Devon)

Tel: **01271 870848**. Email: **goodtimes@woolacombe.com**

Set in the grounds of an attractive Edwardian country house, Twitchen Parc is owned by Woolacombe Bay Holiday Parcs. Its main concern lies in holiday caravans and apartments, although it also provides marked pitches, all for touring units, at the top of the park, with some views over the rolling hills to the sea. With a more recently developed touring field, they include 228 pitches with 16A electricity, many with tarmac hardstanding (not always level), mostly arranged around oval access roads in hedged areas. Further non-electric pitches are behind in two open, unmarked fields which are sloping (blocks are thoughtfully provided, stored in neat wooden boxes next to water points). A smart, modern entertainment complex incorporates a licensed club and family lounge with snacks, a restaurant, teenage disco room, cartoon lounge, outdoor pool and smart indoor pool complex. Twitchen is very popular for families with children. If they become bored, there are always the excellent beaches nearby with a footpath down to the sea.

Facilities

There are two toilet blocks. Dishwashing and laundry facilities at each block plus a good modern launderette at the central complex. Motorcaravan service point. Shop and takeaway. Club, bars, restaurant and entertainment for adults and children, day and evening. OFSTED approved creche for children (charge). Outdoor pool (heated mid May - mid Sept). Attractive indoor pool with sauna, paddling pool, fountain and a viewing area. Putting green. Games rooms for table tennis, pool and arcade games. Good adventure play area. ATM. American motorhomes are accepted (up to 30 ft). Off site: Beach 1 mile. Golf 1 mile. Fishing, riding and bicycle hire 2 miles.

Open: Easter- end October.

Directions

From Barnstaple take A361 towards Ilfracombe and through Braunton. Turn left at Mullacott Cross roundabout towards Woolacombe and then right towards Mortehoe. Park is on the left before village. O.S.GR: SS465451. GPS: N51:11.081 W04:11.862

Charges 2007

Per caravan or motorcaravan	£ 15.00 - £ 50.00
with services	£ 18.00 - £ 52.00
tent - person	£ 5.00 - £ 16.00
tent - child (5-15 yrs)	£ 2.50 - £ 8.00
Special offers available.	

UK0690 Stowford Farm Meadows

Berry Down, Combe Martin, Ilfracombe EX34 0PW (Devon)

Tel: **01271 882476**. Email: **enquiries@stowford.co.uk**

Stowford Farm is a friendly, family park set in 500 acres of the rolling North Devon countryside, available for recreation and walking, yet within easy reach of five local beaches. The touring park and its facilities have been developed in the fields and farm buildings surrounding the attractive old farmhouse and provide a village like centre with a comfortable spacious feel. There are over 710 pitches (including 238 used by seasonal units) on five slightly sloping meadows separated by Devon hedges of beech and ash. Unseparated, the numbered and marked pitches, some with hardstanding, are accessed by tarmac or hardcore roads, most have electricity (10/16A) and there are well placed water points. The Old Stable Bar offers entertainment in high season including barn dances, discos, karaoke and other musical evenings. There is also much for children to do, from the indoor heated pool and under cover mini-zoo (Petorama) where they can handle many sorts of animals (on payment), to the wide range of organised activities on offer. In low season some facilities may only open for limited hours. Stowford also provides plenty to keep the whole family occupied without leaving the park, including woodland walks and horse riding from the park's own stables. However, it is also a good base for exploring the North Devon coast and Exmoor. Some very smart wooden lodges with wonderful views are now being built for sale.

Facilities

Five identical toilet blocks, each looked after by resident wardens, are fully equipped and provide good, functional facilities, each block with laundry facilities and dishwashing sinks under cover. The newest block (in field 5) has under-floor heating and includes facilities for disabled visitors. Extra good facilities for disabled visitors and private family washrooms are beside reception. Well stocked shop (with holiday goods and gas). Good value takeaway with restaurant area. Bars and entertainment in season. Swimming pool (22 x 10 m; heated Easter - Oct) at a small charge (£1.25). Riding. 18-hole pitch and putt. Crazy golf. Bicycle hire. 'Kiddies kar' track (all charged). Games room. Large play area. Games and activities organised in high season. ATM. Woodland walks. Dogs welcome in three sections (max. 2 per pitch). Summer parking and winter caravan storage. Caravan workshop, sales accessories and repair centre. Off site: Fishing and boat launching 4 miles.

Open: All year.

Directions

From Barnstaple take A39 towards Lynton. After 1 mile turn left on B3230. Turn right at garage on A3123 and park is 1.5 miles on the right. O.S.GR: SS565438. GPS: N51:10.499 W04:03.285

Charges 2007

Per unit and car incl. 2 persons and electricity	£ 8.50 - £ 24.50
extra person	free - £ 4.00
child (5-12 yrs)	free - £ 2.00
dog	£ 1.50 - £ 2.50

Low and mid season discounts for over 50s.

UK0725 Warcombe Farm Camping Park

Station Road, Mortehoe EX34 7EJ (Devon)

Tel: **01271 870690**. Email: **info@warcombefarm.co.uk**

This park is set in a quiet position on a hill above Woolacombe. It is a large, fairly open site on gently sloping land. There are 250 level or fairly level pitches, some secluded, others extra large with hardstanding and with electricity, and others fully serviced. Shrubs and trees help to divide some of the pitches. Two hardstanding pitches are designed to provide facilities and access for disabled campers. In total, 160 pitches have electricity hook ups (16A). The site has panoramic views across to the sea and at its centre has a fully fenced lovely well kept lake that is a haven for wildlife. Fishing is permitted in the lake with free lessons sometimes available for those who want to learn. An adjoining, newly planted wood of 14 acres is available for walks and dog walking. There is an adventure playground for children under 14 and space for ball games. The reception area also acts as a small shop with basics including bread and milk, also providing internet access.

Facilities

Two modern toilet blocks are spotlessly clean, with free preset showers. En-suite facilities in one block. Family bathrooms and facilities for disabled visitors (coded locks). Laundry with washing machines, dryers and iron. Motorcaravan services. Shop. Takeaway (w/ends only in low season). Play area. Fishing. Torches useful. Off site: Woolacombe beach is 1.5 miles. Public footpaths and cycle trails (the Tarka Trail is on the doorstep). Riding and golf 1 miles. Bicycle hire 4 miles.

Open: 15 March - 31 October.

Directions

Approaching from Barnstaple on A361 follow signs for Ilfracombe. At Mullacott Cross (10 miles from Barnstaple) turn left and follow B3343 for Woolacombe. After 1.8 miles turn right for Mortehoe. Park is the first on the right in 500 yards. O.S.GR: SS477457.

Charges 2007

Per unit incl. 2 adults, 2 children	£ 9.00 - £ 23.00
incl. electricity	£ 11.00 - £ 26.00
extra person	£ 3.00
child	£ 1.50

UK0680 Channel View Caravan & Camping Park

Manor Farm, Barbrook, Lynton EX35 6LD (Devon)

Tel: **01598 753349**. Email: **relax@channel-view.co.uk**

Channel View is a quiet, family run park situated in a sunny, south-facing position overlooking Lynton and Lynmouth. The gently sloping ground provides fairly level pitches which are mostly on hardstandings. The park is divided into two areas, an open area that is sheltered by bushes and trees and one that is more exposed but has views. There are 15 serviced pitches with electricity, water and a drain, and 60 with electricity (16A). The grass is well cared for and there is site lighting, although a torch would be useful. There is a café on the site that also offers takeaways. A small shop is located with reception and is well stocked. There is a freezer for ice packs, a public telephone and a children's play area. The Country Inn pub is nearby with bar food available.

Facilities

The modern and very clean toilet and shower block is partly tiled. Showers are free (here are three steps down to the ladies showers from the toilets). Baby changing and family washroom. Facilities for disabled visitors (Radar key). Laundry with washing machines, dryers and iron. Café. Small shop. Play area. Off site: Lynton and Lynmouth, Exmoor and the Doone Valley are nearby. Many walks can be started from the site. Riding 1 mile. Fishing 1 mile. Golf 15 miles. Beach 2 miles.

Open: 15 March - 15 November.

Directions

Take the A399 from Ilfracombe. Turn left on the A39 and continue past the turn for Lynton to site on the left after 2 miles. It is not advisable to approach from Lynton and Lynmouth. O.S.GR: 724482.

Charges 2007

Per unit incl. 2 persons	£ 10.00 - £ 15.00
incl. electricity	£ 12.00 - £ 14.00
extra person	£ 3.00 - £ 4.00
child (6-16 yrs)	£ 1.00 - £ 3.00

UK0700 Greenacres Touring Caravan Park

Bratton Fleming, Barnstaple EX31 4SG (Devon)

Tel: **01598 763334**

A neat, compact, rural park on the edge of Exmoor, Greenacres is managed and run alongside, but separately from, the farm owned by the family. Drive through the farm access to the park (clearly signed) – you will need to go back and call at the house to book in. No tents are taken. The site has 30 very large, well drained pitches (all with 16A electric hook-ups) with connecting gravel paths to the road – in theory you can get to your unit without stepping on the grass. The top area is level, the lower part next to the beech woods is semi-terraced to provide six hardstandings and some hedged places. There are marvellous views outside the beech hedge that shelters the site. To the west of Exmoor, the park is very suitable for the coast at Ilfracombe and Combe Martin, or for exploring the moor. The family has opened up a woodland walk through newly planted trees and across the fields to a secluded valley picnic area beside a stream to take advantage of the marvellous views and surroundings. The West Country cycle way passes within a mile of the park and the area is the setting for the classic novel, 'Lorna Doone'.

Facilities

The neat, clean toilet block with showers (1M, 1F) on payment (20p). Units for disabled visitors (and general use in peak times). Laundry room, with sink, spin dryer, iron and board, and dishwashing room. Washing lines provided. Gas supplies. Tourist information kiosk. Area for children with football and volleyball nets and swings, separated by a Devon bank from the 2 acre dog exercise field. Recycling centre. Off site: Fishing 3 miles. Riding 6 miles. Golf 12 miles. Pubs, restaurants and takeaways within 3 mile radius.

Open: Easter/1 April - 31 October.

Directions

From North Devon link road (M5, exit 27) turn north at South Molton onto A399. Continue for 9 miles, past turning for Exmoor Steam Centre and on to Stowford Cross. Turn left towards Exmoor Zoological Park and Greenacres Farm is on the left. O.S.GR: SS660404. GPS: N51:08.858 W03:55.051

Charges 2007

Per unit incl. 2 persons	£ 5.50 - £ 9.25
incl. electricity	£ 7.75 - £ 11.00
extra person	£ 1.50 - £ 2.00
child (under 7 yrs)	free

No credit cards.

UK0710 Hidden Valley Touring & Camping Park

West Down, Ilfracombe EX34 8NU (Devon)

Tel: **01271 813837**. Email: **relax@hiddenvalleypark.com**

The owners, Martin and Dawn Fletcher, run this aptly named award-winning, family park to high standards. In a sheltered valley setting between Barnstaple and Ilfracombe beside a small stream and lake (with ducks), it is most attractive and is also convenient for several resorts, beaches and the surrounding countryside. The original part of the park offers some 74 level pitches of good size on three sheltered terraces. All have hardstanding, electricity hook-ups (16A) and free TV connections (leads for hire), with a water point between each pitch. Kingfisher Meadow, a little way from the main facilities and reached by a tarmac road, provides a further 60 pitches entirely on grass (so suitable for campers with tents), all with electricity, water, waste water and TV hook-ups. Two good adventure play areas have wooden equipment and safe bark surfaces (one near a fast flowing stream which is fenced). There is a well-stocked shop with off-licence, a coffee shop, bar with good value food three times a week (high season) including takeaway, plus a games room. Essentially this is a park for those seeking good quality facilities in very attractive, natural surroundings, without too many man-made distractions – apart from some traffic noise during day time. It provides a relaxed setting with woodland walks direct from the site.

Facilities

Two modern toilet blocks (one for each area, one heated) are tiled and have non-slip floors. Some washbasins in cubicles, some en-suite with toilets in the Kingfisher Meadow block. Bathroom (tokens). Baby room. Laundry facilities including washing machine, dryer and iron. Dishwashing sinks under cover. Complete facilities for people with disabilities. Supplementary clean 'portacabin' style facilities in the original area. Motorcaravan service facilities. Gas supplies. Shop, bar and takeaway. Coffee shop open to the public. Play areas. Up to two dogs are accepted (otherwise by prior arrangement). Caravan storage. Off site: Fishing or golf 2 miles. Bicycle hire 4 miles. Riding 5 miles. Beach 5 miles.

Open: All year.

Directions

Park is on A361 Barnstaple - Ilfracombe road, 3.5 miles after Braunton. O.S.GR: SS499408. GPS: N51:08.792 W04:08.733

Charges 2007

Per unit incl. 2 persons	£ 11.00 - £ 28.00
extra person	£ 3.00 - £ 4.00
child (3-15 yrs)	£ 1.00 - £ 3.00
dog	£ 0.50 - £ 2.00

Discounts for over 50s.
Camping Cheques accepted.

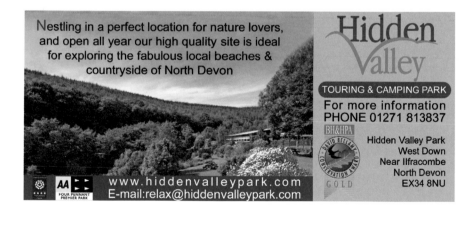

53

UK0735 Woolacombe Sands Holiday Park

Beach Road, Woolacombe EX34 7AF (Devon)

Tel: **01271 870569**. Email: **lifesabeach@woolacombe-sands.co.uk**

With sea views and within walking distance of Woolacombe's lovely sandy beach, this family park has been terraced out of the valley side as you drop down into the village. Apart from its smart entrance, it has been left natural. The pond and stream at the bottom are almost hidden with gated access to the National Trust fields across the valley. The 200 terraced level grass pitches all with 10A electricity are accessed by gravel roads with some good up and down walking needed to the toilet blocks (probably not the best environment for disabled people). Some 50 mobile homes and 14 bungalows are in the more central area, and tents tend to be placed on the bottom terraces. The park boasts both indoor and outdoor pools (accessed by code) with a full time attendant. Evenings see Woolly Bear emerge from his 'shack' to entertain children, with adult family entertainment later. A good plus factor is the fact that all facilities open when the site opens. A useful path leads from the site to the beach via the car park and the walk is said to take 15 minutes.

Facilities

Four basic toilet blocks with good hot water are spread amongst the terraces. The newer shower block has separate toilets opposite. Shop (open 07.00 - 22.00). Self-service food bar providing good value meals and breakfast (main season and B.Hs). Two bars and full entertainment programme. Heated indoor and outdoor pools both with paddling pool areas. Fenced play area on bark with plenty of equipment'. Ball area with nets. Crazy golf. 'Kingpin' bowling Off site: Beach 15 minutes walk or 0.5 miles. Riding next door. Golf, bicycle hire and freshwater fishing 0.5 miles.

Open: 1 April - 1 November.

Directions

Follow A361 from Barnstaple through Braunton towards Ilfracombe. At Mullacott Cross roundabout turn left for Woolacombe (B3343). Site clearly signed on left as you go down the hill into the village. O.S.GR: SS468436. GPS: N51:10.287 W04:11.510

Charges 2007

Per person (incl. electricity)	£ 5.00 - £ 15.00
child (5-16 yrs)	£ 2.50 - £ 7.50
dog	£ 5.00

UK0750 Minnows Touring Caravan Park

Sampford Peverell, Tiverton EX16 7EN (Devon)

Tel: **01884 821770**

Minnows is an attractive, neat small park with views across the Devon countryside, separated from the Grand Western canal by hedging. Easily accessible from the M5, it is suitable as an ideal touring centre for Devon and Somerset, for cycling or walking, or simply for breaking a long journey. A small, neat park, open for nine months of the year, it provides 45 level pitches all with 16A electricity. Of these, 35 are all weather (grass and gravel). A further 3.5 acres have been added to the park providing space for more and larger pitches, a tent area, a playground and a large field for ball games, etc. The village of Sampford Peverell, with pub and farm shop, is only a half mile walk via the towpath, with Tiverton 7.5 miles. In fact, there are 12 miles of level walking on the towpath or one can take a trip on a horse-drawn barge. The site is also on the Sustran cycle route (route 3). Tiverton Parkway station (BR) is one mile and buses run from the village to Tiverton. Coarse fishing permits for the canal are available from reception. A Caravan Club affiliated site, non-members are also very welcome. There could be some road noise from the adjacent A361.

Facilities

The heated toilet block has been refurbished with tiled floors, new pressurised showers and 2 cubicles for ladies. It is clean and comfortable with all modern facilities and constant hot water. Facilities for disabled visitors and babies. Laundry with washing machine, dryer and ironing. Motorcaravan service point. Gas supplies. Newspaper delivery arranged. Play area. Bicycle hire (delivery to site). American RVs accepted (up to 38 ft), advance booking necessary. All year caravan storage. Site gates closed 21.00 and locked 23.00 - 7.30. Off site: Boat slipway and golf driving range 400 yds, full course 4 miles. Riding 6 miles.

Open: 6 March - 6 November.

Directions

From M5 junction 27 take A361 signed Tiverton. After 600 yds take first exit signed Sampford Peverell. After 200 yds. turn right at roundabout and cross bridge over A361 to second roundabout. Go straight ahead and park is immediately ahead. From North Devon on A361 go to M5 junction 27 and return back up the A361 as above. O.S.GR: ST042148. GPS: N50:55.501 W03:21.871

Charges guide

Per person	£ 3.50 - £ 5.00
child (5-16 yrs)	£ 1.30 - £ 2.00
pitch	£ 4.00 - £ 7.00
Credit cards accepted for £10 or more.	

UK0760 Barley Meadow Camping & Caravan Park

Crockernwell, Exeter EX6 6NR (Devon)

Tel: **01647 281629**. Email: **welcome@barleymeadow.com**

This peaceful little park is located on the northern edge of Dartmoor with easy access from the A30. It is sheltered from the weather by good hedging and, although not always visible from the pitches, there are open views across the moorland to the south. The site would be a suitable base for visiting Exeter, Okehampton and Plymouth, hiking over the moors, or just enjoying the local area. The 60 pitches are mostly on level grass, well spaced, most with hardstandings (some taken by seasonal units), and 36 electric hook-ups. Shrubs have now been planted to divide the pitches.

Facilities

The single heated toilet block is well maintained and provides all facilities including a well equipped room for disabled campers and babies. Laundry. Small shop. Games room with pool table and TV. Playground. Small library and information chalet. Only small American RVs (up to 30 ft.) accepted. Off site: Fishing 1 mile (river) or 2 miles (lake). Golf 2.5 miles. Riding 2 miles.

Open: 15 March - 15 November.

Directions

From M5 exit 31, take A30 towards Okehampton. After 10 miles turn left towards Cheriton Bishop. After 0.5 miles pass through village, and continue for 1 mile towards Crockernwell to site.
O.S.GR: SH742924. GPS: N50:43.052 W03:46.995

Charges 2007

Per unit incl. 2 persons	£ 10.00 - £ 14.00
child (3-15 yrs)	£ 1.50

UK0790 Harford Bridge Holiday Park

Peter Tavy, Tavistock PL19 9LS (Devon)

Tel: **01822 810349**. Email: **enquiry@harfordbridge.co.uk**

Harford Bridge has an interesting history – originally the Wheal Union tin mine until 1850, then used as a farm campsite from 1930 and taken over by the Royal Engineers in 1939. It is now a quiet, rural, mature park inside the Dartmoor National Park. It is bounded by the River Tavy on one side and the lane from the main road to the village of Peter Tavy on the other, with Harford Bridge, a classic granite moorland bridge, at the corner. With 16.5 acres, the park provides 120 touring pitches well spaced on a level grassy meadow with some shade from mature trees and others recently planted; 47 pitches have electrical hook-ups and 10 have 'multi-services', 5 with hardstanding. Out of season or by booking in advance you may get one of the delightful spots bordering the river (these are without electricity). Some holiday caravans and chalets are neatly landscaped in their own area. While the river (unfenced) will inevitably mesmerise youngsters, a super central adventure play area on a hilly tree knoll will claim them. In early summer there are chicks to watch (Mr Williamson's hobby) and the park ducks are a feature. To celebrate the park's anniversary, a wonderful wild flower habitat has been created. New this year: seven willow structures resembling wig-wam shaped tents on the main entrance shrub bed.

Facilities

The single toilet block is older in style but fully equipped and well kept, with free hot water and showers all year. Facilities for disabled visitors double for babies. Good launderette and drying room. Freezer. Motorcaravan service point. Games room. TV room. Play area. Tennis (free). Two barbecue areas. Fly fishing (by licence, £3 p/day, £10 p/week). Off site: Bicycle hire, riding and golf, all within 2.5 miles. West Devon cycle way adjacent.

Open: All year.

Directions

Two miles north of Tavistock, off A386 Tavistock - Okehampton road, take the road to Peter Tavy.
O.S.GR: SX504768. GPS: N50:34.278 W04:06.840

Charges 2007

Per unit incl. 2 persons	£ 9.50 - £ 14.50
with electricity	£ 12.50 - £ 16.50
with services	£ 14.00 - £ 18.00

Less 10% for stays over 7 days (not electricity).

UK0800 Higher Longford Caravan Park

Moorshop, Tavistock PL19 9LQ (Devon)

Tel: 01822 613360. Email: stay@higherlongford.co.uk

This attractive well organised, family run park is situated within the Dartmoor National Park boundaries with views up to the higher slopes of the moor. A neat, sheltered field provides 40 level pitches arranged on each side of a circular access road, with three smaller touring areas for a further 12 units, a small terraced camping field with good views and a seasonal camping field for a further 40. Facilities include 65 electrical hook-ups (16A), several multi-serviced pitches and an area of hardstanding for motorcaravans in poor weather. Some attractive converted cottages form a courtyard area with the farmhouse and reception. Within the 14th century farmhouse is a small licensed shop with gas and some farm produce, and a takeaway including breakfast items and fresh bread. It adjoins a pleasant, cosy campers' lounge with pool table and TV which is open all day. Higher Longford is an ideal centre for touring Dartmoor, either by car, on foot, or astride a local pony (riding stables nearby). Plymouth and the cross-channel ferries are a 30 minute drive, Tavistock is 3 miles, with a good market and Goose Fair in October.

Facilities

A heated toilet block provides excellent full en-suite facilities (amongst the best we've seen) plus extra toilets and washbasins. Family bathroom and baby changing. Full laundry facilities. Indoor dishwashing sinks. Motorcaravan services. Ice block service. Shop and takeaway (hours limited in winter). Campers' lounge with pool and TV. Large recreation field with adventure play area in centre. Nature area. Adventure trail for children and walks. Caravan storage. Off site: Bus service outside park. Game or coarse fishing 3 miles, Tavistock golf course 1 mile. Bicycle hire 2.5 miles. Riding 5 miles. Beach 15 miles.

Open: All year.

Directions

Park is clearly signed from the B3357 Princetown road, 2 miles from Tavistock. O.S.GR: SX520747. GPS: N50:33.210 W04:05.623

Charges 2007

Per person	£ 3.50 - £ 6.00
child (5-16 yrs)	£ 1.10 - £ 3.00
pitch incl. electricity	£ 4.50 - £ 10.00
tent pitch	£ 5.50 - £ 7.00

Higher Longford

"nestled in the foothills of Dartmoor"

01822 613360

Book online at
www.higherlongford.co.uk

• Moorshop • Tavistock • Devon • PL19 9LQ

UK0805 Woodovis Park

Woodovis House, Gulworthy, Tavistock PL19 8NY (Devon)

Tel: 01822 832968. Email: info@woodovis.com

Woodovis Park is set in the grounds of Woodovis House, owned in the 19th century by a mine captain in the days when the valley had a thriving copper mining industry. It nestles in a sheltered wooded position covering 14 acres, by the edge of the Tamar Valley (a designated AONB) on the border of Devon and Cornwall. John and Dorothy Lewis have been running Woodovis Park since 1999, helped by their very welcoming staff. There are 50 good sized pitches, all with 10A electricity and 19 with hardstanding. Split over two fields, most are on level, neatly mown grass, some are gently sloping. Landscaped in between are 35 caravan holiday homes, 20 privately owned and 18 for hire. The whole area is sheltered by thick hedges and woodland but in places you can see across the valley to Cornwall. An indoor heated pool complete with spa pool and sauna are a welcome attraction, as are the freshly baked morning croissants or bread ordered the night before at reception. The approach to the site is down a tree lined lane with passing places. This is a peaceful spot with some nice touches, run to a very high standard. A member of the Best of British group.

Facilities

A purpose built, modern toilet block is fully equipped. Bathroom (coin operated) could be used by disabled people or for babies. Family cubicles. Toilet for disabled visitors at the pool. Fully equipped laundry. Motorcaravan service point. Shop. Indoor heated pool. Good games room. Fenced play area. Minigolf. Off site: Pub within walking distance. Fishing 1.5 miles. Golf, riding and bicycle hire 3 miles. Tavistock 4 miles.

Open: 15 March - 1 November.

Directions

From Tavistock follow A390 for Liskeard. After 3 miles turn right at Gulworthy roundabout signed Chipshop, Lamerton and Caravan Park. After 1 mile entrance is signed on left. O.S.GR: SX431743. GPS: N50:32.932 W04:12.951

Charges 2007

Per person (over 5 yrs)	£ 5.00
pitch incl. electricity	£ 5.00 - £ 12.50
awning	£ 2.00

UK0802 Langstone Manor Holiday Park

Moortown, Tavistock PL19 9JZ (Devon)

Tel: **01822 613371**. Email: **web@langstone-manor.co.uk**

Situated on the southwest edge of Dartmoor, this holiday park has been developed in the grounds of the old Langstone Manor house. The touring pitches are tucked into various garden areas with mature trees and flowering shrubs, or in the walled garden area with views over the moor. In all there are 42 level grass pitches which vary in size (20 with 16A electricity). Although they are developing a new camping area. You pass through a number of holiday caravans on the way to reception and the touring pitches where you will also find some holiday cottages and flats for rent. The 'pièce de resistance' is the unexpected traditional bar and restaurant in the Manor House, complete with a terrace that catches the evening sun (try the 'jail ale' made in Princetown). Open in high season and on demand in low season it has an open fire (if needed). Approaching over a short section of the moor, you realise how well Langstone Manor is situated to explore Dartmoor by foot, by car or on bike (the park has direct access). The market town of Tavistock is 3 miles away and there is a wealth of National Trust Houses and Gardens to visit nearby.

Facilities

The toilet block is set to one side of the walled garden area, fully equipped and well maintained. Showers on payment (20p tokens from reception or bar). Fully equipped laundry room and covered dishwashing facilities. Changing mat for babies in the ladies. Basic supplies kept in reception (order bread the day before). Bar/restaurant. Play area. Off site: Leisure centre and pool 2 miles. Golf 1 mile. Fishing 2 miles. Bicycle hire 3 miles. Boat Launching 10 miles. Sailing 15 miles.

Open: 15 March - 29 October.

Directions

From Tavistock take B3357 Princetown road. After about 2 miles turn right at crossroads (site signed). Pass over cattle grid onto the moor and follow site signs. O.S.GR: SX524738.
GPS: N50:32.694 W04:05.050

Charges 2007

Per unit incl. 2 persons	£ 10.00 - £ 12.00
electricity	£ 2.00
child	£ 2.00 - £ 3.00
awning	£ 1.00 - £ 1.50

UK0810 Riverside Caravan Park

Leigham Manor Drive, Marsh Mills, Plymouth PL6 8LL (Devon)

Tel: **01752 344122**. Email: **info@riversidecaravanpark.com**

As you leave the A38 for Plymouth and negotiate the Marsh Mills roundabout you can have no idea that there is a lush green touring park tucked away from the modern, out-of-town shopping units in a quiet green valley. Twenty seven years ago it was a corn field but, with careful development by its owner, it now provides a welcome oasis from which to explore Dartmoor or even to overnight quietly before catching the ferry to France. The wooded valley sides give way to level grass where the trees and shrubs planted all those years ago have matured to give a park-like feel. The River Plym runs down one side of the site but it is carefully fenced. There are 232 pitches for caravans or motorcaravans, 150 of which have electricity (10A) and 60 are on hardstanding – especially useful as the site is open all year round. There is further provision for 60 tents. Hidden behind a high, evergreen hedge is an attractive pool. A play area is nearby and a pleasant restaurant with bar and games room provide welcome facilities and entertainment in high season.

Facilities

Three modern, fully equipped toilet blocks include cubicles with toilets and washbasins. Laundry room. Dishwashing room. Motorcaravan service point. Gas supplies. Basics are kept in reception (more in high season). Bar, restaurant and takeaway (B.Hs and high season). Heated swimming pool and children's pool. Games room with TV. Play area. Off site: Fishing possible in River Plym. Sea fishing 3.5 miles. Golf and riding 5 miles. Bicycle hire 3.5 miles. Beach 10 miles. Dry ski slope and supermarket near. Bus stop 10 minutes.

Open: All year.

Directions

From the A38 Marsh Mills roundabout for Plymouth take the third exit. After a few yards turn left following caravan signs, then right alongside the River Plym to the park. O.S.GR: SX518576.
GPS: N50:23.890 W04:05.240

Charges 2007

Per person	£ 3.25 - £ 5.50
child (3-10 yrs)	£ 1.75 - £ 2.50
pitch incl. electricity	£ 5.50 - £ 7.50
tent pitch	£ 3.50 - £ 6.50

UK0820 Moor View Touring Park

California Cross, Modbury PL21 0SG (Devon)

Tel: **01548 821485**. Email: **info@moorviewtouringpark.co.uk**

Moor View has a gently sloping position with terraced, individual, fairly level grass pitches with marvellous views across to the Dartmoor Tors. It provides 68 pitches of varying size, connected by hardcore roads. All are on hardstanding with 10A electricity, water and drainage. Bushes and shrubs planted between the pitches are growing well giving the park a more mature feel. A two acre field provides space for the odd rally. The amenities have been designed in one block near the entrance, not too far from the furthest pitches. The block includes reception with a shop stocking fresh local produce and some camping accessories. Burgh Island and Bigbury Bay are nearby, Dartmoor is within striking distance. This is a park in a lovely corner of Devon, run personally by the enthusiastic owners, Edward and Liz Corwood. A member of the Countryside Discovery group and an 'adults only' park.

Facilities

Traditional style, heated toilet facilities have access from a courtyard area and are kept clean, providing all necessary facilities including a laundry room and sink, and covered dishwashing sinks. Shop. Takeaway in season (to order, 18.30 - 20.30). TV room. Off site: Golf 5 miles, riding and fishing 6 miles. A local country pub is within walking distance, the small town of Modbury is 3 miles.

Open: All year.

Directions

On the A38 from Exeter, pass exit for A385 (Totnes) and continue for a further 2 miles. Just past Woodpecker Inn leave the A38 at Wrangaton Cross, signed Ermington, Modbury (site signed from here). Turn left and follow straight on at crossroads (Kitterford Cross) signed Modbury, Loddiswell, Kingsbridge for 3 miles to California Cross. Leave garage on left and follow towards Modbury (B3207). Park is 0.5 miles on left. O.S.GR: SX705533.

Charges 2008

Per unit incl. 2 persons and electricity	£ 10.85 - £ 18.85
extra person	£ 3.85 - £ 4.85

UK0826 Higher Rew Caravan & Camping Park

Malborough, Kingsbridge TQ7 3BW (Devon)

Tel: **01548 842681**. Email: **enquiries@higherrew.co.uk**

The Squire family have developed this rural park on their farm which is located about a mile up a single track lane from South Sands, near Salcombe. South Sands is ideal for boating, sailing and windsurfing as well as providing safe bathing. A ferry runs to Salcombe town. The five miles of estuary which stretches between Salcombe and Kingsbridge is a local nature reserve famed for its unique marine habitats and its bird watching opportunities. You can travel the length of it by the 'Rivermaid' ferry. The rural views from the park are amazing but you have to climb a little higher to see the sea. The coastal path can be reached by footpaths from the park. There used to be a dairy herd on the farm but the buildings are now used to provide camping facilities which include a covered play area for children under 11 years. For older children there is a play barn with table tennis, skittle alley and a pool table. A tennis court is available to hire. A large, sloping, open field has been terraced to provide 90 grass pitches, 60 of which have 16A electricity.

Facilities

Toilet facilities have been completley refurbished to a high standard. Unisex showers are in a separate, light and airy part with the laundry and dishwashing sinks. Showers are metered (20p for 4 minutes). Freezer for ice packs. Tourist information. Reception with shop for basics and some camping bits (open main season). Play area. Tennis court. Skittle alley. Caravan storage. Off site: Beach, fishing and sailing 1 mile. Boat launching 3 miles. Riding 5 miles. Golf 4-5 miles.

Open: Easter - October half term

Directions

Park is clearly signed from Malborough. Follow signs to Soar for 1 mile. Turn left at Rew Cross, then first right for Higher Rew. Take care with single track roads, although there are always plenty of passing places. O.S.GR: SX73381.

Charges 2007

Per unit incl. 2 persons	£ 5.00 - £ 14.00
extra person	£ 2.00 - £ 3.00
child (under 2 yrs)	free
child (2-17 yrs)	free - £ 1.00
electricity	£ 2.00

No credit cards.

UK0825 Karrageen Caravan & Camping Park

Bolberry, Malborough, Kingsbridge TQ7 3EN (Devon)

Tel: **01548 561230**. Email: **phil@karrageen.co.uk**

Karrageen is to be found in a wonderful area of Devon, near Kingsbridge and Salcombe, with a mixture of rolling countryside, hidden coves, cliff tops and sandy beaches. You can walk, sail, surf or just relax and enjoy the wonderful scenery. This is a small family park run personally by the Higgin family situated in the hamlet of Bolberry, one mile up the lane from Hope Cove. The family home across the road from the site provides reception, a licensed shop and a takeaway facility which includes vegetarian, Indian or Oriental options. The main camping field slopes gently with either sea or rural views. It has been terraced with hedging to provide 70 grassy pitches with 54 electricity connections (10A). There are some 20 places specifically designed for touring caravans. Six caravan holiday homes to let complete the provision in a separate field which houses the modern toilet block.

Facilities

The attractively decorated toilet block includes two curtained washbasins for privacy. En-suite provision for disabled visitors doubles as a family shower room. Parent and baby room. Laundry room. Separate dishwashing (water metered as it is spring water - 20p). Freezer for ice packs. Shop including some basic camping equipment. Fresh baguettes and croissants daily. Calor and camping gas. Takeaway (evenings only, last orders 19.00). No play area as such but two open areas for ball games. Off site: Fishing, boat launching and beach 1 mile. Golf 4 miles. Riding 6 miles. Salcombe, sailing Mecca and fishing port with sandy beaches 3.5 miles. Kingsbridge, ancient market town 6 miles.

Open: Easter - 29 September.

Directions

Travelling south on the A38, take A3121 (signed Ermington, Modbury). Follow signs to Kingsbridge and Salcombe. At Malborough, turn sharp right through village (Bolberry) for 0.6 mile. Turn right to Bolberry, then after 0.9 miles the park is on the right. Take care with single track lanes, although there are plenty of passing places. O.S.GR: SX692391.

Charges 2007

Per unit incl. 2 adults, 2 children	£ 10.00 - £ 17.00
extra person	£ 3.00 - £ 4.00
child (under 17 yrs)	£ 1.00
electricity	£ 2.00

No credit cards.

Karrageen Caravan & Camping Park
Bolberry, Malborough, Kingsbridge, South Devon, TQ7 3EN
Tel: 01548 561230 Fax: 01548 560192
Email: phil@karrageen.co.uk
www.karrageen.co.uk

UK0830 Slapton Sands Camping & Caravanning Club Site

Middle Grounds, Slapton, Kingsbridge TQ7 2QW (Devon)

Tel: **01548 580538**

This club site is on the road which leads from Slapton Sands, on a well kept meadow overlooking the bay – the sea views are panoramic from some areas of the site, with shelter provided by some large bushes and the surrounding hedge. There are 115 grass pitches, some with a slight slope, and electricity is available for 46 (including 10 with hardstanding). Motorcaravans, trailer tents and tents are accepted without problems but the planners will only permit 8 caravan pitches which are kept for club members. The quaint port of Dartmouth is 7 miles, Kingsbridge 8 miles and a variety of beaches and coves around the beautiful South Hams coastline are within easy reach.

Facilities

The modern toilet block is central, can be heated and is kept very clean. Washing machine and dryer. Reception has a small library, gas and freezer for ice blocks. Small play area. Off site: Riding 0.5 miles. Village 200 yds.

Open: March - October.

Directions

From A38 Exeter - Plymouth road, take A384 to Totnes. Just before town, turn right on A381 to Kingsbridge, then A379 through Stokenham and Torcross to Slapton Sands. O.S.GR: SX825450.

Charges 2007

Per person	£ 4.90 - £ 8.25
child (6-18 yrs)	£ 2.15 - £ 2.25
pitch (non-member)	£ 5.65

UK0835 Little Cotton Caravan Park

Dartmouth TQ6 0LB (Devon)

Tel: **01803 832558**. Email: **enquiries@littlecotton.co.uk**

This lovely, family run park on the outskirts of Dartmouth is ideally situated for exploring this attractive area of South Devon. Well tended and immaculate, the 7.5 acre park is open and grassy. On level and gently sloping ground, it is situated on a hilltop and has views across the other fields. There are 95 pitches, all with electricity (16A) and mostly level with some hardstanding available. The park is divided into four areas with one dedicated to rallies. A dog walking area is to one side. Barbecues are allowed off the ground. Located next to the Dartmouth 'park and ride', it is easy get into Dartmouth (tickets can be bought from reception) and a path leads from the site to the bus stops. Dartmouth has very limited parking so this is really the best way to visit. A site shop in reception is well stocked with foods, camping (including gas) and other items all at very reasonable prices. There is a freezer in the shop for ice packs (small donation to charity). Orders from the bakery, including assorted sandwiches, can be ordered daily.

Facilities

The modern, heated toilet block is centrally situated. It is very clean, light, airy and warm. Some washbasins are in cubicles. Free showers are preset. Excellent facilities for disabled visitors. Indoor dishwashing area and laundry. Unisex baby room. Well stocked shop in reception. Bread and sandwiches to order. Freezer. Off site: Dartmouth Castle and the steam railway can be easily accessed by ferry. Beach 2 miles.

Open: Mid March - late October.

Directions

Park is on the outskirts of Dartmouth on the A3122 next to Dartmouth 'park and ride'. From Totnes take A381 (Kingsbridge) and turn left at Halwell on A3122. Site is on right just before entering Dartmouth. O.S.GR: SX857508.

Charges 2007

Per unit incl. 2 persons	£ 10.50 - £ 15.00
incl. electricity	£ 12.75 - £ 17.25
extra person	£ 3.00
child (3-14 yrs)	£ 2.00

UK0845 Hillhead Caravan Club Holiday Park

Hillhead, Brixham TQ5 0HH (Devon)

Tel: **01803 853204**. Email: **enquiries@caravanclub.co.uk**

Hillhead is a fully refurbished Caravan Club park set in 22 acres of beautiful Devon countryside. Originally developed in the 1960s within what is now a coastal protection area two miles from Brixham, the park has benefited from a £3 million redevelopment. Unusually for a Caravan Club site, it offers a full entertainment programme in peak season. Hillhead comprises 239 pitches, all with electrical hook-ups and many with fine views. Amenities are to a uniformly high standard, notably the main complex based around an attractive courtyard, and housing a shop, bar, games room and restaurant. The children's play area is outstanding with a range of imaginative items including a large wooden fort. Hillhead is rightly proud of its strong commitment to sound environmental practice, with a plan to promote species diversity and the encouragement of good practice by site workers and visitors alike.

Facilities

The two sanitary blocks are new and maintained to a high standard. Each block includes 3 special private family bathrooms (key from reception) and facilities for disabled visitors. Laundry facilities. Motoraravan service point. Shop. Bar and restaurant. Swimming pool (heated May - Sept) with children's pool adjacent. Large play area. Skateboard ramp. Games room. TV. Entertainment in season. Games field. Dog walking area. WiFi. Off site: Nearest beach and coastal path 2 miles. Bus stop at site entrance. River Dart boat trips. Paignton, Torquay and Brixham. Golf (18-hole) and riding 2 miles. Bicycle hire 2.5 miles.

Open: 14 March - 5 January.

Directions

Site is well signed from the A379 Paignton - Dartmouth road and is located on the B3205 (Slappers Hill Road). Entrance is on the left after 400 yards. O.S.GR: SX904534.

Charges 2007

Per person	£ 4.70 - £ 7.50
child (5-16 yrs)	£ 1.80 - £ 4.50
pitch (non-member)	£ 10.90 - £ 17.00

UK0840 Woodlands Leisure Park

Blackawton, Totnes TQ9 7DQ (Devon)

Tel: **01803 712598**. Email: **fun@woodlandspark.com**

Woodlands is a pleasant surprise – from the road you have no idea of just what is hidden away deep in the Devon countryside. To achieve this, there has been sympathetic development of farm and woodland to provide a leisure centre, open to the public and with a range of activities and entertainment appealing to all ages, plus a touring caravan park. Children (and many energetic parents too!) will thoroughly enjoy a huge variety of imaginative adventure play equipment, amazing water toboggan runs, the 'Rock and Roll Tug Boat', the new 'Avalanche' and much more, hidden amongst the trees. Those more peacefully inclined can follow woodland walks around the attractive ponds. The 'Empire of the Sea Dragon', an indoor play centre, provides marvellous wet weather facilities comprising five floors of play areas and amazing slides. With a two night stay, campers on the touring park are admitted free of charge to the leisure park. The camping and caravan site overlooks the woodland and the leisure park, taking 320 units on three sloping, grassy fields, the original terraced one maturing nicely. One of the others has been fully terraced to provide groups of four to eight flat, very spacious pitches (90% with 10A electricity and a shared water tap, drain and rubbish bin). The newest field has 120 pitches (with electricity) designed with a more open feel to provide space for larger groups or rallies. A popular park, early reservation is advisable.

Facilities

Three modern, heated toilet blocks, include private bathrooms (coin-operated, 20p) and 16 family shower cubicles. Two laundry rooms, dishwashing areas and freezer for ice packs. Baby changing facilities. The leisure park café, with terrace, provides good value meals and a takeaway service for campers. Café opening hours and the adjoining gift shop (with gas and a few basic food supplies) vary according to season and demand. TV and games room. Dogs are accepted on the campsite but not in the leisure park (kennels available). Caravan storage. Off site: The charming town of Dartmouth and the South Hams beaches are near. Fishing 4 miles. Golf 0.5 miles. Riding 5 miles. Beach 4 miles.

Open: Easter - 4 November.

Directions

From A38 at Buckfastleigh, take A384 to Totnes. Before the town centre turn right on A381 Kingsbridge road. After Halwell turn left at Totnes Cross garage, on A3122 to Dartmouth. Park is on right after 2.5 miles. O.S.GR: SX813521.

Charges 2007

Per unit incl. 2 persons,	
electricity	£ 14.50 - £ 21.00
extra person over 2 yrs	£ 6.75
awning or extra small pup tent	£ 2.50
large tent or trailer tent (120 sq ft plus)	£ 2.50
dog (contact site first)	£ 2.50

Free entry to leisure park for stays 2 nights or more.

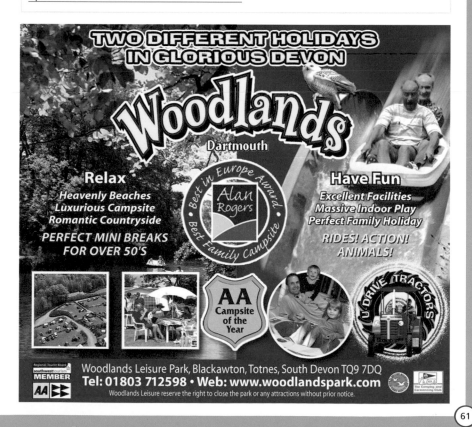

UK0860 Whitehill Country Park

Stoke Road, Paignton TQ4 7PF (Devon)

Tel: **01803 782338**. Email: **info@whitehill-park.co.uk**

Whitehill Country Park is beautifully situated in rolling Devon countryside, just 2.5 miles from the nearest beaches. Extending over 40 acres, a definite sense of space characterises this park and ten acres of ancient woodland are available for walks and attract a great deal of wildlife. Whitehill is a friendly park with 320 large grassy pitches which are located in separate fields around the site with evocative names, such as Nine Acres, Sweethill and Coombe Meadow. Most pitches have electrical connections (16A). Around 60 pitches are used for caravan holiday homes. The park boasts an attractive swimming pool (max. depth 1.3 m) with a children's paddling pool alongside, as well as a good range of other leisure facilities, notably The Hayloft bar (with satellite TV), a café and an extensive decking area for outside eating.

Facilities

Two brand new sanitary blocks include private, individual washing facilities for ladies. Ample laundry facilities. Gas supplies. Shop. Bar. Café (24/5-1/9). Swimming and paddling pools (heated 29/5-4/9). Three play areas. Electronic games. Craft centre for children. Dogs and other pets are not accepted. Off site: Paignton 2.5 miles. Beach 3 miles. Fishing and golf 2 miles. Riding 4 miles. Torquay, Dartmoor, Quay West Aqua Park. Bus stop at site entrance.

Open: Easter - 30 September.

Directions

Turn left at The Parkers Arms off the A385 Paignton to Totnes road, signed Stoke Gabriel. Site is 1 mile along this road. O.S.GR: SX857587.
GPS: N50:25.072 W03:36.540

Charges 2008

| Per unit incl. 2 persons and electricity | £ 13.50 - £ 26.00 |
| tent pitch (no electricity) | £ 11.50 - £ 21.00 |

Camping Cheques accepted.

Beautiful South Devon

- 10 acres of woodland
- Modern touring facilities and holiday homes
- Outdoor heated pool
- David Bellamy Gold Award
- Hayloft Bar & family room
- Children's play areas
- Woodland walks
- Shop, café & takeaway

Whitehill Country Park

Stoke Road, Paignton, South Devon TQ4 7PF
info@whitehill-park.co.uk

01803 782 338
www.whitehill-park.co.uk

UK0850 Galmpton Park

Greenway Road, Galmpton, Brixham TQ5 0EP (Devon)

Tel: **01803 842066**. Email: **galmptontouringpark@hotmail.com**

Within a few miles of the lively amenities of Torbay, Galmpton Park lies peacefully just outside the village of Galmpton, overlooking the beautiful Dart estuary just upstream of Dartmouth and Kingswear. A family park, some 120 pitches (60 marked for caravans) are arranged on a wide sweep of grassy, terraced meadow, each pitch with its own wonderful view of the river. Situated on the hillside, some parts have quite a slope, but there are flatter areas (the owners will advise and assist). There are 90 electrical connections (10A) and 23 pitches have water and drainage. There is a separate tent field. Galmpton is a quiet and simple park in a most picturesque setting, within easy reach of all the attractions of South Devon. A member of the Countryside Discovery group.

Facilities

A central, substantial looking toilet block provides clean facilities including three washbasins in cabins, under 5's bathroom (key), baby unit and hair care areas. Washing machine, dryer and iron. Shop sells basics including gas. Bread to order. Good adventure play equipment. Dogs (max. 2 per unit) are accepted at the owner's discretion and not mid July and Aug. Motorhomes over 21 ft. are not accepted. Off site: Local pub is 5 minutes walk.

Open: Easter - 30 September.

Directions

From Paignton - Brixham coast road. Turn right towards Brixham, then second right into Manor Vale Road. Continue through the village, past the school and site is 500 yds on the right. O.S.GR: SX885558.

Charges 2007

Per unit incl. 2 persons	£ 11.00 - £ 19.40
extra person	£ 2.50
child (5-16 yrs)	£ 1.50

UK0870 Beverley Park Holiday Centre

Goodrington Road, Paignton TQ4 7JE (Devon)

Tel: **01803 661978**. Email: **info@beverley-holidays.co.uk**

Beverley Park is a busy, but good quality holiday centre, attractively landscaped, with marvellous views over Torbay. The pools, a large dance hall, bars and entertainment, are all run in an efficient and orderly manner. The park has 195 caravan holiday homes and 23 lodges, mainly around the central complex. There are 187 touring pitches in the lower areas of the park, all reasonably sheltered, some with views across the bay and some on slightly sloping ground. All pitches can take awnings and have 16A electricity (15 m. cable), 38 have hardstanding and 42 are fully serviced. Tents are accepted and a limited number of tent pitches have electrical connections. The park has a long season and reservations are essential for caravans. Entertainment is organised at Easter and from early May in the Starlight Cabaret bar. There are indoor and outdoor pools, each one heated and supervised. The Oasis fitness centre provides a steam room, jacuzzi, sun-bed and an excellent fitness room. The park is in the heart of residential Torbay, with views across the bay to Brixham and Torquay, and sandy beaches less than a mile away. This popular park has lots to offer and is well maintained and run. A member of the Best of British group.

Facilities

Good toilet blocks are well maintained and heated, include roomy showers, some with washbasins en-suite. Baths on payment. Unit for disabled visitors. Facilities for babies. Laundry. Gas supplies. Motorcaravan service point. Large shop (17/3-31/10). Restaurant, bars and takeaway (all Easter, then 30/5-26/10). Swimming pools. Fitness centre. Tennis. Crazy golf. Playground. Nature trail. Amusement centre. Soft play area. Dogs are not accepted. Off site: Minibus service to Paignton. Fishing, bicycle hire, riding and golf within 2 miles.

Open: January - December.

Directions

Park is south of Paignton in Goodrington Road between A379 coast road and B3203 ring road and is well signed on both. O.S.GR: SX882584. GPS: N50:24.812 W03:34.120

Charges 2008

Per unit incl. 2 persons and electricity	£ 14.00 - £ 35.80
tent pitch incl. 2 persons	£ 10.50 - £ 29.00
extra person	£ 4.50
child (4-14 yrs)	£ 3.00

Max. 6 persons per reservation.

UK0865 Byslades International Touring Park

Totnes Road, Paignton TQ4 7PY (Devon)

Tel: **01803 555072**. Email: **info@byslades.co.uk**

Byslades is a large, well maintained touring park covering 23 acres on the side of a valley. The site is cut into terraces on the steepest slopes, so that most of the pitches are level. Many of the pitches (grass and hardstanding) have a lovely view across the valley to the fields on the other side. There are 190 pitches, 150 with electricity (10/ 16A). There is a security barrier at the entrance to the park and CCTV has been installed. A large heated outdoor swimming pool, with a special area for toddlers. A café is nearby which also sells bread, milk and a few essentials.

Facilities

Two modern toilet blocks are kept very clean, with some washbasins in cubicles and free showers (with dividing curtain). Facilities for disabled visitors. Baby facilities in the Ladies. Laundry. Freezer for ice packs. Motorcaravan point. Café with takeaway and basic supplies. Club house. Swimming pool. Play area. Off site: Beach 3 miles.

Open: May - September.

Directions

Leave Totnes on the A385 signed for Paignton and the site is about 3 miles from Totnes on the left. O.S.GR: SX845597.

Charges 2007

Per unit incl. 2 persons	£ 6.00 - £ 12.50
child (3-12 yrs)	£ 2.00 - £ 3.50
electricity	£ 2.00

63

UK0880 Dornafield

Two Mile Oak, Newton Abbot TQ12 6DD (Devon)

Tel: **01803 812732**. Email: **enquiries@dornafield.com**

The entrance to Dornafield leads into the charming old courtyard of a 14th Century farmhouse giving a mellow feeling that is complemented by the warm welcome from the Dewhirst family. The reception, shop, tourist information/ecology room have been sympathetically converted from farm outbuildings, with the games room from the old milking parlour, complete with stalls. Having booked in, continue down the lane (overlooked by a tree covered bank and alive with wild flowers) to the Buttermeadow, a tranquil valley providing 75 individual, numbered pitches on flat grass, separated by grassy ridges and in some places, wild rose hedges. You pass the walled Orchard area, secluded and cosy for tents. Or take the road up the hill to Blackrock Copse with large luxury pitches with all facilities including a chemical disposal point for each pitch and TV connections, very cleverly concealed and 61 with hardstanding. Electricity points are 10A. Whilst having been carefully designed, the environment remains natural. Both Buttermeadow and Blackrock have super, well maintained woodland adventure play areas. Dornafield is a member of the Caravan Club's 'managed under contract' scheme, with both members and non-members made welcome. Dornafield's rural situation is delightful and, being away from the coast and without any evening activities, it is a haven for those seeking a quiet, restful holiday. A park that is well worth consideration and a member of the Best of British Group.

Facilities

Both modern toilet blocks are excellent and heated, with some washbasins in cubicles and comfortable roomy showers, but the new block up the hill could be said to be 'state of the art' with under-floor heating and a heat recovery system. Both blocks have facilities for disabled visitors and babies and laundry rooms. Shop, Gas supplies. All-weather hard tennis court. Games room with table tennis. Play areas. All year caravan storage. Off site: Local inn 0.5 miles. Fishing 2.5 miles. Golf 1 mile.

Open: 18 March - 1 November.

Directions

Park is northwest of A381 Newton Abbot - Totnes road. Leave A381 at Two Mile Oak Inn, opposite garage, and turn left at crossroads after about half a mile. Entrance is on the right. O.S.GR: SX848683.

Charges 2007

Per pitch incl. 2 persons	£ 11.50 - £ 22.00
tent pitch incl 2 persons	£ 15.50 - £ 19.00
dog	£ 1.00 - £ 1.80

UK0900 Widdicombe Farm Tourist Park

The Ring Road, Compton, Paignton TQ3 1ST (Devon)

Tel: **01803 558325**. Email: **info@widdicombefarm.co.uk**

Widdicombe Farm is only three miles from Torquay and with easy access from the A380, is well situated for the Torbay area. There are 194 numbered pitches, 160 with electricity (10A) of which most have hardstanding and 20 are fully serviced. Surrounded by farmland, the pitches are on terraces with open views across the countryside. Many trees and shrubs have been planted and there are tarmac access roads. There may be some background traffic noise but it is not too intrusive. Touring areas are separated into sections for families, couples, tent campers, etc. A large comfortable bar offers family entertainment and barbecued food is served during most entertainment evenings. The site has a relaxed, friendly feel.

Facilities

Three older style toilet blocks are kept very clean. The original heated block near reception is fully equipped and includes facilities for disabled people, dishwashing area and laundry room. Shop and 'Poppy' restaurant (evening meals, breakfasts, cream teas and takeaway) and family bar (all Easter, then spring B.H - mid Oct). Games room. Play area and recreation field. Certain breeds of dog are not accepted. Caravan storage. Off site: Fishing, bicycle hire, riding and golf, all within 2 miles.

Open: 15 March - mid October.

Directions

From Newton Abbot take A380 south for about 5 miles; site is well signed off this road. O.S.GR: SX874641

Charges 2007

Per unit incl. 2 persons	£ 7.50 - £ 15.50
incl. electricity	£ 9.50 - £ 20.00
extra person	£ 3.50 - £ 3.00
child (3-16 yrs)	£ 2.50
Bargain breaks available.	

UK0910 Ross Park

Park Hill Farm, Ipplepen, Newton Abbot TQ12 5TT (Devon)

Tel: **01803 812983**. Email: **enquiries@rossparkcaravanpark.co.uk**

Ross Park has to be seen to appreciate the amazing floral displays with their dramatic colours, that are a feature of the park. These are complemented by the use of a wide variety of shrubs which form hedging for most of the 110 pitches to provide your own special plot, very much as on the continent. Many pitches have wonderful views over the surrounding countryside and for those who prefer the more open style, one small area has been left unhedged. The owners, Mark and Helen Lowe, continue to strive to provide quality facilities and maintain standards, and this is reflected in the awards they have won. The New Barn provides a comfortable lounge, a mezzanine bar with bar snacks and a restaurant with extra seating in the conservatory which is home to some exotic and colourful plants. The touring area is divided into bays or groups by hedging and shrubs and provides 110 pitches all with electricity (16A). Some 82 of these have a hardened surface, some made larger with a further gravel area. An orchard area alive with daffodils in the spring and a conservation area with information on wild flowers and butterflies, and with extended views, completes these environmentally considered amenities. Barn dances are organised on Sundays in high season. A well cared for park worthy of consideration, now a member of the Best of British group.

Facilities

Seven well equipped, heated en-suite units, one with baby facilities, two suitable for disabled people. Further separate shower, washbasin and toilet facilities. Laundry room. Utility room with dishwashing, freezer and battery charging. Dog shower. Motorcaravan services. Reception with licensed shop. Gas supplies. Bar, bar snacks and restaurant with a la carte menu (all April - end Oct, plus Christmas and New Year). Conservation and tourist information room. Games room. Seven acre park area for recreation. Croquet green. Large playground. Caravan storage. Off site: Dainton Park 18-hole golf course is adjacent. Fishing 3 miles. Riding 1 mile. Beach 6 miles.

Open: All year excl. January and February.

Directions

From A381 Newton Abbot - Totnes road, park is signed towards Woodland at Park Hill crossroads and Jet filling station. O.S.GR: SX845671.

Charges 2007

Per unit incl. 2 persons	£ 10.50 - £ 20.00
incl. electricity	£ 11.50 - £ 21.00
extra person	£ 3.25 - £ 5.30
child (4-16 yrs)	£ 1.50 - £ 2.50

Christmas packages available. No credit cards.

UK0950 River Dart Country Park

Holne Park, Newton Abbot TQ13 7NP (Devon)

Tel: **01364 652511**. Email: **enquiries@riverdart.co.uk**

Once part of a Victorian estate with mature woodland on the edge of Dartmoor in the beautiful Dart valley, the park and its activities are now open to the public on payment. It features a variety of unusual adventure play equipment arranged amongst and below the trees, 'Lilliput Land' for toddlers, Jungle Fun, and woodland streams and a lake with a 'pirate ship' for swimming and inflatables, fly fishing and marked nature and forest trails – all free to campers except fishing. It does become busy at weekends and school holidays with supervised activities for children, such as climbing and canoeing. The camping area is in the more open parkland overlooking the woods and is mainly on a slight slope with some shade from mature trees. There are 185 pitches of very reasonable size, marked by lines on the grass, some slightly sloping, with 105 electrical connections (10/16A).

Facilities

Two wooden toilet blocks, one quite smart, the older a little tired, can both be heated. Washbasins in cubicles, baby facilities, laundry and dishwashing, freezer, en-suite unit for disabled visitors, family bathroom. Motorcaravan service point. Shop (all season). Restaurant, bar (all season) and takeaway (20/7-31/8). Large TV and games room. Small, heated pool (all season). Tennis. Max. two dogs. Off site: Bicycle hire or riding 4 miles. Golf 6 miles.

Open: 1 April - 30 September.

Directions

Signed from the A38 at Peartree junction, park is 1 mile west of Ashburton, on the road to Two Bridges. Disregard signs 'no caravans' as access to the park is before narrow bridge. O.S.GR: SX734701.

Charges 2007

Per unit incl. 2 persons	£ 10.50 - £ 19.00
incl. electricity	£ 13.50 - £ 22.00
extra person (over 3 yrs)	£ 5.00 - £ 6.50

Camping Cheques accepted.

UK0940 Holmans Wood Holiday Park

Harcombe Cross, Chudleigh TQ13 0DZ (Devon)

Tel: **01626 853785**. Email: **enquiries@holmanswood.co.uk**

Close to the main A38 Exeter - Plymouth road, with easy access, this attractive, neat park makes a sheltered base for touring south Devon and Dartmoor. The hedged park is arranged on well kept grass surrounding a shallow depression, the floor of which makes a safe, grassy play area for children. Many attractive trees are growing and the park is decorated with flowers. In two main areas and accessed by tarmac roads, there are 116 level pitches (including a number of seasonal pitches) and 25 smart mobile homes in a private area. There are 100 pitches with electrical hook-ups (10A) and 70 with hardstanding, electricity, water and drainage. A picturesque 8 acre meadow is provided for tents. Adventure play equipment is provided for children, with badminton and tennis nets and an extra meadow for recreation. There may be some traffic noise on pitches to the west of the park. This is a pleasant, well run park and with no other on-site amenities would suit couples or families who prefer a peaceful stay.

Facilities

The single, good quality toilet block includes facilities for babies and disabled visitors, a dishwashing room and a laundry room. Children's play area. Caravan storage. Dogs are not accepted. Off site: Pub/restaurant nearby in Chudleigh village. The beach or Dartmoor are 7 miles and Haldon Forest for walks is 2 miles. Sunday market at Exeter Racecourse (2 miles). Fishing 1 mile, golf or riding 4 miles.

Open: Mid March - end October.

Directions

From Exeter on A38 Plymouth road, 0.5 miles after the racecourse and just after a garage, take the Chudleigh exit (signed). Park is immediately on the left. From Plymouth turn off A38 for Chudleigh/Teign Valley, then right for Chudleigh. Continue through the town and park is 1 mile. O.S.GR: SX882811. GPS: N50:37.191 W03:34.970

Charges 2007

Per unit incl. 2 persons and electricity	£ 12.00 - £ 17.00
de-luxe pitch	£ 13.00 - £ 18.00
extra person	£ 2.20 - £ 3.00
child (4-14 yrs)	£ 1.90 - £ 2.00

" So easy to get to - so easy to explore from "

Our park is surrounded on all sides by rolling Devon countryside. Ideally situated for Dartmoor, Exeter, Torbay and Newton Abbot. Storage/Seasonal pitches available.

Tel: 01626 853785   **www.holmanswood.co.uk**

UK0960 Parkers Farm Holiday Park

Higher Mead Farm, Ashburton, Newton Abbot TQ13 7LJ (Devon)

Tel: **01364 654869**. Email: **parkersfarm@btconnect.com**

Well situated with fine views towards Dartmoor, Parker's Farm is a modern touring site on a working farm. Close inspection reveals a unique chance to experience Devon country life at first hand, with pigs, sheep, goats, calves and rabbits to feed and touch, or the milking to get involved with. In addition the Parker family have added a family bar which provides entertainment during the season (live singers and music) and a restaurant using locally sourced ingredients. Farm walks are very popular and take place three evenings a week in high season, on request at other times. The 90 touring pitches are set directly above the farm buildings on broad terraces giving groups of flat pitches, all with good views across the valley (over the A38 which may give some road noise). Electricity (12A) is provided throughout and hardstandings are available. Trees and hedges have matured nicely on the lower terraces, with many more planted. Parker's Farm provides a warm welcome – in the words of one camper, 'You come here and feel you belong'.

Facilities

Two modern and clean shower and toilet blocks provide good facilities with two family shower rooms, baby bathroom, room for disabled visitors and laundry. Small shop (Easter - mid Oct). Restaurant, comfortable bar with family room (Whitsun - mid Sept.) and entertainment. Games room. Indoor play and TV area. Large play area. Trampolines. Caravan storage. Rallies welcome. American motorhomes accepted by prior arrangement. Off site: Bicycle hire 5 miles. Golf 4 miles. Riding 5 miles.

Open: Easter - 31 October.

Directions

From Exeter on A38, 26 miles from Plymouth, turn left at Alston Cross signed 'Woodland Denbury'. Site is 400 yards. O.S.GR: SX757702. GPS: N50:31.667 W03:43.451

Charges 2008

Per unit incl. 2 persons	£ 7.00 - £ 16.00
incl. electricity	£ 9.00 - £ 18.00
extra person	£ 3.00
child (3-15 yrs)	£ 2.00
dog	£ 1.20

UK0970 Cofton Country Holidays

Starcross, Dawlish EX6 8RP (Devon)

Tel: **01626 890111**. Email: **info@coftonholidays.co.uk**

see advertisement on the back cover

A popular, family run park for families only, Cofton is 1.5 miles from a sandy beach at Dawlish Warren. It has space for 450 touring units on a variety of fields and meadows with beautiful country views. Although not individually marked, there is never a feeling of overcrowding. The smaller, more mature fields, including a pleasant old orchard for tents only, are well terraced. While there are terraces on most of the slopes of the larger, more open fields, there are still some quite steep gradients to climb. There are some 300 electrical connections (10A) and a few hardstandings. One area has 66 park-owned, holiday homes for let. A well designed, central complex overlooking the pool and decorated with flowers and hanging baskets, houses reception, a shop and off-licence and a bar lounge, the 'Cofton Swan', where bar meals are usually available (all Easter - 30 Sept). A family room and bar are on the first floor of this building and there is an outdoor terrace and some light entertainment in season. The adjacent supervised kidney-shaped heated pool with paddling pool, has lots of grassy space for sunbathing. Coarse fishing is available in three lakes on the park. The adjoining unspoilt woodland of 50 acres provides wonderful views across the Exe estuary and a woodland trail of 2 miles to Dawlish Warren.

Facilities

Toilet facilities comprise four blocks, well placed for all areas, and another new one of very high standard has just been completed. Facilities for disabled visitors and babies. Hair dryers. In addition three 'portacabin' style units with basic toilet facilities are provided for the peak season. Two launderettes. Gas available. Ice pack hire service. Bar lounge. TV. Shop. Fish and chip shop - breakfast possible. Swimming pool (overall length 100 ft. open Spr. B.H - mid Sept). Games room (busy in high season). Adventure playground in the woods overlooking the pools and two other well equipped play areas. Pony rides in high season. Coarse fishing (from £20 per rod for 7 days, discount for senior citizens outside July). Winter caravan storage. Off site: Golf 3 miles. Beach 1.5 miles. Woodland walks/pub 0.5 miles.

Open: 1 April - 31 October.

Directions

Access to the park is off the A379 road 3 miles north of Dawlish, just after Cockwood harbour village. O.S.GR: SX965797. GPS: N50:36.756 W03:27.628

Charges 2007

Per unit incl. 2 persons	
and electricity	£ 13.00 - £ 23.00
hardstanding pitch	£ 15.00 - £ 25.00
extra person (over 2 yrs)	£ 2.00 - £ 3.50

Small low season discount for Senior Citizens.

Camping Cheques accepted.

UK1000 Forest Glade Holiday Park

Cullompton EX15 2DT (Devon)

Tel: **01404 841381**. Email: **enquiries@forest-glade.co.uk**

Forest Glade, owned and run by the Wellard family, is set in the Blackdown Hills (designated an area of outstanding natural beauty), deep in mid-Devon away from the hectic life on the coast. A sheltered site set amongst woodland with extensive walking without using your car, there are 80 level touring pitches, 68 of which have 10/16A electricity connections, 4 have full services and 24 have hardstanding. There is a small heated, covered pool with a paddling pool and patio area outside, and a large games room (up a flight of steps, so not suitable for visitors with disabilities). The surrounding forest makes this a dog lover's paradise (dogs are accepted). Touring caravans must book in advance and the easiest route for them will be explained then (phone bookings accepted). Although set in the country, the beaches of East Devon are a fairly easy drive away.

Facilities

There is one main toilet block, heated in cold weather, with some washbasins in cubicles. Separate suite for visitors with disabilities. Laundry with washing machines and dryers. Baby room. Extra facilities of 'portacabin' style with toilets, washbasins and showers are at the swimming pool. Drain for motorcaravan tanks. Shop (all season) is quite well stocked including gas, bread and pastries with a takeaway (open evenings except Sunday). Microwave in kitchenette. Adventure playground. Games room. Swimming pool (free). Sauna. All weather tennis court. Separate area for ball games. WiFi internet access. Caravan storage. Off site: Fishing or riding 1.5 miles. Golf 6 miles. Beach 17 miles.

Open: Mid March - end October.

Directions

Park (at the top of a steep hill) is 5.5 miles from M5 exit 28. Take A373 for 3 miles, turning left at camp sign, just past thatched pub on right, towards Sheldon. Park is on left after 2.5 miles. This access is not suitable for touring caravans owing to a steep hill - phone the park for alternative route details. O.S.GR: ST101073. GPS: N50:51.470 W03:16.651

Charges 2007

Per unit incl. 2 persons	
and electricity	£ 12.00 - £ 16.50
extra person	£ 2.40
child (4-9 yrs)	£ 1.20
dog	£ 0.50

Caravan & Camping Park

A small country estate surrounded by forest and situated in an Area of Outstanding Natural Beauty. Large, flat, sheltered camping/touring pitches. Modern facilities building. Luxury 6 berth full service holiday homes. Shop/takeaway. Central for touring S.W. Easy access coast and moors.

FOREST GLADE HOLIDAY PARK

CULLOMPTON DEVON
EX15 2DT

Motor caravans welcome. Facilities for the disabled. Dogs welcome. Tourers please book in advance.

COLOUR BROCHURE AVAILABLE ON REQUEST

FREE Indoor Heated Pool

Tel: (01404) 841381 (Evgs to 8pm) • Fax: (01404) 841593 • www.forest-glade.co.uk • email: enquiries@forest-glade.co.uk

UK0980 Lemonford Caravan Park

Bickington, Newton Abbot TQ12 6JR (Devon)

Tel: **01626 821242**. Email: **mark@lemonford.co.uk**

Lemonford is a well run, neat and tidy site for all ages and families on the southern edge of the National Park, some three miles from both Ashburton and Newton Abbot. It has the look and atmosphere of the 'cultivated' caravan park, close to the main road, yet set in a sheltered, peaceful dip bordered by the pretty River Lemon. There are 85 pitches (around 40 used as seasonal pitches) on level grass and grouped in four areas. Most pitches have electricity, over 55 have hardstanding. A good pub is within walking distance, along the banks of the river.

Facilities

Two modern toilet blocks, one new, can be heated and provide some large private cabins, a ladies' bathroom (£1 payment) and a family bathroom. Facilities for disabled visitors. Laundry facilities. Shop. Gas. Freezer service. Play area. Putting green. Off site: Fishing 4 miles, riding and bicycle hire 3 miles, golf 2 miles.

Open: End March - 31 October.

Directions

Turn off A38 Plymouth road at A382 (Drumbridges) exit signed Newton Abbot. At roundabout take third exit to Bickington. Park is 3 miles on left. O.S.GR: SX793723. GPS: N50:32.346 W03:42.240

Charges 2007

Per unit incl. 2 persons	£ 9.00 - £ 14.00
electricity	£ 2.50
Special low season offers. No credit cards.	

UK1020 Oakdown Touring & Holiday Caravan Park

Weston, Sidmouth EX10 0PH (Devon)

Tel: **01297 680387**. Email: **enquiries@oakdown.co.uk**

Oakdown is a very attractive, well planned park and the Franks family and their team continue to work hard to provide a warm welcome. The attention to detail is evident at this award-winning park as soon as you arrive. The park has easy access, beautiful floral displays and a spacious feeling. The 100 level touring pitches are arranged in landscaped bays, screened by a growing range of trees and shrubs and linked by a circular road. All have 16A electricity, all have hardstanding and many have water and drainage. Two bays have 16 caravan holiday homes for rent and Oak Grove, a neat area contains 46 privately owned holiday homes. Waste water is dealt with by a Victorian style reed bed which has encouraged more birds and a hide has been established. The field trail, a haven for wild flowers and birds leads to the nearby renowned Donkey Sanctuary. Recent additions include a lake, dew pond and further wild flower areas and there is a 9-hole, par 3 Approach golf course. Continual improvements make this park an excellent choice for visitors with disabilities. A Best of British Group member.

Facilities

The central toilet block provides well maintained, fully equipped, heated sanitary facilities. One private cabin for ladies. Two unisex family bathrooms (bath, shower, toilet, washbasin and coin operated entry), double as units for disabled people. Dishwashing sinks. Laundry facilities plus free freezer and microwave. Motorcaravan service point. Recycling point. Fax service. TV room. Adventure style play equipment and castle. No cycling, skate-boarding or kite flying is permitted. Caravan storage. Off site: Riding 6 miles. Golf adjacent. Swimming 1 mile. Beach 2 miles.

Open: 14 March - 2 November.

Directions

Turn south off the A3052 (Exeter - Lyme Regis) road between Sidford and Colyford, 2.5 miles east of the A375 junction and park is on left.
O.S.GR: SY167902.

Charges 2008

Per pitch incl. 2 persons	£ 10.80 - £ 16.60
with electricity	£ 14.30 - £ 20.25
incl. mains services	£ 20.00 - £ 26.00
extra person (5 yrs and over)	£ 2.95
awning	£ 2.95

Less 70p for senior citizens in low season.

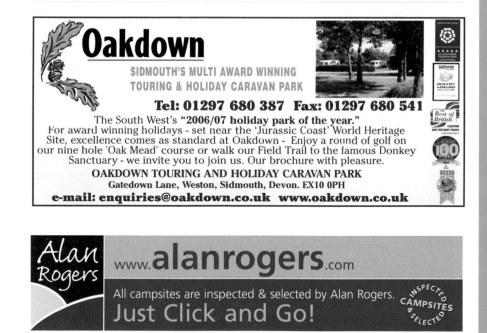

UK1090 Peppermint Park

Warren Road, Dawlish Warren, Dawlish EX7 0PQ (Devon)

Tel: **01626 863436**. Email: **info@peppermintpark.co.uk**

Peppermint Park is a green oasis in a popular holiday area. Extensive, green, sloping fields edged with mature trees have been partly terraced to give level pitches for caravans and some more informal areas catering for tents. There are 60 privately owned holiday homes (10 available to rent) along with some timber lodges to rent close to a small fishing lake. There are 250 touring pitches, 200 with 16A electricity, which are marked and numbered. Tarmac roads thread through the site giving easy access to all areas. A heated outdoor pool includes a water slide in the larger pool. Nightly entertainment is staged in the Peppermint Club in high season. This site's 'jewel in the crown' is the walking distance (700 yards) to the large, safe Blue Flag beaches of Dawlish Warren and its associated pleasure complex – ideal for families. For others, there is the adjacent coastal footpath or the city of Exeter (7 miles) with its cathedral, museums and historic Quay complex. A passenger ferry operates from Starcross (2 miles) across the estuary to Exmouth during high season. Dawlish Warren nature reserve is adjacent and includes an 18-hole links golf course.

Facilities

The two well kept sanitary blocks can be heated. Two units (WC, washbasin and shower) for disabled visitors. Fully equipped mother and baby room. Laundry (washing machines, dryers and free irons) and dishwashing. Shop with gas. Coffee shop. Bar with entertainment programme. Restaurant and takeaway (28/5-10/9). Swimming pools (28/5 - early Sept). Adventure playground on a hill. Field for ball games. Small coarse fishing lake (£5 for adult day ticket). Off site: Golf at Dawlish Warren (links course), 9-hole course at Starcross.

Open: 15 March - 28 October.

Directions

Leave M5 at junction 30 and take A379 Dawlish road. After passing through Starcross (7 miles) turn left to Dawlish Warren just before Dawlish. Continue for 1.5 miles down hill and park is on left in 300 yards. O.S.GR: SX978788.
GPS: N50:35.962 W03:26.818

Charges 2007

Per unit incl. 2 persons	£ 12.00 - £ 20.00
incl. electricity	£ 14.00 - £ 24.00
extra person (2 yrs and over)	£ 2.00 - £ 4.00
dog	£ 2.00 - £ 6.00

UK1010 Lady's Mile Holiday Park

Exeter Road, Dawlish EX7 0LX (Devon)

Tel: **01626 863411**. Email: **info@ladysmile.co.uk**

Lady's Mile is a popular, large family touring park that caters well for children. It has extensive grassy fields (with some trees for shade), in addition to the main, landscaped camping area which is arranged in broad terraces. There are 486 pitches, mostly marked by lines but with nothing between them, and most with electricity (10A). It is a 20 minute walk to a good sandy beach at Dawlish Warren and 10 minutes to Dawlish beach, but the park also has a good sized, free outdoor swimming pool with 200 ft. plus slide, paddling pool and a paved surround, plus a super indoor pool with flume and separate paddling pool (both with lifeguards). A large and attractive bar complex has a family area overlooking the indoor pool and an entertainment programme. Below is a spacious games room and a separate disco and bar. A sloping recreation field is ideal for kite flying and the large adventure playground has a safe, sand surface. A 9-hole golf course is on site (free but with small charge for hire of clubs). The park is popular over a long season, with reservation necessary for high season.

Facilities

Four toilet blocks of various ages and styles, but of a good standard, are well spaced around the main areas of the park with an additional newer block. Facilities for disabled people. Four family bathrooms (50p). Two launderettes. Mini-market. Fish and chip takeaway. Bars and entertainment. Restaurant and carvery (half-board option). All these Easter - mid Sept. Indoor (Easter - Oct) and outdoor (May - Sept) pools. Adventure play area. Games room. Golf (9-hole). Winter caravan storage. Off site: Riding and bicycle hire 1 mile. Fishing 3 miles.

Open: 13 March - 31 October.

Directions

Park is 1 mile north of Dawlish with access off the A379 (Exeter - Teignmouth) road.
O.S.GR: SX969778. GPS: N50:35.715 W03:27.568

Charges 2007

Per unit incl. 2 persons	£ 11.00 - £ 24.00
incl. electricity	£ 11.00 - £ 25.00
extra person over 2 yrs	£ 1.50 - £ 3.25
dog	£ 1.50 - £ 3.25
Low season special offers.	
Low season discount for OAPs.	

UK1060 Yeatheridge Farm Caravan Park

East Worlington, Crediton EX17 4TN (Devon)

Tel: **01884 860330**. Email: **yeatheridge@talk21.com**

Yeatheridge is a friendly, family park with riding, fishing lakes, and indoor pools. Based on a 200 acre farm, 9 acres have been developed over many years into an attractive touring park. Around the site there are views of the local hills and Dartmoor away to the south, and Exmoor lies to the north. You can explore three woodland walks ranging from 1 to 2.5 miles and the banks of the River Dalch. There are two deep coarse fishing lakes (bring your own rod), the top one offering family fishing and the lower one for serious fishing (age 14 or over and free of charge). Horse riding is available on site (best to bring your own hat) with hour-long and park rides available. The ponies and goats are also popular with adults and children alike. The touring area is very neat and tidy with a spacious feel to it as units are sited around the perimeter or back onto hedges, leaving open central areas. The 85 numbered, grass pitches are flat, gently sloping or on terraces and are sufficiently large, 80 with electricity connections (10A). Seasonal tourers take up 25 pitches and in addition there are 4 caravan holiday homes. The owners, Geoff and Liz, are constantly upgrading the park (recently opening a new reception and amenity building) and they try very hard to make everyone feel at home.

Facilities

Two toilet blocks provide family rooms, washbasins in cubicles, showers and facilities for babies. En-suite room for disabled visitors. Dishwashing (hot water 10p) and laundry. Motorcaravan service point. Shop. Bar, restaurant and snack bar (hours vary acc. to season). Unsupervised indoor swimming pools, toddlers' pool and water slide open daily, 10.00 - 20.00. Fenced play area with fort for under 10s (parental supervision). Football field. TV room. Pool table, table tennis and skittles. Fishing. Riding.

Open: 22 March - 29 September.

Directions

Park is off the B3042 Witheridge - Chawleigh (not in East Worlington). From M5 exit 27 take A361 to Tiverton. Turn left on A396 for 0.5 miles then right on B3137 almost to Witheridge, then left on B3042 for 3 miles to site, well signed. O.S.GR: SS770114. GPS: N50:53.322 W03:45.006

Charges 2007

Per unit incl. 2 persons	£ 7.50 - £ 13.50
extra person over 4 yrs	£ 2.20
electricity	£ 1.30
dog (first two)	£ 0.50 - £ 1.00

Yeatheridge Farm Caravan & Camping Park

01884 860330

www.yeatheridge.co.uk

If you are a country lover, there is everything to interest you here. 2 ½ miles of wood & riverside walks. If you wish to explore beautiful Devon, then there could not be a better location.

NEW ON-SITE RESTAURANT

UK1065 Smytham Manor Leisure

Smytham Manor, Little Torrington EX38 8PU (Devon)

Tel: **01805 622110**. Email: **info@smytham.co.uk**

A family owned, rural retreat of 25 acres, Smytham Manor is hidden away in its own valley, some 10 miles south of Bideford and 18 miles north of Okehampton. Part landscaped with neat grass and magnificent trees, the house is to one side of the valley with some privately owned mobile homes and more to the other side with pretty gardens. Tents have space in the walled garden where the swimming pool is situated and caravans go on terraced grass opposite. There is room for 45 units, of which 31 can have 16A electricity connections. Some pitches have gravel hardstanding. Lower down, the valley becomes more natural and wooded, with a series of lakes and a path leading down to the Tarka trail which can be explored on foot or by bike. Three smart, wooden chalets are available to let and another houses the bar and reception.

Facilities

Very smart, heated toilet block with every modern facility, including provision for disabled visitors which double as a baby room. Recycling pavilion. Bar with terrace overlooking the valley (open evenings, weekends only low season). Milk, bread and daily essentials at reception. Swimming pool (solar heated May - Sept). Adventure playground. Games room. Walks from site.
Off site: Fishing, golf and bicycle hire 2 miles. Riding 4 miles. Beach 8 miles. Boat launching/sailing 9 miles. Restaurants and pubs at Great Torrington 2 miles or along the Tarka Trail.

Open: March - October.

Directions

From Bideford follow A386 Okehampton road through Great Torrington. Turn right to park after 2 miles. From A30 pick up A386 south of Okehampton and go north for 18 miles towards Great Torrington. O.S.GR: SS484163.

Charges 2007

Per unit incl. 2 persons	£ 8.00 - £ 18.00
extra person	£ 1.00 - £ 2.00
electricity	£ 2.00
awning	£ 2.00

UK1110 Salcombe Regis Camping & Caravan Park

Salcombe Regis, Sidmouth EX10 0JH (Devon)

Tel: **01395 514303**. Email: contact@salcombe-regis.co.uk

On the edge of Salcombe Regis village, 1.5 miles from Sidmouth and less than a mile from the sea. Salcombe Regis Park covers 16 acres of land. It is surrounded by farmland with views of the combe and the sea beyond. The focal point of the main camping area is a large 'village green' where the play area and pitch and putt are located. The reception and pitches are arranged around the green, all connected by a tarmac road. The 110 pitches are level and have their own water supply, with 98 electricity hook-ups (16A). A 25 minute walk across fields takes you to a small secluded beach, although the walk there is fairly steep – we are told there are 129 steps that take you down to the beach! There are many footpaths and coastal walks nearby, protected by the National Trust and with views of Sidmouth and Weston Mouth. Sidmouth town, originally a small fishing town but now a seaside resort, is host to the annual International Folk Festival, where for one week in summer the town is filled with folk artists from all over the world.

Facilities

The traditional style toilet block (to one side of the side and a longer walk for some) is kept spotlessly clean by the resident wardens and includes a bathroom for families and disabled visitors. Licensed shop at reception selling basic supplies and local produce. Dishwashing area under cover. Laundry room with washing machines, dryers and ironing board. Motorcaravan service point. Play area. Pitch and putt. Caravan storage. Torches useful. Off site: Fishing, bicycle hire and golf 1.5 miles. Riding 3 miles. Sidmouth and beach 1.5 miles.

Open: Easter - 28 October.

Directions

Park is well signed on the A3052 Exeter - Lyme Regis road. From the east, take first left after Donkey Sanctuary. From the west proceed up the hill out of Sidford. Do not take first road signed Salcombe Regis, but take the next right at top of hill. Follow road round to site on left after golf range. O.S.GR: SY149892. GPS: N50:41.743 W03:12.322

Charges 2007

Per unit incl. 2 persons	£ 10.00 - £ 14.95
with electricity	£ 13.25 - £ 18.20
extra person	£ 3.35
child (5-15 yrs)	£ 2.10

UK1100 Webbers Caravan & Camping Park

Castle Lane, Woodbury, Exeter EX5 1EA (Devon)

Tel: **01395 232276**. Email: **reception@webberspark.co.uk**

Set in a lovely location in East Devon, with rural views, this family run park has developed over 20 years to one that can boast spacious, modern facilities, yet still retain its relaxed, rural atmosphere. The 115 marked, grass pitches are large, with the majority level and a few gently sloping. Some of the higher pitches have marvellous views across the Exe river valley. There are 100 pitches with electricity connections (10/16A). The park is surrounded by fields and visitors can watch the wildlife and grazing sheep from a fenced walk around the park perimeter. Within the park is a 'pets paddock' with a friendly donkey, Shetland pony and goats. A short drive takes you to the two miles of glorious sand at Exmouth or the delightful pebble beach at Budleigh Salterton. Woodbury Common for excellent heathland walks is just over a mile away whilst, for a little city life, Exeter is also nearby. A member of the Countryside Discovery and Best of British groups.

Facilities

There are three modern toilet blocks, one is a light and airy building with 4 family shower rooms, a bathroom (£1) and a unit for disabled visitors (WC, shower and washbasin). Dishwashing and laundry facilities. Unusual in terms of number, are seven chemical disposal points, located at each water point (and adequately separated). Motorcaravan service point. Small shop at reception for essentials. Ice pack service. Gas supplies. Play area and games field. All year caravan storage. Off site: Woodbury village within walking distance with excellent pub restaurant, post office, etc. Exeter 6 miles. Fishing or golf (Woodbury Park Golf Club) 1 mile. Riding 4 miles. Bicycle hire or boat launching 5 miles.

Open: Mid March - end October.

Directions

From M5 exit 30 take A3052 (Sidmouth) for 5 miles and turn right at Halfway Inn. From A30, Daisymount exit, take B3180 for 3 miles to Halfway Inn and go straight across at crossroads. All routes then follow B3180 (Budleigh Salterton). After 2 miles turn right into lane (Woodbury). Follow downhill for 1 mile to park on left just before Woodbury village. O.S.GR: SY017874. GPS: N50:40.685 W03:23.521

Charges 2007

Per pitch incl. 2 persons, electricity	£ 12.00 - £ 17.00
extra person (over 2 yrs)	£ 3.00

Min. booking of 4 nights in high season.

UK1130 Hoburne Torbay

Goodrington, Paignton TQ4 7JP (Devon)

Tel: **01803 558010**. Email: **enquiries@hoburne.co.uk**.

Situated to the south of central Paignton, with a short, signed walk to the sea and some sea views of Torbay, this Hoburne-owned park's major interest is a complex of 504 holiday homes (135 to let). There are 137 touring pitches (no tents) in two sections. One, probably the quieter of the two, is on flat grass by the entrance. The other is on higher ground, through the holiday homes at the top of the park with the sites large shop and café (with bakery) close by. It is on a gentle slope with some views. Pitches are of reasonable size, though with some variation, and all have 10A electricity. For those who like entertainment, the central club complex is the parks best feature, with a good sized heated outdoor pool (80 x 40 ft). and a super indoor pool with views across the bay, complete with flume, sauna and steam room. The clubhouse has a large club lounge with dance floor, a separate bar/restaurant (with views of Torbay). Entertainment is organised in season.

Facilities

Three toilet blocks, two of modern design in lower touring field, third block is of older design at the top touring field. Large launderette. Motorcaravan service point. Well stocked shop. Gas. Club room. Restaurant/bar. Takeaway. Café. Heated outdoor pool. Indoor pool with flume, sauna and steam room (all free). Amusement arcade. TV room showing cartoons. Crazy golf. Adventure playground. Indoor play area. Daily children's entertainment. Up to 30 American motorhomes accepted (25 ft. max). No dogs or pets are accepted.

Open: 14 February - 15 January excl. 2 weeks at Xmas.

Directions

Park is signed from the outer Paignton ring road. Look for left turn into Goodrington Road, then left into Grange Road. O.S.GR: SX890585.

Charges guide

Per unit incl. up to 6 persons	£ 11.00 - £ 27.00

73

UK1120 Napps Touring Holiday Park

Old Coast Road, Berrynarbor, Ilfracombe EX34 9SW (Devon)

Tel: **01271 882557**. Email: **info@napps.fsnet.co.uk**

Set in an idyllic location in North Devon, this popular, family-run site offers peace and quiet on site, with plenty to see and do off site. A path just outside the gates leads down to a private beach with safe bathing; although it is only 200 yards to the gate, there are 200 steps down to the beach so it is not suitable for wheelchair users. Combe Martin and Ilfracombe beaches are also close by. The local pub (300 yards down the lane) offers snacks, a beer garden, restaurant and entertainment. The 170 touring pitches, most with views of Watermouth Bay, are terraced and spacious, many are serviced with electricity, water tap and waste point, and over 70 more have a 10A hook-up. An outdoor heated swimming pool with shallow section for children is unsupervised, but there is a terrace with table and chairs for non-swimmers to watch or enjoy a light meal from the snack bar. Light entertainment is organised during the high season. All the services are at the bottom of the site and it can be quite a climb back up, especially to the terraces and tent area.

Facilities

Modern toilet block includes open plan washbasins and refurbished showers. Laundry. Dishwashing. Licensed shop. Gas supplies. Bar with terrace and light entertainment during high season. Heated outdoor pool with paddling pool and small toddlers' slide. Tennis. Ceramic studio for children. Games room. Adventure play area and 5-a-side football pitch. Caravan storage. Off site: Beach and fishing 200 yds. Golf and boat launching 1.5 miles. Bicycle hire and riding 5 miles. Coombe Martin 1.5 miles. Ilfracombe 3.5 miles.

Open: 1 March - 15 November.

Directions

Leave M5 at junction 27, take A361 to South Molton and then A399 to Combe Martin. Site is 1.5 miles west of Combe Martin on the A399 (signed). O.S.GR: SS559475. GPS: N51:12.511 W04:03.845

Charges 2007

Per unit incl. 2 persons	£ 8.00 - £ 17.00
incl. electricity	£ 9.00 - £ 24.00
extra person over 5 yrs	free - £ 3.00
awning	£ 1.00 - £ 2.00

UK1140 Lobb Fields Caravan & Camping Park

Saunton Road, Braunton EX33 1EB (Devon)

Tel: **01271 812090**. Email: **info@lobbfields.com**

Braunton village, Saunton Sands, the famous Tarka Trail for cycling, Baggy Point for walking, the biosphere at Braunton Burrows (one of only 13 similar special reserves in the country), Marwood Gardens, and wind surfing and water skiing on the Taw estuary are just some of the many attractions within a short distance of Lobb Fields. If you just want to sit and relax, then the pitches at the park offer views of the Taw estuary and Saunton, as well as magnificent sunsets. Lobb Fields has two camping areas providing 180 pitches on sloping grass, with a few hardstandings. Twelve pitches are reserved for seasonal caravans, and 61 have 16A electricity hook-ups. A third field is open for campers for 28 days only in high season. The pitches are marked and grass roads lead to the amenities. As the two toilet blocks are at the very bottom or very top of the fields, some up and down walking is inevitable. Lobbs Fields may be close to many holiday activities, but it is also a peaceful retreat for those wanting a quiet holiday.

Facilities

Two elderly toilet blocks (one in each field) have all the usual facilities. Two family/baby rooms. Laundry. Dishwashing sinks under cover. Cleaning and maintenance can be variable. The lower block can be heated and has good facilities for disabled visitors. Hair dryers and irons available from reception (£5 returnable deposit). Play area. Surf shop. Off site: Nearest shops less than a mile. Fishing, golf, riding and bicycle hire 1 mile. Boat launching 1.5 miles.

Open: 29 March - 29 October.

Directions

Take A361 Barnstaple to Braunton road, then B3231 (signed Croyde) to Braunton. Park is 1 mile from Braunton on the right - take care through Braunton as roads are quite narrow and busy. O.S.GR: SS474370. GPS: N51:06.699 W04:10.874

Charges 2007

Per unit incl. 2 persons	£ 6.00 - £ 18.00
prime pitch	£ 9.00 - £ 23.00
extra person	£ 3.00 - £ 5.00
dog	£ 1.00 - £ 2.00

UK1145 Hele Valley Holiday Park

Hele Bay, Ilfracombe EX34 9RD (Devon)

Tel: **01271 862460**. Email: **holidays@helevalley.co.uk**

Hele Valley is a well-established park which has been in the same family for over 30 years. Located a mile from Ilfracombe in a wooded valley, it is only a few minutes walk from Hele Bay beach. Here, quaint coves and coastal paths reveal a genuine smuggler's cave. Apart from the 80 attractively laid out caravan holiday homes (20 available for rent), the park caters for tents and motorcaravans only because of the difficult access. Some 50 pitches are set in two lush green fields surrounded by trees and hedges. Being in a valley, some of the pitches are terraced. Eight dedicated grass pitches for motorcaravans have electricity and 20 for tents (12 large ones) have hookups. This is a great centre for touring North Devon with Lynmouth, Porlock (Lorna Doone country), Exmoor, the pretty market town of Barnstaple and Great Torrington, famous for Dartington Glass. Nature lovers can enjoy walks on Exmoor or along the coast, including the Tarka Trail and, for bird watchers, Lundy Island is but a boat ride away (trips from Ilfracombe). A path leads from the park to nearby Chambercombe Manor with its association with Lady Jane Grey, a tunnel and a mysterious visitor – open to the public.

Facilities

The bright, airy and modern toilet block (access by key with deposit required) provides a mixture of open and enclosed washbasins; plus long mirrors and free hairdryers. Separately, a deluxe baby changing room, complete with pretty freize and chiming mobiles and a well-fitted unit for disabled visitors. Dishwashing and laundry areas, both enclosed. Modern reception with tourist information. Two good adventure play areas and a play field. Parents must keep children away from the steep-sided stream running the length of the park. Off site: Mini-market, pubs and cafés 5 minutes walk. Fishing, sea fishing, sailing, many shops in Ilfracombe 1 mile. Beach and golf 400 yards. Riding 4 miles. Bus service in main road.

Open: Whitsun - 10 September.

Directions

From Ilfracombe, take A399 east towards Combe Martin. With Ilfracombe swimming pool on the left, proceed down the hill for a further 400 m. and, at brown Hele Valley sign, take a very sharp right turn (would be easier to approach from Combe Martin). Go down steep road and continue to T-junction (right-angled and narrow). Turn right to the park. From Combe Martin follow A399 west for 8 miles, past golf course on left. Continue down the hill and turn left at the brown sign and continue as above. O.S. GR: SS533474. GPS: N51:12.667 W04:06.000

Charges 2007

Per tent or motorcaravan	
incl. 2 persons	£ 11.00 - £ 18.00
with electricity	£ 15.00 - £ 27.00
extra person	£ 4.00 - £ 6.00
child (3-14 yrs)	£ 3.00 - £ 5.00

UK1150 Ruda Holiday Park

Parkdean Holidays, Croyde Bay, Croyde EX33 1NY (Devon)

Tel: **01271 890477**. Email: **enquires@ruda.co.uk**

Ruda Holiday Park is the latest addition to Parkdean Holidays, now comprising 12 parks in Scotland, Wales and southwest England. Ruda is right beside a Blue Flag beach and provides 313 camping and touring pitches in two distinct areas. A large camping area divided into four sections is reserved for tent campers and motorcaravans (there are some electricity hook-ups around the perimeter and it is served by two toilet blocks that are aging but clean). Touring caravan and motorcaravan pitches, all with 13A connections, are in a separate field across the road and have direct access to the beach. Here, the toilet facilities are modern with coded entry to stop day visitors using them. A central complex (well away from the camping fields) houses a supermarket, laundry, food outlets, and all of the entertainment clubs and bars. The Cascade Tropical Pool, a fun pool with flume and water features is supervised at all times (children under five must wear arm bands which are provided free of charge). A large adventure play area, a tennis court and a sports field are also a short distance from the camping fields so that visitors are not disturbed. There's plenty of walking on the sand dunes and around the park, and Croyde Bay is renowned for surfing.

Facilities

Two blocks in the camping fields provide toilets, showers with preset controls, and communal washbasins; these are aging but were clean at the time of visit. A separate bathroom with toilet has a door wide enough for wheelchairs. A third, modern building provides all facilities in the touring field. Laundry. Bar, restaurant, snack bar and takeaway. Amusement arcade. Cascade Tropical pool. Adventure playground. Tennis. Sports field. Fishing lake. Supermarket, boutique and hire centre. Direct access to sheltered beach. Caravan holiday homes and lodges for hire. Off site: Surfing. Lundy Island excursion.

Open: March - November.

Directions

From Barnstaple, take A361 signed Braunton and Ilfracombe. At Braunton, take sharp left (narrow road) towards Croyde (signed) and follow the road all the way to the beach. Entrance to Ruda is on the right. O.S.GR: SS561331. GPS: N51:08.111 W04:14.112

Charges 2007

Per pitch incl. 4 persons	£ 9.00 - £ 30.00
pitch with services	£ 12.00 - £ 38.00

Prices are for pitch and up to four persons; maximum eight persons per pitch.

UK1250 Woodland Spring Touring Park

Venton, Drewsteignton EX6 6PG (Devon)

Tel: **01647 231695**. Email: **enquiries@woodlandsprings.co.uk**

Hidden away in a corner of the Dartmoor National Park, Woodlands Springs is a haven of peace and tranquillity. Set in a dip, it is sheltered by woodland with some views across the rural countryside. It provides 85 fairly level, grass pitches (20 with hardstanding) and 52 with electricity (10A), with a circular gravel access road and a central toilet block. Bare essentials are kept in reception, and a large field provides good dog walking. The resident owners provide a warm welcome on this quiet park that only accepts adults. With 600 miles of public right-of-way on Dartmoor, there is plenty to keep walkers busy. Over 50 species of birds have been seen on the park over the last few years so it would also be a good base for bird watching.

Facilities

The fairly old toilet block is fresh and white inside and fully equipped. Chemical disposal. Recycling including composter. Fishing, riding and bicycle hire can be arranged. Off site: Local pub within 1 mile. Castle Drogo and the Mythic garden nearby.

Open: All year.

Directions

From the M5 exit 31 follow the A30 towards Okehampton. After about 15 miles at Whiddon Down junction turn on A382 Moretonhampstead road. Stay on A382 for 0.5 miles then turn left at roundabout. After 1 mile turn left at brown caravan sign, then left and park is 150 yds down drive. O.S.GR: SX694911. GPS: N50:42.385 W03:51.040

Charges 2007

Per unit incl. 2 persons	£ 9.50 - £ 14.00
incl. electricity	£ 12.00 - £ 17.50

No credit cards.

UK1257 Watermouth Cove Holiday Park

Ilfracombe EX34 9SJ (Devon)

Tel: **01271 862504**. Email: **info@watermouthcoveholidays.co.uk**

This park is set in a lovely position, being at the side of a stream as it flows into the harbour and sea at Watermouth Cove. It has its own private beach from where there are lovely views across the sea to Hangman's Hill. Part of the park is arranged on the fairly level valley floor, whilst the tent area is on the side of the private headland with beautiful views of the coast from the higher ground. Electricity hook-ups (10A) are available. Children will enjoy fishing from the rocks, there is an adventure play area and during high season activities are organised for them. A heated outdoor pool is open from May - September. During peak season and at weekends at other times entertainment is arranged in the bar. A shop can be found in the reception area and this stocks a wide range of supplies including bread, milk and camping gas. There is lighting in the park but a torch is useful for the tent area. There are no sanitary facilities for disabled visitors and the paths down to the beach and on the hillside are probably not easily accessible.

Facilities

New heated facilities are provided in good quality 'portacabin' style units arranged in a U-shape with decking and seating joining them together. Showers are preset, have non-slip bases and a glass partition. The camping field has its own toilets. Laundry with washing machines, dryers and a free iron and board. Drinks machines, one providing hot drinks. Shop. Bar, restaurant and takeaway (weekends only in low season). Play area and activities for children (high season). Entertainment. Off site: Ilfracombe is nearby, Lynton and Lynmouth, Exmoor and Combe Martin within easy reach. Coastal roads and paths are numerous.

Open: 16 March - 28 October.

Directions

From M5 junction 27 follow signs for Barnstaple A361. At South Molton roundabout turn right signed A399 and continue for 16 miles following signs to Combe Martin. Go through Combe Martin on A399. After 2 miles Watermouth Cove is clearly signed on the right. O.S.GR: SS557482.

Charges 2007

Per unit incl. 2 persons	£ 7.50 - £ 23.00
incl. services	£ 10.50 - £ 26.00
extra person	£ 2.00
child (under 8 yrs)	free - £ 1.00

UK1340 Cornish Farm Touring Park

Shoreditch, Taunton TA3 7BS (Somerset)

Tel: **01823 327746**. Email: **info@cornishfarm.com**

This neat little park, which opened for its first full season in 2006, is on level ground and conveniently located close to the M5 motorway. There are 44 pitches, all with 10A electricity, of which 25 are on gravel hardstanding. Most pitches are accessed from a gravel road (one-way system) with plenty of fresh water taps, site lighting and some picnic tables. A separate area for tents is close to the toilet block. With its colourful flowerbeds and old apple trees this makes a very pleasant stop-over. Light power cables cross the site and there is some background motorway noise. Maximum length for motorhomes is 30ft, unless by arrangement with the wardens. Off to the left are the barns that house the Van Bitz workshops producing security systems for motorcaravans. The centrally situated, modern toilet block is of a high standard including under-floor heating, designed by the owners who are campers and caravanners themselves. There are no other facilities on the park but a cycle path and a footpath will take you into Taunton town centre. Taunton, the county town of Somerset, is worth a visit with its Castle, museum, a variety of livestock and produce markets and an annual flower show. The site would make a good base from which to visit Cheddar Gorge, Wookey Hole, and Clarke's shopping village at Street.

Facilities

One central block with underfloor heating and modern fittings. Large dual purpose room providing facilities for disabled visitors and small children. Dusk to dawn low energy lighting. Laundry room. Dishwashing sinks outside under cover at one end of the building. Motorcarvan service point. Off site: Level cycle/footpath into Taunton (2 miles) which has a castle, museum, and markets. Tesco Express 1 mile. Golf 2 miles. Bicycle hire 2 miles.

Open: All year.

Directions

From M5 exit 25 follow signs for Taunton. At first set of traffic lights (Creech Castle) turn left signed Corfe (B3170). Take third left (traffic lights) into Ilminster Road following signs to Corfe. Bear right at roundabout onto Blackbrook Way. Bear left at next roundabout and follow to T-junction (B3170). Turn right then next left (Killams Drive). Take second left (Killams Ave), pass through housing estate and cross motorway bridge. Site entrance is immediately after the bridge (second entrance) on the left.
O.S.GR: ST 234 219. GPS: N50:59.520 W03:05.554

Charges 2008

Per unit incl. 2 persons and electricity	£ 15.00
extra person	£ 2.00

UK1350 Quantock Orchard Caravan Park

Crowcombe, Taunton TA4 4AW (Somerset)

Tel: **01984 618618**. Email: qocp@flaxpool.freeserve.co.uk

Quantock Orchard, nestles at the foot of the Quantocks in quiet countryside, close to many of the attractions of the area. Attractively developed, mature apple trees, recently planted trees, shrubs and pretty flower beds with a nice use of heathers, make a pleasant environment and the clock tower on the wooden sanitary block adds interest. With access from fairly narrow gravel roads, there are 55 touring pitches, part separated by growing shrubs and hedging, of which 20 are for tents. Of various sizes, all touring pitches have 10A electricity hook-ups, 20 have hardstanding, 4 have TV hook-up and 5 are fully serviced (two extra large, with patio and barbecue). Levelling blocks may be required on some pitches. Only 'air-flo' style groundsheets are permitted on grass pitches. A leisure suite provides a sauna, steam room, jacuzzi, mini gym and conservatory rest area (this facility is open to the public; visitor membership optional with a range of tariffs; children under 16 not admitted). It is complemented by the outdoor heated swimming pool, open to all, which is walled with paved sunbathing surrounds.

Facilities

The central, heated sanitary block, refurbished in 2005, is very well maintained. Two showers each for ladies and men. Some washbasins in curtained cubicles for ladies, excellent family bathroom and separate mother and baby rooms. Good dishwashing provision, microwave, and laundry facilities. Drain for motorcaravan waste water tanks. Well stocked licensed shop includes camping accessories. Mountain bike hire (some with buggies for children). Fish and chip van visits (twice weekly in summer). Swimming pool (40 x 20 ft. open May - Sept). Leisure suite. Games room, Sky TV. Fenced safe-based play area. Caravan storage Oct. - March. Off site: West Somerset Steam Railway in Crowcombe 1 mile, The Carew Arms serves meals.

Open: All year.

Directions

Park is west off A358 road (Taunton - Minehead), about 1 mile south of Crowcombe village. O.S.GR: ST140363. GPS: N51:06.504 W03:13.587

Charges guide

Per unit incl. 2 persons	
and electricity	£ 12.95 - £ 17.95
tent and car incl. 2 persons	£ 11.95 - £ 16.95
extra person	£ 3.49
child (3-15 yrs)	£ 1.49 - £ 2.49
backpacker or cyclist	£ 3.95 - £ 7.00

UK1360 Halse Farm Touring Caravan & Camping Park

Winsford, Minehead TA24 7JL (Somerset)

Tel: **01643 851259**. Email: ar@halsefarm.co.uk

A truly rural park with beautiful, moorland views, you may be lucky enough to glimpse red deer across the valley or be able to see ponies and foals grazing outside the main gate which is adjacent to the moor. Two open, neatly cut fields (level at the top) back onto traditional hedging and slope gently to the middle and bottom where wild flowers predominate. One field provides electricity points (10A) and is used for motorcaravans and caravans, the other is for tents. There is no reception – you leave your unit by the toilet block and walk down to the farm kitchen to book in. The pretty village of Winsford is one mile (footpath from farm) with a post office, shop, pub and restaurant. Mrs Brown has laminated maps available (at a small cost) detailing six walks of varying distances, starting and finishing at the farm. Also available is a list of the wild birds, flowers, etc. to be found on the site. A member of the Countryside Discovery group.

Facilities

The central toilet block is of good quality and heated. Well equipped and maintained, it includes a toilet, washbasin and shower for visitors with disabilities, washing machine, dryer and iron, and tourist information. Gas is available at the farm. Play equipment. Off site: Fishing 4 miles, bicycle hire 5 miles, riding 2 miles. Tarr Steps and Barle Valley 3 miles. Winsford village 1 mile.

Open: 18 March - 1 November.

Directions

Turn off A396 Tiverton - Minehead road for Winsford (site signed). In Winsford village turn left in front of the Royal Oak (not over ford) and keep on uphill for 1 mile (go slowly round the sharp bend at the bottom). Cross cattle grid onto moor and turn immediately left to farm. Caravans should avoid Dulverton - keep to the A396 from Bridgetown (signed). O.S.GR: SS898342. GPS: N51:05.863 W03:34.799

Charges 2007

Per unit incl. 2 persons	£ 10.00 - £ 12.00
with electricity	£ 12.00 - £ 14.00
extra person	£ 5.00 - £ 6.00
child (5-16 yrs)	£ 1.30 - £ 1.80

UK1355 Lowtrow Cross Caravan Site

Upton, nr. Wiveliscombe, Taunton TA4 2DB (Somerset)

Tel: **01398 371199**. Email: **info@lowtrowcross.co.uk**

Situated just inside Exmoor National Park, Lowtrow Cross is a small park for adults only. It is quietly located on a hillside giving lovely views north towards the Brendon Hills. There are 23 generously sized pitches, of which two are occupied by caravan holiday homes and two are seasonal. An adjacent meadow can be used for tents. There are four hardstandings otherwise the pitches are on sloping grass. There are 17 electricity hook-ups (16A) each with a TV socket (aerial cables on loan). Although there is no bar or restaurant on site there is a pub at the gate with local cask beers and excellent food. Lowtrow Cross is well situated for walking and cycling in the beautiful Exmoor countryside with its wide variety of wildlife. Close by Haddon Moor, with its own herd of ponies and buzzards overhead, overlooks Wimbleball Lake where one can enjoy boating, fishing and nature trails. Not far away are Dunster Castle, Porlock and the West Somerset Steam railway. The area is well known for its cider and there is a museum of cider-making at Taunton.

Facilities

Traditional heated, well equipped, toilet block but no facilities for disabled visitors. Excellent laundry room. Freezer and microwave. Small shop in reception; basic foodstuffs, milk, bread, free range eggs, frozen ready meals, toiletries. Off site: Lowtrow Cross Inn at gate. Garage 750 m. Fishing and boating 3 miles. Golf and riding 10 miles.

Open: 16 March - 31 October.

Directions

From M5 junction 25 follow signs for Minehead (A358) through Taunton, then 5 miles from Taunton turn west (left) on B3224 signed Raleigh Cross. Shortly after passing Raleigh Cross Inn turn south on B3190 signed Bampton. Site is on right in 4 miles just before Upton village. O.S.GR: ST007292.

Charges 2007

Per unit incl. 2 adults	£ 10.00 - £ 13.00
extra adult	£ 4.00
electricity (16A)	£ 2.50
awning	£ 0.50 - £ 1.00

Lowtrow Cross
Upton, Nr. Wiveliscombe, Taunton Somerset, TA4 2DB
A small, quiet, adults only site set in a secluded area on the edge of Exmoor National Park
Email: info@lowtrowcross.co.uk
www.lowtrowcross.co.uk
• Hot showers/ toilet block
• Electric hook up
• TV points
• Laundry
• Dishwashing facilities.
• Small shop
• Pay phone
• Dogs welcome
Tel: (01398) 371199

UK1380 Hoburne Blue Anchor

Blue Anchor Bay, Minehead TA24 6JT (Somerset)

Tel: **01643 821360**. Email: **enquiries@hoburne.com**

Although mainly a holiday park, with almost 300 caravan holiday homes, Blue Anchor nevertheless offers good facilities for 103 touring units. Trailer tents are accepted but not other tents (other than pup tents with a touring booking). Virtually in a separate touring area, the level pitches all have 16A electricity and hardstanding for cars and motorcaravans (with caravans going on the adjacent grass). A feature of the park is a good sized, irregularly shaped indoor swimming pool with an area for small children, complete with a mushroom shaped fountain. With views of the sea from the pool, it is heated and supervised. Although not actually within the park itself, there are restaurants and takeaways within easy walking distance. The park's situation, directly across the small road from the beach, is unusual and gives some beautiful views across the Bristol Channel to South Wales, although not visible from the pitches. Exmoor, the Quantocks and Minehead are close and the West Somerset Steam Railway runs along one side of the park. Part of the Hoburne Group.

Facilities

Toilet facilities provide large, free hot showers (with push-button), dishwashing and laundry sinks under cover, and a fully equipped launderette in a single, modern block serving just the touring area. Indoor heated pool (free). Excellent adventure-style play area in a copse. Note: an unfenced river runs along one boundary. Crazy golf. Small supermarket/shop with coffee shop. American motorhomes accepted (max. 36 ft). Dogs are not accepted. Off site: Beach 100 yds. Riding and bicycle hire 5 miles. Golf 6 miles.

Open: 1 March - 31 October.

Directions

From M5 junction 25, take A358 signed Minehead. After 12 miles turn left onto A39 at Williton. After 4 miles turn right onto B3191 at Carhampton signed Blue Anchor. Park is 1.5 miles on right. O.S.GR: ST024535. GPS: N51:10.932 W03:23.837

Charges 2007

Per unit incl. up to 6 persons, electricity and awning	£ 9.50 - £ 19.50
Weekend breaks available.	

79

UK1390 The Old Oaks Touring Park

Wick Farm, Wick, Glastonbury BA6 8JS (Somerset)

Tel: **01458 831437**. Email: **info@theoldoaks.co.uk**

The Old Oaks, an 'adults only' park, is tucked below and hidden from the 'Tor', in a lovely secluded setting with views across to the Mendips. In total there are 100 large pitches in a series of paddocks, the majority with 10A electricity, hardstanding and several with fully serviced (including sewage). Mainly backing on to hedges, they are attractively arranged and interspersed with shrubs and flowers in a circular development or terraced with increasing views. A quiet orchard area or a separated hedged paddock for camping and a larger field with chemical disposal facilities complete the provision. Mature trees and hedging combine with the mellow farm buildings to give a sense of timelessness, tranquillity and peace. Whether you fish or not, the pond which is well stocked with carp, roach and tench is worth a visit not only for its view of the Tor, but also to see the ducks and the chickens on your way. There is parking for disabled visitors within 25 yards of the pond. In an area steeped in history and legend, this is a very well equipped and maintained park which should meet the needs of the discerning camper or caravanner. A member of the Best of British group.

Facilities

The heated toilet block, converted from the old stables, is of excellent quality and well equipped. Neatly paved outside, it has digital security locks (a public footpath from the Tor passes through the farm). Some washbasins are in cubicles. Two en-suite rooms and a bathroom (£1). Disabled visitors have two rooms. Fully equipped laundry room. Motorcaravan service facilities. Two recycling points. Freezer for ice packs (free). Useful dog wash. Licensed shop for basics (limited hours). Pool table, TV and library room. Bicycle hire (with helmets). Fishing. Adults only accepted (18 yrs and over). Internet access at reception. Off site: Riding 5 miles and golf 6 miles. Market day is Tuesday.

Open: 1 March - 20 November.

Directions

Park is north off A361 Shepton Mallet - Glastonbury road, 2 miles from Glastonbury. Take narrow unclassified road signed Wick for 1 mile and park is on the left. O.S.GR: ST521394. GPS: N51:09.158 W02:40.818

Charges 2008

Per unit with 2 persons	£ 12.50 - £ 19.00
with electricity (10A)	£ 13.00 - £ 16.00
awning with breathing groundsheet	£ 1.00
dog	£ 1.00

UK1420 Southfork Caravan Park

Parrett Works, Martock TA12 6AE (Somerset)

Tel: **01935 825661**. Email: **southforkcaravans@btconnect.com**

Don't be put off by the address which is historic – this was once a 17th century flax mill. Michael and Nancy Broadley now own and run this excellent, modern, well drained site just outside the lovely village of Martock. With 27 touring pitches on grass with a gravel access road (21 with 10A electrical hook-ups and 2 with water and waste water), it is an orderly, quiet park on two acres of flat, tree lined meadow near the River Parrett. All the expected facilities are close to the entrance and as the owners live on the premises, the park is open all year. Most things are available, including an NCC-approved caravan repairs/servicing centre. Despite the rural setting, the A303 trunk road is just five minutes away. This area of South Somerset contains much of interest, including gardens, historic houses and sites, the Fleet Air Arm Museum, Haynes Motor Museum and Cricket St Thomas Wildlife Park. Information about access to many cycle routes and numerous walks, including the Parrett Trail, is available from reception.

Facilities

The heated well maintained toilet block is fully equipped and includes some washbasins in cabins. Laundry room with washing machine and dryer, plus dishwashing sink. Shop and limited off-licence with gas and comprehensive camping accessories. Play area. Off site: Fishing (with licences) on the River Parrett a few yards from the park. Golf 5 miles. Bicycle hire 8 miles. Riding 10 miles. Pubs with good food in South Petherton and Martock, less than 2 miles in each direction.

Open: All year.

Directions

From A303 between Ilchester and Ilminster turn north at the roundabout signed for South Petherton. At T-junction in middle of village, turn right towards Martock. Park is at Parrett Works mid way between the two villages (about 1.5 miles from South Petherton). O.S.GR: ST446187. GPS: N50:57.922 W02:47.389

Charges 2007

Per unit incl. 2 persons	£ 9.00 - £ 13.00
with electricity (10A)	£ 11.50 - £ 15.50
extra person	£ 1.75
child (under 5 yrs)	free
dog	£ 1.00

UK1370 Burrowhayes Farm Caravan & Camping Site

West Luccombe, Porlock, Minehead TA24 8HT (Somerset)

Tel: **01643 862463**. Email: **info@burrowhayes.co.uk**

This delightful park with riding stables on site, is on the edge of Exmoor. The stone packhorse bridge over Horner Water beside the farm entrance sets the tone of the park, which the Dascombe family have created over the last thirty years having previously farmed the land. The farm buildings have been converted into riding stables with escorted rides available (from 7/4). Touring and tent pitches are on partly sloping field with marvelous views or a flatter location in the clearing by the river, while 20 caravan holiday homes are in a separate area. Electrical hook-ups are available (10A), although some long leads may be needed. With walking, birdwatching, plenty of wild life to observe, pretty Exmoor villages and Lorna Doone country nearby there is much to do. Children can ride, play in the stream or explore the woods at the top of the site. Limited trout fishing is available in Horner Water (NT permit) alongside the park.

Facilities

The heated toilet block provides controllable hot showers, one washbasin cubicle for each sex, hairdressing and shaving areas. In the reception and stable block area are a laundry room, unit for disabled visitors and babies, and an indoor dishwashing room. A second older block is opened in high season with extra WCs and washbasins. Motorcaravan service point. Well stocked shop doubles with reception (from 1/4). Dogs must be kept on leads at all times and exercised off site. Off site: Beach 2 miles. Fishing 2 miles. Bicycle hire 5 miles. Golf 6 miles. Minehead 5 miles. Local pub 20 minutes walk.

Open: 15 March - 31 October.

Directions

From A39, 5 miles west of Minehead, take first left past Allerford to Horner and West Luccombe. Site is on right after 400 yards. O.S.GR: SS899461. GPS: N51:12.212 W03:34.668

Charges 2007

Per unit incl. 1 or 2 persons	£ 8.50 - £ 12.00
with electricity	£ 10.50 - £ 14.00
extra person	£ 3.50 - £ 4.50
child (3-15 yrs)	£ 2.00 - £ 2.50
dog	free

IN THE HEART OF EXMOOR COUNTRY

Burrowhayes Farm Caravan & Camping Site & Riding Stables

Popular Site in delightful National Trust setting on Exmoor.
A walkers paradise. Pony trekking from site. Sites for touring caravans, tents & motorhomes. Caravans for hire. Heated toilet & shower block with disabled facilities

Tel: 01643 862 463 www.burrowhayes.co.uk

UK1430 Cheddar, Mendip Heights Camping & Caravanning Club Site

Priddy, Wells BA5 3BP (Somerset)

Tel: **01749 870241**. Email: **cheddar@campingandcaravanningclub.co.uk**

Historic Priddy is the highest village in the Mendips and is famed for its annual Sheep Fair in August. Nearby are extensive Roman lead-workings, Bronze Age burial mounds, the Priddy Circle and access to Swildons Hole, one of the popular cave systems in the Mendips. Formerly Mendip Heights Caravan Park, this well kept site is half a mile from the village with tranquil views across the Mendip fields, characterised by dry stone walling. It has a simple charm with field margins left natural to encourage wildlife and nest boxes in the mature trees edging the three fields which comprise the site. These provide space for 90 units on mostly slightly sloping short grass with 56 electric hook-ups (16A), 36 with hardstanding, 8 serviced pitches with electric and water and 5 seasonal pitches. The park is also on the Padstow-Bristol Sustran Route 3. Many tourist attractions are within a 20 mile radius.

Facilities

The refurbished toilet block with all facilities is bright, cheerful and heated. Two family rooms (one with high and low toilet and shower). Facilities for disabled visitors. Dishwashing and laundry facilities. The reception/licensed shop doubles as the village shop and is therefore open all season selling groceries, Calor gas, etc. Tourist information. Motorcaravan service point. Wendy house, swings and table tennis for children. Torches useful. Off site: Two traditional village pubs with very different characters stand by the village green within walking distance (0.5 miles). Bicycle hire and golf 5 miles. Fishing 6 miles, riding 2 miles.

Open: 2 March - 14 November.

Directions

From M5 exit 21 take A371 to Banwell. Turn left on A368, right on B3134 and right on B3135. After 2 miles turn left at camp sign. From M4 westbound exit 18, A46 to Bath, then A4 towards Bristol. Take A39 for Wells and right at Green Ore traffic lights on B3135; after 5 miles turn left at camp sign. O.S.GR: ST522518. GPS: N51:15.816 W02:41.123

Charges guide

Per person	£ 6.05 - £ 8.40
child	£ 2.25 - £ 4.80
pitch with services incl. electricity	£ 3.25

UK1440 Baltic Wharf Caravan Club Site

Cumberland Road, Bristol BS1 6XG (Somerset)

Tel: **0117 926 8030**. Email: **balticwharf@caravanclub.co.uk**

This excellent Caravan Club site in Bristol's redeveloped dockland, is well laid out and maintained to a high standard. It is screened from the road by a high wall with a boatyard on one side and residential apartments on the other, with access via a lockable gate to the Baltic Wharf dockside. The view across the dock towards Clifton village and Bristol is unique and you can even glimpse the suspension bridge. The 55 pitches are accessed by a circular tarmac road, all on stone chippings and ideal for all year round use (steel pegs are sold at reception). Awnings are prohibited on 16 pitches to meet fire regulations. All have electricity (16A) and TV aerial points (reception is poor). It is a 30 minute walk to the city centre, a daily ferry runs throughout the year or there's a regular bus service. An extra ferry runs from the SS Great Britain to Templemeads. This is a popular site in a popular location so advance booking is essential. Arrive between 12.00 and 20.00. There is no space for trailers, boats, etc. and tents and units over 28 ft. are not accepted.

Facilities

The toilet block provides good clean facilities including controllable showers and washbasins in cubicles (heated in winter). Good facilities for disabled visitors, plus toilets and showers for the walking disabled in the main block. Dishwashing under cover. Fully equipped laundry room. Motorcaravan service point. Tourist information room. Dogs are welcome but there is no dog walk. Wardens live on the site. Off site: Fishing and boating (permits from Harbour Master's office) 400 yards.

Open: All year.

Directions

From M5, J18, take A4 (signed Bristol West). Follow signs for Historic Harbour and SS Great Britain under Clifton Suspension Bridge and through Hotwells (about 5.5 miles). Cross over Dock bridge and site is about 500 yds. on left. From opposite direction (from East) follow signs for Historic Harbour and SS Great Britain. Site on right just to the west of SS Great Britain. Look carefully for the Caravan Club sign – site is behind a high wall and there are no brown signs. O.S.GR: ST574721.
GPS: N51:26.792 W02:36.855

Charges 2007

Per person	£ 4.70 - £ 6.20
child (5-16 yrs)	£ 1.50 - £ 3.00
pitch (non-member)	£ 10.90 - £ 15.30

UK1460 Newton Mill Camping Park

Newton Road, Bath BA2 9JF (Somerset)

Tel: **01225 333909**. Email: **newtonmill@hotmail.com**

In a peaceful valley two miles from the centre of the historic city of Bath and with direct access to the local cycle track network, Newton Mill is an excellent base from which to explore the city and the area. The site has been created around an old mill, the bar and restaurant now occupying part of the original building, and there is a modern timber chalet style reception building with a small, well stocked shop. The restaurant (open evenings all year) serves good value, speciality meals. Breakfasts are available (weekends Easter - October, daily in summer). The tent meadow is in an elevated position, or alternatively you may prefer the paddock, a small field alongside the stream which is a car free zone with a separate parking area. The site accepts 105 tents and also has 90 caravan pitches (with 30 long stay) which are located at the other end of the valley. All of these have hardstandings, with 16A electricity and satellite TV hook-ups. This end of the park is closest to the main Bristol - London railway line, not visually obtrusive but occasional rail noise may be noticeable.

Facilities

Two new heated toilet blocks provide excellent modern facilities with some washbasins in cubicles, free hot showers, bathrooms (on payment), baby rooms, dishwashing rooms and a good suite for disabled campers. Launderette. Basic motorcaravan service point. Shop, bar, restaurant with garden seating area. Play area. Boules court. Fishing. Off site: Bus service into Bath runs every 10 minutes from Twerton village (10 minute walk). Nearby Bristol and Bath Railway Path (a traffic free cycle way) links to the West Bath Riverside Path, and the Kennet and Avon towpath. Thursday market in Twerton.

Open: All year.

Directions

Site is 2 miles west of Bath city centre, about 1 mile southeast of the roundabout where the A4 meets the A39. From the north take M4 exit 19, turn on to M32 and almost immediately take A4174 (Avon ring road) for 7.5 miles to the A4. Turn left towards Bath and after 5 miles at second roundabout, take second exit signed Newton St Loe and pass The Globe public house. Site entrance is on the left after about 1 mile. O.S.GR: ST713647. GPS: N51:22.688 W02:24.649

Charges guide

Per person	£ 5.00
child (3-16 yrs)	£ 2.50
pitch incl. car	£ 3.00 - £ 8.00
awning	£ 2.00
dog	£ 0.75

82

UK1480 Home Farm Holiday Park & Country Club

Edithmead, Burnham-on-Sea TA9 4HD (Somerset)

Tel: **01278 788888**. Email: **SITE@hfhp.co.uk**

Home Farm is neatly and attractively laid out covering 44 acres, and is convenient for those using the M5. The 780 level pitches (including 180 privately owned holiday homes and a number of seasonal units) laid out on level mown grass are all clearly marked, accessed by tarmac roads and divided into various sections, for example an area for those with pets. Including 183 pitches with hardstanding, there are 20 serviced pitches for RVs and motorcaravans. Electrical connections (10A) are available everywhere. A large, modern pool with paved surrounds and a paddling section is neatly walled. There is early evening entertainment for children, plus amusement machines and pool tables for those interested. The club house (with free membership) is a feature of the site providing meals, a range of entertainment, wide screen TV, an attractive conservatory and outside barbecue area. In all, it is an excellent provision and Burnham-on-Sea is only a mile away – there is a footpath from the site crossing the railway line. With Berrow Sands and Brean Down there is over seven miles of beach to choose from! There is some road and rail noise but this quietens at night. Tents are not accepted.

Facilities

Two main, refurbished toilet blocks are heated and well situated for touring areas. Hot showers in one block are larger, but minus dividers. Bathrooms (key with £5 deposit). Baby room. Laundry. Facilities for disabled visitors. Shop. Bar. Restaurants, takeaway (all in club house, hours vary according to season). Swimming pool (May-Sept, lifeguard w/ends, B.Hs and school holidays). Play area. ATM. Internet access and WiFi zone. Off site: Golf 2 miles. Riding 3 miles. Beach 3 miles.

Open: 10 February - 6 January.

Directions

Home Farm is 400 yards from M5 junction 22 and the A38. It is signed from the B3140 into Burnham-on-Sea. O.S.GR: ST328493.
GPS: N51:14.325 W02:57.850

Charges 2007

Per pitch incl. 2 persons, electricity and awning	£ 7.50 - £ 22.50
extra person	£ 3.00 - £ 5.25
child (4-17 yrs)	£ 1.50 - £ 4.50

Club membership free. Special breaks available.

UK1500 Long Hazel Park

High Street, Sparkford, Yeovil BA22 7JH (Somerset)

Tel: **01963 440002**. Email: **longhazelpark@hotmail.com**

Pamela and Alan Walton are really enthusiastic about their neat, small, adult only park in the Somerset village of Sparkford where they will make you most welcome. This level, landscaped park is surrounded by attractive beech hedging, silver birches and many other ornamental trees and the park has a relaxed, comfortable feel. It provides 50 touring pitches for all types of units with electrical hook-ups (16A), 40 pitches with hardstanding, some extra long with grass lawns at the side, and the entrance has been widened for easier access. Part of the park near the road is being developed with pine holiday lodges for private ownership.

Facilities

The well equipped toilet block is neat, tidy and heated in winter. Well planned facilities for visitors with disabilities. Washing machine and dryer. Motorcaravan discharge. Gas supplies. Long hardstanding pitches suitable for American style motorhomes. Off site: Bus service. Village inn 100 yds. Riding or fishing 8 miles. Golf 5 miles.

Open: 16 February - 16 January.

Directions

At roundabout on A303 take road into village of Sparkford and park is signed on the left.
O.S.GR: ST604263. GPS: N51:02.064 W02:34.118

Charges 2008

Per unit incl. 2 persons	£ 16.00 - £ 18.00
extra person	£ 2.00

No credit cards.

83

UK1490 Greenacres Camping

Barrow Lane, North Wootton, Shepton Mallet BA4 4HL (Somerset)

Tel: 01749 890497

Greenacres is a rural site in Somerset countryside for tents, trailer tents and small motorcaravans only. Hidden away below the Mendips and almost at the start of the 'Levels', it is a simple green site – a true haven of peace and quiet. The grass is neatly trimmed over the 4.5 acres and hedged with mature trees, though there is a view of Glastonbury Tor in one direction and of Barrow Hill in the other. All of the 30 pitches are around the perimeter of the park, leaving a central area safe for children to play. At the narrower neck end, 5 pitches have electricity hook-ups (16A) and are ideal for those without children or birdwatchers. Wild life abounds. A speciality of the park is the 'Turf Rider' that tows the cart used to give children an evening ride. There are many nearby attractions should you tire of the peace and quiet, such as Wookey Hole, Cheddar Caves and Gorge, Longleat, the beautiful small city of Wells (with leisure centre), Clarks Village, etc. You can cycle into both Wells and Glastonbury using Sustran Route 3.

Facilities

The central wooden toilet block is simple but perfectly acceptable and kept clean. Hot showers are accessed directly from the outside. Two dishwashing sinks, two laundry sinks (H&C) and a spin dryer, with and iron, board and hairdryer available from the park office. Play equipment, badminton net and play house. The park office is across the lane (gate is usually keep shut), at the owner's bungalow. Here too are fridges and freezers for campers' use (free), a library, tourist information and bicycle hire. Batteries may be charged or borrowed. Dogs are not accepted. Off site: North Wootton (under 1 mile) with large pub/restaurant and a vineyard. Fishing and riding nearby.

Open: March - October.

Directions

From A39 Glastonbury - Wells road turn east at Brownes Garden Centre and follow camping signs. From A361 Glastonbury - Shepton Mallet road follow camp signs from Pilton or Steanbow. (Roads are narrow with few passing places). O.S.GR: ST553416. GPS: N51:10.342 W02:38.513

Charges 2007

Per person	£ 6.00
child (4-16 yrs)	£ 2.00
No credit cards.	

UK1510 Bath Chew Valley Caravan Park

Ham Lane, Bishop Sutton BS39 5TZ (Somerset)

Tel: 01275 332127. Email: enquiries@bathchewvalley.co.uk

A small and secluded garden site for adults only, Chew Valley has been developed with much tender love and care by the Betton family. The result is that caravans are sited by neat lawns amongst colourful beds of flowers and the cars are tucked away on the nearby car park, providing a tranquil and restful atmosphere. An area of woodland has been planted adjacent to the tent field along with an enclosed dog walking area. The warden will assist you in placing your caravan. Groundsheets are not permitted on the grass in order to protect it. There are neat hardstandings and 17 spacious, fully serviced pitches and, again to protect the lawns, motorcaravans must always use them. This park will particularly appeal to garden lovers; a very nice touch is the small nursery 'Gone to Pot' where those staying on the site can purchase some of the plants found on-site. Next to reception there is a good library, also providing tourist information. Chew Valley lake is a walk of about half a mile with trout fishing available and Blagdon lake is popular for birdwatching. There are several circular walks in the area – visitors may borrow the route plans and a walking stick from reception. Bristol and Bath are within an easy distance and Cheddar Gorge or Longleat make excellent days out. A Best of British group member.

Facilities

The heated toilet block (it has a 'home from home' feel), provides all the fittings that make life comfortable. Eight separate en-suite units each with WC, basin and shower. One unit has facilities for disabled visitors. Useful utility room for dish or hand washing with a spin drier and ironing facilities, together with a washing machine and tumble drier for service washes only. Motorcaravan service point. Internet access and WiFi. Off site: Village 100 yds. with useful general store, newsagent, two pubs and a post office. Supermarkets within 15 minutes drive. Fishing 1 mile. Golf 5 miles. Riding 8 miles. Beach 15 miles.

Open: All year.

Directions

From Bath direction on A368 turn right opposite the Red Lion pub in Bishop Sutton. Road appears a little narrow but continue past a small track to the left (50 yds) for a further 50 yds. Park entrance appears on your left with neat, clear entrance. O.S.GR: ST584599. GPS: N51:20.195 W02:35.831

Charges 2007

Per person	£ 4.00
standard pitch incl. electricity, awning and pets	£ 10.00
serviced pitch	£ 12.00
tent	£ 8.00

UK1520 Waterrow Touring Park

Wiveliscombe, Taunton TA4 2AZ (Somerset)

Tel: **01984 623464**

Beside the River Tone in a pretty part of South Somerset, Tony and Anne Taylor have enthusiastically developed Waterrow into a charming, landscaped touring park for adults only. Nestling in a little sheltered valley, it is very peaceful and possible for an overnight stop (just over 30 minutes from the M5) or ideal as a base for exploring nearby Exmoor and the Brendon Hills. There are 48 touring pitches, all of which are on level hardstandings, including 5 with full services. The remainder are on flat or gently sloping grass with little shade as yet but bushes and trees are maturing. All have electricity (16A), spring and mains water are available and TV aerial points have been installed (your own lead is required, sometimes quite long). A small area has been set aside for tent campers. Converted barns have been put to good use, providing local tourist information, a small library and a visual record of the park's development. Further down the park, below the touring area, wide steps lead to a private nature reserve where you can find the Otter Holt, go fly fishing for wild brown trout (tuituion available), take a riverside walk or just relax and watch the birds. This 'adult only' site is open all year. A member of the Best of British group.

Facilities

A modern, clean toilet unit, well fitted out and with heating, provides WCs and washbasins, some in curtained cubicles. New heated shower block. Facilities for disabled people (key). Dishwashing. Washing machine and dryer. Motorcaravan service point. Limited provisions are available in reception. Order jacket potatoes before lunchtime for the evening for just £1. The Taylors will 'dog sit' if you are visiting somewhere your pet is not allowed (£5 per day). Water colour, drawing and fly fishing holidays arranged at certain times. WiFi. Caravan storage with 'store and stay' system. Site is not suitable for American motorhomes. Luxury Holiday Home for hire. Off site: Golf and fishing 7 miles. Bicycle hire 10 miles. Riding 12 miles. The Rock Inn is a short walk and provides good meals and real ales. Wiveliscombe 3 miles.

Open: All year.

Directions

From M5 exit 25 take A358 (signed Minehead) round Taunton for 4 miles, then at Staplegrove onto the B3227 for 11.5 miles to Wiveliscombe where straight over at lights to Waterrow (still on B3227). Park is on left shortly after the Rock Inn. Do not use satellite navigation for this site as it takes you on roads unsuitable for caravans. O.S.GR: ST052250.

Charges 2007

Per unit incl. 2 persons (adults only) and electricity	£ 11.00 - £ 20.00
extra person	£ 5.00

UK1530 Slimeridge Farm Touring Park

Links Road, Uphill, Weston-super-Mare BS23 4XY (Somerset)

Tel: **01934 641641**

This small touring site is next to the beach in Uphill village at the southern end of Weston Bay. There are 56 pitches (many taken on seasonal lets), on level grass with electricity (16A) available, separated from the beach by stone walling. The view across the bay is quite something, with Brean Down and Steep Holm Island standing out. However it is worth noting that, because of its close proximity to the beach, the site could be affected by the tide in extreme adverse winter weather conditions. A circular tarmac road connects the marked and numbered pitches (allocated by the wardens) which include eight hardstandings for motorcaravans. Arrive betweeon 11.00 and 17.00 hrs only. Weston-super-Mare with all its leisure activities and entertainment is 2 miles, Cheddar Gorge, Wooky Hole and Glastonbury are within easy driving distance.

Facilities

A modern toilet block with electronic code entry system is well equipped and includes en-suite shower facilities that are also provided for handicapped visitors. Laundry room and washing up sinks. Chemical disposal unit also used for waste water. Off site: Post office, general stores and pubs within close walking distance. Golf (note: golfers have right of way to cross the park as the golf course is split by the site).

Open: 1 March - 30 October.

Directions

Site is south of Weston-super-Mare. From the A370 follow sign for Uphill village and sands. O.S.GR: ST312588. GPS: N51:19.433 W02:59.342

Charges guide

Per unit incl. 2 persons, electricity and awning	£ 10.00 - £ 20.00
extra person	£ 1.50 - £ 3.00
child (4-9 yrs)	£ 1.00 - £ 2.50
dog	£ 0.50 - £ 1.00

Min. stay 2 nights at B.Hs. No credit cards.

UK1540 Batcombe Vale Campsite

Batcombe Vale, Shepton Mallet BA4 6BW (Somerset)
Tel: **01749 831207**. Email: **gary.butler1@virgin.net**

Set in a secluded valley with fields gently rising around it, contented cows grazing with watchful buzzards cruising above and views across the distant hills, this is a very special place. Batcombe Vale House is a mellow, attractive building covered with wisteria, to one side of the valley overlooking the lakes and the 'wilder' landscape. Trees and shrubs have been skilfully placed to enhance the natural environment providing a range of colour and shape. Designated an 'area of outstanding natural beauty', there are 120 acres around the valley where you are welcome to wander and picnic in the fields – a haven for wild flowers, birds and butterflies. For those who fish, two of the lakes have carp and tench up to 18lbs but you must have a current licence. Descending slowly down the narrow entrance drive you see the pitches attractively set and terraced where necessary, in an oval with the lakes below. The grass is left natural around the 32 pitches (20 have 10A electricity) and paths mown where needed. If you tire of the views and the fishing there is a range of circular walks from the site or you can potter about in one of the four small rowing boats. There are many places to visit nearby, from Glastonbury with the Tor, to Cheddar Gorge and the Caves.

Facilities

The small rustic toilet block covered in honeysuckle meets all needs, including a freezer and dishwashing sinks. Groundsheet awnings must be lifted daily. Fishing. Caravan storage. One dog per pitch is welcome (no dangerous breeds). Bed and breakfast available in Batcombe Vale House. Off site: Golf, riding and bicycle hire 5 miles. Bruton (for shops, etc.) is 2 miles. Launderettes at Shepton or Frome.

Open: Easter - End of September.

Directions

Bruton is south of Shepton Mallet and Frome and north of Wincanton where the A359 intersects the B3081. About 2 miles north of Bruton on B3081 turn on bend (site signed) into narrow lane. Turn left at T-junction and follow signs to site 500 yds on left. Access drive is steep. O.S.GR: ST684376. GPS: N51:08.188 W02:27.190

Charges 2007

Per unit incl. 2 persons	£ 14.50
extra person	£ 4.20
child (4-16 yrs)	£ 2.10 - £ 2.50
electricity	£ 2.75

No commercial vehicles. Family groups only. No credit cards.

UK1545 Cheddar Bridge Touring Park

Draycott Road, Cheddar BS27 3RJ (Somerset)
Tel: **01934 743048**. Email: **enquires@cheddarbridge.co.uk**

Within easy walking distance of Cheddar village, this is an adult only (over 18 yrs) park. A compact site, there are 50 pitches, mostly on level grass, with 45 electric hook-ups (16A) and 10 gravel hardstandings. A separate area for a few tents is on the river bank. Reception keeps basic supplies and gas cylinders. Note: the site access is over a fairly narrow bridge with low stone walls, passable for double axle caravans, but more difficult for American RVs and very large motorcaravans. Cheddar village has a small supermarket with ATM, garage, pubs, restaurants and a leisure centre with an indoor pool. Cheddar Gorge is a little further and would make a good day's hike with a packed lunch, without the problems of parking a vehicle in the Gorge itself where most parking is on payment.

Facilities

Attractive heated sanitary block (close to site entrance, some distance from most of the pitches) with washbasins in cubicles, large showers, and family bathroom with shower over the bath. Utility room with dishwashing and laundry sinks, and washer/dryer. Hot water is restricted to 0700-1200 and 1600-2100. Fishing. Off site: Cheddar Gorge and village. Swimming pool 0.5 miles. Golf 3 miles. Riding 3 miles.

Open: 1 March - end October.

Directions

Site entrance is about 100 yards south of village on A371, on right hand side, next to Cheddar Football Club. O.S.GR: ST461530. GPS: N51:16.389 W02:46.475

Charges 2007

Per unit incl. 2 persons and electricity	£ 7.00 - £ 17.00
extra person	£ 2.00
dog	£ 1.00

UK1550 Bucklegrove Caravan & Camping Park

Wells Road, Rodney Stoke, Cheddar BS27 3UZ (Somerset)

Tel: **01749 870261**. Email: **info@bucklegrove.co.uk**

Bucklegrove is set right in the heart of Somerset on the southern slopes of the Mendip Hills and close to the tourist attractions of Cheddar Gorge, Wookey Hole, and Wells. The 125 touring pitches, 80 of which have 10A electricity connections, are split between two fields joined by a woodland walk. The top slightly undulating field is more suitable for tents and caravans, while the lower field with some short hardstandings is a little more level and would be suitable for caravans and smaller motorhomes. The play area (for under 14s) includes a fort, swings and obstacle course. Campers also have a games room and a heated indoor swimming pool (adult only sessions 10.00 - 11.00 daily). Adjoining the pool is a licensed bar with terrace providing simple bar menus and low-key entertainment mainly during high season or depending on the number of campers on site.

Facilities

Two bright and cheerful toilet blocks house all the usual amenities including some washbasins in cubicles and some spacious showers. The larger, heated block near reception also provides bathrooms (50p) with baby changing facilities, and a room for visitors with disabilities. Dishwashing and laundry rooms. Freezer for ice packs. Well stocked shop. Indoor swimming pool and paddling pool with terrace bar. Games room. Play area. Dogs are accepted in low season only. Off site: Riding 2 miles. Golf 3 miles. Fishing 5 miles. Beach at Weston-Super-Mare 12 miles. A bus to Wells and Cheddar stops at the park entrance.

Open: 1 March - 2 January.

Directions

Take A371 Wells to Cheddar road. Park is on right about 1 mile past Westbury village. Take care as the road between Wells and Cheddar is rather narrow through some of the villages. O.S.GR: ST490496. GPS: N51:14.599 W02:43.938

Charges guide

Per unit incl. 2 persons	
and electricity	£ 7.50 - £ 19.00
pup tent	£ 1.00 - £ 1.50
extra person	£ 2.50
child (4-14 yrs)	£ 1.00 - £ 1.50
dog (off peak only)	£ 1.00

THE FAIRWAYS INTERNATIONAL TOURING CARAVAN & CAMPING PARK

Clive and Cathy warmly welcome visitors old and new. We are situated 2 miles off Junction 23 in the Glastonbury direction, off B3141 behind Bawdrip Service Station. Facilities include comprehensive accessory centre in shop, clean toilet block and laundry room etc. Family and pet friendly, seasonal pitches, rallies welcomed. Caravans, motorhomes, trailer tents and tents charged according to size - online booking. Special offer pensioners' weeks, over 60s and Force Camping Card holders: 7-day bookings (consecutive) in March, June, September and October for £55 a week. ACSI, ADAC and NKC Camping Card holders at only 14 euros daily.

Bath Road, Bawdrip, Bridgwater, Somerset, TA7 8PP

01278 685 569 Web: *www.fairwaysint.btinternet.co.uk* Email: *fairwaysint@btinternet.com*

UK1560 The Fairways International Touring Park

Bath Road, Bawdrip, Bridgwater TA7 8PP (Somerset)

Tel: **01278 685569**. Email: **holidays@fairwaysinternational.co.uk**

Fairways, a level 5.5 acre park set in rural Somerset, is owned and run by the Walker family. Gravel roads lead to the unmarked pitches that have been developed on well-drained grass – Clive Walker ensures that units are pitched sensibly. Of the 200 pitches about 50 are seasonal and 132 have electricity (10A). There are plans for major upgrading and expansion over the next few years. The central toilet block has won awards annually since 1994, although its age is beginning to show through. Families with young children are directed to pitches close to the play area, also in the centre of the park. Adjacent to the shop is a games room to keep older children occupied. The reception is in the shop that is stocked with a good selection of provisions and camping products. Being located so close to the M5, Fairways is ideal for stopovers as well as sightseeing and, if you visit in November, you will be able to see the famous Bridgwater Carnival.

Facilities

A central toilet block houses both washbasins in cubicles and open plan, showers (push-button control) and baby bath/shower room. A unit for disabled visitors with a cubicle for toilet and washbasin and a second for a shower. A wheelchair is provided for visitors to use if required. Good laundry facilities and room for dishwashing. Shop with gas. Freezer and microwaves (free of charge). Central play area. Games room with pool table, television and electronic games. Off site: Beaches at Burnham-on-Sea 8 miles; walking in the Quantock Hills within 10 miles.

Open: 1 March - mid November.

Directions

From M5, junction 23, take A39 in the direction of Glastonbury. Turn left just before Texaco garage on B3141 towards Woolavington and site is about 50 yards on the right. O.S.GR: ST348402. GPS: N51:09.416 W02:56.091

Charges 2007

Per unit incl. 2 persons	
and electricity	£ 11.50 - £ 16.50
extra person	£ 2.00
child (3-13 yrs)	£ 1.00
awning	£ 1.00 - £ 2.50
Euros accepted.	

UK1570 Northam Farm Touring Caravan Park

Brean Sands, Burnham-on-Sea TA8 2SE (Somerset)

Tel: **01278 751244**. Email: **enquiries@northamfarm.demon.co.uk**

Brean has been a popular holiday destination for decades and many large campsites have evolved. Northam Farm is one of them; it is a large family park with good facilities and an ongoing programme of improvements. Of the 750 pitches, 350 are for seasonal units and these are separated from the four tourist fields. Pitches are large so you won't feel cramped and 154 have block paved hardstanding. There are two play areas for youngsters, a sports field, bicycle track, and cricket pitch for teenagers, and fishing on the lake for adults. The owners and staff are always available to help visitors enjoy their stay. About 500 yards down the road is The Seagull, which is also owned by Northam Farm. Here you'll find an excellent restaurant, bar and nightly live entertainment, even during the low season. A bus stops at the park entrance, or visitors can book a free ride on the bus to Cheddar, famous for its gorge and caves. Alternatively, just down the road is Brean Leisure Park with its swimming complex, funfair, golf and much more.

Facilities

Three good toilet blocks, well maintained and within reasonable distance of all pitches, provide ample toilets, washbasins (newest block has curtained cubicles) and spacious showers (50p pull cord operation). Bathrooms (£1 charge). Baby room, hair washing and drying. Rooms for visitors with disabilities (key). New laundry. Motorcaravan service point. Dog shower. Licensed shop well stocked with food, holiday gear and accessories. Snack bar/takeaway. Free entry to live entertainment at The Seagull. Games room. Two play areas. Sports field. Fishing lake. Caravan workshop for repairs and servicing. Caravan storage. Dogs are not accepted in one field. Off site: Burnham-on-Sea and Weston-Super-Mare nearby. Golf and riding 0.5 miles.

Open: March - October.

Directions

From M5 junction 22 follow signs to Burnham-on-Sea, Berrow and then Brean. Continue through Brean and Northam Farm is on the right, half a mile past Brean Leisure Park. O.S.GR: ST297556. GPS: N51:17.694 W03:00.610

Charges 2007

Per unit incl. 2 persons	£ 6.25 - £ 14.50
with electricity	£ 8.25 - £ 20.00
extra person	£ 2.00 - £ 2.50
child	£ 0.75 - £ 1.00
dog, awning, fishing	free

UK1575 Holiday Resort Unity

Coast Road, Brean Sands TA8 2RB (Somerset)

Tel: **01278 751235**. Email: **rjh@hru.co.uk**

Holiday Resort Unity offers everything for everyone, from young children to the 'young at heart'. Apart from the extensive on-site amusements and entertainment programme, campers can also use the swimming pools, funfair and other leisure pursuits at the adjoining Brean Leisure Centre (owned by the same family), some free of charge and others by paying a small fee. Access to the five mile stretch of sandy beach is via a footpath opposite the site entrance. Fishing (with a licence) is permitted from Unity Lake in the Yellow Field. RJ's is a club with bars, food and entertainment for the whole family. Sarah's Pantry offers takeaway or sit-down meals (including the Sunday roast), while fish and chips are available at Porkers Bar. Three large touring fields provide pitches that are flat and open, mostly grass but some on concrete hardstandings (motorcaravans up to 30 ft. can be accommodated). Most pitches have 16A electricity hook-ups. A separate warden looks after each camping field. Ready equipped tents and a substantial number of caravan holiday homes are available for rent.

Facilities

Three good toilet blocks provide ample facilities and include en-suite units. Some toilets and washbasins have been adapted for people with disabilities (key from reception). Well equipped laundries. Dishwashing and hair care rooms. Motorcaravan service point. Well stocked shop. Gas exchange. RJ's Club, Sarah's Pantry and Porkers fish and chip bar. Large adventure play area. Cyber Zone (high season; £1 for 10 minutes). Buster's Work Out Gym, Sally's sun beds. Monday market, Sunday car boot sales. All facilities open in high season, most open during mid season and at weekends in low season. Torches advisable. Off site: Walking access from park to Brean Leisure Centre (pool, funfair etc); riding, cycling, cinema, walks, golf all within walking distance. Bus to Weston-super-Mare stops at park gates. Beach 100 m.

Open: 10 February - 20 November.

Directions

From M5 exit 22, follow signs for Burnham-on-Sea (B3140), Berrow and Brean. Holiday Resort Unity is on right along the main street of Brean – it is well signed. Take care as road through Berrow and Brean is rather narrow. O.S.GR: ST290539. GPS: N51:16.829 W03:00.733

Charges guide

Per standard pitch	£ 6.00 - £ 28.00
serviced pitch	£ 8.00 - £ 30.00
with hardstanding	£ 10.00 - £ 32.00

Price includes unit, 4 persons, awning, entertainment/swimming and 'Piglet Club'. Deduct 25% if only two people occupy the pitch.

UK1590 Exe Valley Caravan Site

Bridgetown, Dulverton TA22 9JR (Somerset)

Tel: **01643 851432**. Email: **paul@paulmatt.fsnet.co.uk**

Occupying a prime position in a wooded valley alongside the River Exe, within the National Park. Exe Valley Caravan Site is ideally situated for visiting the Doone Valley, Tarr Steps, Dulverton and many other beautiful venues in the area. This four acre 'adult only' campsite is owned and managed by Paul and Christine Matthews, and reception forms part of their home. This is an old mill, complete with water wheel and grindstones which are in working order (open for visits every Sunday at 10.00). Reception also houses a small shop stocking basic provisions. CCTV has been installed so campers may watch the bat colony in the loft from a screen in the mill. Set beside the River Exe or the millstream, there are 30 large pitches (mostly grass but with some hardstandings at the top end), all with 10A electricity and TV hook-ups. Fly fishing along the River Exe is possible from the site or at Wimbleball Reservoir just over four miles away. This part of Somerset is a haven for walking, cycling, pony trekking, or as a place to just sit and relax.

Facilities

The refurbished toilet block houses the usual facilities and an en-suite room for disabled visitors (quite short steep ramp to enter). Excellent laundry with domestic washing and drying machines, plus a microwave (free). Small shop with basic provisions. Bicycle hire. Gas supplies. Free fly fishing. This is an adult-only park. Off site: Riding 4 miles. Golf 12 miles. Pub at Bridgetown. Winsford village has a general stores, pub and tea rooms.

Open: 14 March - 13 October.

Directions

Bridgetown is roughly midway between Dunster and Tiverton on the A396. As you enter Bridgetown from Tiverton, look for site sign and turn left on minor road. Site is 100 yards on the right. O.S.GR: SS923332. GPS: N51:05.292 W03:32.325

Charges 2007

Per unit incl. 2 persons	£ 8.00 - £ 13.00
extra person	£ 3.00
electricity (10A) and TV hook-up	£ 2.50
dog	£ 1.00

No credit cards.

UK1580 Warren Farm Holiday Centre

Warren Road, Brean Sands, Burnham-on-Sea TA8 2RP (Somerset)

Tel: **01278 751227**. Email: **enquiries@warren-farm.co.uk**

Warren Farm is a popular venue for family campers who want the beach, fun and entertainment. With over 1,000 pitches, the park is divided into several fields, with touring and seasonal pitches kept well apart; Sunnyside, part of Warren Farm, is about 200 yards further down the road and has its own warden. Access roads are wide and all the 565 touring pitches are grassy and level, with 16A electric hook-ups. There are no hardstandings so motorhomes may have difficulties in extremely wet weather. Play equipment is located in a line through the centre of the camping fields – ranch-style wooden fences break up the fields and couples usually park around the perimeter overlooking fields and views of the Mendip Hills. A fabulous Play Barn incorporates an indoor play centre, bowling alley, bouncy tractor, ball pit, large-screen TV, and electronic games. Warren Farm's Beachcomber Inn offers a variety of facilities including a bar, restaurant (with good value excellent food), Pirate's Cove for youngsters, and cabaret room for live entertainment. With its on-site fishing, direct access to the beach, sports field and walks, this is a holiday park that caters for everyone.

Facilities

Several toilet blocks of varying styles provide WCs, showers (on payment) and mostly communal washbasins. Facilities for disabled visitors in the block in fields 2,4,5 and 6 (plus pitches which may be reserved nearby). Three laundries. Motorcaravan service points. Two shops, snack bar and Chinese takeaway (opening times vary). Fish bar. Beachcomber Inn. Play equipment for toddlers. Play barn. Fishing. WiFi. Off site: Golf and riding 1.5 miles.

Open: 28 March - 31 October.

Directions

Leave M5 at junction 22 and follow the B3140 to Burnham-on-Sea, then to Berrow and Brean. Continue through Brean and Warren Farm is on the right about 1.5 miles past Brean Leisure Park. O.S.GR: ST297564. GPS: N51:18.149 W03:00.590

Charges 2007

Per unit incl. 2 persons	£ 6.50 - £ 14.00
extra person over 3 yrs	£ 2.00
electricity (16A)	£ 2.50

UK1630 Brokerswood Country Park

Brokerswood, Westbury BA13 4EH (Wiltshire)

Tel: **01373 822238**. Email: **info@brokerswood.co.uk**

This countryside campsite is located in an 80 acre country park, with ancient broadleaf woodland, plenty of marked walks, a woodland railway which also runs 'Santa Specials' (bookings taken from 1 August). The gift shop has a special Christmas theme from the end of October. The park also has adventure playgrounds and play trails amongst its many activities for the family. Most are free for campers, except for the train. Fishing in the lake is available, ask at reception. Cycling in the park is forbidden. The campsite has 65 pitches arranged around an open meadow area, served by a circular gravel roadway, with low level site lighting. There are 25 hardstanding pitches, and 44 electricity hook-ups (10A). Although fairly recently laid-out, the site is maturing well. In the interest of environmental conservation it has its own biological waste management system. There are also recycling bins for glass, paper and metal cans. American RVs and other large units should use the coach entrance and they (and all other arrivals after 18.00) are asked to phone ahead so that arrangements can be made for the barrier.

Facilities

Two well insulated and heated, timber clad buildings are at one end of the site. Some washbasins in cubicles, large, controllable hot showers. Family rooms (on payment). Fully equipped suite for disabled people with ramped approach and alarm. Laundry and ironing facilities. Motorcaravan services. Gas. Milk, bread, newspapers to order from reception/shop. Broadleaf Café serving meals and refreshments all day. Fishing. Off site: Golf 6 miles. Pub with meals 400 yds. Nearest shops at Dilton Marsh and Westbury. Longleat 6 miles. Bath 12 miles.

Open: All year.

Directions

From Trowbridge take A361 south for 2 miles, turning left (east) at Southwick, and follow signs to Country Park. O.S.GR: ST840524.
GPS: N51:16.217 W02:13.885

Charges 2007

Per pitch	£ 10.00 - £ 25.00
incl. electricity	£ 12.00 - £ 25.00
extra person	£ 2.50 - £ 3.00
dog	£ 1.00

UK1650 Coombe Touring Park

Coombe Nurseries, Race Plain, Netherhampton, Salisbury SP2 8PN (Wiltshire)

Tel: **01722 328451**

A true touring park with outstanding views over the Chalke Valley, Coombe is adjacent to Salisbury racecourse. There are 100 spacious pitches all on level, well mown grass, 50 with electric hook-ups (10A). The tent pitches are generally around the outer perimeter. Many pitches are individual and sheltered by hedging. Reception also has a small shop, there are supermarkets in Salisbury (4.5 miles), and pubs in Netherhampton and Coombe Bissett (2 miles) both serving meals.

Facilities

Well built, modern, centrally heated sanitary unit. Family room (with bath) has facilities for disabled persons, babies and toddlers. Laundry. Small shop (May-Sept). Open grass play area. Gas. Off site: Nearby attractions include Wilton House, Salisbury Cathedral, Stonehenge. Golf 400 yards. Riding and tennis in Wilton 2.5 miles.

Open: 1 January - 20 December.

Directions

From A36 two miles west of Salisbury (just east of Wilton roundabout), turn south on A3094 towards Netherhampton and Harnham. After 0.5 miles on sharp left hand bend, turn right to Stratford Tony and Racecourse (site signed). O.S.GR: SU098282.

Charges 2008

Per unit incl. 2 persons	£ 11.00 - £ 13.00

No credit cards.

UK1640 Greenhill Farm Camping & Caravan Park

New Road, Landford, Salisbury SP5 2AZ (Wiltshire)

Tel: **01794 324117**. Email: **greenhillcamping@btconnect.com**

On the northern edge of the New Forest National Park, this is an attractive, uncommercialised, hide-away for adults only (over 18 yrs), set around two small lakes, one of which is reserved for coarse fishing. The 100 level pitches, 35 hardstanding (the rest on grass), come complete with 16A electric hook-ups, and are attractively spread around the 14 acre site. An area for tents is in a separate hill-top meadow with views over the nearby forest and its own fishing lake. There is also a separate area set aside for pets. Several local pubs serving meals are close by and a bus stop outside the site entrance provides services to Salisbury or Southampton. Local attractions include Paultons Park, Breamore House, Downton Moot and the New Forest.

Facilities

Portacabin-type units of varying ages located around the site perimeter provide basic facilities and can be heated when necessary. Showers are free, but a token is issued with a refundable £1 deposit. No dedicated facilities for disabled persons. Laundry with washing machine and dryer. Gas supplies. Milk, eggs, gifts, maps etc. stocked. Tourist information from public telephone. Coarse fishing lakes (£3 per rod per day). Torches useful. One vehicle only per camping unit (others to remain in car park). CCTV on access road and car park areas. American motorhomes not accepted. Off site: Landford village has a bakery, post office, off-licence and general stores (15 minute walk). Golf 3 miles.

Open: 25 January - 22 December.

Directions

From M27 exit 2 take A36 north towards Salisbury for about 6 miles. Pass through West Wellow and after passing a B.P. garage on left, take next left into New Road, and continue for under 1 mile to site entrance on left. O.S.GR: SU264184.
GPS: N50:57.867 W01:37.545

Charges 2007

Per unit incl. 2 persons,	
awning and electricity	£ 15.00
tent incl. 2 persons	£ 10.00
extra person	£ 4.00

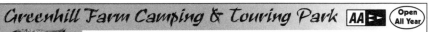
UK1655 Church Farm Caravan & Camping Park

Sixpenny Handley, Salisbury SP5 5ND (Wiltshire)

Tel: **01725 552563**. Email: **churchfarmcandcpark@yahoo.co.uk**

Church Farm offers 35 spacious pitches (including two hardstandings), all with 16A electricity hook-ups, arranged around the perimeter of two fields, plus a tent field. Although the site is fairly open the farm buildings and thick hedges do give some shelter from the prevailing wind. Breakfasts are available in the main season from a recently created snack bar. Sixpenny Handley is a Saxon hilltop village and St Mary's church dates back some 900 years. From the site you can hear the bells and the chimes of its clock. The Roebuck Inn in the High Street offers a varied menu. This is a quiet corner right on the Wiltshire - Dorset border but within day trip distance of many of the area's finest attractions. There are some fine country walks available on nearby Cranborne Chase.

Facilities

A small modern building provides clean facilities and a dedicated room for disabled campers. Laundry with washing machine and dryer in a separate building. Breakfast snack bar. Rather basic motorcaravan service point (may be difficult to access for some units). Recycling centre just outside the main gate. Off site: The village has a bus stop, a number of small shops including a butchers selling fresh meat, sausages and deli foods, a small supermarket and Post Office. Gas available in village. Golf 4 miles. Riding 5 miles. Fishing 10 miles.

Open: All year.

Directions

To avoid the village centre, 1 mile south of Handley Hill roundabout on A354 turn towards Sixpenny Handley, then right by the School and site 300 yards by the Church. O.S.GR: ST996173.
GPS: N50:57.319 W02:00.413

Charges 2007

Per person	£ 5.00 - £ 5.50
child (3-14 yrs)	£ 1.50
serviced pitch	£ 2.25
awning	£ 1.00

91

UK1660 Piccadilly Caravan Park

Folly Lane West, Lacock, Chippenham SN15 2LP (Wiltshire)

Tel: **01249 730260**. Email: **piccadillylacock@aol.com**

Piccadilly Caravan Park is set in open countryside close to several attractions, notably Longleat, Bath, Salisbury Plain, Stourhead, and Lacock itself. It is a small, quiet family owned park that is kept neat and tidy. Landscaped shrubs and trees are maturing, giving the impression of three separate areas. There are 40 well spaced, clearly marked pitches, 12 of which have hardstanding, and two good areas for tents. Electrical connections (10A) are available on 34 pitches. Lacock Abbey was once the home of Henry Fox-Talbot, pioneer of photography, and there is now a museum in the village. A bus service runs from Lacock village to Chippenham (entry to the Chippenham museum and Heritage centre is free of charge).

Facilities

The one toilet block is well maintained and equipped, should be adequate in size for peak periods and can be heated in cool weather. Laundry room with baby changing facilities. Ice pack service. Small, bark-based playground and a large, grass ball play area. Limited gas supplies. Papers can be ordered. Off site: Fishing 1 mile. Bicycle hire 6 miles. Riding 4 miles. Golf 3 miles.

Open: Easter/1 April - October.

Directions

Park is signed west off A350 Chippenham - Melksham road (turning to Gastard with caravan symbol) by Lacock village. 300 yds. to park. O.S.GR: ST911683. GPS: N51:24.828 W02:07.781

Charges 2007

Per unit incl. 2 persons	£ 11.50
extra person over 5 yrs	£ 2.00
electricity	£ 2.00

No credit cards.

UK1670 Alderbury Caravan & Camping Park

Southampton Road, Whaddon, Salisbury SP5 3HB (Wiltshire)

Tel: **01722 710125**. Email: **alderbury@aol.com**

At the southern end of Alderbury/Whaddon village, this small, simple touring park is conveniently located for visiting Salisbury and the New Forest. Situated on level ground, there is a gravel access road to the 39 numbered pitches; 26 with electricity (10A) and 12 on hardstanding. The park has some mature trees for shade, as well as younger trees, shrubs and flowers. The village shop and post office, a pub serving meals and a bus stop are within easy level walking distance of the entrance. There are hourly bus services to Salisbury, Southampton and Romsey. The country lanes around the area are good for cycling and walking. Salisbury Museum, the Cathedral and its Close are all well worth a visit. There is some road noise, most noticeable at the far end of the park.

Facilities

The central toilet block is practical, but has hard use all year round and would benefit from some refurbishment. Showers in cubicles with curtain, separate unit for disabled visitors, dishwashing sink, freezer, washing machine and microwave also in a separate room. Gas supplies. New childrens pool. Music room (1/7-30/8). In high season childrens entertainment and sporting activites. American motorhomes accepted by prior arrangement. Off site: Fishing 1 mile. Bicycle hire 3 miles. Riding 2 miles. Golf 5 miles.

Open: All year.

Directions

From Salisbury take A36 towards Southampton and, after 3 miles (at far end of the dual-carriageway), turn left (Alderbury and Whaddon), then right, over bridge, and left for park entrance. From Southampton on A36 towards Salisbury, continue past A27 (Romsey) junction and over Pepperbox Hill. At end of a downhill straight, left on slip road marked Alderbury, park is signed. O.S.GR: SU198263. GPS: N51:02.072 W01:43.169

Charges 2007

Per unit incl. 2 persons	£ 11.00 - £ 12.00
electricity (16A)	£ 14.00 - £ 15.00
extra person	£ 2.25 - £ 2.50
child (under 14 yrs)	£ 1.25 - £ 1.50
awning	£ 2.00

No credit cards.

UK1680 Plough Lane Caravan Site

Plough Lane, Kington Langley, Chippenham SN15 5PS (Wiltshire)

Tel: **01249 750146**. Email: **ploughlane@lineone.net**

Catering for adults only, this is a good example of a well designed, quality, modern touring site. The 50 pitches (all for touring units) are attractively laid out over four acres, access roads are gravel and the borders are stocked with well established shrubs and trees. The pitches are half grass, half hardstanding and all have electricity (16A), with 25 having full services. The site entrance has a barrier system for security. This site is an ideal base for visiting Bath, Westonbirt Arboretum, Abbey House Gardens at Malmesbury, Castle Combe and the many attractive villages of north Wiltshire.

Facilities

The sanitary building is heated, spacious, light and airy, and has all the usual facilities including some washbasins in cubicles, with a hairdressing area for ladies. Separate en-suite room for disabled visitors with ramp access. Dishwashing under cover. Fully equipped laundry with two further dishwashing sinks. Max. 2 dogs per unit. Adults only (over 18 yrs). Off site: Supermarket, two pubs, and two garages (both with gas). Golf less than 1 mile.

Open: Easter - 30 September.

Directions

From M4 junction 17 turn south on A350 for 2 miles, then left at lights (site signed). From Chippenham head north on A350 (towards M4), approaching lights (signed site and Kington Langley) use right hand lane. O.S.GR: ST914764. GPS: N51:29.182 W02:07.542

Charges 2007

Per unit incl. 2 persons	£ 14.00 - £ 16.00

No credit cards.

UK1690 Longleat Caravan Club Site

Warminster BA12 7NL (Wiltshire)

Tel: **01985 844663**

What a magnificent situation in which to find a caravan park, amidst all the wonders of the Longleat Estate including the Elizabethan House, gardens designed by Capability Brown and the Safari Park. Visitors can roam the woodlands and enjoy the views, watch the wildlife and marvel at the azaleas, bluebells, etc. according to the season or listen to the occupants of the Safari Park. The site itself is situated in 10 acres of lightly wooded, level grassland within walking distance of the house and gardens. There are 165 generous pitches (101 with hardstanding and 64 on grass), all with electricity. Two new buildings provide immaculate facilities, whilst the former toilet block now houses further services, a family room and tourist information. Tents are not accepted (except trailer tents).

Facilities

Two heated toilet blocks provide washbasins in cubicles, controllable showers and a vanity section with mirrors and hairdryers. Baby/toddler room, suite for disabled visitors, laundry and dishwashing room and a family room. Two motorcaravan service points. Play area. Office is manned 09.00 - 18.00 and stocks basic food items. Fish and chip van calls some evenings. Off site: Longleat House and its attractions. Frome 7 miles.

Open: 17 March - 30 October.

Directions

The main entrance to Longleat which caravans must use is signed from the A362 Frome - Warminster road near where it joins the A36 Warminster bypass. O.S.GR: ST806434. GPS: N51:11.442 W02:16.711

Charges 2007

Per person	£ 4.70 - £ 6.20
child (5-16 yrs)	£ 1.50 - £ 3.00
pitch (non-member)	£ 10.90 - £ 15.30

UK1700 Devizes Camping & Caravanning Club Site

Spout Lane, Seend, Melksham SN12 6RN (Wiltshire)

Tel: **01380 828839**

First opened in 1998, this site occupies a level field with gravel roads and centrally located facilities. It is also adjacent to the Kennet and Avon Canal and the towpath now provides a traffic-free route passing the Caen Hill flight of 29 locks into Devizes (4 miles). There are 50 hardstanding and 40 grass pitches, 80 with electricity (16A). The Millennium Wood on the site contains more than 1,000 trees. The site is central for visiting many places of interest including the stone circles at Stonehenge and Avebury. The Vale of Pewsey cycle route can be accessed from the canal towpath.

Facilities

The modern, heated toilet block provides spacious hot showers, washbasins in cubicles, laundry, dishwashing room, and a baby room. Facilities for disabled visitors are by reception. Motorcaravan services. Small playground. Reception opens 09.00-10.00 and 16.00-17.30, and stocks basic foods and drinks, snacks and gas supplies.

Open: All year.

Directions

From Devizes take A361 westbound, and 0.5 miles before Seend village, take A365 towards Melksham. Take next left by 'Three Magpies' to site. O.S.GR: ST950620. GPS: N51:21.390 W02:04.335

Charges 2007

Per person	£ 6.30 - £ 7.25
pitch fee (non-members)	£ 5.65

93

UK1760 Wood Farm Caravan Park

Axminster Road, Charmouth DT6 6BT (Dorset)

Tel: **01297 560697**. Email: **holidays@woodfarm.co.uk**

Wood Farm is an excellent, family run park, maintained to high standards and with an indoor swimming pool. Situated on the western side of Charmouth beside the A35 (some road noise may be expected) but only a mile or two from Lyme Regis and its beaches. This area is now part of England's first natural World Heritage site, the Jurassic Coast. Wood Farm is part of the Caravan Club's 'affiliated' scheme (non-members are also very welcome). On sloping, well landscaped ground, it has splendid rural views across the Marshwood Vale. There are 200 pitches for touring units of which 180 are neat, level all-weather pitches with hardstanding, electricity (10A) and TV connections, and provision for awnings. Some are divided by neat, box-like leylandii hedging, some are terraced. Water and waste water hook-ups are also available. One grassy terraced field takes about 25 tents and there are 80 caravan holiday homes in separate areas. Wood Farm makes excellent provision for disabled visitors, although there is considerable up and down walking due to the terrain. A member of the Best of British group.

Facilities

Four modern, well equipped toilet blocks can be heated and include some washbasins in cubicles, en-suite family rooms, 3 with showers and 1 with bath (charged). Excellent facilities for disabled people. Baby unit. Two laundry rooms. Motorcaravan service point. Shop by reception. Fish and chip van 2-4 times a week (acc. to season). Good heated indoor pool (27 x 54 ft; £2 per session, under 3s free). Recreation hall with two pool tables and family games area with table tennis, TV, 'soft play' and table football. Internet access. Bridge club. Outdoor draughts. Outdoor tennis court. Play field. Two coarse fishing ponds (carp, rudd, roach, tench, perch) adjacent - day and weekly tickets (rod licence required). Dog wallk area. Off site: Golf 1 mile. Riding 4 miles. Beaches and shops 1 and 2 miles.

Open: 29 March - 28 October.

Directions

Park is 0.5 miles west of Charmouth village with access near the roundabout at the A35 and A3052 (Lyme Regis) junction. O.S.GR: SY356940.

Charges 2007

Per person	£ 4.50 - £ 6.50
child (5-16 yrs)	£ 2.00 - £ 3.00
pitch incl. 10A electricity	£ 5.00 - £ 9.50
incl. water and drainage	£ 9.00 - £ 13.50
pup tent, dog, extra car	£ 2.00

Special senior citizens low season discounts.

- Breathtaking countryside views
- Superb indoor swimming pool
- Idyllic fishing ponds
- Tennis court

WOOD FARM
CHARMOUTH • DORSET
www.woodfarm.co.uk

TEL: (01297) 560697
THE CARAVAN CLUB

BEST OF BRITISH   AA

UK1730 Monkton Wyld Farm Caravan Park

Monkton Wyld Farm, Charmouth DT6 6DB (Dorset)

Tel: **01297 631131**. Email: **holidays@monktonwyld.co.uk**

Since Simon and Joanna Kewley opened Monkton Wyld in 1991, it has matured into an attractive, comfortable, garden-like park, with trees and flowering shrubs such as hydrangea and lavender creating a colourful, scented backdrop. A woodland walk has been created in 80 acres of the beautiful countryside surrounding the park. Mature trees around the perimeter of the park provide shade and plenty of space between the 180 pitches gives a feeling of spaciousness. All pitches have 16A electricity and around 70 have hardstanding. On site facilities are limited but an area at the top of the park has been turned into a play area, with a good space for ball games.

Facilities

The well built, heated toilet block is fully equipped. Family room with baby changing facilities (can also be accessed by wheelchairs). Washing machine and dryer. Dishwashing is under cover. Gas supplies. Play area. Caravan storage. Gate locked at 23.00. Off site: Fishing or riding 2 miles, bicycle hire, golf and boat launching 3 miles. Shops and local pubs are within a mile's walking distance. The X53 Jurassic Coast bus stops at the end of the lane.

Open: Easter - end October.

Directions

Park is signed on A35 between Charmouth and Axminster, approx. 2.5 miles west of Charmouth. Turn right at Greenway Head (B3165 signed Marshwood) and park is 600 yds on the left past the Club site. Don't go to Monkton Wyld hamlet - the road is very steep. O.S.GR: SY329966. GPS: N50:45.920 W02:57.150

Charges 2007

Per unit incl. 2 persons	£ 6.30 - £ 8.25
electricity	£ 2.75

UK1810 Newlands Caravan Park

Charmouth DT6 6RB (Dorset)

Tel: **01297 560259**. Email: **enq@newlandsholidays.co.uk**

Newlands is well situated on the Jurassic Coast, the first natural world heritage site in England. A family owned park, it is run with care and enthusiasm, occupying a prominent position beside the road into Charmouth village with rural views southwards to the hills across the valley. The terrain is terraced in two fields to provide over 200 well spaced places for touring units, some for seasonal units and over 80 for caravan holiday homes (some for hire). The mainly sloping tent field also has super views towards the sea and Lyme Regis. Electricity (10A) is provided on 160 pitches and 30 have hardstanding, water and drainage. Other accommodation includes smart pine lodges, apartments and motel rooms. All the facilities are located in a modern building to one side of the wide tarmac entrance. The club bar opens each evening and lunch times to suit. Family entertainment includes a children's club during school holidays with Dino Dan dinosaur. The indoor pool adjoins the bar area and an adjacent outdoor pool is walled, paved and sheltered. A large play area in the field below the tent field is open dawn to dusk. This is a comfortable site for families with the beach and village within easy walking distance, with some evening and family activity.

Facilities

Two modern, heated toilet blocks (both refurbished) provide roomy showers and adjoining covered dishwashing areas and laundry rooms. Baby room. Well stocked shop (March-Nov). Licensed club bar (limited hours Nov-March). Restaurant (open evenings 18.00-21.00 March-Nov plus Xmas/New Year) including takeaway. Outdoor heated pool (supervised in high season; the entrance is key coded). Indoor pool and jacuzzi (small charge, open all year, limited hours Nov-March). Nine-pin bowling alley for hire at £5 per half hour. Play area. Off site: Beach 0.5 miles. Fishing 1 mile. Riding 3 miles. Golf 2 miles. Charmouth is known for its fossil finds and its connection with Jane Austen

Open: 1 February - 1 December (also 27 Dec. - 3 Jan).

Directions

Approaching from Bridport leave the A35 at first sign for Charmouth at start of the bypass and site almost directly on your left. O.S.GR: SY373935. GPS: N50:44.310 W02:53.390

Charges 2007

Per unit incl. up to 6 persons	
and awning	£ 10.00 - £ 25.00
incl. electricity	£ 15.00 - £ 27.00
serviced pitch	£ 14.00 - £ 30.00
dog (max. 2)	£ 1.00 - £ 3.00
extra pup tent	£ 5.00

Camping Cheques accepted.

UK1740 Golden Cap Holiday Park

West Dorset Leisure Holidays, Eype, Bridport DT6 6AR (Dorset)

Tel: 01308 422139. Email: holidays@wdlh.co.uk

Golden Cap, named after the adjacent high cliff (the highest in southern England) which overlooks Lyme Bay, is only 150 metres from a shingle beach at Seatown and is surrounded by National Trust countryside and the Heritage Coastline. The park is arranged over several fields on the valley floor, sloping gently down towards the sea. It is in two main areas, having once been two parks, each separated into fields with marvellous views around and providing 108 touring pitches. All have electricity and 30 also have hardstanding with drainaway and gravel awning area. An extra sloping tent area is used for peak season (torch useful), although it is a five minute walk from here to the toilet blocks and shop. There are 219 caravan holiday homes in their own areas. A coarse fishing lake has been opened and the heated indoor pool at Highlands End (under the same ownership, 3 miles away) is open for campers at Golden Cap on payment. Beaches are nearby, sea fishing or fossil hunting are possible in the area, plus good walks including access to the coastal path.

Facilities

The modern toilet block is of good quality with spacious shower cubicles (some with toilet and washbasin). Baby room. Two other smaller blocks around the park. Laundry room. Motorcaravan service point. Useful and well stocked shop (all season). Gas supplies. Small play area. Fishing lake (day tickets from shop). American motorhomes are not accepted. Off site: Pub with food service close. Golf 2 miles. Beach 150 yds.

Open: 17 March - 5 November.

Directions

Turn off A35 road at Chideock (a bigger village) 3 miles west of Bridport, at sign to Seatown opposite church. Park is less than 1 mile down narrow lane. O.S.GR: SY423919. GPS: N50:42.920 W02:49.300

Charges 2007

Per unit incl. 2 persons and electricity	£ 12.50 - £ 21.00
extra person	£ 3.50 - £ 4.00
child (4-17 yrs)	£ 2.00 - £ 2.50
all service pitch plus	£ 14.50 - £ 23.00

UK1750 Highlands End Holiday Park

West Dorset Leisure Holidays, Eype, Bridport DT6 6AR (Dorset)

Tel: 01308 422139. Email: holidays@wdlh.co.uk

On slightly sloping ground with superb open views, both coastal and inland, Highlands End is quietly situated on the Dorset Heritage Coastline. With access to the coastal path, a path in front of the park runs along the cliff top and then leads down to a shingle beach a little further along. It is a good quality park with 180 caravan holiday homes, mostly privately owned, and 195 touring pitches in two areas nearest to the sea – one has to travel through the holiday homes to reach them. All have electricity and 45 also offer water, drainage, hardstanding and a gravel awning area. A further area is used for tents in high season. A modern, attractive building houses a lounge bar, good value restaurant with takeaway facility, family room and games room with some musical evenings in high season. The park's amenities also include an excellent, air-conditioned indoor heated pool, a tennis court and pitch and putt (all charged). The owners have a long term interest in the fire brigade and an historic fire engine (1936 Leyland Pump Escape) along with memorabilia make an interesting display in the bar. Member of the Best of British group.

Facilities

Two toilet blocks near the touring sections are well maintained and can be heated. Some washbasins in cubicles with toilets, large, roomy showers. Facilities for disabled visitors. Baby room. Laundry. Motorcaravan service point. Well stocked shop (opening times vary). Bar and restaurant/takeaway (evenings and Sunday lunch). Tennis (charged). Indoor pool (20 x 9 m), gym, sauna/steam room. Games room. 9-hole pitch and putt. Two play areas. All facilities open all season. Off site: Golf 2 miles. Fishing 3 miles. Beach 0.5 miles.

Open: 14 March - 2 November.

Directions

Follow Bridport bypass on A35 around the town and park is signed to south (Eype turning), down narrow lane. There is a new exit road. O.S.GR: SY452914. GPS: N50:43.520 W02:46.620

Charges 2007

Per unit incl. 2 persons and electricity	£ 12.50 - £ 21.00
all services and hardstanding	£ 14.50 - £ 23.00
extra person	£ 3.50 - £ 4.00
child (4-17 yrs)	£ 2.00 - £ 2.50
dog	£ 2.00 - £ 2.50

UK1780 Freshwater Beach Holiday Park

Burton Bradstock, Bridport DT6 4PT (Dorset)

Tel: **01308 897317**. Email: **enquiries@freshwaterbeach.co.uk**

Family run parks for families with direct access to their own private beach are rare in Britain and this one has the added advantage of being in beautiful coastal countryside in West Dorset. The site is next to the sea and a beach of fine pebbles, sheltered from the wind by pebble banks. The River Bride edges the park and joins the sea here. Approached by a fairly steep access road, the park itself is on level, open ground. The 500 plus touring pitches, 400 with 10A electricity, are on an open, undulating grass field connected by tarmac or hardcore roads. Caravan pitches (10 x 11 m.) are marked and evenly spaced in lines. Some tent pitches are in the main field, with others well spaced on a newly terraced extra field. In separate areas there are 270 caravan holiday homes, with 40 for hire. This lively holiday park has an extensive range of facilities which include an outdoor pool, a good value licensed restaurant and newly refurbished bars with an evening entertainment programme in season. Daytime entertainment caters for all ages – don't miss the donkey derby! Footpaths lead to the thatched village of Burton Bradstock or West Bay. The overall impression is of a large, busy holiday park with a friendly reception and happy atmosphere.

Facilities

Two fully equipped toilet blocks serve the caravan fields and a third newer block is in the tent field. It is a good provision for a busy beach park. Facilities for disabled people (Radar key), and a baby care room (key system). Laundry and dishwashing sinks cope well at peak times. Launderette. Bars with wide variety of entertainment and evening shows. Licensed restaurant (weekends only in late season). Good value supermarket and takeaway. Heated and supervised outdoor swimming and paddling pools (15/5-30/10) with lessons available. New indoor games room with pool table, music, TV, amusements and soft drinks bar. Activities for children. Two play areas. High season pony trekking (stables on site). Off site: Golf course 0.5 miles. Fishing possible from Chesil Bank. Abbotsbury Sub-Tropical Gardens and Swannery 17 miles.

Open: 17 March - 12 November.

Directions

Park is immediately west of the village of Burton Bradstock, on the Weymouth - Bridport coast road (B3157). O.S.GR: SY980898. GPS: N50:42.300 W02:44.320

Charges 2007

Per unit incl. up to 6 persons, car and awning	£ 11.00 - £ 31.00
extra person, car or boat	£ 2.00
electricity	£ 2.00
small tent incl. 2 persons walking or cycling	£ 4.00 - £ 15.50
dog	£ 2.50

Single sex groups not admitted.

FreshwaterBeach HOLIDAY PARK — **family seaside fun!**

Free entertainment
Free club membership
Own private beach on Dorset's world renowned Jurassic Coast

Dorset's Golden Coast — A World Heritage Destination

AA HOLIDAY CENTRE

Family-owned park with large touring and camping field

- Ideal holiday base for many sights and attractions in Dorset
- Club Complex with licensed restaurant and bars
- Nightly Family Entertainment (*Spring BH – Mid Sept)
- Children's activities and amusements
- Heated outdoor swimming pools
- Beach fishing and wind-surfing
- Fine country and cliff walks
- Self-catering holiday homes
- Pony-trekking & horse and cart rides
- Golf course adjoining park
- Caravan Sales

www.freshwaterbeach.co.uk
01308 897317
Freshwater Beach Holiday Park,
Burton Bradstock, Bridport, DT6 4PT

UK1770 Binghams Farm Touring Park

Melplash, Bridport DT6 3TT (Dorset)

Tel: **01308 488234**. Email: **enquiries@binghamsfarm.co.uk**

Binghams is a small, purpose built park, for adults only. In a pleasant, rural situation two miles from the market town of Bridport, with views seaward towards West Bay and inland across Beaminster Downs and Pilsdon Hill. The park provides an area of individual pitches with 10A electricity and over 50 hardstandings, nicely landscaped with shrubs and trees growing between the pitches, plus an open sloping field overlooking the valley. The entrance to the park is neatly tarmaced and a cottage has been converted into two flats to let. A path is provided to the river which links with the main footpaths for Bridport (20 minutes) or local hostelries. A limited bus service runs on the main road. The Brit Valley is an unspoilt area of West Dorset with an ancient heritage and coastal West Bay is only a couple of miles.

Facilities

The original farm buildings have been sympathetically converted to provide reception, a good heated toilet block and the other amenities. The toilet block, with under floor heating for winter use, provides well fitted, tiled, curtained showers, hairdryers, a separate, fully equipped room for the less able with ramped access and a laundry room. The former games room has been converted into five luxury shower rooms with washbasins (four with toilet as well). Dishwashing under cover. The restaurant serves home cooked food at weekends and weekdays depending on the season. Gas available. Only adults are accepted. Off site: Sea fishing and golf 3 miles.

Open: Easter - October, Xmas and New Year.

Directions

At the roundabouts on the A35 road, on the east side of Bridport, follow signs for Beaminster on the A3066. After about 2 miles watch for site entrance on the left. O.S.GR: SY482963.

Charges 2007

Per unit incl. 2 persons and electricity (10A)	£ 11.50 - £ 20.00
tent pitch incl. 2 persons	£ 11.00 - £ 18.50
extra person	£ 5.00
awning	£ 2.00
dog	£ 2.00

UK1800 East Fleet Farm Touring Park

Fleet Lane, Chickerell, Weymouth DT3 4DW (Dorset)

Tel: **01305 785768**. Email: **enquiries@eastfleet.co.uk**

East Fleet Farm has a marvellous situation on part level, part gently sloping meadows leading to the shores of the Fleet, with views across to the famous Chesil Bank with the sea beyond. Part of the World Heritage Jurassic Coast, the Fleet is a lagoon renowned for its wildlife and popular with bird watchers. This park has been developed by the Whitfield family within the confines of their 300 acre organic working dairy and arable farm in keeping with its surroundings, yet with modern amenities. It is maturing well as bushes and trees grow. The 350 pitches back onto hedges and are a comfortable size so there is no feeling of crowding. Of these, 200 are level and marked with 10/16A electric hook-ups, 40 also having hardstanding. The terraced bar with views over the Fleet, (open from Easter to Sept. with meals), was converted from the barn, and features original beams and brick work. The busy resort of Weymouth with its safe bathing beaches and many watersports facilities is only 3 miles away (bicycle hire and boat launching possible). In peak season a bus runs three times a day from the top of the lane (about half a mile) and Abbotsbury Swannery and Gardens are nearby.

Facilities

Two fully equipped toilet blocks include family rooms. The newest one is very smart in a Norwegian log cabin. En-suite unit for disabled visitors. Laundry room. Motorcaravan service point. Reception plus shop with basic groceries, bread, papers and gas, etc. opens longer in high season. Bar serving food with terrace overlooking the Fleet (Easter - Sept). Games room with pool table. Fenced play area (remember, elsewhere this is a working farm). Games field. Nature watch boards. Off site: Riding and golf 2 miles. Access to the Fleet and coastal path.

Open: 15 March - 31 October.

Directions

Park is signed at traffic lights on B3157 Weymouth - Bridport road, about 3 miles west of Weymouth beside Territorial Army base. Fleet Lane has been widened with plenty of passing places and speed bumps (20 mph). O.S.GR: SY639798.

Charges 2007

Per unit incl. 2 persons	£ 8.00 - £ 18.00
incl. electricity	£ 10.00 - £ 21.00
extra person	£ 1.00 - £ 4.50
child (5-12 years)	£ 0.25 - £ 0.50
Senior citizen discount in June (10%).	

UK1820 Bagwell Farm Touring Park

Chickerell, Weymouth DT3 4EA (Dorset)

Tel: **01305 782575**. Email: **ar@bagwellfarm.co.uk**

A pleasant, large, family park, Bagwell Farm is situated between Weymouth and Abbotsbury, close to Chesil Beach. In a valley, yet with an open aspect, there are 280 numbered touring pitches, some taken up by seasonal units. There are 260 electricity connections (10A) and 9 serviced pitches. Some of the terraced pitches have views of Chesil Bank and the sea. In addition there is a traditional camping field with a campers' shelter and a barbecue, plus a rally field with electric hook-ups. An attractive bar has been converted from farm buildings serving meals with a patio overlooking a pets corner (also open to the public). Only 4 miles from Weymouth, the 'Blue Flag' beaches and other attractions of the resort are easily accessible. This is a useful site, open all year.

Facilities

Traditional style toilet blocks are to be supplemented by a new heated block. Unisex bathrooms on payment. 'Portacabin' style toilets in the camping field for high season. Dishwashing sinks and laundry. Motorcaravan service point. Mini-market with off-licence opposite reception. Fast food takeaway, bar and grill. All facilities open Easter – end Sept. Games room. Play area and pets corner. Off site: Riding and golf 3 miles. Weymouth beach 5 miles with bus service. Abbotsbury with Swannery and Tropical Gardens 4 miles. Two pubs are within walking distance, one in the direction of the marvellous walk from the site to the sea.

Open: All year.

Directions

Follow B3157 from Weymouth in direction of Bridport. Park is 2 miles after passing Chickerell village. The entrance is on the brow of a hill - care is needed. O.S GR: SY627816.

Charges 2007

Per unit incl. 2 persons	
and electricity	£ 11.00 - £ 19.50
incl. services	£ 13.50 - £ 22.50
extra person	£ 3.00 - £ 4.00
child (5-16 yrs)	£ 1.00 - £ 1.50
dog	£ 1.00

UK1830 Sea Barn & West Fleet Holiday Farms

Fleet, Weymouth DT3 4ED (Dorset)

Tel: **01305 782218**. Email: **enquiries@seabarnfarm.couk**

Sea Barn and West Fleet are located just half a mile apart in delightful countryside overlooking the Fleet Lagoon, Chesil Bank and Lyme Bay – all part of the Jurassic coast. Only tents, trailer tents and motorcaravans with tents and awnings are accepted. The parks share some facilities. An outdoor pool and clubhouse are at West Fleet, along with the new smart toilet block. Both have their own reception with well stocked shops. Sea Barn is quieter and popular over a longer period with spectacular views, whereas West Fleet attracts families. Both are popular with birdwatchers, walkers and fishermen. West Fleet has 250 pitches, 60 with electricity, Sea Barn the same number of pitches but only 45 electric hook ups. These are situated in grassy meadows some sloping, some protected by trees and hedging, many with wonderful views.

Facilities

Traditional simple toilet blocks, brightly painted and clean. New block at West Fleet with en-suite room for disabled visitors and two bathrooms (free). Laundry facilities at both sites. Heated pool at West Fleet (May - Sept). Bigger shop offering wider range at West Fleet which also has the Club House (evenings), in reality an open ended barn and outdoor area which works well (home produced steaks the speciality). Breakfast served. Family entertainment. Games field. Adventure play area at Fleet and smaller area at Sea Barn. Torches useful. Off site: Access to South West Coastal path. Fishing Chesil Bank. Riding 1 mile. Golf, bicycle hire, boat launching and beach all at Weymouth 5 miles. Abbotsbury with Swannery and Sub-tropical Gardens 7 miles.

Open: March - October.

Directions

From Wemouth take the B3157 coast road for Bridport. Pass Chickerell and turn left at mini-roundabout to Fleet. Pass church on right and continue to top of hill. Sea Barn is to the left, West Fleet to the right. O.S.GR: SY626805.

Charges 2007

Per unit incl. 2 persons	
and electricity	£ 12.00 - £ 18.00
extra person	£ 3.00 - £ 4.50
child (2-15 yrs)	£ 1.00 - £ 2.50
dog (max 2)	£ 1.00 - £ 2.00

You might also like to consider...

MAP 2

Southern England

Rich in maritime heritage and historical attractions, the Southern region comprises tranquil English countryside boasting picture-postcard villages, ancient cities and towns, formidable castles and grand stately homes, coupled with a beautiful coastline and lively seaside resorts.

THIS REGION INCLUDES: EAST DORSET, HAMPSHIRE, ISLE OF WIGHT, OXFORDSHIRE, BERKSHIRE AND BUCKINGHAMSHIRE

The south coast is a popular holiday destination for those looking for a beach holiday. Seaside resorts include Swanage, and Bournemouth, with its seven miles of golden sand. Also along this coastal stretch is Durdle Door, a natural arch that has been cut by the sea, and Europe's largest natural harbour at Poole Bay. Nearby, the Isle of Purbeck is not actually an island, but a promontory of low hills and heathland that juts out below Poole Harbour. Across the water is the Isle of Wight, easily reached via a short ferry trip across the Solent. Rural Southern England comprises green rolling hills and scenic wooded valleys, with numerous walking and bridle paths passing through picturesque villages with quintessential English pubs. The New Forest, well known for its wild roaming ponies, is a distinctive, peaceful retreat. The River Thames weaves its way through the Thames basin and Chilterns area, passing charming riverside villages, castles, stately homes and beautiful countryside, including that around Oxford. This city of dreaming spires has lovely scenic walks, old university buildings to explore, plus a huge selection of restaurants, pubs and shops. Along the river you can go punting, hire a rowing boat, or take one of the many river-boat trips available.

Places of interest

East Dorset: Monkey World in Wareham; village of Cerne Abbas, with Cerne Giant.

Hampshire: historic Winchester; Portsmouth, home of the Mary Rose; Southampton maritime museum.

Isle of Wight: Cowes; Sandown with Dinosaur Isle; Shipwreck Centre in Ryde; Smuggling Museum in Ventnor; Carisbrooke Castle in Newport.

Oxfordshire: Blenheim Palace; Didcot Railway Centre; historic market town of Chipping Norton.

Berkshire: Windsor, with Legoland, Windsor Castle; Reading.

Buckinghamshire: Bletchley Park near Milton Keynes; county town of Aylesbury; Beaconsfield, once home to Enid Blyton, and now housing the world's first model village.

Did you know?

The Cerne Giant is thought to have represented a pagan god dating back to pre 13th century.

Gosport is home to one of the worlds largest sundials covering 40 metres.

T.E Lawrence 'Lawrence of Arabia' was a fellow of All Souls College in Oxford and lived in Dorset.

Remains of over 20 species of dinosaur have been recovered on the Isle of Wight.

The annual Olney Pancake Race in Bucks has been running since around 1445.

Author Charles Dickens was born in Portsmouth, the house where he was born is now a museum.

Windsurfing was invented on Hayling Island by Peter Chilvers in 1958.

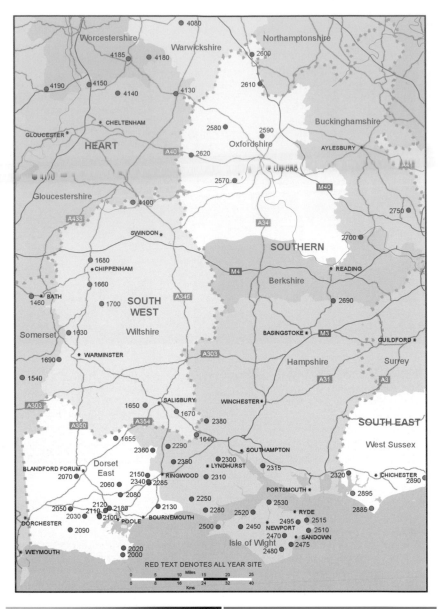

RED TEXT DENOTES ALL YEAR SITE

Map labels:
4080, 4185, 4180, Worcestershire, Warwickshire, Northamptonshire, 2600, 4190, 4150, 4140, 4130, 2610, CHELTENHAM, Buckinghamshire, GLOUCESTER, HEART, Oxfordshire, 2580, 2590, AYLESBURY, 2620, A40, 4170, UXFORD, 2570, M40, Gloucestershire, 4100, 2750, A433, 2700, SWINDON, A34, 1680, SOUTHERN, CHIPPENHAM, 1660, READING, M4, Berkshire, SOUTH WEST, A346, 2690, BATH, 1460, 1700, Somerset, 1630, Wiltshire, BASINGSTOKE, M3, GUILDFORD, 1690, WARMINSTER, A303, Hampshire, Surrey, 1540, A31, A3, A303, SALISBURY, 1650, WINCHESTER, 1670, A350, A354, 2380, SOUTH EAST, 1655, 1640, West Sussex, 2360, 2290, BLANDFORD FORUM, Dorset East, 2350, 2300, SOUTHAMPTON, 2070, 2150, RINGWOOD, LYNDHURST, 2315, 2320, CHICHESTER, 2060, 2340, 2285, 2310, 2890, 2080, PORTSMOUTH, 2895, 2050, 2120, 2130, 2250, 2530, 2885, 2030, 2110, 2180, 2280, RYDE, 2100, POOLE, BOURNEMOUTH, 2520, 2495, 2515, DORCHESTER, 2500, 2450, NEWPORT, 2510, 2090, 2470, SANDOWN, Isle of Wight, 2475, 2480, WEYMOUTH, 2020, 2000

Miles 0 5 10 15 20 25
Kms 0 8 16 24 32 40

UK2020 Ulwell Cottage Caravan Park

Ulwell, Swanage BH19 3DG (Dorset)

Tel: **01929 422823**. Email: **enq@ulwellcottagepark.co.uk**

Nestling under the Purbeck Hills on the edge of Swanage, in the Dorset and East Devon Coast World Heritage Site, Ulwell Cottage is a family run holiday park with an indoor pool and wide range of facilities. A good proportion of the park is taken by caravan holiday homes (140), but an attractive, undulating area accessed by tarmac roads is given over to 77 numbered touring pitches interspersed with trees and shrubs. All have electricity (16A) and 8 are fully serviced. The colourful entrance area is home to the Village Inn with a courtyard adjoining the heated, supervised indoor pool complex (both open all year and open to the public) and modern reception. The hill above the touring area, Nine Barrow Down, is a Site of Special Scientific Interest for butterflies overlooking Round Down. It is possible to walk to Corfe Castle this way. With Brownsea Island, Studland Bay, Corfe village and the Swanage Railway close by, Ulwell Cottage makes a marvellous centre for holidays.

Facilities

The modern, cheerful toilet block at the top of the site is heated and includes a unit for disabled visitors. An older block in the holiday home section has been converted to family rooms. Both are well equipped. Laundry room and baby sinks in the upper block. Dishwashing under cover. Well stocked shop with gas (Easter - mid Sept). Bar snacks and restaurant meals with family room. Takeaway (July/August). Indoor pool with lifeguard (times vary acc. to season). Playing fields and play areas. Off site: Beach 1 mile. Fishing and golf 1 mile. Bicycle hire, sailing and riding 2 miles.

Open: 1 March - 7 January.

Directions

From A351 Wareham - Swanage road, turn onto B3351 Studland road just before Corfe Castle. Follow signs to right (southeast) for Swanage and drop down to Ulwell. Park is on right about 100 yards after 40 mph. sign. O.S.GR: SZ019809. GPS: N50:37.567 W01:58.267

Charges 2007

Per unit incl. up to 6 persons	£ 18.50 - £ 36.70
full services with hardstanding	£ 21.00 - £ 39.00
extra tent, car or boat	£ 2.50

Less £2 for two persons only, less £1 for three persons.

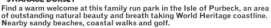

For a brochure call:
01929 422823
website: www.ulwellcottagepark.co.uk
e-mail: enq@ulwellcottagepark.co.uk

CARAVAN PARK
SWANAGE DORSET

Find a warm welcome at this family run park in the Isle of Purbeck, an area of outstanding natural beauty and breath taking World Heritage coastline. Nearby sandy beaches, coastal walks and golf.
● **77 Touring Pitches** with hard standings, electric, water and drainage hook-ups and views of the surrounding hills
● **Superb meals at the 'Village Inn'** ● **Heated Indoor Pool** ● **General Shop**

UK2050 Rowlands Wait Touring Park

Rye Hill, Bere Regis BH20 7LP (Dorset)

Tel: **01929 472727**. Email: **enquiries@rowlandswait.co.uk**

Rowlands Wait is in a designated area of outstanding natural beauty (AONB) and part of the park is officially of special scientific interest (SSSI). The top of the park, edged by mature woods (full of bluebells in spring) is a haven for tents (and squirrels) with marvellous views and provides 30 places in three descending fields. The rest of the park is a little more formal – and nearer to the central toilet block. Most pitches back on to hedging or trees and they are generally level. There are 71 pitches in total with 23 seasonal pitches. Many walks are possible from the park with information leaflets available from reception. It is also possible to walk into the village of Bere Regis. The owners Ivor and Stevie Cargill are keen to welcome nature lovers who enjoy bird watching, walking, and cycling. Sightings of various owls and two pairs of buzzards have been reported on the park. The park is a member of the Countryside Discovery group and is open in winter by arrangement. Rallies are welcome.

Facilities

The refurbished toilet block is fully equipped. New family room and facilities for disabled visitors. Laundry room. Covered dishwashing area. Recycling bins. Shop (reduced hours in low season) providing basic essentials and a freezer for ice packs. Play area. Games room with pool table and table tennis. Bicycle hire in Bovington. Torch useful. Off site: Village (10 minute walk) with shops, two pubs, etc. plus a bus service for Dorchester and Poole. Fishing 5 miles. Golf 3 miles. Riding 9 miles.

Open: 16 March - 31 October, winter by arrangement.

Directions

Park is south of Bere Regis, just off the road to Wool, well signed from A35/A31 roundabout. O.S.GR: SY842933. GPS: N50:44.621 W02:13.443

Charges 2007

Per unit incl. 2 persons	£ 10.00 - £ 13.00
incl. electricity	£ 12.00 - £ 15.00
extra person	£ 3.00 - £ 4.00
child (under 16 yrs)	£ 1.50 - £ 2.00
dog	£ 1.00 - £ 2.00

UK2060 Wilksworth Farm Caravan Park

Cranborne Road, Wimborne BH21 4HW (Dorset)

Tel: **01202 885467**. Email: **rayandwendy@wilksworthfarmcaravanpark.co.uk**

First opened 34 years ago by the parents of the present owners, the careful and sympathetic development of Wilksworth continues with the aim of providing all the 'mod cons' yet remain in keeping with the environment. It is a spacious, quiet park, well suited for families with a heated outdoor pool. The rural situation is lovely, just outside Wimborne and around 10 miles from the beaches between Poole and Bournemouth. With a duck pond at the entrance, the park has been well planned on good quality ground with fairly level grass and some views. It takes 65 caravans and 25 tents mainly on grass. All pitches have electrical connections, 10 also have water and drainage. There are some 77 privately owned caravan holiday homes in a separate area. Facilities are in attractively converted farm buildings designed to be in keeping with the listed status of the other buildings. The heated swimming pool and a tennis court are on the far side of the touring area.

Facilities

The central, well equipped toilet block has under-floor heating, washbasins in cubicles, a family bathroom and baby changing. Facilities for disabled visitors. Laundry. Modern reception and shop (basics only Easter - 30 Sept). Gas supplies. Freezer. Attractive coffee shop serving simple meals with takeaway service (weekends and B.Hs. only outside the main season). Heated swimming pool (unsupervised, but fenced, open May-Sept) with small paddling pool. Play area. BMX track. Golf practice net. Two tennis courts, one full and one short size. Games room. Winter caravan storage. Off site: Golf, fishing and riding 3 miles. Kingston Lacy (NT) 3 miles and Wimborne (with its Minster) 1 mile. Beach 12 miles.

Open: Easter/1 April - 30 October.

Directions

Park is 1 mile north of Wimborne, west off the B3078 road to Cranborne. O.S.GR: SU010019. GPS: N50:49.002 W01:59.424

Charges 2007

Per unit incl. 2 persons	
and electricity	£ 12.00 - £ 22.00
extra person	£ 3.00
child (3-16 yrs)	£ 1.50
full services	£ 2.00
dog	£ 1.00

No credit cards.

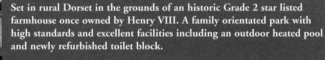

UK2090 Whitemead Caravan Park

East Burton Road, Wool BH20 6HG (Dorset)

Tel: **01929 462241**. Email: **whitemeadcp@aol.com**

The Church family continue to make improvements to this attractive little park which is within walking distance of the village of Wool, between Dorchester and Wareham. Very natural and with open views over the Frome Valley water meadows, it provides 95 numbered pitches on flat grass sloping gently and is orchard-like in parts. There are no caravan holiday homes but 20 pitches are seasonal. The park is 4.5 miles from the beach at Lulworth and is handily placed for many attractions (railway station 400 yards). There may be some rail noise but this is not intrusive at night.

Facilities

The toilet block provides showers and private cubicles. Baby room. Laundry. Shop with off-licence, gas supplies and information room/library. Takeaway with breakfasts at weekends. Games room. Playground. Caravan storage. WiFi in games room. Off site: The Ship Inn is 300 yards. Riding, fishing and golf 3 miles. Bicycle hire 2 miles.

Open: 15 March - 31 October.

Directions

Turn off main A352 on eastern edge of Wool, just north of level crossing, onto East Burton road. Site is 350 yards. on right. O.S.GR: SY841871.

Charges 2007

Per person (over 5 yrs)	£ 2.00
pitch	£ 8.50 - £ 16.50

No credit cards.

UK2030 Wareham Forest Tourist Park

North Trigon, Wareham BH20 7NZ (Dorset)
Tel: **01929 551393**. Email: **holiday@wareham-forest.co.uk**

Under the enthusiastic ownership of Tony and Sarah Birch, this peacefully located, spacious park on the edge of Wareham Forest continues to improve. Reception and the shop have been relocated to beside the pool, making this area the central focus of the park. There is a choice of formal pitching, with or without hardstanding, for caravans or natural pitches for tents in pine wood or open field. There is space for 200 units on large pitches with electrical connections (16A), including 102 with hardstanding and 8 luxury pitches on hardstanding with water, drainage, TV aerial, dustbin and light (available 1/3-31/10 only). It is possible to walk in the forest or use the seven miles of the Sika cycle trail. The lovely market town of Wareham is accessible by bike without having to use the roads. This park has an almost continental feel, with plenty of space. Even when it is busy, it is calm and peaceful in its forest setting. In low season you may be lucky enough to spot the herd of Sika deer which live in the forest. The park is well situated to explore the Dorset coast and Thomas Hardy country. A member of the Best of British Group.

Facilities

Two well maintained toilet blocks are of a good standard with some washbasins in cubicles for ladies. The block used in the winter months is centrally heated. Facilities for disabled people. Well equipped laundry rooms and deep sinks for washing up. Motorcaravan service point. Small licensed shop with gas. Open-air swimming pool (60 x 20 ft), heated Spring B.H. to early Sept. Large adventure play area. Entrance closed 23.00 - 07.00. Resident wardens on site. Caravan storage.
Off site: Fishing 5 miles. Bicycle hire and golf 3 miles. Riding 8 miles. Cycle trail and walking in the forest.

Open: All year.

Directions

Park is north of Wareham between Wareham and Bere Regis, located off the A35 road.
O.S.GR: SY899903. GPS: N50:43.304 W02:09.373

Charges 2007

Per person	£ 2.50 - £ 4.00
child (5-15 yrs)	£ 1.75 - £ 3.00
standard pitch	£ 6.50 - £ 12.75
serviced pitch	£ 9.00 - £ 14.75
'superior' pitch	£ 11.00 - £ 16.00

Couples and families only.

For further details and free colour brochure write or phone:
Tel: (01929) 551393 Fax: (01929) 558321
Tony and Sarah Birch, Wareham Forest Tourist Park, North Trigon, Wareham, Dorset BH20 7NZ
email: holiday@wareham-forest.co.uk
www.wareham-forest.co.uk
Credit cards accepted.

UK2000 Swanage Coastal Park

Priestway, Swanage BH19 2RS (Dorset)

Tel: **01590 648331**. Email: **holidays@shorefield.co.uk**

With wonderful views over Swanage Bay and the Purbeck hills, Swanage Coastal Park is now part of Shorefield Holidays who own other parks in the New Forest. It offers a quiet holiday on the hills above Swanage with its lovely sandy beach (it is quite a steep climb up from the town). Over 100 holiday caravans are terraced up the hillside, of which two-thirds are privately owned. For touring units there are six hardstandings with 10A electricity, plus they four grass pitches on a small plateau. The other 52 grass pitches are unnumbered without electricity and in nooks and crannies on various levels, split by trees and shrubs. Swanage is at the start of the Jurassic Coast World Heritage Site and there is direct access to the coastal paths and to Durlston Country Park and Castle.

Facilities

One older type toilet block at the bottom of the site is clean but basic. Laundry facilities. Dishwashing sinks. Play area. Membership of the Health and Fitness Club at the next door park allows use of the indoor pool, gym, sauna, solarium, bar and restaurant as paying customers (open all year). It also has a shop (open B.Hs. and high season). Off site: Beach and town 1 mile. Golf 3 miles. Bicycle hire, fishing and boat launching 1 mile. 'Hop on Hop off' bus allows you to explore the whole of the Jurassic Coast.

Open: 14 March - 30 October.

Directions

From A351 Wareham - Swanage road turn right just after 'Welcome to Swanage' sign into High Street then immediately right again into Bell Street. At the top turn left into Priests Road then first right up hill towards Priestway. O.S.GR: SZ018783.
GPS: N50:36.363 W01:58.499

Charges 2007

Per pitch	£ 7.50 - £ 15.00
incl. electricity and hardstanding	£ 8.50 - £ 20.00
dog	£ 1.50

UK2080 Merley Court Touring Park

Merley, Wimborne BH21 3AA (Dorset)

Tel: **01590 648331**. Email: **holidays@shorefield.co.uk**

Merley Court is the latest addition to the Shorefield Group. All aspects of this well planned, attractively landscaped park are constantly maintained to the highest of standards. Tarmac roads connect 179 touring pitches, 162 of which have 16A electricity, on neat lawns or one of the many hardstandings. This provision includes 20 serviced pitches with water, waste disposal and satellite TV. The entire park is interspersed with a variety of shrubs, plants and the odd ornamental urn. Some attractive tent pitches are to be found in a small wooded valley. A well-furnished club complex provides a lounge bar where meals are available, snack bar, takeaway, large games room with pool tables and a family room leading onto a spacious sheltered patio. This in turn leads to the paved walled swimming pool area. There are woodland walks (including dog walks) directly from the site connecting to the disused railway line where nature has returned with an abundance of wild flowers, which in turn leads to Delph woods with designated nature trails. A member of the Best of British group.

Facilities

Three heated toilet blocks, two with showers, are of good quality. Separate facilities for disabled visitors and babies. Dishwashing and laundry facilities. Motorcaravan service point. Shop with caravan accessories and gas. Café and takeaway. Bar with food (limited hours in low and mid season). Outdoor pool (30 x 20 ft) with children's section open mid May - mid Sept. Tennis and short tennis courts. Table tennis. Play areas. Games room with pool tables. Tourist information. Barrier card £5 deposit.
Off site: Fishing, riding and golf all within 2 miles. Bicycle hire 5 miles. Poole 5 miles. Bournemouth 8 miles. Tower Park leisure and entertainment centre is nearby, Kingston Lacy House, Knoll Gardens, Brownsea Island and the Moors Valley Country Park are also near.

Open: All year excl. 4 January - 7 February.

Directions

Site clearly signed at the junction of the A31 and A349 roads (roundabout) on the Wimborne bypass. O.S.GR: ST008984. GPS: N50:47.144 W01:59.115

Charges 2008

Per pitch incl. 2 persons	
and electricity	£ 13.50 - £ 33.00
all service pitch	£ 17.50 - £ 36.50
extra person	£ 4.00

No extra pup tent as well as awning.

UK2070 The Inside Park Touring Caravan & Camping Park

Blandford Forum DT11 9AD (Dorset)

Tel: **01258 453719**. Email: **inspark@aol.com**

The Inside Park is set in the grounds of an 18th century country house that burned down in 1941. Family owned and carefully managed alongside an arable farm, this is a must for those interested in local history or arboriculture and it is a haven for wildlife and birds. The reception/toilet block and games room block are respectively the coach house and stables of the old house. The nine acre camping field, a little distant, lies in a sheltered, gently sloping dry valley containing superb tree specimens – notably cedars, with walnuts in one part – and a dog graveyard dating back to the early 1700s under a large Cedar of Lebanon. In total there are 125 spacious pitches, 90 with electricity (10A) and some in wooded glades. The six acres adjoining are the old pleasure gardens of the house. No vehicle access to the park is allowed after 22.30 pm. (there is a separate late arrivals area and car park). Extensive, marked walks are provided through the farmland (guide available in the shop).

Facilities

The toilet block provides some washbasins in cubicles, comfortably sized showers and facilities for disabled visitors or mothers and babies. Dishwashing sinks. Laundry room. Recycling bins. Shop with basics, gas and camping provisions (limited opening in low season). Mobile fish and chips twice weekly. Spacious games room with pool tables, table tennis, etc. Safe based adventure play area. Day kennelling facilities for dogs. Mountain bike course. Winter caravan storage. Off site: Blandford leisure and swimming centre (temporary membership possible) 2 miles. Fishing and riding 2 miles, golf 3 miles. Beach 15 miles.

Open: Easter - 31 October.

Directions

Park is about 2 miles southwest of Blandford and is signed from roundabout junction of the A354 and A350 roads. If approaching from the Shaftesbury direction, do not go into Blandford but follow the bypass to the last roundabout and follow camping signs. O.S.GR: ST864045.
GPS: N50:50.480 W02:11.709

Charges 2007

Per person	£ 3.00 - £ 3.85
child (5-16 years)	free - £ 1.35
pitch	£ 5.00 - £ 6.95
electricity	£ 2.80
dog	£ 0.60 - £ 1.00

UK2120 South Lytchett Manor Caravan & Camping Park

Dorset Road, Lytchett Minster, Poole BH16 6JB (Dorset)

Tel: **01202 622577**. Email: **joannebridgen@aol.com**

Close to Poole, the Isle of Purbeck and the Jurassic Coast, Lytchett Manor is a quiet, attractive, rural campsite with views over the surrounding countryside. There are 150 pitches laid out in fields at either end of the site – one for tents, one for tents or caravans – and a long main drive connecting them. It has been extensively renovated by the new owners, Joanne and David Bridgen, over the winter of 2006/07 with new hardstandings, toilet blocks and electricity system. There are 25 hardstandings (some used by seasonal units). All pitches have electricity (10A) and 78 have TV aerial connections. Water points are plentiful and the three heated toilet blocks have facilities for all needs. This park will suit those who are looking for a quiet holiday or to visit the many attractions in this part of Dorset. Although there are no such facilities on site, there are two pubs within a mile and a local craft centre (300 yards) has some evening events.

Facilities

Three modern, heated toilet blocks include private cabins, en-suite facilities for disabled people, family rooms and dishwashing sinks. Motorcaravan service point. Laundry. Shop in reception for basics, off licence and gas. Takeaway (B.Hs and July/Aug). Games room with TV. Internet. Large grass playing field. Small play area. Off site: Shops, pubs, ATM 1 mile. Golf 3 miles. Beach, sailing and fishing 5 miles. Ferry port 3 miles.

Open: 15 March - 14 October.

Directions

At the roundabout at the end of dual-carriageway on the A35 to the west of Poole turn north on B3067 to Lytchett Minster. Go through village and site is on the left half a mile past the church, through imposing wrought iron gates. O.S.GR: SY966934.

Charges 2007

Per person	£ 4.50 - £ 6.00
child (3-14 yrs)	£ 2.00 - £ 3.00
pitch incl. electricity	£ 6.00 - £ 7.00

UK2100 **Sandford Caravan Park**

Holton Heath, Poole BH16 6JZ (Dorset)

Tel: **0870 0667793**. Email: **touring@weststarholidays.co.uk**

Sandford Park is an 'all singing, all dancing' park with a wide range of facilities near the popular coastal areas of Dorset. It has a large permanent section with 320 caravan holiday homes and lodges. However, the touring section is in an attractive secluded area and can accommodate around 450 units of any type. The pitches are mainly on level grass, either with mature evergreen hedging, or in a more open style area broken up by shrubs. All have 10A electrical connections and 14 are fully serviced. Early booking is advisable. Sandford is a large, very busy holiday park with a wide range of entertainment. The central complex, the Plaza, contains a variety of bars and restaurants (book in busy periods) and a large hall with stage and dance floor. The daily entertainment programme caters for different tastes and age groups. There is provision for simple hot meals and takeaways elsewhere on site in peak season. The 25 m. heated and supervised outdoor swimming pool and a very large play pool, ideal for children, are attractively situated with a snack bar and terraced area close by. There is also an impressive, heated and supervised indoor pool.

Facilities

Three toilet blocks also include facilities for disabled visitors and babies. Large launderette. Ladies' hairdresser. Bars, restaurants. TV lounges. Large supermarket and other shops, including well stocked camping accessory shop. Outdoor swimming pool (May-Sept) and indoor pool. Supervised soft indoor play area (April - Oct and Christmas). Playground. Tennis court. Multisport court. Table tennis. Two short mat bowling greens (outdoor). Crazy golf. Bicycle hire. Riding lessons available at stables on site. Two dog walks. Off site: Beach 9 miles. Golf 3 miles.

Open: February - January.

Directions

From the A351 (Wareham - Poole) road turn west at traffic lights in Holton Heath (signed Organford and Sandford Park). Park is on left after about 50 yards. Touring pitch reception is at the top of the park. O.S.GR: SY940913. GPS: N50:43.204 W02:05.132

Charges 2007

Per pitch incl. up to 6 persons	£ 12.75 - £ 29.00
incl. electricity	£ 15.75 - £ 32.00
serviced pitch	£ 17.25 - £ 33.50
dog (max 2)	£ 5.00

UK2110 Pear Tree Touring Park

Organford Road, Holton Heath, Poole BH16 6LA (Dorset)

Tel: **01202 622434**. Email: **info@visitpeartree.co.uk**

Pear Tree is a neat, landscaped and well cared for park welcoming families with young children and couples only. Set in 7.5 acres, with mature trees and views across to Wareham Forest, there are 125 pitches, of which 26 are hardstanding and the remainder grass. All have electricity (10A) and 50 have full services (water, waste water and electricity). Only breathable groundsheets are permitted for awnings. The tent area is a tranquil, secluded spot with many mature trees. Reception, incorporating tourist information and a small shop supplying milk, bread, gas and other basics, is at the park entrance where the gates (with key) are closed at dusk, although latecomers are admitted. A large, hedged, separate play field is at the top of the park with swings, climbing frame, trampolines and ball games area, all for younger children. A bus service stops outside for Wareham (2.5 miles) or Poole (5 miles).

Facilities

The main heated toilet block (opened by key) provides some washbasins in cubicles, baby changing unit and two WCs for disabled visitors. Separate small block near the tent area. All is kept spotlessly clean. Shop (basics only). Play area. All year caravan storage. Off site: The Clay Pipe Inn 500 m. Bicycle hire 0.5 miles. Golf 2.5 miles. Riding 5 miles. Beach 9 miles.

Open: 1 May - 30 September.

Directions

From the A351 (Wareham - Poole) road, turn west at traffic lights in Holton Heath (signed Organford and Sandford Caravan Park). Park is on left after about 550 m. - past Sandford Park and the Clay Pipe Inn. O.S.GR: SY940915. GPS: N50:43.442 W02:05.218

Charges 2007

Per unit incl. 2 persons, electricity and awning	£ 12.50 - £ 20.00
incl. services	£ 14.00 - £ 24.00
extra person	£ 3.50 - £ 5.00
child (2-15 yrs)	£ 2.00 - £ 4.50
dog	£ 1.50 - £ 3.50

PearTree **www.visitpeartree.co.uk**

All bookings and information through the website

TOURING PARK ● Low season discounts ● Quiet after 10.30 in the evening
● Close to beaches and Pool ● Peaceful (no bar or entertainment) ● Small family touring park
● Excellent facilities, include ,modern toilets & showers ● Large play area for young children
● Well controlled dogs are welcome ● Website discounts available ● On local bus routes

AA DE LUXE PARK

UK2130 Grove Farm Meadow Holiday Park

Meadowbank Holidays, Stour Way, Christchurch BH23 2PQ (Dorset)

Tel: **01202 483597**. Email: **enquiries@meadowbank-holidays.co.uk**

Grove Farm Meadow is a quiet, traditional park with caravan holiday homes and a small provision for touring units. The grass flood bank which separates the River Stour from this park provides an attractive pathway. The river bank has been kept natural and is well populated by a range of water birds. It is popular with bird watchers and there is fishing in the river. There are just under 200 caravan holiday homes (75 for hire), sited in regular rows. For touring units there are 41 level pitches, all clearly numbered with electricity (10A), backing on to fencing or hedging and accessed by tarmac roads. Twenty one are fully serviced (with hardstanding, shingle base for awnings and chemical disposal point), the other grass pitches share service points. The impressive modern reception has a good collection of tourist information. The Littledown Centre, said to be the south coast's premier leisure facility is nearby. Bournemouth is 10 minutes by car, Christchurch 5.

Facilities

The well kept toilet block provides a bathroom for each sex (50p). Separate toilet and washbasin with ramped access for disabled visitors. Baby room. Dishwashing sinks, together with spin dryer, iron and board and washing lines provided. Launderette near reception. Well stocked shop (limited hours in low season). Games room with pool table and electronic games. Adventure play area beside the river bank. Fishing (permits from reception). No dogs or other pets are accepted. Off site: Golf 0.5 miles. Large supermarket 1.5 miles. Beach, boat launching and sailing 2 miles. St Catherine's nature reserve.

Open: 1 March - 31 October.

Directions

From A388 Ringwood - Bournemouth road take B3073 for Christchurch. Turn right at the first roundabout and Stour Way is the third road on the right. O.S.GR: SZ136946. GPS: N50:45.027 W01:48.524

Charges 2007

Per 'luxury' pitch incl. 2 persons, electricity	£ 14.00 - £ 26.00
large pitch	£ 11.00 - £ 22.00
standard pitch (no awnings)	£ 8.00 - £ 17.00
extra person over 5 yrs	£ 1.00 - £ 2.00
extra car or boat	£ 1.00 - £ 2.00

UK2150 Woolsbridge Manor Farm Caravan Park

Three Legged Cross, Wimborne BH21 6RA (Dorset)

Tel: **01202 826369**. Email: **woolsbridge@btconnect.com**

Close to the Moors Valley Country Park, this friendly, family run site is within easy reach of the south coast, the resorts of Christchurch, Bournemouth and Poole, and the ancient market town of Wimborne Minster. Entry is restricted to couples and families. The seven acre camping meadow has 101 large level pitches (51 seasonal) all with electricity (16A) and arranged on either side of a central tarmac road. Reception has a well stocked shop and a good selection of tourist information. The site is part of a working beef cattle farm, so parents should be aware of moving farm machinery and tractors. A cycleway/footpath crosses the fields to the Country Park – very safe for children – where amenities include coarse fishing, golf, steam railway, bicycle hire, a tea room and a country shop.

Facilities

The neat, refurbished toilet block is well maintained and has ample facilities. Four newly built family rooms each with shower, WC, basin, handrails and ramped access provided for disabled people, babies and toddlers. Washing machine, dryer and ironing facilities. Covered dishwashing sinks. Shop. Gas. Playground. Fishing. American RVs accepted, advance booking appreciated. Torches useful. Caravan storage. Off site: Old Barn Farm inn and restaurant 400 m. Riding, golf and bicycle hire 0.5 miles. Boat launching and sailing 5 miles.

Open: Easter - 31 October.

Directions

From Ringwood take A31 southwest to large Ashley Heath roundabout (A31/A338 to Bournemouth). Take left hand slip road up to roundabout, avoiding underpass, and turn right (north) on unclassified road signed Horton and Moors Valley Country Park. Follow signs to Country Park (2 miles), pass park entrance on right, continue for 400 yards to site entrance (well signed on right). O.S.GR: SZ 099052. GPS: N50:50.615 W01:51.450

Charges 2007

Per unit incl. 2 persons and electricity	£ 15.50 - £ 20.50
extra person	£ 5.50 - £ 6.00
child (under 16 yrs)	£ 3.50 - £ 4.00

UK2180 Beacon Hill Touring Park

Blandford Road North, Poole BH16 6AB (Dorset)

Tel: **01202 631631**. Email: **bookings@beaconhilltouringpark.co.uk**

Beacon Hill is located in a marvellous, natural environment of partly wooded heathland, with certain areas of designated habitation for protected species such as sand lizards and the Dartford Warbler, but there is also easy access to main routes. Wildlife ponds encourage dragonflies and other species but fishing is also possible. Conservation is obviously important in such a special area but one can ramble at will over the 30 acres, with the hilltop walk a must. Grassy open spaces provide 170 pitches, 151 with 10A electricity, on sandy grass which is sometimes uneven. Of these, 50 are for tents only and a few are seasonal. The undulating nature of land and the trees allows for discrete areas to be allocated for varying needs, e.g. for young families near the play area, families with teenagers close to the bar/games room, those with dogs near the dog walking area, and for young people further away. The park provides a wide range of facilities, including an open air swimming pool and a tennis court. It is well situated for beaches, Poole harbour and ferries for France or the Channel Isles.

Facilities

Two fully equipped toilet blocks include facilities for disabled people. Laundry facilities and washing up sinks. Well stocked shop at reception. Coffee bar and takeaway (main season). Bar (July-Aug, B.Hs, half-terms). Heated swimming pool (mid May - mid Sept). All weather tennis court (charges). Adventure play areas. Games room with pool tables and amusement machines. TV room. Internet (WiFi). Fishing (charges). Off site: Poole harbour and ferries 3 miles. Riding 2 miles. Bicycle hire 3 miles. Brownsea Island, Studland beach with Sandbanks ferry and the Purbecks near.

Open: 17 March - end September.

Directions

Park is 3 miles north of Poole. Take A350 (towards Blandford) at roundabout where A350 joins the A35. Park signed to the right (northeast) after about 400 yards. O.S.GR: SY977945.

Charges 2007

Per person	£ 3.50 - £ 6.25
child (under 16 yrs)	£ 2.50
pitch	£ 3.00 - £ 18.00
awning	£ 1.00 - £ 2.50
electricity	£ 2.00

UK2280 Lytton Lawn Touring Park

Lymore Lane, Milford-on-Sea SO41 0TX (Hampshire)

Tel: **01590 648331**. Email: **holidays@shorefield.co.uk**   *see advertisement on page 107*

Lytton Lawn is the touring arm of Shorefield Country Park, a holiday home park and leisure centre. Set in eight acres, Lytton Lawn provides 135 marked pitches. These include 53 'premier' pitches (hardstanding, 16A electricity, pitch light, water and waste water outlet) in a grassy, hedged area – this section with its heated toilet block is open for a longer season. The rest of the pitches, all with electricity, are in the adjoining, but separate, gently sloping field, edged with mature trees and hedges and with a further toilet block. The new larger reception and well stocked shop make this a good, comfortable, self-sufficient site. Visitors to Lytton Lawn are entitled to use the very comprehensive leisure facilities at Shorefield itself (2.5 miles away). These include a very attractive indoor pool, solarium, sauna and spa, fitness classes and treatments, all weather tennis courts, minibus pools, restaurant facilities including a bistro (Easter - 2 Nov), and entertainment and activity programmes. The comprehensive facilities at Shorefield are of a very good standard and are mostly free (extra charges are made for certain activities). These include a spa and hair salon.

Facilities

Two purpose built, modern toilet blocks are tiled and well fitted. Dishwashing, washing machine and dryer in each block. Baby changing facilities in one block and facilities for disabled visitors (Radar key). New shop (all year). Small fenced play area and hedged field with goal posts. Only one dog per pitch is accepted. Off site: Village pub 10 minutes walk. Golf, riding, coarse fishing (all within 3 miles), sailing, windsurfing and boat launching facilities (1.5 miles). The New Forest, Isle of Wight, Bournemouth, Southampton and the beach at Milford on Sea are near.

Open: 8 Feburary - 2 January.

Directions

From M27 follow signs for Lyndhurst and Lymington on A337. Continue towards New Milton and Lytton Lawn is signed at Everton; Shorefield is signed at Downton. O.S.GR: SZ293937.

Charges 2008

Per pitch incl. all persons and electricity,	£ 10.50 - £ 34.00
premier pitch incl. water, drainage and TV connection	£ 10.50 - £ 34.00
dog (1 only)	£ 1.50 - £ 3.00

Less 40% Mon - Thurs in certain periods.
Min. weekly charge at busy times.

UK2285 Forest Edge Touring Park

229 Ringwood Road, St Leonards, Ringwood BH242SD (Hampshire)

Tel: **01590 648331**. Email: **holidays@shorefield.co.uk**   *see advertisement on page 107*

This popular family park is the latest addition to the Shorefield Group. Offering 40 pitches for touring holidays, it is complemented by the leisure facilities available at Oakdene Forest Park (which is no longer taking any touring units). There is easy access to the level, marked pitches, each with 16A electricity hook-ups. In addition, there are pitches for 20 seasonal units and 140 caravan holiday homes. The cheerful, flowery reception and well stocked shop help create a friendly and relaxed atmosphere. Picnic tables are dotted about the park giving it a country feel. A short walk through Hurn Forest (less than a mile) leads to Oakdene and its new clubhouse and entertainment centre. Visitors at Forest Edge may use the bar, restaurant, large pools, games room and other entertainment free of charge which is ideal for families not wishing to travel too far. The location of Forest Edge is ideal for visiting Bournemouth (beaches, shops and shows), the New Forest and all the attractions of Dorset.

Facilities

The toilet block provides clean but fairly standard facilities. Unit for disabled visitors. Baby area. These facilities may be under pressure in high season. Laundry in a separate room near the play area. Gas supplies. Shop with off-licence. Off site: Riding 1 mile. Fishing 2 miles. Golf 3 miles. Beach 5 miles.

Open: All year except 3 January - 15 February.

Directions

Take the A31 westbound from Ringwood. After 3 miles and two roundabouts, turn left at the second roundabout into Boundary Lane (before you get to Oakdene). Site is signed. O.S.GR: SU105024.

Charges 2007

Per unit incl. 6 persons	£ 7.50 - £ 23.00
incl. electricity	£ 9.50 - £ 28.00
incl. full services	£ 11.50 - £ 31.00
dog	£ 1.50 - £ 3.00

UK2290 Sandy Balls Holiday Centre

Godshill, Fordingbridge SP6 2JZ (Hampshire)

Tel: **01425 653042**. Email: **post@sandy-balls.co.uk**

Sandy Balls sits high above the sweep of the Avon river near Fordingbridge, amidst woodland which is protected as a nature reserve. It well deserves the entry it has maintained in these guides for over 30 years and continues to improve and develop, with a multimillion pound improvement project currently well under way. Very well run and open all year, the park covers an extensive area of woodland and fields, providing 131 lodges and caravan holiday homes (many for rent), some tent areas with unmarked pitches, and 233 serviced pitches for touring units. These pitches are separated by hedges on part-hardstanding, part-grass, with 10A electricity and TV connections. In winter only 50 pitches are available. The central village area with all the amenities is designed to blend with the forest surroundings. Once the investment project is complete, this area will be completely traffic free and new facilities will include a drive-through check-in system and guest services centre. The leisure centre provides for all round family entertainment. It includes a solar heated outdoor pool, a large indoor pool with exercise facilities and Tempus, a brand new mind and body treatment centre with qualified therapists. Here too are bars, restaurants and shops, plus high season entertainment and varied activities for adults and children. A woodland leisure trail allows wild animals and birds to be observed in their natural surroundings and the attractions of the New Forest are close at hand. A member of the Best of British Group.

Facilities

Three modern toilet blocks have under-floor heating and washbasins in cubicles. One 'portacabin' style unit remains as an overflow in the tent field. Toilets for disabled visitors and baby facilities. Excellent central launderette. Motorcaravan service point. Supermarket with bakery. Takeaway. Restaurants, bars and family room. Entertainment (high season). Outdoor pool (25/5-30/8). Indoor pool (66 x 30 ft). Well equipped gym, jacuzzi, sauna and solarium. Tempus therapy centre. Games room. Play areas. Soft play area. Clay modelling tuition and story telling. River fishing (permit). Riding stables. Bicycle hire. Archery. Off site: Golf 6 miles. Beach 20 miles.

Open: All year.

Directions

Park is northwest off B3078 (Fordingbridge - Cadnam) just west of Godshill village, and about 1.5 miles east of Fordingbridge. O.S.GR: SU168147. GPS: N50:55.816 W01:45.612

Charges 2007

Per person	free - £ 3.50
child (12-17 yrs)	free - £ 2.00
child (3-11 yrs)	free - £ 1.50
pitch	£ 14.00 - £ 22.00
dog	free - £ 3.00

UK2250 Hoburne Bashley

Sway Road, New Milton BH25 5QR (Hampshire)
Tel: **01425 612340**. Email: **enquiries@hoburne.co.uk**

This is an attractive, well run park with many holiday homes (380), but it also has a very sizeable tourist section and can take 300 touring units. However, tents, trailer tents and pup tents are not accepted. Spread over three flat meadows the numbered touring pitches are large, divided by hedging or low fencing, and include 20 'super' pitches. These are of mixed grass and hardstanding with electricity. Set in pleasant park-like surroundings not far from beaches, Bournemouth and the New Forest, the park has a good clubhouse with excellent facilities. This overlooks an 18 m. circular outdoor swimming pool and 18 m. paddling pool, a sensible size and great fun with its geysers, clown and beach effect. An impressive indoor pool complex houses a water flume, sauna, solarium, spa bath and steam room, all well supervised by lifeguards. The club facilities are comprehensive, with a ballroom, large lounges and bars, and a wide range of entertainment from cabaret, talent shows, bingo, quizzes and competitions to discos (Spring B.H to mid-Sept). Children's entertainment covers sports and games for the teens and Sammy the Seahorse club for under 12s. The Hungry Woodcutter provides simple hot food and takeaway all day. A popular park with lots going on, Bashley is part of the Hoburne group.

Facilities

Three well constructed toilet blocks, one central to each area, are fully tiled with modern fittings in cheerful yellow and blue with washbasins in cabins. Showers are preset (no dividers, but shower heads are set fairly low). Baby changing facilities. Covered dishwashing sinks. Launderette. Clubhouse with bars, restaurant and takeaway (1/3-31/10). 10-pin bowling. TV room. Video arcade and games room with snooker tables, plus two pool tables, table tennis and darts in other rooms. Children's club. Shop (1/3-31/10). Indoor pool. Outdoor pools (June - mid-Sept). Crazy golf. Golf course (9-hole, par 3). Tennis courts (3). Adventure play area. Soft ball play area. Only one dog or pet permitted per unit. American motorhomes accepted. Off site: Fishing and riding 1 mile. Mudeford beach 8 miles.

Open: 10 February - 30 October plus weekends.

Directions

Park is on the B3055 about 400 yards east of the crossroads with the B3058 in Bashley village. O.S.GR: SZ246969.

Charges 2006

Per unit incl.up to 6 persons and electricity	£ 13.00 - £ 36.50
multi-service pitch	£ 15.00 - £ 38.50
2 car pitch	£ 15.00 - £ 38.50
pet (1 only)	£ 2.00

Weekend breaks available.

UK2340 Shamba Holidays

Ringwood Road, St Leonards, Ringwood BH24 2SB (Hampshire)
Tel: **01202 873302**. Email: **enquiries@shambaholidays.co.uk**

Shamba is a family run, very modern park, although the aim remains to create a relaxed, pleasant atmosphere. There are 150 pitches, most of which are used for touring units, 20 are on a seasonal basis. Surrounded by trees, the camping area is on flat, open grass with electricity (10-16A) available on all pitches. A Scandinavian style building forms the focal point and here you will find reception, a bar/restaurant, takeaway and a shop. The indoor swimming pool has walls and a roof which can be opened in good weather. Bournemouth with its shops and beaches is 8 miles, while the delights of the New Forest and Dorset are within easy reach. The park's location is excellent for a short stop-over but well worth a longer stay for a family holiday.

Facilities

Sanitary facilities with under-floor heating include modern showers, washbasins and toilets and family changing rooms. Baby rooms with bath and facilities for disabled visitors. Launderette. Motorcaravan service point. Bar with meals and takeaway. Indoor swimming pool (12 x 6 m.) and children's pool. Large children's play area. Amusements room. Off site: Riding 1 mile. Golf 2 miles. Fishing and bicycle hire 2.5 miles. Ringwood 2.5 miles. Moors Valley Country Park 1 mile. Beach 8 miles.

Open: 1 March - 31 October.

Directions

Take the A31 westbound from Ringwood, after 3 miles, at second roundabout, turn back on yourself and after only 20 m. turn left at the park sign. O.S.GR: SU104026. GPS: N50:49.504 W01:51.187

Charges 2007

Per pitch incl. 2 persons and electricity	£ 16.00 - £ 26.00
extra person	£ 3.25
child (6-11 yrs)	£ 2.25
dog	£ 2.25

A minimum advance booking policy applies at peak periods.

Camping Cheques accepted.

UK2315 Riverside Holidays

Satchell Lane, Hamble, Southampton SO31 4HR (Hampshire)

Tel: **023 8045 3220**. Email: **enquiries@riversideholidays.co.uk**

What makes Riverside so special is its location; close to the River Hamble, Mecca for the international yachtsman. Hamble village, one mile away, with its cobbled streets, pubs and restaurants, is famed the world over for its association with yachting. This is an ideal base for the Southampton Boat Show, Cowes Week and its very own Hamble Week Regatta. It is also home to the Royal Yachting Association. On the marina adjacent to the site, a mere two minutes walk, is Oyster Quay with a bar and restaurant overlooking hundreds of yachts worth millions. Where the Hamble river enters Southampton Water, visitors can see all the great liners as they pass in and out of nearby Southampton port. The site is family-owned and covers five acres surrounded by trees and hedges; it has 114 pitches of which 75 are level for touring caravans and tents with 53 electricity hook-ups (16A). The remaining pitches are used for lodges and residential and static caravans on slightly rising ground, but so well spaced and with plenty of grass they are not too obtrusive. A warden-run log cabin reception is at the entrance. Currently the amenities block comprises an old 'Portakabin', screened by fencing and butterfly shrubs. It is clean but not quite up to standard. However, this is to be replaced with a new reception, shop, clubroom, toilet block and a pool in the next two years.

Facilities

The old 'Portakabin' unit is clean but not quite up to standard, with a baby changing area but no unit for the disabled. However, an additional amenities block has recently been installed. Small laundry room alongside. All these facilities could be under pressure in high season. Bicycle hire. Caravan storage. Off site: Buses and trains 1 mile. Fishing, sea fishing, sailing, supermarket, 1 mile in village. Riding 2 miles. Golf 5 miles. You can catch a small ferry across to Warsash on the other bank or take a boat up to the Upper Hamble Country Park. The New Forest, Winchester and Portsmouth are nearby.

Open: 1 March - 31 October.

Directions

From the M27 take exit 8 and follow signs for Hamble. Taking B3397 with Tesco on the left, continue 1.9 miles through traffic lights until Hound roundabout. After 50 yds turn left into Satchell Lane (signed Mercury Marina) and site is on left in 1 mile. Q,S. GR: SU484082. GPS: N50:52.200 W01:18.667

Charges 2007

Per unit incl. 2 persons	£ 11.50 - £ 29.00
extra person	£ 3.50
child (4-16 yrs)	£ 2.50

Camping Cheques accepted.

UK2300 Forest Holidays Ashurst

Forest Holidays, Lyndhurst Road, Ashurst SO4O 7AR (Hampshire)

Tel: 02380 292097. Email: info@forestholidays.co.uk

An attractive Forestry Commission site on the fringe of the New Forest, Ashurst is set in a mixture of oak woodland and grass heathland which is open to the grazing animals of the Forest. Smaller than the Hollands Wood site (23 acres), it provides 280 pitches, 180 of which have been gravelled to provide semi-hardstanding; otherwise you pitch where you like, applying the 20 ft. rule on ground that can be uneven. There are no electricity connections. Some noise must be expected from the adjacent railway line – the station is just five minutes walk away.

Facilities	Directions
The single central toilet block has been refurbished and provides everything necessary, including hairdryers, a well equipped unit for visitors with disabilities (key required) and a good laundry room. It could be under pressure when the site is full in the main season. Motorcaravan service point. Bread and milk to order. Dogs are not accepted. A torch is useful. Off site: Local garage sells gas. Nearby pub by footpath across an adjacent field. Shops and local buses within a five minute walk. Golf 4 miles. **Open:** March - September.	Site is 2 miles east of Lyndhurst, set back from the A35 Southampton - Bournemouth road, 5 miles southwest of Southampton. O.S.GR: SU344099.

Charges 2007

Per unit incl. 2 persons	£ 9.40 - £ 19.70
extra person	£ 3.80 - £ 7.90
child	£ 1.90 - £ 4.00

Less 20% all year for disabled guests and outside 7/7-28/8 for senior citizens.

UK2310 Forest Holidays Hollands Wood

Forest Holidays, Lyndhurst Road, Brockenhurst SO43 7QH (Hampshire)

Tel: 01590 622967. Email: info@forestholidays.co.uk

Forest Holidays is a partnership between the Forestry Commission and The Camping and Caravanning Club. This is a large, spacious 168 acre secluded site in a woodland setting (mainly oak). It is set in the heart of the New Forest, with an abundance of wildlife. The site is arranged informally with 600 level unmarked pitches but it is stipulated that there must be at least 20 feet between each unit. There are no electrical connections and traffic noise is possible from the A337 which runs along one boundary. Brockenhurst village is only about half a mile where there are shops for supplies and gas, etc, plus trains and buses. Barbecues are not permitted in dry weather. The site can get very busy.

Facilities	Directions
Two large utilitarian toilet blocks (and a third smaller, older one) are fully equipped if somewhat basic. Facilities for disabled people. Two laundry rooms. These facilities are under pressure at peak times. Motorcaravan service point. Bread and milk to order. Torches essential. Off site: Bicycle hire and riding 2 miles. Golf 3 miles. **Open:** 29 March - 25 September.	Site entrance is on east side of A337 Lyndhurst - Lymington road, half a mile north of Brockenhurst. O.S.GR: SU303034.

Charges 2007

Per unit incl. 2 persons	£ 8.70 - £ 17.40
extra person	£ 3.60 - £ 7.00
child	£ 2.00 - £ 3.60

UK2360 Hill Cottage Farm Camping & Caravan Park

Sandleheath Road, Alderholt, Fordingbridge SP6 3EG (Hampshire)

Tel: 01425 650513. Email: hillcottagefarmcaravansite@supanet.com

This is a newly constructed, modern site set in 47 acres of beautiful countryside on the Dorset and Hampshire border. The 32 pitches, all on hardstandings with electric hook-ups (16A) and water taps are arranged around a circular gravel roadway. Secluded and sheltered, they have views across the surrounding countryside. A field alongside the camping area is used for tents and rallies, and has space for ball games and a small playground. Also on site is a lake for coarse fishing, and there are many woodland walks in the area. Overall this site is more suitable for adults and younger children.

Facilities	Directions
A large modern barn-style building provides excellent heated facilities. Laundry room. Facilities for disabled people and babies. The first floor has a games room and a separate function room. Motorcaravan services. Playground. Off site: Village centre with pub, church, Post Office and store is a 20 minute woodland walk. Rockbourne Roman Villa, Cranborne Chase. **Open:** 1 March - 31 December.	From Fordingbridge take B3078 west for 2 miles to Alderholt. On entering the village, at left hand bend, turn right towards Sandleheath (site signed) and site entrance is about 300 yards on the left. O.S.GR: SU120130. GPS: N50:55.141 W01:49.967

Charges 2007

Per unit incl. 2 personS	£ 12.00 - £ 16.00
extra person	£ 5.00
child (0-15 yrs)	£ 1.50 - £ 3.00

UK2350 Red Shoot Camping Park

Linwood, Ringwood BH24 3QT (Hampshire)

Tel: **01425 473789**. Email: **enquiries@redshoot-campingpark.com**

Red Shoot is set on three acres of open, slightly sloping, level grass, in the heart of the New Forest. A simple, rural retreat with panoramic views of the surrounding countryside and forest, it is very popular in high season. There are around 130 good sized pitches, 45 with electrical hook-ups (10A), served by a circular gravel road. There is no site lighting so a torch would be useful. The adjacent Red Shoot Inn (under separate ownership) serves hot or cold meals and brews its own real ales – Forest Gold and Tom's Tipple. There are ample opportunities for walking, cycling and naturalist pursuits in the area, and nearby Ringwood has a market on Wednesday. Local attractions include watersports at the New Forest Water Park near Ringwood, a Doll Museum in Fordingbridge, cider making in Burley, and Breamore House just north of Fordingbridge.

Facilities

The sanitary facilities have been extended and refurbished and, as well as under-floor heating, include a family shower room, baby bath and changing area. Dishwashing sinks under cover. Well equipped laundry room. Good unit for disabled visitors. Very well stocked, licensed shop. Fenced adventure style playground. Mountain bike hire. Off site: Fishing 5 miles. Riding 6 miles. Golf 7 miles. Beach 12 miles.

Open: 1 March - 31 October.

Directions

From A338 about 1.75 miles north of Ringwood, turn east (signed Linwood and Moyles Court). Follow signs, over a staggered crossroads, and continue straight on for another 1.75 miles to Red Shoot Inn. O.S.GR: SU188095. GPS: N50:53.035 W01:44.082

Charges 2007

Per person	£ 5.90
child (5-14 yrs)	£ 3.75
child (0-4 yrs)	£ 1.25
pitch incl. car	£ 2.00 - £ 5.00
electricity	£ 3.50
Min. pitch charge £11.50.	

Linwood,
Near Ringwood,
Hampshire,
BH24 3QT

Set in the heart of the New Forest and close to Bournemouth and Ringwood, this is a first class family-run park. Excellent facilities, cycle hire service, children's play area and adjacent to Red Shoot Inn. See our website for full details and saving discounts.

www.redshoot-campingpark.co.uk
01425 473789
Email: enquiries@redshoot-campingpark.com

UK2320 Chichester Camping & Caravanning Club Site

345 Main Road, Southbourne PO10 8JH (Hampshire)

Tel: **01243 373202**

This small, neat site is just to the west of Chichester and north of Bosham harbour. Formerly an orchard, it is rectangular in shape with 58 pitches on flat, well mown lawns on either side of gravel roads. All pitches have 16A electricity, 42 with level hardstanding. Although the A27 bypass takes most of the through traffic, the site is by the main A259 road so there may be some traffic noise in some parts (not busy at night). Opposite the park are orchards through which paths lead to the seashore. Unfortunately there is no parking outside or overnight area for late arrivals. Arrival must be before 20.00. unless prior arrangements have been made with the site manager. Portsmouth is nearby with its ferry port and historic Naval Dockyard. Other attractions include Goodwood (racing), Chichester (Festival Theatre) and Fishbourne Roman palace, with Southampton and the New Forest a little further afield.

Facilities

The well designed, brick built toilet block is of first class quality. Fully tiled and heated in cool weather, with facilities for people with disabilities (access by key). Washing machines and dryers. Gas supplies. No ball games permitted on the park. Dogs can be walked in the lane opposite the entrance. Off site: Shops, restaurants and pubs within easy walking distance in the nearby village and the park is on a main bus route. Chichester has a leisure centre and market day is Wednesday. Excellent caravan shop nearby. Bicycle hire 1 mile. Fishing or golf 5 miles, riding 6 miles.

Open: February - November.

Directions

Park is on A259 Chichester - Havant road at Southbourne, 750 yards west of Chichester Caravans. Coming from the west, it is 2.8 miles from the A27/A259 junction near Havant. O.S.GR: SU774056.

Charges 2007

Per person	£ 6.30 - £ 8.25
child (6-18 yrs)	£ 2.15 - £ 2.25
pitch (non-member)	£ 5.65

UK2380 Hill Farm Caravan Park

Branches Lane, Sherfield English, Romsey SO51 6FH (Hampshire)

Tel: **01794 340402**. Email: **gjb@hillfarmpark.com**

This 11 acre rural park is ideal for those seeking a quiet base but one that is within easy reach of all the main tourist attractions of Hampshire and Dorset. There are 92 pitches, of which 30 for seasonal units are located in a separate area. The touring area is a large open field surrounded by trees and hedges. All pitches are well marked, numbered and mainly level. All have electricity hook-ups (6/10A), 12 pitches are fully serviced and some are available with hardstanding. Adding to the attractiveness of the site is a pitch and putt golf course, set in a sizeable and well-landscaped area. For anyone interested in roses, nearby Mottisfont Abbey (National Trust) has a unique collection of old-fashioned varieties and during the summer open-air plays, films and concerts take place here. The New Forest with Beaulieu Estate and National Motor Museum is just a short drive away. A trip to the Isle of Wight makes a good excursion – the ferry terminal is within a thirty minute drive.

Facilities

Two very clean traditionally built toilet blocks include washbasins, both open style and in cubicles, and controllable showers. Facilities for babies and disabled visitors. Motorcaravan service point. Shop in reception for gas supplies and basics. Bread and pasties are cooked on the premises. Snack bar serves breakfast and takeaway meals. Play area. Pitch and putt golf. Off site: Riding and fishing 3 miles. Bicycle Hire 15 miles. Bournemouth and Southampton for shopping, leisure and family entertainment nearby.

Open: 1 March - 31 October.

Directions

From Romsey, drive north on the A27 for 3.5 miles, turning right into Branches Lane and site is a further 0.5 miles on right. O.S.GR: SU235300.

Charges 2007

Per unit incl. 2 persons and 2 dogs	£ 14.00 - £ 36.00
extra person	£ 4.00
child (4-17 yrs)	£ 1.50 - £ 2.50

Minimum booking for B.Hs, July/Aug. weekends. No credit cards.

UK2470 Southland Camping Park

Newchurch, Sandown PO36 0LZ (Isle of Wight)

Tel: **01983 865385**. Email: **info@southland.co.uk**

Southland was opened in 1981 in the grounds of a former nursery and it has matured nicely with many attractive shrubs and trees. The pleasant surroundings have won many awards. In the peaceful country setting of the Arreton valley, it is a sheltered and well run park with 120 large, level pitches backing on to and separated by high hedging. Comfortable and spacious, all have electricity hook-ups (10/16A) and some water points. Two acres of land on the western edge of the park overlooking the valley have been developed as a nature area. Nearby Arreton and Newchurch have craft shops and in August there is the National Garlic Festival. Sandown and Shanklin are 3 miles, the beach at Lake, 2.5 miles.

Facilities

The excellent toilet block is well maintained - the ladies' is modern, with washbasins in spacious cubicles, low level washbasins for children, three en-suite basin and shower cubicles, and a hairdressing area. Bathroom (on payment), baby room, a good unit for disabled people, and two family shower rooms also suitable for disabled visitors. Laundry and dishwashing sinks. Motorcaravan service point. Shop (1/4-30/9). Fenced play area – no ball games are permitted on the park. Only raised barbecues are permitted. More than one dog per pitch by prior arrangement only. Off site: Main bus route stops at the top of the road, two pubs are within walking distance and there is access to walks and bridleways. Fishing 1 mile. Riding 2 miles. Bicycle hire and golf 3 miles. Beach 2.5 miles.

Open: 1 April - end September.

Directions

Park is signed from A3055/6 Newport-Sandown road, southeast of Arreton. O.S.GR: SZ558848. GPS: N50:39.588 W01:12.718

Charges 2008

Per person	£ 5.60 - £ 8.50
child (3-15 yrs)	£ 2.00 - £ 4.50
dog	£ 1.10

Electricity incl. Packages incl. ferry travel available. Special low season offers.

UK2450 The Orchards Holiday Caravan & Camping Park

Newbridge, Yarmouth PO41 0TS (Isle of Wight)

Tel: **01983 531331**. Email: **info@orchards-holiday-park.co.uk**

In a village situation in the quieter western part of the island, The Orchards, 'a park for all seasons', is a busy and lively family holiday park combining 70 caravan holiday homes (in a separate area) with a neat touring area. Recent developments include complete recycling facilities and the inclusion of two butterfly gardens. A good place from which to explore, the beaches and Yarmouth are only four miles away. There are 171 marked touring pitches, arranged on gently sloping meadow, broken up by apple trees, mature hedges and fences. All have electricity and 84 have hardstanding. In addition, there are 20 'all-service' pitches, 10 with hardstanding. The large reception provides useful tourist information. A meeting room (up to 50 persons) is suitable for small rallies. There are walking and cycling routes from the park with leaflets available. Part of the Caravan Club's affiliated scheme, non-members are also very welcome, the park is also a member of the Best of British group.

Facilities

Three toilet blocks are ample. A few washbasins are in private cubicles. Baths on payment. The latest block, a smart mobile unit, provides en-suite facilities (shower, WC and basin). Facilities for disabled visitors (a hardstanding pitch close by can be reserved). Full laundry facilities. Motorcaravan service point. Ice pack and battery charging services. Gas supplies. Well stocked shop and takeaway (mid March - Oct, limited opening at quiet times). Indoor pool (Feb - Dec). Outdoor heated pool (late May - Sept). Play areas. TV and amusements rooms (no evening entertainment on site). Coarse fishing on site (no closed season). Bicycle hire can be arranged. Hire a metal detector to seek treasure! Off site: Bus stop at entrance. Membership is available for the village social club and a small discount at Freshwater golf course (4 miles) - ask at reception. Boat launching 4 miles. Riding 1 mile.

Open: All year excl. 3 January - 15 February.

Directions

Park is in Newbridge village, signed north from B3401 (Yarmouth - Newport) road.
O.S.GR: SZ411878. GPS: N50:41.278 W01:25.198

Charges 2007

Per unit incl. 2 persons and electricity	£ 12.10 - £ 17.00

No pitch fee for hikers or cyclists.
Packages incl. ferry travel available
- ring park for best deal.

Camping Cheques accepted.

UK2480 Appuldurcombe Gardens Holiday Park

Wroxall, Ventnor PO38 3EP (Isle of Wight)

Tel: **01983 852597**. Email: **info@appuldurcombegardens.co.uk**

Originally part of the grounds of an historic house, this pretty family holiday park is situated in 14 acres of beautiful countryside in the valley of Stenbury Downs and St Martin's Downs, close to the sandy beaches at Sandown, Shanklin and Ventnor. The camping field is set in a grassy meadow through which a stream meanders, with a tranquil seating area close by. With hard access roads, there are 100 spacious marked pitches for touring units and tents, 70 of which have electricity hook-ups (10A). The old walled orchard contains 40 good quality caravan holiday homes, the access friendly Orchard Lodge (all accommodation on one level with ramp access to outside), plus two self contained apartments. In an area of outstanding natural beauty, it is an ideal spot for birdwatching and horse riding. For walkers and cyclists there is an excellent network of footpaths and cycle paths.

Facilities

Two good toilet blocks (access by key) are fully tiled with free hot water throughout. Facilities for visitors with disabilities. Launderette. Shop (fresh baguettes baked daily) and café. Bar and family entertainment room. All amenities open from Spring B.H. Large outdoor swimming pool and toddlers' pool (May - early Sept). Play area. Pitch and putt. Crazy golf. Off site: Fishing, golf, riding, bicycle hire, boat launching, beach, sailing, all within 2-3 miles.

Open: All year excl. mid December - mid January.

Directions

Do not use Sat Nav instructions, road with restricted access nearby. From Newport take A3020 towards Shanklin and Ventnor. Travel through Blackwater, Rookley, Godshill and Sandford. At Whiteley Bank roundabout turn right towards Wroxhall (B3320). Pass Donkey Sanctuary and turn right into Appuldurcombe Road. Park entrance is second on the right, 150 yards along this road. O.S.GR: SZ548803.

Charges 2007

Per person	£ 5.00 - £ 7.50
child (3-14 yrs)	£ 1.50 - £ 3.75
serviced pitch	£ 2.50
dog	£ 1.00 - £ 1.50

UK2500 Heathfield Farm Camping

Heathfield Road, Freshwater PO40 9SH (Isle of Wight)

Tel: **01983 756756**. Email: **web@heathfieldcamping.co.uk**

Heathfield is a pleasant contrast to many of the other sites on the Isle of Wight, in that it is a 'no frills' sort of place, very popular with tenters, cyclists and small camper vans. Despite its name, it is no longer a working farm. A large, open meadow provides 60 large, level pitches, 30 with electricity (10A). Two small fenced areas provide traffic free zones for backpackers and cyclists' tents. A play field for ball games also has two picnic tables and two barbecues, and there is a wild flower meadow with the perimeter mown for dog walking. There is no shop as you are only eight minutes walk from the centre of Freshwater. The site overlooks Colwell Bay and across the Solent towards Milford-on-Sea and Hurst Castle. It is ideal for visiting attractions on the western side of the island including Totland and Freshwater Bays, The Needles and Old Battery, Compton Down, and Mottistone Manor Garden. The Military road which runs from Freshwater Bay to St Catherine's Point gives spectacular coastal views.

Facilities

The main toilet unit is housed in a modern, ingeniously customised, 'portacabin' type unit including one washbasin cubicle for ladies and a baby room. Showers are slightly different in that they have two pushbutton controls, one for pre-mixed hot water, the other for cold only (provided at the special request of some of the regular customers). A second similar unit has WCs and washbasins in cubicles, plus facilities for disabled visitors. Laundry with washing machine and dryer, ironing. Motorcaravan service point. Gas supplies. Ice pack service. Play field. Bicycle hire. No commercial vehicles are accepted. Gate locked 22.30-07.00 hrs. Off site: Bus stop 200 m. Beach 0.5 miles. Fishing 0.5 miles. Golf 1.25 miles. Riding 3 miles.

Open: 1 May - 30 September.

Directions

From A3054 north of Totland and Colwell turn into Heathfield Road where site is signed. Site entrance is on right after a short distance. O.S.GR: SZ336879.

Charges 2007

Per person	£ 4.00 - £ 5.00
child (3-15 yrs)	£ 1.75 - £ 2.75
pitch	£ 8.75 - £ 13.50
with electricity	£ 10.00 - £ 15.00
dog (max. 1, 16/7-31/8)	£ 1.50

Min pitch fee July/Aug £12.00 (no fee for backpacker pitches). One night booking supplement £2.00.

No credit cards.

UK2495 Whitefield Forest Touring Park

Brading Road, Ryde PO30 1QL (Isle of Wight)

Tel: **01983 617069**. Email: **pat&louise@whitefieldforest.co.uk**

This new, family run park, opened in May 2007, has been sympathetically developed by the owners working closely with the Forestry Commission to maintain the natural beauty of the ancient woodland, Whitefield Forest. There is a mixture of well drained all-weather hardstanding and grass pitches, (70 in total) all with 16A electricity hook up. Varying in size (100-170 sq.m), the pitches are level and sheltered withsome on terraces. They are all suitable for tents, caravans and motorcaravans. There is good access to the park and the pitches. Some slight road noise is audible from a few pitches. The park is suitable for families and pre-teen children who want a peaceful relaxing holiday. The nearby towns of Ryde, Shanklin and Sandown provide evening entertainment.

Facilities

The excellent well appointed heated toilet block has private cubicles, hairdryers and razor points. Family shower rooms. Baby changing and facilities for people with disabilities. Laundry room with free ironing (iron from reception). Motorcaravan service point. Paperback book exchange. Adventure type play area with bark surface for children over 5 yrs. Suitable for American style motorhomes and twin axle caravans. Off site: Network of public footpaths from the site. Golf 1 km. Riding, fishing and boat launching 3 km. Bicycle hire 4 km. Beach 3 km. Supermarket 1 km.

Open: Easter - October.

Directions

From Fishbourne and East Cowes follow A3054 to Ryde. Follow the A3055 to Brading. Site is 800 yds. on left (signed) after Tesco roundabout. From Yarmouth follow A3054 to Newport, then to Ryde. Follow the A3055 to Brading and as above. O.S.GR: SZ606894.

Charges 2007

Per person	£ 5.00 - £ 7.50
child (3-14 yrs)	£ 1.50 - £ 3.75
dog	£ 1.00 - £ 1.50

UK2515 Nodes Point Holiday Park

St Helens, Ryde PO33 1YA (Isle of Wight)

Tel: **01983 872401**. Email: **holiday.sales@park-resorts.com**

In a spectacular position, Nodes Point overlooks Bembridge Bay and is set in 65 acres of parkland running down to the beach. This is a park of 200 holiday homes with a separate area for 70 touring caravans. There is a further large dedicated field for up to 200 tents which runs down to the beach. The caravan pitches are large, level and numbered, all with electricity hookups (16A) and including 25 fully serviced (hardstanding, water, electricity and TV point). A one-way circular tarmaced road leads you round the site which is landscaped and has has been cultivated with wildlife in mind. A permanent warden lives in this same area to assist. Alongside are 30 park-owned rented tents, all well sited and maintained. The latest modern toilet block supplements two older ones and a 'Portakabin' unit – together these are ample. The rest of the facilities and entertainment are in the holiday home area, a few minutes walk away. There is a large stage area for discos and spectacular cabaret shows. With these and the park's location by the beach, Nodes Point makes for a good family holiday.

Facilities

Together, the toilet blocks have WCs, open washbasins, showers, a family shower room and two baths. Baby room. Suite for disabled persons. Launderette. Shop. Bar. Restaurant and takeaway. Indoor pool. Adventure playground. Children's clubs. Entertainment. Archery. Riding. ATM. Off site: Fishing and boat launching 2 miles. Golf 3 miles.

Open: Easter - 29 October.

Directions

From Ryde, take the A3055. At Bishop Lovett School (on the left), go straight ahead onto B3330 towards St Helens. After about 2 miles, as road curves right, turn left into signed entrance. O.S.GR:SZ631896. GPS: N50:42.325 W01:06.317

Charges 2007

Per unit incl. up to 6 persons	£ 3.00 - £ 29.00
hardstanding pitch	£ 8.00
dog	£ 1.00 - £ 3.00

UK2520 Thorness Bay Holiday Park

Thorness Bay, Cowes PO31 8NJ (Isle of Wight)

Tel: **01983 523109**. Email: **holiday.sales@park.resorts.com**

Spread over a large area of rural down and woodland that slopes down to the beach at Thorness Bay, this is a large site with more than 500 holiday homes. The touring area has around 90 pitches, most with electricity (16A) including 27 multi-serviced pitches on gravel hardstandings with electricity, water, drain and TV points. These and some grass pitches are on terraces served by tarmac roads. The remainder are on sloping open grassland either divided by ranch style rails or in an open tent area, and all have views of the surrounding countryside. The main activity centre is located in the holiday home area, a short walk from the touring site. Outdoor sporting activities on-site include a multi-court, soccer, archery, and fencing. The indoor pool provides snorkelling, scuba diving and adult only swimming sessions. There is evening entertainment for all the family.

Facilities

New toilet block providing showers, WCs and washbasins. Suite for disabled visitors. Baby changing. Dishwashing area. Laundry facilities. Shop. Indoor pool. Indoor playroom for small children. Adventure playground. Multisport court. Children's club. Off site: The beach is easily accessed from the main entertainment complex. All the attractions of the Island are within easy day-trip distances. Riding within 1 mile. Golf 4 miles.

Open: Easter - 29 October.

Directions

Thorness Bay is southwest of Cowes. From East Cowes ferry follow signs to Newport. Follow the A3054 (Yarmouth). Continue for about 2.5 miles to crossroads, turning right (north) to Thorness Bay. After approx. 2 miles, on sharp right hand bend, turn left, site signed. O.S.GR: SZ452926. GPS: N50:43.868 W01:21.628

Charges 2007

Per unit incl. electricity and up to 6 persons	£ 6.00 - £ 30.00
tent pitch	£ 3.00 - £ 27.00
hardstanding pitch, plus	£ 5.00
dog	£ 1.00 - £ 3.00

UK2475 Lower Hyde Holiday Park

Landguard Road, Shanklin PO37 7LL (Isle of Wight)

Tel: **01983 866131**. Email: **holiday.sales@park-resorts.com**

This site is located on the edge of Shanklin, within walking distance of shops and services and only 1.5 miles from the beach. Lower Hyde is a large holiday park complex with around 200 caravan holiday homes for rent and 114 privately owned. The separate touring area has 115 well-spaced and numbered pitches, 85 with electric hook-ups (16A) of which 26 are fully serviced with hardstanding, water, waste-water drain, electricity and TV hook-up. This area is in an elevated position with good views over the surrounding countryside. The pitches are large and flat, easily accessed, with tarmac roads and low-level lighting. Landscaping is good, with much wildlife planting throughout. There is a permanent warden for the tourers. This section has a modern toilet block but the rest of the facilities and entertainment are in the holiday home area, near reception, a few minutes walk. This is a lively site with a large dedicated stage area for discos and spectacular cabaret shows. With all the activities, lots of young staff, security personnel and lifeguards, it is excellent for a family holiday.

Facilities

The new toilet block has WCs, open washbasins, showers, a family shower room and two bathrooms. Separate baby room. Suite for disabled persons. Launderette. Shop. Bar. Restaurant and takeaway. Indoor and outdoor pools. Adventure playground. Children's clubs. Entertainment. Multicourt. Soccer. Archery. Fencing. Tennis. ATM. Off site: Fishing and boat launching 1.5 miles. Golf 2.5 miles. Riding and bicycle hire 5 miles.

Open: 2 April - 29 October.

Directions

From East Cowes ferry terminal take A3021 for about 2.5 miles to roundabout and turn right on A3054 to Newport. From Newport take A3020 towards Sandown and Shanklin. After 1.5 miles (at Blackwater) continue straight on joining A3056 to Sandown. Keep on this road until you pass Safeway on the left, and shortly afterwards, turn right into Whitecross Lane (signed Landguard Camping). Keep straight on, past Landguard and site is on right after 1 mile. O.S.GR:SZ576817. GPS: N50:37.999 W01:10.859

Charges 2007

Per unit incl. up to 6 persons	£ 3.00 - £ 32.00
hardstanding	£ 5.00
dog	£ 1.00 - £ 3.00

UK2510 Whitecliff Bay Holiday Park

Hillway, Whitecliff Bay, Bembridge PO35 5PL (Isle of Wight)

Tel: **01983 872671**. Email: **holiday@whitecliff-bay.com**

Whitecliff Bay is a very large complex divided by a road, with a holiday home and chalet park on the right hand side, and a touring site on the left hand side. The large touring site is on a sloping hillside with commanding views over the surrounding countryside. The 659 pitches are spread over three fields, the top and second fields are terraced, but field three (the only one in which dogs are permitted in low season only) is quite level. Half of the pitches have electric hook-ups (16A), and there are around 44 gravel hardstandings, 12 in the top field, the remainder in lowest field. There are 13 individual hedged multi-serviced pitches available, so book early. On the opposite side of the lane, in the holiday home park, you will find all the main entertainment and leisure facilities. These include The Culver Club with a bar and evening entertainment, several snack bars and takeaways, supervised swimming pools (indoor and outdoor), a sauna and sunbed, small gym and soft 'playzone' (under 8s). Close to the outdoor pool a very steep path leads down to a sandy beach, where there is a small café. It is possible to launch a boat from this beach (4-wheel drive vehicle essential, advance booking necessary).

Facilities

Three sanitary units, one on the lower part of the site. The other two are fairly close together, not far from reception and both of these have been refitted to a good standard. Showers (on payment) and a suite (with shower) for disabled people. Laundry. Motorcaravan service point. Small mini-market with reception. Playground. At the holiday home park: Launderette, hairdresser and second larger shop. The Culver Club. Snack bars. Swimming pool (18 x 18 m, Whitsun - end Aug). Indoor funpool with jacuzzi, a sauna and sunbed, small gym, a soft playzone (under 8 yrs). Most facilities open March - Oct. Dogs only accepted in lower field outside 20/7-31/8. Off site: Normal bus service from park entrance on weekdays, site runs a minibus at weekends to Bembridge and Sandown. Golf 5 miles. Bicycle hire 4 miles. Riding 2 miles.

Open: 30 March - 1 November.

Directions

Bembridge is at the eastern end of the island. From the A3055 between Ryde and Sandown, turn east at Brading on B3395 for approx. 2 miles passing the Airfield and Propeller Club, fork right (site signed). Follow signs to site, first entry on right is static area, touring entrance is on left immediately after. O.S.GR: SZ635865.

Charges 2007

Per pitch incl. 2 persons	£ 9.85 - £ 17.35
incl. electricity	£ 13.15 - £ 21.25
incl. full services	£ 16.15 - £ 25.50
extra person	£ 4.30 - £ 6.70
child (5-13 yrs)	£ 2.85 - £ 4.40

UK2530 Waverley Park Holiday Centre

51 Old Road, East Cowes PO32 6AW (Isle of Wight)

Tel: **01983 293452**. Email: **sue@waverley-park.co.uk**

This pleasant small family owned and run site is set in the grounds of an old country house, once owned by Dr Arnold, the author of Tom Brown's Schooldays. There are magnificent views over the Solent and just five minutes from the Cowes ferry terminal. The 45 touring pitches are in short rows, back to back on sloping grassland, whilst tents are pitched on the lower half nearer to the promenade and sea. The 28 electricity hook-ups (10A) are tightly packed at the top. To one side of the site is an area housing 75 private and rental holiday homes. At the bottom of the park a gate leads onto the promenade which provides good walks, and the pebble beach which is popular with sailors, windsurfers, etc. The site is an ideal vantage point for Cowes Week, and has good views of the ocean liners sailing in and out of Southampton.

Facilities

At the top of the park, a recently built toilet block provides the usual facilities, including some spacious cubicles with washbasins en-suite. Good suite for disabled people with a baby changing deck. Basic chemical disposal point in the static area. Laundry facilities. Dishwashing room. Small well stocked shop. Heated outdoor pool with sun terrace. Club with restaurant and bar serving good value meals, plus family entertainment in season (all Whitsun - early Sept). Small adventure style playground. Games room. 9-hole putting green. Boats accepted by prior arrangement - public slipway nearby. Off site: Tennis courts close to lower end of site, key available, ask at reception. East Cowes, with its basic shops and services is within walking distance. Bus stop outside the site entrance.

Open: 29 March - 30 September (statics all year).

Directions

Immediately after leaving Southampton - Cowes ferry, take first left, then right into Old Road, and park entrance is 300 yds on left. O.S.GR: SZ505958.

Charges 2007

Per person	£ 4.00 - £ 7.00
child (5-13 yrs)	£ 2.00 - £ 4.00
pitch	£ 3.00
dog	£ 0.50 - £ 1.50

During Cowes Week min. pitch fees apply (£12.00 - £14.50). Packages incl. ferry travel and other offers available.

UK2570 Lincoln Farm Park

High Street, Standlake, Witney OX29 7RH (Oxfordshire)

Tel: **01865 300239**. Email: **lincolnfarm@btconnect.com**

From its immaculately tended grounds and quality facilities, to the efficient and friendly staff, this park is a credit to its owner. Situated in a small, quiet village, it is well set back and screened by mature trees, with wide gravel roads, hedged enclosures, brick pathways and good lighting. All 90 numbered, level touring pitches are generously sized and have electrical connections (10/16A), 75 with gravel hardstanding and grass for awnings, and 22 are fully serviced (fresh and waste water, electricity and satellite TV). Gazebos or extra tents are not permitted on pitches. Although only a relatively small site its leisure facilities are quite outstanding. The indoor leisure centre boasts two heated pools plus a pool for toddlers, spa pools, saunas, steam room, sun bed and a fitness suite. Charges for all of these are modest, and outside of the open sessions everything can be hired privately by the hour. Oxford and the Cotswolds are conveniently close.A member of the Best of British group.

Facilities

Two heated toilet blocks are well maintained and exceptionally clean, with showers and washbasins in cubicles. A well equipped, separate unit for disabled people. Two family bathrooms (with baby bath and changing facilities). Laundry and dishwashing facilities, freezers, fridges and microwaves. Motorcaravan service point. Shop (basic supplies). Information kiosk. Outdoor chess/draughts, putting green and adventure play area. Indoor swimming pools. Off site: Fishing (lake and river) 300 yds - 5 miles, riding centre and water sports nearby.

Open: 1 February - mid November.

Directions

Take A415 Witney - Abingdon road and turn into Standlake High Street by garage; park is 300 yds. on the right. O.S.GR: SP396029.
GPS: N51:43.392 W01:25.727

Charges 2007

Per pitch incl. 2 persons and electricity	£ 13.00 - £ 24.00
extra person	£ 2.25
child (5-14 yrs)	£ 1.75
dog	£ 1.25

Low season offers.

UK2580 Cotswold View Caravan & Camping Park

Enstone Road, Charlbury OX7 3JH (Oxfordshire)

Tel: **01608 810314**. Email: **bookings@cotswoldview.co.uk**

On the edge of the Cotswolds and surrounded by fine views, this well-run family park offers a warm welcome. Originally a working farm, the touring park and self catering country cottages are situated amonst 54 acres of farmland. Wide gravel or tarmac roads ensure easy access to the 125 pitches (all with 10A electricity) in the 10-acre touring area. The park has been thoughtfully separated by hedges into different areas to enable those with children to be close to play areas, and quiter areas for those wanting to enjoy the peaceful surroundings. The small reception also serves as a licensed shop selling freshly baked bread and homemade cakes. Farmhouse breakfasts (ordered the night before) are served in the farmhouse itself with B&B also offered. Extensive tree planting has been undertaken to create well defined and maintained grass trails in the forest. There is also a farm trail where small animals, pigs, sheep and donkeys in enclosures can be observed. Convenient for touring the Cotswolds, there is also a good train service for day trips to London.

Facilities

Two well maintained heated toilet blocks provide washbasins in cubicles, showers, two family shower rooms (free), bathrooms (50p) and hairdryers. Good units for disabled people. Baby changing area. Laundry and dishwashing facilities. Motorcaravan service point. Shop and off-licence. Bar. Play areas. Games room. Tennis. Outdoor chess and draughts. Skittles. American motorhomes accepted. Security barrier (£5 deposit). Off site: Fishing 1 mile. Golf 7 miles. Riding 10 miles. Boat launching 1 mile.

Open: 1 April (or Easter if earlier) - 31 October.

Directions

From A44 Oxford - Chipping Norton road, take B4022 to Charlbury, just south of Enstone. Park is 2 miles on left. O.S.GR: SP365210.
GPS: N51:53.170 W01:28.248

Charges 2007

Per unit incl. 2 persons and electricity	£ 15.00 - £ 19.50
extra person	£ 2.25
child (6-16 yrs)	£ 2.00
dog	free

UK2590 Greenhill Farm Caravan & Camping Park

Bletchingdon OX5 3BQ (Oxfordshire)

Tel: **01869 351600**. Email: **info@greenhill-leisure-park.co.uk**

On a working farm in a rural setting, this is a newly established site. The approach is a half mile gravel track down into the valley, past recently planted woodlands, fields and the farm. The reception office with a shop and tourist information is located in the farmhouse. A gravel path continues round the park giving access to 40 pitches, all with 16A electricity hook-up and 25 with hardstanding. Newly planted trees and hedges partition the site and screen the water stands. An adjacent field is available for rallies and there is a second smaller field for tents. One barn is a games room and another has been converted into a toilet block. Many trees and hedges have been planted and as these mature the aspect will be less open giving more shade and walks through the woodland. This is a quiet, pleasant park with modern facilities, a variety of animals and convenient for visiting various local attractions including Blenheim Palace and Stratford.

Facilities

Two new toilet blocks, one in a converted barn with ramp access for facilities for disabled visitors and families. The newer block has 3 covered dishwashing sinks. Separate laundry room. Shop (April - Sept). Play area with assault course and basketball hoop. Games room which can also be used for meetings. Off site: Golf 2 miles. Boat launching and canal walks 1 mile.

Open: All year.

Directions

From M40 exit 9 take A34 to Newbury and Oxford. After 5 miles turn left on B4027 signed Bletchingdon. After 2.5 miles park is on left just past the village. O.S.GR: SP488177.

Charges 2007

Per unit incl. 2 persons	£ 10.00
extra person (over 4 yrs)	£ 2.00
electricity	£ 2.00
dog	£ 2.00

No credit cards.

UK2610 Bo Peep Caravan Park

Aynho Road, Adderbury, Banbury OX17 3NP (Oxfordshire)

Tel: **01295 810605**. Email: **warden@bo-peep.co.uk**

Set amongst 85 acres of farmland and woodland, there is an air of spacious informality about this peaceful, friendly park and it blends perfectly with the surrounding views. Extensive planting of trees, shrubs and hedges along marked grass trails have enhanced the natural environment of the touring areas. There are 104 numbered pitches all with 16A electricity for caravans and motorhomes. A separate 4 acre field for tents provides a further 40 pitches, including 4 electric points. Gravel road connects the various touring areas which are screened by hedges and trees. Most pitches are on grass but there are plans to increase the number of hardstandings. A network of circular walks along well kept grass trails have been developed around the park, including a pleasant river walk. Bench seats and waste bags and bins for dogs are provided. A 15 acre field is available for recreation use. Children are welcome but there is no play area or baby changing facilities.

Facilities

The original toilet block has been supplemented by a larger, purpose-built unit, all clean and heated. Large showers and hairdryers. Dishwashing sinks. Laundry rooms. Motorcaravan service point. Low level lighting. Small shop with off-licence, gas and basic supplies. Information centre. Fishing. Caravan storage. Caravan cleaning area. Internet access. Off site: Golf course next door. Banbury 3 miles. Blenheim Palace 15 miles. Silverstone 16 miles. Day trips to Stratford-upon-Avon and Warwick.

Open: 18 March - 31 October.

Directions

Adderbury village is on the A4260 Banbury - Oxford road. At traffic lights in Adderbury turn on B4100 (Aynho). Park signed, 0.5 miles on the right (0.5 mile drive). O.S.GR: SP482355. GPS: N52:00.951 W01:17.966

Charges 2007

Per unit incl. 2 persons	
with electricity	£ 14.00 - £ 18.00
extra person	£ 3.00
child (5-15 yrs)	£ 2.50
tent incl. 2 persons	£ 13.00 - £ 15.00

No credit cards.

UK2600 **Barnstones Caravan & Camping Park**

Great Bourton, Banbury OX17 1QU (Oxfordshire)

Tel: **01295 750289**

Three miles from Banbury and open all year round, this small, neat park provides an excellent point from which to explore the Cotswolds. There are 49 level pitches of which 44 have hardstanding with a grass area for awnings (no groundsheets are allowed) and 10A electricity; 20 of these are fully serviced. A further 36 pitches are available on a rally field, all with 10A electricity. Shrubs, flowers and an oval tarmac road convey a tidy impression throughout. The park provides a pleasant environment for couples and young families, but is near the main road, so some traffic noise is to be expected.

Facilities

The upgraded toilet block is small, but well maintained and quite adequate for the number of people it serves. Adjustable, unisex showers. Separate dishwashing and laundry rooms. Gas supplies. Play area. Boules. American motorhomes accepted by prior arrangement. Off site: Pub 150 yds. Nearest shop 1 mile. Supermarket, fishing, bicycle hire, golf and riding, all within 3 miles.

Open: All year.

Directions

From M40 take exit 11 for Banbury. Follow signs for Banbury and Southom. At two small roundabouts follow signs for Southom and Great Bourton. At third roundabout turn right on A42, Southom is 2.5 miles. Turn right (Great Bourton and Crofredy) Site is 100 yds. on right. O.S.GR: SP454454.

Charges 2008

Per unit incl. 2 persons and electricity	£ 10.00
child (5-12 yrs)	£ 1.00

OAPs less 50p per night. No credit cards.

UK2620 **Wysdom Touring Park**

The Bungalow, Burford School, Burford OX18 4JG (Oxfordshire)

Tel: **01993 823207**

You'll have to go a long way before you find anything else remotely like this site! The land is owned by Burford School and the enterprising caretaker and his wife, caravanners themselves, suggested that they create this wonderful place to raise money for the school. Beautifully maintained, it really is like stepping into their own private garden. This 'adults only' park is screened from the main school grounds by trees and provides 25 pitches (6 seasonal), separated by hedges, all with electricity and some have a tap. Tents are accepted for short stays by arrangement. The turn into the site off the school drive is narrow. It is best to avoid school pick-up and drop-off when it can be congested.

Facilities

The older sanitary building is clean and well maintained with two unisex showers (20p token) - there may be a queue at peak times. (Max. 2 dogs per pitch). Tennis courts. Off site: Burford is yards away with its famous hill full of antique shops, old coaching inns and all those 'interesting' shops it is so much fun rooting about in. Burford Golf Club is next door.

Open: All year.

Directions

From roundabout on A40 at Burford, take A361 towards Lechdale on Thames. Park is a few yards on right signed Burford School. Once in drive watch for narrow entrance to site on right in about 100 yards. O.S.GR: SP250115. GPS: N51:48.119 W01:38.362

Charges 2007

Per unit incl. 2 persons	£ 9.00 - £ 10.50
dog (max. 2)	free

No credit cards.

UK2750 **Highclere Farm Country Touring Park**

Newbarn Lane, Seer Green, Beaconsfield HP9 2QZ (Buckinghamshire)

Tel: **01494 874505**. Email: **highclerepark@aol.com**

Only 25 miles from London and 12 miles from Legoland and Windsor, this is a peaceful park that backs onto fields and woodland. Originally developed around a working farm, the park continues to keep chickens. There are 95 level pitches all with 10A electricity. 60 are reserved for caravans and motorhomes, some with gravel hardstanding and the remainder are for tents. A bus service to Uxbridge passes the site, London is 35 minutes by train, whilst Windsor Castle and Thorpe Park are also within easy reach. A member of the Countryside Discovery group.

Facilities

The toilet and shower block is fully equipped and can be heated. Large showers (20p). Unit with toilet and washbasin for disabled people. New launderette. Fridge and freezer. Shop. Play area. Off site: Inn serving food 0.25 miles. Golf 0.5 miles. Riding 2 miles. Bicycle hire 3 miles. Fishing 8 miles. Bekonscot Model Village and Milton's Cottage are close.

Open: All year excl. February.

Directions

From M40 take exit 2. At first roundabout take Beaconsfield exit, at second, take A40 (Denham). Take first left for Seer Green, then follow site signs. Site is 1 mile after village centre on left. O.S.GR: SU977927. GPS: N51:37.537 W00:35.452

Charges 2008

Per unit	£ 15.00 - £ 18.00
tent	£ 10.00 - £ 19.00

UK2700 Hurley Riverside Park

Hurley, Maidenhead SL6 5NE (Berkshire)

Tel: **01628 824493**. Email: **info@hurleyriversidepark.co.uk**

On the banks of the river Thames, not far from Henley-on-Thames, you will find the picturesque village of Hurley where some buildings date back to 1086. Just outside the village is Hurley Riverside Park. The touring area is flat and separated into smaller fields. With the pitches arranged around the outside edges of each field and the centre left free, the park has a very spacious feel. There are 138 pitches with 10A electricity including 12 fully serviced. A camping field provides a further 62 pitches including 6 electric hook-ups. A very popular park, there is also a large rally field. You can enjoy walks along the banks of the Thames or visit the various pubs and restaurants in the village for a good meal and a pint. Nearby Windsor has its famous castle or for younger members of the family, Windsor is the home of Legoland. At Henley you can watch the regatta. Alternatively, you can just relax in the peaceful settings of the site.

Facilities

Three wooden clad toilet blocks (raised on legs) include showers (a little cramped) and separate shower and toilet facilities for disabled visitors. Baby changing area. Laundry. Dishwashing. Motorcaravan service point. Shop. Re-cycling point. Off site: Golf, riding 3 miles. Bicycle hire 4 miles. Legoland at Windsor.

Open: 1 March - 31 October.

Directions

From M4 exit 8/9 take A404M. After 3 miles take A4130 (Henley). Go down steep hill (Hurley village signed on right) - ignore this turning and take next right (site signed from here). O.S.GR: SU825838. GPS: N51:32.796 W00:49.488

Charges 2007

Per unit incl. 2 persons	£ 8.50 - £ 15.00
extra person	£ 2.00
child (5-17 yrs)	free - £ 1.50
electric (10A)	£ 10.00 - £ 17.00
multi-services	£ 11.50 - £ 18.00

UK2690 Wellington Country Park

Riseley, Reading RG7 1SP (Berkshire)

Tel: **01189 326444**. Email: **info@wellington-country-park.co.uk**

Wellington Country Park is open to all on payment of an entry fee (entry for campers included in pitch fee) and many visit it for a day out. It contains play areas for children, nature trails, deer park, crazy golf and miniature railway. The camping site is situated in a wood within the 350 acre park. It has 72 pitches, 10 with hardstanding and 56 with electricity hook-ups (10A). Some 'Premium' pitches are larger and have barbecues and picnic tables. There are several individual pitches and some small groups all within woodland clearings which gives a very rustic and casual feel to this site. It is a very pleasant setting and once the Country Park closes at 17.30. all is very quiet. You should aim to arrive before 17.30 when the main park reception centre closes. Access to the site is through a locked gate (key from reception).

Facilities

The toilet block provides comfortable facilities including washbasins in cubicles and well equipped showers with good dry areas. Dishwashing sinks, and ample laundry. Shop stocks basics (from 1/5). Gas supplies. Fishing. Family events. Torch useful. Off site: Bus service at Risley 2 miles. Legoland and Windsor 30 minutes drive. Riding 1 mile. Golf 6 miles.

Open: Mid February - early November.

Directions

Park is signed at Riseley, off A32/A33 road between Reading and Basingstoke, and from M4. It is 4 miles south of M4 exit 11 and 7 miles north of M3 exit 5. O.S.GR: SU727628. GPS: N51:21.552 W00:57.670

Charges 2007

Per unit incl. up to 2 adults and 2 children	£ 18.00 - £ 21.00
extra person	£ 3.00
child	£ 2.00
electricity	£ 25.00
dog	£ 1.00

MAP 3

Land of 1066, the South East is brimming with historical sights as castles, stately homes and cathedrals abound. It also boasts miles of footpaths and cycle routes through some of the best landscapes in England, passing chalk downland, wooded valleys and dramatic white-faced cliffs.

THE SOUTH EAST COMPRISES: EAST SUSSEX, WEST SUSSEX, SURREY AND KENT

The chalk countryside of golden downland in Sussex offers many opportunities for an active holiday, from walking and cycling to more adventurous pursuits such as rock climbing or ballooning. Once an ancient forest, much of the Weald is now taken up with farmland, but some areas still remain, including Ashdown Forest, a walker's paradise with stunning views of the High Weald and South Downs. The many rivers of the county have cut their way through gaps in the chalk landscape, ending spectacularly in white cliffs on the coast. Here you will find the Regency resorts of Bognor Regis and Brighton, with its Royal Pavilion, famous pier and quirky shops. Often referred to as the 'Garden of England', Kent is a richly fertile region flourishing with hop fields, fruit orchards and flowers. It is also home to the world renowned Canterbury Cathedral, several splendid castles, hidden towns, and quaint villages with oast houses. Surrey too boasts a rich heritage with numerous stately homes and National Trust sites plus large areas of ancient woodland. With a network of rivers, an enjoyable way to explore the beautiful countryside is by boat, stopping off at a riverside pub – or two!

Places of interest

East Sussex: Runnymede; Thorpe Park in Chertsey; Bexhill; historical towns of Hastings and St Leonards.

West Sussex: Eastbourne; Chichester; Bognor Regis; Arundel, with castle; Littlehampton.

Surrey: Guildford castle and cathedral; Mole Valley; Royal Horticultural Society's gardens at Wisley; Chessington World of Adventures; Dorking, a renowned centre for antiques.

Kent: Leeds Castle and gardens, the oldest stately home in the country; Canterbury, a designated World Heritage Site; Dover, with museum and castle; traditional seaside resort of Folkstone; Hever Castle in Sevenoaks; market town of Maidstone; Isle of Thanet incorporating Margate, Broadstairs and Ramsgate.

Did you know?

Hastings is home to Britain's first Norman castle, built by William the Conqueror.

Some of England's finest writers have found inspiration from living in Sussex – Rudyard Kipling, Sir Arthur Conan Doyle and A.A.Milne.

Bexhill housed one of the country's first cinemas and was the first to permit 'risqué' mixed sea bathing.

The world famous Mclaren F1 racing team has its base in Woking.

Runnymede takes its name from the meadow where the Magna Carta, the great charter of English liberties, was sealed by King John in 1215.

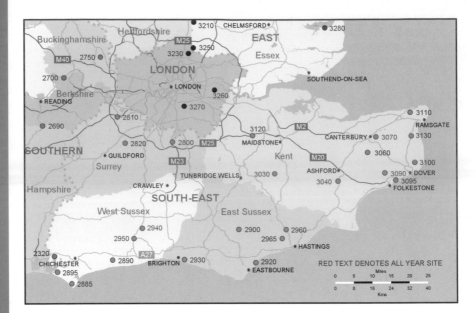

UK2885 Warner Farm

Warner Lane, Selsey, Chichester PO20 9EL (West Sussex)

Tel: **01243 604499**. Email: **touring@bunnleisure.co.uk**

This site is a member of the Bunn Leisure Group, owners of several large holiday home parks which surround the pretty holiday town of Selsey. Warner Farm however is a top quality touring park with 250 large grassy pitches, 165 of which have electrical connections. Pitches have a generally open aspect and there is a large area at the back of the site, the 'artichoke field', which offers an unmarked camping area, as well as providing a number of picnic tables and barbecues. 35 super pitches are available with electricity, water and waste water. The site is modern and well-maintained, and benefits from free access to the extensive leisure facilities on offer at the neighbouring holiday home parks. These include the Oasis swimming and leisure complex with a large covered pool, a fun fair, a number of bars and restaurants and a lively entertainment programme. Surprisingly perhaps, the site retains a pleasant rural feel with plenty of space and open countryside to the rear.

Facilities

Modern toilet block with facilities for disabled visitors. Preset showers in large cubicles. Dishwashing sinks outside but under cover. Washing machines and dryers. Small shop. Heated indoor pool (all season). Outdoor pool (subject to weather). Children's play area and multisport area. Communal barbecues, picnic area and dog walking area. Free shuttle bus to neighbouring parks.
Off site: Nearest beach 900 m. Oasis swimming and leisure complex, fun fair, bars, restaurants and entertainment. Bicycle hire. Tennis. Children's clubs.

Open: 1 March - 30 October.

Directions

Follow the A27 Chichester by-pass and join the B2145 heading south to Selsey. After 8 miles you will reach Selsey. Shortly after entering the town turn right into West Street and follow signs to the site. O.S.GR: SZ846939.

Charges 2007

Per pitch incl. up to 4 persons and electricity	£ 18.50 - £ 32.00
incl. services	£ 26.00 - £ 42.00

UK2890 White Rose Touring Park

Mill Lane, Wick, Littlehampton BN17 7PH (West Sussex)

Tel: **01903 716176**. Email: **snowdondavid@hotmail.com**

Situated about midway between the imposing castle at Arundel and the beaches of Littlehampton, White Rose makes an excellent base from which to enjoy the many attractions of this popular district. Watersports centres, race courses, beaches, historical and cultural interests, downland walks and the resorts of Bognor and Brighton are within easy reach. There are 118 pitches for tourists, 88 with electricity (10/16A). The flat grassy meadow is surrounded by trees and divided into two areas. The first part has individually hedged pitches, as on the continent, on either side of concrete access roads, with electricity hook-ups and shared water/waste water connections. The second area includes 14 'super' pitches (each having electricity, fresh and waste water and sewage connections, TV aerial socket and night light), further full sized pitches with no electricity, plus a few special pitches for small tents and small motorcaravans. A busy road runs along one side of the park and road noise could be disturbing in the early mornings during the week to a few pitches.

Facilities

The central toilet block is heated and fully equipped, with two rooms for disabled people, one with shower, the other with WC and basin (key from reception). Reception has a few basic supplies and gas. Central play area for children. Trailered boats by prior arrangement only. Off site: Supermarket 400 yds. Fishing, boat launching, bicycle hire, riding and golf within 2 miles.

Open: All year excl. 15 December - 15 March.

Directions

Take A284 Littlehampton road from A27 just to the east of Arundel station (ignore campsite behind the pub at this junction) and park is signed along on the left. O.S.GR: TQ026041.

Charges 2007

Per unit incl. up to 2 people	
and electricity	£ 16.00 - £ 18.00
pitch with no services	£ 14.00 - £ 16.00
full service pitch	£ 18.00 - £ 20.00
extra person	£ 2.00 - £ 4.00

UK2940 Honeybridge Park

Honeybridge Lane, Dial Post, Horsham RH13 8NX (West Sussex)

Tel: **01403 710923**. Email: **enquiries@honeybridgepark.co.uk**

Honeybridge's owners, Jeff and Val Burrows, continue to develop this good 15 acre park which includes gravel hardstandings and the majority of pitches with electric hook-ups (16A). Some pitches are hedged for privacy, others are on slightly sloping grass, well spaced and generously sized. The reception building houses a licensed shop. A large wooden, adventure-style playground is provided for children away from the pitches, and simple family entertainment is organised on special occasions. A large games room provides darts, table tennis, pool, free use of many board games and a library. The tourist information centre is also here. This site is ideally situated for visiting the South Downs with its many attractive villages.

Facilities

Modern, heated toilet facilities are heated in cool weather and include spacious facilities for disabled visitors (radar key). Dishwashing and laundry sinks, washing machines and dryers. Motorcaravan service point. Licensed shop. Play area. Games room with library. Security barrier (card access) is locked 23.00 - 07.00. Off site: Bus 0.5 miles. Pub in nearby Dial Post village. Old Barn Nurseries serves meals during the day. Billingshurst and Horsham are both 8 miles. Fishing 1 mile. Golf 10 miles. Riding 5 miles. Beach at Worthing 10 miles.

Open: All year.

Directions

Two miles south of the junction of A24 and A272 at Dial Post, turn east by Old Barn Nurseries. Follow signs to site (0.5 miles approx). O.S.GR: TQ153183.

Charges 2008

Per person	£ 4.00 - £ 6.00
child (5-14 yrs)	£ 2.50
pitch	£ 7.00
incl. electricity	£ 9.00 - £ 11.00
2 man small tent (incl. pitch fee)	£ 9.50
Senior citizen discounts.	
Barrier pass (£10 deposit).	

UK2950 Washington Caravan & Camping Park

Old London Road, Washington RH20 4AJ (West Sussex)

Tel: **01903 892869**. Email: **washcamp@amserve.com**

Washington is a pleasant campsite to the north of Worthing with a bias towards tenting families. It provides only 21 hardstanding pitches for caravans or motorcaravans, and a large gently sloping grassy field with enough space for 80 tents. The 23 electric hook-ups (16A) are on slot meters (50p). Security is good, but unobtrusive. There is some road noise from the A24. There is an equestrian centre adjacent to the campsite offering stabling and paddock facilities. There are excellent riding opportunities on the bridle paths of the South Downs Way. Local attractions (all with free admission, check opening times) include Highdown Chalk Gardens at Worthing, Nutbourne Vineyard near Pulborough, and Steyning Museum.

Facilities

A heated chalet style building houses sanitary facilities of an excellent standard, including spacious shower rooms (20p) and indoor dishwashing and laundry facilities. No on-site shop but eggs, bread, butter and milk can be obtained from the reception office. Drinks machine and freezer. Off site: Bus stop 200 yds in village. Eating out options include the local pub and a nearby restaurant. Beach 9 miles.

Open: All year.

Directions

Site entrance is just east of the junction of A24 and A283 at Washington, 6 miles north of Worthing. O.S.GR: TQ122134. GPS: N50:54.525 W00:24.336

Charges 2007

Per caravan or motorcaravan incl. 2 persons	£ 15.00
extra person	£ 3.50
tent	£ 4.00
electricity on meter	£ 0.50

Weekly terms acc. to time of year.

Washington

Caravan & Camping Park

Bring your horse on holiday
01903 892869

• Beautiful landscaped grounds
• Superb Equestrian facilities
• Close to many attractions

@washcamp@amserve.com: www.washcamp.com

UK2895 Nunnington Farm Campsite

Rookwood Road, West Wittering PO20 8LZ (West Sussex)

Tel: **01243 514013**. Email: **hunningtonfarm@hotmail.com**

This no-frills, basic, family run farm site for touring units only can be found on the coast a mere seven miles from Chichester. There are 200 pitches, 130 with 15A electricity connections. The pitches are large, level and grassy, which leads to a comfortable feeling, even when the site is full. The safe, sandy beaches of The Witterings, only a mile away, make this an especially good venue for families in the holidays and a quieter one for off-season visitors. The easily accessible pets corner is an attraction for children of all ages. Visitors with tents are very welcome here and a second field is opened in busy periods, but with no electricity.

Facilities

Three, very clean, central toilet blocks provide all facilities including showers in cubicles, open washbasins, baby bath, washing machines and ramped facilities for disabled visitors (key access). Gates closed 23.00-07.00. Off site: Local shops 300 yds. Bus service to Chichester every 30 minutes. Beach and boat mooring 1 mile. Bicycle hire 2 miles. Golf 3 miles.

Open: Easter - 2nd week October.

Directions

From A27 at Chichester, take A286 signed The Witterings and continue to roundabout. Take second exit on B2179 for West Wittering and site is on left after 7 miles. O.S.GR: SZ785988.

Charges 2007

Per unit incl. 2 persons	£ 13.00 - £ 18.00
extra person	£ 2.00
child (under 17 yrs)	£ 0.50
boat	£ 1.00

No credit cards.

UK2900 Horam Manor Touring Park

Horam, Heathfield TN21 0YD (East Sussex)

Tel: **01435 813662**. Email: **camp@horam-manor.co.uk**

In the heart of the Sussex countryside, this rural touring park is part of (but under separate management from) Horam Manor which has a farm museum, nature trail and several fishing lakes. The 90 pitches, 54 with electrical connections, are on two open meadows joined by a tarmac/gravel access road. The field nearer reception has an undulating surface, the second field is flatter but slopes – levelling blocks are needed for motorcaravans. Pitches are of generous size, and all numbered and marked. Both areas are ringed with a variety of mainly tall trees. The whole park, back from the main Eastbourne to Tunbridge Wells road, is a haven of peace and tranquility, although in high season it naturally becomes very busy. The site has no shop but the village is close, with supermarkets in Heathfield (3 miles). Two inns are within walking distance and the Lakeside cafe at the Farm Centre serves drinks and snacks (9.30 - 17.00). The Craft Centre to the side of the site has some interesting exhibits, farm machinery and riding stables. The nature trail has walks ranging from 30 to 90 minutes in length (written guide available). Fishing is possible in 10 lakes on the estate (adults £4).

Facilities

The modern, well built toilet block (unheated) is fully equipped and is said to be cleaned four times daily. There are some curtained cubicles. Family room (access by key from reception) with shower, washbasin, toilet and baby bath, suitable also for disabled visitors (not ideal for wheelchairs). Laundry and dishwashing sinks. Washing machine. Gas supplies. Simple fenced play area. Up to two dogs per unit are accepted. Off site: Tennis (small fee) 200 yds. Golf within 1 mile. The coastal towns of Brighton, Hastings and Eastbourne are within easy reach, as is the famous Pantiles at Tunbridge Wells.

Open: 1 March - 31 October.

Directions

Horam is on the A267 between Tunbridge Wells and Eastbourne and entry to the park is signed at the recreation ground at southern edge of the village. O.S.GR: TQ577169. GPS: N50:55.907 E00:14.410

Charges 2007

Per unit incl. 2 adults and 2 children under 18)	£ 14.50
extra person	£ 5.00
extra child	£ 2.00
electricity	£ 1.95 - £ 2.85

No credit cards.

UK2930 Sheepcote Valley Caravan Club Site

East Brighton Park, Brighton BN2 5TS (East Sussex)

Tel: **01273 626546**

Brighton is without doubt the South of England's most popular seaside resort and the Caravan Club's Sheepcote Valley Site is a first class base from which to enjoy the many and diverse attractions both in the town and this area of the south coast. The site occupies a quiet situation in an almost fully enclosed valley in the South Downs, a mile north of the town's interesting Marina which has a superstore and good variety of shops and restaurants. A wide tarmac road winds its way through the site from reception, with gravel pitches on either side, leading to terraces with grass pitches on the lower slopes of the valley. With a total of 275 pitches, 169 have electricity (16A), 85 have hardstanding and 11 have water, drainage and TV sockets. Three grass terraces are for tents and these have hard parking nearby as a low fence prevents cars being taken onto the camping areas. Although there are a number of trees, many are young so do not yet provide shade. Flower beds add to the attractiveness of the site. The site fully lives up to the very high standards expected from the Caravan Club and provides a first class venue both for a quiet holiday and as a base from which to explore.

Facilities

Two well built, brick, heated sanitary blocks have excellent facilities including all washbasins in private cabins. In the main season a third timber clad building provides additional services near the tent places. Well equipped room for wheelchair users, another one for walking disabled and two baby and toddler wash rooms. Laundry facilities. Motorcaravan service point. Gas available. Milk and bread from reception. Play area with safety base. Off site: Brighton is 2 miles with a bus service from the entry road. Extensive recreation grounds adjacent.

Open: All year.

Directions

Site is in eastern part of Brighton and signed from A259 coast road. From west on A259: at Palace Pier roundabout continue on A259 towards Newhaven for 1.25 miles, join dual carriageway and after 100 yards turn left at sign into Arundel Road. At mini-roundabout turn right into Wilson Avenue. After 100 yards, turn right into East Brighton Park. Continue for 0.5 miles, site on left. From east on A259: immediately after Roedean School take right hand slip road and turn into Roedean Road. Continue towards traffic lights and turn right into Wilson Avenue, then as above. O.S.GR: TQ341043.

Charges 2007

Per person	£ 4.70 - £ 6.20
child (5-16 yrs)	£ 1.50 - £ 3.00
pitch (non-member)	£ 10.90 - £ 15.30

UK2920 Bay View Park

Old Martello Road, Pevensey Bay BN24 6DX (East Sussex)
Tel: **01323 768688**. Email: **holidays@bay-view.co.uk**

Under new ownership, this friendly beachside park is located at the end of a private road right beside the beautiful Sussex coast. There are 5.5 acres of grass (some areas are a little uneven) divided into two separate areas and surrounded by a low bank and hedges to give shelter if it is windy. The 94 touring pitches (80 sq.m, most with 16A electricity and some with hardstanding) are neatly marked out by numbered posts, the majority divided by low wooden rails. Several caravan holiday homes for hire are at the back of the park. It is an ideal site for a family beach holiday.

Facilities

Toilet facilities are housed in two superior 'portacabin' style buildings which are kept very clean and are heated when necessary. Laundry room with washing machine, powder dispenser, dryer, spin dryer, iron and board, plus tourist information. Motorcaravan services. Well stocked shop. Gas available. Fenced play area with bark surface and adventure equipment (10 years and under). Winter caravan storage. Off site: Sailing club. Sea fishing. Indoor swimming pool 1 mile. Golf 2 miles.

Open: 1 March - 31 October.

Directions

Park is 1 mile west of Pevensey Bay and 3 miles east of Eastbourne, off the A259 Pevensey Bay road. O.S.GR: TQ648028. GPS: N50:48.000 E00:20.279

Charges 2007

Per unit incl. 1or 2 persons	£ 13.50 - £ 15.50
incl. electricity	£ 16.50 - £ 18.50
extra person	£ 2.50
child (2-16 yrs)	£ 2.00

Couples and families only.
No commercial vehicles, large vans or pick-ups.

UK2960 Crazy Lane Tourist Caravan Park

Crazy Lane, Sedlescombe, Battle TN33 0QT (East Sussex)
Tel: **01424 870147**. Email: **info@crazylane.co.uk**

Formerly known as Whydown Farm, this peaceful, traditional style, two acre park has just 36 pitches arranged on grassy terraces, all with electric hook-ups (5/10A) and 4 with hardstanding. It may be best to phone to make sure space is available before travelling long distances. Set in the heart of '1066 country' with its historical links, other local attractions within easy reach include the very pretty village of Sedlescombe, two steam railways, an organic vineyard, Rye with its quaint cobbled streets and of course Battle itself. This is an ideal park for couples.

Facilities

The tiny but well maintained sanitary unit (unheated) includes controllable hot showers (on payment), laundry facilities, dishwashing sinks and a suite for disabled visitors. A new block is planned for 2008. Shop at reception. Caravan storage. Off site: Bus stop and pub in the village. The fascinating towns of Battle and Rye, plus Hastings (6.5 miles) with its beaches, markets and Heritage Shipwreck Centre.

Open: March - October.

Directions

From A21, 100 yards south of junction with B2244 (to Sedlescombe) turn into Crazy Lane, where site is signed on the right hand side. O.S.GR: TQ782170.

Charges 2007

Per unit incl. 2 persons with electricity	£ 14.50 - £ 17.50
tent pitch incl. 2 adults	£ 12.00 - £ 15.00

No credit cards.

UK2965 Brakes Coppice Park

Forewood Lane, Crowhurst, Battle TN33 9AB (East Sussex)
Tel: **01424 830322**. Email: **brakesco@btinternet.com**

Brakes Coppice Park is a small and secluded site set in woodland just a mile away from historic Battle. Reached by an uneven, winding private track, it is signed to prevent visitors taking a wrong turn to the nearby farm of the same name. The site has 30 grassy pitches, 21 with 6A electricity and TV aerial points, in a gently sloping field. An adjacent area of 15 small pitches has been set aside for adults only. A further area near a small fishing lake provides a few extra pitches. As well as fishing, visitors can enjoy walking in the surrounding woods and there is an attractive new wooden play area.

Facilities

The single toilet block is very basic but clean with coin operated showers (one for men, one for ladies). There are plans to add new facilities for disabled visitors. Washing machine, dryer, iron and board. Dishwashing sinks with hot water are outside but under cover. Shop. Gas supplies. Fishing permits from reception. Off site: Pubs and shops in Crowhurst and Battle. Crowhurst station 10 minutes walk.

Open: 1 March - 31 October.

Directions

From Battle follow A2100 to Hastings for 2 miles. Turn right on Telham Lane (signed Crowhurst). Continue into Foreword Lane. Turn left on private track shortly after sign for Crowhurst village. O.S.GR: TQ764131. GPS: N50:53.439 E00:30.425

Charges 2007

Per pitch with 2 persons	£ 12.00 - £ 14.00
incl. electricity	£ 14.00 - £ 16.00
child (5-15 yrs)	£ 0.50

UK3030 Tanner Farm Touring Caravan & Camping Park

Goudhurst Road, Marden TN12 9ND (Kent)

Tel: **01622 832399**. Email: **enquiries@tannerfarmpark.co.uk**

Tanner Farm is a top class, 5 star quality park, developed as part of a family working farm in the heart of the Weald of Kent. It is surrounded by orchards, oast houses, lovely countryside and delightful small villages and the owners are much concerned with conserving the natural beauty of the environment. Visitors are welcome to walk around the farm and see the Shire horses and other animals. The park extends over 15 acres, most of which is level and part a gentle slope. The grass meadowland has been semi-landscaped by planting saplings, etc. which units back onto, as the owners do not wish to regiment pitches into rows. Places are numbered but not marked, allowing plenty of space between units which, with large open areas, gives a pleasant, comfortable atmosphere. There are 100 pitches, all with 16A electricity, 38 with hardstanding, 27 with water tap and 1 with waste water point also. The farm drive links the park with the B2079 and a group of refurbished oast houses (listed heritage buildings) with a duck pond in front, along with pigs, pygmy goats, lambs, etc. make a focal point. The park is a member of the Caravan Club's 'Affiliated Site' scheme although non-members are also very welcome. Best of British and Countryside Discovery groups.

Facilities

Two heated, well cared for sanitary units include some washbasins in private cubicles in both units. Purpose built facilities for disabled visitors. A bathroom (£1 token) and baby facilities have been added in the newer block (this block is not opened Nov - Easter). Small launderette. Dishwashing sinks. Motorcaravan service point. Small shop/reception (opening hours and stock limited in winter) and reception. Gas supplies. Off site: Riding and golf within 6 miles, leisure centres and sailing facilities near and good shopping facilities at Maidstone and Tunbridge Wells. Many National Trust attractions in the area (Sissinghurst, Scotney Castle, Bodiam Castle).

Open: All year.

Directions

Park is 2.5 miles south of Marden on B2079 towards Goudhurst. O.S.GR: TQ732417.

Charges 2007

Per person	£ 3.90 - £ 5.40
child (5-16 yrs)	£ 1.30 - £ 2.15
pitch incl. electriciry	£ 4.30 - £ 8.10
tent pitch	£ 4.50 - £ 5.50

Only one car per pitch permitted.

UK3040 Broadhembury Caravan & Camping Park

Steeds Lane, Kingsnorth, Ashford TN26 1NQ (Kent)

Tel: **01233 620859**. Email: **holidaypark@broadhembury.co.uk**

In quiet countryside just outside Ashford and within easy reach of Dover, Folkestone and the Kent coast, this sheltered park is attractively landscaped. It takes 65 touring units of any type with several seasonal units and 25 caravan holiday homes (5 for hire) in separate areas. The well kept pitches are on level grass and backed by tall, neat hedges, with over 50 electricity connections (10A). In addition, 4 pitches are fully serviced including16A electricity and 8 more have double hardstanding plus a grass area for an awning. The welcome is friendly at this popular park and it is often full in the main season, with a good proportion of continental visitors, so reservation is advisable. Thoughtfully considered amenities include a very good toilet block, well equipped campers' kitchen and provision for children of all ages. Security arrangements are excellent – with coded entry through gates and onto park. For those who would like a trip to France, the International railway terminal is at Ashford (Paris in two hours) – take your passport. A member of the Best of British group.

Facilities

The recently upgraded toilet block is well equipped including under-floor heating and is kept very clean. Private cabins. High quality facilities for disabled visitors (can also be used as a family bathroom). Well equipped laundry room. Good campers' kitchen, fully enclosed with dishwashing sinks, microwaves, fridge and freezer, all free of charge. Motorcaravan service point. Well stocked shop (bread and papers to order) and comprehensive tourist information. Internet access. TV and pool room, games room. Two play areas (one for children under 7 yrs) with wood-chip bases. Play field away from the touring area. Dog exercise field - up to two dogs per pitch are accepted. Off site: Fishing 300 m. Golf 1 mile. Riding 2 miles. Bicycle hire 3 miles. Beach 12 miles.

Open: All year.

Directions

From M20 junction 10 take A2070. After 2 miles follow sign for Kingsnorth. Turn left at second crossroads in Kingsnorth village. O.S.GR: TR010382.

Charges 2007

Per unit incl. 2 persons	£ 18.00 - £ 20.00
with services	£ 22.00 - £ 24.00
tent incl. 2 persons	£ 14.00 - £ 16.00
extra person	£ 5.00
child (5-16 yrs)	£ 3.50

Less 10% for bookings of 7 nights or more.

135

UK3060 Yew Tree Park

Stone Street, Petham, Canterbury CT4 5PL (Kent)

Tel: **01227 700306**. Email: **info@yewtreepark.com**

Yew Tree Park is a small, quiet site located in the heart of the Kent countryside overlooking the Chartham Downs. Just 5 miles south of Canterbury and 8 miles north of the M20, it is ideally placed either to explore the delights of the ancient city or the many attractions of eastern and coastal Kent. Its nearness to the Channel ports also makes it useful for a night stop on the way to, or on return from, the continent. If catching a late evening ferry you may remain on site after 12 noon for a small payment. With some caravan holiday homes, the site also has 45 pitches for tourers and tents. The 20 with electricity (10A) are marked on mainly level grass either side of the entrance road, the remainder unmarked on a rather attractive, sloping area, left natural with trees and bushes creating cosy little recesses in which to pitch. There are mobile homes and apartments to rent. This neat, tidy park, created by resident proprietors Derek and Dee Zanders, makes an excellent base away from the hurly-burly of life where you can enjoy the rural scenery and also have the opportunity for walking, riding, visiting local places of interest or for Cross-Channel excursions.

Facilities

Two brick-built sanitary blocks (one for each sex) can be heated. Washbasins (H&C) and four showers (on payment). Extra toilets on the edge of the camping area. Toilet/shower room for families or disabled visitors. Laundry and dishwashing sinks, plus a washing machine, dryer and iron. Gas supplies. Outdoor swimming pool (60 x 30 ft. open June-Sept). Play area. WiFi. Torches may be useful. Dogs are not accepted. Off site: Riding 4 miles. Golf 6 miles. Bicycle hire 5 miles. The County cricket ground is 4 miles.

Open: Easter - mid October.

Directions

Park is on B2068 Canterbury-Folkestone road. From south, take exit 11 from the M20. From Canterbury, ignore signs to Petham and Waltham on B2068 and continue towards Folkestone. From either direction, turn into road beside the Chequers Inn, turn left into park and follow road to owners' house/reception. O.S.GR: TR138507. GPS: N51:13.008 E01:03.491

Charges 2007

Per unit incl. 2 persons	£ 11.00 - £ 16.20
serviced pitch	£ 13.00 - £ 18.50
extra person	£ 4.00 - £ 5.00
child (2-16 yrs)	£ 2.00 - £ 2.50

UK3070 Canterbury Camping & Caravanning Club Site

Bekesbourne Lane, Canterbury CT3 4AB (Kent)

Tel: **01227 463216**. Email: **canterbury@campingandcaravanningclub.co.uk**

Situated just off the A257 Sandwich road, about 1.5 miles from the centre of Canterbury, this site is an ideal base for exploring Canterbury and the north Kent coast, as well as being a good stop-over to and from the Dover ferries, and the Folkestone Channel Tunnel terminal. There are 200 pitches, 86 with electric hook-ups (10A) and, except at the very height of the season, you are likely to find a pitch, although not necessarily with electricity. Most of the pitches are on well kept grass with hundreds of saplings planted, but there are also 21 pitches with hardstanding (more are planned). Some pitches do slope so blocks are advised. A good sized overnight area for late arrivals can be reached even when the barriers are down. The site is adjacent to Bekepond nature reserve and within 3 miles of Howletts Zoo. Although the busy A257 is close, there is minimal noise from the traffic. Note: power lines cross the site.

Facilities

Two modern toilet blocks, the main one with a laundry room, a room for dishwashing, an outside vegetable preparation area, and recycling bins. Motorcaravan service point. Reception stocks a small range of essential foods, milk and gas. Excellent tourist information room. Children's play area with equipment on bark chippings. Off site: Golf adjacent. Bicycle hire 2 miles.

Open: All year.

Directions

From A2 take Canterbury exit and follow signs for Sandwich - A257. After passing Howe military barracks turn right into Bekesbourne Lane opposite golf course. O.S.GR: TR172577. GPS: N51:16.614 E01:06.812

Charges 2007

Per person	£ 4.90 - £ 7.25
child (6-18 yrs)	£ 2.15 - £ 2.25
pitch (non-member)	£ 5.65

UK3090 Black Horse Farm Caravan Club Site

385 Canterbury Road, Densole, Folkestone CT18 7BG (Kent)

Tel: **01303 892665**

This neat, tidy and attractive six acre park, owned by the Caravan Club, is situated amidst farming country in the village of Densole on the Downs just 4 miles north of Folkestone, 8 northeast of Dover and 11 south of Canterbury. This makes it ideal for an overnight stop travelling to or from the continent via the Channel Ports or the Tunnel, or as a base for visiting the many attractions of this part of southeast England. Accessed directly from the A260, the tarmac entrance road leads past reception towards the top field which has gravel hardstanding pitches with a grass area for awnings (possibly some road noise), past hedging to the smaller middle area with 8 hardstandings, then to the large bottom field which has been redeveloped to give 140 large pitches, all with electricity (16A). A late arrivals area and pitches for 'one-nighters' are now located in the top field. Opposite the entrance is a general store and newsagent and within 100 m, a pub and filling station.

Facilities

The carefully thought out and well constructed toilet blocks, one below reception and the other at the far end of the site, have washbasins in private cabins with curtains, good sized shower compartments, a baby room and facilities for disabled visitors, laundry and washing-up facilities, all well heated in cool weather. Motorcaravan service point. Gas supplies. Play area. A fish and chip van calls April to September. Caravan storage. Off site: Riding 1 mile. Golf and fishing 5 miles.

Open: All year.

Directions

Directly by the A260 Folkestone - Canterbury road, 2 miles north of junction with A20. Follow signs for Canterbury. O.S.GR: TR211418.
GPS: N51:07.957 E01:09.509

Charges 2007

Per person	£ 3.90 - £ 5.40
child (5-16 yrs)	£ 1.30 - £ 2.15
pitch (non-member)	£ 10.30 - £ 14.10

UK3120 Gate House Wood Touring Park

Ford Lane, Wrotham Heath, Sevenoaks TN15 7SD (Kent)

Tel: **01732 843062**. Email: **gatehousewood@btinternet.com**

This sheltered park, which opened for its first season in '98, has been created in a former quarry where all the pitches are on well drained grass. A spacious paved entrance with a new reception building and well stocked shop, leads on to the park itself. The 60 pitches are level and open with a few small trees, two brick built barbecue units, and 40 electric hook-ups (10A). A playground has swings, seesaw and a slide, all set on a safety base, and the entire site is enclosed by grassy banks on three sides, with a wild flower walk around the top. Local attractions include Brands Hatch Circuit (4 miles), the International Karting Circuit at Buckmore Park (7 miles), and the nearby Country Park at West Malling.

Facilities

Comprehensive toilet facilities are smart and well maintained, including a well equipped family room, which is also designed for disabled people. The laundry and dishwashing room is at one end of the modern heated building. No dogs or other pets. Caravans/motorcaravans greater than 25' overall are not admitted. Commercial vehicles are not accepted. Off site: Within walking distance are three pubs and a good Cantonese restaurant. Trains run to London Victoria from Borough Green (2 miles). Golf 1 mile. Riding 3 miles. Fishing 7 miles.

Open: 1 March - 30 November.

Directions

From M26 junction 2a, take A20 eastwards towards Wrotham Heath and Maidstone. Just past junction with A25, and opposite the Royal Oak pub, turn left into Ford Lane, and park is immediately on left. O.S.GR: TQ630580. GPS: N51:18.008 E00:20.723

Charges 2007

Per unit incl. 2 persons	£ 11.00 - £ 12.50
with electricity	£ 13.00 - £ 14.50
extra person	£ 1.50
child (3-12 yrs)	£ 1.00
No credit cards.	

UK3130 Sandwich Leisure Park

Woodnesborough Road, Sandwich CT13 0AA (Kent)

Tel: **01304 612681**. Email: **info@coastandcountryleisure.com**

A pleasant well kept site, with modern facilities, this park is in one of England's historic old Cinque Ports and within walking distance of all its attractions, shops and services. From the entrance barrier by reception, you drive through the area of privately owned holiday homes, to reach the two touring fields which have 190 pitches, all on grass with electric hook-ups (10A). There are 80 multi-service pitches with electricity, TV, water and waste water drain, nine of which have hardstandings. The site is encouraging wildlife in the newer second field by planting hedges of native varieties and these will give greater privacy as they develop. A railway runs along one side of the site and there is a little rail noise at times during the day but it is quiet at night. The site is well lit at night and all roads are well surfaced. Children will love the large, fenced adventure playground with its tube slides etc. which is on a bark surface.

Facilities

Stylish sanitary building provides washbasins in cubicles, controllable hot showers, plus a room which can be heated with some family suites and a full suite for disabled people (radar key). Dishwashing sinks under cover at each end of the building. Laundry in reception building with washing machines, dryers, spin dryer and ironing facility. Adventure playground. Note; skateboarding, rollerblading, skating, scooters and cycling are not permitted on site. Off site: Supermarket 5 minutes walk. Sandwich has a market on Thursdays. In and around the town are a folk museum, Roman fort, nature reserve, swing bridge, the old gaol, weavers, a sports and leisure centre and further afield is the Dreamland Fun Park. Fishing 3 miles, golf and beach 2 miles.

Open: 1 March - 31 October.

Directions

Sandwich is mid way between Ramsgate and Deal, with access from the A256. The town's streets are narrow and there is a one-way system in operation. Follow the brown campsite signs from anywhere in the town centre, the site is to the west of town, just after a railway level crossing. O.S.GR: TR 330575. GPS: N51:16.443 E01:19.935

Charges 2007

Per pitch incl. up to 4 people	
and electricity	£ 15.00 - £ 20.00
extra person	£ 2.00
awning	£ 1.00
one man tent	£ 10.00 - £ 15.00

UK3095 Little Satmar Holiday Park

Winehouse Lane, Capel-le-Ferne, nr. Folkestone CT18 7JF (Kent)

Tel: **01303 251188**. Email: **info@keatfarm.co.uk**

Capel-le-Ferne is a relatively little known seaside town mid way between Dover and Folkestone. Little Satmar is a quiet site a short walk from the delightful cliff top paths which run between these towns and which offer fine views across the English Channel. The site is a member of the Keat Farm group and is located about a mile from the village. There are 61 touring pitches, 51 of which have electricity (10A). The pitches generally have a sunny, open setting, a few with rather more shade. Privately owned mobile homes occupy 78 pitches between the entrance to the site and reception, but these are quite separate from the touring field.

Facilities

Two toilet blocks (one in a 'Portakabin' style unit) are modern and kept very clean and the main block has now been fitted with heating. Washing and drying machines. Shop (with gas). Play area. For more than 1 dog per unit, contact park. Off site: Bus at end of lane to Dover and Folkestone. Port Lympne Zoo, seafront funpark nearby.

Open: 1 March - 31 October.

Directions

Leave A20 Dover - Folkestone road at Capel-le-Ferne exit and follow signs to the village. Site is clearly signed to right afer approx. 0.75 miles. O.S GR: TR256393. GPS: N51:06.115 E01:13.376

Charges 2007

Per pitch incl. 2 persons	£ 11.50 - £ 14.50
incl. electricity	£ 14.00 - £ 17.00
extra person	£ 3.00 - £ 3.50
child (5-16 yrs)	£ 1.50 - £ 2.00
dog	£ 1.00

UK3100 Hawthorn Farm Caravan & Camping Site

Martin Mill, Dover CT15 5LA (Kent)

Tel: **01304 852658**. Email: **info@keatfarm.co.uk**

Hawthorn Farm is a large, relaxed park close to Dover. Set in 27 acres, it is an extensive park taking 250 touring units of any type on several large meadows which could accommodate far more, plus 160 privately owned caravan holiday homes in their own areas. Campers not requiring electricity choose their own spot, most staying near the two toilet blocks leaving the farthest fields to those liking solitude. There are 100 pitches with electricity (10/16A), 46 of which are large pitches separated by hedges, the remainder in glades either side of tarmac roads. A well run, relaxed park with plenty of room, mature hedging and trees make an attractive environment. A torch would be useful. Being only 4 miles from Dover docks, it is a very useful park for those using the ferries and is popular with continental visitors. Close to the sea at St Margaret's Bay, it is a fairly quiet situation apart from some rail noise (no trains 23.30 - 05.30). A member of the Best of British group.

Facilities

The heated toilet blocks are well equipped and of good quality, including facilities for disabled visitors and a baby room. Dishwashing and laundry sinks. Launderette. Motorcaravan services. Breakfast and other snacks are served at the shop (all season) and a pub is nearby. Gates close at 20.00 (22.00 in July and August) - £10 deposit for card. Caravan storage. Off site: Riding 0.5 miles. Golf 3 miles. Bicycle hire, fishing and boat launching 4 miles.

Open: 1 March - 31 October.

Directions

Park is north of the A258 road (Dover - Deal), with signs to park and Martin Mill where you turn off about 4 miles from Dover. O.S.GR: TR341464. GPS: N51:10.113 E01:20.780

Charges 2007

Per unit incl. 2 persons	£ 11.50 - £ 14.50
incl. electricity	£ 14.00 - £ 17.00
child (5-16 yrs)	£ 1.50 - £ 2.00

Less 10% for 4 nights booked (paid for on arrival).

UK3110 Quex Caravan Park

Park Road, Birchington CT7 0BL (Kent)

Tel: **01843 841273**. Email: **info@keatfarm.co.uk**

Although there are a fair number of privately owned holiday homes at Quex, they do not intrude on the touring area which is in a sheltered glade under tall trees. There are 40 touring pitches all with electric hook-ups (16A). This park does not accept tents. Local attractions include Quex House and gardens, the model village and motor museum at Ramsgate, whilst in the seaside resort of Margate you can walk through 1,000 years of history at the Caves, or visit the Hollywood Bowl. Reception can provide you with a map of the local area. A member of the Best of British group.

Facilities

The central sanitary unit is in a heated chalet style building with all the usual facilities. Dishwashing sinks under cover. Laundry room with sink, washing machine and dryer. Well stocked shop. More than one dog per pitch is accepted by prior arrangement only. Off site: Supermarkets close by. Fishing, golf and riding 3 miles.

Open: 7 March - 7 November.

Directions

From roundabout at junction of A28 and A299, take A28 east towards Birchington and Margate. At Birchington carry straight on at roundabout by church, then next right, then right again, and left at mini-roundabout. Site on right in half a mile (signed). O.S.GR: TR320685. GPS: N51:22.055 E01:19.944

Charges 2007

Per unit incl. 2 persons	£ 11.50 - £ 14.50
incl. electricity	£ 14.00 - £ 17.00
extra adult	£ 3.00 - £ 3.50
child (5-16 yrs)	£ 1.50 - £ 2.00

Less 10% for 4 nights booked (paid for on arrival).

UK2810 Chertsey Camping & Caravanning Club Site

Bridge Road, Chertsey KT16 8JX (Surrey)

Tel: **01932 562405**

This long-established site (1926) is splendidly located on the banks of the River Thames, only a few minutes walk from the shops and amenities of Chertsey. A flagship site for the Club, it was totally redeveloped in 2004 at a cost of over £1 million pounds. There are 200 pitches including 50 new serviced pitches with hardstanding and 16A electricity and 15 'super service' pitches which have TV aerial points, water and waste drainage. The work included a new road system, heated toilet blocks with facilities for disabled visitors, recreation hall and much more. There has been extensive landscaping and the existing Thames creek has been extended to flow through the site with marshland areas to support the local wildlife environment. When possible, energy saving devices have been used. Squirrels, rabbits and ducks abound and trees and plants create a pretty site with views across the water and towards Chertsey bridge. Unfortunately there is some road noise and, depending on flight paths, aircraft noise. The rail station for London is at Chertsey or Weybridge. Fishing is possible and canoeing can be arranged (Chertsey is the main base of the Club' Canoe section).

Facilities

The well equipped toilet blocks can be heated and include washbasins in cabins and facilities for disabled visitors. Hairdryers. Laundry. Dishwashing area. Motorcaravan service point. Well stocked shop for essentials and gas (8.00-11.00 and 16.00-18.00). Recreation hall. Play area on bark. Fishing (adults £1.30, NRA licence needed). Short dog walk areas. Caravan storage. Torches are necessary. Off site: Bus service in Chertsey 1.5 miles. Golf and bicycle hire 1 mile.

Open: All year.

Directions

Suggested: from M25 use junction 11. Turn left at roundabout on A317 towards Shepperton and continue to second set of traffic lights. Turn right then almost immediately left watching for green Club camp sign just before Chertsey bridge; the opening is narrow. O.S.GR: TQ052667.

Charges 2007

Per person	£ 6.35 - £ 8.80
child (6-18 yrs)	£ 2.35 - £ 5.05
non-member pitch fee	£ 5.65

UK2820 Horsley Camping & Caravanning Club Site

Ockham Road North, East Horsley KT24 6PE (Surrey)

Tel: **01483 283273**

London and all the sights are only 40 minutes away by train, yet Horsley is a delightful, quiet unspoilt site with a good duck and goose population on its part lily covered lake (unfenced). It provides 130 pitches, of which 83 have 10A electrical connections and 42 are all weather pitches (most with electricity). Seventeen pitches are around the bank of the lake, the rest further back in three hedged, grass fields with mostly level ground but with some slope in places. There is a range of mature trees and a woodland dog walk area (may be muddy). The soil is clay based so rain tends to settle – sluice gates remove extra water from the lake area when the rain is heavy. A recreation hall with table tennis (bats to hire) is sometimes used for bingo. Basic provisions, gas and books are kept in reception and resident managers will make you comfortable. Guildford and the R.H.S. gardens at Wisley are close by.

Facilities

Two purpose built, heated toilet blocks with good design and fittings, with some washbasins in cabins, a Belfast sink and parent and child room with vanity style basin, toilet and wide surface area. Dishwashing sinks, laundry room and new drying areas. Well designed facilities for disabled people. Papers and milk can be ordered the day before at reception. Play area. Fishing is possible from May (£5 per day, NRA licence required). Off site: Shops and the station are 1 mile. Pubs 1.5 - 2 miles. Golf 1.5 miles. Riding 2 miles.

Open: March - October.

Directions

From M25 junction 10, in the direction of Guildford, after 0.5 miles take first left B2039 to Ockham and East Horsley, continuing through Ockham towards East Horsley. After 2 miles start to watch for brown site sign - not easy to see - and site is on right in 2.5 miles. O.S.GR: TQ083552.

Charges 2007

Per person	£ 4.90 - £ 8.25
child (6-18 yrs)	£ 2.15 - £ 2.25
non-member pitch fee	£ 5.65

UK2800 Alderstead Heath Caravan Club Site

Dean Lane, Merstham, Redhill RH1 3AH (Surrey)

Tel: **01737 644629**

Alderstead Heath is a surprisingly rural site given that it lies just 25 minutes from central London by train. It is also well located for exploring the North Downs and is situated on the Pilgrim's Way. There are 240 pitches, of which 79 are reserved for touring, all with 16A electrical connections. There are plans to increase the number of touring pitches in future years. Most pitches are on well kept grass, but there are also 59 hardstandings. An attractive wooded area surrounds the site and concrete tracks there were laid during the war for tanks in prepartion for the D-Day landings. Given the proximity of the M25 and M23 motorways, there is a certain amount of background traffic noise in parts of the site.

Facilities

Two well-maintained toilet blocks, include a parent and toddler bathroom. The main block houses facilities for disabled visitors. Motorcaravan service point. Reception stocks a small range of essential foods, milk and gas. Small playing field. Good tourist information room. Off site: Golf 2 miles, Fishing 3 miles.

Open: All year.

Directions

Leave M25 at junction 8 and join A217 (signed Reigate). Fork left after 300 yards (signed Merstham). After a further 2.5 miles turn left at T-junction and join the A23. After 500 yards turn right into Shepherd's Hill and after a mile turn left into Dean Lane. Site is on the right after 175 yards. O.S.GR: TQ290557.

Charges 2007

Per person	£ 3.90 - £ 5.40
child (5-16 yrs)	£ 1.30 - £ 2.15
pitch (non-member)	£ 10.70 - £ 14.10

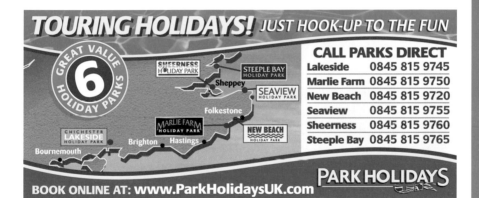

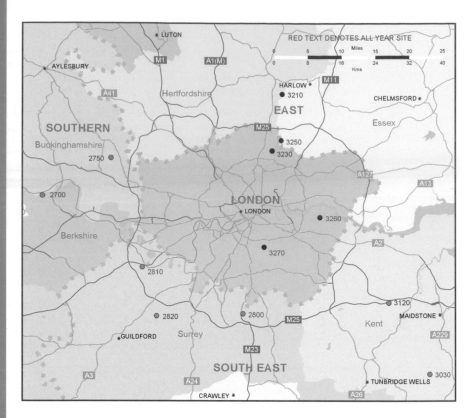

Map of South East England with campsite locations:

RED TEXT DENOTES ALL YEAR SITE

LUTON, AYLESBURY, M1, A1(M), M11, A41, Hertfordshire, HARLOW * 3210, EAST, CHELMSFORD *, SOUTHERN, Essex, M25, Buckinghamshire, 3250, 2750, 3230, A127, A13, 2700, LONDON, LONDON, 3260, Berkshire, A2, 3270, 2810, 3120, MAIDSTONE *, 2820, 2800, M25, Kent, GUILDFORD, Surrey, A229, M23, A3, SOUTH EAST, 3030, A24, TUNBRIDGE WELLS *, A26, CRAWLEY *

MAP 3 and region map opposite

London

The largest city in Europe, covering over 600 square miles, London is jam packed with hundreds of magnificent museums, impressive art galleries, historic buildings and monuments, beautiful parks, bustling shopping centres and markets; it really has something to offer everyone.

WE HAVE CHOSEN FIVE PARKS WHICH HAVE EASY ACCESS TO CENTRAL LONDON, INCLUDING ONE IN HERTFORDSHIRE

Despite its size, London is relatively easy to explore, largely thanks to the efficient underground service. Buses are also very useful and allow you to see the famous sights as you travel, in particular, the open-top tourist buses which ply the streets offer a good introduction to the city. Among London's many landmarks are the Tower of London, Trafalgar Square, Piccadilly Circus, Buckingham Palace, Big Ben and the Houses of Parliament, to name but a few! Running through the heart of London is the River Thames, dividing north and south; over the years many attractions, restaurants and chic bars have appeared along its banks. Being one of the most multicultural cities in the world, there is a huge choice of restaurants offering a diverse variety of cuisine; food markets are dotted all around the capital. Shopping is another major feature of the city, from the famous Harrods store and Harvey Nichols, to commercial Oxford Street and the street markets of Camden town and Portobello Road. If all the crowds become too much then head to one of London's beautiful parks such as St James' Park next to Buckingham Palace, or Hyde Park, where you can take a boat trip along the Serpentine.

Places of interest

London Eye: world's highest observation wheel, reaching 450 feet. With 32 capsules, carrying 25 passengers in each, it offers breathtaking views.

Madame Tussaud's: huge collection of wax figures.

Tate Modern: contemporary art gallery housed in a transformed Bankside Power Station.

Victoria & Albert Museum: decorative art and design from around the world.

Kew Gardens: beautiful botanical gardens, with over 40,000 varieties of plants.

London Dungeon: a grisly house of horrors.

Hampton Court Palace: one the best palaces in Britain, with maze.

British Museum: houses a treasure trove of objects from all over the globe.

Did you know?

One in eight of the UK population live in London and over 200 languages are spoken.

The London Underground dates back to 1863 when the first underground railway was opened, from Paddington to Farringdon Street. Today, 150,000 people an hour enter the Tube network.

Founded in 1753 the British Museum is the oldest public museum in the world.

With 345 steps to the top, the Monument marks the start of the Great Fire of London.

London has over 18,000 Licensed Taxis.

At over 900 years old, the Tower of London has been a palace, prison, treasury, arsenal and even a zoo. It is now home to the Crown Jewels, which have been housed there since the 14th century.

143

UK3210 Lee Valley Caravan Park

Essex Road, Dobbs Weir, Hoddesdon EN11 0AS (Hertfordshire)

Tel: **01992 462090**. Email: **caravanpark@leevalleypark.org.uk**

Right on the banks of the River Lee and with easy access to the 1,000 acre River Lee Country Park, this site offers a large open touring field which is very level. Pitches are well spaced around the outer edge of the field, with a tent area in the centre, with an additional small tent field on the river bank for the keen angler. Of the 100 touring pitches, 48 have 10A electricity. There is a private mobile home area adjacent. Although the site has very few trees, those that are there give some shade and the perimeter trees are tall enough to help keep out any noise from the nearby industrial area. The managers work hard to keep the site clean and tidy. Just outside the site and across the road is the Weir with a large picnic area, river walks and a pub – at weekends and holiday times this spot can get very busy. The nearby Lee Valley Park is being developed for white water rapids for the 2012 Olympics.

Facilities

The large toilet block is old but has been refurbished to provide clean and tidy facilities. Parent shower room with WC and baby changing. Good facilities for disabled visitors. Dishwashing and laundry area. Motorcaravan service point. Shop with camping accessories and sweets. Play area. Barbecue area. Fishing. Off site: Pub and restaurant 100 yards. Supermarket 1 mile. Hoddesdon 1.5 miles. Swimming pool 2 miles. Rye Meads Nature Reserve. Hatfield House and Hertford within easy access.

Open: 1 March - 30 November.

Directions

Take exit 25 from M25 and then north on A10 for 4 miles; take Hoddesdon exit, turn left at second roundabout. Follow Camping and Caravanning Park signs. Over bridge then at next roundabout turn right (Dobbs Weir). Park on right. O.S.GR: TL383082. GPS: N51:45.231 E00:00.071

Charges 2007

Per person	£ 6.40
child (under 16 yrs)	£ 2.60
electricity	£ 2.70

Min charge £8.40 (but not appled to backpackers). Checking out time 12 noon.

UK3250 Lee Valley Campsite

Sewardstone Road, Chingford, London E4 7RA (London)

Tel: **020 8529 5689**. Email: **scs@leevalleypark.org.uk**

This attractive site provides an excellent base from which to visit London, having both easy access to the M25 and excellent public transport links into the centre of London. Close to Epping Forest in the heart of the Lee Valley, this site is on a hillside overlooking the King George reservoir in a very pleasant and relaxed setting. Like its sister sites, it is understandably very popular with foreign tourers. With capacity for 200 units the site is mostly level, with several bush sheltered avenues and plenty of trees throughout providing shade. There are 20 pitches with tarmac hardstanding and 100 with electricity (10A). American motorhomes are not accepted. Just outside the gate is the bus stop (reception have full details of good value Travel Card schemes). The bus (no. 215) will take you to Walthamstow Central Underground station from where a frequent service runs to central London. Alternatively you can park at South Woodford or Chingford stations and use the train for London visits. Staff are very pleasant and helpful.

Facilities

Three blocks offer good facilities (one is heated in low season), all recently totally refurbished. Good en-suite room for disabled visitors. Baby changing area. Dishwashing, Laundry. Motorcaravan service point. Well stocked shop. Gas available. Playground. Off site: Fishing 500 yards. Shops within 2 miles. Riding 1 mile. 9-hole golf 1 mile, 18-hole golf 3 miles. Waltham Abbey 3 miles. River Lee Country Park and Epping Forest nearby.

Open: 1 April - 4 November.

Directions

From M25 take exit 26 on A112 to Chingford and site is on right in 3 miles. From A10 take the A110 (Chingford). After passing between reservoirs, at next traffic lights turn left on A112. Site on left after 2 miles. O.S. GR: TQ378970. GPS: N51:39.239 W00:00.391

Charges 2007

Per person	£ 6.45
child (under 16 yrs)	£ 2.90
electricity	£ 2.80
dog	£ 1.65

Min charge £8.60 per unit/night

UK3230 Lee Valley Camping & Caravanning Park

Meridian Way, Edmonton, London N9 0AS (London)

Tel: **020 8803 6900**. Email: **leisurecentre@leevalleypark.org.uk**

Certainly one of the only sites in this guide with a multiplex cinema just outside the gate, you are greeted here by a very attractive entrance with flower displays. The site offers 140 spacious level pitches, with hardstandings and 100 with electricity hook-ups. The pitches are well laid out around a large field and there is a tent area just behind two grassy mounds. The grass and gardens are well trimmed and kept very tidy. There is a small kitchen facility and eating area with TV, set out under a gazebo. The site also offers hook-up points for tents. The adjacent sports complex is being rebuilt and will be used for the 2012 Olympics. The cinema complex incorporates a pizza restaurant, and from here you can hop on a bus to Edmonton Green or Ponders End station from where there is a regular service into central London (journey time around 40 minutes). The friendly site managers have detailed information about the various Travel Card schemes available. Alternatively, historic Waltham Abbey, Epping Forest and the 1,000 acre River Lee Country Park are all within easy access. This is a popular site, very well looked after and kept clean and tidy by site managers, this is a peaceful stop within easy reach of the city.

Facilities

Two modern, heated toilet blocks include spacious showers and two large en-suite units for disabled people. Baby changing area. All facilities are accessed by combination locks. Dishwashing. Laundry. Motorcaravan service point. New barbecue area. Kitchen. Shop. Play area. Table tennis, tennis and badminton. Tents for hire. Off site: Cinema with pizza restaurant at entrance. Supermarket 0.5 miles. Fishing 0.5 miles. Golf adjacent. Riding 4 miles.

Open: All year excl. Christmas, Boxing and New Year's Day.

Directions

From M25 take exit 25. Follow signs for the city. At first set of traffic lights turn left (Freezywater). Continue on for approximately 6 miles. Follow signs for Lee Valley Leisure Complex. After roundabout (where A110 crosses), turn left at second set of traffic lights onto the complex. Follow site signs. O.S.GR: TQ357940. GPS: N51:37.943 W00:02.303

Charges 2007

Per person	£ 6.40
child (under 16 yrs)	£ 2.90
electricity	£ 2.70
Min. charge £ 9.60	

UK3260 Abbey Wood Caravan Club Site

Federation Road, Abbey Wood, London SE2 0LS (London)

Tel: 0208 311 7708

Situated close to Abbey Wood, it is hard to believe that this park is in London and the wardens have made every effort to create an attractive environment. There are 120 level caravan pitches all with 16A electricity and TV aerial connections. Of these, 64 have hardstandings. A large tent area provides an additional 100 pitches. Many pitches benefit from shade by mature trees. A secure fence around the perimeter is linked to close circuit TV cameras for security and just outside is a late arrivals area with electric and toilets; also protected by cameras. This park attracts many UK and overseas visitors as it offers a very good base from which to visit central London. A train service runs every 15 minutes from Abbey Wood station (5 minutes walk) to either Charing Cross or Cannon Street.

Facilities

Three modern, fully equipped toilet blocks, two with under-floor heating, one designed to be open all year, include washbasins in cubicles, generous showers, baby/toddler washroom, laundry equipment and dishwashing sinks. Good private facilities for disabled visitors. Motorcaravan service point. Gas. Bread, milk and cold drinks from reception (high season). Play area. Good travel and information centre (08.30-11.00 hrs) can provide tickets for travel and tourist attractions. Off site: Sports centre 1 mile. Golf 4 miles.

Open: All year.

Directions

From east on M2/A2 or from central London: on the A2 (third exit) turn off at A221 into Danson Road (signed Bexleyheath, Welling and Sidcup). Follow sign Bexleyheath to Crook Log (A207 junction); at traffic lights turn right and immediately left into Brampton Road. In 1.5 miles at traffic lights turn left into Bostal Road (A206); in 0.75 miles at traffic lights turn right into Basildon Road (B213). In 300 yds. turn right into McLeod Road, in about 0.5 miles at roundabout turn right into Knee Hill; in 100 yds. turn right (second right) into Federation Road. Site on left in 50 yds. From M25, north, west or south approach: leave at junction 2 onto A2 (signed London), then as above. O.S.GR: TQ472785.

Charges 2007

Per person	£ 4.70 - £ 6.20
child (5-16 yrs)	£ 1.50 - £ 3.00
pitch (non-member)	£ 10.90 - £ 15.30

UK3270 Crystal Palace Caravan Club Site

Crystal Palace Parade, London SE19 1UF (London)

Tel: 020 8778 7155

The Caravan Club's site at Crystal Palace in south London provides easy access to the city centre and all its many attractions. The pitches are pleasantly arranged in terraces overlooking the ruins of the old Crystal Palace, its park and National Sports Centre. It is surprisingly quiet given its location (with the exception of police sirens and over-flying aircraft). In peak season advance booking is always necessary. Most pitches are on gravel hardstanding, so it is particularly useful for out of season stays. There are places for 84 caravans or motorcaravans, all with electricity (16A). Tents are placed on the site's well mown lawns near reception, where there are four additional electric points. The Crystal Palace park is extensive and provides open spaces for strolls or picnics and plenty of activities for children. The Sports Centre has two swimming pools, tennis and squash courts and gym facilities, with national events in a variety of sports to watch at certain times. An area at the site entrance should be used for arrivals after 20.00.

Facilities

The main toilet block can be heated in cool weather with curtained washbasins for ladies. Another block provides basic unisex showers and toilets. Facilities for disabled visitors. Laundry room. Dishwashing sinks and rubbish bins. Motorcaravan service facilities. Gas available. Off site: Shops, pubs, etc. 400 yards. Many buses stop outside the site, including services to central London.

Open: All year.

Directions

On A205 South Circular road travelling east, pass Dulwich College and golf course on right, turn right at traffic lights. Within 400 yards, at traffic lights, turn right into Sydenham Hill. In 350 yds. at roundabout turn left. Site is 1 mile opposite mini-roundabouts. Travelling west on A205 South Circular, immediately after passing under Catford railway bridge, keep left onto A212 (Crystal Palace). After 2.75 miles, site is on left. O.S.GR: TQ341724.

Charges 2007

Per person	£ 4.70 - £ 6.20
child (5-16 yrs)	£ 1.50 - £ 3.00
pitch (non-member)	£ 10.90 - £ 15.30

MAP 4

The East of England is a perfect mix of soft and gentle countryside, ancient cities, historical towns, and storybook villages. Its coastline is largely untouched and studded with nature reserves, ideal for bird-watching, while the traditional beach resorts offer old-fashioned seaside fun.

East of England

THIS REGION INCLUDES THE COUNTIES OF ESSEX, SUFFOLK, NORFOLK, CAMBRIDGESHIRE, HERTFORDSHIRE AND BEDFORDSHIRE

Bedfordshire and Hertfordshire are the smallest counties in the region, with peaceful canals, undulating countryside with chalk downs, and some of the greatest stately homes in the country. Essex is full of quaint villages with a smattering of old towns and traditional seasides resorts, including Colchester and Southend-on-Sea. The river Cam winds its way through Cambridgeshire; punting along the river in Cambridge is a good way to relax and take in the many famous university buildings that dominate the waterfront along the 'Backs'. Further along the river is the ancient cathedral city of Ely, once an island before the Fen drainage. The flat Fenland has a network of rivers and canals, ideal for narrowboat trips, as are the Norfolk Broads. Norfolk itself is very flat, sparsely populated and tranquil, popular with walkers and cyclists, while the numerous nature reserves attract a variety of wildlife. It also has a beautiful coastline; the seaside towns of Great Yarmouth and Hunstanton are major draws. This unspoilt coastline stretches into Suffolk, 'Constable Country'. Full of space, with picturesque villages set amongst lush green countryside, dotted with timbered cottages and ruined abbeys, the county is home to Newmarket, the horse racing capital of the world.

Places of interest

Essex: Clacton-on-Sea; Walton-on-the-Naze, with nature reserve; Colchester, Epping; Chelmsford.

Suffolk: Ipswich; Felixstowe; Lowestoft; Bury St Edmonds; village of Clare with country park.

Norfolk: Norwich, seaside resort of Cromer; old fishing village of Sheringham, Sandringham Palace near King's Lynn; Banham Zoo.

Cambridgeshire: King's College and Chapel in Cambridge plus Fitzwilliam Museum; Peterborough; Imperial War Museum in Duxford; Huntingdon; Wildfowl & Wetland Trust near Wisbech.

Hertfordshire: St Albans; stately homes and gardens of Knebworth House and Hatfield House.

Bedfordshire: Bedford, Woburn with Abbey and safari park; Whipsnade Wild Animal Park; Shuttleworth Collection near Biggleswade.

Did you know?

Newmarket has been recognised as the Headquarters of Racing for over 300 years.

The highest point of the East of England is the Dunstable Downs at 244 metres.

Colchester is Britain's oldest recorded town with Europe's largest Norman Castle keep.

The artist John Constable was born in 1776 in the village of East Bergholt. Nearby Flatford Mill, was portrayed in his most famous scene 'The Haywain'.

Peterhouse is the first Cambridge college, founded in 1284 by the Bishop of Ely.

Epping Forest was the haunt of the renowned highwayman, Dick Turpin.

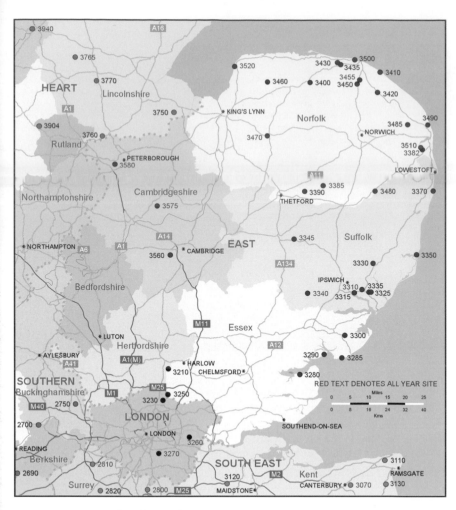

UK3300 Homestead Lake Park

Thorpe Road, Weeley, Clacton-on-Sea CO16 9JN (Essex)

Tel: **01255 833492**. Email: **lakepark@homesteadcaravans.co.uk**

This well laid out, 25 acre park was opened in 2002. It is hidden from the road at the rear of Homestead Caravans sales areas and workshops in the countryside of the Tendring district, at Weeley near Clacton. It offers 50 fully serviced hardstanding pitches on gently sloping ground overlooking a fishing lake and recently built holiday lodge accommodation on the other side of the lake. Tents accepted for short stays only on a limited number of pitches.The park makes an ideal spot to stay either for fishing or a relaxing weekend, or as a base for touring this part of Essex. A special area has been added to allow wheelchair users to fish. You could even arrange for your caravan to be serviced or repairs to be made while you stay. Homestead also have a large accessories superstore. Breakfast is recommended at the café as a start to your day.

Facilities

The toilet block offers clean and spacious facilities including an en-suite unit for disabled visitors. Baby changing facilities. Shop. Coffee shop and snack bar. Fishing lake. Woodland walks. Caravan sales, workshops and accessory shop.

Open: 1 March - 31 October.

Directions

From Colchester take A120, then A133 signed Clacton. At roundabout, turn left on B1033 into Weeley and site and showrooms are on left just past council offices. O.S GR: TM149225.

Charges 2007

Per unit incl. 2 persons and electricity	£ 13.00 - £ 18.00
extra person	£ 3.00
child (under 18 yrs)	£ 1.00
dog	£ 1.00

UK3280 Waterside Holiday Park

Main Road, St Lawrence Bay, Southminster CM0 7LY (Essex)

Tel: **0871 664 9794**

With views over the Blackwater estuary, this large park is a member of the Park Resorts chain, which specialises in caravan holiday homes. Touring units are accepted and are located within two main areas within the mobile home park. Campers have access to the park's amenities including an indoor swimming pool, bar, café and launderette. In high season there is a programme of entertainment including children's clubs. The toilet and washing facilities are situated reasonably close to the main touring area, but are a long walk from the other area which is located on the far side of the park.

Facilities

There are two toilet blocks within the main reception and entertainment complex. A smaller block provides some showers and toilets, as well as an older style 'portacabin' style unit providing additional showers and toilets. Facilities for disabled visitors with key access. Launderette. Fresh water points throughout the park. Shop. Café and takeaway. Lounge bar. Entertainment complex. Indoor pool, spa and sauna. Play area.

Open: 7 April - 27 October.

Directions

From the A12, take A414 towards Maldon. Follow the B1010 and take turning to Latchingdon. Drive through Latchingdon and follow signs for St Lawrence. On driving through St Lawrence, pick up signs for park. O.S.GR: TL955056.

Charges 2007

Per touring pitch	£ 5.00 - £ 23.00
tent pitch	£ 3.00 - £ 20.00
dog	£ 1.00 - £ 3.00

UK3290 Fen Farm Caravan & Camping Site

East Mersea, Colchester CO5 8UA (Essex)

Tel: **01206 383275**. Email: **fenfarm@talk21.com**

Tents were first pitched at Fen Farm in 1923 and since then the park has 'grown rather than developed' – something of which owners Raph and Wenda Lord are proud. Most of the 90 pitches are unmarked, on grass and within two touring areas, either side of an area for over 80 holiday homes. All pitches have electricity connections and some have hardstanding and are fully serviced. A limited number of touring pitches are available on the smaller field, with outstanding views and direct access to the beach. This is an attractive well laid out site with trees and two ponds. The site provides facilities for launching boats from the seashore and it is popular with water skiers and windsurfers. Jet skis are not allowed. There are also many opportunities for walking, either inland or along the beach.

Facilities

New shower block in main touring field. Laundry room. Family room and shower and toilet for disabled visitors. Older facilities, recently redecorated, in Heron Bay area also with facilities for disabled visitors. Recycling. Play area. Basic supplies from van from local shop (daily high season, weekends low season). Mobile shop for papers, bread and milk (weekends in summer). Gas supplies. Caravan and boat storage. Off site: Shop and post office 1.5 miles. 'Pick your own' fruit farm and tea room.

Open: 1 March - 31 October.

Directions

From Colchester, take B1025 to Mersea Island. After crossing causeway bridge, take left fork to East Mersea. Follow road for 2.75 miles to 'Dog and Pheasant' pub. Site entrance is next right. O.S.GR: TM058144.

Charges 2007

Per pitch	£ 17.00 - £ 25.00
awning	£ 2.00
extra car	£ 5.00

149

UK3285 Martello Beach Holiday Park

Belsize Avenue, Jaywick, Clacton-On-Sea CO15 2LF (Essex)

Tel: 08712 501010

Situated on the outskirts of Jaywick and adjacent to a small sandy beach and the Martello tower, this large park is a member of the Park Resorts chain which specialises in caravan holiday home parks. On the far side of the park a large touring field provides 110 unmarked pitches, 70 of which have access to electricity. Tourers have access to the park's entertainment complex providing children's clubs, an arcade and evening entertainment. An outdoor swimming pool is due to be replaced with a new indoor pool. However, facilities for tourers here are very limited indeed, with one toilet block providing showers and toilets, very limited fresh water provision and a very restricted dishwashing area.

Facilities

An older style toilet block provides showers and toilets, restricted dishwashing and a chemical disposal point. The toilet block has two outside fresh water points for tourers. No baby changing or facilities for disabled visitors. Launderette. Shop. Café. Outdoor pool (indoor pool planned). Entertainment complex with clubs for children, entertainment and arcade. Off site: The centre of Jaywick is a short drive from the park and the seaside resort of Clacton-on-Sea is about 4 miles.

Open: 7 April - 27 October.

Directions

From A12 take A133 to Clacton-on-Sea. On outskirts of Clacton, turn right into B1077 (St John's Road). Continue for 1.5 miles, turn left into Jaywick Lane. Continue for 3 miles, then follow road signs for park. O.S.GR: TM138128.

Charges 2007

Per touring pitch	£ 6.00 - £ 29.00
tent pitch	£ 3.00 - £ 26.00

UK3310 Low House Touring Caravan Centre

Buchlesham Road, Foxhall, Ipswich IP10 0AU (Suffolk)

Tel: **01473 659437**. Email: **low.house@btinternet.com**

Set in a sheltered 3.5 acres, this site has 30 level, grass pitches and an abundance of shrubs and flowers. The park has been divided into two areas bordered by mature trees and the grounds are well maintained by the wardens, Brian and Mary Saunders. All the pitches have electrical connections (10/16A) and they back onto trees that provide plenty of shade and the opportunity to observe a range of wildlife. The wardens live on site and manage the park from the reception in a mobile office near the entrance. Low House lies between Felixstowe (8 miles) and Ipswich (4 miles) and would be a useful stopover for the Felixstowe port or Harwich.

Facilities

The older style, heated sanitary block is spotlessly clean with hot showers (50p). Chemical disposal facilities. Dishwashing sink. No on-site provisions but a supermarket is 2 miles (towards Ipswich). Frozen goods can be stored. Calor gas is available. Small, secure play area. Pet area with rabbit, hens and guinea fowl. Off site: Pub in Bucklesham village (1.5 miles) and other good pubs nearby. Golf 2 miles.

Open: All year.

Directions

Turn off A14 (was A45) Ipswich ring road (south) via slip road onto A1156 (signed Ipswich East). Follow road over bridge crossing over the A45 and almost immediately turn right (no sign). After 0.5 miles turn right again (signed Bucklesham) and site is on left after 400 yards. O.S.GR: TM225423.

Charges 2007

Per unit incl. 2 adults and children	£ 13.00 - £ 16.00
extra person	£ 3.00
child (5-14 yrs)	£ 2.00

No large commercial vehicles. No credit cards.

UK3315 Orwell Meadows Leisure Park

Priory Lane, Ipswich IP10 0JS (Suffolk)

Tel: **01473 726666**

This popular, family park is set on the edge of the Orwell Country Park near Ipswich with its many miles of walks and the famous Orwell Bridge with views of the Suffolk countryside. The park is run by David and Sally Miles and offers an ideal spot for a family holiday with an outdoor swimming pool and a good clubhouse with a bar, restaurant and a shop. Spacious pitches are around the edges of several separate meadows (surrounded on three sides by earth banks), all offering 16A electricity hook-ups. There is lots to see and do in the area, from towns such as Ipswich and Colchester to villages such as Framlingham (with its castle) and Aldeburgh, plus the rest of Constable country.

Facilities

The modern toilet block includes clean and spacious showers. It is kept to a very high standard. En-suite facilities for disabled visitors. Dishwashing area. Well stocked shop. Bar and restaurant. Outdoor pool. Play area. TV/family room. Max. two dogs per unit.

Open: March - January.

Directions

From A14 Ipswich bypass take Nacton/Ipswich exit (north of the A14) and follow signs for Orwell Country Park (narrow lane). Cross single track bridge over A14 to site entrance 20 yards on left. Follow signs past house/reception up hill. Park on left and walk back to reception. O.S.GR: TM190408.

Charges 2007

Per unit incl. 2 persons	£ 12.00 - £ 14.00
incl. electricity	£ 14.00 - £ 16.00
extra person	£ 4.00 - £ 6.00
Weekly specials available.	

UK3330 Moat Barn Touring Caravan Park

Dallinghoo Road, Bredfield, Woodbridge IP13 6BD (Suffolk)

Tel: **01473 737520**

Mike Allen opened this small touring park in April 2000 on the Suffolk Heritage Cycle Route, and also the Hull - Harwich National Cycle Route. The main touring area is bordered by established hedging and incorporates a circular roadway. The park currently provides 25 level grass pitches, all with electricity (10A), and there are plans to extend the number of pitches to 34, by 2008. The park is popular with both walkers and cyclists and provides a tranquil environment to explore the area. Limited provision for large units (e.g. American motorhomes). There are no facilities for children.

Facilities

The well equipped sanitary block can be heated. A separate unit houses a dishwashing sink. Motorcaravan service point. Bicycle hire. Laundry and shop planned. Off site: Nearby pub serving food. Public footpath.

Open: 1 March - 15 January.

Directions

Park is midway between Woodbridge and Wickham Market. From A12 take turning signed Bredfield. At village pump in Bredfield turn right. Follow road past public house and church. Continue through S-bends. After 200 yards, site on left. O.S.GR: TM270537.

Charges 2007

Per unit incl. 2 persons and electricity	£ 13.00
extra person	£ 2.00

UK3335 Westwood Park Caravan Park

Old Felixstowe Road, Bucklesham, Ipswich IP10 0BN (Suffolk)

Tel: **01473 659637**. Email: **julie@westwoodcaravanpark.co.uk**

This brand new park opened in Easter 2007 and has been developed on land previously owned by the neighbouring farm. The park is situated between Felixstowe and Ipswich and is within easy reach of the River Deben and Woodbridge. The enthusiastic managers, Justin Rich and Julie Freeland have undertaken extensive planting throughout the park which promises to bring benefits and shade over time. The 90 level grass pitches are of varying size to accommodate both small and large caravans and motorhomes. All pitches have 16A electricity. Families are welcome.

Facilities

A brand new, but traditionally built, toilet block in the centre of the park includes facilities for disabled visitors (£5 deposit for key). Laundry. Reception provides local information and sells a limited range of provisions e.g. milk (plus bread and papers at B.Hs and high season). Recycling facilities planned. Off site: Free range eggs from a farm (short walk). Pubs serving meals. Fishing 2 miles. Golf 4 miles. Beach 5 miles. Bus to Ipswich.

Open: All year excl. 16 January - 28 February.

Directions

Site is near Bucklesham. From the A12 (south) or A14(12) (north) take A14 towards Felixstowe. Continue for 5 miles and turn left signed Kirton, Bucklesham and Brightwell. Continue for about 1 mile: Park is on the right, immediately after Tenth Road on the left. O.S.GR: TN253411.

Charges 2007

Per unit incl. 2 persons and electricity	£ 15.00
extra person	£ 2.50

UK3325 The Oaks Caravan Park

Chapel Road, Bucklesham, Ipswich IP10 0BT (Suffolk)

Tel: **01394 448837**. Email: **oakscaravanpark@aol.com**

Situated between Felixstowe and Ipswich and with views over open farmland, this pleasant adult only touring park provides access to the surrounding countryside and towns, including the River Deben, Woodbridge and the Suffolk Heritage coast. Since opening in the summer of 2003, the park continues to attract many repeat visitors. Trees and shrubs are now maturing, creating screening and shade for the 89 marked touring pitches. There are 79 electricity hook-ups and the well maintained grass pitches are laid out either side of an oval gravel path. A summer house contains local information, newspapers and a small patio with tables and chairs where visitors can sit and read.

Facilities

The single modern sanitary block provides bright and clean toilet and shower facilities, as well as a covered dishwashing area and motorcaravan point. Facilities for disabled people are planned. Gas is available at reception. Bicycle hire. Off site: Bus service outside park. Minibus service in the evenings by prior arrangement to nearby local pubs/restaurants, fish and chips Friday evenings. Riding 1 mile. Fishing less than 1 mile. Golf 4 miles. Beach 5 miles.

Open: 1 April - 31 October.

Directions

Site is between Bucklesham and Kirton. From the A12 (south) or A14(12) (north) take the A14 towards Felixstowe. Continue for 5 miles and turn left signed Bucklesham and Brightwell. Continue for 1 mile, take next right signed Kirton and Newbourne. Park is on the right in 550 yds. O.S.GR: TM261411.

Charges 2008

Per unit incl. 2 persons and electricity	£ 13.00 - £ 15.00
extra person	£ 2.50

UK3340 Polstead Touring Park

Holt Road, Bower Housetye, Polstead CO6 5BZ (Suffolk)

Tel: **01787 211969**. Email: **polsteadtouringpark@hotmail.co.uk**

This lovely adult only touring park in the peaceful Suffolk countryside is an ideal base from which to explore many places of interest. These include Flatford Mill, the scene for Constable's famous painting, Sudbury (birthplace of Gainsborough), Long Melford with its Hall and Colchester, Britain's oldest town. The very neat and well cared for park offers 30 level pitches all with electricity (10A). Well established hedges separate the pitches, 27 of which have gravel hardstanding. The enthusiastic new owners plan to create an additional 20 pitches, including 4 super pitches.

Facilities

The toilet block is well cared for with freshly laundered hand towels. Spacious showers. Facilities for disabled visitors are provided (showers large enough for wheelchair access), plus separate toilets. Laundry. Reception sells basic supplies. Fish and chips delivered by arrangement Saturdays. Rally field. Caravan storage. Off site: Fishing and golf. Pub 3 minutes walk. Farm shop 100 yards.

Open: All year.

Directions

From A1071 Hadleigh - Sudbury road, just past the 'Brewers Arms' public house, turn left just before a water tower towards Polstead; park is 250 yards on the right. O.S.GR: TL985403.

Charges 2007

Per unit incl. 2 persons	£ 14.00 - £ 17.50
extra person	£ 4.00 - £ 5.00
No credit cards.	

UK3345 The Dell Caravan & Camping Park

Beyton Road, Thurston, Bury St Edmunds IP31 3RB (Suffolk)

Tel: **01359 270121**. Email: **thedellcaravanpark@btinternet.com**

Close to the A14 and surrounded by farmland, this small touring site, four miles east of Bury St Edmunds, provides a convenient base to explore the area or as a stopover point. The owners have created 60 spacious pitches within the main touring area, divided into two sections – one of which is reserved for adults only. All pitches have electricity (10A). A separate field with a further 10 pitches is available for contractors working locally, as well as any visitors who prefer shaded areas. The main touring field has some shade from well maintained hedges and the trees bordering the site. All pitches have access to the site's facilities. There is some noise from the nearby A14.

Facilities

Excellent and ample toilet and spacious shower facilities. Ladies' toilets include a private bathroom and toilet. Family bathroom with bath, shower and baby changing facilities (charged). Separate toilet/shower for disabled visitors. Laundry room. Off site: Bus to Bury St Edmonds from outside park. Fishing, golf and riding 3 miles. Pubs and restaurants in Thurston and neighbouring villages.

Open: All year.

Directions

From the A14 take exit for Thurston and Beyton, 4 miles east of Bury St Edmunds. Follow signs to Thurston. Park is on the left, shortly after arriving at Thurston and signed from Beyton. O.S.GR: TL928640.

Charges 2008

Per unit incl. 2 persons	£ 11.00
incl. electricity	£ 13.00 - £ 15.00

UK3350 **Church Farm Holiday Park**

Church Farm Road, Aldeburgh IP15 5DW (Suffolk)

Tel: **01728 453433**. Email: **aldeburgh@amberleisure.com**

This area of the Suffolk coast has always been a popular destination for visitors and Church Farm Holiday Park has an enviable location on the outskirts of Aldeburgh. The park lies opposite a shingle beach (to the south of Thorpeness) and is adjacent to a nature reserve, a haven for birds and other wildlife. The park includes a large area designated for caravan holiday homes as well as a separate touring area situated to the front of the park. The touring area provides 85 pitches for caravans and motorhomes (tents and trailer tents are not accepted). Pitches are separated by attractive hedging that blends in well with the natural environment. 60 pitches have access to 16A electricity, as well as own water taps and a shared waste outlet (one between two pitches). This is a quiet park with no facilities for children on site, but close to the beach and amenities in Aldeburgh.

Facilities

The single toilet block has been fully refurbished with heating, free showers, toilets and washbasins. Access to the toilets and showers are via two steps, making it unsuitable for wheelchair users. Laundry room. Gas supplies. Off site: Bus service 0.5 - 1 mile. Shops, pubs, etc. 15 minutes walk. Beach 5 minutes walk. Fishing, and bicycle hire 1 mile. Riding 2 miles.

Open: Easter - 31 October.

Directions

On arrival at Aldeburgh, site is signed at roundabout in the direction of Thorpeness. Where road meets seafront, site is on left. From town centre follow road along seafront to site on left at end of town. O.S.GR: TM465572.

Charges 2007

Per pitch	£ 18.00 - £ 22.00
with services	£ 22.00 - £ 26.00

UK3370 **Kessingland Beach Holiday Park**

Kessingland, Lowestoft NR33 7RN (Suffolk)

Tel: **01502 740636**

Set near the most easterly point in the UK, this park offers all you need for that total family holiday experience, including, bowling, pool tables, an amusement arcade and indoor and outdoor swimming pools. If you so wish you need never leave Kessingland Beach until your holiday ends. There is evening entertainment, as well as a selection of bars and restaurants. Although mainly a large park for static caravan holiday homes, there is a touring area to the west of the park with quite spacious pitching. Electricity hook-ups are available. The toilet block is older in style but has been refurbished. There is lots to see and do here on the Suffolk coast, in nearby Lowestoft and further along the coast in Great Yarmouth, as well as neaby Oulton Broad.

Facilities

The toilet block has been refurbished, but access is unsuitable for wheelchairs. Laundry. Bars, restaurants, fish and chips. Entertainment complex. Indoor and outdoor swimming pools. Adventure play area. Shop. Tennis courts. Amusements. Crazy golf. Bicycle hire. Off site: Beach and sea fishing 100 yds. Golf and riding 3 miles.

Open: 20 March - 26 October.

Directions

From Lowestoft, north, on A12 ignore first turning to Kessingland village and continue along A12 to next roundabout. Take left turning on roundabout signed Kessingland Beach. From A12 south, turn right at roundabout signed Kessingland Beach. At beach take sharp right continuing along to park entrance (narrow road). O.S.GR: TM535859.

Charges 2007

Per caravan or motorcaravan	£ 6.00 - £ 28.00
tent pitch	£ 3.00 - £ 25.00
dog	£ 1.00 - £ 3.00

UK3382 Rose Farm Touring Park

Stepshort, Belton, Great Yarmouth NR31 9JS (Norfolk)

Tel: **01493 780896**. Email: **myhra@rosefarmtouringpark.fsnet.co.uk**

This part of Norfolk is well known for its seaside attractions and the campsites which combine caravan holiday homes and touring pitches. Rose Farm caters for another type of camping holiday, offering space with the peace and tranquillity that you may not be expecting in this particular area! With nearby attractions such as Fritton Lake Country Park, Pleasure Wood Hills Theme Park and of course Great Yarmouth with its fun fair and amusement arcades, your holiday in Norfolk could be full of busy days. Sue and Tora Myhra are very proud of Rose Farm and what they have achieved in the few years since taking over what was quite a run-down campsite. Spread over eight acres, the park is split into two separate fields. The first is large and open, surrounded by fencing and hedges, with pitches around the edge. It is very spacious with a very good toilet/shower block. The second field is long with pitching on either side. A new toilet/shower block here offers top quality facilities. Both blocks are immaculate with thoughtful decor. Several hardstanding pitches are also available. Recent landscaping of the site includes a new walkway along the bank with picnic tables.

Facilities

The two excellent blocks offer super facilities. The newer block is in Norwegian style, with a very modern fresh and spacious interior. Showers are good with changing space, washbasins are open or in cubicles. The laundry is in the first block along with an iron and ironing board. Facilities for disabled visitors (pitching can be arranged in advance). Adventure playground by reception. Pool table, TV room, library and tourist information. Dog walk. Internet access. Off site: Shops nearby. Fishing and golf 3 miles. Riding and bicycle hire 4 miles. Beach 5 miles.

Open: All year.

Directions

From Great Yarmouth and Gorleston take the A143 signed Beccles and Diss. At dual carriageway (Bradwell) take immediate right to Burgh Castle, take next right, site on right in 25 yards. O.S.GR: TG486033

Charges 2007

Per unit incl. 2 persons	£ 10.00 - £ 15.00
incl. electricity	£ 12.50 - £ 17.00
extra person	£ 2.50
pup tent	£ 2.00

Special offers available. No credit cards.

UK3385 Applewood Caravan & Camping Park

Banham Zoo, The Grove, Banham NR16 2HE (Norfolk)

Tel: **01953 888370**. Email: **info@banhamzoo.co.uk**

Applewood is a 13 acre touring park, adjacent to the famous Banham Zoo, the residents of which are the only thing that may disturb your relaxation while on this park (but they do not usually rise until 08.00). Visitors to the park receive a special price for addmission to the Zoo. At weekends, one of Norfolk's largest car boot sales is held at the arena area alongside the site. Applewood has 100 pitches, 70 with electric hook-ups (10A). They are spread amongst thirteen areas, each separated by high, established hedges which offer privacy and seclusion. There is a large rally field and a function room. The Appleyard, two minutes walk from the park provides a Spar shop, Huckleberry's restaurant and gift shops. The village with its pub is also within walking distance.

Facilities

Two toilet blocks, one new and one refurbished provide good, clean and spacious facilities. Room for disabled visitors. Laundry. Motorcaravan service point. Accessory shop, rally field and function room. Gas supplies. Off site: Zoo and The Appleyard with shop and restaurant. Snetterton race circuit 3 miles. Norwich 15 miles.

Open: All year.

Directions

From Attleborough on the A11 take B1077 to New Buckenham and Banham Zoo. Follow road to T-junction with B1113 and turn right signed Banham. Follow through village and park is on the left at top of hill. O.S.GR: TM058871.

Charges guide

Per person (4 yrs and over)	£ 1.50
pitch incl. electricity	£ 15.00
tent	£ 7.75

UK3390 The Dower House Touring Park

Thetford Forest, East Harling NR16 2SE (Norfolk)

Tel: **01953 717314**. Email: **info@dowerhouse.co.uk**

Set on 20 acres in the heart of Britain's largest forest on the Suffolk and Norfolk borders, The Dower House provides quiet woodland walks and cycle ways, with an abundance of wildlife. David and Karen Bushell, owners for many years, continue to upgrade the facilities without compromising the park's natural features. There are now 160 really large pitches with electricity available (10A). Most are level, although given the forest location there are a few tree roots. A fourth field provides 60 pitches for tents. Six pitches for visitors with mobility problems are linked by a path to the main facilities. The Dower House, as well as being the owners' home, houses a pleasant bar that also serves bar food (weekends only in low season) and a takeaway. A pleasant patio area is used for occasional entertainment at weekends. A torch is necessary as there is no lighting other than at the facilities.

Facilities

Two toilet blocks - a small, refurbished one near the entrance, and a larger one with a baby room. A separate building houses the showers (5 for each sex and 20p) and a unit for disabled people. Dishwashing room, including a lower sink for children or disabled people. Laundry room with washing machine and dryer. Separate licensed shop doubling as reception and open daily in the season, on request at other times. Gas supplies. Information room. TV and quiet rooms (no games machines). New heated outdoor swimming pool (25/5-2/9, under 15s must be with an adult). Paddling pool. Caravan storage. Off site: Fishing nearby (1.5 miles). Snetterton motor racing circuit and Sunday market (2-3 miles).

Open: 15 March - 29 September.

Directions

From A11 (Thetford - Norwich) road, 7 miles from Thetford, turn right on B1111 towards East Harling. Turn right at church and right at T-junction; park is on right. From A1066 Thetford-Diss road take left fork signed East Harling. Ignore signs for Forestry Commission site and park is next on left. Follow long drive (unmade road) for approx. 1 mile - keep speed down. O.S GR: TL969853.

Charges 2007

Per unit incl. 2 persons	£ 10.95 - £ 18.95
with electricity	£ 13.75 - £ 21.95
extra person	£ 2.25
child (4-17 yrs)	£ 1.00

No charge for awnings or dogs.

UK3400 The Old Brick Kilns Caravan & Camping Park

Little Barney Lane, Barney, Fakenham NR21 0NL (Norfolk)

Tel: **01328 878305**. Email: **enquiries@old-brick-kilns.co.uk**

This tranquil, family run park is under new ownership and further improvements are taking place. The park's development on the site of old brick kilns has resulted in land on varying levels. This provides areas of level, well drained pitches (e.g. the Dell, the Orchard) which include some hardstandings. There are 65 pitches in total, all with electricity (16A), including a new area with serviced pitches. Banks around the park and a wide range of trees and shrubs provide shelter and are home for a variety of wildlife. There are garden areas, including a butterfly garden, and a conservation pond is the central feature. Drinking water is supplied by a 285 ft. bore and excellent roofed service areas provide water and waste disposal. Amenities include a large, comfortable bar area and restaurant, open at weekends. A friendly, helpful atmosphere prevails and as the park is 8 miles from the coast, it is ideally situated to explore North Norfolk. A member of the Best of British group.

Facilities

Smart, heated toilet blocks provide very good, clean facilities with washbasins in curtained cubicles and a baby room. Facilities for disabled people (unisex; Radar key). Laundry room. Motorcaravan service point. Good shop with gas supplies. Bar/restaurant (weekends) with patio area outside with barbecue. New TV and games room. Table tennis, giant chess and mini-library. Fenced play area with bark surface. Fishing (with purpose-built platforms). Caravan storage. Internet access. B&B also available. Strictly no arrivals until after 13.00. Off site: Riding 6 miles. Golf 5 or 8 miles. Thursford collection 2 miles.

Open: All year excl. 7 January - 1 March.

Directions

From Fakenham take A148 Cromer road. After 6 miles, at Thursford, fork right on B1354 Melton Constable road. In 300 yds, turn right, signed Barney, and then first left along a narrow country lane with passing places, for 0.75 miles. O.S.GR: TG004332.

Charges 2007

Per pitch incl. 2 persons and electricity	£ 13.50 - £ 17.50
'super pitch' plus	£ 2.50 - £ 3.50
extra person	£ 3.00
child (up to 15 yrs)	£ 1.00 - £ 2.00
dog (max. 2)	£ 0.75

UK3410 Sandy Gulls Caravan Park

Cromer Road, Mundesley NR11 8DF (Norfolk)

Tel: **01263 720513**

This is a super, adults only clifftop hideaway on the outskirts of Mundesley-on-Sea. One of the only clifftop parks with space for touring units on this coastline, there are panoramic views from every pitch. All 35 pitches have electricity and TV aerial hook-ups. Some are on hardstanding, others are slightly sloping on grass (chocks advised). Primarily a caravan holiday home park, there are units to rent. Facilities are excellent and well maintained. Access to the Blue Flag beach is via a large tarmac ramp. The village of Mundesley is ony a mile away with a 9-hole golf course and a wide variety of shops and pubs, plus an amusement arcade. There is much to see and do in this area of Norfok with a steam railway further along the coast. North Walsham is within easy reach and has a good array of shops and supermarkets.

Facilities

The toilet block is modern and spacious offering large shower rooms and open washbasins, all kept very clean. Facilities for disabled visitors planned. Shops, pubs and restaurants nearby. Off site: Village 1 mile. Tennis, boat launching, riding and golf nearby.

Open: March - November.

Directions

Site is 1 mile north of Mundesley (4 miles south of Cromer) on the main coast road. O.S.GR: TG302373.

Charges 2007

Per unit incl. up to 4 peraons	£ 11.00 - £ 20.00
extra person	£ 3.00

Sandy Gulls Caravan Park. Tel: 01263 720 513. Nestling on the Mundesley cliffs is the area's only cliff top touring park, affording panoramic views of the coastline. Norfolk Broads National Park is only a short drive away. The park offers easy access to clean, sandy, Blue Flag beaches. Mundesley has been voted one of the country's best kept seaside villages. The park offers good local amenities, including a great golf course, and fly, coarse and sea fishing. Electric & TV hookups. This small, family-operated park has been owned and run for more than twenty five years by the current family. SANDY GULLS CARAVAN PARK, CROMER ROAD, MUNDESLEY, NORFOLK, NR11 8DF.

UK3420 Two Mills Touring Park

Yarmouth Road, North Walsham NR28 9NA (Norfolk)

Tel: **01692 405829**. Email: **enquiries@twomills.co.uk**

Two Mills is a quiet site for adults only. Set in the bowl of a former quarry, the park is a real sun trap, both secluded and sheltered, with bird song to be heard at all times of the day. Neatly maintained with natural areas, varied trees, wild flowers and birds, the owners, Barbara and Ray Barnes, want to add their own touches to this popular park. There are 55 level marked pitches for tourers, 48 all weather gravel, including 12 serviced pitches (hardstanding, patio, water and waste water drainage). All are generously sized and have electricity (10/16A). This is a good centre from which to explore the north Norfolk coast, the Broads or for visiting Norwich and a footpath from the park joins the Weavers Way. A member of the Best of British group.

Facilities

Neat, clean central toilet block can be heated and includes some washbasins in cabins, en-suite facilities for disabled people, laundry and dishwashing rooms. Small shop at reception. TV room with tea and coffee facilities. Dogs are accepted by arrangement only. Only adults are accepted. Off site: Hotel/pub 100 yds. Town 20 minutes walk. Fishing or golf 5 miles. Bicycle hire 1.5 miles. The coast is 5 miles.

Open: All year excl. 2 January - 1 March.

Directions

From A149 Stalham - North Walsham road, watch for caravan sign 1.5 miles before North Walsham (also signed White Horse Common). The road runs parallel to the A149 and site is on right in 1.25 miles. From North Walsham take Old Yarrmouth road past hospital, and park is on left after 1 mile. O.S.GR: TG292287.

Charges 2007

Per unit incl. 2 persons	£ 13.00 - £ 18.00
'panorama' pitch	£ 15.00 - £ 19.00
extra person	£ 2.50
Senior citizen discounts.	

UK3430 **Kelling Heath Holiday Park**

Weybourne, Holt, Sheringham NR25 7HW (Norfolk)

Tel: **01263 588181**. Email: **info@kellingheath.co.uk**

Not many parks can boast their own railway station and Kelling Heath's own halt on the North Norfolk Steam Railway gives access to shopping in Holt or the beach at Sheringham. Set in 250 acres of woodland and heathland overlooking the north Norfolk coast, this spacious holiday park offers freedom and relaxation with 300 touring pitches, all with electricity (16A) in four different zones. Pitching is good on quite firm, level grass (no hardstanding). Together with 384 caravan holiday homes (36 to let, the rest privately owned), they blend easily into the part-wooded, part-open heath. A wide range of facilities provides activities for all ages. 'The Forge' has an entertainment bar, an adult only bar and a family room, with comprehensive entertainment all season. 'Fitness Express' provides an indoor pool, spa pool, sauna, steam rooms and gym. An adventure playground with assault course is near. The central reception area is attractively paved to provide a 'village store' and an open air bandstand where one can sit and enjoy the atmosphere. The park's natural environment allows for woodland walks, a nature trail and cycling trails, and a small lake for fishing (permit holders only). Other amenities include two hard tennis courts, a small, outdoor heated fun pool and play areas (some rather hidden from the pitches).

Facilities

Three toilet blocks serve the touring pitches, one heated and with a conservatory providing covered access all year to disabled people, baby room and dishwashing and laundry sinks. All blocks have a few washbasins in private cubicles, baby baths and, in season, a nappy disposal service. Laundry facilities. Shop. Gas supplies. Bar, restaurant and takeaway. Indoor leisure centre with pool (19 x 9 m), gym, etc. with trained staff (membership on either daily or weekly basis). Outdoor pool (main season). Adventure play area. Tennis. Fishing. Bicycle hire. Entertainment programme. Special environmental 'Acorn Club' for children. Torches useful. Off site: The Norfolk coast, Felbrigg Hall, the Walsingham Shrine and the Norfolk Broads National Park are nearby.

Open: 10 February - 10 December.

Directions

On A148 road from Holt to Cromer, after High Kelling, turn left just before Bodham village (international sign) signed Weybourne. Follow road for about 1 mile to park O.S.GR: TG11/418.

Charges 2007

Per unit incl. electricity	£ 16.00 - £ 27.00
awning	£ 2.00 - £ 5.00
dog (max. 2)	£ 3.00 - £ 5.00

Min 7 day stay in high season. No single sex groups.

Escape the normal routine...

KELLING HEATH
THE NATURAL ESCAPE

Enjoy the beauty of Kelling Heath from your touring pitch set amongst rare open heathland with backdrops of pine and native woodland. A magnificent range of facilities and environmental activities await you. Lodges and holiday homes available for hire.

Bookings or **brochure 01263 588 181**
or online **www.kellingheath.co.uk**
Kelling Heath, Weybourne, Holt,
Norfolk NR25 7HW

UK3435 Woodlands Caravan Park

Holt Road, Upper Sheringham NR26 8TU (Norfolk)

Tel: **01263 823802**. Email: **enquiries@woodlandscaravanpark.co.uk**

This pleasantly wooded caravan park is set in the beautiful surroundings of North Norfolk's protected heathland, next to Sheringham Park (National Trust). There are many lovely walks all around the area, including one to the beach (1.5 miles). The park is within easy reach of Holt, Cromer and Sheringham, with the major bird watching areas of Blakeney, Cley and Salthouse also within 30 minutes drive. There are 225 touring pitches in two main areas for caravans and motorcaravans (tents are not accepted). Electricity (10A) is available to most. The excellent Pinewood Park Leisure Club is adjacent to the park offering swimming and other fitness facilities at a discounted rate for those staying at Woodlands.

Facilities

Three well maintained toilet blocks provide good facilities and include facilities for disabled visitors, baby changing and laundry. Well stocked shop. Gas supplies. Lounge bar and family bar with musical entertainment most weekends. Barbecues. Play area (2 acres, fenced and gated). Pinewood Park Leisure Club with indoor pool, gym, sauna. etc (all year). Off site: Golf and bicycle hire 1.5 miles. Fishing and riding 3 miles.

Open: March - October.

Directions

From Cromer on the A148 towards Holt, pass signs for Sheringham Park and site is on right just before Bodham village. From Holt on A148 just after Bodham, site is on left, well signed. O.S.GR: TG130409.

Charges 2007

Per pitch incl. electricity	£ 15.50 - £ 18.50
awning	£ 2.50

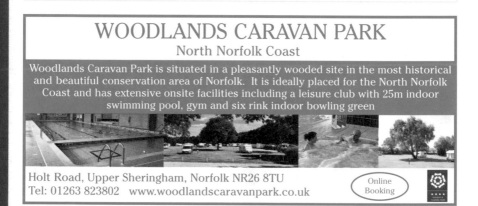

WOODLANDS CARAVAN PARK
North Norfolk Coast

Woodlands Caravan Park is situated in a pleasantly wooded site in the most historical and beautiful conservation area of Norfolk. It is ideally placed for the North Norfolk Coast and has extensive onsite facilities including a leisure club with 25m indoor swimming pool, gym and six rink indoor bowling green

Holt Road, Upper Sheringham, Norfolk NR26 8TU
Tel: 01263 823802   www.woodlandscaravanpark.co.uk

Online Booking

UK3450 Little Haven Caravan & Camping Park

The Street, Erpingham, Norwich NR11 7QD (Norfolk)

Tel: **01263 768959**. Email: **patl@haven30.fsnet.co.uk**

Within easy reach of the coast and the Broads, this is an attractive, peaceful little site with good facilities. Only adults are accepted. There are 24 grassy pitches, all with electricity (16A) and 6 with hardstanding. They are arranged around the outside of a gravel access road with a central lawn and decorative pergola, a neat little garden and a seating area. There is no shop, but two pubs serving food and traditional ales are within walking distance. An ideal base for cycling and walking (the Weavers Way footpath is within half a mile) or just relaxing. Also close by is magnificent Blickling Hall with its superb state rooms, gardens and park, or a short drive takes you to the historic market town of Aylsham.

Facilities

The well maintained toilet unit is heated and includes spacious hot showers and a covered dishwashing and laundry area. Facilities for disabled people are planned. Gas available. Site is unsuitable for American motorhomes. Note: This is an adults only park. Off site: Bus service on the main A140 road. Riding 1 mile. Fishing 3 miles. Bicycle hire 5 miles. Beach 6 miles. Golf 10 miles.

Open: 1 March - 31 October.

Directions

From A140 Cromer - Norwich road, going south towards Aylsham and 3 miles south of Roughton, past the Horseshoes pub and Alby crafts, take first turning right signed Erpingham 2 miles (narrow road). Site is 175 yards on right. O.S.GR: TG190320.

Charges 2007

Per unit incl. 2 persons, electricity and awning	£ 11.00
No credit cards.	

UK3485 Clippesby Hall

Clippesby, Great Yarmouth NR29 3BL (Norfolk)

Tel: **01493 367800**. Email: **holidays@clippesby.com**

Set in the heart of the Broads National Park this is an unusual park in the grounds of a private estate where one can wander at will. Clippesby offers the choice of pitching amongst the shady woodland or on the gently sloping lawns of the hall with colourful mature trees and shrubs. The 100 pitches are well spaced and clearly numbered (70 have 10A electricity). A new area, 'The Meadow' offers serviced pitches for motorcaravans with hardstandng and 16A electricity. There is a friendly welcome from the Lindsay family who have lived in the single storey Hall for many years and the opportunity to enjoy the mature gardens and facilities. These include a sunken grass tennis court, a small heated pool with mellow flagstone patio area behind the Hall, a timber adventure playground, and family golf with a seaside theme. The Muskett Arms with an attractive and comfortable family bar and a sheltered courtyard outside, provides home-cooked meals, music nights and other ntertainment and Susie's Coffee Shop has a good selection of food during the day. Children can roam at will, and in safety, and parents can relax and unwind at this comfortable park, never mind all the attractions of the Broads and Great Yarmouth on your doorstep and only the peacocks to disturb you!

Facilities

Three timbered heated toilet blocks provide clean and modern facilities. Some washbasins in cabins and 10 showers in total. New en-suite room for disabled visitors. Family room with bath and baby changing. Hot water for dishwashing is charged (20p) – the park is not on mains services. Laundry. Gas. Shop (Easter - end Sept). Café and family bar/restaurant, pizza takeaway. Swimming pool (all end May - end Sept). Adventure play area. Bicycle hire. Dog walk (max. 1 per pitch). New measures in place for recycling. Off site: Bus service 1.5 miles. Fishing 2 miles. Riding 3 miles. Golf 5 miles. Great Yarmouth 7 miles. Norwich 15 miles. Beach 5 miles.

Open: 1 April - 31 October.

Directions

From the A47 Norwich - Great Yarmouth road at Acle roundabout take exit for Filby (A1064). After 1.5 miles take left fork on B1152 signed Potter Heigham. Take first left and park is 100 yards on the right. O.S.GR: TG423145.

Charges 2007

Per unit incl. 2 persons	£ 14.00 - £ 21.00
extra person	£ 5.00
child	£ 2.00
dog (max. 1)	£ 3.50 - £ 2.00
electricity	£ 2.00

UK3490 The Grange Touring Park

Ormesby St Margaret, Great Yarmouth NR29 3QG (Norfolk)

Tel: **01493 730306**. Email: **info@grangetouring.co.uk**

The appealing appearance of this family touring site is that of a garden, with hanging baskets, flower beds, bluebells and daffodils under the trees in spring, all carefully tended by the resident wardens. The 70 level pitches are on well trimmed grass arranged around tarmac access roads, 60 with electricity (16A). Adjacent to the campsite is The Grange itself – a free house offering a wide range of meals, beers and real ale, plus children's play equipment (open all year). The site owner also has a holiday campsite at Hemsby (4 miles) with its own wide sandy beach, which guests at The Grange are welcome to use. The nearest beach is a mile away and local attractions include Caister Castle and Motor Museum and Norfolk Rare Breed Centre. Great Yarmouth Centre with many attractions and The Broads are within 5 miles.

Facilities

A modern toilet building is spacious and well maintained, housing all the usual facilities including free showers, a baby changing room in the ladies' and a laundry room with washing machine and dryer. Washing lines are provided at the rear of the building. Gas supplies. Swings for children. Internet café (£2 per hour) and WiFi. Off site: Bus service 250 yds. Beach, shops and supermarket 1 mile. Golf 3 miles. Fishing 4 miles.

Open: 20 March - 1 October.

Directions

From A149 Great Yarmouth - North Walsham road, on the Caister bypass, at roundabout take B1159 road signed Hemsby. Park is on left just before next roundabout. O.S.GR: TG515140.

Charges 2007

Per unit incl. up to 4 persons	£ 8.00 - £ 13.50
extra person	£ 2.50
awning	£ 3.00
electricity	£ 3.00

UK3455 Deer's Glade Caravan & Camping Park

White Post Road, Hanworth, Norwich NR11 7HN (Norfolk)

Tel: **01263 768633**. Email: **info@deersglade.co.uk**

As it's name suggests, you would not be surprised to wake and see deer wandering on this park and in the surrounding woodland areas. If you do miss them, a short walk will take you to Gunton Park where deer are bred and wander in herds. In 2003, David and Heather Attew decided that they had an area that would make a superb setting for a caravan park and that they could give up farming. In early 2004 after much hard work, they opened this top quality park and it has since developed into a very popular site. Not far from the Norfolk Broads and close to the East Anglian coast, the park is open all year round. There are 125 level pitches (some with hardstandings), all with 16A electricity and 100 with TV aerial points. New hedging between pitches is becoming established. Internet access is possible from all the pitches. Amenities are of a high standard and include two toilet blocks, a play area, small shop and a popular, well stocked fishing lake.

Facilities

Two spacious new toilet blocks are of a high standard and include vanity style washbasins for ladies, a room for disabled visitors or families, dishwashing room and a laundry. Motorcaravan service point. Licensed shop (all year). Play area. Fishing lake (charge). Bicycle hire. Caravan velet service. Free minibus to local tavern. Off site: Bus service under 1 mile. Pub 1.5 miles. Woodland walks. Riding 2 miles. Beach, golf 5 miles.

Open: All year.

Directions

From Norwich take A140 towards Cromer and 5 miles after Aylsham turn right towards Suffield Park (White Post Road). Park is 0.5 miles on the right. O.S.GR: TG214340.

Charges 2007

Per person	£ 5.00 - £ 7.50
child	£ 1.75 - £ 2.75
awning	£ 1.75
dog	£ 1.00
Family deals available.	

UK3500 Woodhill Park

Cromer Road, East Runton, Cromer NR27 9PX (Norfolk)

Tel: **01263 512242**. Email: **info@woodhill-park.com**

Woodhill is a seaside site with good views and a traditional atmosphere. It is situated on the cliff top, in a large gently sloping open grassy field, with 300 marked touring pitches. Of these, 210 have electricity (16A), 7 are fully serviced and many have wonderful views over the surrounding countryside. A small number of holiday homes which are located nearer to the cliff edge have the best sea views, although perhaps at times a little bracing! Although the site is fenced there is access to the cliff top path (watch young children). Nearby attractions include boat trips to see the seals off Blakeney Point, the Shire Horse Centre at West Runton and the North Norfolk Steam Railway.

Facilities

The three sanitary units are fully equipped but could be a little short of showers at peak times. Laundry with washing machines and dryer (iron from reception). Fully equipped unit for disabled persons. Well stocked mini-market (19/3-31/8). Good, large adventure playground and plenty of space for ball games. Crazy golf. Giant chess and golf course adjacent to the site. Off site: Beach 0.5 miles. Fishing 1 mile. Bicycle hire, golf and riding 2 miles.

Open: 19 March - 31 October.

Directions

Site is beside the A149 coast road between East and West Runton. O.S.GR: TG190420.

Charges 2007

Per person	£ 2.50
child (4-16 yrs)	£ 1.00
small pitch (no electricity)	£ 6.20 - £ 8.60
pitch with electricity	£ 9.50 - £ 11.80
multi-service pitch	£ 12.75 - £ 15.25

UK3460 The Garden Caravan Site

Barmer Hall, Syderstone, Kings Lynn PE31 8SR (Norfolk)

Tel: **01485 578220**. Email: **nigel@mason96.fsnet.co.uk**

In the quiet Norfolk countryside, this imaginative touring park is set in an enclosed walled garden. Sheltered from the winds by the high walls and a sun trap, visitors can relax in peace and tranquility. Attractive mature trees, shrubs and climbers provide shade at various times of the day. The Mason family run the site in a relaxed way and the atmosphere is superb. There are 30 pitches, all with electricity (16A) and TV hook-up. Some are slightly slopping and will require blocks. Reception is housed in a small kiosk (not always manned, so pitch yourself and pay later). Barmer Hall is not far from Sandringham, and there are plenty of peaceful lanes to explore on your bicycle or take a woodland walk from the little door in the wall at the rear of the site.

Facilities

The single toilet block (heated when necessary) includes very spacious hot showers and free hot water. Dishwashing sinks are under cover at one end of the building. No shop, but gas, ices, soft drinks and free range fresh eggs are usually available. Off site: Bicycle hire 4 miles, riding 6 miles, golf 10 miles. Maybe visit Norfolk Lavender, Langham Glass or the Thursford collection of steam engines and mechanical organs.

Open: 1 March - 1 November.

Directions

About 6 miles west of Fakenham turn off A148 at Fourwinds Garage to Docking and Hunstanton on B1454. After a further 4 miles turn to Barmer Hall (site signed). Road is marked 'unsuitable for motor vehicles' but ignore and follow past and behind the Hall and farm buildings. O.S.GR: TF810330.

Charges 2007

Per person	£ 6.50 - £ 8.50
child (under 15 yrs)	£ 2.00
pitch incl. electricity	£ 2.00
TV aerial hook-up	£ 1.00
No credit cards.	

UK3470 Breckland Meadows Touring Park

Lynn Road, Swaffham PE37 7PT (Norfolk)

Tel: **01760 721246**. Email: **info@brecklandmeadows.co.uk**

Within easy reach of the historic market town of Swaffham, this 'adult only' park offers peace and tranquility and would make a good base to explore East Anglia and the local area. There are just 45 pitches, 25 on hardstanding, the remainder on fairly level, neat grass. All have 16A electricity hook-ups. There are two main roads close to the park but well established hedges and trees help minimise any noise. The Swaefas Way runs alongside the park and from this walkers can access the famous Peddars Way. Swaffham (0.5 miles) has a popular Saturday market.

Facilities

The neat, well cared for toilet block provides all the usual facilities, including spacious showers and a separate toilet and washbasin unit for disabled visitors. Laundry room. Gas supplies. Off site: Town 0.5 miles. Bicycle hire 1 mile. Golf 2 miles. Riding 4 miles. Fishing 5 miles.

Open: All year.

Directions

Park is just west of Swaffham on the old A47, about 1 mile from the town centre. O.S.GR: TF809094.

Charges 2007

Per unit incl. 2 persons and electricity	£ 11.75 - £ 16.00
extra person	£ 3.00

No credit cards.

UK3480 Little Lakeland Caravan Park

Wortwell, Harleston IP20 0EL (Norfolk)

Tel: **01986 788646**. Email: **information@littlelakeland.co.uk**

This peaceful hideaway with its own fishing lake is tucked behind the houses and gardens that border the village main street. It is a traditional, mature little park with just 58 pitches. There are several caravan holiday homes and long stay units, but there should always be around 22 places for tourers. The pitches are mostly individual ones separated by mature hedges and trees. Fishing in the attractive lake is free of charge and solely for the use of campers (bream, tench, roach, perch and carp). A member of the Countryside Discovery group.

Facilities

A modern, heated toilet block provides washbasins all in cubicles for ladies, and one for men. Fully equipped laundry. Separate en-suite room for disabled visitors also has facilities for baby changing. A further unit (also heated) by reception provides a shower, WC and basin per sex and is used mostly in the colder months. Reception stocks gas and some basic essentials. Small play area. Fishing (max. 4 rods per unit). Off site: Bus service on the main road 250 yds. Golf 4 miles. Riding 6 miles.

Open: 15 March - 31 October.

Directions

Approaching from Diss, leave A143 at roundabout signed Wortwell. Continue to village, pass 'The Bell' pub, then a garage on the right, after which turn right at first bungalow (Little Lakeland Lodge) watching carefully for signs. Site is down lane, 250 yards on right. O.S.GR: TM270850.

Charges 2008

Per unit incl. 2 persons	£ 10.80 - £ 15.80
extra person	£ 1.50 - £ 2.75

No credit cards.

UK3520 Searles Leisure Resort

South Beach Road, Hunstanton PE36 5BB (Norfolk)

Tel: **01485 534211**. Email: **bookings@searles.co.uk**

This 'all-in' family holiday park on the North Norfolk coast offers everything you need for that seaside family holiday. With the beach within walking distance, the covered 'town plaza' including a sports bar, Chinese restaurant and Mediterranean café, pools, a golf course, fishing lakes and bowling greens, there should be something to entertain everyone. Although now a major caravan holiday home park, for more than fifty years touring pitches have remained important on this site. Spacious pitches separated by hedges, either fully serviced, with electricity or not, are set in seven different areas of the park. Security is important for safety and peace of mind and 24 hour CCTV operates.

Facilities

Three large toilet blocks offer clean and tidy facilities with background music adding that little extra. Washbasins in cubicles. En-suite rooms in all blocks for disabled visitors. Baby room. Laundry. Dishwashing facilities on the side of each block. Food hall. Restaurants, bars and cafés. Hair and beauty salon. Indoor and outdoor swimming pools. Gym. Tennis. Soft play area. Golf (9-hole course, driving range and putting course). Fishing lake. Bicycle hire. Off site: Nearest beach 200 yards. Hunstanton 0.5 miles.

Open: All year.

Directions

On the A149 from Kings Lynn take Hunstanton exit at roundabout. At next roundabout take second exit then immediate left into site. O.S.GR: TF670401.

Charges guide

Per pitch	£ 11.00 - £ 30.00
pitch with electricity	£ 16.00 - £ 33.00
fully serviced pitch	£ 14.00 - £ 37.00
awning	£ 3.00

UK3510 Breydon Water Holiday Park

Butt Lane, Burgh Castle, Great Yarmouth NR31 9QB (Norfolk)

Tel: **01493 780357**. Email: **breydon.water@park-resorts.com**

Owned by the Park Resorts group, these well established holiday parks (formerly Liffens Holiday Park and Welcome Holiday Centre) are in a semi-rural area on the edge of the Norfolk Broads within easy reach of Great Yarmouth. Breydon Water Holiday Park comprises the two parks, now named Bure Village (caravan holiday homes only) and Yare Village, which are just a short walk apart along a country lane. Visitors at each park may use the facilities at the other. Yare Village has over 300 pitches which include 178 touring pitches (123 with 16A electricity, 2 fully serviced) on a separate open, level and grassy area. The remaining pitches are used for caravan holiday homes, most privately owned, some for rent. A large restaurant/bar providing club style entertainment in season and a takeaway service (12.00-19.00) overlooks a heated outdoor pool. The excellent playground and new all-weather sports court are far enough from the pitches to preserve peace and quiet. The amenities here would contribute to an enjoyable family holiday.

Facilities

Two toilet blocks offer clean, spacious, but fairly standard facilities. Unit for disabled persons. Baby room. Laundry. Dishwashing sinks. Shop and post office. Entertainment complex with restaurant, two bars and takeaway. Swimming and paddling pools (29/5-31/8). Play area and play field. Tennis. Off site: At Bure Village: indoor pool, gym, solarium, amusements and supermarket. Fishing 400 yds. Golf 3 miles. Riding 8 miles. Bus stop outside.

Open: 1 March - 31 October.

Directions

From Great Yarmouth take A143 signed Beccles. From the dual-carriageway at Bradwell turn right signed Burgh Castle into New Road. At mini-roundabout turn right into Butt Lane and follow this road for 1 mile to park on the left (care needed due to parked vehicles). O.S.GR: TM490050.

Charges 2007

Per pitch	£ 5.00 - £ 28.00

Special offer breaks available.

You might also like to consider...

UK3575 Stroud Hill Park

Fen Road, Pidley PE28 3DE (Cambridgeshire)
Tel: **01487 741333**. Email: **stroudhillpark@btconnect.com**

Opened in 2003 as an all year round, adult only site Stroud Hill Park is a well designed, high quality park; a credit to its owners, David and Jayne Newman. Developed from existing farmland where David grew up, the park has been landscaped to create a terraced effect and now incorporates a large fishing lake (well stocked with carp, tench, bream, rudd and roach) plus a superb tennis court. The attractive, timber framed barn that dominates the site is all the more impressive when you know that David built most of it; even to the canopy over the open fireplace. There are no half measures here, from the quality of the building itself through to the fittings throughout, everything has been well thought out and it adds up to a gem of new site. The barn is the hub of the site where you will find reception, shop, terrace, bar and a 44 seat restaurant (open Weds. to Sunday incl.) There are 60 large, slightly sloping pitches, of which 44 are hardstanding, and fully serviced with electricity (16A), fresh water and drainage. The hedges and shrubs around the site are young and need time to mature, but an atmosphere and character has quickly developed and already many return regularly. Affiliated to the Caravan Club, non-members are equally welcome.

Facilities

Toilets and spacious en-suite shower facilities are located in the main building along with a very well equipped room for disabled users. Good size laundry room plus vegetable preparation and dishwashing room, all spotlessly clean. Small, licensed shop stocks basic provisions, home-made cakes, local produce, gas and camping accessories. Attractive bar and café/restaurant. Fishing (£4 per day). All-weather tennis court.
Off site: Golf course, ten-pin bowling and paintball adjacent to site. Rding 0.5 miles. Peterborough, Ely, Cambridge, Huntingdon and St Ives all within easy reach.

Open: All year.

Directions

Leave A1 near Huntingdon, take A14 east. Leave A14 at A141, signed March. In Warboys, at roundabout, turn right on B1040 signed Pidley. In Pidley turn left just beyond church, Fen Road. Site is approx. 1 mile on right. O.S.GR: TL335787. GPS: N52:23.529 W00:02.226

Charges 2007

Per unit incl 2 persons, electricity	£ 21.00
tent incl. 2 persons	£ 15.00
extra person	£ 2.50
dog	£ 1.00

UK3580 Ferry Meadows Caravan Club Site

Ham Lane, Peterborough PE2 5UU (Cambridgeshire)
Tel: **01733 233526**

Three miles from bustling Peterborough and closer still to the East of England Showground, the immaculate Ferry Meadows is an ideal family holiday site occupying 30 acres of the 500 acre Nene Country Park. Meadows, lakes and woodlands provide ample opportunities to sample the facilities. These include water sports, fishing, golf, nature reserves, miniature railway and 60 miles of footpaths, bridleways and cycleways, all off road, even into the town centre. Open all year the site provides 254 pitches (16A electricity) – 160 grass pitches on one side of the park, informally laid out in small groups and surrounded by a variety of mature trees, and 94 gravel hardstandings just across the road for caravans and motorcaravans. A very small area (no electricity) is reserved for up to 10 tents. Families with children may prefer the grass area, from where they can keep a watchful eye on the well equipped playground.

Facilities

Two modern, well appointed and heated toilet blocks are of the usual high standard, with en-suite facilities for disabled visitors in one block. Baby/toddler washroom. Dishwashing sinks under cover, as well as a laundry room. Motorcaravan service point. The office stocks basic provisions. Tourist information room. Good play areas. TV socket and lead. WiFi in one area. Off site: Wheelchair hire in Nene Park. Steam railway 500 yards. Bus Service 800 yards. Pitch and put 800 yards. Nearest shops 1 mile. Restaurants within 0.5 miles. Peterborough, lido, night clubs and supermarkets 3 miles.

Open: All year.

Directions

From south on A1, do not turn onto A1139, but turn left, 1 mile on, at next junction (signed Showground, Chesterton, Alwalton) and immediately left onto A605, signed Peterborough. Continue straight on at three roundabouts, signed Nene Park. At fourth roundabout turn left into Ham Lane, signed Nene Park and Ferry Meadows. Site is on left 300 yards beyond level crossing. From the east follow the many Nene Park signs around Peterborough onto the A605 and then to the site. O.S.GR: TL151972.

Charges 2007

Per person	£ 3.90 - £ 5.40
child (5-16 yrs)	£ 1.30 - £ 2.15
pitch (non-member)	£ 10.30 - £ 14.10

UK3560 Highfield Farm Touring Park

Long Road, Comberton, Cambridge CB23 7DG (Cambridgeshire)
Tel: **01223 262308**. Email: **enquiries@highfieldfarmtouringpark.co.uk**

Situated five miles from Cambridge, this eight acre park is set in a delightfully quiet touring location yet close to major routes around Cambridge. The welcome is always warm from the friendly family owners. The facilities are of high quality and the grass and hedges are well cared for. Divided into five enclosures by conifers hedges, there are also shady glades for those who wish to retreat even further; plus one enclosure is reserved for those without children. Offering 60 numbered pitches for caravans or motorcaravans, and 60 for tents, pitching is around the outer edges. As a result, the park never looks crowded even when fully booked (which is frequently the case). All pitches have 10A electricity, 50 have gravel hardstanding, and most are level. A good dog walk is provided, which can be extended to a pleasant 1.5 mile walk, with seats, around the farm perimeter. A member of the Best of British group.

Facilities

Three heated toilet blocks provide more than adequate coverage and good facilities (showers 10 pence), all very clean and well maintained. Baby room but no dedicated provision for disabled visitors, although one block has extra wide doors and easy access. Laundry room. Small play area. Good shop. Motorcaravan service point. Excellent tourist information room. Bicycle hire. Gates closed midnight to 7.30. Off site: Comberton village 0.5 miles. Golf 2 miles. Fishing 3.5 miles. Cambridge 5 miles. Duxford War Museum and National Trust properties.

Open: 23 March - 31 October.

Directions

From M11 exit 12, take A603 towards Sandy. After 0.5 miles turn right, B1046 to Comberton. Turn right just before village signed Madingley (also caravan sign). Site on right just north of village. O.S GR: TL391571. GPS: N52:11.676 E00:02.020

Charges 2007

Per unit incl. 2 persons	£ 9.50 - £ 12.00
hiker or cyclist incl. tent	£ 8.25 - £ 9.75
extra person	£ 3.00
child (5-16 yrs)	£ 2.00
electricity	£ 2.50

No credit cards.

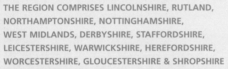

MAP 4

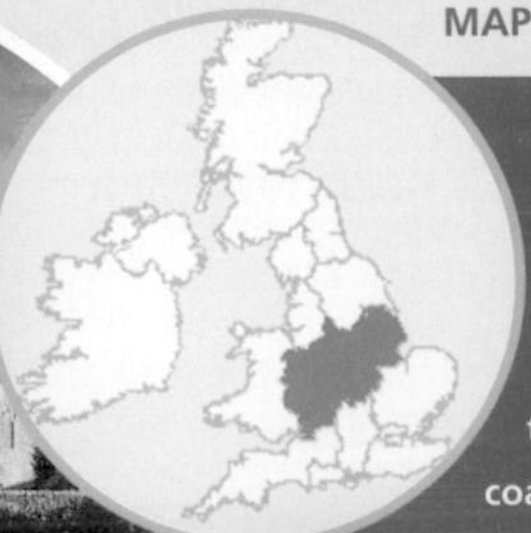

Spanning central England, from the ancient borders of Wales on the west across to Lincolnshire on the east coast, the Heart of England is rich in glorious rolling countryside, magnificent castles, fine stately houses and beautiful gardens.

THE REGION COMPRISES LINCOLNSHIRE, RUTLAND, NORTHAMPTONSHIRE, NOTTINGHAMSHIRE, WEST MIDLANDS, DERBYSHIRE, STAFFORDSHIRE, LEICESTERSHIRE, WARWICKSHIRE, HEREFORDSHIRE, WORCESTERSHIRE, GLOUCESTERSHIRE & SHROPSHIRE

The charming and diverse countryside of the Heart of England includes: the Lincolnshire Wolds, with the dramatic open landscape of the Fens; the ragged crags, dales and moorland of the Peak District National Park in Derbyshire and Staffordshire; the heathered hilltops of Shropshire; the famous Sherwood Forest, in the heart of Nottinghamshire; and the miles of lush green countryside of Herefordshire, dotted with black and white timber houses. Rutland Water is a mecca for watersports and the whole region offers superb opportunities for walking, cycling and more daring activities such as rock climbing and caving. The Cotswolds to the west of the region is the largest area of Outstanding Natural Beauty in England and Wales. Here you will find many traditional English villages, with charming country pubs and cottage gardens. Another significant feature of the region are the rivers and canals. Passing pretty towns and villages, a large canal network threads its way through the area, weaving through the Lincolnshire Fens, past the waterside bars and restaurants of Birmingham and along to estuaries of the rivers of Severn and Avon.

Places of interest

Lincolnshire: Belvoir Castle near Grantham.

Rutland: market towns of Oakham and Uppingham.

Northamptonshire: Silverstone; Althorp House.

Nottinghamshire: Nottingham Castle.

West Midlands: Birmingham; Cadbury World.

Derbyshire: Bakewell; Buxton; Chatsworth House.

Staffordshire: Alton Towers; Stoke-on-Trent.

Leicestershire: Snibston Discovery Park; Twycross Zoo.

Warwickshire: Warwick Castle; Stratford-upon-Avon.

Herefordshire: Hereford Cathedral.

Worcestershire: West Midland Safari Park.

Gloucestershire: Sudeley Castle; Cheltenham.

Shropshire: Shrewsbury and Whitchurch.

Did you know?

Herefordshire is one of the largest apple cider producers in the world.

The World Toe Wrestling Championship, held every June in Wetton, is a registered international sport.

The hollow trunk of the 'Mighty Tree' in Sherwood Forest is reputedly where Robin Hood and his Merry Men hid from the Sheriff of Nottingham.

Quite different from the more familiar tart, the Bakewell pudding was first created in the 1860s.

Rutland is the smallest county in Britain, measuring just 16 miles by 16 miles.

The Peak District contains over 50 reservoirs, including Ladybower, where the bouncing bomb used in World War II was tested.

UK3650 Cherry Tree Site

Huttoft Road, Sutton-on-Sea LN12 2RU (Lincolnshire)

Tel: **01507 441626**. Email: **info@cherrytreesite.co.uk**

This is a delightful, tranquil, adult only site and is a fine example of a small, good value touring park. It is a 15 minute walk from a Blue Flag beach and a short drive from some of the attractive villages of the Lincolnshire Wolds. A very warm welcome awaits from Geoff and Margaret Murray whose attention to detail is evident everywhere. The site is level, the grass is neatly trimmed and well drained, and screening is provided by lines of evergreen hedging. There are 60 good sized pitches of which 40 are for touring, all with 10A electricity and 10 'super pitches' with hardstanding. Buses stop outside hourly, and a shop and pub are within ten minutes walk. Mablethorpe beach is just 4 miles away and Skegness, with all its popular attractions is just down the road.

Facilities

The brick built toilet block can be heated and is immaculately kept, providing controllable hot showers, hairdryers and an en-suite unit for disabled visitors (Radar key required). Combined dishwashing and laundry room with washing machine, spin dryer and tumble dryer. Neat reception and separate tourist information. Gas available. Off site: Bicycle hire, tennis, bowls and fishing 1.5 miles. Golf 1 mile. Riding adjacent.

Open: 11 March - 29 October.

Directions

Sutton-on-Sea is 15 miles north of Skegness. The site is 1.5 miles south of the town on A52 coast road, with the entrance leading off a lay-by on the east. O.S.GR: TF518828. GPS: N53:17.568 E00:17.999

Charges 2007

Per unit incl. 2 persons and electricity	£ 13.00 - £ 16.00
extra person	£ 3.00
awning or extra pup tent	£ 1.00
dog	£ 0.50

Min. stay 3 nights at B.Hs.

UK3660 Walesby Woodlands Caravan Park

Walesby, Market Rasen LN8 3UN (Lincolnshire)

Tel: **01673 843285**. Email: **walesbywoodlands@talk21.com**

Surrounded by mature Forestry Commission woodland, this small family-owned, touring park is mainly very peaceful (if the wind is in a certain direction trains may be heard in the distance). The owners, Paul and Christine Burrows will make you very welcome. About a mile away is the small town of Market Rasen, but further afield and within easy driving distance, are Lincoln, the east coast including Skegness and, of course, the Lincolnshire Wolds. There are 60 well spaced pitches, 52 with 10A electricity, marked out on a single, mainly flat, grassy field divided by a central gravel road and with a double row of trees providing useful visual screening. The Viking Way passes through Walesby and there are many other shorter walks in the forest and surrounding area.

Facilities

The single, heated toilet block (£5 deposit charged for the key) is spacious and ample for the site. It has toilet facilities for disabled people and outside, covered, dishwashing sinks. Laundry room. Small shop with information section (all season). Coffee shop is planned. Battery charging. Gas supplies. Play area. No kite flying (overhead wires). Winter caravan storage. Off site: Market Rasen racecourse 2 miles. Golf 1.5 miles. Riding 2 miles. Fishing 3 miles.

Open: 1 March - 31 October.

Directions

Market Rasen is on the A46, 17 miles north east of Lincoln. Park is a mile northeast of the town, just off the B1203, and is signed from all the main approach roads. O.S.GR: TF117907.
GPS: N53:24.081 W00:19.260

Charges guide

Per unit incl. 2 persons	£ 10.00 - £ 12.00
with electricity	£ 12.00 - £ 13.50
extra person	£ 1.50
child (under 12 yrs)	£ 1.25
awning	£ 1.25 - £ 1.50

UK3675 Willow Holt Camping & Caravan Park

Lodge Road, Tattershall LN4 4JS (Lincolnshire)

Tel: **01526 343111**. Email: **enquiries@willowholt.co.uk**

Willow Holt is a pleasant park with plenty of potential. It will appeal, in particular, to fishing enthusiasts and to those who would like a quiet location from which to explore this interesting corner of Lincolnshire with its RAF associations. It covers some 25 acres of woodland and former gravel pits, with the camping areas on flat land alongside the large lake. There are 60 pitches occupied on a seasonal basis but a further 47 are available for touring units. All have 10A electricity and water taps close by. An area without electricity is available for tents. There are a few privately owned mobile homes along the lakeside. The young owners are working hard to improve the facilities; the roads have been resurfaced with gravel and a new reception building is under construction. There are plenty of interesting places to visit nearby, including Tattershall Castle, the Battle of Britain Memorial Flight, Woodhall Spa, with its Kinema in the Woods, and Horncastle. Further afield are Lincoln, Boston, Skegness and the Lincolnshire coast.

Facilities

The toilet block is small and must be under considerable pressure at busy times. Showers are preset and hot water is free to the open style basins. Motorcaravan service point. Laundry room with washing machines, dryers and iron/ironing board. No facilities for disabled visitors or for babies and young children. Free fishing (permit required). Off site: Golf and riding 2.5 miles. Shops, pubs and restaurants in Tattershall (1.5 miles) and Woodhall Spa (2.5 miles). Beaches 30 miles.

Open: 15 March - 31 October.

Directions

Tattershall is 20 miles southeast of Lincoln on the A153 Sleaford - Horncastle/Louth road. Site is 1.5 miles north of town; from Market Place follow brown campsite sign along Lodge Road. Entrance is on left before junction with B1192 to Woodhall Spa. O.S.GR: TF201592. GPS: N53:07.190 W00:12.474

Charges 2007

Per unit incl. 2 persons	£ 10.00 - £ 14.00
incl. electricity	£ 12.00 - £ 16.00
extra person	£ 2.00
child	£ 1.00

UK3680 Ashby Park

West Ashby, Horncastle LN9 5PP (Lincolnshire)

Tel: **01507 527966**. Email: **ashbyparklakes@aol.com**

Ashby Park is a pleasant, well run site located in 70 acres of former gravel pits that now provide seven attractive fishing lakes. There is a series of clearings occupied by privately owned caravan holiday homes and by 77 touring pitches. Most are on grass, but some have hardstanding. All have access to electricity (16A) and 12 super pitches also have hardstanding, water tap and waste water drain. Lakeside pitches will no doubt appeal to anglers, whereas families with young children will probably prefer to be further away from the lakes, which are inevitably unfenced. This is a peaceful site in an interesting area. The market town of Horncastle is just down the road, whilst nearby are Tattershall Castle, the Battle of Britain Memorial Flight and Woodhall Spa with its 'Kinema in the Woods'. Further afield are Lincoln, Boston, Skegness and the Lincolnshire coast.

Facilities

Three toilet blocks are well maintained and equipped, with open style washbasins and controllable showers; all hot water is metered (20p). Good en-suite facilities for disabled visitors. Laundry room with washing machine and dryer. Limited dishwashing (in new block – a long walk from lakeside pitches). Motorcaravan service point. Gas sales. Tourist information. Fishing (day ticket £4.50). Off site. Golf 0.5 miles. Riding 5 miles. Sailing and lakeside beach 6 miles. Seaside beaches 20 miles. Shops, pubs and restaurants in Horncastle 2 miles.

Open: 1 March - 30 November.

Directions

Horncastle is 20 miles east of Lincoln on the A153 Sleaford - Louth road. Turn west off the A153 1.6 miles north of the town along Docking Lane and follow signs to site in 0.8 miles. O.S.GR: TF251724. GPS: N53:14.126 W00:07.585

Charges 2007

Per unit incl. 2 adults, 2 children	£ 11.50
incl. electricity	£ 15.00
serviced pitch	£ 18.50 - £ 20.00

UK3690 Bainland Country Park

Horncastle Road, Woodhall Spa LN10 6UX (Lincolnshire)

Tel: **01526 352903**. Email: **bookings@bainland.co.uk**

A family park with many amenities, Bainland has 170 spacious, level pitches in hedged bays (120 touring pitches) grouped in circles and islands and linked by curving roads. There are 51 fully serviced pitches with hardstanding, honeycombed for awning, individual water, drainage and chemical disposal, electricity and TV aerial hook-ups. The remainder of the pitches are either on gravel hardstanding or level grass, all with 16A electricity. The friendly reception is housed in a pleasant Swiss-style building together with the heated indoor pool and jacuzzi, a bistro and spacious bar area. These overlook the 18-hole, par 3 golf course and outdoor bowls area. Bainland is 1.5 miles from Woodhall Spa, with its old fashioned charm and Dambusters associations, yet deep in the heart of the Lincolnshire Wolds, surrounded by mature trees and with direct access to woods for walking dogs. A member of the Best of British group.

Facilities

Three modern, well equipped, heated toilet blocks including a baby room, unisex en-suite shower rooms, family bathroom, fully equipped unit for disabled people. Laundry room. Enclosed dishwashing and separate laundry sinks. Motorcaravan service points. Licensed shop (Feb-Dec). Bistro and bar (all year). Indoor pool (under 16s must be accompanied by an adult). Adventure playground. Trampolines. Crazy golf. Croquet. TV and games room. Soft play area. Floodlit tennis dome with 3-4 courts including badminton (the dome comes off in the summer). Leisure activities, including the pool, are individually booked and paid for at reception. Some entertainment in high season. Winter caravan storage. Off site: Fishing 3 miles. Riding 6 miles.

Open: All year (in winter, 'super' pitches only).

Directions

Woodhall Spa is 18 miles southeast of Lincoln. Entrance to park is off B1191 Horncastle road 1.5 miles northeast of the village by 50 mph sign. O.S.GR: TF214637. GPS: N53:09.517 W00:11.011

Charges 2007

Per unit incl. electricity	£ 15.00 - £ 30.00
serviced pitch	£ 16.00 - £ 36.00
pup tent	free - £ 4.00
dog	£ 2.00 - £ 4.00

Special rate for firework display (min. 2 nights, 4/5 Nov). Discounts for senior citizens.

UK3692 Glen Lodge Touring Park

Glen Lodge, Edlington Moor, Woodhall Spa LN10 6UL (Lincolnshire)

Tel: **01526 353523**

This quiet, modern site is ideal for couples and families who enjoy the rural lifestyle, yet it is only just over a mile from the thriving village of Woodhall Spa which retains much of its old-fashioned charm. All 35 pitches have hardstanding and 10A electricity hook-ups (one or two appeared to need long leads) and are served by shingle roads with some street lighting. The grass and flowerbeds are obviously tended by someone who enjoys gardening. In fact, the whole park has a much-loved feel. Places to visit include the Battle of Britain Memorial Flight, Tattershall Castle, Horncastle with its antiques centre and the city of Lincoln. Skegness is only 26 miles away.

Facilities

The modern heated toilet block (key-pad access) is spotlessly clean with vanity style washbasins and piped music. Facilities for disabled visitors. Washing machine and dryer. Off site: Pub 0.5 miles, golf 2 miles, fishing 5 miles, riding 6 miles.

Open: 1 March - 30 November.

Directions

Woodhall Spa is 18 miles southeast of Lincoln. From mini-roundabout in village turn northeast towards Bardney on B1190 (Stixwould Road) past Petwood Hotel. In about 1 mile at sharp left bend, turn right. Site is 300 yards on left. O.S.GR: TF189647. GPS: N53:09.974 W00:13.200

Charges 2007

Per unit incl. 2 persons and electricity	£ 13.00
extra person (over 4 yrs)	£ 2.00
No credit cards.	

UK3730 Skegness Sands Touring Site

Winthorpe Avenue, Skegness PE25 1QZ (Lincolnshire)

Tel: **01754 761484**. Email: **info@skegness-sands.com**

This very well organised touring site is part of a much larger caravan holiday home park, but has its own entrance. It is a modern, well appointed site adjacent to the promenade and beach. There are 85 pitches, all level and with electricity (16A). 48 are grass (3 tents only) and 37 gravel hardstandings, four of which are fully serviced. Site lighting is good throughout and there are regular security patrols. The gate to the promenade is kept locked at all times, campers getting a key. Local attractions include Funcoast World, Fantasy Island, Hardy's Animal Farm, a seal sanctuary and Gibraltar Point National Nature Reserve. The site is a member of the Caravan Club's 'managed under contract' scheme, members and non-members are all made very welcome.

Facilities

The good quality, heated toilet block includes washbasins in curtained cubicles plus three family shower rooms with WC and washbasin and a well equipped room for disabled people. Two dishwashing sinks are outside under cover. Laundry room. Gas supplies on site. Hairdressing salon. Indoor heated swimming pool (Spring B.H - 30 Sept; adult £3, child £2). Small modern playground. Off site: Well stocked shop/post office 200 m. Pubs, fast food outlets and a supermarket are all within easy walking distance. 'Hail and ride' bus service to Skegness and Ingoldmells at 200 m. Fishing 1 mile. Golf 2 miles. Riding 5 miles. Also stock car racing and 10-pin bowling.

Open: All year.

Directions

Site is off the A52 Boston - Skegness - Mablethorpe road, 1.75 miles north of Skegness town centre. Turn east opposite 'Garden City' public house into Winthorpe Avenue and site entrance is on the left at far end of road. Note: This entrance is locked from 17.00 - 8.00. At other times, access is by the Roman Bank entrance, a short distance further north on A52. New arrivals please contact site if unable to arrive before 17.00. O.S.GR: TF570640. GPS: N53:10.008 E00:20.970

Charges 2007

Per person	£ 4.50 - £ 5.80
child (5-16 yrs)	£ 1.50 - £ 2.50
pitch	£ 4.80 - £ 8.00
'super' pitch supplement	£ 3.00

UK3750 Foreman's Bridge Caravan Park

Sutton St James, Spalding PE12 0HU (Lincolnshire)

Tel: **01945 440346**. Email: **foremansbridge@btconnect.com**

Foreman's Bridge is an extremely pleasant and compact park and the new owners are now well established. It makes an excellent base from which to explore the Fens, including Spalding, famous for its annual flower festival held at the beginning of May. Fishing and cycling are popular pastimes in the area, indeed bicycle hire and fishing licences are both available from the site, with fishing possible in the river that runs just past the entrance. Occupying a large, level and grassy meadow surrounded by trees and high hedges which give it a very secluded feel, the park has 40 level pitches, of which 28 are touring pitches, all with electricity (10A) and 20 with gravel hardstanding. There are now holiday homes for sale on site. Fruit trees, flower beds, hanging baskets and planted troughs provide bursts of vibrant colour. At times there can be noise from military aircraft.

Facilities

The modern, brick built toilet unit is spacious and kept very clean, providing really large individual shower rooms with seats and washbasins (showers on payment). Dishwashing room. Laundry room with washing machine, dryer and ironing. Recycling of glass, cans and paper. Basic provisions and gas are kept. Fishing. Bicycle hire. Site barrier (£5 deposit for card). Winter caravan storage. Off site: Small shop in village 1 mile. Golf 3 miles. Riding 8 miles. Coast 12 miles (The Wash); nearest beach 32 miles.

Open: 1 March - 15 January.

Directions

Sutton St James is 26 miles northeast of Peterborough and 17 miles west of Kings Lynn. From A17 Spalding - Kings Lynn road turn south on the B1390 at Long Sutton towards Sutton St James for about 2 miles. Site entrance is on the left immediately after the bridge. O.S.GR: TF410198. GPS: N52:45.471 E00:05.280

Charges 2007

Per unit incl. 2 persons	£ 10.00 - £ 14.00
extra person	£ 3.00
child	£ 2.00
electricity	£ 2.00
No credit cards.	

UK3760 Tallington Lakes Camping & Caravanning

Barholm Road, Tallington, Stamford PE9 4RJ (Lincolnshire)

Tel: **01778 347000**. Email: **info@tallington.com**

The 160 acre site spreads around a series of lakes that provide for many watersport activities including water-ski (slalom and jump courses), jet-ski, sailing (sailboards and dinghies) and angling. The touring campsite has 118 pitches, of which 106 have electric hook-ups (10A), and 11 are on hardstandings. Major roads are tarmac, with gravel roads serving the pitches, and maturing hedges and shrubs separate the rows. The complex also has eight mobile homes for hire and there are some 200 privately-owned holiday homes. Local places of interest are Stamford Museum, Burghley House, Sacrewell Farm and Country Centre and the Nene Valley Railway.

Facilities

The heated sanitary unit has facilities for babies, small children and disabled visitors. Additional WCs and showers (also used by the water skiers). Laundry and dishwashing facilities. Motorcaravan service point. Bar and restaurant. Swimming and paddling pools. Climbing wall. Go-karting. Watersports. Fishing. Dry-ski slope, snowboard centre and tennis. Small, well fenced, adventure style playground (age 5-12 yrs). Key-card for toilet unit and barrier (£10 refundable deposit). Off site: Bus stop 1 mile. Golf, riding and bicycle hire 5 miles.

Open: 1 March - 31 January.

Directions

From A16, midway between Stamford and Market Deeping, just east of the railway crossing at Tallington, turn north into Barholm Road and site entrance is on the right. (site is signed). O.S.GR: TF085090.

Charges guide

Per person	£ 2.00
pitch	£ 6.00
electricity	£ 2.00
awning or pup tent	£ 1.50
dog (max. 2 per unit)	£ 1.00

171

UK3765 Woodland Waters

Willoughby Road, Ancaster, Grantham NG32 3RT (Lincolnshire)

Tel: **01400 230888**. Email: **info@woodlandwaters.co.uk**

This attractive holiday park occupies 70 acres of woodland, gently sloping grassland and lakes, with the caravan park itself taking up about 20 of them. Although the site has a capacity of 120 pitches, only 60 (all with 10A electricity and water taps nearby) are regularly used. A further 20 with electricity are kept for rallies and there are areas for camping and those not requiring hook-ups. The main pitches are numbered but not marked (jockey-wheels go on the number pad). The land slopes gently down to the 14 acre lake and the pitches nearer the water are more level, although probably not suitable for those with younger children since there is no fencing. Reception is housed in a neat modern building at the entrance to the park, the welcome is warm, fishing tickets are sold and tourist information is available. The pleasant bar and restaurant (open to the public) occupy a chalet-style building near the lake; the menu seemed varied and reasonably priced. There are four fishing lakes (plus a junior pool), with carp, tench, bream, roach, rudd and pike. Walking and birdwatching are other featured attractions of the park, while days out could include Nottingham, Lincoln and even Skegness (50 miles). Some aircraft noise is possible.

Facilities

A single, modern, heated toilet block provides clean, well maintained toilets, washbasins (in cubicles for ladies) and free showers (controllable for ladies, push-button for men). These facilities might possibly be under some pressure if the additional camping areas were fully occupied, but regular visitors had nothing but praise for them. Dishwashing sinks under cover. Small laundry room with washing machine, tumble dryer and iron, but no laundry sinks. Motorcaravan service point. Bar and restaurant with takeaway (all year). Play area. Off site: Limited bus service in Ancaster. Shop in village (1 mile). Go-karting and paint-ball 1 mile. Golf 3 miles. Riding 6 miles.

Open: All year.

Directions

Ancaster is 8 miles northeast of Grantham and 19 miles south of Lincoln. The park entrance is off the A153 Grantham - Sleaford road, 600 yards west of the junction with B6403 High Dyke road (Ermine Street). O.S.GR: SK973437.

Charges 2007

Per unit incl. up to 4 persons	£ 11.00 - £ 12.00
with electricity	£ 14.50 - £ 16.00
extra person	£ 2.00
child	£ 1.00
dog	£ 1.00

UK3770 Low Farm Touring Park

Spring Lane, Folkingham, Sleaford NG34 0SJ (Lincolnshire)

Tel: **01529 497322**

This quiet secluded park is a lovely spot either just to relax or to tour the Lincolnshire countryside. Jane and Nigel Stevens are working hard to make this site a pleasant place to stay and have a well laid out park offering good quality facilities which are very clean and tidy. The site is on the edge of the village of Folkingham with a pub (currently serving food at lunch time only) and a couple of small shops. There are some pleasant walks around the village which is set in attractive Lincolnshire countryside. The site offers 36 touring pitches, 35 of which have electric hook-ups. Larger shops and places of interest are in and around Bourne (9 miles), Sleaford (10 miles), Grantham (14 miles), Lincoln and Peterborough (both 26 miles).

Facilities

Controllable free showers. Dishwashing and laundry sinks. Washing machine. Tourist information. Large field where children can play (also sometimes used by tenters). Off site: Fishing 2 miles. Golf 6 miles. Riding 7 miles.

Open: Easter - 30 September.

Directions

Folkingham is on the A15 Lincoln - Peterborough road, 2 miles south of the roundabout junction with the A52 (Nottingham/Grantham - Boston). Park is on southern edge of village; at foot of hill at campsite sign, turn west and site is at end of lane. O.S.GR: TF070333. GPS: N52:53.211 W00:24.670

Charges guide

Per unit incl. 2 persons	£ 8.00 - £ 10.00
extra person	£ 2.00
extra child (over 5 yrs)	£ 1.00
electricity	£ 2.00
awning	£ 0.50
No credit cards.	

UK3850 Rivendale Caravan & Leisure Park

Buxton Road, Alsop-en-le-Dale, Ashbourne DE6 1QU (Derbyshire)

Tel: **01335 310311**. Email: **enquiries@rivendalecaravanpark.co.uk**

This is an unusual park, recently developed in the bowl of a hill quarry that was last worked 50 years ago. The steep quarry walls shelter three sides with marvellous views over the Peak National Park countryside to the south. A wide access road passes the renovated stone building which houses reception, a shop, bar and a café/restaurant. It gently climbs to a horseshoe shaped area providing 100 pitches, most of generous size, with 16A electricity. The pitches, a mixture of hardstanding and half grass, half hardstanding, are divided by shrubs which are now maturing well with a further, open, marked grass area accessed by hard core roads. All pitches are within easy reach of the central stone-built toilet block which is in keeping with the environment and thoughtfully provided with under-floor heating. The park takes up about 11 acres and a further 26 acres belong to the owners with certain parts suitable for walking – a must to appreciate the Derbyshire countryside with its dry stone walls, wild flowers and a little more of the quarry history. The park is situated almost on the Tissington Trail for walking or off road cycling and linking with the High Peak and Monsal Dale Trail. Other spectacular walks and cycle rides run along the Manifold, Wye and Dove valleys.

Facilities

First rate toilet facilities include some washbasins in cubicles for ladies, and an excellent en-suite room for disabled visitors. Laundry room. Glass and paper recycling bins. Bar (evenings) and café with home-made and local food (open mornings, lunch times and evenings, both with limited opening in low season). Special events monthly and games in main season. Shop (all essentials). Off site: Bicycle hire and riding 5 miles. Sailing and boat launching 8 miles. Fishing and golf 10 miles. Alton Towers 35 minutes drive. Chatsworth House and Gardens, Heights of Abraham and Guillivers Kingdom near.

Open: All year excl. 9 January - 2 February.

Directions

Park is about 7 miles north of Ashbourne on the A515 to Buxton, on the eastern side of the road. It is well signed between the turnings east to Alsop Moor and Matlock (A5012), but take care as this is a very fast section of the A515. O.S.GR: SK161566. GPS: N53:06.383 W01:45.634

Charges guide

Per unit incl. 2 persons	
and electricity	£ 12.30 - £ 14.50
extra person	£ 2.00
child (4-15 yrs)	£ 1.50
dog	£ 1.00
Camping Cheques accepted.	

Beautiful surroundings in the Peak District National Park. Open all year except 8 Jan – 1 Feb. Ideal for cycling, walking, outdoor and adventure sports. Convenient for Chatsworth, Alton Towers & Dove Dale. Holiday homes for sale.

www.Rivendalecaravanpark.co.uk Tel: +44 (0)1335 310311 or 310441

UK3815 Lickpenny Touring Park

Lickpenny Lane, Tansley, Matlock DE4 5GF (Derbyshire)

Tel: **01629 583040**. Email: **lickpenny@btinternet.com**

This spacious caravan park on a hill above Matlock has 122 terraced pitches, all on hardstandings (tents are not accepted) and with 16A electricity. Of these, 100 are touring pitches and 27 are fully serviced. Looking at the rows of mature trees and bushes, it seems hard to believe that this site was only created for the 2003 season; the enthusiastic owners have taken full advantage of the fact that this was previously a market garden and are continuing to work very hard to maintain high standards and improve facilities. Pitches are large and separated by shrubs and bushes. Buildings are of natural stone and well equipped. Recreational grassy areas and attractive flower borders are well tended, whilst the top corner of the park has been kept as woodland. Reception incorporates a small shop (basics only at present) and tourist information. Local attractions include Matlock Bath and the Heights of Abraham, Chatsworth House, Haddon Hall, Hardwick Hall, Eyam and Castleton.

Facilities

Two well equipped, heated toilet blocks include free controllable showers and some washbasins in cubicles. Good facilities for disabled people. Family room with small bath, toilet and washbasin. Laundry room with washing machines, dryers, irons and ironing boards. Chemical disposal points. Motorcaravan service point. Security barrier with keypad access at all times. Off site: Bus service from end of the road. Riding 1 mile. Fishing 3 miles. Golf 4 miles. Bicycle hire 6 miles. Woodland walk to Garden Centre with restaurant serving snacks and lunches (200 yards).

Open: All year.

Directions

Matlock is 18 miles west of the M1 at exit 28. From motorway, follow signs for Matlock on the A38, A61 and A615. After 5 miles on A615 turn north on Lickpenny Lane to site (signed). From Matlock take A615; after Tansley fork left on B6014 (Clay Cross) and turn right at top of hill after Garden Centre. O.S.GR: SK339598. GPS: N53:08.072 W01:29.429

Charges 2007

Per unit incl. 2 persons	£ 17.00 - £ 19.00
extra person	£ 4.00
child (0-14 yrs)	£ 1.50

UK3840 Lime Tree Park

Dukes Drive, Buxton SK17 9RP (Derbyshire)

Tel: **01298 22988**. Email: **info@limetreeparkbuxton.co.uk**

A select park with high quality, modern facilities, Lime Tree is in a convenient, edge of town location that makes a very good base for touring the Peak District. There are 99 pitches including some for seasonal and rental units, the 64 for tourists with 10A electricity (hardstandings available) and an area for tents (some terracing but mainly sloping ground) are on the two upper terraces which have the best views but are slightly more exposed. Below are areas set aside for late arrivals and the caravan holiday homes (most privately owned, some for rent). On site is a small shop for gas and basics, and a recently extended children's playground. Buxton town centre is a comfortable stroll away.

Facilities

A modern toilet building serves the caravan and motorcaravan area, including some washbasins in cubicles, controllable showers, a baby room with the very latest design of baby bath, and a family room with facilities for disabled people, whilst the refitted original unit serves the tent area. Both units can be heated and have top quality fittings. Dishwashing sinks are outside under cover. Laundry room with washing machine and dryer. Motorcaravan service area. Shop. Play area. Games/TV room. Off site: The nearest pub serving food is just around the corner. Riding and golf 1 mile, fishing, bicycle hire, sailing and boat-launching 5 miles. Alton Towers 22 miles.

Open: 1 March - 31 October.

Directions

Park is on outskirts of Buxton and is signed from A515 Buxton - Ashbourne road 1 mile south of town. From town, immediately after hospital bear sharp left into Dukes Drive, go under railway viaduct and site is on the right. From south watch out for sharp turn right at foot of hill (signed in advance). O.S.GR: SK069725.

Charges 2007

Per unit incl. 2 persons	£ 13.00
with electricity	£ 17.00
extra person	£ 5.00
child (5-15 yrs)	£ 2.00
awning	£ 2.00

UK3980 Longnor Wood Caravan & Camping Park

Longnor, nr. Buxton SK17 0NG (Derbyshire)

Tel: **01298 83648**. Email: **info@longnorwood.co.uk**

A secluded rural location, deep in the heart of the Peak District, Longnor Wood is an ideal environment for a relaxing break from the outside world. It is a good base for walking, red deer and bird watching (barn owls) and serious cycling – the area is very hilly. There are 47 touring pitches plus an additional 14 pitches for holiday homes. Pitches are level, some on small terraces, all with 10A electric hook-ups. There are 17 with multi-services (electricity, water, waste water and TV aerial connections) and 40 on hardstanding. The tenting area is at the top of the site with wonderful views over the National Park, but you may have a problem with tent pegs as the topsoil can be rather thin in places. There is a well appointed late arrivals area at the entrance. Reception has a brochure with the history of the old market town of Longnor (where 'Peak Practice' was filmed), which includes several places worth visiting. This is an adult only park (over 18 yrs).

Facilities

The single heated building has been recently refurbished and includes cubicles with a toilet and washbasin, spacious showers and has dishwashing sinks under cover, and a microwave oven (donations to charity). Laundry with washing machine, tumble dryer and spin dryer. Reception stocks basic requirements. Gas supplies. Putting green, badminton and boules courts. Dogs accepted, max. 2 per unit. Site is not suitable for American RVs. Off site: Markets in Buxton (Tues/Sat), Leek (Wed). Sightseeing opportunities include Dove Dale and the Manifold Valley, Arbor Low Stone Circle, and Flash, at 1,580 ft. is the highest village in England. Fishing 5 miles, golf 8 miles, riding 8 miles.

Open: All year excl. 11 January - 28 February.

Directions

Longnor village is on the B5053, about 6 miles south of Buxton. Site is west of village (where it is signed) on a minor road (1 mile). Also signed from the A53 between Leek and Buxton, turning next to the Winking Man public house. O.S.GR: SK072640.

Charges 2007

Per unit incl. 2 persons and electricity	£ 15.50
serviced pitch incl 2 persons	£ 17.00
extra person	£ 3.50
tent incl 2 persons	£ 13.50

LONGNOR WOOD
CARAVAN & CAMPING PARK

Longnor Wood is a small select park just for adults. A warm welcome awaits all our visitors who will find peace and tranquility. We are located in the heart of the Peak National Park, an area of outstanding natural beauty, with unspoilt, dramatic rolling countryside and charming villages. Facilities include electrical hook-ups, heated toilet and shower blocks, Laundry Room, Putting Green, Boules Court and Badminton.
Open 1st March - 10th January.

Longnor Wood Caravan & Camping Park, Longnor, Nr Buxton, Derbyshire, SK17 0NG
Tel: 01298 83648   www.longnorwood.co.uk

UK3904 Greendale Farm Caravan & Camping Park

Pickwell Lane, Whissendine, Oakham LE15 7LB (Rutland)

Tel: **01664 474516**. Email: **enq@rutlandgreendale.co.uk**

This is a delightful little, adult only park set in rolling countryside, ideal for those seeking peace and tranquillity. It is very eco-friendly and extremely well appointed for such a small site. Reception, the shop and the toilet facilities are in a modern building adjoining the owners' house. The shop is well stocked with essentials and local produce. It also has one of the most comprehensive information displays we have seen on any campsite. This includes charts for visitors to record birds seen on the park – the list is impressive – walking and cycle routes and pub menus. There are weekly meetings for birdwatchers, would-be artists (the office is decorated with the paintings produced by visitors over the past five years) and photographers. Cooked breakfasts are available on Sundays. There are only 15 pitches, 14 with 10 or 16A electricity, so it's worth checking availability!

Facilities

Each of the two rooms of the toilet block has a power-shower, WCs and two washbasins (cubicles for the ladies). All is beautifully appointed and immaculately kept. Washing machine and dryer. Small open air swimming pool (6 x 3 m; £1 charge), heated by solar-panels, with summer house. Two bicycles for hire. Off site: Village with bus service 0.5 miles. Riding 4 miles. Fishing 6 miles. Golf 8 miles. Sailing, bird-watching, walking, cycling (and bicycle hire) and fishing at Rutland Water 8 miles.

Open: Easter - end Spetember.

Directions

Whissendine is just off the A606 Oakham - Melton Mowbray road. Approach from this road and not through the village. From Oakham ignore first turn to Whissendine, continue 2 miles and turn right at site sign. From Melton ignore first two turns to Whissendine; turn left 0.6 mile after Rutland sign. Park is on right in 0.6 mile. O.S.GR:SK819133. GPS: N52:42.710 W00:47.317

Charges 2007

Per unit incl. two persons and electricity	£ 15.00 - £ 18.00
extra person	£ 4.00

175

UK3910 Shardaroba Camping & Caravanning Club Site

Silverhill Lane, Teversal NG17 3JJ (Nottinghamshire)

Tel: **01623 551838**

In a peaceful village location, and yet surprisingly close to the motorway network, this attractive, six acre campsite has 100 pitches. It is beautifully kept and has recently won awards. Many of the spacious touring pitches are on hardstandings, arranged in well spaced rows surrounded by areas of grass and flower beds. All have electric hook-ups (16A), and 20 are multi-serviced. A grassed area for campers has a covered patio nearby with tables and chairs. Adjacent is an attractive country park.

Facilities

Excellent, well equipped, heated toilet block with spacious showers, and brand new family room. Shower room and toilet/wash room for disabled visitors. Separate laundry. Separate building with six full suites (WC, washbasin, shower) and unisex toilet/washbasin next to camping area. Motorcaravan service point. Shop with basics. Calor gas. Playground. Off site: Golf 800 yds. Riding 200 yds. Fishing, bicycle hire, pub, bakery, chip shop and general stores all within 1 mile. Sailing 2 miles.

Open: All year.

Directions

Teversal is central in a triangle formed by M1 junctions 28 and 29, and Mansfield. Site is signed off B6014 at western end of the village, turning north by the Carnarvon Arms into Silverhill Lane. Site entrance is 300 yds. on left. O.S.GR: SK485625. GPS: N53:08.911 W01:17.750

Charges guide

Per person	£ 6.00 - £ 6.90
child (3-14 yrs)	£ 2.05 - £ 2.15
pitch (non member)	£ 5.40

UK3920 Riverside Caravan Park

Central Avenue, Worksop S80 1ER (Nottinghamshire)

Tel: **01909 474118**

A town centre touring park, adjacent to the Worksop cricket ground, this excellent site is attractive and surprisingly peaceful. Riverside is within easy walking distance of the town centre pedestrian precinct and shops, and the Chesterfield Canal runs close to its northern side offering delightful towpath walks or fishing. For those who cannot resist the thwack of leather on willow, this site is ideal. Of the 60 marked level pitches, 50 are for touring, mainly on gravel hardstanding, others are on grass and some are separated by trees and low rails, and all have electric hook-ups (10A).

Facilities

The modern sanitary unit near reception can be heated and has all the usual facilities, although showers are on payment (20p). No laundry, but a launderette is close by in the town. Off site: Fishing 0.5 miles. Several golf courses 1 mile. Bicycle hire 4 miles. Squash and flat or crown green bowling nearby. Campers are made very welcome at the cricket ground clubhouse.

Open: All year.

Directions

Easiest approach to Park is from A57/A60 roundabout west of the town – third roundabout from the A1. Turn east (at Little Chef) on B6024 towards town centre. Site is well signed: in 400 yds. O.S.GR: SK580790. GPS: N53:18.360 W01:07.720

Charges 2007

Per pitch incl. 2 persons,	£ 6.00
child (5-13 years)	£ 2.00
No credit cards.	

UK3940 Smeaton's Lakes Touring Caravan & Fishing Park

Great North Road, South Muskham, Newark-on-Trent NG23 6ED (Nottinghamshire)

Tel: **01636 605088**. Email: **lesley@smeatonslakes.co.uk**

This 82 acre site is really ideal for anglers, with four fishing lakes (coarse, carp and pike) and river fishing on the Trent. Smeaton's Lakes has tarmac access roads and a modern building near the entrance housing reception and the original sanitary facilities. There are 130 pitches of which 100 have electricity (16A). Non-anglers might choose this park if visiting events at nearby Newark Showground, or Newark town (1 mile) with its castle and various weekly markets.

Facilities

Two toilet blocks (with keypad access) are heated and include a good unit for disabled people, but no laundry room. Laundry and dishwashing sinks are outside. Reception keeps gas, soft drinks, dairy produce, etc. and newspapers can be ordered. On-site concessions for lake and river fishing. Security cameras and night-time height barrier (about 6 ft). Off site: Bus stop at the end of the entry lane – buses run into Newark every hour until 22.00. Riding 2 miles.

Open: All year.

Directions

Park is just over a mile north of Newark on the Great North Road (to the east). From south on A1, take A46 west (signed Newark, then Leicester) and at next roundabout turn north on A6065/A616 (Ollerton) towards South Muskham. From north on A1 leave B6325 (Newark). GPS: N53:05.616 W00:49.240

Charges 2007

Per unit incl. 2 persons	£ 12.00 - £ 17.00
extra person	£ 2.00

UK3950 Orchard Park

Marnham Road, Tuxford, Newark NG22 0PY (Nottinghamshire)

Tel: **01777 870228**. Email: **info@orchardcaravanpark.co.uk**

This well established family run touring and caravan park has been created in an old fruit orchard in a quiet location, yet is very convenient for the A1. It has a friendly feel, with just 65 pitches, including 34 with hardstanding, 20 of which were occupied by seasonal units at the time of our visit. All pitches have access to electricity (10A). There is also a spacious camping field with views and plenty of room for ball games. Reception is at the owner's house with a nearby information cabin and at the far end of the park is a picnic area, an excellent children's adventure trail and a nature walk.

Facilities

The heated toilet block (with piped music) includes a well equipped room for disabled persons. Laundry with washing machines, dryer and dishwashing sinks, free spin dryer, iron and freezer for ice-packs. Small shop with basics and gas. Apples, pears and blackberries can be picked in season. WiFi available on most of site (£3 per weekend). Off site: Pub 0.5 miles, shops 1 mile. Riding 3 miles. Fishing 4 miles. Bicycle hire and golf 10 miles.

Open: March - October.

Directions

The park lies to the east of the A1. Leave at signs for Tuxford and turn east on A6075 towards Lincoln (A57), continue through village to the outskirts and turn south towards Marnham. Site is on right 0.5 miles after railway bridge (well signed in village). O.S.GR: SK750710. GPS: N53:13.776 W00:52.170

Charges 2007

Per unit incl. 2 persons	£ 15.00 - £ 20.00
child (4-12 yrs)	£ 1.00

UK3970 Glencote Caravan Park

Station Road, Cheddleton, Leek ST13 7EE (Staffordshire)

Tel: **01538 360745**. Email: **canistay@glencote.co.uk**

At the entrance to the Churnet Valley, three miles south of the market town of Leek, Glencote is a pleasant, family run park of six acres. It has 88 numbered touring pitches set on flat grass, all have patio style hardstandings with tarmac access roads, electrical connections (16A) and a dedicated water supply. Pretty flowerbeds and trees make a very pleasant environment. An attractive, sunken play area, on grass and bark with an abundance of shrubs and flowers, sits alongside the small (fenced) coarse fishing pool. There is also a refurbished barbecue area complete with gazebo.

Facilities

The toilet block is centrally situated and can be heated. Facilities include one private cabin for ladies, a combined shower and toilet for disabled visitors, a small laundry room. Mobile shop visits daily (except Sunday). Gas supplies. Max. 2 dogs per unit. Off site: Small supermarket and post office in Cheddleton 0.5 miles. Golf 4 miles. Bicycle hire 5 miles. Riding 10 miles.

Open: 1 February - end December.

Directions

Park is signed off A520 Leek - Stone road, 3.5 miles south of Leek on northern edge of Cheddleton Village. O.S.GR: SJ982524.

Charges 2007

Per unit incl. 2 persons and awning	£ 17.50
child (5-16 yrs)	£ 2.00
electricity	£ 2.00

Min. stay of 3 nights at B.Hs.

UK4040 Clent Hills Camping & Caravanning Club Site

Fieldhouse Lane, Romsley, Halesowen B62 0NH (West Midlands)

Tel: **01562 710015**

Conveniently close to Birmingham and only a couple of miles or so off the M5/M42 intersection, this site is a real surprise in terms of being quiet and peaceful and very pretty with good views. Its only disadvantage is that it is on sloping ground. There are some level pitches and these are all earmarked for motorcaravans. The 95 pitches are all of a good size, 74 with electricity (10/16A) and 17 with hardstanding. Generally this is a well run and attractive site, very usefully situated.

Facilities

The central sanitary toilet block can be heated and provides the latest facilities, including washbasins in cabins, hairdryers, baby room and a toilet and shower for disabled people. It was spotless when last visited. Washing machine, dryer and ironing facilities. Small play area with rubber safety surface. Gas supplies. Caravan storage. Off site: Riding 1 mile. Fishing 3 miles. Golf 7 miles.

Open: March - November.

Directions

From M5 junction 4 take A491, branch right to Romsley on B4551 and watch for site signs in Romsley village by shops. Site is on left. O.S.GR: SO955795.

Charges 2007

Per person	£ 4.90 - £ 7.25
child (6-18 yrs)	£ 2.15 - £ 2.15
non-member pitch fee	£ 5.65

UK4070 Somers Wood Caravan Park

Somers Road, Meriden CV7 7PL (Warwickshire)

Tel: **01676 522978**. Email: **somerswoodcpk@aol.com**

Somers Wood is a quiet, peaceful park, attractively situated amongst pine trees. It is beside an 18-hole golf corse and a fishing lake, both of which may be used by visitors and next to a bridle path which can be used to exercise dogs. From the reception building at the entrance, an oval gravel road provides access to 48 pitches, all on hardstanding and with 10A electricity hook-ups. Areas of woodland, carpeted with flowers in summer, surround the site and partition it into small intimate areas that create a rural feel. Log buildings blend comfortably into the surroundings providing reception, the owners' home, separate sa1nitary facilities and tourist information. There are also wooden table and chairs. This is a very pleasant park which only accepts adults and does no take tents. It is especially useful for those visiting the various shows at the NEC when it can get very busy.

Facilities

The central, heated sanitary block is fully equipped. Shower cubicles are especially large. Two dishwashing sinks on the veranda area. Laundry service at reception. Off site: Local shops and restaurant less than 1 mile and visitors also welcome to use the bar and restaurant at the golf club next door.

Open: 1 February - 12 December.

Directions

From M42 junction 6 (NEC) take A45 towards Coventry. Keep in left lane down to roundabout and exit on A452 (signed Leamington/Meriden), then turn left into Hampton Lane at the next roundabout. Site is signed with golf and fishing centres on the left. O.S.GR: SP228819.

Charges 2007

Per pitch incl. 2 persons and electricity	£ 17.00
extra person	£ 3.00
Special offers for some weeks.	

UK4075 Hollyfast Caravan Park

Wall Hill Road, Allesley, Coventry CV5 9EL (Warwickshire)

Tel: **024 7633 6411**. Email: **sales@hollyfastcaravanpark.co.uk**

Hollyfast is situated in beautiful countryside on the outskirts of Coventry, part of the park being set within a lovely woodland area giving peace and tranquillity all year round. Located on the Birmingham side of Coventry, this means a five minute drive into the centre of Coventry and just a ten minute drive to Birmingham's National Exhibition Centre. You will receive a friendly welcome and be directed to a very clean and well spaced site with 35 pitches of varying sizes with 6A electricity connections. You may be asked to park your car on a nearby car park. A new toilet block provides very clean facilities, along with a laundry room and games room. Rallies are welcome and a club house is provided with a stage, television and kitchen areas for these groups. Under the same ownership, a motorcaravan sales centre with caravan and motorhome storage, LPG and a children's play area are reached through the site.

Facilities

The modern toilet block provides simple clean facilities with good sized showers (3 per sex) and open washbasins. Toilet and shower for disabled campers. Laundry. Games room. Club house for rallies. Deposit for barrier (£25). Off site: The local area has shops, three pubs (hot and cold food), a golf course and a riding centre. Bus stop 1 mile for Coventry. Interesting British Road Transport museum. Birmingham, Stratford upon Avon, Leamington Spa and Warwick are within driving distance.

Open: All year.

Directions

From M1/M45 (or the M40/A46, or M69/A46) take A45 towards Birmingham. Turn right on A4114 and follow brown and white caravan signs. After turning by the White Lion pub, site is 0.5 miles on the left. From the north take M6 north of Birmingham or the M1 north (Nottingham) follow M42 to NEC, A45 towards Coventry and onto A4114 and as above. O.S.GR: SP303831.

Charges 2007

Per unit incl. 2 persons and electricity	£ 11.00 - £ 15.00
extra person	£ 2.50
child (5-15 yrs)	£ 1.50
dog	£ 1.00

UK4080 Riverside Caravan Park

Tiddington Road, Tiddington, Stratford-upon-Avon CV37 7AB (Warwickshire)

Tel: **01789 292312**. Email: **info@stratfordcaravans.co.uk**

On the bank of the River Avon, this spacious site has about 250 pitches in total, and about 100 privately owned mobile homes. The 125 touring pitches (no tents) are on level grass, all with electric hook-ups (16A) and some with TV aerial sockets. There is a small shop and cafe on site, which serves breakfasts and takeaways in addition to stocking a good selection of basic supplies. A clubhouse that incorporates a bar, restaurant, playground, games room and TV room is on the adjacent Rayford Park which is under the same management. There is a possible flood risk during periods of inclement weather. A river taxi runs to Stratford.

Facilities

The main toilet unit has been re-fitted to modern standards and is bright and comfortable with central heating. Spacious preset showers, some washbasins in cubicles, with a child-size toilet and shower in the ladies. Facilities for disabled guests. Washing machines and dryers. Slipway and fishing on-site. Courtesy river launch to Stratford. Gas supplies. No commercial vehicles are accepted. Off site: Shakespeare.

Open: 1 April - 31 October.

Directions

From Stratford take B4086 towards Wellesbourne. Site entrance is on left, after one mile, just before Tiddington village (ignore entrance to Rayford Park C.P.). O.S.GR: SP219559.

Charges 2007

Per unit incl. 4 persons	£ 20.00
extra person	£ 1.00
dog	£ 1.00

UK4090 Island Meadow Caravan Park

The Mill House, Aston Cantlow B95 6JP (Warwickshire)

Tel: **01789 488273**. Email: **holiday@islandmeadowcaravanpark.co.uk**

This peaceful, traditional, family run site is in a rural location, surrounded by the River Alne and its mill race. A good base for walking, cycling and birdwatching, it has 80 pitches in total, with 56 holiday homes (4 for rent) located around the perimeter. The 24 touring pitches are on the spacious, central area of the site, all have 10A electricitys. The small shop has an adequate stock of basic requirements and gas supplies, and a good stock of local information. Note: The site is on an island with obvious hazards for small children.

Facilities

Two sanitary units, both heated. The original provides adequate WCs and washbasins for men, and the more modern unit has been provided for women, with a separate access shower unit for the men, and a suite for disabled people on one end. Laundry. The millpond and its weir offer good coarse fishing. Off site: Golf 3 miles, riding 4.5 miles, bicycle hire 6 miles.

Open: 1 March - 31 October.

Directions

From A46 (Stratford - Alcester) follow signs for Mary Arden's House. At Wilmcote follow signs to Aston Cantlow and site. O.S.GR: SP136598.

Charges 2007

Per unit incl. 2 persons and electricity	£ 16.00
extra person	£ 1.00
child (5-10 yrs)	£ 0.50
No credit cards.	

UK4130 Moreton-in-Marsh Caravan Club Site

Bourton Road, Moreton-in-Marsh GL56 0BT (Gloucestershire)

Tel: **01608 650519**

This excellent, busy, but rural, tree-surrounded site in the heart of the Cotswolds offers most one would hope for from a camping holiday. Only 250 yards from the town, there is plenty of choice for food and pubs. The site has 182 pitches, all with electricity and TV sockets, 172 with hardstanding. Milk, and ice-cream are available from reception. Moreton-in-Marsh is famous for its Tuesday street market and is always a busy town, being only a few miles from the pretty villages of Bourton-on-the-Water and Stow-on-the-Wold, just two of the many interesting Cotswold villages worthy of a visit in this lovely area of England. Tents are not accepted.

Facilities

The two toilet blocks have been completely renovated and offer excellent facilities. Both have a large room for disabled people and babies. Small toilet and bath with seat for children. Large laundry area. Play area. Boules. Internet access. Off site: Shops, pubs and restaurants 400 yards. Golf 7 miles.

Open: All year.

Directions

From Evesham on A44, site on left after Bourton-on-the-Hill village. From Moreton-in-Marsh take the A44 towards Evesham and site is on right. O.S.GR: SP200323. GPS: N51:59.325 W01:42.650

Charges 2007

Per person	£ 4.70 - £ 6.20
child (5-16 yrs)	£ 1.50 - £ 3.00
pitch (non-member)	£ 10.90 - £ 15.30

(179)

UK4150 Croft Farm Water & Leisure Park

Bredon's Hardwick, Tewkesbury GL20 7EE (Gloucestershire)

Tel: **01684 772321**. Email: **enquiries@croftfarmleisure.co.uk**

Croft Farm is an AALA licensed Watersports Centre with Royal Yachting Association approved tuition available for windsurfing, sailing, kayaking and canoeing. The lakeside campsite has around 96 level pitches, with 80 electric hook-ups (10A), but there are many seasonal units, leaving around 36 pitches for tourists, plus some tent pitches. There are 36 gravel hardstandings but very little shade or shelter. 'Gym and Tonic' is a fully equipped gymnasium with qualified instructors, sunbed and sauna. Sports massage, aromatherapy and beauty treatments are available by appointment. Activity holidays for families and groups are organised. Campers can use their own non-powered boats on the lake with reduced launch fees and there is free fishing. Climb Bredon Hill (2 miles) for a panoramic view of the Severn and Avon Valleys. Places of interest include Bredon Barn, pottery and church, Beckford Silk Mill and Tewkesbury Abbey.

Facilities

A new building (opened during the summer) has excellent facilities with spacious hot showers, plus some dishwashing sinks. A heated unit in the main building is always open and best for cooler months; this provides further WCs, washbasins and showers, laundry and facilities for disabled persons. Gas. Cafe/bar (Fri-Sun low season, daily at other times). Takeaway. Gym. Playground. Fishing. Barrier and toilet block key (£5 deposit). Off site: Pub opposite. Tewkesbury 1.5 miles. Golf 3 miles. Riding 8 miles.

Open: All year, excl. January and February.

Directions

Bredon's Hardwick is midway between Tewkesbury and Bredon on B4080. Site opposite 'Cross Keys Inn'. From M5 exit 9 take A438 (Tewkesbury), at first traffic lights turn right into Shannon Way. Turn right at next lights, cross motorway bridge. Turn left (housing estate) and cross second bridge. At T-junction turn right on B4080, site is on left. O.S.GR: SO912353. GPS: N52:00.958 W02:07.816

Charges 2007

Per unit incl. 2 persons and awning	£ 14.00
extra person (over 3 yrs)	£ 3.00
electricity	£ 2.00
Discount 10% for 8 nights or more (excl. July, August and B.Hs).	

CROFT FARM WATER PARK

BREDONS HARDWICK, TEWKESBURY, GLOS. GL20 7EE
TEL 01684 772321
www.croftfarmleisure.co.uk
Lakeside caravan and camping park - water sports centre
log cabin clubhouse - modern facilities

UK4100 Hoburne Cotswold

Broadway Lane, South Cerney, Cirencester GL7 5UQ (Gloucestershire)

Tel: **01285 860216**. Email: **enquiries@hoburne.co.uk**

Since this park is adjacent to the Cotswold Water Park, those staying here will have easy access to the varied watersports available. On the park itself there is a lake with pedaloes and canoes for hire. Its wide range of other amenities includes outdoor and indoor heated swimming pools and an impressive, large indoor leisure complex. There are 200 well marked touring pitches for any type of unit, all with hardstanding (only fairly level) and a grass surround for awning or tent; 90 are serviced 'super' pitches. Of good size but with nothing between them, all have electricity (some need long leads). There are also 210 holiday units, mainly for letting. The large, refurbished clubhouse has a big general lounge with giant TV screen, entertainment at times, food service (or food bar in lounge), big games room and a lounge bar which overlooks the outdoor pool and lake with a patio. This is a very secure park which is being continually updated. Part of the Hoburne group.

Facilities

Six small toilet blocks are clean and well maintained with preset showers and background heating. Baby changing facilities. Basic facilities for disabled visitors. The site has heavy weekend trade. Launderette. Supermarket. Indoor leisure complex including pool with flume, spa bath, sauna, steam room and sun bed. Outdoor pool (Whitsun - early Sept). Clubhouse with bar, food and entertainment. Football field. Tennis. Adventure playground. Crazy golf. Fishing lake. Dogs or pets are not accepted.

Open: March - October.

Directions

Three miles southeast of Cirencester on A419, turn west towards Cotswold Water Park at new roundabout on bypass onto B4696. Take second right and follow signs. O.S.GR: SU055957.

Charges guide

Per pitch incl. max. 6 persons and electricity	£ 12.50 - £ 30.00
serviced 'super' pitch	£ 13.50 - £ 32.00
Weekly rates and weekend breaks available.	

UK4170 Tudor Caravan & Camping Park

Shepherds Patch, Slimbridge GL2 7BP (Gloucestershire)

Tel: **01453 890483**. Email: **info@tudorcaravanpark.co.uk**

This traditional style campsite is adjacent to the Gloucester - Sharpness Canal. Located behind the Tudor Arms public house, a gate clearly identifies the entrance and reception is up a short path on the left. There are many trees and hedges, particularly surrounding the site, so the canal is not visible. Attractively laid out on two separate fields, there are 75 pitches, all with electric hook-ups (16A), and 35 with hardstanding. The old orchard is for long stay or 'adult only' units, with some concrete wheel track hardstands, and a more open grassy meadow is for family touring units. The adjacent pub has a restaurant and bar (2007 CAMRA award winner) and just across the road, beside the canal, is a café and shop where boats can be hired. This is a delightful, peaceful park with plenty to offer: walking, fishing and boating, not to mention ornithology as the Wildfowl and Wetlands Centre founded by Sir Peter Scott at Slimbridge is only 800 yards away.

Facilities

The toilet building located to one side of the orchard, provides all the usual facilities including push-button hot showers and it can be heated in cool weather. No facilities for disabled persons at present but a new block is planned in the meadow which will include facilities for disabled people and babies. Gas available. Some site lighting but a torch would be useful. Gate locked 22.30 - 07.00. Off site: Meals at the Tudor Arms pub. Shop and cafe in boatyard opposite the site (Easter-Sept), also serves breakfasts. Fishing adjacent. Towpath walks. Berkeley Castle, Frampton and Stroud.

Open: All year.

Directions

From A38 by the junction with A4135 (Dursley), turn west, signed WWT Wetlands Centre Slimbridge. Continue for 1.5 miles turning left into car park of the Tudor Arms. Site entrance is at rear of car park. O.S.GR: SO728042. GPS: N51:44.132 W02:23.749

Charges 2007

Per unit incl. 2 persons	£ 11.00 - £ 15.00
extra person	£ 2.00
child (under 12 yrs)	£ 1.00
electricity	£ 2.25 - £ 2.50

No credit cards.

UK4140 Winchcombe Camping & Caravanning Club Site

Brooklands Farm, Alderton, Tewkesbury GL20 8NX (Gloucestershire)

Tel: **01242 620259**

This is a popular, quiet site in a rural location, close to the Cotswold attractions. Some pitches surround a small coarse fishing lake, with others in a more recently developed area with open views over the surrounding countryside. In total there are 80 pitches, 53 with electric hook-ups (10A) and 42 with gravel hardstanding. The reception building flanks a small gravel courtyard car park and late arrivals area approached from a tarmac drive. Future plans include the addition of lodges, an extended camping area and a new toilet block. Places to visit include Gloucester Docks and the National Waterways Museum, whilst south of Gloucester are Owlpen Manor near Uley, and the Painswick Rococo Garden. The Wildfowl and Wetlands Trust at Slimbridge, first opened in 1946 by Sir Peter Scott is also well worth a visit. Much closer to the site is the GWR (Gloucester Warwickshire Railway) at Toddington or Winchcombe.

Facilities

The main, heated sanitary unit, kept very clean and tidy by the wardens, is well equipped. To the rear of the site is a small, 'portacabin' style sanitary unit (also heated). Well equipped unit for disabled people. Laundry facilities. Gas supplies. Large games room with bowling alley, table tennis and pool table. Small outdoor play area. Off site: Several pubs and restaurants in the area. Golf 7 miles.

Open: 16 March - 15 January.

Directions

From M5 exit 9, take A46 Evesham road for 3 miles to Toddington roundabout, then the B4077 towards Stow-on-the-Wold for a further 3 miles to the site entrance. Ignore signs for Alderton village. O.S.GR: SP 007324. GPS: N51:59.424 W01:59.441

Charges 2007

Per person	£ 6.30 - £ 7.25
child (5-16 yrs)	£ 2.15 - £ 2.25
non-member pitch fee	£ 5.65

UK4180 Ranch Caravan Park

Honeybourne, Evesham WR11 7PR (Worcestershire)

Tel: **01386 830744**. Email: **enquiries@ranch.co.uk**

Set in the Vale of Evesham, Ranch lies not far from both Evesham and Broadway in quiet rural surroundings of 50 acres and just half an hour's drive from Stratford-on-Avon. The park takes 120 touring units – caravans, motorcaravans or trailer tents, but not other tents – on flat, partly undulating, hedged meadows with well mown grass and a spacious feel. The pitches are not marked but the staff position units. All have electrical connections (10A) and there are 20 hardstandings including 8 fully serviced pitches (electricity, TV, water and drainage). There are 169 caravan holiday homes in their own section. The Vale of Evesham is noted for being a sheltered area growing fruit and other produce from early spring through to late autumn.

Facilities

Two very well appointed, modern sanitary blocks with free hot showers and heating. Motorcaravan service point. Shop. Clubhouse (weekends only in early and late season) offering a range of good value meals and entertainment is arranged at B.H weekends and Saturdays in school holidays. Heated pool (55 x 30 ft; June - Sept). Gym and sauna. Games room with TV, video machines and pool table. Playground. Off site: Riding and bicycle hire 2 miles. Fishing 4 miles. Golf 6 miles.

Open: 1 March - 30 November.

Directions

From A46 Evesham take B4035 towards Chipping Campden. After Badsey and Bretforton follow signs for Honeybourne down unclassified road (Ryknild Street, Roman road). Park is through village on left by station. O.S.GR: SP112444.

Charges 2007

Per unit incl. 2 persons	
and electricity	£ 16.50 - £ 21.00
with water and drainage	£ 20.00 - £ 34.50

One free night for every 7 booked.
Note: tents are not accepted.

UK4160 Forest Holidays Christchurch

Bracelands Drive, Christchurch, Coleford GL16 7NN (Gloucestershire)

Tel: **01594 837258**. Email: **info@forestholidays.co.uk**

Forest Holidays is a partnership between the Forestry Commission and The Camping and Caravanning Club. With 280 unmarked pitches, this 20 acre site occupies an undulating, open grassy area in the heart of the Forest of Dean. There are around 60 seasonal units, seven hardstandings and 95 pitches with electrical hook-ups (10A). The reception also houses a well stocked licensed shop and has a good selection of tourist information. Tenters will appreciate the large pavilion in the centre of the site, a large common room with a wood burning stove, tables and chairs – an ideal retreat if the weather proves inclement. Symonds Yat Rock is within walking distance with spectacular views over the Wye Valley and also nearby are Clearwell Caves, ancient iron mines and Dean Forest Railway.

Facilities

Four sanitary units, two fairly modern with spacious well equipped showers, some vanity style basins with dividers, plus two much older units with WCs and washbasins only. The central block has a laundry room. Units for disabled people and baby changing in two blocks. Adventure playground. Dogs are not accepted. Off site: Fishing and swimming 1 mile. Coleford 1.5 miles. Golf 2 miles. Bicycle hire 3 miles. Ross-on-Wye 8 miles. Riding 10 miles.

Open: All year excl. 14 Jan - 28 Feb.

Directions

From Monmouth take A4136 east for 5 miles turning north at at Pike House Inn, site on left after 0.5 miles. From centre of Coleford take road towards Monmouth, turn right to Symonds Yat and Berry Hill. O.S.GR: SO569129. GPS: N51:48.800 W02:37.641

Charges 2007

Per unit incl. 2 persons	£ 7.60 - £ 14.60
extra person	£ 3.10 - £ 5.90
child (5-14 yrs)	£ 1.60 - £ 3.00

UK4185 Weir Meadow Holiday Park

Lower Leys, Evesham WR11 3AA (Worcestershire)

Tel: **01386 442417**

On entering this park you drive through neat caravan holiday homes surrounded by flowers and shrubs, but his does not prepare you for the view which opens in front of you of 27 touring pitches set out on the banks of the river Avon with splendid vistas of the narrow boats on the river and of the weir itself. The park has 130 caravan holiday homes, 8 caravans for hire and 27 touring pitches. Pitches are clearly marked off the tarmac roads and all have electricity. Units over 9 m. may have access problems. A central barbecue area is provided beside the river. Visitors to the park should be aware of the dangers of the river and these are clearly signed and the necessary safety equipment provided. Altogether a gem of a site, but advance booking is necessary most of the year.

Facilities

A well kept toilet block includes provision for disabled visitors. Excellent laundry area. Barbecue area. Fishing is available (in season with the necessary licence) at £5 per day. Off site: All town centre facilities nearby. River walks.

Open: 1 March - 31 October.

Directions

From the A44 follow signs for Evesham town centre. Go straight across two roundabouts, turn right at second set of traffic lights, then in 80 m. turn left. O.S.GR: SP041438. GPS: N52:05.629 W01:56.342

Charges guide

Per unit incl. 2 persons and electricity	£ 16.00 - £ 21.00
extra person	£ 2.00

UK4210 Lickhill Manor Caravan Park

Lower Lickhill Road, Stourport-on-Severn DY13 8RL (Worcestershire)

Tel: **01299 871041**. Email: **excellent@lickhillmanor.co.uk**

Lickhill Manor is a well managed touring and holiday site within easy walking distance of the town centre via a footpath along the River Severn which lies a short distance below the site. There are opportunities for fishing and boating. The touring area has 70 marked, level, pitches accessed via tarmac roads, all with electricity (10/16A). The 124 holiday homes, well screened from the touring area, are not visually intrusive, and there is a separate rally field (with 64 hook-ups). There is an excellent play area for children and the park has recently created wildlife ponds and planted over 1,000 native trees and shrubs. This park has matured into one of the best in the area.

Facilities

A second sanitary building serves the touring pitches and complements the older unit at the other end of the park. This heated building provides good, modern facilities including a well equipped suite for disabled guests which doubles as a family washroom with facilities for baby changing. Drive over motorcaravan service point. Recycling bins. Gas supplies. Children's play park in separate family area. Off site: Shops and pub 10 minutes walk. Riding 1 mile. Bicycle hire 3 miles. Golf 5 miles.

Open: All year.

Directions

From the A451 in Stourport take B4195 northwest towards Bewdley. After 1 mile turn left at crossroads (traffic lights), into Lickhill Road North where site is signed. O.S.GR: SO790730.

Charges 2007

Per unit incl. 4 persons and electricity	£ 12.00 - £ 18.50
extra person over 2 yrs	£ 1.50
dog	£ 1.00

Weekly rates available. Senior citizen discounts.

UK4190 Kingsgreen Caravan Park

Kingsgreen, Berrow, Malvern WR13 6AQ (Worcestershire)

Tel: **01531 650272**

A friendly and extremely well kept site with views of the Malvern Hills, Kingsgreen has an attractive rural location. An ideal site for adults who like the quiet life, there are no amusements for children. The surrounding countryside is ideal for walking or cycling, and the small, fenced fishing lakes on the site are well stocked (£4 per day). There are 45 level, grass and gravel pitches, all with 16A electricity, plus an additional area for tents. Some old orchard trees provide a little shade in parts.

Facilities

Modern heated toilet facilities (key on deposit) provide hot showers (25p token from reception) and a separate unit for disabled people (WC and washbasin). Laundry room. Gas and barbecue fuels are stocked and a milkman calls daily with milk, eggs, bread, soft drinks, etc. Off site: Nearest shop and pub 1.5 miles. Bicycle hire 2 miles. Riding 3 miles. Golf 5 miles.

Open: 1 March - 31 October.

Directions

From M50 exit 2, take A417 towards Gloucester, then first left, back over the motorway. Site is 2 miles from the M50. O.S.GR: SO767338.

Charges 2007

Per unit incl. 2 persons	£ 10.00 - £ 12.00
electricity	£ 2.00

No credit cards. VAT not included.

UK4310 Lucksall Caravan & Camping Park

Mordiford, Hereford HR1 4LP (Herefordshire)

Tel: **01432 870213**. Email: **karen@lucksallpark.co.uk**

Set in around 17 acres on the bank of the River Wye and benefiting from improvements by the new owners, Lucksall has 80 large, well spaced and level touring pitches, of which 80 have 16A electricity and 30 have hardstanding. The river is open to the site but lifebelts and safety messages are in evidence. Canoes are available for hire – or bring your own – and fishing permits may be obtained from reception. A larged, fenced new playground and a large grassy area for games are provided. The site shop is well stocked with a variety of goods and gas (a mini-market is within 1.5 miles). Amongst the local places worthy of a visit are the Cider Museum and King Offa Distillery in Hereford, Belmont Abbey and Queenswood Country Park. The park is also a good base for touring the Wye Valley. A member of the Countryside Discovery group.

Facilities

The main sanitary facilities provide showers (20p) and a separate unit for disabled visitors with ramped entrance, WC, washbasin, shower, hairdriers and hand-dryer. New laundry room. A smaller, refurbished, now c/heated open all times shop (basics only). Fishing. Canoeing. Site barrier (2.13 m. height limit) locked 21.00 - 09.00 hrs. Only 'breathable' groundsheets are permitted. Off site: Golf 5 miles. Bicycle hire 9 miles.

Open: 1 March - 30 November.

Directions

Between Mordiford and Fownhope, 5 miles southeast of Hereford on B4224, the park is well signed. O.S.GR: SO571355.

Charges 2007

Per unit incl. 2 persons	£ 11.00 - £ 14.50
extra person (over 5 yrs)	£ 2.00 - £ 3.00
awning	£ 1.50 - £ 2.00

Mordiford, Hereford, HR1 4LP Tel 01432 870213
Email karen@lucksallpark.co.uk
Web www.lucksallpark.co.uk

- Your touring caravan is welcome at Lucksall.
- Tents can be pitched on smooth mown grass.
- A separate rally field provides room for larger club gatherings of tents & caravans.
- Open March 1st to November 30th (weather permitting)

UK4300 Poston Mill Caravan Park

Peterchurch, Golden Valley HR2 0SF (Herefordshire)

Tel: **01981 550225**. Email: **enquiries@poston-mill.co.uk**

Poston Mill Park is a pleasant, neat park in farmland a mile from Peterchurch in the heart of the Golden Valley. There are currently 43 touring pitches which are set on level grass or hardstanding, including some very pleasant ones near the River Dore, with mature trees and conifers around the perimeter. All pitches have electricity (10/16A), water and TV connections (leads to hire), and a few have waste water and sewage outlets. An attractive walk along one side of the park, edging the River Dore (fishing available), follows the line of the old Golden Valley railway. There is a footpath from the park over the fields. Next to the park is 'The Mill' restaurant for lunches, evening meals, takeaway meals and a TV room. Peterchurch village is only 1 mile. A member of the Best of British group.

Facilities

There is one central sanitary block with a smaller block near the holiday home area which has just undergone a vast refurbishment, including private cubicles. They are fully equipped and include a unit for disabled people (toilet and basin only) and a baby changing room. 2 laundry rooms. Motorcaravan service point. Laundry room. Gas. Mobile shop calls 10.00. Mondays and Thursdays. Play area. Pitch and putt. Tennis, petanque and croquet. Golf driving range. Football pitch. Games room. Winter caravan storage. Off site: Riding 3 miles.

Open: All year.

Directions

Park is 1 mile southeast of Peterchurch on the B4348 road. O.S.GR: SO356371.

Charges 2007

Per unit incl. 2 persons and electricity	£ 14.00 - £ 18.00
extra person	£ 3.00
child (4-10 yrs)	£ 1.50
awning	£ 2.00
dog	£ 1.00
Min. charge at B.Hs. 5 nights.	

UK4320 Broadmeadow Caravan & Camping Park

Broadmeadows, Ross-on-Wye HR9 7BW (Herefordshire)

Tel: **01989 768076**. Email: **broadm4811@aol.com**

This modern, spacious park with open views and its own fishing lake, is conveniently located for the town of Ross-on-Wye. The town centre is within easy walking distance. The approach to the site is unusual, but persevere and you will find one of the best laid out, immaculately maintained sites with facilities of the very highest quality. There are 150 large pitches on level, open grass, and the site is especially good for tents. Each set of four pitches has a service post with water, drain, electricity points (16A) and lighting. Although the A40 relief road is at the eastern end of the site, the traffic noise should not be too intrusive (but tenters be aware).

Facilities

Two superb modern sanitary buildings are fully equipped, including hairdryers, baby rooms, family bathrooms each with WC, basin and bath, and a comprehensive unit for disabled visitors. Laundry at each building. Motorcaravan service point. Small part-fenced playground. Well fenced fishing lake. Off site: Supermarket 200 m. Bicycle hire in town. Golf 3 miles. Riding 8 miles.

Open: Easter/1 April - 30 September.

Directions

From A40 relief road turn into Ross at roundabout, take first right into industrial estate, then right in 0.5 miles before supermarket, where site is signed. O.S.GR: SO610240.

Charges 2007

Per person	£ 4.00
child (2-9 yrs)	£ 2.50
pitch with electricity	£ 11.00 - £ 12.50

UK4330 The Millpond Touring Caravans & Camping

Little Tarrington, Hereford HR1 4JA (Herefordshire)

Tel: **01432 890243**. Email: **enquiries@millpond.co.uk**

This peaceful little site with its own fishing lake is set in 30 acres of countryside. Opened for the first time in 1997, it has 40 large pitches on open grassland, all with electricity (10A) and 15 pitches for tents in an adjacent field. Special attention has been made to providing good facilities for disabled visitors. The large fishing lake (unfenced) is well stocked with coarse fish, has facilities for disabled fishermen and offers reduced rates for campers. Site lighting is minimal (local authority regulations) so a torch might be useful for tents. There may be a little noise at times from a railway track nearby.

Facilities

A modern building houses heated sanitary facilities, laundry and dishwashing sinks, baby changing surface, an upgraded unit for disabled visitors (with wet room shower) and a common room with tourist information and walking guides. Site is currently not really suitable for American motorhomes. Off site: Local pub is a 10 minute walk, but there is no shop in the village.

Open: 1 March - 31 October.

Directions

Little Tarrington is midway between Hereford and Ledbury. Site is just north of A438 on eastern edge of Tarrington village. O.S.GR: SO627409.

Charges 2007

Per unit incl. 2 persons, awning, electricity and 1 pet	£ 13.00 - £ 16.00
extra person	£ 3.00

UK4360 Doward Park Camp Site

Great Doward, Symonds Yat West HR9 6BP (Herefordshire)

Tel: **01600 890438**. Email: **enquiries@dowardpark.co.uk**

Created around 1997 in a disused quarry, this is a very pleasant, peaceful little site, partially terraced, and in a sheltered location. The access roads and the physical proportions of the site make it suitable only for tents, trailer tents and camper vans. A site that is popular with couples and young families, but has nothing to offer teenagers. The 33 pitches are mostly on grass (with 6 hardstandings used by seasonal units when we visited) and there are 11 electric hook-ups (16A) for tourers. There are two new motorcaravan hardstanding pitches for units up to 23 feet.

Facilities

A neat timber clad building provides the usual facilities including hot showers, dishwashing sinks and a freezer for ice packs. Small shop selling basic supplies. Torches are advisable. Off site: Variety of inns at both Symonds Yat West and East all offering meals. Shops and services in Monmouth 4 miles.

Open: Mid March - 31 October.

Directions

From A40 between Ross-on-Wye and Monmouth, turn for Symonds Yat West, and follow signs for Doward Park. Turn into narrow lane for 1 mile and site is on right, on sharp left hand bend. O.S.GR: SO548157. GPS: N51:50.311 W02:39.420

Charges 2007

Per unit incl. 2 persons	£ 14.50 - £ 16.50
extra person	£ 2.50
child (4-15 yrs)	£ 1.75

UK4345 Townsend Touring & Caravan Park

Townsend Farm, Pembridge, Leominster HR6 9HB (Herefordshire)

Tel: **01544 388527**. Email: **info@townsend-farm.co.uk**

Opened in 2002, this is a modern, family run campsite. It provides tarmac roads, good site lighting, well spaced pitches and a drive-over motorcaravan service point, with plenty of open space and a small fishing lake (with ducks and completely unfenced). There are 60 pitches in total, 20 with gravel hardstanding, the remainder on grass, and all have access to electricity (16A), water and drainage. Reception is at the Farm Shop by the entrance. This is a real treat as it stocks a wide variety of fresh fruit and vegetables, eggs and has a butchery section with farm produced meats. Pembridge is known as the capital of the Black and White Villages and holds its Farmer's Market on the first Saturday of each month. This is a short stroll from the site. A member of the Best of British group.

Facilities

A modern building with blown air heating, accessed through a foyer with public telephone and tourist information. It is surrounded by wide decking with ramps giving good access for wheelchairs to all facilities including the dishwashing area, laundry room and chemical disposal point. Inside are spacious controllable showers, some washbasins in cubicles, a suite for disabled guests, family bathroom and baby changing facilities. Off site: Riding and bicycle hire 0.5 miles. Kington 5 miles, Leominster 7 miles. Golf 7 miles.

Open: 1 March - 15 January.

Directions

Site is beside the A44, 7 miles west of Leominster. Site is just inside the 30 mph speed limit on the eastern edge of Pembridge village. O.S.GR: SO385580.

Charges 2007

Per unit incl. 2 persons	£ 9.00 - £ 15.00
incl. electricity, water and drain	£ 12.00 - £ 18.00
extra person	£ 3.00
child (5-15 yrs)	£ 1.50
awning or pup tent	£ 2.00

Townsend Touring Park

Townsend Farm, Pembridge, Leominster, Herefordshire. HR6 9HB
Tel: 01544 388527 email: info@townsend-farm.co.uk
www.townsend-farm.co.uk

Spacious 12 acre 62 pitch Caravan Park. Luxurious heated facilities block comprising showers, wash cubicles, toilets, disabled room, family room, laundry and washing up area. Fully serviced pitches inc electricity, water, waste water hook-ups, hard standings. Onsite award winning farm shop and butchery. Minutes walk from the centre of the medieval village of Pembridge.

October /November /December (Excluding New Year) Stay Mon to Fri ~ pay for three nights and get one free.
For Terms & Conditions please call 01544 388 527

UK4390 Westbrook Park

Little Hereford, Ludlow SY8 4AU (Shropshire)

Tel: **01584 711280**

A beautifully kept, traditional, quiet touring campsite in a 'working' cider apple orchard, Westbrook Park is bordered on one side by the River Teme and within walking distance of the village and pub. There are 52 level pitches with 16A electric hook-ups, some on well mown grass, and 35 on gravel or concrete and gravel all-weather hardstandings with water and waste water drain. Some pitches have semi-shade, other have none. Satellite TV hook-ups are available to all pitches. A footpath along the river bank in one direction leads to the Temeside Inn which serves hot meals. There is a pleasant riverside walk and dog walk in the other direction.

Facilities

A modern, timber clad, heated toilet block provides spacious hot showers (20p for 5 minutes), washbasins in curtained cubicles, a basic laundry room and dishwashing sinks. Limited facilities for disabled people (WC and basin) - the current steps need to be replaced with a ramp. Gas supplies. Playground. Fishing (£4 per day). Riverside walks. No gazebos. No cycling. Off site: Burford House Gardens. Croft Castle. Market towns of Tenbury Wells, Leominster, Ludlow. Golf 3 miles. Riding and bicycle hire 5 miles.

Open: 1 March - 30 November.

Directions

From A49 midway between Ludlow and Leominster, turn east at Woofferton on A456 (Tenbury Wells, Kidderminster). After 2 miles turn right just before river bridge and Temeside Inn. Turn left after 150 yds. Park is on left. O.S.GR: SU547679. GPS: N52:18.490 W02:39.955

Charges 2007

Per unit incl. 2 persons and electricity	£ 14.00 - £ 18.00
extra person	£ 3.00
child (4-10 yrs)	£ 1.50
dog	£ 1.00

UK4380 Fernwood Caravan Park

Lyneal, Ellesmere SY12 0QF (Shropshire)

Tel: **01948 710221**. Email: **enquiries@fernwoodpark.co.uk**

Fernwood is set in an area known as the Shropshire 'Lake District' – the mere at Ellesmere is the largest of nine meres – and the picturesque Shropshire Union Canal is only a few minutes walk. The park itself is a real oasis of calm and rural tranquillity with its floral landscaping, the setting and the attention to detail, all of a very high standard with planted and natural vegetation blending harmoniously. In addition to 165 caravan holiday homes, used normally only by their owners, the park takes 30 caravans, motorcaravans or trailer tents (but not other tents) in several well cut, grassy enclosures (including 30 seasonal long stay). Some are in light woodland, others in more open, but still relatively sheltered situations. All pitches have electricity (10A) and six also have water and drainage. One area is set aside for units with adults only. Siting is carried out by the management and there is always generous spacing, even when the site is full.

Facilities

The small toilet block for tourers has background heating for cooler days and includes some washbasins in cabins and limited facilities for disabled people. No dishwashing sinks. Basic motorcaravan services. Laundry room near shop and adjacent are WCs for ladies and men. Shop doubles as reception (from 1/4, hours vary). Coarse fishing lake. Forty acres of woodland for walking. Play area on grass.

Open: 1 March - 30 November.

Directions

Park is just northeast of Lyneal village, signed southwest off the B5063 Ellesmere - Wem road, about 1.5 miles from junction of the B5063 with the A495. O.S.GR: SJ452338.
GPS: N52:53.950 W02:48.961

Charges 2007

Per unit incl. electricity	£ 16.50 - £ 21.00
multi-service pitch	£ 3.50
awning	free - £ 3.00

One night free for every 7 booked in advance.

UK4440 The Green Caravan Park

Wentnor, Bishop's Castle SY9 5EF (Shropshire)

Tel: **01588 650605**. Email: **info@greencaravanpark.co.uk**

Remotely situated in a pleasant valley, in a designated 'area of outstanding natural beauty', and sandwiched between the Stipperstones and The Long Mynd, the Green would make an ideal base for some serious walking or cycling. The 15 acre site is very natural, and is divided into several fields. There are 160 pitches, taking 40 seasonal units, and around 20 holiday homes, with approximately 140 pitches for tourists (42 with 16A electric hook-ups). The main field has some hardstandings. The East Onny is a small, shallow river which runs through the site, much enjoyed by the youngsters, who can spend many hours catching minnows.

Facilities

One main sanitary block, rather austere in appearance, built into the side of a large barn. However it provides adequate and plentiful facilities with spacious new hot showers (on payment), dishwashing and laundry facilities, but there is no dedicated unit for disabled people. Small shop with reception. Playground. Off site: Four pubs within 3 miles. Fishing 3 miles. Riding 4 miles. Bishops Castle with museums. Leisure Centre. Stapely Hill historic trail. Gliding club.

Open: Easter - 31 October.

Directions

From Shrewsbury take A488 south for 21 miles. At Lydham Heath turn east on A489 for 0.75 miles, then north on minor road (Wentnor). Follow signs for 3 miles. Site immediately after The Inn on the Green. O.S.GR: SO381933. GPS: N52:32.025 W02:54.825

Charges 2007

Per unit incl. 2 persons	£ 10.00 - £ 12.00
extra person	£ 2.50
child (3-14 yrs)	£ 2.00
electricity	£ 2.25

187

UK4400 Stanmore Hall Touring Park

Stourbridge Road, Bridgnorth WV15 6DT (Shropshire)

Tel: **01746 761761**. Email: **stanmore@morris-leisure.co.uk**

This good quality park is situated in the former grounds of Stanmore Hall, where the huge lily pond, fine mature trees and beautifully manicured lawns give a mark of quality. There are 135 generously sized pitches, 130 with 16A electricity including 30 hardstanding 'super' pitches with TV connections. A limited number of 'standard' hardstanding pitches are also available, but the majority are on grass. Some pitches are reserved for adult only use (over 18 years). Access and internal roads are tarmac; site lighting is adequate and reassuring. Reception is located within the shop. The adjacent conservatory and patio overlook the lake, accommodating everything from humbler ducks to the resident peacocks who strut proudly around their domain. But there's something else too; this is a peaceful site with personality. Little wonder it needs advance booking and people keep returning to enjoy its atmosphere. Open all year round, there are even groups who spend Christmas and New Year at Stanmore Hall. The Severn Valley is full of interest – Bridgnorth nearby, the Clee Hills and Ironbridge Gorge Museum are just a few suggestions. The site is a member of the Caravan Club's managed under contract scheme but non-members are also very welcome.

Facilities

Access to the centrally heated sanitary block is by key. Facilities are excellent and provide washbasins in cubicles and a room for disabled people and baby care. Full laundry facilities. Motorcaravan service points. Shop, including caravan accessories and repair items. Play area. Dogs are limited to two per unit. Off site: Fishing at Bridgnorth 1.5 miles. Golf and Riding 2 miles.

Open: All year.

Directions

Site is 1.5 miles from Bridgnorth on the A458 (signed Stourbridge). O.S.GR: SO744922. GPS: N52:31.629 W02:22.717

Charges 2007

Per person	£ 5.50 - £ 5.90
child (5-15 yrs)	£ 2.20
pitch	£ 7.60 - £ 9.50
awning or pup tent	£ 1.25
full services, plus	£ 2.50 - £ 3.00

UK4410 Beaconsfield Farm Caravan Park

Battlefield, Shrewsbury SY4 4AA (Shropshire)

Tel: **01939 210370**. Email: **mail@beaconsfield-farm.co.uk**

Just north of the historic market town, a drive of half a mile through open fields lead to this purpose-designed park for adults only (21 yrs). It is neatly laid out in a rural situation, with a well stocked trout fishing lake and a small coarse pool forming the main feature. The ground has been levelled and grassed to provide 80 well spaced pitches, 50 are 'de-luxe' hardstanding pitches. All have electricity connections (10A). Two further areas accommodate 36 caravan holiday homes. The park is well lit with a circular tarmac access road. A large timber chalet-style building provides reception and a coffee shop that is open during reception hours. Recent additions are the bowling green and the popular 'Bothy' a la carte restaurant. Limousins and pedigree Suffolk sheep graze in neighbouring fields and a 'park and ride' scheme operates nearby for those interested in Shrewsbury and its medieval past, bought to life by the Brother Cadfael novels. This is a top class park, maturing by the year. A member of the Best of British Group.

Facilities

Heated toilet facilities (£2 key deposit) are of excellent quality, with roomy, preset showers and hairdryers. Excellent suite for disabled visitors. Dishwashing and laundry facilities. Motorcaravan services. A la Carte Restaurant. Indoor heated swimming pool with daily open sessions (£3.00 inc. steam room per person) and to hire privately at other times. Small library. Security barrier and CCTV. WiFi. Only two dogs per unit are accepted. An adult only park. Car hire available. Off site: Bicycle hire and golf 2 miles. Riding 7 miles.

Open: All year.

Directions

Site is north of Shrewsbury and off the Whitchurch road (A49) just before Hadnall. Turn opposite the New Inn at camping sign towards Astley and park entrance is 400 m. on right. O.S.GR: SJ525195. GPS: N52:46.255 W02:42.289

Charges 2007

Per grass pitch incl. unit, 2 persons and electricity	£ 15.00 - £ 18.00
hardstanding pitch	£ 18.00 - £ 20.00
extra person	£ 4.00
awning	£ 1.50

No credit cards. Last arrivals 7 pm. (8 pm. Fridays).

UK4415 Green Lane Farm

Whitchurch SY13 2AH (Shropshire)

Tel: **01948 840460**

Green Lane Farm is a small family run site in the heart of the countryside. Pitches are set on a flat open field, surrounded by trees and hedges and provide a relaxing and really quiet place to stay with no traffic noise to disturb the tranquillity. A gravel track leads into the site and after 30 yards becomes grass encircling the field. The 20 grass pitches are situated around the outside with an attractive group of shrubs beside each electric hook-up stand. There is space for tents in the central area together with play equipment and picnic tables. Although this is a secluded site with the nearest shop being over 1 mile away, it is convenient for the many nearby attractions. On-site facilities are limited but can be found in the nearby village or in the town of Whitchurch 5 miles away.

Facilities

The recently built sanitary block provides washbasins and showers (only one toilet for men and two for ladies). Large separate toilet and shower for disabled visitors. Dishwashing sinks. Play area. Football. Basketball. Tourist information. Torches useful. Off site: Pubs, shop, garage, takeaway, and club in Prees village, just over a mile away. The site is central to many attractions and activities. Fishing and golf 2 miles. Ironbridge, Telford, Shrewsbury and RAF Cosford are nearby.

Open: April - October

Directions

The easiest route is from the A41. 4 miles south of Whitchurch turn west signposted Prees. In 200 yards turn right. The site is on the right in 200 yards. On the A49 turn east to Prees. At the crossroads in Prees turn right towards the church. Turn left at the church. Site is 1 mile on the left.

Charges 2007

Per unit	£ 10.00
electricity	£ 2.00
awning	£ 1.00

No credit cards.

Green Lane Farm
Camping and Caravan Site
Green Lane, Witchurch, Shropshire. SY13 2AH   Tel: 01948 840460

Small, quiet, countryside site. 20 pitches with electrical hook up.
Toilet and shower room, Childrens play area.

UK4430 Oxon Hall Touring Park

Welshpool Road, Shrewsbury SY3 5FB (Shropshire)

Tel: **01743 340868**. Email: **oxon@morris-leisure.co.uk**

Oxon Hall is a purpose-built park, well situated for visiting Shrewsbury. It is under the same ownership as Stanmore Hall (no. 4400) and has been developed from a green field site by an experienced park operator to a very high standard. The site has matured well and the trees and shrubs now provide some shade and shelter. Of the 120 pitches, half are all weather, full service pitches (fresh and waste water facilities, TV hook-up), the others being either grass or with hardstanding. An area is set aside as an 'adults only' section. Most pitches have 16A electricity, some pitches for large units have 32A. Some extra long hardstandings are provided for American motorhomes. Entry to the park is controlled by electronic barriers. Virtually adjacent to the park is the Oxon 'park and ride' which makes a trip into Shrewsbury some 2 miles away very simple. The famous Ironbridge Gorge Museum and the mysteries of the Welsh Borders are all easy day trips from this excellent base. A member of the Best of British group.

Facilities

Toilet facilities here are first rate with washbasins in cubicles, ample showers, baby room, facilities for disabled visitors, dishwashing room and laundry, all situated at the entrance in a centrally heated building which also houses reception and the shop - perhaps a hike from some of the pitches. Motorcaravan service point. Up to two dogs per pitch. Deposit for toilet block key £5. Off site: Golf, riding and fishing nearby. Supermarket within walking distance.

Open: All year.

Directions

From junction of A5 and A458, west of Shrewsbury, follow signs for Oxon 'park and ride'. Park is signed just 0.5 miles from junction. O.S.GR: SJ457134. GPS: N52:42.924 W02:48.295

Charges 2007

Per person	£ 5.50 - £ 5.90
child (5-15 yrs)	£ 2.20
standard grass pitch	£ 7.60 - £ 9.50
dog (max. 2)	£ 1.00

189

MAP 5

A beautiful and varied region of rolling hills and undulating moors, Yorkshire has an historic past with a wealth of new attractions. Its landscape has inspired famous authors and been the setting for some of Britain's best-loved television programmes.

THE REGION IS DIVIDED INTO NORTH, SOUTH, EAST AND WEST YORKSHIRE

The major attractions of this region are the parks: the Yorkshire Dales National Park is comprised of 680 square miles of unspoilt countryside with high fells, winding rivers, ancient castles and outstanding views of the surrounding landscapes; the Peak District is noted for its rocky peaks and limestone plateau; while the North York Moors National Park has miles of open, heather covered moorland and pretty villages in its valleys. These areas are ideal places for walking, cycling, horse riding and climbing. Or if you prefer to relax and take in the scenery, the North Yorkshire Moors Railway, starting at Pickering, is one of the many steam railways in the region. On the coast, traditional family resorts like Scarborough, Bridlington and Cleethorpes offer the holidaymaker a wide range of activities. Also by the sea is Kingston Upon Hull, a maritime city with powerful links to Britain's proud seafaring tradition, and the picturesque fishing port of Whitby, once home to Captain James Cook. Elsewhere in the region are the vibrant cities of York, with its wealth of ancient sites including the Minster, Leeds and Sheffield plus the busy market town of Doncaster.

Places of interest

North: Harrogate; Wensleydale Creamery in Hawes; Jorvik Viking Centre in York; Lightwater Valley Theme Park, near Ripon; Castle Howard near York: Flamingo Land Theme Park and Zoo in Malton; Skipton Castle.

South: Hatfield Waterpark near Doncaster; Tropical Butterfly House and Wildlife Centre in Anston; Sheffield Ski Village, Europe's biggest artificial ski resort; Magna science adventure centre in Rotherham.

East: Bempton Cliffs RSPB Nature Reserve near Bridlington, England's largest seabird colony; market town of Beverly; Captain Cook Museum in Whitby; Scarborough Millennium.

West: Bolling Hall in Bradford; Royal Armouries Museum in Leeds; 'Brontë Country' and village of Haworth; Pontefract.

Did you know?

The comedy series Last of the Summer Wine is filmed in the Pennine town of Holmfirth and its surrounding countryside.

York is the oldest city in Yorkshire, founded in AD71. The Minster is the largest Gothic Cathedral in Northern Europe.

Pontefract has been growing liquorice since medieval times, it is believed that Pontefract cakes were made by the monks for medicinal purposes.

The Tan Hill Inn is the highest pub in England at 528 metres above sea level.

Dick Turpin, the notorious 17th century highwayman, lived in Pontefract.

Rudston is said to be the oldest inhabited village in England, named after the Rood Stone, a mysterious 4000 year old monolith.

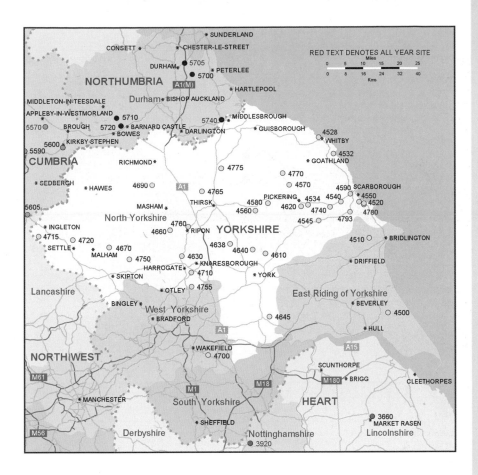

UK4500 Burton Constable Holiday Park & Arboretum

The Old Lodges, Sproatley, Hull HU11 4LN (East Yorkshire)

Tel: **01964 562508**. Email: **info@burtonconstable.co.uk**

This park is in the grounds of the stately home of Burton Constable, and consequently the entrance is most impressive – one of the gatehouses acts as reception and tourist information room. The 40 acre campsite is part of the 300 acre park which was landscaped by Capability Brown in the 18th century and with well trimmed grass and hedges, it has a spacious feel. All 180 touring pitches have 10A electricity, there is a separate field for tents and a large hardstanding area providing electricity, water and drainage for six motorcaravans. All the pitches overlook two small lakes (unfenced), both of which are used for fishing (permits at reception), one for boating (bring your own, but no engines). Privately owned caravan holiday homes are quite separate and do not intrude.

Facilities

Two heated toilet blocks - one older and small with unisex showers, the central newer block including a laundry room with baby changing. Well equipped room for disabled visitors (Radar key). Shop in the mobile home area. Bar with family room and tables outside overlooking the lakes. Good adventure play area. Off site: Sproatley (1 mile) has pubs, a shop and the occasional bus. Hull 7 miles. Golf 4 miles. Riding 3 miles.

Open: 1 March - 31 October.

Directions

From south via the M62 or Humber Bridge, take A63 into Hull, then follow signs to A165 Bridlington. On eastern outskirts of Hull follow B1238 signed Aldborough. At Sproatley, site is signed to left. From the north and Beverley, take A1035 to Hornsea. At roundabout with A165 (Hull - Bridlington) follow signs to Burton Constable for about 8 miles. Pass the Hall to Sproatley, then follow caravan signs. O.S.GR: TA186357. GPS: N53:48.159 W00:11.948

Charges 2007

Per unit incl. 2 persons and electricity	£ 13.00 - £ 24.00
tent incl. 2 persons	£ 13.00 - £ 20.00
extra person	£ 1.50

(191)

UK4532 Middlewood Farm Holiday Park

Middlewood Lane, Fylingthorpe, Robin Hood's Bay YO22 4UF (North Yorkshire)

Tel: **01947 880414**

Middlewood Farm is a level park, surrounded by hills and with views of the sea from some of the pitches. A short walk through the farm fields and wild flower conservation areas leads to the picturesque old fishing village of Robin Hood's Bay and the sea. The park has 22 touring pitches for caravans and motorcaravans with 10A electricity, 17 with hardstanding and the remainder on grass. There is space for around 130 tents in two areas with 12 electricity connections (10A) available and 30 caravan holiday homes to rent. A good beach is only ten minutes walk through the fields and the nearby village of Fylingthorpe with a post office, stores and a pub is a level walk. This is a very tidy farm park.

Facilities

The central toilet block has clean facilities and is modern, heated and tiled with free showers. Another new block is planned. Fully equipped laundry room including iron and board. Facilities for babies and disabled persons. Two private family shower rooms to rent. Play area with bark base set amongst the tents. Off site: Sandy beach with fishing 0.5 miles. Boat launching 2 miles. Golf 7 miles. Shop in village 5 minutes walk.

Open: Easter - early November.

Directions

From the A171 Scarborough - Whitby road turn right signed Robin Hood's Bay and Fylingthorpe (site signed). Just past the 30 mph sign bear right and after 100 yds. turn right into Middlewood Lane (site signed). From Whitby on the A171 turn left on B1447 signed Robin Hood's Bay and Fylingthorpe. After 1.5 miles turn right signed Fylingthorpe and brown site sign. Follow for 1 mile to crossroads and shops and straight on to Middlewood Lane (site signed). O.S.GR: NZ945045.

Charges 2007

Per unit incl. 2 persons and electricity	£ 12.50 - £ 20.00
extra person	£ 3.00
dog	£ 1.50

UK4510 Thorpe Hall Caravan & Camping Site

Rudston, Driffield YO25 4JE (East Yorkshire)

Tel: **01262 420393**. Email: **caravansite@thorpehall.co.uk**

Just outside the village of Rudston, in the grounds of Thorpe Hall, this pleasant small touring park is 4.5 miles from the sea at Bridlington. Enthusiastically managed by Jayne Chatterton, it is set on flat grass, largely enclosed by the old kitchen garden wall. The 90 pitches are numbered and well spaced with 78 electrical hook-ups (16A) and TV connections. A separate area takes tents and there are no caravan holiday homes. There is always a chance of finding space, though it is best to book for B.Hs and peak weeks. Information sheets on a range of local walks are provided and Sir Ian Macdonald takes visitors on walks around the estate.

Facilities

The solid, central toilet block can be heated. The ladies facilities have been refurbished and those for men should now also be complete. Some washbasins are in cabins. Bathroom for disabled visitors and families with young children (deposit for key). Launderette. Covered dishwashing sinks. Small shop with gas, essentials and local produce. Games room with pool table, table football and table tennis. TV room. Coarse fishing lake. Off site: Bicycle hire, golf and boat launching at Bridlington (4.5 miles). Riding 2 miles. Footpath to the village with a shop, post office, garage, a pub serving bar meals and a restaurant, plus a twice weekly bus service to Bridlington.

Open: 1 March - 31 October.

Directions

Site is by the B1253 road, 4.5 miles from Bridlington, on east side of Rudston. O.S.GR: TA105676. GPS: N54:05.629 W00:18.750

Charges 2007

Per unit incl. all persons and electricity	£ 12.00 - £ 24.00
tent pitch incl. 2 persons	£ 8.00 - £ 20.00
Less 10% on booked stays of 7 days or more.	

UK4528 Sandfield House Farm Caravan Park

Sandsend Road, Whitby YO21 3SR (North Yorkshire)

Tel: **01947 602660**. Email: **info@sandfieldhousefarm.co.uk**

Although it is set on a hill in undulating countryside on the low cliffs near Whitby, this park provides 200 level pitches, all with electricity. There are 60 pitches for touring caravans, all on hardstanding, and these are mainly set to the front of the park giving wonderful views over the golf course and the sea. Tents are not accepted here. Whitby is only a mile away and a quarter of a mile walk down a gently sloping track from the park brings you to a two mile long sandy beach. From here it is a gentle stroll along the new promenade to Whitby harbour. Whitby offers a variety of attractions to interest all the family, from fishing trips and amusement arcades, to the Spa theatre, plus all the famous fish and chips.

Facilities

Two toilet blocks, one older and one new and very good, have free hot showers. Laundry room with washing machines, dryers and iron. Dishwashing area. No facilities for disabled visitors. Tents are not accepted. Off site: Shops 800 yards. Hourly bus service to town centre. Fishing 400 yds. Golf 200 yds. Boat launching 800 yds.

Open: 18 March - 30 October.

Directions

From Whitby follow signs for Sandsend on the A174. The park is on the landward side of the road, opposite the golf course and well signed. O.S.GR: NZ872117. GPS: N54:29.503 W00:38.566

Charges 2007

Per unit incl. up to 4 persons	
and electricity	£ 13.00 - £ 15.50
extra person	£ 2.00
awning	£ 2.00
dog (max.2)	£ 1.00
No credit cards.	

UK4534 Overbrook Caravan Park

Maltongate, Thornton-le-Dale, Pickering YO18 7SE (North Yorkshire)

Tel: **01751 474417**. Email: **enquiry@overbrookcaravanpark.co.uk**

Situated in the very pretty village of Thornton-le-Dale, Overbrook has been developed on the site of the old railway station. With the line dismantled, the station building now provides holiday cottages and the caravan park toilet facilities. This is a level site with 50 pitches (20 for tourers, the remainder used for seasonal units) arranged either side of a tarmac access road and backed by trees. All are on hardstanding and all have electricity connections (16A). Neither children nor tents are accepted at this 'adult only' park. The owners will do all they can to assist you during your stay. A half mile, level walk brings you to the village which is very convenient for shops, pubs, tearooms and even a chocolate factory. There is a good bus service to York, Pickering and Scarborough. The beck which runs through the village and down under the railway property is home to kingfishers, herons, ducks and trout. There are plenty of footpaths for walking in this lovely area. Many local attractions are within half an hour's drive from the park. Dalby Forest is nearby with a visitor centre, walks and mountain bike trails.

Facilities

The toilet facilities and reception are situated in the old station house. Dishwashing sinks and laundry sink with ironing board. Gas supplies. Battery charging (£1). No tents accepted. Children are not admitted. Off site: Village with bus stop, shops, pubs, fish and chips 800 yds. Bicycle hire 800 yds. Fishing 3 miles. Golf courses within 10 miles.

Open: 1 March - 31 October.

Directions

Thornton-le-Dale is on the A170 Pickering - Scarborough road. In the village follow sign for Malton and park is 800 yds. on the left (follow the stream on the left). O.S.GR: SE833821. GPS: N54:13.712 W00:43.374

Charges 2007

Per unit incl. 2 persons	
and electricity	£ 13.00 - £ 14.00
incl. awning	£ 14.50 - £ 15.50
extra person	£ 2.50
dog (max. 2)	free
No credit cards.	

UK4520 Flower of May Holiday Park

Lebberston Cliff, Scarborough YO11 3NU (North Yorkshire)

Tel: **01723 584311**. Email: **info@flowerofmay.com**

Situated on the cliff tops, 4.5 miles from Scarborough and 2.5 miles from Filey, Flower of May is a large, family owned park for both touring caravans and caravan holiday homes. There is a cliff walk to the beach but it is only suitable for the reasonably active – there is an easier walk down from a car park a mile away. The entrance to the park is very colourful and the reception office is light and airy. The park is licensed for 300 touring units and 184 caravan holiday homes (45 to hire, the remainder privately owned). The touring pitches are pretty level, arranged in wide avenues, mainly on grass and divided by shrubs. There are 270 with electricity (10A), including 45 'star pitches' with water and drainage also. The range of leisure facilities grouped around reception includes an indoor pool with areas for both adults and children, a water flume and a jacuzzi. In the same building are two squash courts, 10 pin bowling, table tennis and amusement machines. The leisure centre is also open to the public (concessionary rates for campers) but during high season is only available to local regulars and the caravanners and campers on the park. Riverside Meadows at Ripon and Rosedale Country Caravan Park near Pickering are under the same ownership.

Facilities

Three toilet blocks, all refurbished in a light and colourful style, are fully tiled with washbasins in both cabins and vanity style. Baby rooms. Facilities for disabled visitors. Well stocked and licensed shop (closes end Sept) near the leisure centre, as is the laundry room. Two modern bar lounges, one for families and one for adults only, with discos in season. Café and takeaway fish and chips. Games room with TV. Large adventure playground. Pay and play golf course (£5 a round). Indoor swimming pool. Skateboard ramps. Basketball. Dog exercise area, but numbers and breeds are limited (one per pitch) and not allowed at all at B.Hs and the six week summer holiday. Off site: The Plough Inn near the park entrance offers good bar meals. Fishing, boat slipway or riding 2 miles. Bicycle hire 4 miles.

Open: Easter - 28 October.

Directions

Park is signed from roundabout at junction of the A165 and B1261 from where it is 600 yds. O.S.GR: TA088836. GPS: N54:13.752 W00:20.550

Charges 2007

Per unit incl. up to 4 persons	
and electricity	£ 14.00 - £ 19.00
tent (no electricity)	£ 11.50 - £ 15.50
extra person (over 3 yrs)	£ 3.00
awning	£ 4.00
dog (see above)	£ 1.00

10% discount on pitch fee for weekly bookings.

UK4770 Rosedale Caravan & Camping Park

Rosedale Abbey, Pickering YO18 8SA (North Yorkshire)

Tel: **01751 417272**. Email: **info@flowerofmay.com**

In a beautiful location below Rosedale Moor and on the edge of a popular village, this is a campsite that is highly suitable for walkers. The surrounding hillsides are a maze of public footpaths and these and nearby Cropton Forest can all be reached without using your car. The site itself has a wide entrance on the edge of the village and as it is within the National Park, the buildings are in the local stone and in keeping with the area. The site is reasonably level, with 200 pitches, a few with hardstanding and with 28 electricity connections (10A). There are some caravan holiday homes (private) and seasonal touring pitches in their own areas, with the remainder for touring caravans and motorcaravans. The majority have superb views of the surrounding hills. One field is set aside for tents only and many are sited near the river which runs along the edge of the park. In summer the Dales bus runs through the village, connecting several of the popular villages. The 13 mile Rosedale circuit follows the route of the old iron-ore railway, giving magnificent views and reminders of bygone industries. There is a glass blower at the village blacksmith's and the Ryedale Folk Museum at Hutton-le-Hole is 3.5 miles.

Facilities

Fully refurbished sanitary facilities with under-floor heating include free showers and hairdressing units. Facilities for disabled visitors and baby changing. Dishwashing and laundry facilities. Reception provides maps and a small selection of camping accessories, plus gas supplies. Games room with pool and video games. Large play area with space for ball games. Entrance barrier controlled by card (£10 deposit). Off site: The village has a general store with daily papers, a post office, bakery, pubs and a restaurant. Nine 9-hole golf course (set on a picturesque hillside) 200 yards.

Open: Easter - 28 October.

Directions

Rosedale is signed from the A170, 2 miles west of Pickering. Site is in the village of Rosedale Abbey, 8 miles north of the A170. O.S.GR: SE725958.

Charges 2007

Per unit incl. up to 4 persons	
amd electricity	£ 14.00 - £ 19.00
tent incl. up to 4 persons	£ 11.50 - £ 15.50

10% discount on pitch fee for weekly bookings.

UK4545 Wolds Way Caravan Park

West Farm, West Knapton, Malton YO17 8JE (North Yorkshire)

Tel: **01944 728463**. Email: **info@ryedalesbest.co.uk**

This new park, opened in 2004, is located along the top of the Yorkshire Wolds with super panoramic views across the Vale of Pickering to the North Yorks Moors. The one and a half mile gravel track from the road to the park is well worth while to reach this peaceful location set amongst glorious countryside. There are 80 level pitches (50 for touring units), most with 16A electricity and some with water points. There are 34 pitches with hardstanding. Seating areas, picnic benches and barbecues are provided on the park. As well as the obvious attractions of walking the Wolds Way national trail and the many other footpaths and cycle ways the area has to offer, the park is well placed for visiting all the local attractions which include Scarborough, Bridlington, Sledmere House and Scampston Hall.

Facilities

A brand new toilet block is very well appointed and heated. Family bathrooms. Laundry facilities. Very large heated room with dishwashing sinks and tourist information. Room for disabled visitors. Reception also provides a small shop selling basic supplies. Play area and football field for children and many places to walk dogs. Caravan storage. Off site: Fishing 3 miles. Golf and riding 5 miles. Beach 15 miles.

Open: 1 March - 31 October.

Directions

Park entrance is on the south side of the A64 York - Scarborough road, just past the B1258 turn off and it is well signed. O.S.GR: SE896744. GPS: N54:09.969 W00:39.242

Charges 2007

Per unit incl. 2 persons, electricity	£ 11.00 - £ 15.50
tent incl. 2 persons and car	£ 9.00 - £ 12.00
extra person (over 14 yrs)	£ 2.00
awning	£ 1.50
dog	free

The park is peacefully located adjacent to Wolds farmland and large areas of woodland providing peace and tranquillity, meaning visitors are able to relax amidst wildlife, flora and fauna.

Yorkshire
WOLDS WAY
CARAVAN & CAMPING

West Farm, West Knapton, Malton, North Yorkshire, YO17 8JE
Telephone/Fax 01944 728 463

www.ryedalesbest.co.uk

Landscaped site situated on a working farm with outstanding views over the Vale of Ryedale and North Yorkshire Moors.

Full Facilities including:-

Fantastic Shower/Toilet block with Family Bathroom Miles of scenic walks and cycle tracks over adjoining farm and woodland
Electric Hook-Ups and Water to all pitches
Laundry facilities
Shop

UK4540 Saint Helens in the Park

Wykeham, Scarborough YO13 9QD (North Yorkshire)

Tel: **01723 862771**. Email: **caravans@wykeham.co.uk**

St Helens is a high quality touring park with pleasant views, set within 30 acres of parkland. The site is divided into terraces with trees screening each area (one of which is set aside for adults only) and the 250 mainly level pitches have a spacious feel. Electrical hook-ups (16A) are available on 240 pitches, also in the late arrivals area. Set on a hillside, the park's buildings are built in local stone and all is maintained to a high standard. The Downe Arms, a short stroll away, is known for its good food and family friendly atmosphere. Scarborough is only 5 miles with its beaches and summer shows and buses pass the site gates.

Facilities

Four heated toilet blocks are well equipped and maintained to a high standard. Some washbasins in cabins, free showers and baby baths. Unit for disabled visitors. Dishwashing sinks under cover. Good central laundry room. Well stocked shop. Café and takeaway. Internet café. WiFi. Bicycle hire. Small games room. Tourist information cabin. Caravan storage. Off site: Nearby Wykeham Lakes offer fishing (trout and coarse), scuba diving, windsurfing and sailing (in your own boat), 1 mile. Golf or riding 2 miles.

Open: All year excl. 15 January - 13 February.

Directions

Park access road leads off the A170 (Pickering - Scarborough) road in Wykeham village 2 miles west of junction with B1262. O.S.GR: SE963835. GPS: N54:14.282 W00:30.028

Charges 2007

Per unit incl. 2 persons	£ 10.30 - £ 13.00
electricity	£ 3.50
extra person (over 3 yrs)	£ 1.50
awning	£ 2.30
dog	£ 1.50

UK4550 Cayton Village Caravan Park

Mill Lane, Cayton Bay, Scarborough YO11 3NN (North Yorkshire)

Tel: **01723 583171**. Email: **info@caytontouring.co.uk**

Cayton Village Caravan Park can only be described as a gem. Just three miles from the hustle and bustle of Scarborough, it is a peaceful, attractive haven. Originally just a flat field with caravans around the perimeter, years of hard work have produced a park which is very pleasing to the eye and of which the owner, Carol, can be justly proud. The entrance is a mass of flowers. The late arrivals area here has electrical hook-ups, very handy as the gates are locked at night and anyone leaving early is also expected to use it, so as not to disturb others. Newly tarmaced entrance with electrical barriers. The 200 pitches are numbered and everyone is taken to their pitch. All of the 190 for touring units, have electricity (many with hardstanding) and there are 91 fully serviced pitches. A short walk across a field takes you to Cayton Village which has a popular pub providing excellent meals, a post office stores and a church, and Cayton Bay is half a mile. The North York Moors are a short distance away, as is the Forestry Commission's Dalby Forest with its scenic drive, mountain bike trails and way-marked walks.

Facilities

Three toilet blocks (key code locks) can be heated and have high quality tiling and fittings. Some showers are preset, others controllable. Two family shower rooms, family bathroom and baby changing facilities. Reception and shop with comprehensive range including gas and caravan spares. Adventure playground with safety surface. Superb dog walk (an enormous well mown field, floodlit at night). Caravan storage. Off site: Fishing and bicycle hire 0.5 miles. Riding 4 miles. Golf 3 miles. Regular bus service from the village to Scarborough or Filey.

Open: 1 March - 31 October.

Directions

From A64 Malton - Scarborough road turn right at roundabout (with MacDonald's and pub) signed B1261 Filey. Follow signs for Cayton, in Cayton Village take second left after Blacksmiths Arms down Mill Lane (at brown tourism sign) and park is 200 yds. on left. From roundabout to park is 2.25 miles. From A165 turn inland at Cayton Bay traffic lights and park is 0.5 miles on right. O.S.GR: TA057837. GPS: N54:14.144 W00:22.567

Charges 2007

Per unit incl. 2 persons, electricity and awning	£ 13.00 - £ 24.00

Special offers available.

UK4560 Golden Square Caravan & Camping Park

Oswaldkirk, York YO62 5YQ (North Yorkshire)

Tel: **01439 788269**. Email: **barbara@goldensquarecaravanpark.freeserve.co.uk**

Golden Square is a popular, high quality, family owned touring park. Mr and Mrs Armstrong are local farmers who have worked hard to turn an old quarry into a very attractive caravan park with a number of level bays that have superb views over the North York Moors. The 130 pitches are not separated but they do have markers set into the ground and mainly back on to grass banks. In very dry weather the ground can be hard, steel pegs would be needed (even in wet weather the park is well drained). All pitches have electrical connections (10A), 24 have drainage and 6 are 'deluxe' pitches (with waste water, sewage, electricity, water and TV aerial connection). The licensed shop is very well stocked, selling home-made fresh bread and cakes, dairy produce, fresh vegetables and groceries, newspapers, gas and gifts. Visitors may use the Ampleforth College sports centre (charged), with its indoor pool, tennis and gym, etc. The area abounds with footpaths and three well known long distance footpaths are near. Dog owners are well catered for with two or three enormous fields for exercising alongside the park.

Facilities

Two heated toilet blocks have been refurbished and are of excellent quality, with some washbasins in private cabins. Showers are free. Bathroom (£1) also houses baby changing facilities. Both ladies and men have full facilities for disabled visitors. Laundry with washing machines, dryers, spin dryer and iron and board. Motorcaravan service point. Tourist information room also houses a microwave. Shop. Two excellent play areas. Games field and a barn with table tennis and pool table. Bicycle hire. All year caravan storage. Off site: Riding 2 miles. Golf 3 miles. Fishing 5 miles. Outdoor pool at Helmsley, sports centre at Ampleforth with indoor pool, both have shops and pubs with food.

Open: 1 March - 31 October.

Directions

From York take B1363 to Helmsley. At Oswaldkirk Bank Top turn left on B1257 to Helmsley. Take second left turn signed Ampleforth to site. O.S.GR: SE605797. GPS: N54:12.560 W01:04.427

Charges 2007

Per unit incl. 2 persons and electricity	£ 13.00 - £ 17.00
incl. full services and awning	£ 21.00 - £ 26.00
extra person (14 yrs or over)	£ 2.00
extra child (5-14 yrs)	£ 1.00
awning	£ 2.00

No credit cards.

UK4580 Foxholme Touring Caravan & Camping Park

Harome, Helmsley YO62 5JG (North Yorkshire)

Tel: **01439 771696**

Foxholme is now an 'adult only' park. With only 60 pitches for caravans and a large field for tents, it is unusual in that nearly all the pitches are individual ones in clearings in the quite dense coniferous plantation. The trees give much shade and quite a lot of privacy (manoeuvring may be difficult on some of the pitches). All pitches have electricity (6A, a few need long leads) and six places have hardstanding. Some picnic tables are provided. There are 30 pitches for tourers, the remainder being taken by seasonal units. The site is managed by a warden, with limited reception opening times. Very basic provisions are kept. The park is set in quiet countryside and would be a good base for touring, being within striking distance of the moors, the coast and York. There are no on site activities but campers may use the indoor pool at the Pheasant Hotel in Harome. There is lighting, but a torch would be useful.

Facilities

The toilet block is an older style building and is clean but basic. Laundry facilities and a washing up area. Two further small blocks provide WCs only in other parts of the park. Motorcaravan service point. Caravan storage. Off site: The nearest shops are at Helmsley and Kirkbymoorside, both about 4 miles away, where there is also bicycle hire. Riding and golf also 4 miles.

Open: Easter - 31 October.

Directions

Turn south off the A170 between adjoining villages of Beadlam (to west) and Nawton (to east) at sign to Ryedale School, then 1 mile to park on left (passing another park on right). From east ignore first camp sign at turning before Nawton. From west turn right 400 yards east of Helmsley, signed Harome, turn left at church, go through village and follow camp signs. O.S.GR: SE661831. GPS: N54:14.247 W00:59.420

Charges 2007

Per unit incl. 2 persons	£ 12.50
extra person	£ 1.50
electricity	£ 2.50

No credit cards.

UK4570 Forest Holidays Spiers House

Cropton Forest, Cropton, Pickering YO18 8ES (North Yorkshire)

Tel: **01751 417591**. Email: **info@forestholidays.co.uk**

Forest Holidays is a new partnership between the Forestry Commission and The Camping and Caravanning Club. The Spiers House site is set in a sunny clearing in the middle of Cropton Forest. It is an ideal location for a cycling or walking holiday without having to move your car. The site buildings, built in local stone, are set around a central courtyard with a pedestrian archway leading to the pitches. The welcoming reception also incorporates a well stocked shop. Sloping fields provide for 150 pitches, which include 74 with 10A electricity and 19 with hardstanding.

Facilities

The tiled toilet block is spacious, if a little spartan, with open plan washbasins and roomy, preset showers (refurbishment is planned). Unit for disabled campers. Laundry room. Well stocked shop. Large adventure playground and games field set under tall pines. Raised barbecues are permitted. Off site: Pub with home-brewed beer 1 mile. Riding 5 miles. Fishing 7 miles. Golf 12 miles.

Open: All year excl. 14 January - 28 February.

Directions

From A170 Pickering head west towards Helmsley. Turn right (Cropton and Rosedale) (do not go into Cropton village). Forest and park signed in 4 miles. O.S.GR: SE758918. GPS: N54:18.459 W00:50.776

Charges 2007

Per unit incl. 2 persons	£ 8.70 - £ 13.50
electricity	£ 3.00
child (5-15) yrs	£ 1.80 - £ 2.70

UK4590 Jacobs Mount Caravan Park

Stepney Road, Scarborough YO12 5NL (North Yorkshire)

Tel: **01723 361178**. Email: **jacobsmount@yahoo.co.uk**

Situated just two miles from the centre of Scarborough, on the edge of the Forge Valley National Park, Jacobs Mount is well placed. The sea and the sand are the main attractions, but this is also on the doorstep of the North York moors. In addition to caravan holiday homes in separate areas of the park, there are 142 touring pitches, all with electricity. Of these 131 are fully serviced on well spaced gravel hardstandings. In sunny locations, some pitches have good views. There is a bar with a pleasant lounge (no children), plus a family room and a games/TV room. Bar meals and a quite extensive range of takeaways can be purchased. There is an activity centre and play area for children.

Facilities

The heated toilet block is new and of a high standard. Washbasins in cubicles with WCs, large shower cubicles (free) and a family bathroom (metered hot water) and baby facilities. Motorcaravan service point. Small shop. Bar with bar meals and takeaway. Two play areas. Caravan storage. No gazebo style tents allowed. Off site: Scarborough centre and beach 2 miles. Golf, fishing and bicycle hire 2 miles. Riding 5 miles.

Open: 1 March - 6 November.

Directions

Site entrance is on the A170 Pickering - Scarborough road, about 2 miles west of Scarborough (on the right as you start to drop down into the town). O.S.GR: TA021877. GPS: N54:16.037 W00:26.073

Charges 2007

Per unit incl. 4 persons and electricity (16A)	£ 10.50 - £ 17.50
extra person 3 yrs and over	£ 2.00
dog (max. 2)	£ 2.50

UK4610 Moorside Adult Caravan Park

Lords Moor Lane, Strensall, York YO32 5XJ (North Yorkshire)

Tel: **01904 491208**

Strensall is only a few miles from York, one of England's most attractive cities and Moorside will provide a peaceful haven after a day's sightseeing. It will impress you with its pretty fishing lake, masses of flowers and the tranquillity (except for the odd passing daytime train). There are 57 marked pitches on neat well trimmed grass, most with electricity (5/10A) and 18 with paved hardstanding. A small lake is well stocked for coarse fishing and the pitches bordering the lake are the most popular. York golf course is almost opposite. Children (under 16 years) are not accepted.

Facilities

The purpose built toilet block can be heated and houses immaculately kept facilities with washbasins in cubicles for ladies. One WC is suitable for use by disabled visitors. Fully equipped laundry room. Dishwashing area. Tourist information and books to borrow. Coarse fishing (£2 per day). Caravan storage. Off site: Strensall village with shops and places to eat is less than a mile. Golf 0.5 miles. Riding 3 miles.

Open: March - end October.

Directions

From A1237 York outer ring road follow signs for Earswick and Strensall. At Strensall follow Flaxton road. The park entrance is on the left past signs to Strensall village and York Golf Club. O.S.GR: SE647614. GPS: N54:02.564 W01:00.701

Charges 2007

Per unit incl. 2 persons	£ 8.00 - £ 12.50
electricity	£ 2.00
No credit cards.	

UK4620 Upper Carr Chalet & Touring Park

Upper Carr Lane, Malton Road, Pickering YO18 7JP (North Yorkshire)

Tel: **01751 473115**. Email: **harker@uppercarr.demon.co.uk**

With a central location in the Vale of Pickering, Upper Carr is well placed for the many attractions the area has to offer. Now under new ownership, the enthusiastic manager is keen to develop it into a family friendly park, introducing themed weekends and nature trails. The park is surrounded by a high, well trimmed hedge which protects it from the wind and deadens the road noise. Upper Carr's six acres provide 80 level pitches, 75 with 10A electricity and some with hardstanding. Seasonal units use 25 pitches. The picturesque village of Thornton Dale can be reached on foot.

Facilities

The heated toilet blocks are dated (in 'chalet' style building) but clean. Showers are charged for. Baby facilities. Separate room with WC and washbasin for disabled visitors. Laundry room. Motorcaravan service point. Small shop. Play area. Bicycle hire. Nature trail. Off site: Pub 100 yards. Golf (9-hole) adjacent to park. Pickering within 2 miles. Riding 6 miles. Fishing 5 miles.

Open: 1 March - 31 October.

Directions

Travelling on the Pickering - Malton A169 road, park is on the left about 1.5 miles south of Pickering. O.S.GR: SE804815. GPS: N54:13.378 W00:46.140

Charges 2007

Per unit incl. 2 adults, 2 children and electricity	£ 13.00 - £ 18.90
extra adult	£ 2.50
extra child	£ 1.50

199

UK4640 Goose Wood Caravan Park

Sutton-on-the-Forest, York YO61 1ET (North Yorkshire)

Tel: **01347 810829**. Email: **edward@goosewood.co.uk**

A family owned park in a natural woodland setting, Goose Wood provides a quiet, relaxed atmosphere from which to explore York itself or the surrounding Yorkshire Dales, Wolds or Moors. The park has a well kept air and a rural atmosphere, with 100 well spaced and marked pitches, all with electricity (16A) on hardstanding (four also have water and drainage). No tents are accepted. For children, there is a 'super plus' adventure playground in the trees at one side of the park and for adults, a small coarse fishing lake and attractive, natural woodland for walking, plus a large scale chess set. A new health suite has been added with pool, sauna, hot tub and exercise machines. The park is popular with families in high season when it can be busy at weekends. A 'park and ride' scheme for York operates from nearby all year, six days a week or there is a local bus every two hours, six days a week. The park is just over a mile from Sutton village. A member of the Best of British group.

Facilities

Tiled and heated, the modern toilet block is well maintained. Bathroom (£1). An additional unit provides shower rooms, WC and washbasins in cubicles and extra dishwashing sinks. Full facilities for disabled visitors. Laundry room. Motorcaravan service point. Small shop (with gas). Health Suite (can be hired for 45 minutes, max. 8 people at a time). Fishing lake. Large adventure playground. Games room with pool and TV. Outdoor table tennis. Dogs (max. two per pitch), to be exercised in nearby woodland. No tents are accepted. Off site: Riding or golf 1 mile. Bicycle hire 6 miles. York 6 miles.

Open: All year excl. 15 - 31 January.

Directions

Park is 6 miles north of York; from the A1237 York outer ring-road take the B1363 for Sutton-on-the-Forest and Stillington, taking the first right after the Haxby and Wigginton junction and follow park signs. O.S.GR: SE595636.

Charges 2007

Per unit incl. 1 or 2 persons,	
car and electricity	£ 12.50 - £ 20.00
extra person	£ 2.00
awning or extra pup tent (1 only)	£ 2.00
fully serviced pitch plus	£ 3.00

UK4630 Ripley Caravan Park

Ripley, Harrogate HG3 3AU (North Yorkshire)

Tel: **01423 770050**. Email: **ripleycaravanpark@talk21.com**

Peter and Valerie House are the friendly, resident owners of Ripley Park, an 18 acre grass caravan park with an indoor heated pool. It accommodates 100 touring units and 40 caravan holiday homes on fairly level grass which undulates in parts. Connected by a circular gravel road, some pitches are marked, others carefully spaced (allowing the grass to recover). There are 130 electricity connections (10A) and 20 hardstandings. The owners have planted 2,000 trees and these are developing well to provide individual areas and shelter. A pond with ducks provides an attractive feature. The park is situated at the gateway to the Yorkshire Dales National Park and almost midway between the spa town of Harrogate and historic Knaresborough. The village of Ripley, dominated by its castle, is within walking distance.

Facilities

The central, attractively designed toilet block can be heated and provides smart facilities including washbasins in curtained cubicles, 4 new individual wash facilites, a baby bath and a separate unit with a shower for disabled people. Small laundry. Dishwashing sinks under cover. Motorcaravan service point. Recycling bins. Shop with gas (limited hours in low seasons). Games room with TV. Nursery playroom. Adventure play equipment and football area. Heated indoor pool (75p per person) and sauna. Up to two dogs per unit are welcome unless by prior arrangement. Winter caravan storage.
Off site: Fishing, riding and golf 3 miles. Bus stop 150 yds.

Open: Easter - 31 October.

Directions

About 4 miles north of Harrogate, park access is 150 yds. down the B6165 Knaresborough road from its roundabout junction with the A61. O.S.GR: SE291601. GPS: N54:02.214 W01:33.530

Charges 2007

Per unit incl. 2 persons and electricity	£ 13.00 - £ 15.00

UK4645 The Ranch Caravan Park

Cliffe Common, Cliffe, Selby YO8 6EF (North Yorkshire)

Tel: **01757 638984**. Email: **contact@theranchcaravanpark.co.uk**

The Ranch is a small, family run caravan park set in six acres of woodland. There are 55 pitches in total, with 39 for touring units on well draining land with some hardstandings available. All have electricity (10/16A) and 4 also have water and a drain. Several pitches are most suitable for American style motorhomes and these are welcomed. The reception has a tiny shop that sometimes stocks UHT milk. This is a well maintained park with two areas of open grass, one surrounded by a gravel road. Most of the site is surrounded by trees. There is a security gate at the entrance. There is a slightly overgrown wooded area with some adventure playground equipment amongst it. A large function hall is attached to the toilet block with a small bar, lounge area, tables and a dance floor. Light meals and takeaways are offered on Friday and Saturday evenings. A hut near reception houses a sauna and jacuzzi (accessed by key but the heat needs to be turned on). There is a log cabin for rent with a few more planned.

Facilities

Heated toilet block has free showers (with dividing curtains). Facilities for disabled visitors that doubles as a family bathroom and baby room. Motorcaravan service point. Small laundry. Function hall with bar and lounge area. Light meals and takeaway (Friday and Saturday). Sauna and jacuzzi. Off site: Selby 4 miles. York 12 miles. Fishing 2 miles. Golf and riding 15 miles.

Open: All year excl. 5 January - 5 February.

Directions

Leave M62 at exit 37 (Goole) and take A63 towards Selby. At Cliffe turn right and after 1 mile, turn left at crossroads. Park is 80 yards on the right. O.S.GR: SE663338.

Charges 2007

Per unit incl. 2 persons and electricity	£ 13.00
extra person	£ 1.50
child (2-16 yrs)	£ 1.00

THE RANCH CARAVAN PARK

CLIFFE COMMON SELBY NORTH YORKSHIRE YO8 6EF

TEL: 01757 638 984   WWW.THERANCHCARAVANPARK.CO.UK

Ideal base for the city of York. Small, Peaceful, idyllic family run site. Level hardstand pitches with electric. Excellent toilet and shower facilities including disabled/family room. Laundry, Sauna and Jacuzzi. Lounge bar serving food open at weekends. Open all year except January. Telephone for a brochure or see us on the web at *www.theranchcaravanpark.co.uk*

UK4638 Alders Caravan Park

Home Farm, Alne, York YO61 1RY (North Yorkshire)

Tel: **01347 838722**. Email: **enquiries@homefarmalne.co.uk**

The Alders is located in the village of Alne, only nine miles from the centre of the ancient city of York. Carefully developed on a working farm in historic parkland, the drive to reach the pitches gives a real feeling of space. On reaching the 87 level pitches (25 for tourers, the rest for seasonal units), you will find an area of well trimmed grass and a pitch layout designed to give as much privacy and space as possible. Arranged in small bays, each group is named after a Yorkshire Abbey or Dale. Newly planted woodland with woodland walks and a water meadow with wild flowers enhance the wonderful peace and tranquillity. The site overlooks the village cricket pitch where you can watch summer matches or enjoy a drink at the club bar at weekends. This park would suit couples or young families (no play area). The village centre is only a short stroll away. Alders is also well placed for visiting the many attractions of the area, for example York, Harrogate and Castle Howard.

Facilities

The central toilet block is heated with family sized shower rooms, one also has a bath (£1 charge). A new block includes en-suite bathrooms with bath or shower, laundry and dishwashing facilities. Provision for disabled visitors. Gas is sold at reception (shop in the village). Off site: Floodlit tennis courts in the village. Fishing 2 miles. Golf 3 miles. Riding 4 miles.

Open: 1 March - 31 October.

Directions

From the north on the A19: after leaving Easingwold bypass take next right turn signed Alne. From the south (A19), 5 miles north of Shipton turn left at sign for Alne. In 1.5 miles at T-junction turn left and in about 0.5 miles, site is signed in the centre of the village. O.S.GR: SE496651.
GPS: N54:04.911 W01:14.463

Charges 2007

Per unit incl. 2 persons and electricity	£ 11.50
extra person	£ 2.50
awning	£ 1.50
No credit cards.	

UK4660 Woodhouse Farm Caravan & Camping Park

Winksley, Ripon HG4 3PG (North Yorkshire)

Tel: **01765 658309**. Email: **woodhouse.farm@talk21.com**

This secluded family park on a former working farm, is only six miles from Ripon and about four from the World Heritage site of Fountains Abbey. It is a very rural park with a spacious feel and various pitching areas are tucked away in woodland areas or around the edges of hedged fields with the centres left clear for children. There are hard roads and most of the 160 pitches have 16A electricity. There are 56 acres in total, 17.5 devoted to the site and 20 acres of woodland for walking, with a good area where dogs can run free. The 2.5 acre fishing lake (day tickets from reception) is a big attraction and provides a pleasant area for picnics or walks. The tastefully developed bar (daily) and restaurant (weekends only) offers reasonably priced menus. Woodhouse Farm has a quiet, secluded location from which many excursions can be made – the Yorkshire Dales of Nidderdale, Wharfedale, Wensleydale and Swaledale are all within easy reach. As in most parts of the Dales, the peace is occasionally disturbed by passing jets, but happily not very often.

Facilities

The clean toilet block near the touring pitches has been upgraded and includes heating, roomy showers (20p) and some washbasins in cabins. Covered dishwashing sinks. Two bathrooms. Facilities for disabled visitors. Extra facilities are in the farm buildings along with a well equipped laundry, reception and shop. Gas supplies. Motorcaravan services. Bar (daily) and restaurant (weekends). Takeaway on request. Games room, table tennis, pool table and TV. Play equipment around the park. Fishing. Mountain bike hire. Caravan storage. Deposit for amenity block key £10. Off site: Twice daily bus service passes gate. Many attractive villages with inns supplying food and drinks. The small historic city of Ripon has a beautiful cathedral. Riding 3 miles. Golf 6 miles.

Open: 1 March - 31 October.

Directions

From Ripon take Fountains Abbey - Pateley Bridge road (B6265). After approx. 3.5 miles turn right to Grantley and then follow campsite signs for further 1-2 miles. O.S.GR: SE241715.
GPS: N54:08.245 W01:38.080

Charges 2006

Per unit incl. 2 persons	£ 11.00 - £ 14.00
with electricity	£ 12.50 - £ 15.50
extra person	£ 2.50
child (5-16 yrs)	£ 0.75
small tent incl. 2 persons	£ 9.50 - £ 12.50

UK4670 Wood Nook Caravan Park

Skirethorns, Threshfield, Skipton BD23 5NU (North Yorkshire)

Tel: **01756 752412**. Email: **enquiries@woodnook.net**

Wood Nook is a family-run park in the heart of Wharfedale, part of the Yorkshire Dales National Park. The access road is narrow for a short distance, so care should be taken. The site includes six acres of woodland with quite rare flora and wildlife. Reception is in the farmhouse, as is the small shop. The gently sloping fields have gravel roads and provide 20 touring pitches with gravel hardstanding. All have electricity (10A) and nearby water and chemical disposal points. There is also room for 24 tents and there are some caravan holiday homes to let. The Thompson family are very friendly, always willing to have a chat, although Wood Nook is still a working farm producing beef cattle. The park itself adjoins the fells, with direct access from the top of the site. Nearby is the village of Grassington, with its cobbled main street and quaint gift shops. This is a delightful and peaceful base from which to explore the Yorkshire Dales.

Facilities

Converted farm buildings provide modern, clean sanitary facilities which can be heated. Washbasins in cubicles for ladies. Roomy showers (in another building - coin operated). Laundry facilities. Motorcaravan service points. Licensed shop for basics and gifts (from Easter). Gas. Small play area. American motorhomes are taken by prior arrangement. Internet access. WiFi coverage (charged). Off site: Fishing and bicycle hire 2 miles. Riding 3 miles. Golf 9 miles. Leisure centre.

Open: 1 March - 31 October.

Directions

Threshfield is 9 miles north of Skipton on the B6265. Continue through village onto B6160 and after garage turn left into Skirethorns Lane. Follow signs for 600 yds, keeping left up narrow lane, then turn right up track for 300 yds. The last 900 yds. is single track – on arrival you could phone ahead to make sure it is clear. O.S.GR: SD974641.

Charges 2007

Per person	£ 3.00
child (5-15 yrs)	£ 1.50
serviced pitch incl. electricity	£ 8.00
hiker or cyclist incl. tent	£ 5.00

Payment also accepted in Euros.

UK4690 Constable Burton Hall Caravan Park

Constable Burton Hall, Leyburn DL8 5LJ (North Yorkshire)
Tel: **01677 450428**

This tranquil park is in beautiful Wensleydale and the emphasis is on peace and quiet, the wardens working to provide a relaxing environment. Being in the grounds of the Hall, it has a spacious, park-like feel to it. On part level, part sloping, well trimmed grass, the 120 pitches (40 for touring units) are of a good size and all have electrical connections (10A). There are no pitches for tents. The gardens of the Hall are open to the public, with a collection of maples and terraced gardens developed by Mrs Vida Burton. There is no shop on site but nearby Leyburn will provide all your needs. Opposite the park entrance is the Wyvill Arms for bar meals.

Facilities

Two toilet blocks built of local stone and blending in with the local surroundings, have been refurbished recently, are well tiled, kept very clean, and can be heated. New facility for disabled visitors and baby room. Gas supplies.
Off site: Irregular bus service from site gate. Fishing and golf within 5 miles.

Open: Late March - 31 October.

Directions

Park is by the A684 between Bedale and Leyburn, 0.5 miles from the village of Constable Burton on the Leyburn side. O.S.GR: SE152907.
GPS: N54:18.750 W01:45.250

Charges 2007

Per unit incl. 2 persons	£ 14.00 - £ 17.00
extra person	£ 5.00 - £ 6.00
child (5-16 yrs)	£ 3.00

UK4710 Rudding Holiday Park

Follifoot, Harrogate HG3 1JH (North Yorkshire)
Tel: **01423 870439**. Email: **holiday-park@ruddingpark.com**

The extensive part wooded, part open grounds of Rudding Park are very attractive, peaceful and well laid out. One camping area is sloping but terraces provide level pitches and further pitches are in the very sheltered old walled garden. All 141 touring pitches have electricity and 49 'super pitches' are fully serviced. Further pitches are let on a seasonal basis and a separate area contains 96 owner-occupied caravan holiday homes and chalets. On the outer edge of the park is 'The Deer House', a family pub serving bar meals. There is also an 18-hole golf course and driving range.

Facilities

Two toilet blocks (heated when necessary and may be under pressure at peak times), some washbasins in cabins, baby room. Laundry Facilities for disabled visitors. Motorcaravan services. Shop (1/3-4/11), sometimes limited hours). Gas. Restaurant and bar. Heated outdoor pool (25/5-30/8 supervised (extra charge). Adventure playground. Golf. Off site: Buses to Harrogate and Knaresborough. Riding 1 mile. Fishing 2 miles.

Open: 1 March - 31 January.

Directions

Park is 3 miles south-east of Harrogate, clearly signed north of the A658 and west of the A661. O.S.GR: SE333528.

Charges 2007

Per pitch with electricity	£ 15.00 - £ 30.00
Special offers - contact park.	

UK4720 Knight Stainforth Hall Caravan & Camping Park

Little Stainforth, Settle BD24 0DP (North Yorkshire)
Tel: **01729 822200**. Email: **info@knightstainforth.co.uk**

In a very attractive setting, this park is located in the heart of the Yorkshire Dales. The camping area is on slightly sloping grass, sheltered by mature woodland. There are 100 touring pitches, 50 with electricity (10A) and 10 with hardstanding, and a separate area contains 60 privately owned caravan holiday homes. A gate leads from the bottom of the camping field giving access to the river bank where the Ribble bubbles over small waterfalls and rocks and whirls around deep pools where campers swim in warm weather. Fishing permits and licences are available from reception and one can fish for trout (or salmon when available).

Facilities

A new building provides all new facilities including some washbasins in cubicles. Dishwashing sinks. Laundry room with washing machine and dryers. Shop. Games/TV room. Play area with safety base. Fishing. Security barrier at entrance. Deposit for key to toilet block and barrier £10. Off site: Bicycle hire and golf 3 miles. Riding 6 miles. The Dales Falconry and Conservation Centre at Felzor.

Open: 1 March - 31 October.

Directions

From Settle, drive west towards Giggleswick. Ignore turn marked Stainforth and Horton, and in 200 yards turn right into Stackhouse Lane (Knight Stainforth). After 2 miles turn right at crossroads. O.S.GR: SD815671. GPS: N54:06.015 W02:17.090

Charges 2007

Per unit incl. 2 persons	£ 12.00 - £ 14.00
extra person	£ 1.50 - £ 2.50

UK4750 Howgill Lodge Caravan & Camping Park

Barden, Skipton BD23 6DJ (North Yorkshire)

Tel: **01756 720655**. Email: **info@howgill-lodge.co.uk**

Howgill Lodge is a traditional family site set in the heart of the Dales. Arranged on a sloping hillside, the terraced pitches have fantastic views. It is a small park catering for the needs of walkers, tourers and the people who like to just relax. The whole area is a haven for both experienced walkers or the casual rambler, without having to move your car. All the pitches at the upper part of the park are on hardstanding and have electricity (10A), the lower ones are mainly on grass (40 in total). Picnic tables and chairs are provided. Pretty villages abound in the area, all with attractive inns.

Facilities

Heated toilet facilities are at the entrance. Showers are large and adjustable (on payment). Fully equipped laundry room. Two small blocks housing WCs are lower down the site. Shop. No play area. Fishing licences from reception. B&B is available. Off site: Bus service within walking distance (3 per day). Skipton, an agricultural market town, is 8 miles and the well known Bolton Abbey, with its beautiful riverside walks is 3 miles. Fishing 1 mile. Golf, riding and bicycle hire 7 miles.

Open: 1 April - 31 October.

Directions

Turn off A59 Skipton - Harrogate road at roundabout onto B6160 Bolton Abbey, Burnsall road. Three miles past Bolton Abbey at Barden Towers, bear right signed Appletreewick and Pateley Bridge. This road is fairly narrow for 1.25 miles (with passing places). Park is signed on right at phone box. O.S.GR: SE065593. GPS: N54:01.546 W01:54.590

Charges 2007

Per unit, 2 persons and electricity	£ 14.00
family unit with electricity	£ 19.50

UK4755 Maustin Caravan Park

Kearby with Netherby, Wetherby LS22 4DA (North Yorkshire)

Tel: **0113 2886234**. Email: **judith@maustin.co.uk**

A tranquil site for couples only, this well manicured park is set within the North Yorkshire National Park. It offers 25 well spaced pitches sited on grass, all with peaceful, scenic views of the surrounding area. Caravan holiday homes are in a separate area. A bowling club on the site offers membership to all visitors and competitions are held throughout the season. Relax in the comfortable lounge or in the tasteful bar and restaurant area. The attentive park managers ensure that the luxury facilities are spotlessly clean so that you have a pleasant stay.

Facilities

One heated, purpose built toilet block has luxury showers, free hairdryers and roomy toilet and washing cubicles, all with non slip flooring. Designated facilitiy for disabled visitors. Laundry room. Kitchen area with freezer. Milk, newspapers, etc. to order. Internet facilities. Off site: Riding 2 miles. Golf 4 miles.

Open: All year excl. February.

Directions

From A1 North take exit 47 for Harrogate (A59), then after three roundabouts (9 miles) turn left on A61 (Leeds). In 2 miles turn left (Kirkby Overblow) then right to Kearby and park. O.S.GR: SE331468.

Charges 2007

Per unit incl. 2 persons	£ 15.50 - £ 17.50
extra person	£ 2.00

UK4760 Riverside Meadows Country Caravan Park

Ure Bank Top, Ripon HG4 1JD (North Yorkshire)

Tel: **01765 602964**. Email: **info@flowerofmay.com**   *see advertisement on page 195*

Riverside Meadows is a rural park, although the approach to it belies that fact. The short approach from the main road passes a row of houses and a factory, but once they are passed, the park opens up before you and you are once again back in the countryside. There are plenty of caravan holiday homes here but they are, on the whole, quite separate from the 64 touring pitches. These pitches, practically all with electrical hook-ups, are mainly on gently sloping grass with a few hardstandings. A meadow separates the park from the River Ure, a favourite place for strolling and fishing (licences available). There is lots to see and do on and off the park for both families and couples.

Facilities

The tiled toilet block is quite new and includes a baby room, dishwashing room, a fully fitted shower room for disabled visitors. Laundry facilities. Shop. Bar with snacks. Games room. Well equipped play area. An indoor pool is planned. Off site: Fishing, bicycle hire and riding 800 yds. Golf 1.25 miles. The delightful market town (city) of Ripon with its ancient cathedral is only 20 minutes walk.

Open: Easter - 31 October.

Directions

At the most northern roundabout on the Ripon bypass (A61), turn onto the A6108 signed Ripon, Masham and Leyburn. Go straight on at mini-roundabout and park is signed on right. O.S.GR: SE317727. GPS: N54:09.027 W01:30.900

Charges 2007

Per unit incl. up to 4 persons	£ 11.50 - £ 19.00
extra person (over 3 yrs)	£ 3.00
dog (max. 2)	£ 1.00

UK4715 Riverside Caravan Park

High Bentham LA2 7FJ (North Yorkshire)

Tel: **01524 261272**. Email: **info@riversidecaravanpark.co.uk**

Riverside nestles on the banks of the River Wenning, owned and managed by the Marshall family since its first development from a grass field site 30 years ago. The 206 privately owned caravan holiday homes are quite separate and located away from the main touring and tent areas. These include 12 'super' pitches on tarmac hardstanding (excellent for motorcaravans and early and late touring) and 49 marked, level grass touring pitches with 10A electricity and TV aerial points, divided by mature trees and hedges. At the far end of the park a new area has been developed for 50 seasonal pitches on gravel hardstanding designed not to be too regimented and a large fenced field for ball games adjoining. The reception is smart and comfortable with weekly local 'what's on' notices. Fishing is possible from their stretch of the river (permits and tickets from reception). High Bentham 18-hole golf course is nearby. There are plenty of walks in the area and, for the more adventurous, there are the three peaks of Ingleborough, Whernside and Pen-y-Ghent.

Facilities

An all new toilet facilities with under-floor heating are centrally located. Toilets and washbasin cubicles in separate sections opening from a spacious hall, large, well equipped, unisex showers in a separate area. Fully equipped toilet and shower room for disabled visitors (Radar key) which doubles as a family shower room (charged). Large airy utility room and campers' kitchen. Chemical disposal. Motorcaravan services. A new building will house a laundry and internet access point. Children's room with TV, table tennis and video games. Small outdoor play area. Dinghies can be put onto the river where you can also swim. Caravan storage.

Open: 1 March - November.

Directions

From B6480 in High Bentham, at Black Bull hotel, follow caravan signs and turn sharp right after crossing the river bridge. O.S.GR: SD662687. GPS: N54:06.787 W02:30.640

Charges 2007

Per person	£ 4.50
child (2-16 yrs)	£ 2.50
pitch incl. electricity	£ 6.00 - £ 7.50
dog	£ 1.50

Min. charge per night £8.75.
Less 10% for bookings over 7 nights.

UK4740 Jasmine Park

Cross Lane, Snainton, Scarborough YO13 9BE (North Yorkshire)

Tel: **01723 859240**. Email: **info@jasminepark.co.uk**

Jasmine is a very attractive, quiet and well manicured park with owners who go to much trouble to produce many plants to decorate a very colourful entrance. Set in the Vale of Pickering, the park is level, well drained and protected by a coniferous hedge. The 106 pitches (54 for touring units) are on grass, with electricity connections (10A) for all caravans and some tents. There is no play equipment for children, although a field is provided for games. Much tourist information is provided in a log cabin and the owners are only too happy to advise. The market town of Pickering and the seaside town of Scarborough are both 8 miles. Many local attractions are within easy reach, including Castle Howard, Dalby Forest, Sledmere House, Nunington Hall, Goathland (the setting for ITV's 'Heartbeat') and the North York Moors Railway. Some privately owned log cabins and seasonal tourers are also on the site. This is an award-winning, peaceful park for a restful holiday. A member of the Countryside Discovery group.

Facilities

The heated toilet block has been refurbished to a high standard and is kept very clean. It includes a large room for families or disabled visitors containing a bath, shower, WC and washbasin (access by key). Laundry room with dishwashing sinks, washing machine, dryer and iron (hot water metered). Motorcaravan service point. Licensed shop selling essentials and gas. Dogs are welcome but there is no dog walk. Caravan storage. Off site: Bus service in village 0.5 miles. Riding 2 miles. Golf driving range and 9-hole course 2 miles. Fishing and bicycle hire 5 miles.

Open: 1 March - 31 December.

Directions

Snainton is on the A170 Pickering - Scarborough road and park is signed at eastern end of the village. Follow Barker GPS: N54:13.115 W00:34.534

Charges 2007

Per unit incl. 4 persons	£ 14.00 - £ 20.00
extra person	£ 1.50
child (5-14 yrs)	£ 1.00
awning	£ 2.00

Min. stay at Easter 4 nights, other B.Hs 3 nights.

UK4765 Otterington Park

Station Farm, South Otterington, Northallerton DL7 9JB (North Yorkshire)

Tel: **01609 780656**. Email: **info@otteringtonpark.com**

This family owned, five acre park is located near a farm and the entrance to the park is via stables, paddocks and the farm itself. Between Thirsk and Northallerton, in the Vale of York, it is ideally placed to visit the moors and dales of Yorkshire along with local market towns, theme parks and stately homes. Predominantly it is a flat grass site with pebble hardstanding providing 40 touring pitches, each with 16A electricity. There is a separate paddock for tents or visitors not needing electricity. The park is shared with seasonal caravans and some privately owned luxury chalets. At present, landscaping offers limited shade. Unmade roads throughout may cause dust problems. A family oriented park, there is a children's playground and grassy play areas. The owners have supplied good tourist information and local nature walks for visitors. There is course fishing in a well stocked, spring fed, one acre lake located 200 m. from the site. The main London - Edinburgh railway line runs to the rear of the park, so some train noise may be experienced.

Facilities

One purpose built, clean block in a heated building. Unisex en-suite style shower rooms with free showers. Laundry. Facilities for disabled visitors incorporating a baby area. Small shop in reception. Play areas. Fishing. Off site: Large supermarket 3 miles. Local bus service to Thirsk and Northallerton run every 2 hours from park entrance (not Sunday) Several local country pubs serving meals within 1 mile. Riding 1 mile. Golf 3 miles.

Open: 1 March - 31 October.

Directions

From A1M join A684 for Leeming Bar and Morton-on-Swale. At roundabout bear right on A167 signed South Otterington and Topcliffe. At South Otterington crossroads (pub) turn left signed Thornton-le-Dale to park in 500 yards.

Charges 2007

Per unit incl. 4 persons and electricity	£ 15.00 - £ 19.00

Otterington Park   Northallerton (01609) 780656   www.otteringtonpark.com

South Otterington, Northallerton,

A quality, purpose built, 11 acre park for up to 40 touring units and 40 mobile homes/lodges, with water and 16/32 amp electricity, heated amenity block with five individual bath and shower rooms & disabled shower room with toilet and hand basin. Static caravans and holiday lodges for sale. Situated in the Vale of York, Otterington is an ideal base for visiting the moors and dales of Yorkshire including TV locations e.g. Emmerdale, Brideshead Revisited – historic cities, market towns, leisure centres, theme parks, golf courses, equestrian facilities and stately homes. Coarse fishing also available on our own lake.

North Yorkshire DL7 9JB

UK4775 Cote Ghyll Caravan & Camping Park

Osmotherley, Northallerton DL6 3AH (North Yorkshire)

Tel: **01609 883425**. Email: **hills@coteghyll.com**

Jon and Helen Hill are working hard to maintain the good standard and make improvements to their park, and their efforts are evident. The site is set on a secluded hillside with the higher pitches terraced and the lower ones on a level grassy area, bordered by the small Cod Beck stream. Of the 80 pitches, 50 are for tourers. There are also 18 pitches used for caravan holiday homes and 30 are seasonal. All have 10A electricity hook ups. A simple site, Cote Ghyll is highly suited for lovers of peace and quiet, for bird watching or for more energetic hobbies such as cycling and walking. On the western edge of the North York Moors, cycle paths and footpaths lead almost from the site entrance and the three main long distance footpaths, the Lyke Wake walk, the Cleveland Way and the Coast to Coast, all pass close by. A 10 minute stroll takes you to the pretty and popular Osmotherley village, where there is a post office and general store, tea rooms and two pubs and a bistro selling reasonably priced meals.

Facilities

Two heated toilet blocks, one new, provide free power showers, vanity style washbasins and hairdryers and dishwashing. Bathroom and facilities for babies and disabled visitors. Laundry room with washing machine, dryer, iron and board. Drying room. Reception sells gas and basic supplies. Play area. Caravan storage. New reception and shop. Off site: Shop and pubs 10 minutes walk. Fishing 1 mile. Bicycle hire 6 miles. Golf and riding 8 miles. Mount Grace Priory 4 miles. Swimming pool and leisure centre 6 miles. Beach 18 miles.

Open: 1 March - 31 October.

Directions

Osmotherley is east of the A19. Leave the A19 at A684 exit signed Northallerton and Osmotherely. Go to Osmotherley and site is at the northern end of the village, well signed. O.S.GR: SE460983.

Charges 2007

Per unit incl. 2 persons	£ 13.00 - £ 16.00
with electricity	£ 15.00 - £ 18.00
walkers or cyclists (2 persons)	£ 6.00 - £ 7.00
extra person	£ 2.00
child 5-12 yrs (max. 4)	£ 1.00
No credit cards.	

UK4780 Lebberston Touring Park

Filey Road, Lebberston, Scarborough YO11 3PE (North Yorkshire)
Tel: **01723 585723**. Email: **info@lebberstontouring.co.uk**

Lebberston Touring Park is a quiet, spacious touring site and is highly suitable for anyone seeking a quiet relaxing break, such as mature couples or young families (although tents are not accepted). There is no play area or games room, the only concession to children being a large central area with goal posts, so teenagers may get bored. The park itself has a very spacious feel – it is gently sloping and south facing and the views are superb. There are 125 numbered pitches with 75 for touring units. All have 10A electricity and 25 are on hardstanding. The circular access road is tarmac, the grass is well manicured and the entrance a mass of flowers. Reception is part of a farmhouse style new build, also the home of the owners and their young family. The resorts of Filey, Bridlington, Scarborough and Hornsea provide something for everyone, the moors and the Dalby forest are also within a short distance. This being such a popular area, we feel justified in adding another site to this guide, especially one of such quality.

Facilities

Recently upgraded toilet blocks are of high quality and kept very clean. Large shower cubicles and washbasins in cubicles with curtains. Both blocks have dishwashing sinks and one has a family bathroom (20p). Good room for disabled visitors. Laundry with washing machine, dryer, spin dryer, iron and board. A key is supplied for the laundry and bathroom, with radar key acess to the disabled shower room. Reception sells a few supplies, plus papers, ice cream and gas. Only 'breathable' groundsheets are permitted. Off site: Hourly bus 5 minutes walk. Local pub within 5 minutes walking distance. Each new arrival is given details of parking in Scarborough including a parking disc.

Open: 1 March - 31 October.

Directions

From A64 Malton - Scarborough road turn right at roundabout (MacDonald's, pub and superstore) signed B1261 Filey. Go through Cayton, Killerby and in 4.5 miles site is signed on right. O.S.GR: TA082823.

Charges 2008

Per unit incl. 2 persons and electricity	£ 13.00 - £ 21.00
extra person	£ 1.50
child (5-14 yrs)	£ 1.00
trailer tent over 8 sq.m.	£ 2.00
full awning	£ 2.00

UK4793 Spring Willows Touring Park

Main Road, Staxton, Scarborough YO12 4SB (North Yorkshire)
Tel: **01723 891505**. Email: **enquires@springwillows.co.uk**

With good road links to the coast at Scarborough, Whitby or Filey and inland to York, Spring WIllows is ideal for a family visit to this area. The social focus of the park is a well stocked bar with free entertainment every weekend including live acts and themed weekends. An eating area serves meals and hot snacks. A small attractive outdoor beer garden and patio area is situated next to the bar and overlooks a culverted stream. Families with children are well catered for with an abundance of facilities, including a children's club and play areas. A small heated indoor pool is unsupervised (CCTV) with adult only sessions held daily. The park provides 67 flat, terraced touring pitches with some hardstanding, plus a slightly sloping tent field. Thirty caravan holiday homes are in one area with more planned. The enthusiastic new owner is currently renovating this mature park and insists on reduced noise after 23.00. to allow everyone to enjoy their stay.

Facilities

One central older toilet block, plus a heated building near reception with free showers and private wash cubicles. Facilities for disabled visitors in reception area. Laundry. Well stocked shop. Indoor swimming pool. Play areas. Off site: Fishing 2 miles. Beach 5 miles.

Open: All year excl. 4 January - 28 February.

Directions

On A64 at roundabout follow signs for Filey and Flixton on A1039. Immediately after roundabout entrance to park is on the right. O.S.GR: TA024793.

Charges 2006

Per unit incl. 2 persons and electricity	£ 8.00 - £ 15.00
extra person	£ 2.00
child (3-17 yrs)	£ 1.00
awning	£ 2.00

UK4700 Nostell Priory Holiday Park

Nostell, Wakefield WF4 1QD (West Yorkshire)

Tel: **01924 863938**. Email: **info@nostellprioryholidaypark.co.uk**

This tranquil, secluded woodland park is within the Nostell Priory estate. Under new ownership, the site now provides just 25 touring pitches, plus 82 caravan holiday homes in a separate area. In a grassy, flat and sheltered area edged with mature trees, all the touring pitches have electricity connections (5A). There is a hardstanding area suitable for motorcaravans. Amenities are designed to blend into the environment in rustic wood, including the sanitary block. Nostell Priory itself, with its collection of Chippendale furniture and attractive gardens, is well worth a visit. Fishing, golf and watersports are possible locally (details in reception). The park is well cared for and the natural environment is encouraged so there is an abundance of birds and wildlife. The Dales, York and the Peak District are all an easy drive away. Buses pass the end of the drive (a mile long).

Facilities

The toilet block, although older in style, has been refurbished and includes some washbasins in cubicles (coded entry). Separate room for dishwashing. Laundry with two washing machines and a dryer (opening times on the door). Gas supplies. Milk and papers can be ordered at reception. Play area (no ball games on site). Fishing. Up to two dogs are accepted. Off site: Nearest shops 2 miles. Golf 5 miles. Boat launching 8 miles.

Open: 1 March - 31 October.

Directions

Park entrance is off A638 Wakefield - Doncaster road, 5 miles southeast of Wakefield. Follow drive for 0.5 miles keeping the rose nursery on your left. Approaching from the south on A638, the site entrance is almost a mile past the entry to the Priory, on the right. O.S.GR: SE394181. GPS: N53:39.297 W01:23.910

Charges 2007

Per unit incl. 2 persons	£ 14.00 - £ 18.00
2 person tent	£ 12.00 - £ 16.00
extra person (over 5 yrs)	£ 2.00
dog (max. 2)	£ 1.00

You might also like to consider...

MAP 5

The northwest region boasts a wealth of industrial heritage with undiscovered countryside, the vibrant cities of Manchester and Liverpool, the seaside resorts of Blackpool and Morecambe Bay, plus miles of glorious coastline, home to a wide variety of bird species.

THIS REGION INCLUDES: CHESHIRE, LANCASHIRE, MERSEYSIDE, GREATER MANCHESTER AND THE HIGH PEAKS OF DERBYSHIRE

The miles of beautiful, North West countryside offers endless opportunities for recreation. For the more active, the peaceful plains of Cheshire are a walker's haven with endless trails to choose from. Lancashire is also good walking country, with way marked paths passing through the outstanding forest of Bowland, which affords marvellous views over the Lake District in Cumbria and the Yorkshire Dales. Birdwatchers are catered for too, with the coast offering some of the best bird spotting activitiy in the country, most notably along the Sefton coast and around the Wirral Peninsula. The region's cities have their own charm. Manchester, with its fabulous shopping centres and vibrant nightlife, boasts a rich Victorian heritage; the maritime city of Liverpool has more museums and galleries than any other UK city outside London; Lancaster features fine Georgian buildings and an imposing Norman castle; while Chester is renowned for its medieval architecture and shopping galleries. And offering good, old-fashioned seaside fun is Blackpool. England's most popular seaside resort is packed full of lively entertainment and attractions, such as the white knuckle rides at the pleasure beach, amusement games on the pier and the observation decks in the famous Tower.

Places of interest

Cheshire: Tatton Park in Knutsford; Chester Cathedral and Zoo; Cheshire Military Museum; Lyme Park stately home in Macclesfield; Beeston Castle; Boat Museum at Ellesmere Port.

Lancashire: Williamson Park, Castle and Leisure Park in Lancaster; Camelot Theme Park; Museum of Football in Preston; Morecambe Bay; Hoghton Tower and National Museum of Football in Preston.

Merseyside: Liverpool Football Club Museum and Tour Centre; The Beatles Story Museum; Speke Hall Garden and Estate; The Wirral Country Park; Williamson Tunnels Heritage Centre.

Greater Manchester: Imperial War Museum North; Manchester United Football Club Museum; The Lowry; Corgi Heritage Centre in Rochdale; Stockport Air Raid Shelter.

Did you know?

The first public gallery to open in England was in Liverpool in 1877.

Lancaster Castle is infamous as host to the Pendle Witch trials in 1612.

The first passenger railway station was built in Manchester.

Hoghton Tower is where King James I knighted a loin of beef in 1617 – hence the name Sirloin.

To date 300 bird species have been recorded within the boundaries of Sefton.

Chester has the most complete set of city walls in Britain.

Opened in 1894, the Blackpool Tower was copied from the Eiffel Tower; the height to the top of the flagpole is 518 feet 9 inches.

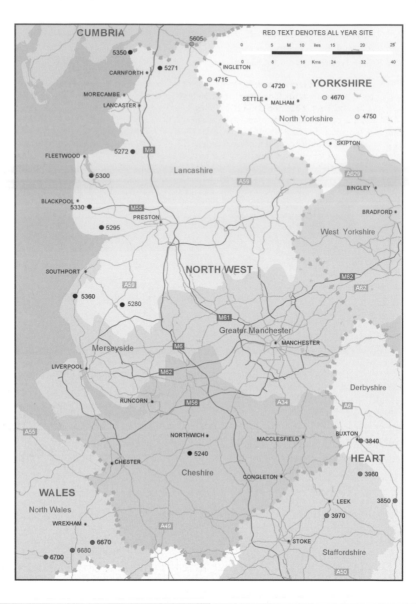

RED TEXT DENOTES ALL YEAR SITE

CUMBRIA

5605
5350
CARNFORTH · 5271
INGLETON
4715
MORECAMBE ·
LANCASTER ·
SETTLE · 4720
MALHAM ·
4670
YORKSHIRE
North Yorkshire
4750

SKIPTON

FLEETWOOD · 5272 · M6
5300
Lancashire
A59
A629
BINGLEY ·
BLACKPOOL · 5330
PRESTON
M55
5295
BRADFORD ·
West Yorkshire

SOUTHPORT · 5360
A58
5280
NORTH WEST
M62
A62
M61
Greater Manchester
MANCHESTER
Merseyside M6
LIVERPOOL
M62
RUNCORN ·
M56
A34
Derbyshire
A6
A55
NORTHWICH · 5240
MACCLESFIELD · BUXTON
3840
CHESTER
Cheshire
CONGLETON ·
HEART
3980
WALES
North Wales
LEEK 3850
WREXHAM · A49
3970
6670
STOKE
6680
Staffordshire
6700
A50

Widely regarded as the 'Bible' by site owners and readers alike, there is no better guide when it comes to forming an independent view of a campsite's quality. When you need to be confident in your choice of campsite, you need the Alan Rogers Guide.

☑ Sites only included on merit
☑ Sites cannot pay to be included
☑ Independently inspected, rigorously assessed
☑ Impartial reviews
☑ 40 years of expertise

INSPECTED CAMPSITES & SELECTED

UK5240 Lamb Cottage Caravan Park

Dalefords Lane, Whitegate, Northwich CW8 2BN (Cheshire)

Tel: **01606 882302**. Email: **lynn@lccp.fsworld.co.uk**

This quiet, family run 'adult only' park is set in the midst of the lovely Vale Royal area of Cheshire. Mike and Lynn Howard are making great improvements with a complete redevelopment of the touring section and new toilet and shower facilities. The entrance road is flanked by 22 privately owned residential caravan holiday homes which are not unduly obtrusive, and a second area beyond has 15 landscaped seasonal caravan pitches. Beyond this again is the touring area which has 25 large pitches, all with 16A electric hook-ups, gravel hardstandings, water and drainage. Only 'breathable' groundsheets are permitted and tents and motorcycles are not accepted. Nearby are Delamere Forest with its walking and mountain biking trails, Whitegate Way walking trail, Oulton Park Motor Racing Circuit, castles at Peckforton and Beeston, and the city of Chester, which is 12 miles.

Facilities

Toilet and shower facilities are housed in a new custom built 'park home' style unit which includes washbasins in cubicles and facilities for disabled guests. Dishwashing area. Laundry room. Recycling of glass and paper. Calor gas stocked. Fenced dog walk (max. 2 dogs per unit permitted). Off site: Pub serving food under 1 mile. Riding 1.5 miles. Golf 2 miles. Supermarket 3 miles. Fishing 3 miles. Bicycle hire 4 miles.

Open: 1 March - 31 October.

Directions

From M6 exit 19 take A556 towards Chester. After about 12 miles turn left at traffic lights (signed Winsford and Whitegate) into Dalefords Lane. Continue for about 1 mile and site entrance is on right between white house and bungalow. O.S.GR: SJ614693. GPS: N53:13.074 W02:34.834

Charges 2007

Per pitch incl. 2 persons and electricity	£ 18.00
extra person	£ 5.00

UK5360 Willowbank Touring Park

Coastal Road, Ainsdale, Southport PR8 3ST (Mersey)

Tel: **01704 571566**. Email: **info@willowbankcp.co.uk**

Well situated for the Sefton coast and Southport, Willowbank is a fairly new park. The touring park is on the edge of sand dunes amongst mature, wind swept trees. Entrance to the park is controlled by a barrier, with a pass-key issued at the excellent reception building which doubles as a sales office for the substantial, high quality caravan holiday home development. The new owners are very well supported on the touring side by the reception team who have considerable experience in managing the touring park. There are 54 touring pitches, 30 on gravel hardstanding and 24 on grass, all with 10A electricity. Motorhomes or caravans longer than 27 feet (8 m) are not accepted. There could be some noise from the nearby main road. This is a good area for cycling and walking and the attractions of Southport with its parks, gardens, funfair and shopping are 4 miles away.

Facilities

The purpose built, heated toilet block is of a high standard including an excellent bathroom for disabled visitors, although the showers are rather compact. Baby room. Small dishwashing room. Laundry with washing machine and dryer. Motorcaravan service point. Play area. Off site: Beach 1.5 miles. Golf and riding 0.5 miles. Fishing 4 miles. Bicycle hire 4.5 miles. Martin Mere nature reserve nearby.

Open: All year excl. 11 January - 28 February.

Directions

Park is 4 miles south of Southport. From Ainsdale on A565 travel south for 1.5 miles to second traffic lights (Woodvale) and turn right into Coastal Road to site on right in 150 yds. From south pass RAF Woodvale and turn left at second set of lights. O.S.GR: SD308108. GPS: N53:35.328 W03:02.640

Charges 2007

Per unit incl. 2 person	£ 11.30 - £ 14.50
hardstanding	£ 1.45
extra person	£ 2.70
child (5-16 yrs)	£ 2.10
dog (max. 2)	£ 1.00
Latest arrival time 21.00 hrs.	

UK5272 Moss Wood Caravan Park

Crimbles Lane, Cockerham, Lancaster LA2 0ES (Lancashire)

Tel: **01524 791041**. Email: **info@mosswood.co.uk**

Moss Wood is a well established park set in a secluded rural location near the village of Cockerham. A sheltered field has 25 touring pitches on level hardstandings (steel pegs required) with 16A electricity. Most also have water and drainage. Screened from the touring area by a high fence so not visually intrusive are 175 privately owned holiday homes. There is a large adventure playground on site and, although well screened by mature trees, it could be lively and noisy at busy times. A purpose-built log cabin houses reception and a shop which sells basic supplies. Although there are passing places, the approach road to the park is narrow so care should be taken.

Facilities

New centrally located sanitary block (key entry) is kept spotlessly clean and provides vanity style washbasins and roomy, preset showers. Fully equipped facilities for disabled visitors. Undercover food preparation area, dishwashing and laundry facilities. Play area. Large sports field and woodland dog walking. Off site: Pubs at Cockerham 1 mile. Garstang, historic Lancaster, seaside town of Morecambe and the Lune Valley all within easy reach. Fishing nearby. Riding 3 miles. Golf 4 miles. Beach 5 miles. Local buses stop at end of lane.

Open: 1 March - 31 October.

Directions

Park is 1 mile west of Cockerham on the A588. Leave M6 at junction 33 and follow signs for Cockerham. A588 is about 4 miles. Site is signed on the left. O.S.GR: SD456498.

Charges 2007

Per unit incl. 2 adults, 2 children and electricity	£ 16.00 - £ 20.00
extra person	£ 3.00
awning	£ 3.00

"*The place to stay*"
North West Tourist Board Award Winner

A secluded, rural, tree lined park, near South East shore of Morecambe Bay, offering easy access to the Fylde Coast, historic Lancaster, Lune Valley and South Lakes.

Holiday homes for sale

Touring pitches available

Crimbles Lane, Cockerham, Lancaster LA2 0ES   Telephone: 01524 791041 www.mosswood.co.uk

UK5271 Old Hall Caravan Park

Capernwray, Carnforth LA6 1AD (Lancashire)

Tel: **01524 733276**. Email: **oldhall@charis.co.uk**

In a woodland clearing, just five minutes drive from junction 35 of the M6, Old Hall Caravan Park is a gem. Approached along a tree-lined road, this secluded park offers peace and tranquility. There are 38 touring pitches which are accessed from a circular roadway, all on marked and level hardstandings and with 15A electricity, water and drainage (shared between two pitches). TV hook-ups are also available for hire. Tents are not accepted on this park. There are 220 privately owned holiday homes which are quite separate from the touring pitches. A new adventure play area is located in a wooded clearing and there are woodland walks for all to enjoy along with the birds and wildlife. Plenty of tourist information is available from the reception building.

Facilities

The central sanitary block (combination lock) is very clean and is heated during cooler months. Vanity style washbasins and large controllable showers. Separate unit for disabled visitors doubles as a family room. Laundry facilities. No shop but a van calls in high season with basic requirements. Gas supplies. Off site: Canal fishing 100 yds. Over Kellet 2 miles. Carnforth 3 miles. Historic Lancaster and the seaside town of Morecambe (15 minutes drive). Trough of Bowland, Yorkshire Dales and Grange-over-Sands (30 minutes drive).

Open: 1 March - 10 January.

Directions

From M6 exit 35 take link road signed Over Kellet. Turn left on B6254. At Over Kellet village green turn left signed Capernwray and follow for 1.5 miles. Park is on the right at the end of a 0.5 mile drive. O.S.GR: SD538718.

Charges 2007

Per unit incl. electricicy	£ 16.50 - £ 18.50
awning	£ 1.00 - £ 2.00

UK5280 Abbey Farm Caravan Park

Dark Lane, Ormskirk L40 5TX (Lancashire)

Tel: **01695 572686**. Email: **abbeyfarm@yahoo.com**

This quiet, well equipped, family park beside the Abbey ruins has views over open farmland. It is an ideal base for a longer stay with plenty of interest in the local area, including Ormskirk parish church, unusual for having both a tower and a spire. Market days are on Thursday and Saturday. The park is divided into small paddocks, one of which is for 30 privately owned seasonal units, one for tents, the others for touring units, plus a rally field for special events. The 60 touring pitches, all with electricity (10/16A), are on neatly mown level grass, separated by small shrubs and colourful flower borders. Some mature trees provide shade in parts. Amenities include a farm walk and a small, free lending library with a good stock of tourist information. The owners organise two annual events – a barbecue in early June and a Bonfire Night in November. They have planned plenty of routes for walkers from the park. Southport with its beach and Pleasureland is 10 miles. Wigan Pier, Aintree for the Grand National, the annual Beatles Festival or Southport Flower Show and Martin Mere Nature reserve are some of the attractions within easy reach. A member of the Countryside Discovery group.

Facilities

The main toilet block is modern, heated and spotless, providing controllable hot showers. Dual purpose family bathroom that includes facilities for disabled people. A second smaller unit has individual shower/WC/basin cubicles. Dishwashing sinks under cover at both units. Laundry room with washing machine, dryer, spinner, ironing board and airing cupboard. Small well stocked shop shares space with reception, with a butcher calling twice weekly. Indoor games room with table tennis and football games machine. Small adventure playground. Field for ball games. Fishing lake (£2 per rod, per day).

Open: All year.

Directions

From M6 junction 27 take A5209 (Parbold) road. After 5 miles turn left (just before garage) onto B5240, and then first right into Hob Cross Lane, following signs to site. O.S.GR: SD433099. GPS: N53:34.188 W02:51.399

Charges 2007

Per unit incl. 2 persons	£ 7.00 - £ 16.60
serviced pitch	£ 15.60 - £ 15.90
extra person	£ 2.50
child (5-15 yrs)	£ 1.50

UK5295 Eastham Hall Caravan Park

Saltcotes Road, Lytham St Annes FY8 4LS (Lancashire)

Tel: **01253 737907**. Email: **info@easthamhall.co.uk**

Eastham Hall is a well established, family run park set in rural Lancashire, between the Victorian town of Lytham and the pretty village of Wrea Green. Entering by an electronic barrier system, one sees an area of 150 caravan holiday homes quite separate from touring areas where there are 150 pitches. These provide open plan, grass pitches for 100 seasonal units and 56 touring units on mostly level ground. All pitches have electricity hook-ups (10A). Tents are not accepted. A recent addition is eight large, fully serviced pitches on hardstanding placed around the perimeter of the touring area. Mature trees border the park and shrubs and bushes separate the various touring areas. The reception is spacious with lots of tourist information and, at one end, is a large well stocked shop. The park has no bar or clubhouse, but Lytham is just five minutes by car or a pleasant twenty minute walk. The flat terrain is also ideal for cycling.

Facilities

Four toilet blocks are old and fairly basic, but are kept clean. Laundry and dishwashing facilities are also old and in need of refurbishment. Plans are in place for a new amenity block. No facilities for disabled visitors. Gas supplies. Well stocked shop. Adventure play area and large sports field. Barrier (£10 deposit). Off site: Excellent pub in Wrea Green. Shops and restaurants in Lytham 2.5 miles. Blackpool 6 miles. Golf and riding 1 mile. Boat launching 2 miles: Local bus stops at entrance to park.

Open: 1 March - 31 October.

Directions

From M55 take exit 3 and turn left for Kirkham. At roundabouts follow signs for Wrea Green and Lytham. Continue on B5259 passing Grapes pub and village green. After 1.5 miles cross level crossing (Moss Side) and park is 1 mile on left. O.S.GR: SD377290. GPS: N53:45.225 W02:56.535

Charges 2007

Per unit incl. 1-4 persons	£ 10.00 - £ 14.00
with electricity	£ 15.00 - £ 20.00
serviced pitch	£ 17.00 - £ 24.00
dog	£ 1.00

UK5300 Kneps Farm Holiday Park

River Road, Stanah, Thornton-Cleveleys FY5 5LR (Lancashire)

Tel: **01253 823632**. Email: **enquiries@knepsfarm.co.uk**

A well established park with top class modern facilities, Kneps Farm is still operated by the family who opened it in 1967. Next to Wyre Country Park, it makes an excellent base from which to explore the area. A barrier system flanks the reception building which also houses a well stocked shop. The 60 marked and numbered touring pitches are generally on hardstandings with electricity (16A) available to most, and all are accessed from tarmac roads. There are also some grassy pitches and a separate area with 70 caravan holiday homes (most privately owned). A path leads through a gate at the back of the site into the country park. Just down the lane is a public slipway and the Wyreside Ecology Centre. A list and map are provided of local services and amenities, including pubs, restaurants, takeaway, etc. Other local attractions include Marsh Mill Village with a restored windmill, the Freeport Shopping and Leisure village at nearby Fleetwood (discount shopping), and several bird-watching sites around the estuary and country park.

Facilities

The excellent, large, centrally heated sanitary building is warm and inviting with ten individual family bathrooms, each providing a WC, basin and bath/shower. Separate toilet facilities with electric hand-wash units for men and women. Well equipped room for disabled visitors. Combined baby care/first aid room. Laundry room. Shop. Small, fenced playground. Up to two dogs are accepted per unit. Off site: Fishing 0.25 miles. Golf 2.5 miles.

Open: 1 March - 15 November.

Directions

From M55 junction 3, take A585 towards Fleetwood. Turn left at traffic lights, then turn right at traffic lights by Shell station (for Thornton-Cleveleys), straight across next traffic lights, then right at the next roundabout by River Wyre Hotel. After one mile (past school) turn right at mini-roundabout into Stanah Road, continue across second mini-roundabout and eventually into River Road with site entrance ahead of you. O.S.GR: SD350430.

Charges 2007

Per unit incl. 2 adults,	
2 children and electricity	£ 31.00 - £ 23.50
tent (2 adults and 2 children)	£ 18.00 - £ 20.50
adult couple	£ 13.00 - £ 17.50
extra person	£ 3.25 - £ 3.75
extra child	£ 2.50 - £ 3.00
Special Senior Citizen rates.	

UK5330 Marton Mere Holiday Village

Mythop Road, Blackpool FY4 4NX (Lancashire)

Tel: **01253 767544**. Email: **sarah.corlett@bourne-leisure.co.uk**

If Blackpool is your holiday destination and your family are looking for lots to do then this Haven Holidays park may well be a suitable choice. Although mainly used for static caravan holiday homes, there are 148 touring pitches with hardstanding, of which 60 are fully serviced. All have electricity hook ups (10/16A). A few trees give a small amount of shade, but as with a lot of coastal sites, it can be a little windy. During the day buses depart every 30 minutes from the main reception area to Blackpool. On site there is plenty of entertainment including three licensed bars, discos and the Rainbow room where children are entertained. For small children (under 12s), there is the Bradley Bear Club with face painting, disco dancing, games and competitions. In the autumn months, the Blackpool illuminations are a must for young and old alike. Other places to visit include the historic towns of Lytham and St Annes, the world of Coronation Street and many fantastic golf courses.

Facilities

Two heated toilet blocks (key pad entry system) have piped music playing and although of older design are clean and well kept with large preset showers and hairdryers. Each block has a suite for disabled people, baby room, family bathroom and launderette. Well stocked supermarket with all day bakery, bars, fast food outlets and restaurants. New outdoor splash pool and heated indoor pool with flume, jacuzzi and sauna. Amusement arcades, multisport court, crazy golf and bowling. Two children's clubs with full entertainment schedule. Off site: Martin Mere nature reserve. Blackpool beach, entertainment, etc.

Open: 24 March - 30 October.

Directions

From M55 junction 4, turn right at roundabout taking A583 towards Blackpool. Pass the windmill, then right at the traffic lights by the Clifton Arms into Mythop Road. Park is on the left O.S.GR: SD344351. GPS: N53:48.171 W02:59.488

Charges 2006

Per unit incl. up to 4 persons	
and electricity	£ 11.00 - £ 57.00
serviced pitch	£ 13.00 - £ 66.00
extra person	£ 2.00 - £ 3.00
Variety of special offers available.	

UK5350 Holgates Caravan Park

Middlebarrow Plain, Cove Road, Silverdale, Carnforth LA5 0SH (Lancashire)

Tel: **01524 701508**. Email: **caravan@holgates.co.uk**

This attractive, very high quality park is in an outstanding craggy, part-wooded, hillside location with fine views over Morecambe Bay. It takes 70 touring units, with 339 privately owned caravan holiday homes and 11 to rent located in woodland away from the touring pitches. With just 5 grassy pitches for tents, the remaining 65 large touring pitches are on gravel hardstandings, all with electricity (16A), free TV connection, individual drainage and water points. The main complex, with reception and the entrance barrier provides a well stocked supermarket, lounge bar, restaurant with good value meals and a terrace with views over the bay. There is also an indoor leisure centre. Children have a choice of two adventure playgrounds and plenty of space for ball games. Also on site is a small but challenging 'pitch and putt' course. Everything is completed to the highest standards.

Facilities

Two modern, heated toilet buildings are fully equipped with top quality fittings and including some private cubicles with WC and washbasin. Dishwashing sinks at each block. Excellent provision for disabled visitors with a reserved pitch and parking bay adjacent. Launderette. Shop. Gas supplies. Bar and restaurant. Indoor pool (17 x 17 m; with lifeguard) with spa pool, steam room and sauna (no unaccompanied under 10s). Playgrounds. Games room with pool table and video games. Pitch and putt course (£2.00 per person). Facilities are limited mid week in January and early February. Admission restrictions include no unaccompanied under 18s or single sex groups, certain breeds of dog or commercial vehicles. Off site: Riding, cycling, walking and fishing all within 9 miles. Morecambe or Lancaster 12 miles. Kendal 15 miles.

Open: All year excl. 6 November - 21 December.

Directions

From traffic lights in centre of Carnforth take road to Silverdale under low bridge. After 1 mile turn left signed Silverdale and after 2.5 miles over level crossing, carry on and turn right at T-junction. Follow Holgates sign from here watching for left then right forks (narrow roads). O.S.GR: SD460755. GPS: N54:10.569 W02:50.154

Charges 2007

Per unit incl. 2 adults	
and 2 children	£ 31.00 - £ 32.50
extra person	£ 7.00
extra child (5-17 yrs)	£ 4.00
awning or pup tent	£ 3.00

Minimum stays apply for all B.H weekends.

215

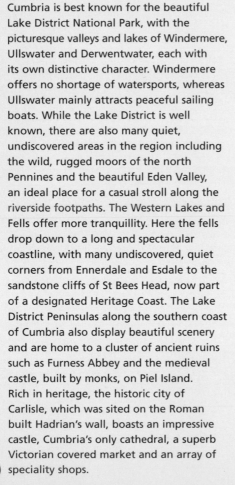

MAP 5

With spectacular lakes, undulating fells, impressive mountains and lush green valleys, Cumbria is ideal for those who wish to get away from it all and unwind in peaceful, natural surroundings, or for the more active who want to participate in a range of outdoor pursuits.

Cumbria is best known for the beautiful Lake District National Park, with the picturesque valleys and lakes of Windermere, Ullswater and Derwentwater, each with its own distinctive character. Windermere offers no shortage of watersports, whereas Ullswater mainly attracts peaceful sailing boats. While the Lake District is well known, there are also many quiet, undiscovered areas in the region including the wild, rugged moors of the north Pennines and the beautiful Eden Valley, an ideal place for a casual stroll along the riverside footpaths. The Western Lakes and Fells offer more tranquillity. Here the fells drop down to a long and spectacular coastline, with many undiscovered, quiet corners from Ennerdale and Esdale to the sandstone cliffs of St Bees Head, now part of a designated Heritage Coast. The Lake District Peninsulas along the southern coast of Cumbria also display beautiful scenery and are home to a cluster of ancient ruins such as Furness Abbey and the medieval castle, built by monks, on Piel Island. Rich in heritage, the historic city of Carlisle, which was sited on the Roman built Hadrian's wall, boasts an impressive castle, Cumbria's only cathedral, a superb Victorian covered market and an array of speciality shops.

Places of interest

Barrow-in-Furness: South Lakes Wild Animal Park; Dalton Castle; Furness Abbey; Piel Island.

Carlisle: 11th century castle; Birdoswald Roman fort; Lanercost Priory.

Ravenglass: Muncaster Castle, an historic haunted castle and Headquarters of the World Owl Trust.

Ulverston: the world's only Laurel and Hardy museum.

Kendal: historic riverside town situated between the Lakes and Dales, famous for its mint cake and castle ruins.

Lake Derwentwater: lakeside theatre open all year hosting plays, music, dance, comedy and film.

Windermere: Steamboat Centre, a collection of Windermere's nautical heritage with boats on display; World of Beatrix Potter.

Grasmere: Dove Cottage and Wordsworth Museum.

Did you know?

Cumbria has the steepest road in England, called the Hardknott Pass.

The Lake District was the inspiration for many poets, writers and artists, including William Wordsworth, Beatrix Potter and John Ruskin.

Ulverston is the birthplace of Quakerism and pole vaulting.

Bassenthwaite is the only real lake in the Lake District! All the others are either meres, (Windermere) or waters (Derwentwater, Coniston Water and Ullswater).

Stretching 73 miles, Hadrian's Wall was built by Romans in the second century.

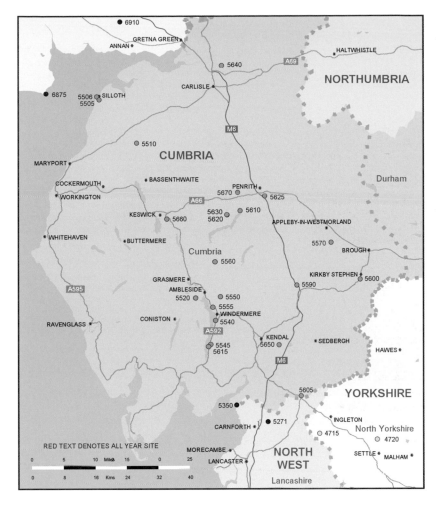

RED TEXT DENOTES ALL YEAR SITE

UK5510 The Larches Caravan Park

Mealsgate, Wigton CA7 1LQ (Cumbria)
Tel: **01697 371379**. Email: **info@larchescaravanpark.co.uk**

Mealsgate and The Larches lie on the Carlisle - Cockermouth road, a little removed from the hectic centre of the Lake District, yet with easy access to it (and good views towards it). It is a quality, family run park which takes 73 touring units of any type and also accommodates 100 privately owned holiday homes. Touring pitches are in different grassy areas with tall, mature trees, shrubs and accompanying wildlife. Some are sloping and irregular, others on marked hardstandings, with electricity (10A), water and drainage. On arrival visitors are loaned very comprehensive tourist information brochures. There are bus routes to Carlisle and Keswick, walks from the park and good restaurants nearby. The Elliott family provide a warm welcome at this peaceful, well organised park. This is an ideal haven for couples – only adult visitors are accepted.

Facilities

Toilet facilities, in two purpose designed blocks, are of good quality providing en-suite facilities for both sexes. Washbasins for ladies are in cubicles, those for men set in flat surfaces. Separate unit for disabled visitors can be heated. Campers' kitchen with cooker and microwave (metered). Laundry room. Well stocked shop incl. camping accessories, gas and off-licence. Small indoor heated pool. Table tennis. Wildlife pond. Caravan storage. Off site: Golf 3.5 miles. Bicycle hire 7 miles. Fishing 8 miles. Riding 10 miles.

Open: 1 March - 31 October.

Directions

Park entrance is south off A595 (Carlisle - Cockermouth road) just southwest of Mealsgate. O.S.GR: NY206415. GPS: N54:45.796 W03:14.148

Charges 2007

Per unit incl. 2 adults	£ 11.50 - £ 13.90
incl. electricity	£ 13.50 - £ 15.90
extra person	£ 2.00 - £ 2.50
awning or extra car	£ 1.00 - £ 2.00
backpacker	£ 6.00 - £ 7.50

Discounts for senior citizens and bookings over 7 nights. No credit cards.

217

UK5505 Stanwix Park Holiday Centre

Greenrow, Silloth, Wigton CA7 4HH (Cumbria)

Tel: **016973 32666**. Email: **enquiries@stanwix.com**

Stanwix Park is a family run holiday park with absolutely everything anyone could want for a memorable holiday all year round. The park has 83 caravan holiday homes and 28 chalets for rent, together with 212 which are privately owned. These are mostly located around the central complex. In addition at either end of the park, there are 121 fully serviced (10A electricity) pitches for touring units and tents, some on grass, some with hardstanding. The central complex holds all the indoor and outdoor amenities (many of which are included in the nightly fees). A warm welcome awaits in the main reception, with lots of local and tourist information. The indoor tropical leisure centre contains a 29 m. fun pool with slides, a steam room, sauna, spa, fitness gym and vertical sun shower (charge). The upper floor has the Sky Bar and Dunes Cabaret Bar (adults only) with the Sunset Inn licensed family club, all enjoying nightly entertainment and special themed weekends from November to March. A giant TV and snooker room are in the Gallery observation area with a state-of-the-art, newly refurbished Astro Bowling Centre (charged) and amusement arcade, with a soft play area and ball pond to one side. Outside are a large, terraced swimming pool, an adventure play area and minigolf, all screened by plants and shrubs, Tennis courts and bicycle hire are also available (charge).

Facilities

The two heated sanitary blocks have been recently refurbished to a high standard and are adjacent to the pitches, kept spotlessly clean and opened by combination lock. Large en-suite bathrooms, showers, vanity style washbasins and a unit in each for disabled visitors. Dishwashing under cover. Campers kitchen. Fully equipped laundry. Gas sales. Well stocked shop (5/3-6/11). Restaurant with takeaway (all year). Bars (adults only and family) with evening entertainment (5/3-6/11). TV and snooker room. Indoor leisure centre. Outdoor swimming pool (31/5-1/9). Ten-pin bowling centre. Amusement arcade. Soft play area. Minigolf. Tennis. Bicycle hire. Off site: Bus service 1 mile in Silloth (easy walk). Silloth golf club, bowling club and sports ground. Beach 1 mile.

Open: All year.

Directions

From the south, take exit 41 from the M6 and follow B5305 through Wigton to Silloth. From north on A74/M6 take exit 44 and the A595 and A596 to Wigton. On entering Silloth, turn left following signs for park. Entrance is on the right. O.S.GR: NY108525. GPS: N54:51.684 W03:23.300

Charges 2007

Per person	£ 3.45 - £ 4.15
child (under 5 yrs)	£ 2.20 - £ 2.65
pitch	£ 10.70 - £ 13.25

Many special offers and short break prices.

UK5506 Hylton Caravan Park

Eden Street, Silloth, Wigton CA7 4AY (Cumbria)

Tel: **016973 32666**. Email: **ericstanwix@stanwix.com**

Owned and managed by the Stanwix family, Hylton Caravan Park was completely refurbished in 2001. Although it is only a short walk away from the livelier Stanwix Leisure Park, it is a peaceful haven for people who prefer the 'quiet life'. The only activity is an adventure park for children which is not visible from the touring area. Divided by a circular road, the 170 privately owned caravan holiday homes are visible but not intrusive. There are 90 open plan, mostly level touring and tent pitches, all fully serviced and with 10A electricity. There is no shop on site as the town and Stanwix Holiday Park are both within walking distance. Club membership for the extensive leisure and entertainment amenities at Stanwix Park is free of charge for the duration of your stay. Local attractions include the Ravenglass - Eskdale Miniature Railway where, the nearby World Owl Centre at Muncaster is a must.

Facilities

A high quality toilet block is superbly fitted out and includes toilets, showers, vanity style washbasins, extra large bathrooms and a separate cubicle for disabled people. Dishwashing under cover. Fully equipped laundry. Gas sales. Off site: Bus stop 1 mile. Entertainment and amenities at Stanwix Park. Silloth golf course. Bowling. Windsurfing and boat launching 1 mile.

Open: 1 March - 15 November.

Directions

On entering Silloth, turn left following signs to Hylton Caravan Park. O.S.GR: NY114534. GPS: N54:52.100 W03:23.901

Charges 2007

Per person	£ 3.45 - £ 4.15
child (under 5 yrs)	£ 2.20 - £ 2.65
pitch	£ 8.55 - £ 10.60

UK5520 Skelwith Fold Caravan Park

Ambleside LA22 0HX (Cumbria)

Tel: **015394 32277**. Email: **info@skelwith.com**

Skelwith Fold has been developed in the extensive grounds of a country estate taking advantage of the wealth of mature trees and shrubs. The 300 privately owned caravan holiday homes and 150 touring pitches are absorbed into this unspoilt natural environment, sharing it with red squirrels and other wildlife in several discrete areas branching off the central, mile long main driveway. Touring pitches (no tents) are on gravel hardstanding and metal pegs will be necessary for awnings. Electricity hook-ups (10A) and basic amenities are available in all areas. Youngsters and indeed their parents will find endless pleasure exploring over 90 acres of wild woodland and, if early risers, it is possible to see deer, foxes, etc. at the almost hidden tarn deep in the woods. This is a fascinating site where you feel at home with nature at any time of the year, but it is particularly beautiful in the spring with wild daffodils, bluebells and later rhododendrons and azaleas. Only caravans, motorcaravans and trailer tents are accepted.

Facilities

Eight toilet blocks, well situated to serve all areas, have the usual facilities including laundry, drying and ironing rooms. Some blocks have facilities for disabled visitors. Well stocked, licensed shop. Battery charging, gas and caravan spares and accessories. Adventure play area. Family recreation area with picnic tables and goal posts in the Lower Glade. Bicycle hire. Off site: Ambleside village 1.5 miles. Pubs within walking distance. Fishing 200 m. Riding 3 miles.

Open: 1 March - 15 November.

Directions

From Ambleside take the A593 towards Coniston. Pass through Clappergate and on the far outskirts watch for the B5286 to Hawkshead on the left. Park is clearly signed 1 mile down this road on the right. O.S.GR: NY358028. GPS: N54:25:029 W02:59.717

Charges 2007

Per pitch	£ 17.50 - £ 20.00
with electricity	£ 20.50 - £ 23.00
awning	£ 3.00

Discounts for weekly or monthly stays.

UK5540 Fallbarrow Park

Rayrigg Road, Bowness, Windermere LA23 3DL (Cumbria)

Tel: **015394 44422**. Email: **enquiries@southlakeland-caravans.co.uk**

Fallbarrow Park is most attractively situated alongside Lake Windermere with a lake frontage of about 600 yards; one can stroll among the lawns and gardens near the lake. The major part of the park is occupied by approximately 260 seasonal holiday homes, with about 85 for letting, the remainder privately owned. In the 'Lake' area (not actually by the lake, but some pitches have lake views), there are 38 fenced or hedged touring pitches, all with hardstanding, fresh and waste water points, electric hook-up (10/16A) and TV aerial connection. Reception is smart and comfortable, with lots of tourist information. The Boathouse pub has a spacious and comfortable lounge with bar meals and snacks, a separate restaurant section with varied menu and table service, and an attractive outdoor terrace. The site has a boat park with winter storage and two launching ramps and three jetties can cater for craft up to 18 ft. in length. The centre of Bowness is only a short walk and facilities for pony trekking and numerous visitor attractions are close.

Facilities

Two excellent toilet blocks serve the touring sections (combination locks) with top quality fittings and heating when required, controllable showers, make-up and hairdressing areas and a baby washroom. Very well equipped laundry which also houses a freezer. Motorcaravan service point. Gas is available at the well stocked supermarket. Restaurant. Bar. Fishing. Adventure play area and sports field. American motorhomes are accepted by prior arrangement. Dogs are accepted, but only one per booking (exercise area provided). Off site: Bicycle hire 1 mile. Riding 2 miles. Golf 3 miles.

Open: 1 March - 14 November.

Directions

Park is beside the A592 road just north of Bowness town centre. O.S.GR: SD401971. GPS: N54:22.007 W02:55.246

Charges 2007

Per unit incl. 2 adults	
and 2 children	£ 18.00 - £ 26.00
extra person	£ 2.00
awning	£ 3.50
dog	£ 3.00

UK5550 Limefitt Park

Windermere LA23 1PA (Cumbria)

Tel: **015394 32300**

Part of the South Lakeland Holiday Group, Limefitt Park is located in a really beautiful Lakeland valley with fine views and ideal for walking and cycling. Four miles from Windermere, it is also centrally located for the attractions of the southern Lake District. With various active pursuits on offer nearby and some evening entertainment, this park is designed for families and couples. Of the 151 touring pitches, 38 are on hardstanding with direct connections for electricity, TV, fresh water and waste water, and a further 85 hardstanding pitches are fully serviced. Pitches for tents are in a separate area. The ground by the beck has been developed for 65 log cabins (for private sale) in addition to some caravan holiday homes (a few for hire). Activities available from the park include fell walking and pony trekking. Away from the camping area by the river is a play field and an adventure playground on grass and a small riverside area with picnic tables. The park is popular throughout the season so advance reservation is recommended.

Facilities

Sanitary facilities are of excellent quality, well equipped with modern fittings, with one large, central block for the tenting area and a smaller block for the caravan area accessed by combination locks. Part of one building is dedicated to three toddlers' rooms with half-size bath and changing facilities. Covered dishwashing and vegetable preparation areas. Campers' kitchen. Launderette. Motorcaravan service point. Gas supplies. Supermarket. Bar (real ales), bar meals and takeaway, all open all season. Weekly entertainment. Games room with many machines. Play area. Riding. Play area. Dogs are not accepted. Off site: Fishing 2 miles. Bicycle hire 4 miles. Golf 5 miles.

Open: 1 March - 15 November.

Directions

Limefitt is 2.5 miles north up the A592 from its junction with the A591 north of Windermere. O.S.GR: NY416030. GPS: N54:25.210 W02:54.210

Charges 2007

Per unit incl. 2 adults,	
2 children and electricity	£ 16.00 - £ 26.00
tent incl. 2 adults, 2 children	£ 18.00 - £ 26.00
extra person	£ 2.00
child (2-14 yrs)	£ 1.00

UK5555 White Cross Bay Leisure Park & Marina

Ambleside Road, Windermere LA23 1LF (Cumbria)

Tel: **015394 43937**. Email: **enquiries@southlakeland-caravans.co.uk**

White Cross Bay Leisure Park and Marina is situated alongside Lake Windermere, a perfect holiday destination for watersports enthusiasts. A large part of the park is occupied by privately owned chalets and holiday homes of which 100 are to let. These are near or overlooking the lake. Of the 356 pitches, there are only 26 currently available for touring units. These are located on large hardstanding areas (steel pegs required), together with many seasonal pitches. When we visited some units were parked quite close together. The busy main road is close by so noise will be a problem in this area. Electricity (10A) is available via a £1 meter card. We are told that the touring area and its toilet block are to be upgraded. The park's amenities otherwise are first class. The main complex provides a large reception displaying tourist information, a well stocked shop, an attractive restaurant and a comfortable bar. There is an indoor pool with sauna, solarium and a gym (charged) and a large games room. There are tennis courts, an adventure play park, picnic areas and woodland walks near the lake. This area is well known for low flying aircraft.

Facilities

Two toilet blocks (combination locks). The one adjacent to the touring area is heated and clean, but rather old (renovation planned). Open style washbasins and preset showers with curtains only. Baby changing. Laundry. The other block (Marina) is a new purpose built chalet type building quite close to the lake. It provides facilities for disabled visitors. Shop. Restaurant. Bar and games room. Indoor pool complex. Tennis. Play area. Fishing. Boat launching. Off site: Golf, riding and bicycle hire 5 miles.

Open: 1 March - 14 November.

Directions

From M6 exit 36, take A591 to Windermere. Continue on A591 towards Ambleside and park is 2 miles on the left. O.S.GR: NY395004. GPS: N54:23.788 W02:55.891

Charges 2007

Per unit incl. 2 adults and 2 children	£ 16.00 - £ 22.00
extra person	£ 2.00
child	£ 1.00
dog	£ 3.00

UK5560 Sykeside Camping Park

Brotherswater, Patterdale, Penrith CA11 0NZ (Cumbria)

Tel: **017684 82239**. Email: **info@sykeside.co.uk**

This small touring park is located in a really beautiful, quiet spot in the northern Lakes area (it is just 400 yards from Brotherswater). The site is surrounded by the fells and is ideal for active outdoor holidays with walking or climbing on the high hills. With views up the Dovedale valley, the park has 100 pitches in the valley floor, including several hardstandings. Caravans are now permitted and the access road has been improved. Pitches are not marked and campers arrange themselves to best enjoy the superb views. There are 19 electrical connections (5/10A).

Facilities

The toilet block includes hot showers and has been refurbished. Small launderette and dishwashing room. Self-service shop with camping equipment, gas and an ice-pack service, doubles as reception. Cosy, licensed bar and restaurant (daily in summer, weekends only in winter). Bunkhouse accommodation for 30 persons. Fishing nearby. Off site: Bicycle hire 3 miles. Riding 8 miles. Golf 10 miles. The Brotherswater Inn is adjacent (open all year).

Open: All year.

Directions

On west side of A592, 2 miles south of Patterdale, which lies at the southwestern end of Ullswater - entrance is just behind the Brotherswater Inn. O.S.GR: NY396005. GPS: N54:29.910 W02:55.530

Charges 2007

Per tent incl. 2 persons and car	£ 12.00 - £ 20.00
caravan or motorcaravan	£ 16.00 - £ 22.00
child (5-16 yrs)	£ 2.00

Min. charge for motorcaravan £15 per night.

221

UK5570 Wild Rose Park

Ormside, Appleby-in-Westmorland CA16 6EJ (Cumbria)

Tel: **01768 351077**. Email: **reception@wildrose.co.uk**

Set in the Eden Valley within easy reach of the Lake District and the Yorkshire Dales, Wild Rose is a well known park now under new ownership. The entrance is very inviting with its well mown grass, trim borders and colourful flower displays and impressive. It is immediately apparent that this is a much loved park, and this is reflected throughout the site in the care and attention to detail. There are 226 touring pitches, two areas with their own warden to ensure that everything is always neat and tidy. The top areas have been upgraded to provide neat, level, fully serviced pitches. These are separated by hedges (plus a small fence until the hedge grows) and many have views. The lower touring area, on a slightly sloping field, caters for both tents and caravans. Next to this are six individual 'super' pitches, fenced or hedged with full services, some including patio, barbecue, picnic table, grass area and satellite TV connections. Privately owned caravan holiday homes (316) occupy their own areas and do not intrude. There are also a number of wigwams for hire. This area is used for training by military jets – there may be some noise at times. Wild Rose deserves its excellent reputation, which the owners strive to maintain and improve. Nothing is overlooked from recycling bins, electric buggies to keep the noise down, 'sac-o-mat' special bags in the dog walk and cycle racks placed around the park. A member of the Best of British group.

Facilities

Three toilet blocks (two heated) are of excellent quality and kept spotlessly clean. Most washbasins are in cubicles. Hair washing basins, baby baths and bottle warmers. Full facilities for disabled visitors. Fully equipped laundry with lines and drying rooms. Motorcaravan service point. Exceptionally well stocked shop (with gas). Licensed restaurant with takeaway and conservatory/coffee lounge (all 1/4-5/11). Outdoor pool (heated mid May - mid Sept and open 10.00-22.00). Well kept, fenced play area. Indoor playroom for under 5s. Games room with video games for older children and two TV rooms, one with a cinema style screen. BMX track. Half court tennis. Certain breeds of dog are not accepted. Caravan storage. Off site: Fishing 2 miles. Golf and riding 3 miles.

Open: All year.

Directions

Park is signed south off B6260 road 1.5 miles southwest of Appleby. Follow signs to park, in the direction of Ormside. O.S.GR: NY697165. GPS: N54:32.644 W02:28.197

Charges 2007

Per unit incl. 2 persons 'super pitch' incl.	£ 16.00 - £ 25.00
mains services and awning	£ 19.50 - £ 31.00
extra person (over 4 yrs)	£ 3.00 - £ 4.00
walker or cyclist	£ 6.50
dog	£ 1.50

Less 10% for 7 nights or more. Special winter or long-stay rates. Low season discounts.

UK5545 Park Cliffe Camping & Caravan Estate

Birks Road, Windermere LA23 3PG (Cumbria)

Tel: **015395 31344**. Email: **info@parkcliffe.co.uk**

Set in the heart of the Lake District National Park, this attractive park has been recently acquired by the Holgates family. Sitting high in open countryside it has spectacular views over the Lakeland Fells and Lake Windermere. Well managed, the park offers touring pitches which are numbered gravel hardstandings with electricity, water and drainage. There are also 24 seasonal pitches. Two areas have been set aside for tents, one unmarked and undulating on the hillside divided by an original stone wall and adjacent to the tourers and one across the road for tents that require electricity.

Facilities

The central main building includes two blocks of toilets and showers, heated and very clean. Vanity style washbasins. Full facilities for disabled visitors and excellent baby room. Five rooms with bath, WC and washbasin, 4 for hire. Laundry. Motorcaravan service point. Bar. Restaurant and takeaway. Small shop. Games room. Adventure play area. Off site: Fellfoot Park. Walking, climbing and cycling. Lake cruises.

Open: 1 March - 14 November.

Directions

From M6 exit 36 take A590 to Newby Bridge. Turn right on A592 for 3.6 miles and turn right. Site is signed shortly on the right. Caravans and trailers must approach from Newby Bridge on the A592. O.S.GR: SD391911. GPS: N54:18.751 W02:56.250

Charges 2007

Per unit incl. 2 persons and electricity	£ 23.00
extra person	£ 4.00
child (2-14 yrs)	£ 2.00

UK5590 Westmorland Caravan Park

Tebay, Orton, Penrith CA10 3SB (Cumbria)

Tel: **01539 711322**. Email: **caravans@westmorland.com**

For caravans, motorhomes and trailer tents only, this is the ideal stopover for anyone heading either north or south, near the M6 motorway, but far enough away for the traffic noise not to be too disturbing. There are 70 level pitches on gravel, divided into bays of about six or seven units (30 are for touring units). All touring pitches have electricity (10/16A). The bays are backed by grassy banks alive with rabbits and birds – a long list in the office describes the large variety of birds to be seen on the site. There is good site lighting and a late arrivals area.

Facilities

The heated toilet block is kept very clean. Showers. Facilities for disabled visitors planned. Sinks for laundry and dishwashing. Laundry. Reception sells gas. WiFi connections. Off site: Shops and restaurants five minutes walk away at the motorway service area.

Open: 30 March - 29 October.

Directions

From the M6, just north of junction 38, exit for Tebay Services (site signed). Site is accessible from the services travelling north or south. O.S.GR: NY607060. GPS: N54:26.862 W02:36.388

Charges 2007

Per unit incl. 4 persons	£ 15.00 - £ 17.00

Special rates for 3, 5 or 7 days.
Discount on hotel and café meals and farm shop.

UK5600 Pennine View Caravan & Camping Park

Station Road, Kirkby Stephen CA17 4SZ (Cumbria)

Tel: **017683 71717**

Suitable for night halts or longer breaks to visit the Lake District or the Yorkshire Dales, Pennine View is a super small park, well managed and well maintained. The whole site is very neat and tidy with level, numbered pitches on gravel hardstandings arranged around the perimeter with grass pitches in the centre. The pitches are of a good size (some especially large) and are all are supplied with electricity hook-ups (16A). Pennine View was opened in 1990 and is built on reclaimed land from a former railway goods yard. One end of the park adjoins the River Eden with steps leading down huge projecting stone slabs on the river bank. There are trout but a licence is needed for fishing.

Facilities

Built of local stone, the modern toilet block is accessed by a digital keypad and includes individual wash cubicles and deep sink for a baby bath. Both ladies and men have large en-suite units for disabled visitors. Well equipped laundry room. Gas available. Play area. Off site: Nearby hotel offers bar meals. Kirkby Stephen 1 mile. Bicycle hire 300 m. Golf 4 miles.

Open: 1 March - 31 October.

Directions

Park is on the A685 on the southerly outskirts of Kirkby Stephen (just under a mile from the town centre). Turn left at small site sign opposite the Croglin Castle hotel. Site is 50 yds. on right. O.S.GR: NY772075. GPS: N54:27.700 W02:21.202

Charges 2007

Per person	£ 5.10 - £ 5.50
child (4-15 yrs)	£ 2.00 - £ 2.30
pitch	£ 4.00 - £ 5.00

UK5640 Green Acres Caravan Park

High Knells, Houghton, Carlisle CA6 4JW (Cumbria)

Tel: **01228 675418**. Email: **info@caravanpark_cumbria.com**

Green Acres is a small, family run park situated in beautiful, rural surroundings, yet only two miles from the M6/A74 – perfect for an overnight stop or a longer stay to enjoy Cumbria, Hadrian's Wall and the delights of Carlisle city (4 miles away). Mr and Mrs Brown have developed Green Acres over the last few years into an attractive, well maintained and level touring park. There are 30 numbered pitches arranged in a semi-circle, some on grass but most on large hardstandings. There are 19 electricity connections (10A). Divided by a long beech hedge is a large camping field including on one side 6 new hardstanding 'super' pitches for seasonal letting and, in one corner, a small play area.

Facilities

Small, very clean toilet block with open style washbasins and coin operated showers (50p for 10 minutes). No facilities for disabled people. Dishwashing sinks under cover. Laundry room in farm building. Car wash area. No shop but ices, drinks and sweets from reception. Play area. Caravan storage. Off site: Golf 3 miles. Fishing 8 miles. Riding and bicycle hire 10 miles.

Open: April - end October.

Directions

Leave M6/A74 at junction 44 and take A689 for 1 miles. Turn left towards Scaleby (site signed) and site is 1 miles on left. O.S.GR: NY419615. GPS: N54:56.656 W02:54.572

Charges 2007

Per unit incl. 2 persons and electricity	£ 11.00
extra person	£ 2.00
tent	£ 8.00 - £ 12.00

223

UK5605 Woodclose Caravan Park

Kirkby Lonsdale LA6 2SE (Cumbria)

Tel: **015242 71597**. Email: **info@woodclosepark.com**

Woodclose is an established, nine acre park with new owners. Situated in the Lune Valley and just one mile from the market town of Kirkby Lonsdale, this park offers a peaceful and secluded setting catering for walkers, tourers and people who just want to relax. Access to the park is narrow, so care should be taken. The whole park has a very well cared for appearance with well mown grass, flowering tubs and neat hedges. The upper part contains many privately owned holiday homes with neat terraces built from local stone. Screened by a hedge and placed around the perimeter are several seasonal pitches with touring units being placed in the centre. These pitches are numbered and mostly level, some on hardstanding, some on grass, with 16A electricity and digital TV hook-ups. More seasonal pitches and holiday homes on the lower part of the park, again most attractively terraced with stone walling and paths. Reception is part of the well stocked shop which includes local produce and fresh baked bread; an information room is adjoining with tables and chairs and internet access (£1 per half an hour).

Facilities

Two toilet blocks, the main one central to the touring area. These facilities are all unisex in large, heated, individual rooms with toilets, washbasin and toilet or washbasin and shower, all well equipped and very clean. Indoor dishwashing, well equipped laundry and chemical disposal within the same building. The second block is in the lower part, again all unisex in cubicles together with an indoor dishwashing area. No motorcaravan service point, but facilities for disabled visitors have been installed. Shop. Small adventure play area. Bicycle hire. Internet access. American style motorhomes accepted (limited space). Gates locked midnight - 07.30, warden and telephone on site for emergencies. Off site: Golf 1 mile. Fishing 7 miles. Beach 20 miles.

Open: 1 March - 1 November.

Directions

From M6 exit 36 take A65 to Kirkby Lonsdale. Site is off the A65 in 6 miles. O.S.GR: SD620781. GPS: N54:11.901 W02:35.101

Charges 2007

Per unit incl. 2 persons and electricity	£ 10.00 - £ 20.00
tent incl. 2 persons	£ 12.00 - £ 14.00
extra person	£ 3.75
child (5-16 yrs)	£ 2.00
awning	£ 2.00

Book for 7 nights and receive 1 night free (high season only).

UK5615 Hill of Oaks Caravan Park

Tower Wood, Windermere LA12 8NR (Cumbria)

Tel: **015395 31578**. Email: **enquiries@hillofoaks.co.uk**

This park on the banks of Lake Windermere lives up to its name 'Hill of Oaks'. Set on a hillside in mature woodland, the park offers families a safe natural environment with nature walks through the managed ancient woodlands, as well as six jetties for boat launching and access to watersport activities (jet skis are not allowed). The road into the park passing the farmhouse is long, winding and narrow, so care should be taken especially with long outfits, reception being about half a mile from the entrance. The entrance barrier is open from 08.00 till dusk with a security code being provided for exit. The reception and shop selling basics with a tourist information room adjacent are on the lakeside in wooden chalet-type buildings with an abundance of hanging baskets and flowers. Privately owned caravan holiday homes have been built into the hillside on terraces and are quite unobtrusive, screened by hedges and trees. Although the park is situated on Lake Windermere the touring pitches nestle within the trees, not actually by the lake. All 43 have electricity (16A), digital TV hook-up and hardstanding, most large enough to take a car and boat. Three large super pitches, all hardstanding, have 16A electricity, drain, water and digital TV. Tents are not accepted.

Facilities

The central tiled toilet block, recently refurbished, is very clean and heated. Vanity style washbasins, controllable showers and free hairdryers. Baby changing areas. Fully equipped laundry. Dishwashing area under cover. New unit for disabled visitors (combination lock). Recycling bins. Motorcaravan service point. Shop for basics. Two fenced play areas, one for toddlers and adventure type for over 5s. Picnic areas and nature trails. Fishing (licence required). Off site: Fell Foot Park and Gardens 1 mile, with rowing boat hire or ferry rides to Lakeside or Ambleside. Aquarium of the Lakes (3.5 miles) at Newby Bridge. Golf 4 miles. Riding and bicycle hire 6 miles.

Open: 1 March - 14 November.

Directions

From M6 exit 36 head west on A590 towards Barrow and Newby Bridge. Follow A590 to roundabout signed Bowness and turn right on A592 for about 3 miles. Site is signed on left. O.S.GR: SD384903. GPS: N54:18.453 W02:56.724

Charges guide

Per pitch	£ 10.00 - £ 24.00
car	£ 1.00
awning	£ 3.00
boat	£ 5.00 - £ 10.50

UK5610 Waterfoot Caravan Park

Pooley Bridge, Penrith CA11 0JF (Cumbria)

Tel: **017684 86302**. Email: **enquiries@waterfootpark.co.uk**

Waterfoot is a quiet family park for caravans and motorcaravans only. It is set in 22 acres of partially wooded land, developed in the fifties from a private estate. The 146 private caravan holiday homes are quite separate from the 34 touring pitches. Lake Ullswater is only about 400 yards away and a half mile stroll through bluebell woods brings you to the village of Pooley Bridge. Waterfoot's touring pitches are arranged very informally in a large clearing. Most are level, there are some hardstandings and all have 10A electricity. The park no longer accepts American RVs. There is a bar in a large, imposing mansion, in the past a family home then a golf hotel. Public footpaths lead straight from the park. The regular lake steamer service calls at Pooley Bridge, the Ullswater yacht club is only 10 minutes drive and the market town of Penrith is 5 miles. The historic house and gardens of Dalemain are a short walk.

Facilities

The heated toilet block includes washbasins and preset showers in cubicles. New facilities for disabled visitors. Large, light and airy dishwashing room and fully equipped laundry. Small shop selling basics, gas and newspapers. Bar with strictly enforced, separate family room open weekend evenings in low season and every evening in high season. Large fenced field with play equipment to suit all ages and goal posts for football and a new play park. Off site: Fishing 0.5 miles. Riding 1.5 miles. Golf 5 miles. Pooley Bridge has a post office/general store, hotels and restaurants.

Open: 1 March - 14 November.

Directions

Do not use GPS here – it directs outfits the wrong way, finishing up on farm tracks. Please use the following directions. From M6 junction 40, take the A66 signed Keswick. After 0.5 miles at roundabout take A592 signed Ullswater and site is on right after 4 miles. O.S.GR: NY460245.

Charges 2007

Per unit incl. all persons and electricity	£ 15.00 - £ 21.50

No credit cards.

UK5650 Ashes Exclusively Adult Caravan Park

New Hutton, Kendal LA8 0AS (Cumbria)

Tel: **01539 731 833**. Email: **info@ashescaravanpark.co.uk**

The Ashes is a friendly, small, adult only park in an extremely peaceful setting in the rolling Cumbrian countryside, yet less than three miles from the M6, and only slightly further from Kendal. A very tidy park, the central grass area is attractively planted and there is an open vista (with little shade). There are 25 hardstanding gravel pitches, all with electricity (10A), neatly placed around the perimeter, with an oval access road. The whole area slopes gently down from the entrance, with some pitches fairly level and others with a little more slope. No tents accepted other than trailer tents.

Facilities

A small, purpose built stone building with a slate roof houses two unisex, heated shower rooms and the washing and toilet facilities. New facilities for disabled visitors. Laundry service. No shop. New electronic barrier. Off site: Mr and Mrs Mason have prepared a full information sheet with details of shopping, eating and many other local venues. Fishing 2 miles. Golf and riding 3 miles. Bicycle hire 4 miles. Kendal 4 miles.

Open: 1 March - 9 November.

Directions

From M6 exit 37 follow A684 towards Kendal for 2 miles. Turn sharp left at crossroads signed New Hutton. Site is on right in 0.75 miles at a left bend. Only approach and depart using this road. O.S.GR: SD560908. GPS: N54:18.788 W02:40.500

Charges 2007

Per unit incl. 2 persons and electricity	£ 12.00 - £ 15.00
extra person (over 18s only)	£ 4.50

225

UK5620 Cove Camping Park

Ullswater, Watermillock, Penrith CA11 0LS (Cumbria)

Tel: **017684 86549**. Email: **info@cove-park.co.uk**

Cove Camping is a delightful small site, some of the 50 pitches having great views over Lake Ullswater. A separate area behind the camping field holds 39 privately owned caravan holiday homes. The grass is well trimmed, there are ramps to keep speeds down to 5 mph and the site is well lit. At the top of the park are 17 level pitches with electric hook-ups and 13 with hardstanding suitable for touring caravans and motorcaravans. The rest of the park is quite sloping. Rubbish bins are hidden behind larch lap fencing, as are recycling bins. The park is well situated for walking, boating, fishing and pony trekking activities. The road up from the A592 is narrow, but a self imposed one way system is generally adhered to and the warden will advise on a different way to leave the site.

Facilities

The tiled toilet block is immaculate and heated in cooler months, providing adjustable showers, some washbasins in cabins and, for ladies, a hairdressing area with stool and a baby changing unit. Foyer containing a freezer (free), coffee machine and tourist information. Laundry with washing machine, dryer and an iron. Dishwashing sinks in a separate area. Gas supplies. Small, grass based play area. Off site: Shop nearby. Fishing 1.5 miles. Riding 3 miles. Golf 6 mile. Bicycle hire 7 miles (will deliver).

Open: March - 31 October.

Directions

We would advise using the following directions rather than GPS. From A66 Penrith - Keswick road, take A592 south, signed Ullswater. Turn right at Brackenrigg Inn (site signed) and follow road uphill for about 1.5 miles to park on left. This road is narrow so if you have a larger unit, telephone the park for advice about an alternative route. O.S.GR: NY431236. GPS: N54:36.257 W02:52.913

Charges 2007

Per unit incl. 2 persons and electricity	£ 15.00 - £ 25.00
tent incl. 2 persons	£ 10.00 - £ 22.00
extra person (over 4 yrs)	£ 2.00
dog	£ 1.00

No credit cards.

UK5625 Lowther Holiday Park

Eamont Bridge, Penrith CA10 2JB (Cumbria)

Tel: **017688 63631**. Email: **alan@lowther-holidaypark.co.uk**

Sitting on the banks of the River Lowther this holiday park occupies 50 acres of rural, wooded parkland, home to the rare red squirrel. There are 400 caravan holiday homes and lodges around the park, together with 200 touring pitches. A proportion of these are taken by seasonal lets. Marked and numbered, on mostly level ground between mature trees, they have 10A electricity and hardstanding. A separate elevated grass area is available for tents. There is a small touring office with 24 hour security adjacent to the holiday home sales office. Here too is a well stocked, licensed shop also selling some caravan accessories. The Squirrel Inn is open all season and serves restaurant meals and takeaways. Outside is a large paved seating area with a play area to one side. A lovely riverside walk has been created with many benches to rest and enjoy the birds and other wildlife.

Facilities

Two toilet blocks are central to the touring areas (key entry). Very clean, they provide large, preset showers. Fully equipped bathroom with baby changing. Drive through motorcaravan service. Well equipped laundry. Full facilities for disabled visitors (Radar key). Licensed shop. Squirrel Inn with restaurant, terrace and games room. Play areas. Fly fishing on river (permit from office). Activity weekends. Live entertainment and children's parties. Max. two dogs per unit. Off site: Market town of Penrith 3 miles. Golf, riding and bicycle hire 2 miles. Boat launching 4 miles.

Open: March - November.

Directions

From M6 exit 40 take A66 towards Scotch Corner for 1 mile. At roundabout take A6 south for 1 mile towards Shap. Lowther is on the right as you pass through village of Eamont Bridge. O.S.GR: NY527264. GPS: N54:38.860 W02:44.221

Charges guide

Per unit incl. 1-6 persons and electricity	£ 18.00 - £ 22.00

UK5630 The Quiet Site Caravan & Camping Park

Watermillock, Penrith CA11 0LS (Cumbria)

Tel: **07768 727016**. Email: **info@thequietsite.co.uk**

The Quiet Site is a secluded, family run park, operating as a carbon neutral company. It is situated on a hillside in the National Park with views over the fells and just 1.5 miles from Lake Ullswater. There are 90 unmarked pitches, most with hardstanding and 50 with electricity connections. Most have been terraced to provide level surfaces, but a few are very sloping. The camping area is very undulating (we noticed that some tents were pitched amongst the caravans to find flatter ground). In a separate part of the park, screened by mature trees, are 23 privately owned caravan holiday homes and a cottage for rent. In converted old farm buildings, the amenities are centred around the reception and shop and include a first floor 'Olde-Worlde' bar with oak beams and barrel seats. Many beautiful walks start from right outside the park and the numerous activities and attractions of the Lake District are within a short drive. The owners, the Holder family, are continuing to develop this attractive, well maintained park and a new bathroom and two new shower rooms have been added. A member of the Best of British group.

Facilities

The upgraded toilet block provides preset showers and open style washbasins. Three new bathrooms and two private shower rooms. Bathroom with facilities for disabled visitors (key from reception). Baby changing area. Dishwashing under cover. Laundry facilities. Well stocked shop at reception. Gas supplies. Bar (weekends only in low season), adult only room with pool and darts. TV and games room. Excellent adventure play area. Caravan storage. American motorhomes would find access very difficult. Off site: Fishing 1.5 miles. Riding and bicycle hire 3 miles. Golf 8 miles.

Open: All year excl. 17 January - 28 February.

Directions

We advise using the following directions, rather than GPS. From M6, exit 40, take A66 (Keswick) for 1 mile, then A592 signed Ullswater for 4 miles. Turn right at Lake junction, still on A592 signed Windermere. After 1 miles turn right (at Brackenrigg Inn) and follow for 1.5 miles to site on right (large units should phone for an alternative route). O.S.GR: NY431236. GPS: N54:36.281 W02:52.967

Charges 2007

Per unit incl. 2 persons, awning and electricity	£ 17.00 - £ 27.00
tent incl. 2 persons	£ 12.00 - £ 22.00
extra person	free - £ 3.00
dog	£ 1.00

Camping Cheques accepted.

The Quiet Site Ullswater

Award winning park in idyllic setting. Carbon neutral company.
Also caravan storage in the heart of the lakes.
www.thequietsite.co.uk   *07768 727016*

UK5660 Castlerigg Hall Caravan & Camping Park

Keswick CA12 4TE (Cumbria)

Tel: **017687 74499**. Email: **info@castlerigg.co.uk**

This well laid out park was started in the late 1950s by the Jackson family, who over the years have developed and improved the site whilst maintaining its character. Good use has been made of the traditional stone buildings to house the reception and shop, whilst another building houses a modern amenity block along with a really excellent campers' kitchen. Tarmac roads wend their way around the site to the separate tent area of 110 pitches. Gently sloping with some shelter, these pitches have fine views across Keswick, Derwentwater and the western Fells. The 45 caravan pitches tend to be on terraces, again overlooking the lake. Each terrace has a maximum of eight pitches, all on hardstanding and with 10A electricity and nearly all with a water tap and grey water drain. Places to visit include Keswick (about 20 minutes walk), Derwentwater, Ullswater, Penrith, Carlisle, Hadrian's Wall, Rhegad (the village in the hill) and, quite close to the site, Castlerigg stone circle which is believed to be some 4,000 years old, and of course as much walking as you might want. The Jacksons are committed to conservation.

Facilities

The main toilet block is beautifully fitted out, fully tiled and heated, with showers, vanity style washbasins (2 in cabins) and hair care areas. Unit for disabled visitors (key). Baby area. Fully equipped laundry and dishwashing area. Games room and campers' kitchen complete with microwave, toasters, kettle and hot plates. Two other toilet blocks are older in style but newly decorated and clean. Reception houses tourist information, internet point and a well stocked shop (with gas). Off site: Hotel/pub for meals adjacent to site. Fishing, golf, riding. Bicycle hire and boat launching, all 1.5 miles.

Open: Mid March - November.

Directions

From Penrith take A66 towards Keswick and Cockermouth. Leave at first sign for Keswick (A591) and follow to junction (A5271). Turn left on A591 signed Windermere and after 1 mile, take small road on right signed Castlerigg and Rakefoot. Park entrance is on right after 400 yards. O.S.GR: NY282227. GPS: N54:35.586 W03:06.755

Charges 2007

Per caravan incl. 2 persons	£ 13.50 - £ 15.95
motorcaravan incl. 2 persons	£ 12.00 - £ 14.50
awning	£ 1.90 - £ 2.30

UK5670 Flusco Wood Touring Caravan Park

Flusco, Penrith CA11 0JB (Cumbria)

Tel: **017684 80020**. Email: **admin@fluscowood.co.uk**

Flusco Wood Caravan Park is still being developed but everything is to a very high standard. Set amongst woodland with the touring pitches in bays, this park will meet the needs of those requiring a quiet holiday (with plenty of walks from the site) and also those travelling up or down the M6 looking for a quiet night's rest. All pitches are on hardstanding, with an area near reception with hardstandings for motorcaravans. Recent additions here include new log cabins (privately owned), with a further planned. The area abounds with wildlife including deer and red squirrels, as well as many breeds of birds (we watched a woodpecker taking food from a bird feeder). For a wet day you are about 2.5 miles from Rheged, the 'village in the hill' and, if the weather improves, a short drive from Ullswater, Keswick, Penrith and Carlisle. Member of the Countryside Discovery group.

Facilities

A log cabin style building houses very clean, heated facilities including preset showers and vanity style washbasins (1 cubicle). Large en-suite shower rooms for families or disabled visitors, one in the ladies' and one in the men's. Dishwashing sinks under cover. Laundry, drying room and boot washing sink. Second log cabin serves as reception/shop with basic supplies, gas and daily papers. Play equipment on bark. Grass area for ball games. Off site: Pub and P.O. stores 2 miles. Fishing, bicycle hire and golf 4 miles. Riding 5 miles.

Open: Easter or 1 April - end October.

Directions

From M6 take A66 towards Keswick. Go straight on at first roundabout, then third right at top of hill (signed Flusco, Recycling Centre, Pottery and caravan sign). After 0.5 miles road turns right up hill (narrow, so take care in large units), site is on left at the top. Site is 4 miles from M6. O.S.GR: NY457293. GPS: N54:39.381 W02:50.537

Charges 2007

Per unit incl. 2 persons and electricity	£ 16.00 - £ 19.00
extra person (over 3 yrs)	£ 2.50
No credit cards.	

MAP 5

Northumbria

The most northerly region of England, Northumbria is steeped in history, full of ancient forts and fairytale castles. The great outdoors offers limitless walking with plenty of trails stretching across moorlands and beaches, encompassing views of the beautiful scenery.

THE REGION COMPRISES: NORTHUMBERLAND, DURHAM, TYNE AND WEAR, AND TEESIDE

The 400 square mile Northumberland National Park is one of the most peaceful, remote places in England. With endless walks across moorlands and hills, it stretches south from the Cheviot Hills, through the Simonside Hills, to the crags of Whin Sill, where it engulfs a section of the historic Hadrian's Wall, built by the Romans to mark the northern limit of their empire. The Pennine Way was the country's first official long-distance path and is still the longest. At 268 miles, it stretches from the Peak National Park to the border. The coastline is not to be forgotten, with mile upon mile of deserted, sandy beaches, with resorts that still have an old fashioned feel to them, such as Whitley Bay, South Shields and Seaton Carew. The majestic castles of Bamburgh, and Dunstanburgh can be seen for miles along the Northumberland coast. Surrounded on three sides by the river Wear, the small, historic city of Durham is dominated by England's greatest Norman Cathedral. With cobbled medieval streets and restricted car access it is a popular place with visitors. Further north is the bustling city of Newcastle. Home to an array of cosmopolitan restaurants and bars, music venues, and fabulous architecture, it also boasts a lively nightlife.

Places of interest

Northumberland: Bamburgh Castle; Alnwick Castle and gardens; Berwick-upon-Tweed; bird reserve on Farne Islands, home to large colony of grey seals; Hauxley Nature Reserve; Dunstanburgh Castle; Corbridge Roman sites at Hadrian's Wall.

Durham: Durham Castle and Cathedral; Barnard Castle, a ruined castle overlooking the River Tees; Diggerland at Langley Park; Harperley POW Camp.

Tyne and Wear: New Metroland, Europe's only indoor theme park within a large shopping complex; Newcastle with Life Science Centre, Discovery Museum and Castle Keep; Whitley Bay.

Teeside: Kirkleatham Owl Centre; Darlington Railway Centre and Museum; Guisborough Hall; Hartlepool Historic Quay and HMS Trinacomalee; Butterfly World in Stockton-on-Tees.

Did you know?

Alnwick Castle is used as the setting of Hogwarts in the Harry Potter films.

Stretching from Wallsend to Bowness-on-Solway, Hadrian's Wall is 81 miles long; it is possible to walk the entire length.

Born in Northumbria in 1825, George Stephenson was the first person to design the steam engine that ran on wheels.

In the past 300 years Berwick has changed hands between the Scottish and the English no less than 13 times.

The Angel of The North is made up of 200 tonnes of steel and rises 20 metres from the ground.

Built in 1817, HMS Trinacomalee is the oldest ship afloat in the UK.

SCOTLAND

MELROSE
7030
KELSO

Scottish Lowlands

JEDBURGH

5800

5755   5750

WOOLER

5770

Northumberland

Northumberland

MORPETH

NORTHUMBRIA

5810
HALTWHISTLE   HEXHAM

NEWCASTLE
UPON TYNE

Tyne and Wear

SUNDERLAND

CONSETT   CHESTER-LE-STREET

CUMBRIA

DURHAM   5705

5700   PETERLEE

Durham

HARTLEPOOL

BISHOP AUCKLAND
MIDDLETON-IN-TEESDALE

APPLEBY-IN-WESTMORLAND

5710   A688

5570   5720   BARNARD CASTLE

5740
MIDDLESBROUGH

BROUGH   BOWES   DARLINGTON

KIRKBY STEPHEN   5600

UK5740 White Water Caravan Club Park

Tees Barrage, Stockton-on-Tees TS18 2QW (Teeside)

Tel: **01642 634880**

Being part of the multimillion pound development at the Tees Barrage, this pleasantly landscaped club site caters for all tastes, especially water sports enthusiasts. The Tees Barrage has transformed eleven miles of the Tees, providing clean, non-tidal water for many activities. The adjoining White Water Course (Britain's largest purpose-built canoe course) provides facilities for both advanced and beginner canoeists, and hosts major national and international events. Close to the site are wetlands that provide a home for a variety of birds. The site itself provides 115 pitches, hedged with bushes, all with 16A electricity connections, and includes 21 fully serviced pitches set within bays and hedges (fresh water and waste disposal). The site is well lit, with a security barrier.

Facilities

The central, heated toilet block of high quality includes washbasins in cubicles, baby facilities and a well appointed unit for disabled visitors. Laundry room. Motorcaravan service point. Play area on fine gravel. Heated family room with TV. Off site: Supermarket 6 minutes. Retail and leisure park with 14-screen cinema, 10-pin bowling, shops and fast food. North Yorkshire Moors and the Hartlepool Historic Quay 40 minutes drive.

Open: All year.

Directions

From A1(M) take A66 for Darlington and follow until you pick up signs for Teeside Retail Park and the Tees Barrage. Cross railway bridge and the Barrage bridge, then first right to site on left in 400 yards. O.S.GR: NZ463194. GPS: N54:34.064 W01:17.194

Charges 2007

Per person	£ 3.30 - £ 4.60
child (5-16 yrs)	£ 1.30 - £ 2.00
pitch (non-member)	£ 9.80 - £ 13.20.

UK5700 Strawberry Hill Caravan Park

Running Waters, Old Cassop, Durham DH6 4QA (Co. Durham)

Tel: **01913 723457**. Email: **info@strawberryhf.co.uk**

This park is owned and managed by Howard and Elizabeth who are experienced caravanners. They have terraced their site to offer panoramic views over the fields and woodland from all the pitches. The park is licensed to accommodate more units but the owners prefer to offer space to visitors by providing generous pitches on either grass or hardstanding. There are 44 touring pitches (with 16A electric hook-ups), including 10 on hardstanding, plus a separate terrace for tents. At present the new landscaping on the park offers limited shade. Nature corridors and the surrounding country-side make this a haven for nature lovers and visitors are encouraged to enjoy the tranquillity of the area. The owners supply good tourist information and details of local nature walks. The easy access to the A1M and the proximity of the historic cathedral city of Durham (3 miles) make this an ideal location for visiting local attractions. These include Beamish museum, Gateshead metro centre and the historic Hartlepool Quays.

Facilities

The single toilet block can be heated and is kept immaculately clean. Free showers. Laundry. Facilities for disabled visitors incorporating a baby care area. Small but well stocked shop in reception. Gas. Off site: Country pub with meals 1 mile. Large hypermarket 3 miles. Riding 5 miles. Park and ride (07.00 to 19.00hrs) into Durham city centre operates nearby. Buses (Durham – Hartlepool) from entrance.

Open: 1 March - 31 December.

Directions

From A1M exit 61 follow signs for 177 signed Bowburn and Peterlee. After 200 m. turn right (Peterlee, Sherburn) and watch for brown sign to Bowburn Hall Hotel. Follow this twisting road for 3 miles to crossroads and turn right on the A181 Wheatley Hill, Peterlee road. Approx 1 mile to dual carriageway, entrance to park is 200 m. up the hill (this site can only be approached from the eastbound carriageway). O.S.GR: NZ338399.

Charges 2007

Per unit incl. 2 persons	£ 13.50 - £ 14.50
extra person	£ 2.00
child	£ 1.00

UK5710 Doe Park Touring Caravan Park

Cotherstone, Barnard Castle DL12 9UQ (Co. Durham)

Tel: **01833 650302**

This is Hannah Hauxwell country and the Dales, less frequented than other upland areas, provide wonderful walking country; indeed part of the Pennine Way runs near this peaceful site. The farm and park are close to where the River Balder joins the Tees at Cotherstone and the ancient oak wood beside the river is an SSSI (Site of Special Scientific Interest) for its insects and flowers, but is also a haven for bird-watchers. The park's reception is in a log cabin at the entrance to the pitch area and is well stocked with tourist information guides. The farmhouse, formerly Leadgard Hall, is a mellow three storey, Grade II listed building with a history of its own. The Lamb family will make you very welcome and personally take you to your pitch. The camping fields have a lovely open aspect with wonderful views and the 70 pitches are spacious with well mown grass, all with 10A electricity, over 40 with hardstanding (no tents are taken). A bus service passes the park from Barnard Castle to Middleton and the village of Cotherstone is only half a mile with post office and a restaurant with bar meals, a pleasant walk by road or river bank.

Facilities

With toilet facilities at the farmhouse, two well kept blocks are closer to the pitches. Built in local stone, these are fully tiled with the newest one heated. Washbasins in cabins and adjustable showers. Well appointed unisex unit for disabled visitors. Small laundry. Eggs and milk are available from the farmhouse, plus gas supplies and battery charging. No play area but a large grass area in front of some of the pitches can be used for ball games. River fishing on site. Dogs and pets are accepted by arrangement only. Off site: Reservoirs (sailing, water skiing and fishing) 3 miles. Bicycle hire and golf 4 miles. Riding 2 miles. Local leisure centre with pool 4 miles.

Open: 1 March - 31 October.

Directions

Follow B6277 from Barnard Castle in direction of Middleton in Teesdale. The farm is signed on the left just after Cotherstone village (there is no need to go into Barnard Castle). O.S.GR: NZ005204. GPS: N54:34.693 W01:59.541

Charges 2007

Per unit incl. 2 persons	£ 9.00 - £ 13.50

No credit cards.

UK5705 Grange Caravan Club Site

Meadow Lane, Durham DH1 1TL (Co. Durham)

Tel: **01913 844778**

Fully refurbished and landscaped, this park offers 75 flat spacious pitches suitable for all units. Easy access to the A1M and the A690 make it an ideal stop-over for those travelling north or south or for visiting the historic cathedral city of Durham, Beamish museum or Gateshead Metro centre. A coppice of mature trees and newly planted shrubs mask road noise and make an attractive dog walking area. The park has been redesigned with attention to detail in all areas offering pockets of privacy or a central area with picnic tables and benches. A purpose built central block offers spacious, heated, modern and clean facilities with ample free showers and hairdryers including private washing cubicles and a larger cubicle for families or less able bodied.

Facilities

The single toilet block is a heated building with free showers, hairdryers, and private cubicles. Laundry and food preparation area. Separate baby area and facilities for disabled visitors are available via a key entry system. Shop in reception with limited supplies, bread, milk and newspapers to order. Gas. Secure caravan storage. Off site: Large supermarket 2 miles. Park and ride (07.00-19.00) into Durham city centre 800 yds. Local service buses run from Belmont and Carville.

Open: All year.

Directions

From A1M junction 62 follow signs for Durham city (A690). At roundabout take first exit left and after 20 yds. turn right (across dualcarriageway A690); large units continue along A690 to next roundabout about 2 miles and return on A690 left hand turn (signed just before A1M). O.S.GR: NZ302446.

Charges 2007

Per person	£ 4.40 - £ 5.50
child (5-16 yrs)	£ 1.50 - £ 2.50
pitch (non-member)	£ 10.80 - £ 14.60

UK5720 Barnard Castle Camping & Caravanning Club Site

Dockenflatts Lane, Lartington, Barnard Castle DL12 9DG (Co. Durham)

Tel: **01833 630228**

Welcoming non-members and tents, the Camping and Caravanning Club site at Barnard Castle was opened in 1996. One side of the site is bordered by mature trees and further planting now gives privacy to individual pitches. There are 90 flat pitches, most on grass but including 12 hardstanding pitches (gravel base with room for both car and caravan and space for an awning on grass). There are 56 electrical hook-ups (16A). There is an attractive woodland dog walking area leading to a riverside footpath which takes you into Barnard Castle. There are a number of footpaths and walks in the area and numerous attractions include the market town itself, Bowes Museum, Egglestone Abbey and Raby Castle all within a 10 mile radius of the site.

Facilities

The centrally located toilet facilities are of good quality and kept spotlessly clean. Washbasins are in cubicles and free, controllable showers are roomy. Baby room. Fully equipped unisex unit for visitors with disabilities. Large laundry with outside lines provided. Well stocked shop. Motorcaravan service point. Gas supplies. Central play area with rubber safety base. Caravan storage. Off site: Riding 200 m. Fishing 4 miles. Golf 2.5 miles. Bus service from end of lane.

Open: 30 March - 30 October.

Directions

Follow B6277 from Barnard Castle (towards Middleton in Teesdale) for 1 mile to Lartington. Turn left at club sign into narrow lane with passing places to site entrance on left (there is no need to go into Barnard Castle). O.S.GR: NZ025168. GPS: N54:32.813 W01:57.755

Charges 2007

Per person	£ 4.90 - £ 7.25
child (6-18 yrs)	£ 2.15 - £ 2.25
non-member pitch fee	£ 5.65

UK5755 South Meadows Caravan Park

South Meadows, Belford NE70 7DP (Northumberland)

Tel: **01668 213326**. Email: **g.mcl@btinternet.com**

South Meadows is set in the north Northumberland countryside, within walking distance of the village of Belford with its market cross and old coaching inn. Covering 5 acres of level grass, there are 77 pitches, all with electricity (13A), water and TV aerial point. At present 20 pitches are available for touring units. The manager is environmentally aware and encourages recycling. Determined that visitors have a relaxing holiday, he will site your caravan using his own towing equipment. There is an area especially for disabled visitors with wider paths and safety features including a 24 hour panic telephone directly to the managers home on site. Booking ahead is advised to ensure availability. The park is pleasantly landscaped and two short walks lead into the adjacent Blue Bell woods with streams, wildlife and spring flowers. Just off the A1 road, this would be a convenient stopover but Northumberland is an undiscovered county with castles and stately homes, the Farne Islands, Holy Island and long golden beaches, and you would be made most welcome here for a longer stay. This attractive, well maintained park is already popular with couples and young families and booking is advised.

Facilities

The new, fully tiled toilet block is excellent, heated in cool weather, with washbasins in cabins and roomy showers (free). Hairdryers. Full facilities for disabled visitors. Laundry with washing machines, dryers and iron plus a baby unit. Food preparation and cooking area. Coffee shop (weekends, incl. Sunday roast) and takeaway (daily until 16.00). Play area. Caravan storage and servicing. Off site: Village with pub and shops 0.5 miles. Golf 0.5 miles. Riding 3 miles. Beach 3 miles. Alnwick Castle of Harry Potter fame.

Open: All year.

Directions

Turn off A1 about 15 miles from Alnwick to Belford village and park is signed at the southern end. O.S.GR: NU115331. GPS: N55:35.458 W01:49.355

Charges 2007

Per unit incl. 2 persons	£ 17.00 - £ 30.00
extra person	£ 7.50 - £ 10.00
tent per person	£ 8.00 - £ 10.00
child (2-16 years)	£ 2.00

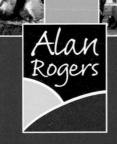

UK5770 Dunstan Hill Camping & Caravanning Club Site

Dunstan Hill, Dunstan, Alnwick NE66 3TQ (Northumberland)

Tel: **01665 576310**

Off a quiet lane between Embleton and Craster this is a rural site with a tree belt to shelter it from the north wind and access to the beach by a level footpath through the fields, across the golf course and past the ruins of Dunstanburgh Castle. This is just over a mile by car. With gravel access roads, the peaceful site has 150 level, well spaced pitches, 80 with 16A electricity. Reception is manned by very helpful managers and there is an area for outside parking and late arrivals at the entrance. This is a wonderful area to visit, with its unspoilt beaches and the whole area is steeped in history with Holy Island, the Farne Islands, Bamburgh, Dunstanburgh, Walkworth and Alnwick castles (featured in many films including Macbeth and Harry Potter). The multimillion pound gardens project at Alnwick is well worth a visit. The site is not suitable for large American motorhomes.

Facilities

Two very clean and well maintained toilet blocks have some washbasins in cubicles, hairdryers (20p) and a washroom for children with deep sinks. Fully equipped facility for disabled visitors in one block, a laundry in the other. Small shop for gas and basic provisions. Bread and milk can be ordered and a mobile shop and the paper man visit. Well stocked tourist information room. Small play area. Torches are useful. Off site: Buses pass the site entrance (request stop) and there are good eating places near including Craster - world famous fish restaurant. Fishing 1.5 miles. Golf 1.5 miles. Beach 1.5 miles. Riding 8 miles. Bicycle hire 10 miles.

Open: March - October.

Directions

From A1 just north of Alnwick take B1340 or B6347 (further north) for Embleton. Site is signed in Embleton village - avoid signs to Dunstanburgh Castle and follow those for Craster. Site is (south) on the left after approx. 0.5 miles. O.S.GR: NU236214. GPS: N55:29.130 W01:37.746

Charges 2007

Per person	£ 4.90 - £ 7.25
child (6-18 yrs)	£ 2.15 - £ 2.25
non-member pitch fee	£ 5.65

UK5800 Ord House Country Park

East Ord, Berwick-upon-Tweed TD15 2NS (Northumberland)

Tel: **01289 305288**. Email: **enquiries@ordhouse.co.uk**

Ord House is 40 acre park for 287 privately owned holiday homes and 74 touring caravan and tent pitches. The park has a very well cared for appearance throughout with well mown grass and colourful arrays of flowering bushes. The touring pitches, all with electricity (10-16A), are in small sections, from the secluded, walled orchard to the more open areas nearer the toilet blocks. There are 39 hardstanding pitches, each with electricity, water and drainage, 12 in the walled garden separated by shrubs and camomile lawns. At the entrance to the park an area with a few pitches is suitable for wheelchair users and close by is a small sanitary unit with WCs and showers plus a large, unisex, well appointed unit (Radar key). The whole site is 'wheelchair friendly' with good access to the airy reception. Ord House itself, an 18th century mansion, has been tastefully converted to provide a bar, lounge bar and family room. Although there are many caravan holiday homes, they are not overwhelming and their presence does mean that other amenities can remain open all season. A member of the Best of British group.

Facilities

The main, modern toilet building is of excellent quality and cleanliness, very well maintained and can be heated. Two good large family bathrooms (with two showers, a bath, WC and washbasin). Two rooms for disabled visitors. Large well equipped laundry. Motorcaravan service point. Gas supplies. Bar, bar food and family room (1/3-10/1). Crazy golf. Table tennis. Draughts. Play area. No commercial vehicles are accepted. Dogs only accepted by prior arrangement. Off site: Post office stores 50 yards from the entrance. Leisure centre with a pool 15 minutes walk. Fishing 1.5 miles. Riding 8 miles. Golf 2 miles. Sea fishing can be booked in Berwick. Beach 1.5 miles.

Open: All year.

Directions

From A1 Berwick bypass take East Ord exit and follow signs. O.S.GR: NT982515.

Charges 2007

Per unit incl. up to 4 persons and electricity	£ 14.00 - £ 21.00
extra person over 6 yrs	£ 2.50
awning	£ 2.50
dog	free - £ 1.50

Discounts for 1- and 2-man tents and for longer stays.

UK5750 Waren Caravan Park

Waren Mill, Bamburgh, Iford NE70 7EE (Northumberland)

Tel: **01668 214366**. Email: **enquiries@warencp.demon.co.uk**

Developed from 100 acres of undulating privately owned heath and woodland, Waren Park is a large, spacious family site with marvellous views over Northumberland's golden beaches and the sea. A large section of caravan holiday homes (for hire) is separate from a self contained four acre touring area. Enclosed by sheltering banks, this provides 170 reasonably level pitches, 100 with electrical connections (10A). As well as the spacious grounds to wander in, there is much to see nearby from historic castles and the Farne Islands to the Cheviot Hills and miles and miles of sandy beaches.

Facilities

The older toilet facilities are poor and in need of refurbishment, whilst a newer block situated in a separate static holiday home section provides good facilities. Laundry room. Dishwashing sinks. Motorcaravan service point. Licensed shop. Bar with terrace serving bar meals (all season). Games room with pool table. Patio area. Children's play park and playing fields. Splash pool (June - Sept). Off site: Beach 500 yds. excellent for birdwatching, unsuitable for bathing. Safe bathing beach 4 miles (Bamburgh). Golf or bicycle hire 2 miles. Riding 5 miles. Birdwatching opportunities nearby.

Open: 20 March - 1 November.

Directions

Follow B1342 from the A1 to Waren Mill towards Bamburgh. After Budle Bay turn right and follow signs. O.S.GR: NU154342.

Charges 2007

Per unit incl. 2 persons	£ 11.00 - £ 19.50
extra person (over 5 yrs)	£ 2.00
1-man tent	£ 7.50 - £ 11.00
dog	£ 1.60

Less 10% for bookings of 7 days or over.

Meadowhead Parks Waren Mill-Bamburgh

A completely self-contained and self-sufficient park, you dont have to go beyond its gates for a perfect off-season break or a satisfying family holiday.

01668 214 366 www.meadowhead.co.uk   Barnburgh, Northumberland, NE70 7EE

UK5810 Fallowfield Dene Caravan & Camping Park

Acomb, Hexham NE46 4RP (Northumberland)

Tel: **01434 603553**

Although only 2.5 miles from Hexham, Fallowfield Dene Caravan Park is very secluded, situated in mature woodland at the end of a no-through road. Set in woodland glades (formerly a Victorian lead mine), each with a Roman name (Hadrian's Wall is close), are 118 seasonal pitches and 32 touring pitches, all with 16A electricity. A further 10 tent pitches have been added, suitable for smaller tents, and a barbecue area with views of woodland and fields. The park entrance, with reception and a small shop, is neat, tidy and very colourful. There is no play area or games field, but the surrounding woods are a paradise for children. Fallowfield Dene itself is a network of tracks and there are footpaths from the site entrance. The site is a haven for wildlife with red squirrels, foxes and badgers to be seen. Hadrian's Wall is only a mile away, with Roman forts such as Housteads Fort and Chesters, being great attractions. The whole area abounds with well preserved Roman remains. Nearby, Hexham market town has its Border History museum, housed in the oldest purpose-built gaol in England, where one can learn about the Border Reivers. This site has a very friendly atmosphere.

Facilities

Brick built toilet blocks (one for each sex) are central and heated in cool weather. Well tiled and kept very clean, there are washbasins in cabins and free hairdryers. Separate, fully equipped room for disabled people. Laundry room with dishwashing sinks. Baby bath. Motorcaravan service point. Small shop for necessities, including gas. Barrier card £5 deposit. Off site: Supermarkets and other shops at Hexham or Corbridge. Good restaurant five minutes walk. Fishing or riding 3 miles. Golf 5 miles.

Open: 17 March - 29 October.

Directions

From A69 Newcastle - Carlisle road, take A6079 north signed Bellingham and Rothbury. At village of Acomb, site is signed to right. Follow site signs for approx. 1.5 miles. The last 0.5 miles is single track with passing places. O.S.GR: NY938676.

Charges 2008

Per unit incl. 2 persons	£ 13.50 - £ 14.50
extra person	£ 3.00
child (5-17 yrs)	£ 1.25
electricity	£ 2.00
dog	£ 0.50

Land of ancient myths and Celtic legends, Wales is a small and compact country boasting a diverse landscape, from lakes and mountains, rivers and valleys to beautiful coastlines and rolling wooded countryside. It offers superb opportunities for an active holiday.

WE HAVE DIVIDED OUR LIST OF CAMPSITES IN WALES INTO NORTH, WEST, MID AND SOUTH REGIONS

Wales' biggest asset is undoubtedly its countryside, home to three National Parks that make up almost a quarter of the country's total area. Snowdonia National Park in the north combines dramatic mountain scenery with glacial valleys, lakes and streams, while in the south the Brecon Beacons boast mountains, moorlands, forests and wooded gorges with deep caves. The surrounding area of the Wye Valley on the borders with England is a designated Area of Outstanding Beauty; as is the Gower Peninsula, the Lleyn Peninsula, the Anglesey Coast and the Clwydian Range. The endless miles of largely unspoilt and beautiful Pembrokeshire coastline in the west has some of the finest long beaches in Europe, with pretty little bays plus the lively traditional seaside resorts of Tenby and Whitesand. Further inland is the secluded and pretty Gwaun Valley. The capital of Wales, Cardiff, has many attractions, including its newly developed waterfront, the Millennium Stadium. Castles can be seen all over Wales, ranging from tiny stone keeps to huge medieval fortresses; some of the best preserved are Caernarfon, Conwy and Harlech, all built by Edward I.

Places of interest

North: Isle of Anglesey; Victorian School of 3R's and Motor Museum at Llangollen; Victorian seaside resort of Llandudno; Colwyn Bay; Caernarfon Castle; Snowdon Mountain Railway at Llanberis.

West: Oakwood Park, Wales' only theme park; the National Botanic Gardens at Aberglasney; Dolaucothi Goldmines; historic, stone-walled Aberaeron.

Mid: Brecon Beacons National Park; the lakes of the Elan Valley; entertaining events all summer at Llanwrtyd Wells; the Centre for Alternative Technology near Machynlleth.

South: Merthyr Tydfil, the Iron Capital of the World; Caerphilly's truly massive medieval castle; Cardiff, capital of Wales; the Wye Valley and the Vale of Usk of the Welsh borderlands with Tintern Abbey.

Did you know?

The origins of the Red Dragon flag may date back to the Roman period, when the dragon was used by military cohorts.

St David's in Pembrokeshire is Britain's smallest city by virtue of its Cathedral to the patron saint of Wales.

There are many sites in Wales linked to the legend of King Arthur: Castell Dinas Brân, near Llangollen, is reputed to be the resting-place of the Holy Grail.

Towering at 1085 metres Mount Snowdon is the highest mountain in England and Wales.

'The Dam Busters' was filmed on location in the Elan Valley.

The Welsh language is one of Europe's oldest languages and shares its roots with Breton, Gaelic and Cornish.

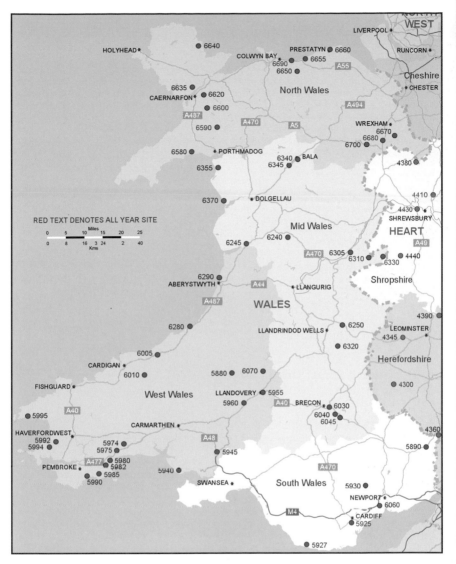

RED TEXT DENOTES ALL YEAR SITE

UK5925 Cardiff Caravan Park

Pontcanna Fields, via Sophia Close, Cardiff CF11 9LB (Cardiff)

Tel: **02920 398362**

Run by the city council, this popular site is set within acres of parkland, one mile from the city centre, ideal for visiting the many attractions of the City of Cardiff. The campsite has 73 pitches which are on a fairly open area, with 43 on a grassed grid surface with electric hook-ups (16A), the remainder are on grass. There is a public right of way through the site. Security is good with an on-site warden 24 hours a day, and security cameras (infra red) constantly scanning the whole area. Remember though that you are in a city centre environment, so lock up your valuables.

Facilities

Two heated buildings each with key code entry. One has a laundry with washer and dryer, and facilities for disabled campers. Both have controllable hot showers. Baby facilities. Bicycle hire (site specialises in cycles adapted for disabled people). Riding can be arranged. Off site: The Millennium Stadium, Glamorgan County Cricket Ground, Cardiff Bay. Local shops and services within easy walking distance. Fishing 400 yds. Golf 4 miles.

Open: All year.

Directions

From the A48 turn south on A4119 (Cardiff Road). Follow signs for Institute of Sport and at next traffic lights turn into Sophia Close and Gardens. Turn left at Institute of Sport and pass County Cricket Ground on right to site on left. O.S.GR: ST171772.

Charges guide

Per person	£ 4.25
child (4-14 yrs)	£ 2.15
vehicle	£ 2.70

UK5890 Glen Trothy Caravan & Camping Park

Mitchel Troy, Monmouth NP25 4BD (Monmouthshire)

Tel: **01600 712295**. Email: **enquiries@glentrothy.co.uk**

Glen Trothy is a pretty park on the banks of the river Trothy and visitors are greeted by an array of colourful flowerbeds and tubs around the entrance and reception area. The owners, Horace and Merle Price, are working hard on their site bringing its facilities up-to-date, recently adding a security gate to the new reception office. Three fields provide 40 level touring pitches. The first and largest field has a circular gravel road with seasonal pitches arranged on the outer side of the road and touring pitches on the inner side. These have slabs for vehicle wheels and electricity hook-ups. The second field, just past the toilet block, has pitches for trailer tents and tents only, whilst the camping field is for tents only (no cars allowed on this area).

Facilities

The sanitary block is old and a little tired (possibly stretched at peak times). Facilities for disabled visitors. Laundry and dishwashing. Tourist information in reception. Bicycle hire. Fishing in the River Trothy (WWA licence required). Dogs are not accepted. Only purpose built barbecues are allowed. Play area. Off site: Golf 2 miles. Shopping and supermarkets at Monmouth. The Wye Valley and the Forest of Dean are nearby for outings.

Open: 1 March - 31 October.

Directions

At Monmouth, take A40 east to Abergavenny. Exit at first junction and at T-junction, where site is signed, turn left onto B4284. Follow signs for Mitchel Troy. Site is on right just past village sign. O.S.GR: SO495105. GPS: N51:47.458 W02:44.046

Charges 2007

Per unit incl. 2 persons	£ 8.00 - £ 13.00
extra person	£ 2.50
electricity	£ 2.50

UK5930 Cwmcarn Forest Drive Campsite

Cwmcarn, Crosskeys, Newport NP11 7FA (Newport)

Tel: **01495 272001**. Email: **cwmcarn-vc@caerphilly.gov.uk**

This forest site, run by Caerphilly Council, is set in a narrow, sheltered valley with magnificent wooded slopes. The park is not only central for the many attractions of this part of Wales, but there is also much of the natural environment to enjoy including a small fishing lake and the seven mile forest drive. The site has a slightly wild feel, but is well located and has 27 well spaced, flat pitches with 15A electricity (3 with concrete hardstanding) spread over three small fields between the new Visitor Centre and the small lake. Wardens are on hand daily and the Visitor Centre and campsite reception are open 09.00 - 17.00 (18.00 at weekends, Oct - Easter Fridays 09.00 - 16.30). The forest drive (open daily in season) has several car parks en-route where visitors can stop to enjoy the great views, many picnic and barbecue areas, wood carvings and a play area. The climb up to the Twmbarlwm ancient hill fort is well worth making with its magnificent views across the Severn to Somerset, Devon and Gloucestershire.

Facilities

The single, heated toilet block (£5 deposit for key) includes toilet facilities for disabled visitors, laundry facilities, small cooker and fridge. Visitor Centre has a coffee shop selling refreshments and snacks. Guided walks and the popular Twrch (9 miles) mountain bike trail. Numeracy trail and 'environmenteering' routes for children. Rallies accommodated. Dogs accepted by prior arrangement. Off site: Shops, leisure centre, pubs and takeaway food in village less than 1 mile. Riding 2 miles. Golf 3 miles.

Open: All year excl. 23 December - 2 January.

Directions

Cwmcarn Forest Drive is well signed from junction 28 on the M4. From the Midlands and the 'Heads of the Valleys' road (A465), take A467 south to Cwmcarn. O.S.GR: ST230935.

Charges 2007

Per pitch	£ 6.50 - £ 10.00
electricity	£ 2.50

UK6060 Tredegar House Country Park Caravan Club Site

Coedkernen, Newport NP10 8TW (Newport)

Tel: **01633 815600**

This immaculate Caravan Club site is ideally situated for breaking a journey or for longer stays. It can accommodate 80 caravans, all with 16A electricity hook-up and 47 with gravel hardstanding. A further grass area is allocated for 20 tents, with its use limited to families and couples – no single sex groups are accepted. The site itself is set within the gardens and park of Tredegar House, a 17th century house and country park which is open to the public to discover what life was like 'above and below stairs'. The park entrance gates are locked at dusk so contact the site reception for details of latest arrival times. Some road noise may be expected at times, but otherwise this is an excellent site.

Facilities

The sanitary block is of an excellent standard with a digital lock system. It includes washbasins in cubicles. Facilities for disabled visitors. Baby and toddler bathroom. Laundry. Good motorcaravan service point. Calor gas available. Tredegar House visitor centre with tea rooms, gift shop and craft workshops (open Easter - Sept). Adventure play area in the park. Off site: Large supermarket 0.5 miles. Newport 3 miles. Cardiff 9 miles. Bus service 10 minutes walk.

Open: 24 March - 10 December.

Directions

From M4 take exit 28 or from A48 junction with the M4 follow brown signs for Tredegar House. The caravan park is indicated to the left at the house entrance. O.S.GR: ST299855.

Charges 2007

Per person	£ 3.90 - £ 5.40
child (5-16 yrs)	£ 1.30 - £ 2.15
pitch (non-member)	£ 10.30 - £ 14.10

UK5927 Acorn Camping & Caravanning

Ham Lane South, Llantwit Major CF61 1RP (Vale of Glamorgan)

Tel: **01446 794024**. Email: **info@acorncamping.co.uk**

A peaceful, family owned, rural site, Acorn is situated on the Heritage Coast, one mile from the beach and the historic town of Llantwit Major. The 105 pitches are mostly on grass, with a few private and rental mobile homes at the far end, leaving around 90 pitches for tourers. These include 10 serviced pitches and 4 gravel hardstandings with 74 electric hook-ups (10A), and a seperate area for tents. Reception houses a very well stocked shop which includes groceries and essentials, souvenirs, children's toys, camping gear, a delicatessen, and takeaway meals cooked to order. There is occasional aircraft noise. Site lighting is kept to a minimum to allow guests to enjoy the night sky – a torch might be useful. The Glamorgan Heritage Coastal footpath Is a short walk from the site and Llantwit Major is also worth a visit, particualrly St Illtud's Church for its wall paintings, medieval altar, and collection of Celtic stones.

Facilities

A warm, modern building houses spacious shower cubicles with washbasins, ample WCs, a family/baby room, and a suite for disabled campers. Dishwashing sinks and laundry facilities. Drinks machine. Shop. Gas. Recycling. Snooker room. Games room (charged). Play area with free trampoline. Off site: Glamorgan Heritage Coastal footpath. Llanerch Vineyard. Cosmeston Lakes Country Park at Penarth. Sea fishing 1 mile. Riding 2 miles. Lake 4 miles. Golf, boat launching 9 miles.

Open: 1 February - 8 December.

Directions

From east: M4 exit 33 follow signs to Cardiff airport, take B4265 for Llantwit Major. Turn left at traffic lights, through Broverton and left into Ham Lane East, finally left into Ham Manor Park and follow signs to site. From west: M4 exit 35, turn south on A473 for 3 miles, then left on A48, turning right at Pentre Meyrick towards Llantwit Major on B4268/70. Left at roundabout on B4265, over mini-roundabout, right at traffic lights into Llanmaes Road, left at mini-roundabout, continue around back of the town, left at mini-roundabout, and right into Ham Lane East and continue as above. O.S.GR: SS974678.

Charges 2007

Per unit incl. 2 persons and electricity	£ 12.00 - £ 13.00
extra person	£ 4.00
dog	£ 0.50

UK5880 Springwater Lakes

Harford, Llanwrda SA19 8DT (Carmarthenshire)

Tel: **01558 650788**

Set in 20 acres of Welsh countryside, Springwater offers a selection of fishing lakes to keep even the keenest of anglers occupied. However, it is not just anglers who will enjoy this site – it is a lovely base to enjoy the peace and tranquillity of this part of Wales. Springwater offers 20 spacious, flat pitches either on grass or gravel hardstanding, all with electricity hook-ups (16A). Malcolm and Shirley Bexon are very proud of their site and welcome all visitors with a smile. This is not a site for children unless they enjoy fishing (no play areas). If you want to learn about fishing Malcolm will be happy to help.

Facilities	Directions
The modern toilet block is very clean and includes facilities for disabled visitors (there is also access to the lakes for wheelchairs). Dishwashing. Baker visits daily. Fishing; tackle/bait shop. Off site: Spar shop and garage 500 yards, other shops 5 miles. Bicycle hire and riding 2 miles. Golf 4 miles.	From A40 at Llanwrda take A482 to Lampeter. After 6 miles go through village of Pumsaint and site is 2 mile further on the left, just before garage shop. O.S.GR: SN642429. GPS: N52:04.045 W03:58.935

Open: March - 31 October.

Charges 2007

Per unit incl. 2 persons and electricity	£ 15.75
extra person (over 2 yrs)	£ 4.00

No credit cards.

UK5960 Abermarlais Caravan Park

Llangadog SA19 9NG (Carmarthenshire)

Tel: **01550 777868**

Apart from the attractions of south or mid Wales for a stay, this sheltered, family run park could also double as a useful transit stop close to the main holiday route for those travelling to Pembrokeshire. In a natural setting, up to 88 touring units are accommodated in one fairly flat, tapering five acre grass field edged by mature trees and a stream. Pitches are numbered, and generously spaced around the perimeter or on either side of a central, hedged spine at the wider end, with 42 electrical hook-ups (10A) and some hardstanding. Backpackers have a small, separate area. The park is set in a sheltered valley with a range of wildlife and nine acres of woodland walks.

Facilities	Directions
The one small toilet block is older in style, but is clean, bright and adequate with controllable showers. Dishwashing sinks but no laundry facilities (nearest about 5 miles). Motorcaravan service point. Shop doubling as reception. Gas supplies. Play area. Tennis. Volleyball. Winter caravan storage. Off site: Restaurants nearby. Pubs, shops, etc. at Llangadog. Fishing 2 miles.	Park is on the A40, between the junctions with the A4069 and A482, between Llandovery and Llandeilo. O.S.GR: SN695298. GPS: N51:57.095 W03:54.018

Open: 14 March - 14 November.

Charges 2007

Per person	£ 1.50
child (over 5 yrs)	£ 1.00
pitch incl. electricity	£ 8.00

UK6070 Rhandirmwyn Camping & Caravanning Club Site

Rhandirmwyn, Llandovery SA20 0NT (Carmarthenshire)

Tel: **01550 760257**

This is a popular site with those who like a peaceful life with no on-site entertainment, just fresh air and beautiful countryside. The site is only a short drive from the magnificent Llyn Brianne reservoir and close to the Dinas RSPB nature reserve, where a two mile trail runs through oak and alder woodland alongside the River Tywi and the wildlife includes many species of birds including red kites. The site is in a sheltered valley with 90 pitches on level grass, 51 electric hook-ups (16A) and 17 hardstandings. The village is within walking distance although there is a fairly steep hill to negotiate (but the return is much easier), and you can take a short cut through the woodland grove dedicated to John Lloyd, a former Chairman of the Club.

Facilities	Directions
The single heated sanitary block is kept very clean and tidy. Some washbasins in cubicles, dishwashing sinks and fully equipped laundry. Drive-over motorcaravan service point. Small playground with rubber base. Off site: The village has a Post Office and general store and the Royal Oak Inn serves good value meals. Farmers' market in Llandovery twice a month. Fishing 6 miles. Golf 7 miles. Riding 11 miles.	From centre of Llandovery take A483 towards Builth Wells, after a short distance turn left by the fire station, signed Rhandirmwyn, continue for about 7 miles along country lanes. O.S.GR: SN779436. GPS: N52:04.621 W03:47.030

Open: March - October.

Charges 2007

Per person	£ 4.90 - £ 7.25
child (6-18 yrs)	£ 2.15 - £ 2.25
non-member pitch fee	£ 5.65

UK5940 Pembrey Country Park Caravan Club Site

Pembrey, Llanelli SA16 0EJ (Carmarthenshire)

Tel: **01554 834369**

This very popular Caravan Club site has a wonderful location on the edge of a 520 acre Country Park with a vast range of outdoor activities, including the use of an eight mile stretch of safe, sandy beach a mile away. This well sheltered site is set in 12 acre grounds and provides 50 large hardstanding pitches and 80 level, grass pitches for caravans and motorcaravans, all with 16A electricity. Tents are not accepted. Thoughtful landscaping has included the planting of many species of tree and a circular, one-way tarmac road provides easy access. Sensibly placed service points provide fresh water and waste disposal of all types. RAF jets do practise in this area (although becoming less frequent and generally not flying at the weekend). There may be occasional noise from the nearby motor racing circuit. However, the real plus for this site is its proximity to the Country Park – access to this is free on foot or cycle direct from the site, or the site can organise a special weekly car pass for around £12. Within the parkland are delightful walks, cycle trails, unlimited flora and fauna, bird hides, an equestrian centre, adventure play area, dry ski slope and toboggan run, crazy golf and pitch and putt, miniature railway, bicycle hire and picnic areas, all fronted by Cefn Sidan, an eight mile stretch of golden sands. The nearest section of beach is a 20 minute walk, whilst car parks place you close to the visitor centre, gift shop and the lifeguard patrolled bathing area.

Facilities

The toilet block is of an excellent standard including washbasins in cubicles, facilities for disabled visitors and a baby room. Fully equipped laundry room. Dishwashing room and further sinks under cover. Motorcaravan service point. Gas available. Local tradesmen visit each morning selling milk, bread and newspapers. Play area. Late arrivals area (with electricity). Off site: Dogs are restricted on the beach May - Sept (follow signs).

Open: 17 March - 5 January.

Directions

Leave M4 at junction 48 onto A4138 (signed Llanelli). After 4 miles turn right onto A484 at roundabout signed Carmarthen. Continue for 7 miles to Pembrey. The Country Park is signed off the A484 in Pembrey village; site entrance is on right 100 yds before park gates. O.S.GR: SN413006. GPS: N51:40.909 W04:17.845

Charges 2007

Per person	£ 4.40 - £ 5.50
child (5-16 yrs)	£ 1.50 - £ 2.50
pitch (non-member)	£ 10.80 - £ 14.60

UK5945 River View Touring Park

The Dingle, Llanedi, Pontarddulais SA4 0FH (Carmarthenshire)

Tel: **01269 844876**. Email: **info@riverviewtouringpark.com**

Keith and Kath Brassnett with their warm welcome and helpful efficiency ensure that this park remains attractive, quiet and friendly. Nestling in the valley of the River Gwili, it is made up of three fields: one by the river which is kept mainly for adults and two on a plateau up a steep slope on the opposite side of the lane. There are 60 level, generously sized pitches of which 45 are touring pitches, the remainder seasonal. Twenty have hardstandings, all have electricity (16A) and five are serviced. This is a popular site with young families and older couples. The park is close to the end of the M40, allowing easy access and there is plenty to do or see in the near vicinity, castles, gardens, beaches, wildfowl reserves and a water park, and there is an SSSI immediately at the back of the site. The bird life visible from the site is varied and includes buzzards and red kites, and dippers on the river. The toilet block, including an en-suite family room with baby changing facilities and one for the disabled, is modern and equipped to a very high standard, including under floor heating and automatic lighting.

Facilities

The modern, heated, toilet block is spotless with spacious showers, family room and suite for disabled visitors. New laundry with sinks, washing machine, tumble dryer, iron and ironing board. Small shop for basics and local fresh produce. Large grassy recreation area on main field. Fishing. Off site: Shop, bar and restaurant 1 mile. Bicycle hire 5 miles. Riding 6 miles. Golf, beach and sailing 7 miles.

Open: 1 March - 6 December.

Directions

From the M4 exit 49 take A483 signed Llandeilo. Take the first turn left (after layby) and park is on left after 300 yds. O.S.GR: SN578086.

Charges 2007

Per unit incl. 2 persons and electricity	£ 12.00 - £ 15.00
incl. services	£ 14.50 - £ 17.50
child	£ 1.00 - £ 1.50
No credit cards.	

UK5955 Erwlon Caravan & Camping Park

Brecon Road, Llandovery SA20 0RD (Carmarthenshire)

Tel: **01550 721021**. Email: **peter@erwlon.fsnet.co.uk**

Just outside Llandovery and on the edge of the Brecon Beacons National Park, Erwlon is an attractive and welcoming campsite. Of the 110 pitches, 7 are used for privately owned caravan holiday homes, 40 have seasonal caravans and 53 are for tourers. Most are on hardstanding with electricity connections and 11 have water and a drain as well. There is a flat field for tents at the bottom of the park with some electrical outlets, an open-sided, covered area for eating, food preparation and bicycle storage. The site has a relaxed atmosphere where consideration for others minimises the need for formal rules. It is ideal for young families, walkers, cyclists and fishermen. Gold mines and the National Showcaves Centre for Wales (including dinosaur park) are within an easy drive.

Facilities

New heated toilet block with washbasins in cabins, 4 family rooms (basin, shower, toilet) and a room for families and disabled visitors which includes a baby unit. Combined, well equipped laundry and dishwashing room. Motorcaravan service point. Fridge freezer. Fishing. Bicycle hire. Off site: Supermarket 500 m. Town amenities (shops, pubs, restaurants and indoor pool) within 1 mile. Riding 1 mile. Fishing 1 mile. Golf 1.5 miles. Beaches 25 miles.

Open: All year.

Directions

Park is about half a mile outside the town boundary of Llandovery on the A40 to Brecon.
O.S.GR: SN778344.

Charges 2007

Per unit incl. up to 4 persons	£ 11.00
incl. services	£ 13.50
extra person	£ 1.00
No credit cards.	

UK5974 Pantglas Farm Caravan Park

Tavernspite, Amroth SA34 0NS (Pembrokeshire)

Tel: **01834 831618**. Email: **pantglasfarm@btinternet.com**

A secluded, rural, family run park with a nice atmosphere, Pantglas Farm is four miles from the coast with extensive views over rolling countryside and down to the sea. Set in three gently sloping paddocks spread over 14 acres, there are 86 generous sized, fairly level pitches most with 10A hook-ups, 52 on gravel hardstanding. Around 86 are available for touring units. This is a popular and attractive site close to the main resorts but enjoying a more tranquil atmosphere. Amenities on site include a well equipped, partially fenced playground and activity centre which includes an aerial ropeway. A football field is located at the very end of the site. The on-site clubhouse also has lounge with TV, a games room with pool table and video machines, and some simple entertainment activities are arranged at Bank Holidays, weekends and in high season. No kite flying or washing lines are allowed on the site and single sex groups are not accepted.

Facilities

Two toilet blocks (one can be heated) have a good standard of facilities including large controllable showers, some washbasins in cubicles, a laundry with washing machine, dryer, indoor washing lines and a baby deck. Washbasin and WC for disabled campers. Dishwashing sinks. Gas supplies. Battery charging and freezer pack services. Licensed clubhouse (evenings only daily for B.Hs and peak season, weekends only low season). Playground. Games field. Games room. TV lounge. Caravan and boat storage. Off site: Supermarket and ATM at Whitland 3 miles. Beaches at Amroth or Pendine 4 miles. Also nearby are Whitland Abbey, Oakwood Adventure and Leisure Park and Colby Woodland Gardens. Fishing 1 mile. Golf 10 miles.

Open: March - 3rd weekend in October.

Directions

Site is 3 miles southwest of Whitland. From the A477 Tenby - Pembroke road turn right at Red Roses crossroads to Tavernspite for 1.25 miles. At the village pump take the middle road and site is about 0.5 miles on left. O.S.GR: SN176122.
GPS: N51:46.699 W04:38.725

Charges 2007

Per unit incl. 2 persons, electricity	£ 12.00 - £ 15.00
tent incl. 2 persons	£ 8.00 - £ 10.00
extra person	£ 2.50
child (2-15 yrs)	£ 1.50

UK6005 Brynawelon Touring & Camping Park

Sarnau, Llandysul SA44 6RE (Ceredigion)

Tel: **01239 654584**. Email: **info@brynawlon.co.uk**

Paul and Liz Cowton have turned Brynawelon into a friendly, attractive and well appointed campsite. It is in a stunning rural location within two miles of the Ceredigion coast with its beaches, and close to the River Teifi with plenty of water based activities. All the 40 pitches have electricity hook-ups and of these 26 are serviced pitches (water and waste) on hardstanding. The remainder are on level grass. The park has ample room for children to play, an enclosed play area, an indoor games room with TV, and a sauna next to reception. Buzzards, red kites, owls and the occasional eagle can be seen from the park. There is also a wide variety of small birds. A wide choice of beaches can be found along the coast, there are dolphin trips from Newquay ten miles away and white water rafting on the Teifi at Llandysul. The Teifi is also a well known canoeing and fishing river.

Facilities

New modern toilet block with toilets, showers, washbasins in cabins, two full suites in each side and a separate room for families and disabled visitors. Laundry/kitchen with washing machine, tumble dryer, ironing board and iron, fridge/freezer, microwave, kettle and toaster. Small shop in reception selling basics. Enclosed play area. Games room with pool, electronic games, TV and library. Sauna. Dog walking area and daytime dog care (charged). Off site: Shops and pub 1 mile. Beaches, fishing, sailing 2 miles. Riding 800 m. Dolphin trips at Newquay 10 miles. White water rafting and canoeing at Llandysul 10 miles.

Open: 1 March - 31 October.

Directions

Travelling north on the A487 from Cardigan turn right (southeast) at the crossroads in Sarnau village, signed Rhydlewis. Site is on the left after 650 yds. Note: the country roads from the south are not suitable for caravans and motorcaravans. O.S.GR: SN322508.

Charges 2007

Per unit incl. 2 adults,	
2 children and electricty	£ 13.50 - £ 15.50
incl. services, hardstanding	£ 15.50 - £ 17.50
extra persoon	£ 1.00

No credit cards.

UK6010 Cenarth Falls Holiday Park

Cenarth, Newcastle Emlyn SA38 9JS (Ceredigion)

Tel: **01239 710345**. Email: **enquiries@cenarth-holipark.co.uk**

The Davies family has developed an attractively landscaped, part wooded holiday home park with 86 privately owned units and 3 for hire. However, a neat well cared for, sheltered grassy area at the top of the park provides 30 touring pitches, accessed via a semicircular tarmac road, and all with sunken grass grid hardstanding and electricity (16A). A sunken, kidney shaped outdoor pool with landscaped surrounds and sunbeds is a focal point. The Coracles Health and Country Club provides an indoor pool, spa, sauna and steam rooms and fitness suite (reduced rates for campers). It also provides a bar, restaurant area, adult-only lounge and a large function room where live entertainment is organised weekly all season. Everything is of a high quality. A footpath leads to the village and the famous Cenarth Falls. The National Coracle Centre is well worth a visit. A member of the Best of British group.

Facilities

The excellent, heated sanitary block has easy ramped access, even to the chemical disposal unit. etc. Accessed by key, it uses a 'P.I.R.' system that controls heating, lighting, water and air freshener on entry - very efficient. Tiled with non-slip floors, both men and ladies have an en-suite provision for disabled visitors (doubling as a family room), spacious well equipped showers and one of the washbasins in a roomy private cabin. Laundry room with two washing machines, two dryers and ironing facilities (used by the whole park). No laundry sinks, but two dishwashing sinks are under cover. Gas supplies. Outdoor pool (mid May - mid Sept). Coracles Health and Country Club (see above). Play area. Games room with pool table and electronic games. No dogs on touring field (16/7-3/9). Off site: Shop 800 yds. Fishing 400 yds. Riding 7 miles. Bicycle hire 8 miles. Golf 10 miles.

Open: 1 March - 9 January.

Directions

Follow A484 Cardigan - Newcastle Emlyn road and park is signed before Cenarth village. O.S.GR: SN265421. GPS: N52:02.994 W04:31.903

Charges 2007

Per unit incl. up to 4 people	
and a car	£ 13.00 - £ 23.00
extra person	£ 2.00
awning	£ 2.00
extra pup tent (space permitting)	£ 2.50

UK6280 Aeron Coast Caravan Park

North Road, Aberaeron SA46 0JF (Ceredigion)

Tel: **01545 570349**. Email: **enquiries@aeroncoast.co.uk**

Aeron Coast is a family holiday park with a wide range of recreational facilities, on the west coast of Wales. Although it has a high proportion of caravan holiday homes (200 privately owned), touring units of all types are provided for in two fields separated from the beach and sea by a high bank (although the best beach is on the south side of this traditional fishing village). Pitches are on level grass with all units regularly and well spaced in lines in traditional style. The main attraction of the park is its excellent provision for families, both in and out of doors.

Facilities

Two modern toilet blocks offer excellent facilities including large family showers. Facilities for disabled people and babies. Basic motorcaravan service point. Swimming pools (1/6-30/9). Club house and bar (from Easter, 12.00-14.00 and from 19.00) with family room serving bar meals and takeaway in school holidays. Entertainment room. Shop at petrol station (at entrance). Only one dog per unit. Off site: Beach, fishing, boat launching 0.5 miles.

Open: 1 March - 31 October.

Directions

Park is on northern outskirts of Aberaeron village with entrance on the right beside a petrol station (not too easily seen). O.S.GR: SN461631. GPS: N52:14.670 W04:15.295

Charges 2008

Per unit incl. 2 persons and electricity	£ 14.00 - £ 20.00
extra person (over 12 yrs)	£ 2.00

UK6290 Glan-y-Mor Leisure Park

Clarach Bay, Aberystwyth SY23 3DT (Ceredigion)

Tel: **01970 828900**. Email: **glanymor@sunbourne.co.uk**

Follow the road to Clarach Bay and on the sea-front is Glan-y-Mor, a busy, holiday-style park with an enviable situation. On a wet day you may not wish to go far with the comprehensive leisure centre on site – it is open eight months of the year with reduced entry fee for campers. Although the balance of pitches is very much in favour of caravan holiday homes (3:1) which dominate the open park and bay, there are 60 touring pitches, 45 with electricity (10A) and 4 new 'super' pitches. They are rather small and are pressed together in two small sections on the lower part of the park. In high season, tents, tourers or motorcaravans can opt for space and fine views (but maybe winds) on a ridge of higher ground above the park.

Facilities

The heated toilet block is on the lower touring area with a toilet for disabled people. A 'portacabin' type block (high season only) is on the ridge ground. Motorcaravan service point. Supermarket. Play area. Swimming pool. Licensed restaurant and takeaway (from Easter). Freezer pack service and gas supplies. No dogs are accepted on touring pitches during B.H and school summer holiday periods. Off site: Reduced rates at local golf courses.

Open: 1 March - 31 October.

Directions

Clarach is signed west from the A487 (Aberystwyth - Machynlleth) in village of Bow Street (take care at narrow bridge). Follow signs to beach and park. Access for caravans on B4572 is difficult. O.S.GR: SN587841. GPS: N52:26.175 W04:04.815

Charges 2007

Per unit incl. 2 persons and electricity	£ 14.00 - £ 22.00
'super' pitch	£ 17.00 - £ 27.00

UK5992 Creampots Touring Caravan & Camping Park

Broadway, Broad Haven, Haverfordwest SA62 3TU (Pembrokeshire)

Tel: **01437 781776**

This peacefully located and beautifully manicured, garden-like park is ideal for couples and families with very young children, and is a convenient base within easy reach of beaches or for touring the local area. Creampots has 72 spacious, level pitches all with 10A electric hook-ups, including 12 with gravel hardstanding, and 10 pitches for tents. These are in two neat well hedged and sheltered paddocks. Around 40 seasonal units are also accommodated. American RVs are accepted (maximum 36 ft. – book in advance). Nearby there are bird sanctuaries and the Pembrokeshire Coastal Path.

Facilities

The single small sanitary unit is a modern building which can be heated. Two free hot showers per sex, open style washbasins. Washbasin and WC for disabled campers. These facilities may come under pressure at peak times. Tiny laundry room. Gas supplies. Bread, milk, newspapers to order. Off site: Summer bus service 500 m. Shop, pub 1 mile. Beach 1.5 miles. Riding 4 miles. Golf 7 miles.

Open: March - October.

Directions

From Haverfordwest take B4341 to Broad Haven, at Broadway turn left (Milford Haven) and park is under half a mile. O.S.GR: SM882132. GPS: N51:46.640 W05:04.337

Charges 2008

Per unit incl. 2 persons	£ 13.00 - £ 15.00
extra person	£ 4.50
electricity (10A)	£ 2.75

UK5975 Little Kings Park

Ludchurch, Amroth SA67 8PG (Pembrokeshire)

Tel: **01834 831330**. Email: **littlekingspark@btconnect.com**

This superb family run park has a number of attributes to make your stay both comfortable and memorable. First there is the stunning view, at its best from the seat on the 9-hole putting green. From here on a good day you can look out over Carmarthen Bay to the Gower and on beyond to the coast of Somerset and North Devon. At night no fewer than seven lighthouses can be seen blinking out their warnings. Then there is the restaurant and bar, which has a conservatory overlooking the well presented, covered, heated swimming pool. The restaurant serves a good range of evening meals and has a children's menu. Last, but by no means least, is the comprehensively stocked shop which has just about everything you might need, including reception, tourist information and a bakery offering fresh bread daily and hot snacks (pasties, sausage rolls, etc.) cooked to order. The park itself provides 111 well spaced, large touring pitches all with 10A electricity, 23 with gravel hardstanding and 17 fully serviced. There are 40 pitches for tents arranged in two paddocks. An attractive playground is in the central open grass area of one of the paddocks, and a games field is at the back of the second. A separate well hedged and screened paddock contains 28 caravan holiday homes. This is an ideal site for a family holiday or for touring the area.

Facilities

The two toilet blocks are modern and well equipped, including controllable hot showers (20p. for 6 minutes 30p. for 9), open style washbasins, a family shower room with basin and WC, baby bath and full suite for disabled campers. Extras include paper towel and soap dispensers, perfumed air fresheners, hand and hairdryers. Laundry. Shop with bakery, Takeaway, bar and restaurant with conservatory (evenings only; low season at B.Hs and weekends only). Covered swimming pool. Games rooms. 9-hole pitch and putt. Playground. Gas supplies. Off site: Supermarket and ATM at Kilgetty 2.5 miles. Tenby and Pendine Sands 7 miles. Oakwood Adventure Park 6 miles. National Botanic Garden of Wales.

Open: 1 week before Easter - first week in January.

Directions

Site is 5 miles southeast of Narberth. From the A477 Carmarthen to Pembroke road turn left towards Amroth and Wiseman's Bridge. Take first right (signed Ludchurch) and park is 300 m. on left. O.S.GR: SN146093. GPS: N51:45.091 W04:41.274

Charges 2008

Per unit incl. 2 persons and electricity	£ 14.00 - £ 20.00
tent incl. 2 persons	£ 13.00 - £ 20.00
extra person (over 2 yrs)	£ 2.00
awning	£ 2.00
dog (max. 2)	£ 2.00 - £ 3.00

Little Kings Park

Quiet family run 5-star Holiday Park offering a high standard of facilities and a warm welcome. Set in an ideal location to explore all that Pembrokeshire has to offer.

- Holiday Homes and Bungalow
- Tourers and Motorhomes
- Tents and Trailer Tents
- Family Bar/Restaurant
- Covered, heated Pool
- Shop and Public Phone
- Games Room
- 2 Amenity Blocks
- 2 Play areas
- Dog walk
- Staff present 24 hrs

Open: March to January (Touring)   Easter to September (Holiday Homes)
Tel: 01834 831330   Fax: 01834 831161
Website: www.littlekings.co.uk email: littlekingspark@btconnect.com
We look forward to welcoming you to our park - we love it here and hope that you will too.

UK5982 Trefalun Park

Devonshire Drive, St Florence, Tenby SA70 8RD (Pembrokeshire)

Tel: **01646 657514**. Email: **trefalun@aol.com**

Only four miles from Tenby and the beaches of Carmarthen Bay, Trefalun Park is an open, well laid out campsite with a friendly atmosphere engendered by the owners. The 100 pitches, including 10 occupied by caravan holiday homes in their own enclave and 22 seasonal units, are mainly level, although the park has gentle slopes. There are 34 hardstandings, of which 12 are serviced pitches. Except for the tent area, pitches are generously sized and have electricity (10/16A). This park will suit those, particularly families, looking for a quiet holiday and also the more active who favour walking, cycling or watersports. A large fenced recreational area has a variety of adventure type play equipment and a football pitch. Pembroke, with its castle is only four miles away.

Facilities

Modern heated toilet block, with some washbasins in cabins. Water to showers and laundry and dishwashing sinks is metered (20p). Separate, fully equipped suite for disabled visitors and families. Separate baby room. Laundry. Play area. Gas sold. Off site: Shop, pub (with food) and outdoor pool 1.5 miles. Fishing, riding and wildlife park 600 yds. Golf 3 miles. Tenby with all town facilities, beach, boat launching and sailing 4 miles.

Open: 16 March - 31 October.

Directions

From the A477 at Sageston (about 4 miles east of Pembroke) turn southeast just to the east of the village on B4318 signed for the Wildlife Park. Trefalun Park is signed to the left after 2.5 miles, opposite the entrance to the Wildlife Park.

Charges 2007

Per pitch	£ 9.50 - £ 15.00
incl. services	£ 11.00 - £ 17.00
'super' pitch	£ 13.00 - £ 19.50

245

UK5980 Moreton Farm Leisure Park

Moreton, Saundersfoot SA69 9EA (Pembrokeshire)

Tel: **01834 812016**. Email: **moretonfarm@btconnect.com**

Moreton Farm has been developed in a secluded valley, a 10-20 minute walk from Saundersfoot and four miles from Tenby. It provides 30 caravan (all with 16A electricity, and including 17 with hardstanding) and 30 tent pitches on two sloping, neatly cut grass fields, with 12 pine holiday lodges and four cottages for letting occupying another field. The site is approached under a railway bridge (height 10 ft 9 ins, width across the top 6 ft 6 ins, but with alternative access over the railway line for slightly larger vehicles just possible). There are a few trains during the day, none at night. An attractive lake at the bottom of the valley is home to ducks, geese and chickens (no fishing).

Facilities

The toilet blocks (which can be heated) are light and airy, providing preset hot showers (on payment), and a ramp to a unit for disabled visitors with toilet and washbasin, a baby bath, dishwashing sinks and laundry facilities. Fenced, outside clothes drying area. Small shop for basics and gas. Playground. Bicycle hire can be arranged. No dogs or other pets are accepted. Off site: Fishing and riding 1 mile. Golf 4 miles.

Open: 1 March - 31 October.

Directions

From A477 Carmarthen - Pembroke road take the A478 for Tenby at Kilgelly. Park is signed on left after 1.5 miles. Watch carefully for sign and park is 0.5 miles up poorly made-up road and under bridge. O.S.GR: SN116050. GPS: N51:42.719 W04:43.661

Charges 2007

Per unit incl. 2 persons and electricity	£ 15.00 - £ 18.00
extra person	£ 2.00

UK5985 Manorbier Country Park

Station Road, Manorbier, Tenby SA70 7SN (Pembrokeshire)

Tel: **01834 871952**. Email: **enquiries@countrypark.co.uk**

This campsite has 103 caravan holiday homes and 28 seasonal units, which leaves only around 22 pitches for tourists. There are seven orderly rows of concrete and gravel hardstanding pitches set into a level grass field; 32 pitches have electric hook-ups (16A), cable TV and a shared water tap, and 4 are multi-service pitches. Cars park away from the caravans on a wide tarmac parking area. A small grassy recreation area is at one end of the touring site, with an adventure playground. The complex offers a bar with family entertainment each evening, a good value restaurant, wellness centre and an indoor pool. Larger units should book in advance and motorhomes over 25 ft. are not accepted.

Facilities

A single building at one end of the car parking area provides all toilet facilities, it can be heated, and has controllable hot showers (on payment), a multi-purpose room suitable for families, babies and disabled campers. Small laundry room. Shop. Bar and restaurant. Indoor pool. Jacuzzi. Sauna and steam room, gym and tennis (all charged). Adventure play area and playground. Dogs are not accepted. Off site: Bicycle hire, boat launching and beach 1.5 miles. Golf and riding 3 miles. Tenby 6 miles.

Open: 1 March - 31 October.

Directions

From Tenby take A4139 towards Pembroke, passing through Penally and Lydstep. At crossroads (Manorbier signed to left) continue straight on following signs to the station. Turn right by Baptist Chapel into Station Road, and continue to site entrance (do not go into Manorbier village). O.S.GR: SS068991. GPS: N51:39.475 W04:47.657

Charges 2007

Per unit incl. up to 4 persons	£ 16.50 - £ 23.50
extra person	£ 2.00

UK5990 Freshwater East Caravan Club Site

Trewent Hill, Freshwater East, Pembroke SA71 5LJ (Pembrokeshire)

Tel: **01646 672341**

This Caravan Club site in the Pembrokeshire Coast National Park is open to non-members. At the bottom of a hill, it has 140 mainly level pitches bounded by trees, 128 with 16A electricity and around half on hardstanding. There are a further 12 pitches for tents. The beach and the Pembroke Coastal Path are about a five minute walk. This is an excellent area for walking with magnificent cliff views and birdwatching. You will find St David's, the smallest cathedral city, well worth a visit.

Facilities

The two heated toilet blocks are modern and clean with washbasins in cubicles, and free hairdryers or sockets for your own. Facilities for disabled visitors. Fully equipped laundry rooms. Waste point for motorcaravans. Gas supplies. Reception keeps basic food items. Small play area. Off site: Shop 0.5 miles. Fishing within 5 miles.

Open: 24 March - 30 October.

Directions

From the east on A477, fork left 1.25 miles past Milton on A4075 Pembroke road. In Pembroke immediately (after bridge) turn left at roundabout on A4139 Tenby road. In Lamphey turn right on B4584 (Freshwater) and follow signs. O.S.GR: SS014980.

Charges 2007

Per person	£ 4.10 - £ 5.40
pitch (non-member)	£ 10.70 - £ 14.10

UK5995 Caerfai Bay Caravan & Tent Park

St Davids, Haverfordwest SA62 6QT (Pembrokeshire)

Tel: **01437 720274**. Email: **info@caerfaibay.co.uk**

About as far west as one can get in Wales, St David's is Britain's smallest city, noted for its Cathedral and Bishops Palace. This cliff-top park in West Wales has direct access to the Pembrokeshire Coastal Path and a magnificent sandy beach is just a few minutes away, down the path from the car park by the site entrance. The camping area is spread over three open and sloping fields, all with magnificent views over St Brides Bay. The caravan field also has a small number of holiday homes and is closest to reception. The second and third fields are for tents and motorcaravans, almost all on grass with a few hardstandings available. Main access roads are tarmac. Altogether there are 105 touring pitches and 45 electric hook-ups (10A). Caerfai Farm Shop is just across the lane (opens end of May), and other shops and services are just 1 mile. Site lighting is deliberately minimal, so torches useful.

Facilities

Two main buildings house the sanitary facilities, one by reception which is heated, contains facilities for disabled visitors and families, and a room with sinks, microwave and hot drinks machine. Also in this block is a useful 'storm shelter' for inclement weather. The second block between the tent fields is new and includes 3 en-suite cubicles. Motorcaravan services. Bicycle storage. Wet suit washing facility and enclosed clothes drying area. Gas stocked. Barbecue stands for hire. Off site: Walk the Pembrokeshire coastal path, visit Ramsey Island Bird and Grey Seal Reserve. Sea fishing 400 yds. Indoor pool and bicycle hire 1 mile. Golf 2 miles. Riding 10 miles. Boat launching 1.5 or 3 miles.

Open: 1 March - 15 November.

Directions

From Haverfordwest take the A487 to St David's. On passing the city boundary, turn left into lane immediately before the National Park Visitor Centre (site signed), and continue on for 0.75 mile to site entrance on right. O.S.GR: SM759244. GPS: N51:52.379 W05:15.414

Charges 2008

Per unit incl. 2 persons	£ 11.00 - £ 15.50
tent incl. 2 persons	£ 9.50 - £ 13.00
extra person	£ 4.25
child (3-12 yrs)	£ 3.00
electricity	£ 4.00

Discounts for early payment, and for senior citizens in low season.

CAERFAI BAY CARAVAN & TENT PARK

Quiet family-run park uniquely situated in St Davids and within Pembrokeshire Coast National Park. The perfect spot to relax on the beach and explore Pembrokeshire.
• Electric Hook-up Points • Launderette • Family Rooms
• Free Hot Showers • Disabled Toilet & Shower • Dogs Allowed
Call: 01437 720274 or visit: www.caerfaibay.co.uk

UK5994 Redlands Touring Caravan & Camping Park

Hasguard Cross, nr. Little Haven, Haverfordwest SA62 3SJ (Pembrokeshire)

Tel: **01437 781300**. Email: **info@redlandscamping.co.uk**

This peaceful, family run site is located in the heart of the Pembrokeshire countryside, close to a lovely sandy beach. Redlands takes around 85 touring units in three areas divided by banks topped with pine trees, 64 with 10A electricity. The first two areas take 60 caravans or motorcaravans and include 20 hardstandings, the third takes 25 tents on a level grassy meadow. There are fine views across rolling countryside to St Brides Bay. A caravan holiday home park has a restaurant and bar. Reception has a small shop which is open only in peak periods. Breathable groundsheets must be used. American RVs – advance booking only. A sandy beach and the Pembrokeshire Coastal Path are 1.5 miles away.

Facilities

The traditional style toilet block is well kept and heated early and late season. It has all the usual requirements including two extra shower, basin and WC suites. Large utility room with washing machine, dryer and spin dryer. Ironing is free, and there are sinks for laundry and dishes. Shop. Freezers. Wet suit washing area. Off site: Shops and ATM in Broadhaven 2 miles. Summer bus service. Fishing and boat launching 1.5 miles. Riding and sailing 5 miles. Golf 6 miles.

Open: 1 March - mid December.

Directions

Site 6.5 miles southwest of Haverfordwest. From Haverfordwest take the B4327 road towards Dale and site is on the right at Hasguard Cross. Do not approach via Broad Haven. O.S.GR: SM853109. GPS: N51:45.334 W05:06.743

Charges 2007

Per unit incl. 4 persons	£ 12.00 - £ 19.00
extra person	£ 4.50
electric hook-up	£ 2.75
awning	£ 1.25 - £ 2.25
dog	£ 0.60

No credit cards.

247

UK6030 Brynich Caravan Park

Brecon LD3 7SH (Powys)

Tel: **01874 623325**. Email: **holidays@brynich.co.uk**

Brynich is a well kept, family run park with a picturesque setting and super views towards the Brecon Beacons, developed over the years by Colin and Maureen Jones to very high standards. Originally farmland near the Brecon bypass, there are now three level, hedged and neatly mown camping fields with tarmac roads and a mixture of hardwood trees and shrubs maturing nicely. These fields provide for 130 touring units of all types with hardstanding on many pitches, 108 electricity points (10/16A) and 39 multi-serviced pitches with grass or gravel hardstandings. In a sloping field leading down to a stream, is an extensive dog walk on one side of the Brynich Brook and, on the opposite side, an adventure play area. The stream is shallow and an added attraction along with the play equipment and there is a large recreation field for ball games. For smaller children there is some play equipment near reception and the Play Barn which provides extensive indoor entertainment for the under-12s (charges apply). In a beautifully converted barn adjacent to the campsite the fully licensed restaurant uses local produce in its good value menus. Being within the Brecon Beacons National Park, this is a good area for hill walking and climbing. A member of the Best of British group.

Facilities

Two modern, heated toilet blocks have well equipped showers, some washbasins in cubicles (one block only), dishwashing sinks and a laundry room. Two fully equipped units for disabled visitors in one block, one providing left handed toilet facilities, the other right handed (key system). Baby unit including bath. Family room with bath, shower, toilet and hand basin. Fridge, freezer and microwave for visitors' use. Motorcaravan service point with bike wash. Reception and well stocked shop (with gas). Play areas. Restaurant and indoor Play Barn open all year. Boules court. Bicycle hire can be arranged. Off site: Local pub within walking distance. Fishing 1.5 miles. Riding 2 miles. Golf 3 miles. Bus stops in car park for Cardiff, Abergavenny and Brecon.

Open: March - October.

Directions

From the A40 Abergavenny road, at roundabout on the Brecon bypass (A40/A470) take A470 north and park is 150 yards on right. O.S.GR: SO069279. GPS: N51:56.526 W03:21.312

Charges 2007

Per unit incl. 2 persons	
and electricity	£ 16.00 - £ 18.00
with services	£ 18.00 - £ 20.00
tent incl. 2 persons	£ 14.00 - £ 16.00
extra person	£ 6.00
child	£ 4.00

Brynich Caravan Park, Brecon
holidays@brynich.co.uk 01874 623325
www.brynich.co.uk

BWRDD CROESO CYMRU WALES TOURIST BOARD
PARC TEITHIO A GWERSYLLA
★★★★★
TOURING & CAMPING PARK

THE Best of British
TOURING AND HOLIDAY PARKS
www.bob.org.uk

UK6240 Cringoed Caravan Park

Cringoed, Llanbrynmair, Newtown SY19 7DR (Powys)

Tel: **01650 521237**

Cringoed is a pleasant, peaceful, small park with a river to one side, hills on the other and trees at either end. There are 50 spacious pitches of which 20 are occupied by seasonal units. These are in a level open field. Some of these have hardstanding and all have electricity (16A). The 31 caravan holiday homes are at both ends of the site, some amongst trees and some in a newer, more open area. There are also 10 tent pitches. This is a relaxing base where you can sit and listen to the river and watch the wildlife, but it is also within easy reach of some of mid-Wales' best scenery and not far from the coast. Paul and Sue Mathers will make you very welcome.

Facilities

The single toilet block is neat, modern and quite adequate. Laundry and dishwashing. Adventure play area. Small tourist information room. Off site: Shops 1 mile. ATM at Spar in Carno 6 miles. Fishing 5 miles. Golf 8 miles. Riding 12 miles.

Open: 7 March - 7 January (ring first in low season)

Directions

From the A470 between Newton and Machynlleth in the village of Llanbrynmair take the B4518 signed Staylittle (caravan signs). After 1 mile just before bridge turn right, go over site bridge and turn right into site. O.S.GR: SH887013.
GPS: N52:35.900 W03:38.663

Charges 2007

Per unit incl. 2 persons	
and electricity	£ 13.00 - £ 18.00

No credit cards.

UK6040 Pencelli Castle Caravan & Camping Park

Pencelli, Brecon LD3 7LX (Powys)

Tel: **01874 665451**. Email: **pencelli@tiscali.co.uk**

Open all year round, this is a quality park with atmosphere and character which continues to improve. Set amidst the Brecon scenery, it offers excellent facilities in peaceful, rural tranquillity. The owners, Liz and Gerwyn Rees, have retained the country charm but have added an all embracing range of spacious, heated, luxury facilities, attractively enhanced by potted plants, etc. There are three touring fields. The 'Orchard' incorporates 15 fully serviced pitches with hardstanding, amongst shrubs, fruit trees and a stone cider mill. The 'Oaks' taking 20 caravans and tents and the 'Meadow' for 40 tents (with boot and bike wash) are bordered by majestic trees and the Monmouthshire and Brecon Canal, where gaily painted barges slip past. All the fields are level with neatly mown grass and tarmac access roads. The historic manor house, that dates back to 1583, is adjacent to arched barns that house an increasing collection of vintage farm machinery including carts and rare tractors. For mountain bikers and walkers, a path leaves the village to reach the top of the Brecon Beacons or there is an easy towpath ramble to Tal-y-Bont where there are pubs, tea rooms and a post office.

Facilities

The toilet block is very well designed and includes some private cubicles, two large fully equipped rooms for families or disabled visitors incorporating double showers, baby changing and bath facilities, all humorously decorated for the young at heart. Laundry. Drying room with lockers (a must as this is walking country). Information and planning room. Internet access and WiFi. Indoor dishwashing and food preparation room. Motorcaravan service point (with washbasin, soap and hand dryer). Small shop at reception (basics). Playground and nature trail for children. Bicycle hire. Dogs are not accepted (except 'assistance dogs'). Off site: Inn with meals 100 m. Buses pass regularly for Brecon, Abergavenny. Riding 2 miles. Golf and bicycle hire 5 miles.

Open: All year excl. 4 - 27 December.

Directions

From A40 south after Brecon bypass take B4558 at signs for Llanfrynach and later Pencelli (narrow bridge). If travelling north on A40, approach via Tal-y-Bont. Site at south end of Pencelli.
O.S.GR: SO095249. GPS: N51:54.887 W03:19.072

Charges 2007

Per unit incl. 2 persons	£ 15.00 - £ 18.00
extra person	£ 6.00 - £ 9.00
child (5-15 yrs)	£ 4.00 - £ 5.00
electricity	£ 3.25
tent - per person	£ 7.50 - £ 9.00

Pencelli Castle Caravan & Camping Park

Peacefully set at the foothills of the Brecon Beacons and within walking distance of the highest peaks. Adjoining Brecon Canal and the Taff Cycle Trail. Village pub 150 yds. Shop, hardstandings, serviced pitches and luxurious shower block. Red deer, vintage farm machinery, and children's play area. On bus route. WiFi and internet access on site. Closed 3rd to 30th December. **Assistance Dogs Only.**

Wales Cymru
Touring & Camping Park
Parc Teithio a Gwersylla
★★★★★

- 2007, 06, 05 & 4 Wales In Bloom Winner
- 2006 & 02 AA - Best Campsite in Wales
- 2005 WTB Wales Tourism Awards - Winner Best Place to Stay
- 2007 to 01 Gold - David Bellamy Conservation Award
- 2005 Practical Caravan Top 100 Family Park - Winner Wales
- 2006, 5, 3 & 2 Loo of the Year - National Winner Wales
- 2003 WTB Wales Tourism Awards - Winner Best Place to Stay
- 2001 Calor Gas - Best Park in Wales

Campsite of the Year
AA
Wales 2006

Pencelli • Brecon • Powys • Wales • UK • LD3 7LX Tel: 01874 665 451
email: pencelli@tiscali.co.uk www.pencelli-castle.com

UK6045 Gilestone Camping & Caravan Park

On A40, Talybont on Usk LD3 7JE (Powys)

Tel: **01874 676236**. Email: **gilestonefarm@aol.com**

Only opened in 2006, Gilestone is situated in the Usk valley within a 300 acre arable and beef farm in the Brecon Beacons National Park. It has 100 pitches, 50 for caravans and 50 for tents, all with electricity, plus 22 fully serviced pitches suitable for large units. Unusually the park can provide horse B&B facilities for those who wish to take their horses and ponies on holiday and has direct access to large areas of trekking country. There is a dedicated area for those with tents which has its own toilet facilities. This rural park caters for all ages and has a four acre play area for children, a well stocked Farm Shop selling local fresh produce and hot tubs to relax in after all those strenuous activities. The owners Chris and Geraint Thomas are extremely knowledgeable about the area and can arrange most requests (with a little advance warning). Ready erected tents can be rented on the site, as can bicycles. Llangorse Lake is only three miles away where windsurfing, sailing and scuba lessons are all on offer. Alternatively, you can just enjoy the peace and tranquillity of the 300 acres where red kite, herons, buzzards, swans and lapwings are readily seen from the lanes.

Facilities

Toilet and shower facilities will be available in the single new main block which is being built to also house reception and the Farm Shop and café. Hot tubs to rent. Facilities for disabled visitors. Laundry room. Motorcaravan service area. Shop with local produce (all year). Play area. Fishing. Bicycle hire. Horse B&B. Teepee hire for woodland camping. Nature trail. Rallies welcome. Off site: Four pubs with meals within 5 minutes walk. Lake for watersports 3 miles. Riding 2 miles. Golf 5 miles. Two local Play Barns for children.

Open: All year.

Directions

From Brecon on the A40 follow brown tourism signs along the 40 to new junction. Site is on right after bridge over the river. O.S.GR: SO120231. GPS: N51:54.104 W03:17.197

Charges 2007

Per unit incl. 2 persons and electricity	£ 16.00 - £ 18.00
incl. services	£ 21.00 - £ 25.00
extra person	£ 6.00 - £ 7.00
child (0-8 yrs	free

Lying in the heart of the Usk valley, at the foothills of the Brecon Beacons, Gilestone is a 300 acre arable and beef farm. Our new park caters for touring caravans, with seasonal pitches available from March 1st to November 1st, motor homes, tents, large parties welcome. We can offer horse B+B and welcome pets (rules apply). Ready-erected tents are available to hire, fishing on the river Usk is also available for hire.
Gilestone Farm, Tal Y Bont On Usk, Brecon, Powys LD3 7JE   Tel: +44(0) 1874 676 236   www.gilestonecaravanpark.co.uk

UK6250 Dolswydd Caravan Park

Dolswydd, Pen-y-Bont, Llandrindod Wells LD1 5UB (Powys)

Tel: **01597 851267**. Email: **Hughes@dolswydd.freeserve.co.uk**

Dolswydd is on the edge of a pretty, traditional working farm. Peaceful and tranquil, with fine views of the Welsh hills and surrounding area, it has modern facilities and 25 good spacious pitches mainly on hardstandings, all with electrical connections (16A). The Hughes family extends a warm and friendly welcome to their little park, surrounded by hills and wandering sheep, which is ideal as a touring base or for a one night stop, but booking is recommended, especially at peak times, Bank Holidays and during the Victorian Festival (last week in August). The park is within walking distance of the local pub which offers good, home cooked food.

Facilities

Modern facilities include lots of hot water, dishwashing, laundry, and a WC/washroom for disabled people. Fishing in the river alongside the site (free, but licence required). Off site: Within walking distance are the local pub, Post Office and garage. Riding 1 mile. Golf and bicycle hire 5 miles.

Open: Easter - end October.

Directions

Pen-y-bont is 2 miles east of the junction of the A44 and A483 roads at Crossgates. Take the A44 (Kington). Go through Pen-y-bont and immediately after crossing cattle grid, site is on right. O.S.GR: SO117639.

Charges 2007

Per unit with 2 persons and 2 children	£ 8.50
extra person	£ 1.00
electricity	£ 1.50
dog	free

UK6245 Morben Isaf Touring & Holiday Home Park

Derwenlas, Machynlleth SY20 8SR (Powys)

Tel: **01654 781473**. Email: **manager@morbenisaf.co.uk**

Machynlleth is a market town, home of Owain Glyndwr's fifteenth century Welsh Parliament building and the Celtica Centre, and is also close to the Tal-y-Llyn Steam Railway, the Centre for Alternative Technology, Corris Craft Centre and King Arthur's Labyrinth. This site is in a convenient location for an overnight halt, or a short stay whilst visiting all these attractions. It provides 16 touring pitches with multi-services, all with electricity (16A), water tap, waste water drain and a satellite TV hook-up. There is further grassy space below the touring pitches beyond the fishing lake which is normally used as a football pitch but can accommodate around 30 tents who do not need any services. On a lower level, behind the site manager's bungalow, and barely visible from the touring site, are 87 privately owned holiday mobile homes. Also on site is an unfenced coarse fishing lake which campers are free to use.

Facilities

A small but well equipped, heated modern toilet block includes spacious controllable showers, baby changing and child seats in both ladies' and men's, and a well equipped laundry and dishwashing facilities. Facilities for disabled campers. Powered motorcaravan service point suitable for American RVs. Off site: Pub serving hot food 1.5 miles. Leisure Centre, shops and services in Machynlleth 3 miles (market on Wednesday). Centre for Alternative Technology 6 miles.

Open: Mid March - 31 October.

Directions

Site is 2.5 miles southwest of Machynlleth beside the A487. O.S.GR: SN706986.
GPS: N52:34.204 W03:54.687

Charges 2007

Per unit incl. 2 adults, 2 children and electricity	£ 14.00 - £ 16.00

Morben Isaf Caravan Park

Morben Isaf Caravan Park, Machynlleth, Powys

Set in a peaceful location, we are ideally located near the historic town of Machynlleth. Fishing and Golf are available and our facilities include a fully serviced laundry room. A selection of holiday homes are also available

For more details please contact us on 01654 781473

UK6305 Smithy Caravan Park

Abermule, Montgomery SY15 6ND (Powys)

Tel: **01584 711280**. Email: **info@bestparks.co.uk**

Smithy Caravan Park is set in four acres of landscaped ground bordered by the River Severn and the Shropshire Union Canal in the tranquil rolling countryside of central Wales. It does have 60 privately owned caravan holiday homes, but the touring area is separate and also has the benefit of being closest to the river with the best views and a small picnic and seating area on the bank. This area has 26 fully serviced hardstanding pitches (16A electricity, water, waste water and satellite TV hook-ups). A newly installed timber chalet provides all the sanitary facilities, and is located in one corner of the touring area. This is a well run site, which is under the same ownership as Westbrook Park, with a resident manager on-site here. The village has two local pubs, a shop and Post Office, and a bus service – all within easy walking distance. American RVs are accepted with prior notice. Kite flying or cycling on the park are not permitted.

Facilities

The new timber clad chalet building provides two good sized showers per sex, washbasins in cubicles, a family room suitable for the less able (there is a step up to the building). Utility room housing a laundry with washing machine, dryer and dishwashing sink. Fishing in the river Severn. Fenced playground. Gas stocked. Off site: Bus stop in village opposite end of site access road. Supermarkets and all other services in Newtown 3 miles. Golf 3 miles. Riding 5 miles.

Open: 1 March - 30 October.

Directions

Site is 3 miles north of Newtown in the village of Abermule. Turn off the A483 into village, and turn down the lane beside the Waterloo Arms, opposite the village shop and Post Office. Site is at end of lane. O.S.GR: SO161948.
GPS: N52:32.653 W03:14.323

Charges 2007

Per unit incl. 2 persons and electricity	£ 14.00 - £ 18.00
extra person	£ 3.00
child (4-10 yrs)	£ 1.50
awning	£ 2.00
dog	£ 1.00

251

UK6320 Fforest Fields Caravan & Camping Park

Hundred House, Builth Wells LD1 5RT (Powys)

Tel: **01982 570406**. Email: **office@fforestfields.co.uk**

This secluded 'different' park is set on a family hill farm in the heart of Radnorshire. Truly rural, there are glorious views and a distinctly family atmosphere. This is simple country camping and caravanning at its best, without man-made distractions or intrusions. The facilities include 80 large pitches on level grass on a spacious and peaceful, carefully landscaped field by a stream. Electrical connections (mostly 16A) are available and there are 13 hardstanding pitches, also with electricity. Several additional areas without electricity are provided for tents. A new reception and toilet block are planned for 2007 and there are two new fishing lakes. George and Kate, the enthusiastic owners, have opened up much of the farm for moderate or ample woodland and moorland trails which can be enjoyed with much wildlife to see. Indeed wildlife is actively encouraged with nesting boxes for owls, songbirds and bats, by leaving field margins wild to encourage small mammals and by yearly tree planting. George and Kate also run a paragliding school where beginners are welcome.

Facilities

The toilet facilities are acceptable with baby bath, dishwashing and laundry facilities including washing machines and a dryer. Milk, eggs and orange juice are sold in reception and gas, otherwise there are few other on-site facilities, but the village of Hundred House, one mile away, has a pub, village stores and post office. Torches are useful. Off site: Fishing 3 miles. Bicycle hire and golf 5 miles. Riding 10 miles.

Open: Easter - 17 November.

Directions

Park is 4 miles east of Builth Wells near the village of Hundred House on A481. Follow brown signs. O.S.GR: SO098535.

Charges 2007

Per person	£ 3.00
child	£ 2.50
pitch incl. electricity	£ 6.50

Special low season rates for senior citizens. No credit cards.

Wonderful walks lead up into the hills from Fforest Fields

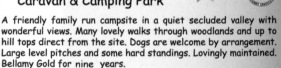

Fforest Fields

Caravan & Camping Park

A friendly family run campsite in a quiet secluded valley with wonderful views. Many lovely walks through woodlands and up to hill tops direct from the site. Dogs are welcome by arrangement. Large level pitches and some hard standings. Lovingly maintained. Bellamy Gold for nine years.

See lots of photos, prices & local info on

www.fforestfields.co.uk

Or phone 01982 570406 for brochure

Four miles from Builth Wells and the Wye Valley (On the A481)

UK6310 Bacheldre Watermill Caravan Park

Churchstoke, Montgomery SY15 6TE (Powys)

Tel: **01588 620489**. Email: **info@bacheldremill.co.uk**

A delightful little site, Bacheldre has just 25 pitches arranged around the perimeter of a grass meadow, with no site road. There is just one lamp on the outside of the toilet block and three small lights on the perimeter so torches are useful. However, there are 18 electric hook-ups (10A) and 10 hardstandings. Ideal for tenters and small units, it is not really suitable for larger units (20 ft. plus) and American RVs. The watermill is fully operational, producing high quality organic wheat flour, which can be purchased from reception, together with eggs and bread. The mill is not normally accessible, although guided tours can be arranged. Note: there are obvious hazards for small children – a deep partially fenced millpond, moving waterwheel and the stream.

Facilities

A portacabin provides the usual facilities including one controllable hot shower per sex with dishwashing sinks in a separate room. Calor gas stocked. Off site: Walking and cycling along Offa's Dyke 800 yards from site. Clun Castle ruins are worth a visit. Steam enthusiasts are well catered for with the Welshpool and Llanfair light railway. Supermarket at Churchstoke 2 miles.

Open: All year.

Directions

Bacheldre is just off the A489 between Newtown and Churchstoke, about 9 miles east of Newtown and 2 miles west of Churchstoke. Turn into narrow lane (signed Bacheldre Mill), over bridge and site is immediately on your right. O.S.GR: SO243929.

Charges 2007

Per unit incl. 2 persons	£ 10.00 - £ 13.00
extra person	£ 2.00

UK6330 Daisy Bank Touring Caravan Park

Snead, Montgomery SY15 6EB (Powys)

Tel: **01588 620471**. Email: **enquiries@daisy-bank.co.uk**

For adults only, this pretty, tranquil park in the Camlad Valley has panoramic views, and is an ideal base for walkers. Attractively landscaped with 'old English' flower beds and many different trees and shrubs, this small park has been carefully developed. The Welsh hills to the north and the Shropshire hills to the south overlook the three fields which provide a total of 55 pitches. The field nearer to the road (perhaps a little noisy) is slightly sloping but there are hardstandings for motorcaravans, while the second field is more level. All pitches have 16A electricity, water and drainage and TV hook up. Although technically in Wales, the park is yards from the Shropshire border, an area rich in history.

Facilities

The well equipped, heated toilet block provides modern, en-suite units (6 with shower, WC and washbasin, 2 with WC and washbasin and facilities for disabled visitors). Laundry facilities. Shop. Gas supplies. Small putting green. Bicycle hire. WiFi (charged). Off site: Supermarket 2 miles. Fishing 3 miles. Golf and riding 10 miles.

Open: All year.

Directions

Site is by the A489 road 2 miles east of Churchstoke in the direction of Craven Arms. O.S.GR: SO302930. GPS: N52:31.795 W03:01.782

Charges 2007

Per unit incl. 2 persons	£ 16.00 - £ 22.00
extra person	£ 5.00
dog	£ 1.00

UK6655 Ty Mawr Holiday Park

Towyn Road, Towyn, Abergele LL22 9HG (Conwy)

Tel: **01745 832079**. Email: **sam.hodgson@park-resorts.com**

Ty Mawr Holiday Park is located close to the many attractions of the North Wales Coast and the Snowdonia National Park. It is an easy walk into the town of Towyn with seaside facilities and Rhyl, some three miles along the coast is a busy resort with a fun fair and holiday amusements on its wide promenade. Ty Mawr is ideal for families seeking plenty of holiday park type activities, with organised children's clubs for 5-11 and 12-16 year olds. The outdoor all-weather multisport courts and the playground are excellent facilities for younger family members and the whole family are catered for in the entertainment complex which provides mini ten-pin bowling, pool and darts. In the evening there are discos and live spectaculars. The heated indoor pool complete with flume is the venue for organised water-based activities. There are two areas for touring units, one on open meadows with facilities provided in 'portacabin' style units, the other in a more well established area near the playgrounds and entertainment area. Both areas are flat with views of open countryside. There is some traffic noise from the road adjacent to the meadow. A large proportion of privately owned and rental caravan holiday homes are neatly sited on well manicured grass.

Facilities

Two well maintained, functional blocks serve the main touring area with 'portacabin' style units (unisex) on the meadows. Baby rooms. Facilities for disabled visitors (key). Launderette. Shop. Bar with meals, cafe and takeaway. Indoor pool. Multisport courts. Excellent play areas and children's clubs. Evening entertainment. Off site: Bicycle hire 0.5 miles. Golf, riding and boat launching 3 miles. Fishing 6 miles. Beach 0.25 miles.

Open: Easter - 30 October.

Directions

Take the A55 in a westerly direction into North Wales and take exit for Abergele. Follow signs for A548 Rhyl towards Towyn. Shortly after Towyn turn right into site. O.S.GR: SH965791

Charges 2007

Per unit incl. electricity	£ 8.00 - £ 36.00
tent	£ 5.00 - £ 33.00
dog	£ 1.00 - £ 3.00

UK6650 Hunters Hamlet Caravan Park

Sirior Goch Farm, Betws-yn-Rhos, Abergele LL22 8PL (Conwy)

Tel: **01745 832237**. Email: **huntershamlet@aol.com**

This small, family owned park is licensed for all units except tents (trailer tents allowed). On a gently sloping hillside providing beautiful panoramic views, one area provides 15 well spaced pitches with hardstanding and 10A electricity hook-ups, with access from a circular, hardcore road. A more recent area has been developed next to this of a similar design but with 8 fully serviced 'super pitches' (water, waste water, sewage, TV and electricity connections). Shrubs and bushes at various stages of growth enhance both areas. A natural play area incorporating rustic adventure equipment set amongst mature beech trees with a small bubbling stream is a children's paradise. Milk and papers can be ordered and the Hunters will do their best to meet your needs, even to survival rations! The park is well located to tour Snowdonia and Anglesey and is within easy reach of Llandudno and Rhyl.

Facilities

The tiny heated toilet block has fully tiled facilities including showers en-suite with toilets for both sexes. A sunroom to the rear houses laundry and dishwashing (hot and cold), washing machine and dryer, iron and board, freezer and fridge. Family bathroom (metered) and basic toilet and shower facilities for disabled visitors. Play area. All year caravan storage. Max. 2 dogs per pitch. Off site: Fishing and golf 2 miles. Riding 10 miles.

Open: 21 March - 31 October.

Directions

From Abergele take A548 south for almost 3 miles; turn onto B5381 in direction of Betws-yn-Rhos and park is on left after 0.5 miles. To date there are no local authority caravan signs so watch carefully for the farm after turning - it can be identified by an artistically painted sign with the house and farm name: 'Sirior Goch Farm' and Hunter's Hamlet. O.S.GR: SH929736. GPS: N53:14.930 W03:36.408

Charges 2007

Per unit incl. 2 persons	
and electtricity	£ 14.00 - £ 19.00
super pitch (fully incl.)	£ 19.00 - £ 24.00
extra person	£ 3.00
child	£ 1.00

UK6690 Bron-Y-Wendon Touring Caravan Park

Wern Road, Llanddulas, Colwyn Bay LL22 8HG (Conwy)

Tel: **01492 512903**. Email: **stay@northwales-holidays.co.uk**

Bron-Y-Wendon is right by the sea between Abergele and Colwyn Bay on the beautiful North Wales coast road. This is a quiet park which, by its own admission, is not really geared up for the family unit – there is no playground here, although there is a games room with table tennis and a TV room. The park is manicured to the highest standards and caters for a large number of seasonal caravans on pitches with gravel bases which are kept very tidy. There are a further 65 grass based, and 20 hardstanding touring pitches, all with electrical hook ups (16A) and tarmac access roads. All pitches have coastal views and the sea and beach are just a short walk away. Colwyn Bay, Conwy, Anglesey, Llandudno, Snowdonia and Chester are all within easy reach, so there is lots to do. Having said how peaceful and quiet everything is (particularly for a seaside park in this area), there is some road noise from the adjacent A55 and during our visit a small train passed on the tracks between the park and the sea (just a few yards) and at night with little else going on it could be just noticeable. Trailer tents are accepted, but not other tents.

Facilities

Two toilet blocks, both with heating, provide excellent facilities including men's and women's shower rooms separate from the toilets and washbasins. Good facilities for disabled visitors. Laundry with washing machines and dryers. Mobile shop visits daily. Gas supplies. Off site: Llanddulas village with shops and several good pubs is very near. Fishing 1 mile. Golf 4 miles. Riding 6 miles. Bicycle hire 15 miles.

Open: All year.

Directions

From A55 Chester - Conwy road turn at Llanddulas interchange (A547), junction 23. Turn right opposite Shell garage and park is 400 yards, signed on coast side of the road. O.S.GR: SH903785.

Charges 2007

Per unit incl. 2 persons	
and electricity	£ 16.00 - £ 20.00
extra person	£ 2.00
child (2 -12 yrs)	£ 1.00
awning	£ 2.00 - £ 3.00

UK6340 Pen-y-Bont Touring & Camping Park

Llangynog Road, Bala LL23 7PH (Gwynedd)

Tel: **01678 520549**. Email: **pennybont-bala@btconnect.co.uk**

This is a pretty little park with 59 touring pitches, 42 of which have hardstanding. Connected by circular gravel roads, they are intermingled with trees and tall trees edge the site. Electricity (16A) is available and there are 24 serviced pitches with hardstanding, electricity, water and drainage. There are also pitches for 25 seasonal units. The park entrance and stone building housing reception and the well stocked shop provide quite a smart image. With views of the Berwyn mountains, Pen-y-bont has a peaceful, attractive and useful location being the closest park to Bala town, 100 yards from Bala Lake and 3 miles from the Welsh National White Water Centre, with Snowdonia on hand.

Facilities

The toilet block includes washbasins in cubicles and spacious hot showers. Two new cubicles with washbasin and WC. Separate laundry room and an en-suite unit for disabled visitors, that doubles as a baby room, operated by key (£2 deposit). Motorcaravan service point. Shop. Bicycle hire. Caravan storage. Off site: Fishing 200 yds. Boat launching, golf and riding 2 miles.

Open: 1 April - 31 October.

Directions

Park is 0.5 miles southeast of Bala village on the B4391. Bala is between Dolgellau and Conwen on the A494. O.S.GR: SH932350.
GPS: N52:54.103 W03:35.407

Charges 2007

Per unit incl. 2 persons	£ 12.00 - £ 18.00
extra person	£ 5.00
child (4-16 yrs)	£ 3.50

UK6345 Glanllyn Lakeside Caravan & Camping Park

Llanuwchllyn, Bala LL23 7ST (Gwynedd)

Tel: **01678 540227**. Email: **info@glanllyn.com**

This 16 acre site lying alongside the southern end of Bala lake has 204 pitches. With around 40 seasonal units, this leaves 164 tourist pitches, 94 of which have electric hook-ups. In this location, virtually all the pitches have wonderful views of the lake or the surrounding mountain sides. The terrain is grassy, fairly open and level, but with natural terraces. There are 19 hardstandings and a further hardstanding area by the beach is a favourite with motorcaravanners. The site is served by main tarmac access roads with speed bumps. Lake swimming is possible and the private beach allows easy access for windsurfing. The park is also an ideal base for some serious walking.

Facilities

A complex of three modern buildings (one can be heated) is at the rear of the site. Preset hot showers, hairdressing and shaver stations, a laundry room, facilities for babies and a suite for disabled people. Motorcaravan service point. Well stocked shop (Easter - Oct). Freezer pack service. Gas supplies. Splendid adventure style playground. Off site: Bus stops outside site gate. Bicycle hire and golf in Bala 3 miles. Riding 18 miles.

Open: Mid March (Easter) - mid October.

Directions

From Bala take A494 southwest towards Dolgellau for 3 miles, entrance is on left, on right hand bend. O.S.GR: SH893324. GPS: N52:52.660 W03:38.799

Charges 2007

Per unit incl. 2 persons	£ 15.00
extra person	£ 4.00
child (3-16 yrs)	£ 2.00 - £ 3.00
dog (max .2)	£ 1.00

UK6580 Llanystumdwy Camping & Caravanning Club Site

Tyddyn Sianel, Llanystumdwy, Criccieth LL52 0LS (Gwynedd)

Tel: **01766 522855**

Overlooking mountains and sea, Llanystumdwy is one of the earliest Camping and Caravanning Club sites. Well maintained with good facilities, it is on sloping grass. However, the managers are very helpful and know their site and can advise on the most suitable pitch and even have a supply of chocks. There are 70 pitches in total (20 ft. spacing), 45 with 10A electricity, spaced over two hedged fields with mainly caravans in the top field with four hardstandings for motorcaravans, and with tents lower down. A shop and pub are in the village and a bus leaves each hour from outside the site to Pwllheli or Porthmadog. This is a good base from which to explore the Lleyn peninsula.

Facilities

A purpose-built toilet block to one side includes excellent, full facilities for disabled visitors including access ramp, one washbasin each in a cubicle for male and female and extra large sinks. Facilities for babies. Laundry (taps with fitting for disabled people). Gas supplies. Off site: Riding or fishing 0.5 miles. Golf 2.5 miles. Beach 3 miles.

Open: March - October.

Directions

Follow A497 from Criccieth west and take second right to Llanystumdwy. Site is on the right. O.S.GR: SH469384. GPS: N52:55.252 W04:16.731

Charges 2007

Per person	£ 4.90 - £ 7.25
child (6-18 yrs)	£ 2.15 - £ 2.25
non-member pitch fee	£ 5.65

255

UK6355 Woodlands Caravan Park

Harlech LL46 2UE (Gwynedd)

Tel: **01766 780419**. Email: **grace@woodlandscp.fsnet.co.uk**

This delightful little site is lovingly tended by its owners and has just 18 pitches for tourists, all with gravel hardstanding and electric hook-up (10A) for caravans and motorcaravans only. Tents are not accepted. There are also 21 privately owned holiday homes, one for rent and a holiday cottage. However, the location of this site certainly makes up for its diminutive size, nestling under the massive rock topped by Harlech Castle, now a designated World Heritage Site. The narrow lane running alongside the site up to the old town above, is the steepest hill in Britain – no wonder the town is considering installing a funicular railway in the future. The coastal railway runs close to the site and the station is just 100 yards away. Railway noise should not be a problem (the small 'Sprinter' trains do not run at night). The 'Blue Flag' beach is only 500 yards, and the Leisure Centre with its indoor pool is 250 yards.

Facilities

The modern stone built toilet facilities are heated, clean and tidy with controllable showers (50p), vanity style washbasins, a small laundry with a baby changing area, but with no dedicated facilities for disabled visitors (£5 deposit for the key to the facilities). Chemical disposal point but no motorcaravan service point. Off site: Harlech Castle. The town also has a theatre and cinema. Nearby is Maes Artro Village with its Museum of Bygone Days. Portmeirion, location of the cult TV series 'The Prisoner', 8 miles. Barmouth (market Thursday and Sunday) 10 miles. Golf 0.25 mile. Fishing 3 miles. Riding 3 miles.

Open: 1 March - 31 October.

Directions

From Barmouth take A496 to Harlech and continue downhill past Royal St David's Golf Course. Fork right immediately before railway crossing, and site is 200 yards on right. DO NOT turn towards town centre which lies on B4573, it is very narrow and congested. O.S.GR: SH582314. GPS: N52:51.693 W04:06.458

Charges 2007

Per unit incl. 2 persons and electricity	£ 14.00 - £ 16.00
extra person	£ 2.50
awning	£ 2.50

No credit cards.

UK6370 Hendre Mynach Touring Caravan & Camping Park

Llanaber, Barmouth LL42 1YR (Gwynedd)

Tel: **01341 280262**. Email: **mynach@lineone.net**

A neat and tidy family park, colourful flowers and top rate facilities make an instant impression on arrival down the steep entrance to this park (help is available to get out if you are worried). The 240 pitches are allocated in various areas, with substantial tenting areas identified. 40 gravel hardstandings are available and around the park there are 110 electricity hook-ups (10A), 20 fully serviced pitches and ample water taps. The quaint old seaside and fishing town of Barmouth is under a mile away, a 15-20 minute walk along the prom. Here you will find 'everything'. The beach is only 100 yards away but a railway line runs between this and the park. It can be crossed by pedestrian operated gates which could be a worry for those with young children. Reception will provide leaflets with maps of local walks. Snowdonia National Park and mountain railway, the Ffestiniog railway, castles and lakes everywhere provide plenty to see and do – this is a classic park in a classic area.

Facilities

Two toilet blocks, one modern and one traditional, both offer excellent facilities including spacious showers (free) and washbasins in cubicles. An extension to the traditional block has added a good unit for disabled visitors with ramp access. Motorcaravan service point. Well stocked shop incorporating a snack bar and takeaway (Easter - 1 Nov; 08.30-21.00 hrs. in peak season, less at quieter times). Off site: Beach 100 m. Fishing, boat launching and bicycle hire within 0.5 miles. Riding 5 miles. Golf 9 miles.

Open: All year excl. 10 January - 28 February.

Directions

Park is off the A496 road north of Barmouth in village of Llanaber with entrance down a steep drive. O.S.GR: SH606171. GPS: N52:43.980 W04:03.971

Charges 2007

Per unit incl. 2 persons and electricity	£ 15.00 - £ 23.00
2 adults and up to 3 children	£ 18.00 - £ 26.00
extra person	£ 4.00
child (2-14 yrs)	£ 2.00
first dog free, extra dog	£ 1.00

Plus £1 per night for certain weekends. Mid-season and Christmas/New Year offers.

UK6600 Bryn Gloch Caravan & Camping Park

Betws Garmon, Caernarfon LL54 7YY (Gwynedd)

Tel: **01286 650216**. Email: **eurig@bryngloch.co.uk**

Bryn Gloch is a well kept and family owned touring park in the impressive Snowdonia area – an unusual feature is the mountain railway which passes through the park. Neat and quiet, it takes some 160 units on five flat, wide meadows with some breathtaking views. With tarmac access roads and free areas allowed in the centre for play, 100 pitches have electricity connections (10A). There are 80 all weather pitches, including 18 'super' pitches and 6 serviced pitches (shared), all with hardstanding. In addition, there are 12 caravan holiday homes. Fishing is possible on the river bordering the park with a barbecue and picnic area, adventure play area and field for ball games. Tourist information is provided in the complex by reception and the park is very popular with walkers and cyclists. Caernarfon with its famous castle is 5 miles.

Facilities

The two main toilet blocks (both recently refurbished) include washbasins in cabins, a family bathroom (hot water £1), baby room and complete facilities for visitors with disabilities (coded access). The far field has a 'portacabin' style unit containing all facilities, for use in peak season. Well equipped laundry and separate drying room. Motorcaravan service point. Shop (1/3-30/10). TV and games rooms with pool tables and amusement machines. Minigolf. Entrance barrier with coded access. Off site: Pub 1 mile. ATM at garage in Ceathro 3 miles. Riding 2.5 miles, bicycle hire and golf 5 miles.

Open: All year, limited facilities 1 November - 1 March.

Directions

From Caernarfon take A4085 signed Beddgelert. Park is just beyond Waunfawr, 4.5 miles southeast of Caernarfon. At Betws Garmon, after crossing river bridge, watch for signs and entrance is opposite St Garmon church. O.S.GR: SH536576. GPS: N53:05.711 W04:11.304

Charges 2007

Per unit incl. 2 persons	£ 15.00 - £ 17.00
incl. electricty	£ 18.00 - £ 20.00
serviced pitch, plus	£ 20.00 - £ 22.00
extra person	£ 4.00
child (3-16 yrs)	£ 2.00

UK6590 Forest Holidays Beddgelert

Caernarfon Road, Beddgelert LL55 4UU (Gwynedd)

Tel: **01766 890288**. Email: **info@forestholidays.co.uk**

Forest Holidays is a partnership between the Forestry Commission and The Camping and Caravanning Club. This well equipped site is in the heart of Snowdonia. Set in a marvellous, natural, wooded environment on the slopes of Snowdon, well equipped and well managed, the site provides 280 pitches – tents in a semi-wooded field area and caravans amongst the trees with numbered hardstandings, and 105 places with 10A electricity. Tents may pitch where they like in their areas leaving 6 m. between units or there are 6 new grass pitches with electrical hook-ups for tents.

Facilities

Two fully equipped modern sanitary toilet blocks clad in natural wood provide large, free hot showers (with good dry areas). Laundry equipment is in one block. A small unit provides extra washbasins and toilets in peak season and there is a toilet and washbasin for disabled visitors. Motorcaravan service point. Shop (Easter - end Sept). Well equipped adventure playground. Off site: Pub within walking distance. Bicycle hire 500 yds. in forest.

Open: All year.

Directions

Site is clearly signed to the left 1 mile north of Beddgelert on A4085 Caernarfon road. O.S.GR: SH579492. GPS: N53:01.245 W04:07.186

Charges 2007

Per unit incl. 2 persons	£ 8.30 - £ 14.00
extra person	£ 3.40 - £ 5.60
child (5-14 yrs)	£ 1.70 - £ 2.80

Less 20% all year for disabled guests and outside 23/7-31/8 for the over 60s.

257

UK6620 Plas Gwyn Caravan & Camping Park

Llanrug, Caernarfon LL55 2AQ (Gwynedd)

Tel: **01286 672619**. Email: **info@plasgwyn.co.uk**

In a beautiful location, this traditional touring site is within the grounds of a house that was built in 1785 in the Georgian style with a colonial style veranda. Of historical interest, Prime Minister Lloyd George was a frequent visitor to Plas Gwyn House. The site is just 2.5 miles from the Llanberis Pass, the Snowdon Mountain Railway, the Electric Mountain Visitor Centre, and this is also good walking country. The 27 touring caravan pitches are set around the perimeter of a slightly sloping grass field, and there are four hardstandings for motorcaravans. The separate tent field has 10 pitches. There are 30 electric hook-ups (16A), and with minimal site lighting on the caravan field and none on the tent field, a torch could be very useful. A further separate small field houses 18 caravan holiday homes. This site is not really suitable for American RVs. A member of the Countryside Discovery Group.

Facilities

An older style building houses the toilet facilities, although the fittings and tiling inside are modern and are kept neat and tidy. Controllable free hot showers, dishwashing sinks, a good laundry room (by reception), but no dedicated facilities for babies or disabled campers. Drive-over motorhome service point. Gas stocked. Reception stocks basic food items, etc. Breakfast 'butties' to order. Internet access possible (ask at reception). Off site: Llanberis and Snowdon Mountain Railway 2.5 miles. Golf 1 mile. Riding 2.5 miles. Bicycle hire 3 miles. Fishing 4 miles.

Open: 1 March - 31 October.

Directions

Site is on A4086, 3 miles from Caernarfon, 2.5 miles from Llanberis, well signed with easy access. O.S.GR: SH522634. GPS: N53:08.804 W04:12.734

Charges 2007

Per person	£ 2.00
child (5-15 yrs)	£ 1.50
child (under 5 yrs)	£ 1.00
pitch incl. awning and electricity	£ 7.50 - £ 11.50
tent pitch	£ 2.50 - £ 9.50

UK6635 Fron Caravan & Camping Park

Brynsiencyn, Anglesey LL61 6TX (Isle of Anglesey)

Tel: **01248 430310**. Email: **mail@froncaravanpark.co.uk**

A traditional, all touring campsite in a peaceful rural location, Fron has panoramic views over the surrounding countryside. From the entrance gate a tarmac drive passes through a two acre level grass paddock, which is reserved for 35 large sized tent and trailer tent pitches. The drive leads up to the old farmhouse which houses reception, a well stocked shop, and plenty of tourist information. Behind the farmhouse is another two acre sloping paddock with 40 caravan and motorcaravan pitches, 5 with hardstandings, and 45 electric hook-ups (10A). An adventure style playground is located in the tent paddock. By the farmhouse a heated swimming pool (30 x 14 ft. and open May - Sept) is well controlled by the owners and is now covered by a dome.

Facilities

Toilet facilities are in three units of varying ages and designs located at both sides of the farmhouse. These include a new unit for ladies with some basins in cubicles, good hot showers with dividers (20p), hairdryers, a baby area with mat and a suite for disabled campers. Laundry with washing machine, dryer and dishwashing sinks. Motorcaravan service point. Outdoor heated swimming pool. Gas stocked. Internet point. Recycling of glass and newspapers. Max. 2 dogs per pitch. No single sex groups are accepted. Torches useful. Breathable groundsheets only. Off site: Nearby are Anglesey Sea Zoo, Plas Newydd House, Foel Farm Park, Anglesey Transport and Agriculture Museum and the Menai Bridges. Brynsiencyn Village (0.5 mile) has a hotel and Spar shop (with ATM). Fishing 1.5 miles. Riding 3 miles. Golf 4 miles.

Open: Easter - end September.

Directions

After crossing the Britannia Bridge, take first slip road signed Llanfairpwll A4080, then next left signed Newborough and Brynsiencyn. Continue on the A4080 for 5 miles, turning right in village at the Groeslon Hotel. Continue through Brynsiencyn to site at western end of village. O.S.GR: SH472668. GPS: N53:10.573 W04:17.271

Charges 2007

Per unit incl. 2 persons and 2 children	£ 18.00
extra person	£ 5.00
extra child	£ 2.50
No credit cards.	

UK6640 Home Farm Caravan Park

Marianglas, Anglesey LL73 8PH (Isle of Anglesey)

Tel: **01248 410614**. Email: **enq@homefarm-anglesey.co.uk**

A tarmac drive through an open field leads to this neatly laid out quality park, with caravan holiday homes to one side. Nestling below what was once a Celtic hill fort, later decimated as a quarry, the park is edged with mature trees and farmland. A circular, tarmac access road leads to the 99 well spaced and numbered pitches. There are 20 hardstanding pitches all with 16A electric hook-ups, including 9 larger pitches with TV hook-ups, water tanks and waste water drain, and 11 normal size pitches with water taps and waste water drain. All the remaining pitches have 10A hook-ups, 33 are on hardstandings, 45 are neatly cut grass. Some areas are slightly sloping. There is a separate area for tents and 15 seasonal units are taken. The 'piece de resistance' of this park must be the children's indoor play area, large super adventure play equipment, complete with tunnels and bridges on safe rubber matting, not to mention an outside fenced play area and fields available for sports and walking. Various beaches, sandy or rocky, are within a mile. A member of the Best of British group.

Facilities

Two purpose built toilet blocks, one part of the reception building, are of similar design and can be heated. En-suite provision for people with disabilities (with key). Excellent small bathroom for children with baby bath and curtain for privacy. Family room (with key). Laundry room and good dishwashing facilities. Motorcaravan service point. Ice pack service. Reception provides basic essentials, gas and some caravan accessories. Indoor and outdoor play areas. TV and pool table. Small library. Hard tennis (extra charge) with racquet hire. Off site: Restaurants, shops and ATM at Benllech 2 miles. Beach 1 mile. Fishing and golf 2 miles. Riding 8 miles.

Open: April - October.

Directions

From the Britannia Bridge take second exit left signed Benllech and Amlwch on the A5025. Two miles after Benllech keep left at roundabout and park entrance is approx. 300 yards on the left beyond the church. O.S.GR: SH499850. GPS: N53:20.433 W04:15.382

Charges 2007

Per unit incl. 2 persons	£ 11.50 - £ 20.50
dog (max. 2)	£ 1.00 - £ 2.00
incl. electricity and hardstanding	£ 17.00 - £ 23.00
incl. full services	£ 18.50 - £ 25.00
extra person	£ 2.50 - £ 5.00

UK6660 Nant Mill Family Touring Caravan & Tenting Park

Prestatyn LL19 9LY (Denbighshire)

Tel: **01745 852360**. Email: **nantmilltouring@aol.com**

The area around Prestatyn on the coast of North Wales is very popular, and this traditional style, family owned and run park of around five acres, takes some 150 units arranged over four fields. There are some distant sea views to be had from many pitches. These are carefully allocated to ensure that the largest, central, sloping field is reserved for families. A smaller more intimate field for tents only is to one side of this and two small paddocks on the other side are for couples who might prefer a quieter, more level location. There are 96 electrical connections (10/16A) but tents are not permitted on pitches with hook-ups. The sanitary buildings are located in the central field and reception is at the farmhouse. Fresh milk and eggs can be purchased. Lighting is fairly minimal, being located at the service points and around the toilet block, it is generally enough but a torch could be useful at times. Children have a designated ball games area and a very good, enclosed adventure playground on a bark surface. Small children might like to visit the duck pond at the rear of the farmhouse. The best beach is the Blue Flag Prestatyn central beach which is about half a mile from the site. Note: The main site gate is locked at night generally around dusk until 08.00 each morning. An alternative entry point is available during these hours.

Facilities

The main toilet block is older in style but well kept. It includes two showers per sex, an ample number of open style washbasins and baby changing in both ladies' and men's rooms. Extra showers are in a small modern 'portacabin' style unit alongside. Showers are charged (50p), with a £1 deposit for the cubicle key (return after each shower). A separate 'portacabin' unit with ramp provides a full suite of services for disabled campers. Large utility room with washing machines, dryers, spin dryer, ironing facilities, together with sinks for hand washing and dishes plus a hairdressing station. Playground and play field. Off site: Beach 1 mile. Town with supermarkets, shops, services and gas supplies 0.5 mile. Sea fishing 0.5 mile.

Open: Easter - mid October.

Directions

Site entrance is 0.5 mile east of Prestatyn on the A548 coast road. O.S.GR: SJ073832. GPS: N53:20.259 W03:23.592

Charges 2007

Per unit incl. 2 persons	£ 13.00
extra person (over 3 yrs)	£ 0.50
electricity	£ 2.00
No credit/debit cards.	

UK6700 Ty-Ucha Farm Caravan Park

Maesmawr Road, Llangollen LL20 7PP (Denbighshire)

Tel: **01978 860677**

Only a mile from Llangollen, Ty Ucha has a rather dramatic setting, nestling under its own mountain and with views across the valley to craggy Dinas Bran castle. It is a neat, ordered park, carefully managed by the owners and providing 40 pitches (30 with 10A electrical hook-up) for caravans and motorcaravans only (tents are not accepted). They are well spaced round a large, grassy field with an open centre for play. One side slopes gently and is bounded by a stream and wood in which a Nature Trail has been made. Because of overhead cables, kite flying is forbidden; no bike riding either. A path leads to various mountain walks, depending on your energy and ability.The world famous Eisteddfod is an international festival of music and dance held for six days starting on the first Tuesday of the first full week in July every year – it is a very busy time for the area.

Facilities

The single toilet block, although of 'portacabin' style, is clean and well maintained and can be heated. It includes two metered showers for each sex (a little cramped). Dishwashing sink with cold water outside. No laundry facilities but there is a launderette in Llangollen. Gas supplies. Games room with table tennis. Late arrivals area. Note: tents are not accepted. Off site: Hotel 0.5 miles with reasonably priced meals. Fishing 1 mile, golf 0.5 miles.

Open: Easter - October.

Directions

Park is signed off A5 road, 1 mile east of Llangollen (250 yds). O.S.GR: SJ228411.

Charges 2007

Per unit incl. 2 persons	£ 9.00 - £ 10.00
extra person	£ 2.00
electricity	£ 3.00

Reductions for OAPs for weekly stays.
No credit cards.

UK6680 James' Caravan Park

Ruabon, Wrexham LL14 6DW (Wrexham)

Tel: **01978 820148**. Email: ray@carastay.demon.co.uk

Open all year, this park has attractive, park-like surroundings with mature trees and neat, short grass. However, edged by two main roads it is subject to some road noise. The old farm buildings and owner's collection of original farm machinery, carefully restored and maintained, add interest. The park has over 40 pitches, some level and some on a slope, with informal siting giving either a view or shade. Electricity (6/10A) is available all over, although a long lead may be useful. Tourist information and a free freezer for ice packs are in the foyer of the toilet block. This is a useful park with easy access from the A483 Wrexham - Oswestry road.

Facilities

The heated toilet block offers roomy showers with a useful rail to help those of advancing age with feet washing. En-suite facilities for visitors with disabilities complete with special 'clos-o-mat' toilet! Motorcaravan service point. Gas available. Off site: The village is 10 minutes walk with a Spar shop, fish and chips, a restaurant, launderette and four pubs. Golf 3 miles.

Open: All year.

Directions

Park is at junction of A483/A539 Llangollen road and is accessible from the west-bound A539. O.S.GR: SJ302434.

Charges 2007

Per unit incl. 2 persons and electricity	£ 12.00
extra person	£ 2.00
awning	£ 2.00
gazebo	£ 5.00
dog	£ 1.00

No credit cards.

UK6670 The Plassey Leisure Park

Eyton, Wrexham LL13 0SP (Wrexham)

Tel: **01978 780277**. Email: **enquiries@theplassey.co.uk**

The Plassey has been carefully developed over the past 45 years. Originally a dairy farm, the park is set in 247 acres of the Dee Valley and offers an extensive range of activities. It has been divided into discreet areas with pitches around the edges. There are 120 touring pitches with electricity connections (16A), including 30 new fully serviced pitches with hardstanding. Five further areas accommodate 120 seasonal caravans. There is much to do and to look at in the rural setting at the Plassey but it is probably best enjoyed midweek, avoiding the busy Bank Holidays. A member of the Best of British group. The Edwardian farm buildings have been tastefully converted to provide a restaurant, coffee shop, health, beauty and hair studio, a small garden centre and 16 different craft and retail units, open all year. Unusually there is also a small brewery on site, producing its own unique Plassey Bitter!

Facilities

Some refurbished toilet facilities are supplemented by a new heated block with individual washbasin cubicles, a room for disabled visitors or families Off site: Riding 2 miles. Bicycle hire 5 miles.

Open: March - October.

Directions

Follow brown and cream signs for The Plassey from the A483 Chester - Oswestry bypass onto B5426 and park is 2.5 miles. Also signed from the A528 Marchwiel - Overton road. O.S.GR: SJ349452.

Charges 2007

Per unit incl. 2 persons and electricity	£ 11.00 - £ 27.00
extra person (over 5 yrs)	£ 3.75
dog or car	£ 2.00

Includes club membership, coarse fishing, badminton and table tennis (own racquets and bats required). B.H. supplement £4 per weekend. Discount for weekly booking.

From gentle rolling hills and rugged coastlines, to dramatic peaks, punctuated with beautiful lochs, Scotland is a land steeped in history that provides superb opportunities to enjoy wild, untamed and spectacular scenery.

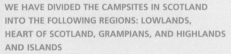

WE HAVE DIVIDED THE CAMPSITES IN SCOTLAND INTO THE FOLLOWING REGIONS: LOWLANDS, HEART OF SCOTLAND, GRAMPIANS, AND HIGHLANDS AND ISLANDS

Probably the most striking thing about Scotland is the vast areas of uninhabited landscape. Southern Scotland boasts beautiful fertile plains, woodlands and wild sea coasts. It also has a rich heritage with ancient castles, abbeys and grand houses. Further north are the Trossachs with their heather-clad hills, home of Rob Roy, the folk hero. The Highlands and Islands, including Skye, Mull and Islay, have some of the most dramatic landscapes in Europe, dominated by breathtaking mountain ranges, such as Ben Nevis and the Grampians, plus deep glistening lochs: the largest being Loch Ness, where the monster reputedly lives. And lying at the very edge of Europe, the islands of the Inner and Outer Hebrides share a rugged natural beauty, with unspoilt beaches and an abundance of wildlife. The two largest cities, Edinburgh and Glasgow, have their own unique attractions. The capital, Edinburgh, with magnificent architecture, comprises the medieval Old Town and the Georgian New Town, with the ancient castle standing proud in the middle. A short distance to the west, Glasgow has more parks and over 20 museums and galleries, with works by Charles Rennie Mackintosh scattered around the city.

Places of interest

Lowlands: Floors Castle near Kelso; Museum of Scotland and Balmoral Castle in Edinburgh; People's Palace, Burrell Collection in Pollock Park, Glasgow; Sweetheart Abbey near Dumfries; New Lanark World Heritage Site; Melrose Abbey.

Heart of Scotland: fishing town of Oban; Stirling Castle and Wallace Monument; Loch Lomond; Pitlochry; university town of St Andrews; Aberdeen; Dunfermline Abbey; fishing villages of Crail and Anstruther; Famous Grouse Experience in Crieff.

Highlands and Islands: Fort William; Eilean Donan Castle near Dornie; the Cairngorms; Highland Wildlife Part at Kingussie; Inverness; Aviemore; Urquhart Castle near Drumnadrochit; Jacobite Steam Train, operates between Fort William and Mallaig; Dunvegan Castle on the Isle of Skye.

Did you know?

Dunfermline Abbey is the final resting place of 22 kings, queens, princes and princesses of Scotland, including Robert the Bruce.

Whales can be seen off the west coast of the Highlands, and the Moray Firth is home to bottle-nosed dolphins.

Arbroath Abbey is the site where Scotland's nobles swore independence from England in 1320.

Since 1861, every day (except on Sundays), the one o'clock gun has boomed out from Edinburgh castle.

Charles Rennie Mackintosh, famous architect and designer, was born in Glasgow in 1868.

Eas Coul Aulin near Kylesku in Sutherland is Britain's highest waterfall at 200 metres – four times the height of Niagara.

Ben Nevis is the highest mountain in the UK.

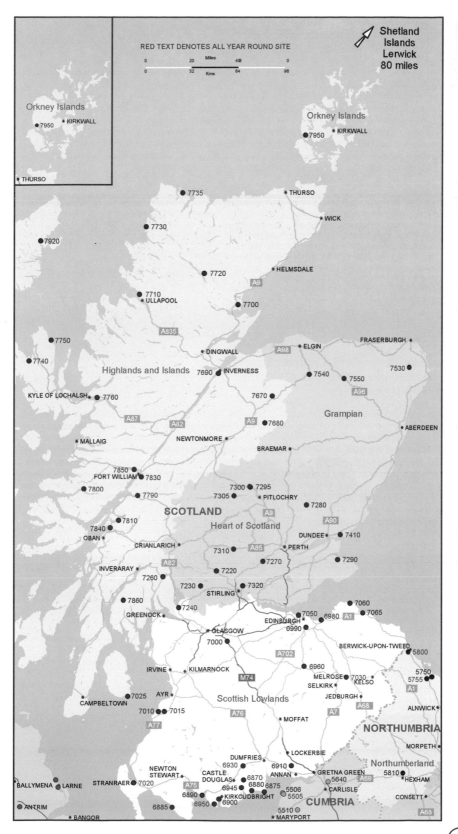

RED TEXT DENOTES ALL YEAR ROUND SITE

Miles
0   20   40   0
0   32   64   96
Kms

Shetland
Islands
Lerwick
80 miles

Orkney Islands
7950 * KIRKWALL

* THURSO

Orkney Islands
7950 * KIRKWALL

7735
* THURSO

7730
* WICK

7920

7720
* HELMSDALE
A9

7710
* ULLAPOOL
7700

A835

7750
DINGWALL
FRASERBURGH *
A98 * ELGIN

7740
Highlands and Islands 7690 * INVERNESS
7540
7550
7530

KYLE OF LOCHALSH * 7760
7670
A96

A87
A82
A9 7680
Grampian

* MALLAIG
NEWTONMORE *
* ABERDEEN

BRAEMAR *

7850
FORT WILLIAM 7830
7300 7295
7280
7800
7790
7305 * PITLOCHRY
SCOTLAND
7810
Heart of Scotland
A9
DUNDEE * 7410
7840
7290
OBAN *
CRIANLARICH *
A85 * PERTH
A90

INVERARAY *
7310
A82
7270
7260
7230 7320
7860
7220
STIRLING
7240
7060
GREENOCK
7050 6980 A1 7065
EDINBURGH *
0990
GLASGOW
BERWICK-UPON-TWEED
7000
5800

IRVINE *
KILMARNOCK *
6960
MELROSE 7030 5750
M74
SELKIRK * KELSO 5755
7025
JEDBURGH * A1
CAMPBELTOWN *
AYR *
7010 7015
A68
ALNWICK *
A77
A76 * MOFFAT A7
NORTHUMBRIA

* LOCKERBIE
MORPETH *
6930 6910 Northumberland
DUMFRIES * * GRETNA GREEN 5810
NEWTON
STEWART * CASTLE ANNAN * 5640 * HEXHAM
DOUGLAS 6870 6875 A69
BALLYMENA * LARNE STRANRAER * 7020 6945 6880 5506 CARLISLE
6890 KIRKCUDBRIGHT 5505 CONSETT *
* ANTRIM 6885 6950 6900 5510 CUMBRIA
* BANGOR * MARYPORT A68

Scottish Lowlands

UK6960 Crossburn Caravan Park

Edinburgh Road, Peebles EH45 8ED (Borders)

Tel: **01721 720501**. Email: **enquiries@crossburncaravans.co.uk**

A peaceful, friendly small park, suitable as a night stop, Crossburn is on the south side of the A703 road, half a mile north of the town centre. The entrance has a fairly steep slope down to reception and the shop which also sells a very large selection of caravan and camping accessories. Passing the caravans for sale and the holiday homes you might think that this is not the site for you, but persevere as the touring area is very pleasant, with attractive trees and bushes. Of the 50 pitches, 46 have electricity (16A), 20 have hardstanding and 8 are fully serviced. There is also a sheltered area for tents. If you decide to stay longer, the area has many places to visit and things to do. From historic homes, abbeys, woodland walks, fishing, horse riding, golf and canoeing – it's all there. Edinburgh is only 40 minutes drive. Perhaps the night halt may turn into a longer visit.

Facilities

There are two toilet blocks, the smaller one (which can be heated) with fairly basic facilities, the other more modern with washbasins in cubicles, free hairdryers and spacious, controllable free showers. Campers' kitchen (key at reception) with free use of an electric hot plate, kettle and fridge. Shop. Adjacent is a large games room with table tennis and games machines. Good play area on bark chippings. Riverside dog walk. Card operated barrier (£10 deposit). Off site: Buses from site gate or in Peebles (a short walk).

Open: Easter/1 April - end October.

Directions

Park is by the A703 road, about 0.5 miles north of Peebles. O.S.GR: NT248417. GPS: N55:39.730 W03:11.600

Charges 2007

Per unit incl. 2 persons and awning	£ 14.00 - £ 16.00
with services	£ 18.00

UK7030 Gibson Park Caravan Club Site

High Street, Melrose TD6 9RY (Borders)

Tel: **01896 822969**

This is an ideal transit park, being so close to the A68, but is also a perfect base for exploring this Southern Scotland area or indeed a trip to Edinburgh, as this is only 35 miles away by car or one of the regular buses which run from the park entrance. This small, three acre park has only 60 touring pitches plus, unusually, an extra 12 tent pitches (summer only) next to the adjacent rugby pitch. All touring pitches have electricity (16A) and TV connections (otherwise it is a bad signal here), 57 have hardstanding and 10 are serviced with water and drainage. A one-way system on the tarmac roads is in operation. This is Sir Walter Scott country – visit Abbotsford House, his romantic mansion on the banks of the River Tweed. Melrose's Abbey ruins are believed to be the final resting place of Robert The Bruce and the starting place of St Cuthbert's Way. A 62 mile, cross border trail leads to Northumberland's Lindisfarne.

Facilities

First rate toilet facilities are in a new building with spacious showers, washbasins in cabins, centrally heated and all fitted out with purpose made faced boarding giving a very pleasing finish. Laundry facilities. Separate room with shower and WC for disabled visitors. Motorcaravan service point. Gas is available. Security barrier (operated by card). Off site: Situated on the edge of the little town of Melrose, a five minute walk, shops, pubs and restaurants are all in easy reach. Play area next to site.

Open: All year.

Directions

Turn left off A68 Jedburgh - Lauder road at roundabout about 2.5 miles past Newton St Boswell onto A6091 Galashiels road. In about 3.25 miles at roundabout turn right onto B6374 to Melrose. Site is on right at filling station opposite Melrose Rugby Club, just before entering town centre. O.S.GR: NT545340. GPS: N55:35.881 W02:43.454

Charges 2007

Per person	£ 4.40 - £ 5.50
child (5-16 yrs)	£ 1.50 - £ 2.50
pitch (non-members)	£ 10.80 - £ 14.60

UK6875 Southerness Holiday Village

Southerness, Dumfries DG2 8AZ (Dumfries and Galloway)

Tel: **01387 880256**. Email: **enquiries@parkdeanholidays.co.uk**

Set beside a two mile stretch of sandy beach, at the foot of the beautiful Galloway Hills, is Southerness Holiday Village. Part of the Parkdean Group, it is a large park with the main emphasis on caravan holiday homes. However, there are also 100 open plan pitches for caravans, motorcaravans and tents. Set away from the static units, these are divided into two areas, some on level hardstanding with water, others on grass and all with 16A electricity. The main leisure complex is a short walk from the touring area. This park is well organised with lots going on for all the family.

Facilities

A modern toilet block provides en-suite facilities throughout (key entry). Well maintained, it is kept very clean. Excellent unit for disabled visitors. Well equipped laundry. Shop. Bar with TV. Bistro, takeaway and coffee shop. Indoor pool. Indoor play area. Bowling (charge). Evening entertainment in the Sunset Showbar. Adventure play area. Crazy golf. Nature trails. Off site: Golf course adjacent. Fishing 2 miles. Bus from outside gate.

Open: Before Easter - 31 October.

Directions

From Dumfries take A710 Solway Coast road for about 10 miles. Sign for Holiday Village is on the left. O.S.GR: NX974545.

Charges 2007

Per pitch incl. up to 8 persons	£ 8.00 - £ 22.00
incl. services	£ 10.00 - £ 26.00
dog	£ 2.00

UK6870 Glenearly Caravan Park

Dalbeattie DG5 4NE (Dumfries and Galloway)

Tel: **01556 611393**

Glenearly is a new park (opened in 2000), owned and managed by Mr and Mrs Jardine. Rurally located, it has been tastefully developed from farmland into a touring and mobile home, all year park. There are 39 marked, open pitches, all with 16A electrical connections (and TV), most on hardstandings. Seasonal units use some pitches. Walls and shrubs divide the touring section from the caravan holiday homes (two for rent), with mature trees around the perimeter. There are attractive views over the hills and forest of Barhill and buzzards, yellow wagtails, woodpeckers and goldfinch are some of the birds that can be seen, along with the park's own donkeys, ponies and sheep. The large games room, converted from an old barn, is excellent – heated and with plenty of chairs for parents to supervise the activities. A super play area suitable for all ages is behind the touring area. A ten minute stroll brings you into the small town of Dalbeattie. Just 6 miles from the park along the Solway coast is Kippford, a well known sailing centre from which you can walk the Jubilee Path to Rockcliffe. Set in a bay, Rockcliffe has a small sandy beach, an excellent tea room and gift shop.

Facilities

Situated in the centre of the touring area, the toilets and showers are fitted out to a high standard. Unit for disabled visitors or families. Laundry room with washing machines and dryer and an outside drying area. Large games room. Play area. Off site: Shops, pubs, restaurants, etc. at Dalbeatie. Bicycle hire at Mabie Forest just 3 miles from Dumfries on the A710.

Open: All year.

Directions

From Dumfries take A711 towards Dalbeattie. Six miles beyond Beeswing, after passing sign for Edingham Farm, park is signed with entrance on right (beside a bungalow). O.S.GR: NX834626. GPS: N54:56.692 W03:49.337

Charges 2007

Per unit incl. 2 persons	£ 11.00 - £ 13.00
extra person over 5 yrs	£ 2.00
electricity	£ 2.00 - £ 2.50

A warm welcome awaits you at

GLENEARLY CARAVAN PARK

We are sure you will enjoy your stay with us and we will do everything we can to ensure that you have a truly happy time.

The site is a peace haven for statics, tourers, motor homes and tents

Nearby attractions and activities
- *Sandyhills and Rockcliffe beaches*
- *Kippford - perfect for sailing*
- *Pony trekking, mountain biking, walking, fishing and sightseeing*

T: 01556 611393

Dalbeattie, Kirkcudbrightshire, Scotland

265

UK6950 Brighouse Bay Holiday Park

Brighouse Bay, Borgue, Kirkcudbright DG6 4TS (Dumfries and Galloway)

Tel: **01557 870267**. Email: **info@gillespie-leisure.co.uk**

Hidden away within 1,200 exclusive acres, on a quiet, unspoilt peninsula, this spacious family park is only some 200 yards through bluebell woods from a lovely sheltered bay. It has exceptional all weather facilities, as well as golf and pony trekking. Over 90% of the 210 touring caravan pitches have electricity (10/16A), some with hardstanding and some with water, drainage and TV aerial. The three tent areas are on fairly flat, undulating ground and some pitches have electricity. There are 120 self-contained holiday caravans and lodges of which about 30 are let, the rest privately owned. On site leisure facilities include a golf and leisure club with 16.5 m. pool, water features, jacuzzi, steam room, fitness room, games room (all on payment), golf driving range and clubhouse bar and bistro. The 18-hole golf course extends onto the headland with superb views over the Irish Sea to the Isle of Man and Cumbria. A 9-hole family golf course is a popular attraction. Like the park, these facilities are open all year. The BHS approved pony trekking centre (April - October) offers treks for complete beginners, slow hacks for the nervous or inexperienced or gallops on the beach for the more experienced. This is a well run park of high standards and a member of the Best of British group.

Facilities

The large, well maintained main toilet block includes 10 unisex cabins with shower, basin and WC, and 12 with washbasin and WC, a launderette and covered dishwashing sinks. A second, excellent block next to the tent areas has en-suite shower rooms (one for disabled people) and bathroom, separate washing cubicles, showers, baby room, laundry sinks, and covered dishwashing sinks. One section is heated in winter. Motorcaravan service point. Gas supplies. Licensed supermarket. Bar, restaurant and takeaway (all year). Golf (new practise area) and Leisure Club with indoor pool (all year). Play area (incl. new one for under 5s). Riding centre. Mountain bike hire. Quad bikes, boating pond, 10-pin bowling, playgrounds, putting. Nature trails. Coarse fishing ponds plus sea angling and an all-tide slipway for boating enthusiasts. Caravan storage. New purpose built chalet for tourist information and leisure facility bookings.

Open: All year.

Directions

In Kirkcudbright turn onto A755 and cross river bridge. In 400 yards turn left onto B727 at international camping sign. Or follow Brighouse Bay signs off A75 just east of Gatehouse of Fleet. O.S.GR: NX630455. GPS: N54:47.250 W04:07.746

Charges 2007

Per unit incl. 2 persons	£ 12.50 - £ 17.60
extra adult	£ 2.10
child (4-15 yrs)	£ 1.40
electricity	£ 3.60
fully serviced pitch	£ 4.60 - £ 5.10

Contact site for full charges.
Golf packages in low season.
Camping Cheques accepted.

UK6880 Sandyhills Bay Leisure Park

Sandyhills, Dalbeattie DG5 4NY (Dumfries and Galloway)

Tel: **01387 780257**. Email: **info@sandyhills-bay.co.uk**

Sandyhills Bay is a small, quiet park beside a sheltered, sandy beach. Reception is on the left through a car park used by visitors either walking the hills or enjoying the beach. Beyond is a large flat camping area, above which, divided by a tree lined hedge, are 60 pitches, half taken by mobile homes situated around the perimeter. The 30 touring pitches, 28 with electrical connection (16A) are in the centre of the all grassed flat area. This is an excellent family park, with the beach and a children's play area at the site, whilst up the hill next to the park is an 18 hole golf course where you can enjoy a bar meal in the clubhouse and within walking distance at Barend is an approved riding centre suitable for all the family. There is a well stocked licensed shop and a takeaway with table and chairs outside from where you can enjoy the well kept garden and splendid views across the Solway.

Facilities

The sanitary facilities are of traditional design, situated in one central block to the side of the touring area. Laundry room (tokens from reception). Shop and small takeaway. New adventure play area by the beach. Visitors can also use the facilities at Brighouse Bay, the largest park in the Gillespie Group. New barrier at entrance and beach car park (returnable deposit). Off site: Cliff-top walk from Sandyhills to Rockcliffe approx. 10 miles. Pleasant drive to Rockcliffe and Kippford, a well known sailing centre.

Open: Easter - 31 October.

Directions

From Dumfries take A710 Solway coast road (approx. 16 miles). Site is on left just after signs for Sandyhills. O.S.GR: NX890549. GPS: N54:52.741 W03:43.862

Charges 2007

Per unit incl. 2 persons	£ 10.25 - £ 14.70
extra person	£ 1.70
child (4-15 yrs)	£ 1.10
electricity	£ 3.60
awning	£ 1.80

UK6945 Barlochan Caravan Park

Palnackie, Castle Douglas DG7 1PF (Dumfries and Galloway)

Tel: **01557 870267**. Email: **info@barlochan.co.uk**

Barlochan Caravan Park is situated on a hillside overlooking the Urr Estuary on the Solway Coast close to Dalbeattie and Castle Douglas, with the small village of Palnackie being a short walk away. Set on terraces, level, marked and numbered, most of the touring and tent pitches are on grass with a limited number of hardstandings available. There are 12 with electrical connections (16A). In addition, 55 mobile homes (5 for rent) are positioned on terraces high above the touring areas and screened by mature shrubs and trees. Just to the left of the entrance there is a minigolf course and an adventure play area screened from the park with mature trees. Through the village, under a mile from the park, there is a course fishing lake which is free for visitors to the park.

Facilities

The refurbished sanitary facilities are kept spotlessly clean. Shower cubicles have recently been made larger suitable for wheelchair entry, but if required there is also a separate unit with WC and basin. Fully equipped laundry with outside drying area. Dishwashing under cover. Reception and well stocked shop. Large games/TV room. Off site: Fishing 400 yds. Bicycle hire 6 miles. Golf 7 miles. Riding 10 miles. Beach 10 miles.

Open: Easter - end October.

Directions

From Dumfries take A711 west to Dalbeattie. Continue through Dalbeattie for 0.5 miles. Bear left at T-junction (Auchencairn). Site is 2 miles on right. O.S.GR: NX819571. GPS: N54:53.757 W03:50.601

Charges 2007

Per unit incl. 2 persons	£ 10.25 - £ 14.70
extra person	£ 1.60
child (4-15 yrs)	£ 1.10
electricity	£ 3.60

UK6900 Seaward Caravan Park

Dhoon Bay, Kirkcudbright DG6 4TJ (Dumfries and Galloway)

Tel: **01557 870267**. Email: **info@seaward-park.co.uk**

Seaward Caravan Park is little sister to the much larger Brighouse Bay Holiday Park, 3.5 miles away. Set in an idyllic location overlooking the bay, this park is suitable for all units. The terrain is slightly undulating, but most of the numbered pitches are flat and of a good size. There are 35 pitches (21 with hardstanding) designated for caravans and motorcaravans, a further 14 for tents, plus 43 caravan holiday homes (6 for hire). Electric hook-ups (16A) are on 32 of the touring pitches and 12 are also serviced with water and drain. This is a quiet park with excellent views ideally suited for that relaxing holiday or for touring the region.

Facilities

The principal, fully equipped toilet block is to the rear of the park. Four rooms with en-suite facilities are also suitable for disabled campers. Well equipped baby room. Laundry and dishwashing room. No motorcaravan service point but the manager can lift a manhole cover to empty waste water tanks. The reception/shop stocks basic provisions, books, gifts, gas, and tourist information. Unsupervised heated outdoor swimming pool with sunbathing area (15/5-15/9). Play area with bark surface and rocking horse. Picnic tables. Excellent games room. Pitch and putt. Off site: Beach and sea angling nearby. Riding or bicycle hire 3.5 miles. Kirkcudbright 2.5 miles.

Open: 1 March - 31 October.

Directions

In Kirkcudbright turn onto A755 signed Borgue. Go over river bridge and after 400 yards turn left onto B727 at international camping sign. Proceed with caution when turning right into site - it is tight. O.S.GR: NX680510. GPS: N54:49.186 W04:04.927

Charges 2007

Per unit incl. 2 persons	£ 10.75 - £ 15.35
extra person	£ 1.70
child (4-15 yrs)	£ 1.30
electricity	£ 3.60
serviced pitch	£ 4.60 - £ 5.10

Less 5-10% for bookings
(not valid with some other discount schemes).

UK6885 Kings Green Caravan Park

South Street, Port William DG8 9SG (Dumfries and Galloway)

Tel: **07988 700880**. Email: **enquiries@portwilliam.com**

Kings Green Caravan Park is now owned and run by the Port William Community Association. Kept very natural and situated beside the sea overlooking Luce Bay and the Mull of Galloway, it is within walking distance of Port William, well known for its harbour and fishing community. The all grass, open site provides 30 marked and numbered pitches for caravans, motorcaravans and tents (21 with 10A electricity). On arrival visitors are given a welcome pack which includes a guide on the history of the area and local information. Second Sands at the northern end of the village is perfect for the launching and recovery of boats at any stage of the tide and provides wheelchair and pushchair access to the beach. When we inspected the park, volunteers were in charge. Reception may not therefore always be open. You are invited to park and details of reserved pitches are placed on the notice board.

Facilities

The small toilet block (key entry) is kept very clean and has vanity style washbasins, free electric showers and hair dryers. Facilities for disabled visitors include WC and washbasin (Radar key). Small basic outdoor dishwashing. No laundry, motorcaravan point or gas sales. Large play and ball game area adjacent. Off site: Shops, restaurants and bars in Port William. Local walks and cycle routes. Fishing 50 yds. Golf 2 miles. Sailing and boat launching 600 yds. Riding 3 miles. Bladnoch distillery and the Isle of Whithorn just a short drive away or further to Stranraer with boats to Ireland.

Open: 30 March - 31 October.

Directions

From Dumfries, take A75 to Newton Stewart. Follow A714 to Wigtown, then B7085 to Port William. O.S.GR: NX337433. GPS: N54:45.358 W04:34.892

Charges 2007

Per pitch	£ 8.00 - £ 9.00
incl. electricity	£ 10.00 - £ 11.00

UK6890 Mossyard Caravan Park

Gatehouse of Fleet, Castle Douglas DG7 2ET (Dumfries and Galloway)

Tel: **01557 840226**. Email: **enquiry@mossyard.co.uk**

Mossyard is a family run park set within a working farm right beside the sea in a sheltered bay. The park and farmhouse appear together suddenly over the horizon and in the distance as you approach, with some breathtaking views across the Solway where the Galloway Hills and the waters of Wigtown Bay meet. On arrival you pass through the farm buildings into the park which is divided into two sections by stone walls. Around the perimeter are several new wooden chalets and holiday homes and self catering holiday cottages. There are 30 grass pitches (15 for tourers), some flat but most on an elevated sloping area, plus 20 for tents or motorhomes on a level camping field which adjoins the beach but is a little way from the sanitary facilities. Electrical connections (10A) are available for caravan and tent pitches. This is a wonderful park for outdoor activities such as watersports and fishing where small craft can be launched from site. Although some of the beaches and tides around the Solway Coast are dangerous, the one around this bay is very safe.

Facilities

Some of the farm buildings around the main farmhouse have been utilised for the toilet facilities, which are of traditional design. Showers are coin-operated (20p). Roomy facilities for disabled visitors can also be used as a family bathroom. New purpose built building with laundry, dishwashing area and information room with freezer and fridge for visitors' use. No shop on site. Off site: Gatehouse of Fleet with shops, pubs and restaurants 4 miles.

Open: 24 March - 28 October.

Directions

Take A75 road from Dumfries towards Stranraer and park is signed to the left, 4 miles west of Gatehouse of Fleet, approx. 1 mile down a single track farm road. O.S.GR: NX547518. GPS: N54:50.411 W04:15.609

Charges 2007

Per unit	£ 11.00 - £ 13.00
tent	£ 11.00 - £ 13.00
electricity	£ 2.00
awning	free - £ 1.00

UK6910 Hoddom Castle Caravan Park

Hoddom, Lockerbie DG11 1AS (Dumfries and Galloway)

Tel: **01576 300251**. Email: **hoddomcastle@aol.com**

The oldest part of Hoddom Castle itself is a 16th century Borders Pele Tower, or fortified Keep. This was extended to form a residence for a Lancashire cotton magnate, became a youth hostel and was then taken over by the army during WW2. Since then parts have been demolished but the original 'Border Keep' still survives, unfortunately in a semi-derelict state. The site's bar and restaurant have been developed in the courtyard area from the coach houses, and the main ladies' toilet block was the stables. The park is landscaped and spacious, well laid out on mainly sloping ground with many mature and beautiful trees, originally part of an arboretum. The drive to the site is just under a mile long, with a one way system. Many of the 120 numbered pitches have good views of the castle and have gravel hardstandings with grass for awnings, most with electrical connections (16A). In front of the castle are flat fields for tents and caravans not needing electricity. Amenities include a comfortable bar lounge with a family room and TV. The park's 9-hole golf course is in an attractive setting alongside the Annan river, where fishing is possible for salmon and trout (tickets available). Coarse fishing is also possible elsewhere on the estate. This is a peaceful base from which to explore historic southwest Scotland.

Facilities

The main toilet block can be heated and is very well appointed, with washbasins in cubicles, 3 en-suite cubicles with WC and basin (one with baby changing facilities) and an en-suite shower unit for disabled visitors. Two further tiled blocks, kept very clean, provide washbasins and WCs only. Each block has dishwashing sinks. Well equipped laundry room at the castle. Motorcaravan service point. Licensed shop at reception (gas available). Bar, restaurant and takeaway (restricted opening outside high season). Games room with pool tables, table tennis and video games. Large, grass play area. Crazy golf. Mountain bike trail. Fishing. Golf. Guided walks organised in high season. Caravan storage. Off site: Tennis nearby.

Open: 1 April - 30 October.

Directions

Leave A74M at junction 19 (Ecclefechan) and follow signs to park. Leave A75 at Annan junction (west end of Annan by-pass) and follow signs. O.S.GR: NY155725. GPS: N55:02.482 W03:18.660

Charges 2007

Per unit incl. 2 persons	£ 7.50 - £ 14.00
extra person	£ 2.00
child (7-16 yrs)	£ 1.00
electricity (10A)	£ 13.00 - £ 17.00
small tent	£ 6.50 - £ 11.50

HODDOM CASTLE CARAVAN PARK

- Fishing
- Walking
- Golf
- Cycle Hire

Scottish HOLIDAY PARK ★★★★

AA ►►

ENQUIRIES: The Warden, Hoddom Castle, Hoddom, Lockerbie DG11 1AS
Tel: 01576 300251 • www.hoddomcastle.co.uk • Email: hoddomcastle@aol.com

UK7020 Aird Donald Caravan Park

London Road, Stranraer DG9 8RN (Dumfries and Galloway)

Tel: **01776 702025**. Email: **enquiries@aird-donald.co.uk**

Aird Donald is a good stopping off place when travelling to and from the Irish ferries, but it is also useful for seeing the sights around Stranraer. This tidy park comprises 12 acres surrounded by conifers, flowering trees and shrubs and the 300 yard drive is lit and lined with well trimmed conifers. There are grass areas for caravans or tents and hardstandings with electricity hook-up (these are very handy for hardy winter tourers). A small play area caters for young children, but the local leisure centre is only a walk away and provides swimming, table tennis, gym, etc, and a theatre that hosts everything from country and western to opera. It also has bar facilities.

Facilities

Two toilet blocks. The new block is modern, heated and very clean with excellent facilities. It is kept locked with a key deposit of £5. Two types of shower - one electric and metered (20p) and two others which are free. Washbasins are in vanity units, ladies having one in a cubicle. Unit for visitors with disabilities has a washbasin and WC. The original block is being renovated but is more basic with free showers (open all the time). Dishwashing sinks. Small laundry. Motorcaravan services. Play area.

Open: All year.

Directions

Enter Stranraer on A75 road. Watch for narrow site entrance on left entering town, opposite school. O.S.GR: NX075605. GPS: N54:54.111 W05:00.373

Charges 2007

Per unit incl. electricity	£ 15.00
tent	£ 12.00
No credit cards.	

UK6930 Park of Brandedleys

Crocketford, Dumfries DG2 8RG (Dumfries and Galloway)

Tel: **01387 266700**. Email: **brandedleys@holgates.com**

Brandedleys is a first class park providing pitches for some 75 caravans and a limited number of tents, plus 55 self-contained caravan holiday homes in three or four flat and variably sloping fields with tarmac access roads, 15 for rent. It has excellent facilities and amenities. Caravan pitches are on lawns or terraced hardstandings, many with a pleasant outlook across a loch. All have electrical connections (10A) and 21 pitches also have water and drainage. Improvements continue with more serviced pitches. A heated outdoor swimming pool is open when the weather is suitable and the heated indoor pool adjacent to the bar/restaurant is open all season with changing room (both pools free) and a sauna. The bar and licensed restaurant are open for lunch and dinner with full menus at reasonable prices and a patio area overlooking Auchenreoch Loch. Walks on the open moors or forest and beautiful sandy beaches 12 miles away from this popular, quality park.

Facilities

The main heated toilet block has been extensively modernised with clean, well appointed shower cubicles with toilet and washbasin (just one for men), in addition to the normal provision. Bathroom for disabled visitors. Laundry room, baby and hair care room. Covered dishwashing sinks. A second block of equal size and standard is in the lower field, also with laundry and dishwashing facilities. Bar and restaurant. Takeaway food to order (18.00-21.30 hrs). Swimming pool. All-weather tennis courts, outdoor badminton court. Play area. Games room, pool table and air-hockey table. Off site: Riding, fishing 1.5 miles. Golf 6 miles. Bicycle hire 9 miles. Beach 12 miles.

Open: All year.

Directions

Park is 9 miles from Dumfries on the south side of the A75 Dumfries - Stranraer road, just west of the village of Crocketford. O.S.GR: NX830725. GPS: N55:01.966 W03:49.898

Charges 2007

Per unit incl. 2 persons and electricity	£ 14.00 - £ 19.50
family unit (5)	£ 17.00 - £ 22.50
serviced pitch	£ 3.00
awning	£ 1.50 - £ 3.00
pup tent	£ 4.00

No single sex groups.

Park of Brandedleys

The Park BRANDEDLEYS

From castles to stately homes, coastal and forest walks, cycling, sailing, golfing and fishing - from Red Deer, Red Kite and Red Squirrel to Golden Eagles and Sea Eagles this tranquil part of Southern Scotland has something for everyone.
The Park is open all year with facilities for Tourers, a choice of Pine Lodges and luxury Holiday Homes for sale or hire. Bar and Restaurant, Indoor pool, sauna, tennis court, games room and fitness trail are all included in the pitch fees.
Tourers from £14.00 to £19.50   Holiday Homes & Lodges from £215.00 to £995.00 pw
Short breaks available

AA Campsite of the year for Scotland

Crocketford, Dumfries, DG2 8RG Tel. 01387 266700 Fax. 01556 690681 www.holgates.com

UK7010 Culzean Castle Camping & Caravanning Club Site

Maybole KA19 8JJ (South Ayrshire)

Tel: **01655 760627**

With wonderful views of the Firth of Clyde and over to the Isle of Arran, this quiet Camping and Caravanning Club site is next door to Culzean Castle (pronounced Kullayne). Visitors are given a pass to walk in the grounds (when open) with their 17 miles of footpaths as many times as they wish. The 18th century, cliff-top castle is built on the site of a former ancient castle and its armoury exhibition is superb. Besides the woodland walks, deer park and aviary, there are three miles of rocky shore and small sandy beaches. A full programme of events is staged at the castle over the season, including special children's weeks, sheepdog trials, bands, battle re-enactments, ranger walks and craft fairs. The campsite has 90 pitches, some level others slightly sloping, and 60 have electrical hook-ups (10A). A few level pitches are suitable for motorcaravans and 20 pitches have hardstanding. American style motorhomes (more than 25 ft.) must contact the site prior to arrival as large pitches are limited.

Facilities

The toilet blocks, kept very clean, can be heated and include some washbasins in cubicles. Unit for disabled visitors has a WC, washbasin and shower - an excellent facility. Dishwashing sinks. Well equipped laundry. Small shop for basics opens for short periods morning and evening. Adventure playground. Units over 25 ft. long only accepted by prior arrangement. Off site: Golf or bicycle hire 4 miles. Fishing 8 miles. Buses pass the gate.

Open: 30 March - 30 October.

Directions

From Maybole follow signs for Culzean Castle and Country Park, turning in the town on B7023 which runs into the A719. Country Park entrance is clearly signed on right after 3.75 miles; entrance to caravan park is on the right in Country Park drive. O.S.GR: NS247103. GPS: N55:21.207 W04:46.167

Charges 2007

Per person	£ 4.90 - £ 7.25
child (6-18 yrs)	£ 2.15 - £ 2.25
non-member pitch fee	£ 5.65

Scotland

UK7015 The Ranch Holiday Park

Culzean Road, Maybole KA19 8DU (South Ayrshire)

Tel: **01655 882446**

This holiday park is situated in the Ayrshire countryside, four miles from the small town of Maybole. The Ranch, a Caravan Club affiliated site, is managed by the McAuley family who moved here in November 2003. Barrier controlled, the park is beautifully set out with 60 spacious touring pitches, all with 16A electricity connections and including 8 super pitches. Most are on level hardstanding with a few level, all grass pitches arranged open plan facing a huge playing field. There are also 65 caravan holiday homes, 1 for rent. There are plans to extend the number of touring pitches and holiday homes. The superb facilities include a private Leisure Centre with an indoor heated pool, sauna, solarium and well equipped gym, complete with changing room, toilets, shower and free hair dryers. To the rear is a small unfenced play park adjacent to the small camping area which has undercover seating for those rainy days. A 'Wee Honesty Shop' offers exchange books and magazines and a kiddies corner for the under 5s. This is an excellent park for relaxing and enjoying the amenities or for touring the area with nearby sandy beaches at Maybole Shore and Croy Bay plus the wonderful freak of nature, where the laws of gravity are turned upside down at the Electric Brae, where you can see water run uphill.

Facilities

The sanitary facilities are away from the touring area and older in style, but kept spotlessly clean, (there are plans for a new block). Washbasins in vanity units, four in cubicles with WCs for ladies. Large preset showers. Individual unit with WC and basin for disabled visitors. Purpose built wooden building housing well equipped laundry with dishwashing area on the end. No shop on site but reception has a good information area. Off site: Golf at Turnberry and fishing at Mochram Loch.

Open: March - October (and weekends).

Directions

From Maybole turn onto B7023 (signed Culzean Maidens) for 1 mile and site is signed on left. O.S.GR: NS286102. GPS: N55:21.358 W04:42.368

Charges guide

Per unit incl. 2 persons	£ 10.60 - £ 16.60
extra person	£ 3.30 - £ 4.80
child	£ 1.10 - £ 1.60

UK7410 Riverview Holiday Park

Marine Drive, Monifieth DD5 4NN (Angus)

Tel: **01382 535471**. Email: **info@riverview.co.uk**

A quiet, family park, Riverview overlooks a long sandy beach and has magnificent views over the River Tay towards the Kingdom of Fife and yet is within walking distance of Monifieth town. Under new ownership (December 2005), the park is neatly set out with flowering shrubs and bushes dividing 40 numbered touring pitches. Some enjoying river views, they are grassy and level, each with 16A electricity and two also with water and drainage. Bordering the park are 46 privately owned caravan holiday homes and 4 to rent. At the entrance to the park is a small reception office and separate tourist information room and a leisure suite with sauna, steam baths and gym (charge). For children, there is an indoor games room with a pool table and a play area for the under 5s, and a small outdoor adventure play area for under 12s with seats alongside for supervision. A member of the Best of British group.

Facilities

The spotlessly clean amenity block (key entry) has open washbasins, one in a cabin with WC, and pre-set showers. Baby bath. Full facility for disabled visitors. Well equipped laundry. Leisure suite. Games room and play area. Adventure play area. Off site: Picnic areas and small boat slipway adjacent. Opposite the Riverview recreation park offers football pitches, putting, crazy golf, tennis, bowling as well as a well equipped adventure play park. Golf 800 yds. Fishing 2 miles. Riding 3 miles. Dundee city 5 miles. Bus service nearby.

Open: 1 April - 31 October.

Directions

From Dundee follow signs for Monifieth on the A930, after passing Tesco. Turn right at sign for golf course and right again under railway bridge. Park is signed on the left. O.S.GR: NO501322. GPS: N56:28.797 W02:48.692

Charges 2007

Per unit incl. 2 adults and 2 children	£ 13.00 - £ 15.00
extra person	£ 2.00
awning	£ 2.00

UK7025 Seal Shore Camping & Touring Site

Kildonan KA27 8SE (North Ayrshire)

Tel: **01770 820320**. Email: **mdeighton@seashore.fsnet.co.uk**

A warm welcome awaits here on the Island of Arran from the resident owners, Sylvia and Maurice Deighton. On the southernmost point of the island, this is a quiet and peaceful park situated along its own private beach with wonderful sea views. The open, grassy area, sloping in parts, takes caravans, motorcaravans and tents with 8 electrical connections (16A). The reception doubles as a shop selling basics with a TV room adjacent. There are communal picnic and barbecue areas. The Kildonan Hotel next door serves restaurant and bar meals. Permits are available for loch fishing and charters available from the owner, a registered fisherman. There is a choice of seven golf courses.

Facilities

The toilet block is basic but clean and tidy. Full facilities for disabled visitors doubles as a baby room. No laundry but you may use the owner's washing machine and iron. Indoor dishwashing with fridge and freezer for campers use. Camping gas only. Fishing. Sailing. Off site: Golf at Whiting 4 miles. Heritage Museum in Brodick and to the North of the Island Lochranza castle and distillery.

Open: March - October.

Directions

From Brodick take A841 south for 12 miles to sign for Kildonan. Site is downhill, on the seashore, next to the Kildonan Hotel. O.S.GR: NS022209. GPS: N55:26.460 W05:06.838

Charges 2007

Per person	£ 6.00
child (6-12 yrs)	£ 2.00
pitch incl. electricity	£ 3.00 - £ 4.00

UK7260 Forest Holidays Ardgartan

Ardgartan, Arrochar G83 7AR (Dunbartonshire)

Tel: **01301 702293**. Email: **fe.holidays@forestry.gsi.gov.uk**

Forest Holidays is a partnership between the Forestry Commission and The Camping and Caravanning Club. Ardgartan is a rugged site in the Argyll Forest Park. Splendidly situated with mountains all around and lovely views of Loch Long, there are lots of sightseeing and activity opportunities. At the northern end of the Cowal Peninsula, the site is on a promontory on the shores of Loch Long, with good sea fishing and facilities for launching small boats. The 70 touring pitches are in sections which are well divided by grass. Most with hardstanding and marked by numbered posts, they are accessed from hard surfaced roads and 54 have electrical hook-ups. There are additional grass areas for tents. Midges can be a problem in this area of Scotland.

Facilities

The main toilet block is opposite the reception and shop. It is a basic, but clean provision with facilities for disabled visitors and a launderette. These facilities may be quite stretched when the park is busy. Play equipment (bark surfaces). Raised barbecues are allowed. Off site: Arrochar village (2 miles) has fuel, general stores and a restaurant.

Open: All year excl. 14 January - 28 February.

Directions

From A82 Glasgow - Crianlarich road take A83 at Tarbet signed Arrochar and Cambletown. Site is 2 miles past Arrochar, the entrance on a bend. O.S.GR: NN275030. GPS: N56:11.327 W04:46.900

Charges 2007

Per unit incl. 2 persons	£ 9.00 - £ 13.70

Less 20% all year for disabled guests and outside 22/7-30/8 for senior citizens.

UK7810 Oban Camping & Caravanning Club Site

Barcaldine, By Connel PA37 1SG (Argyll and Bute)

Tel: **01631 720348**

Owned by the Camping and Caravanning Club, this site at Barcaldine, 12 miles north of Oban, is a small, intimate site taking 75 units. Arranged within the old walled garden of Barcaldine House, there are 23 level, fairly small pitches with hardstanding and 52 electrical hook-ups (16A). (It can be wet underfoot in bad weather). Being a small site, it has a very cosy feel to it, due no doubt to the friendly welcome new arrivals receive. Through the garden gate, one is immediately in the Barcaldine forest with its miles of forest tracks, absolutely perfect for both dog walking and mountain biking. Sea fishing and freshwater lake fishing are both nearby.

Facilities

The central toilet block can be heated and is kept very clean with free hot showers, hair dryers and plenty of washbasins and WCs. Excellent unit for disabled visitors. Laundry. Motorcaravan service point. Small shop open a few hours each day for basics and gas. Bar serving bar meals. Small play area with effective safety base. Off site: Sea Life Centre 2 miles. Bus (hourly) outside gate.

Open: April - end October.

Directions

Site is off the A828 on south side of Loch Creran, 6 miles north of Connel Bridge. From the south, go past Barcaldine House and site is 300 yards on right. O.S.GR: NM966420. GPS: N56:31.590 W05:18.596

Charges 2007

Per person	£ 4.20 - £ 6.60
child (6-18 yrs)	£ 2.05 - £ 2.15
non-member pitch fee	£ 5.65

UK7790 Invercoe Caravan & Camping Park

Invercoe, Glencoe PH49 4HP (Argyll and Bute)

Tel: **01855 811210**. Email: **holidays@invercoe.co.uk**

On the edge of Loch Leven, surrounded by mountains and forest, Iain and Lynn Brown are continually developing this attractively located park in its magnificent historical setting. It provides 63 pitches for caravans, motorcaravans or tents on level grass (can be a bit wet in bad weather) with gravel access roads (some hardstandings). You choose your own numbered pitch, those at the loch side being very popular. The only rules imposed are necessary for safety because the owners prefer their guests to feel free and enjoy themselves. There is much to do for the active visitor with hill walking, climbing, boating, pony riding and sea loch or fresh water fishing in this area of outstanding natural beauty. This is a park you will want to return to again and again.

Facilities

The well refurbished toilet block can be heated. Dishwashing under-cover, excellent laundry facilities with a drying room. New large under-cover eating area. Motorcaravan service point comprising multi-drainage point, fresh water, dustbins, and chemical disposal point. Shop (Easter - end Oct). Play area with swings. Fishing. Off site: The village with pub and restaurant is within walking distance. Visitors' Centre at Glencoe 2 miles. Bicycle hire 2 miles. Golf 3 miles.

Open: All year.

Directions

Follow A82 Crianlarich - Fort William road to Glencoe village and turn onto the B863; park is 0.5 miles along, well signed. O.S.GR: NN098594. GPS: N56:41.194 W05:06.359

Charges 2007

Per unit incl. 2 persons and electricity	£ 17.00
extra person	£ 3.00
child (3-15 yrs)	£ 1.00
awning	£ 2.00

Senior citizens less £1 per person outside July/Aug.

INVERCOE CARAVAN and CAMPING PARK
GLENCOE

A family owned park set amidst spectacular scenery on the shores of Loch Leven. An ideal base for exploring the West Highlands. The park has excellent toilets and wash-up facilities & fully serviced laundrette. Level grassy and hard standing pitches with ample hook-ups available. The park is a short 5 minute stroll from the village of Glencoe. Open all year. Won Best Park in Scotland 2002.

Telephone: 01855 811 210 Email: holidays@invercoe.co.uk www.invercoe.co.uk

UK7860 Glendaruel Caravan Park

Glendaruel PA22 3AB (Argyll and Bute)

Tel: **01369 820267**. Email: **mail@glendaruelcaravanpark.co.uk**

Glendaruel is in South Argyll, in the area of Scotland bounded by the Kyles of Bute and Loch Fyne, yet is less than two hours by road from Glasgow and serviced by ferries from Gourock and the Isle of Bute. There is also a service between Tarbert and Portavadie. Set in the peaceful wooded gardens of the former Glendaruel House in a secluded glen surrounded by the Cowal hills, it makes an ideal centre for touring this beautiful area. The park takes 35 units on numbered hardstandings with electricity connections (10A), plus 15 tents, on flat oval meadows bordered by over 50 different varieties of mature trees. In a separate area are 28 privately owned holiday homes and 2 for rent. The converted stables of the original house provide an attractive little shop selling basics, local produce, venison, salmon, wines (some Scottish!) and tourist gifts. Glendaruel is a park for families with young children or for older couples to relax and to enjoy the beautiful views across the Sound of Bute from Tighnabruaich or the botanical gardens which flourish in the climate. The Craig family provides a warm welcome and will advise you where to eat and what to do – they are justifiably proud of their park and its beautiful environment.

Facilities

The toilet block is ageing but it is kept very neat and tidy and can be heated. Washing machine and dryer. A covered area has picnic tables for use in bad weather and dishwashing sinks. Shop (hours may be limited in low season). Gas available. Games room with pool table, table tennis and video games. Behind the laundry is a children's play centre for under 12s and additional play field. Fishing. Torches advised. Off site: Sea fishing and boat slipway 5 miles, adventure centre (assault courses, abseiling and rafting) and sailing school close. Golf 12 miles.

Open: 28 March - 26 October.

Directions

Entrance is off A886 road 13 miles south of Strachur. Alternatively there are two ferry services from Gourock to Dunoon, then on B836 which joins the A886 about 4 miles south of the park - this route not recommended for touring caravans. Note: the park has discount arrangements with Western Ferries so contact the park before making arrangements (allow 7 days for postage of tickets). O.S.GR: NS001865. GPS: N56:02.038 W05:12.770

Charges 2007

Per unit	£ 12.00 - £ 16.00
tent	£ 6.00 - £ 13.00

Special weekly rates and senior citizen discount outside July/Aug.

UK7060 Tantallon Caravan Park

Dunbar Road, North Berwick EH39 5NJ (East Lothian)

Tel: **01620 893348**. Email: **tantallon@meadowhead.co.uk**

Tantallon is a large park with views over the Firth of Forth and the Bass Rock, which is a popular venue for bird-watchers with its world famous gannet colony. Tantallon and Dirleton Castles are also nearby. Access to the beach is through the golf course and then down the road or via cliff paths. The park has 147 quite large, grass touring pitches in two lower, more sheltered areas (Law Park), with the rest having good views at the top (Bass Park). Many have some degree of slope. There are 75 electrical connections (15A) and 10 pitches also with water and waste water. Each area has its own sanitary facilities, the top block a little way from the end pitches. About 55 caravan holiday homes for sale or hire are in their own areas. This a mature, well managed park with good facilities.

Facilities

Bass Park has 8 unisex units with shower, washbasin and toilet. The other areas have open washbasins. Two heated units for disabled visitors. Dishwashing sinks. Good launderette with spin dryer and free iron. Motorcaravan service point. Reception combines with a small shop. Games room with pool table and TV. Internet access. Good playground and better than average putting green. Dogs are only accepted by prior arrangement. Off site: Golf next door, sea fishing, safe sandy beaches in walking distance. Town (with footpath) 1 mile. Riding 5 miles. Bicycle hire 1 mile.

Open: 20 March - 31 October.

Directions

Park is beside the A198 just to the east of North Berwick, which lies between Edinburgh and Dunbar. O.S.GR: NT567850. GPS: N56:03.345 W02:41.450

Charges 2007

Per pitch	£ 12.00 - £ 17.00
with electricity	£ 14.00 - £ 19.00
with full services	£ 16.00 - £ 21.00
dog	£ 2.50

UK7065 Belhaven Bay Caravan & Camping Park

Belhaven Bay, West Barns, Dunbar EH42 1TU (East Lothian)

Tel: **01368 865956**. Email: **belhaven@meadowhead.co.uk**

Located in the John Muir Country Park, Belhaven Bay Caravan Park is just one mile from the historic town of Dunbar, where the ancient castle ruin stands guard over the town's twin harbours. This is an excellent family park with easy access to the beach and to the cliff-top trail which has spectacular views capturing the beauty of the countryside and seascapes. The park's 67 caravan holiday homes (7 for rent) are located quite separately from the touring and tent areas. These are surrounded by mature trees and are arranged in large open bays. There are 27 reasonably level, mostly grass touring pitches with 10A electricity connections. Two separate areas accommodate 25 pitches for tents. There is much to see nearby with Dunbar's Lifeboat and underground museums, golf courses, a local smokery and the Belhaven Brewery. Attractions for children include the John Muir Country Park, Lauderdale Park and a tropical leisure pool. Some daytime train noise may be heard on the park.

Facilities

Facilities are central, with recently upgraded shower rooms and toilets. Laundry room. Motorcaravan service point and chemical disposal. Reception sells ice cream and cold drinks together with tourist information and internet connection (metered). Recently upgraded small shop. Play area and ball game area. Off site: Golf 1 mile. Riding and boat launching 2 miles. Bus stop at entrance.

Open: March - October.

Directions

From the A1 (north or south) exit at the roundabout west of Dunbar. Park is about 1 mile down the A1087 towards Dunbar. O.S.GR: NT655784. GPS: N55:59.806 W02:32.707

Charges 2007

Per unit incl. 2 persons	£ 10.50 - £ 19.50
extra person	£ 1.30
tent (1 person) with car	£ 6.50
dog	£ 1.20

UK6990 Mortonhall Caravan Park

38 Mortonhall Gate, Frogston Road East, Edinburgh EH16 6TJ (Edinburgh)

Tel: **0131 664 1533**. Email: **mortonhall@meadowhead.co.uk**

Mortonhall Park makes a good base to see the historic city of Edinburgh and buses to the City leave from the park entrance every ten minutes (parking in Edinburgh is not easy). Although only four miles from the city centre, Mortonhall is in quiet mature parkland, in the grounds of Mortonhall mansion, and easy to find with access off the ring road. There is room for 250 units mostly on numbered pitches on a slight slope with nothing to separate them, but marked by jockey wheel points. Over 180 places have electricity (10/16A), several with hardstanding, water and drainage as well, and there are many places for tents. The park is very popular but only part is reserved and tourists arriving early may find space. An attractive courtyard development houses a lounge bar and restaurant, open all year and to all, with good value meals in pleasant surroundings. There are mobile homes (19) and wooden family camping cabins (Wigwams) for rent.

Facilities

Two modern toilet blocks with outside, but covered dishwashing sinks, but the only cabins are in the third excellent facility at the top of the park, which has eight unisex units incorporating shower, washbasin and WC. The courtyard area provides further standard facilities and 'portacabin' type units are added for the high season to serve the large number of tents. Facilities for disabled visitors. Laundry room with washing machines and dryer. Motorcaravan services. Bar/restaurant. Self-service shop. Games and TV rooms. Table tennis. Play area. Internet access. Late arrivals area with hook-ups. Torches useful in early and late season. Security lockers. Off site: Bus from site gate. Golf courses and driving range 2 miles. Riding 2 miles. Bicycle hire 4 miles.

Open: 12 March - 4 January.

Directions

Park is well signed south of the city, 5 minutes from A720 city bypass. Take the Mortonhall exit from the Straiton junction and follow camping signs. Entrance road is alongside the Klondyke Garden Centre. O.S.GR: NT262686. GPS: N55:54.200 W03:10.800

Charges 2007

Per unit incl. 2 persons and children under 5 yrs	£ 11.25 - £ 24.00
extra person (5 yrs and over)	£ 1.50
dog	£ 2.00

UK7840 North Ledaig Caravan Park

Connel, Oban PA37 1RU (Argyll and Bute)

Tel: **01631 710291**

The views over the Sound of Mull here are magnificent and Mr and Mrs Weir have tried to ensure good views by staggering the pitches and not planting many trees. The park provides 260 pitches for caravans, motorcaravans and trailer tents only, all with electricity (10A) and 228 with hardstanding. An award winning 30 acre nature reserve with ponds and walks (strictly no dogs) to attract wildlife has been developed on land across the road. Being well organised and run, this is a quiet park which makes a good base for exploring the area and visiting the islands from Oban. A member of the Caravan Club's 'managed under contract' scheme, non-members are also very welcome.

Facilities

Sanitary block has been refurbished to a high standard. Washbasins (in cabins for ladies). Further excellent amenities include facilities for disabled visitors and babies (access by key). Laundry and dishwashing facilities. Motorcaravan service area. Licensed shop. Play area. Caravan storage. New leisure area. TV, snooker table, mini museum. Off site: Bicycle hire, golf 6 km. Buses at gate.

Open: 27 March - 31 October.

Directions

Park is about 1 mile north of Connel Bridge, on the A828 Oban - Fort William road, 7 miles from Oban. O.S.GR: NM913456. GPS: N56:28.654 W05:23.925

Charges 2007

Per pitch incl. 2 persons and electricity	£ 12.90 - £ 18.90
extra person	£ 3.50 - £ 5.00
child (5-17 yrs)	£ 1.30 - £ 2.00

UK6980 Drum Mohr Caravan Park

Levenhall, Musselburgh EH21 8JS (East Lothian)

Tel: **0131 665 6867**. Email: **bookings@drummohr.org**

This family owned, attractively laid out touring park is on the east side of Edinburgh. It is a secluded, well kept modern park which has been carefully landscaped and there are many plants, flowers and hedging. There are 120 pitches, 40 with hardstanding, for touring units of any type, well spaced out on gently sloping grass in groups of 12 or more, marked with white posts. Most have electric hook-ups and 13 are fully serviced with water and waste water connections. Managed personally by the owner, Mr Melville, this is a well run park and is a member of the Best of British group.

Facilities

The two toilet blocks are clean, attractive, of ample size and can be heated. Free hot water to washbasins (one cabin for men, two for ladies in each block) and to four external washing-up sinks. Hot water is on payment for the showers (outside the cubicle) and laundry sinks. Laundry facilities. Motorcaravan service point. Well stocked, licensed shop (gas available, bread and papers to order). Playground on sand. Excellent dog walk. Security barrier. Caravan storage. Off site: Golf course adjacent.

Open: 1 March - 31 October.

Directions

From Edinburgh follow A1 signs for Berwick on Tweed for 6-7 miles. Turn off for Wallyford and follow camp and Mining Museum signs. From south follow A1 taking junction after Tranent village (A199 Musselburgh) and follow signs. O.S.GR: NT371732. GPS: N55:57.002 W03:00.700

Charges 2007

Per unit incl. 2 persons	£ 14.00 - £ 17.00
serviced pitch	£ 17.00 - £ 20.00
extra person (over 5 yrs)	£ 2.00

UK7050 Edinburgh Caravan Club Site

35-37 Marine Drive, Edinburgh EH4 5EN (Edinburgh)

Tel: **0131 312 6874**

Situated as it is on the northern outskirts and within easy reach of the city of Edinburgh, this large, busy Caravan Club site (open to non-members) provides an ideal base for touring. Buses (numbers 8A and 28A stop just outside the gates) take you right into the centre of the city and within walking distance of many of its attractions. There are 147 large flat pitches (103 hardstandings, 12 with water tap and waste water disposal) with electric hook-ups (16A) and TV aerial and provision for 50 tents in a separate field (hook-ups available) with a covered cooking shelter and bicycle stands close by.

Facilities

Two heated, well kept toilet blocks provide washbasins in cubicles, hair and hand dryers, an en-suite room for campers with disabilities, plus a baby and toddler room. Dishwashing and vegetable preparation area. Laundry. Drying room. No shop, but milk, bread, and newspapers can be ordered. Ices and gas from reception. Fenced play area. Boules. Dog walk. Off site: Bicycle hire nearby. Health club 400 yds; ask at site for introduction card.

Open: All year.

Directions

From A720 (signed City Bypass North), turn right at Gogar roundabout onto A8 and follow international camping signs. O.S.GR: NT212768. GPS: N55:58.653 W03:15.870

Charges 2007

Per person	£ 4.40 - £ 5.50
child (5-16 yrs)	£ 1.50 - £ 2.50
pitch (non-member)	£ 10.80 - £ 14.60

UK7290 Craigtoun Meadows Holiday Park

Mount Melville, St Andrews KY16 8PQ (Fife)

Tel: **01334 475959**. Email: **craigtoun@aol.com**

This attractively laid out, quality park has individual pitches and good facilities and although outnumbered by caravan holiday homes, the touring section is an important subsidiary. Its facilities are both well designed and comprehensive. With 67 units taken on gently sloping land, caravans go on individual hardstandings with grass alongside for awnings on most pitches. All caravan pitches are large (130 sq.m) and are equipped with electricity (16A), water and drainage. There are 15 larger 'patio pitches' with summer house, barbecue patio, picnic table and chairs, partially screened. Tents are taken on a grassy meadow at one end, also with electricity available. The 157 caravan holiday homes stand round the outer parts of the site; 27 are owned and let by the park. Buses pass the entrance and Craigtoun park with boating pond and miniature railway, etc. Is within walking distance. This is a well run park, two miles from St Andrews with its golf courses and long, sandy beaches, from where there is a picturesque view of St Andrews and its ruined Abbey and Castle.

Facilities

An excellent, de-luxe, centrally heated sanitary building serves the touring area. All washbasins are in cabins and each toilet has its own basin. Showers are unisex, as are two bathrooms, with hand and hair dryers. Facilities for disabled people and babies. Dishwashing room. Launderette. Shop and licensed restaurant (both restricted hours in low seasons), also providing takeaway. Games room. Well equipped playground, play field and 8 acres of woodland. Barbecue area. Tennis. Information room. Dogs and other pets are not accepted. Off site: Golf or bicycle hire 1.5 miles. Fishing 5 miles. Riding 6 miles.

Open: 15 March - 15 November.

Directions

From M90 junction 8 take A91 to St Andrews. Just after sign for Guardbridge (to left, A919), turn right at site sign and sign for Strathkinness. Go through village, over crossroads at end of village, left at next crossroads, then 0.75 miles to park. O.S.GR: NO482151. GPS: N56:19.477 W02:50.247

Charges 2007

Per unit	£ 18.00 - £ 24.50
tent	£ 18.00

Only 'breathable' type groundsheets may be used in awnings.

UK7000 Strathclyde Country Park Caravan Site

Strathclyde Country Park, 366 Hamilton Road, Motherwell ML1 3ED (North Lanarkshire)

Tel: **01698 266155**. Email: **strathclydepark@northlan.gov.uk**

The 1,200 acre Country Park is a large green area less than 15 miles from the centre of Glasgow. Well kept and open to all, it provides nature trails, children's adventure play area, sandy beaches and coarse fishing, with an 18-hole golf course two miles away. In addition there is a large water sports centre offering sailing, water skiing, windsurfing, canoeing, rowing (all with craft for hire), a water bus, a selection of family 'fun boats' and bicycle hire, plus Scotland's own theme park nearby. The touring site, part of the park, is suitable for both overnight or longer stays (max. 14 days) and has 80 numbered pitches for caravans or tents, 70 with electrical connections (10A). Arranged in semicircular groups on flat grass they are served by made-up access roads and the site is well lit. As it is close to the motorway, there may be some traffic noise.

Facilities

Four solidly built toilet blocks make a good provision. Enclosed sinks for dishwashing or food preparation. Laundry in two blocks (irons from reception). Block 4 has facilities for visitors with disabilities, block 3 has a baby changing room. Motorcaravan services. Shop within reception sells basic provisions. Play equipment. Bicycle hire. American motorhomes accepted up to 22 ft. Barrier card and toilet block key £10 deposit. Off site: Bar and restaurant facilities (100 yds) in the Country Park. Fishing 400 yards. Bus 1 mile.

Open: Easter - 18 October.

Directions

Take exit 5 from the M74 and follow sign for Strathclyde Country Park. Turn first left for site. O.S.GR: NS720584. GPS: N55:48.235 W04:02.804

Charges 2007

Per caravan pitch incl. 2 persons and electricity	£ 13.00
tent pitch (4 persons)	£ 8.70
extra person	£ 1.25
child	£ 1.00

No credit cards.

277

Scotland

UK7220 The Gart Caravan Park

Stirling Road, Callander FK17 8LE (Perth and Kinross)

Tel: **01877 330002**. Email: **enquiries@theholidaypark.co.uk**

Gart Caravan Park is situated within the Loch Lomond and Trossachs National Park, just a mile from the centre of Callander. Surrounded by mature trees, this attractive, family run park is peaceful and spacious. All is kept in a pristine condition and a very warm welcome awaits on arrival with a superb information pack given to all. The 128 all grass touring pitches are reasonably level, open plan and marked, with electricity (10A), water and drain. Tents or pup tents are not accepted, groundsheets are not permitted. Privately owned caravan holiday homes are located away from the touring section near the river which runs for 200 m. along the park boundary. There is some daytime road noise.

Facilities

Modern heated facilities are kept spotlessly clean with toilets and showers. Separate facilities for disabled visitors. Laundry facilities. Motorcaravan service point. Gas sales. No shop, but a breakfast car at 09.00 sells papers and basics. Play field. Adventure play area. Fishing (not on Sundays). Max. two dogs. Off site: Golf, bicycle hire 1 mile. Riding 6 miles.

Open: 1 April - 15 October.

Directions

From the south take M9. Near Stirling, leave at exit 10 and follow A84 through Doune. Park is on the left, 1 mile before Callander town centre. O.S.GR: NN643070. GPS: N56:14.190 W04:11.346

Charges 2007

Per pitch incl. services	£ 18.00
awning	£ 1.50
Reduced rates for the over 50s.	

UK7230 Trossachs Holiday Park

Aberfoyle FK8 3SA (Perth and Kinross)

Tel: **01877 382614**. Email: **info@trossachsholidays.co.uk**

Nestling on the side of a hill, three miles south of Aberfoyle, this is an excellent base for touring this famously beautiful area. Lochs Lomond, Ard, Venachar and others are within easy reach, as are the Queen Elizabeth Forest Park and, of course, the Trossachs. This park specialises in the sale and hire of top class mountain bikes. Very neat and tidy, there are 45 well laid out and marked pitches arranged on terraces with hardstanding. All have electricity and TV connections and most also have water and drainage. There is also a large area for tents. You will receive a warm welcome from Joe and Hazel Norman at this well run, family park. A member of the Best of British group.

Facilities

Sanitary facilities provide a satisfactory supply of toilets, showers and washbasins, the ladies' area being rather larger, with two private cabins. Laundry room. Well stocked shop and bike shop. Games room with TV. Play equipment. Off site: Nearby golf, boat launching and fishing (3 miles). A passport scheme arranged with a local leisure centre (10 miles, 8 passes) for swimming, sauna, solarium, badminton, tennis, windsurfing, etc.

Open: 1 March - 31 October.

Directions

Park is 3 miles south of Aberfoyle on the A81 road, well signed. O.S.GR: NS544976. GPS: N56:08.408 W04:21.330

Charges 2007

Per unit incl. 2 persons and electricity	£ 14.00 - £ 18.00
with all services	£ 16.00 - £ 20.00
extra person	£ 2.00

UK7270 Auchterarder Caravan Park

Nether Coul, Auchterarder PH3 1ET (Perth and Kinross)

Tel: **01764 663119**. Email: **info@prestonpark.co.uk**

This is a charming small park, purpose designed and landscaped by the owners Stuart and Susie Robertson. It is in a sheltered position and within walking distance of the village (1 mile). The 21 original pitches, all with electricity (6A) and hardstanding, 12 with drainage, are well spaced around the edge of the elongated, level grass park. Marked pitches with grass frontage back on to raised banks which are planted with trees. Further pitches have been developed to one side of the site, along with a trout fishing pond and a woodland walk.There is easy access from the nearby A9 road which does create some background road noise, although it is peaceful at night.

Facilities

Toilet facilities (with key system) include controllable, well equipped hot showers. A toilet for disabled people is provided in both the male and female units. Laundry room with sink and washing machine; an iron can be provided. Dishwashing is under cover. Caravan storage. Off site: Village 1 mile. Golf 1 mile. Bicycle hire and riding 4 miles. The historic cities of Perth and Stirling.

Open: All year.

Directions

Park is between the A9 and A824 roads east of Auchterarder village, only 2 miles from the main road. It is reached by turning on to the B8062 (Dunning) road from the A824. O.S.GR: NN964138. GPS: N56:18.260 W03:40.570

Charges 2008

Per unit incl. up to 4 persons	£ 11.50 - £ 13.00
No credit cards.	

UK7280 Nether Craig Caravan Park

By Alyth, Blairgowrie PH11 8HN (Perth and Kinross)

Tel: **01575 560204**. Email: **nethercraig@lineone.net**

Nether Craig is a family run touring park, attractively designed and beautifully landscaped, with views across the Strathmore valley to the long range of the Sidlaw hills. The 40 large pitches are accessed from a circular, gravel road; 26 have hardstanding (for awnings too) and 10A electrical connections. The majority are level and there are 9 large tent pitches on flat grass. There is a personal welcome for all visitors at the attractive wooden chalet beside the entrance (with a slope for wheelchairs) which doubles as reception and shop providing the necessary essentials, gas and tourist information. A one mile circular woodland walk from the park has picnic benches and a leaflet guide is provided. Otherwise you can just enjoy the peace of the Angus Glens by hill walking, birdwatching, fishing or pony trekking. Alyth with its Arthurian connections is only 4 miles away and Glamis Castle, the childhood home of the Queen Mother, is nearby, as is the beautiful Glenshee and Braemar with its castle.

Facilities

The central, purpose built toilet block is modern, well equipped and maintained, and can be heated. Unit for disabled visitors (entry by key). Separate sinks for dishwashing and clothes are in the laundry room (metered hot water), plus a washing machine, dryer and iron, and clothes line. Shop. Play area. Small football field. Bicycle hire. Caravan storage. Off site: Fishing 2 miles. Riding 4 miles. Golf within 4 miles. Boat launching 6 miles.

Open: 15 March - 31 October.

Directions

From A926 Blairgowrie - Kirriemuir road, at roundabout south of Alyth join B954 (Glenisla). Follow caravan signs for 4 miles and turn right onto unclassified road (Nether Craig). Park is on left after 0.5 miles. O.S.GR: NO265528. GPS: N56:39.684 W03:11.988

Charges 2008

Per unit incl. 2 persons and electricity	£ 14.00 - £ 16.00
tent per person	£ 7.00
extra person	£ 1.50 - £ 5.00

UK7295 The River Tilt Park

Golf Course Road, Blair Atholl, Pitlochry PH18 5TB (Perth and Kinross)

Tel: **01796 481467**. Email: **stuart@rivertilt.co.uk**

This good quality, family owned park is set on the banks of the River Tilt, a short walk from the village of Blair Atholl, where the 16th Century Blair Castle stands proud. There are 51 caravan holiday homes including 3 for rent. Two central areas have been set aside for touring caravans, motorcaravans and tents, with 31 pitches mostly with hardstanding. Divided by mature shrubs and hedges, all have 10A electricity connections, 18 have water and a drain. One of the areas is reserved for dog owners and their pets. The Steadings Spa provides an indoor pool, solarium, steam room, spa pool and gym, plus Waves hair salon. Also open to the public, there are charges for these facilities. The park also has an award winning restaurant. Adjacent are a riverside walk and a golf course. There may be some noise from the railway line that runs alongside the park.

Facilities

The purpose built toilet block is centrally situated (with key entry) and provides en-suite toilet and washbasin cabins and individual large preset showers, one suitable for disabled visitors. Baby facilities. Well equipped laundry. Motorcaravan service point. Bar and restaurant. Leisure spa complex with indoor pool, etc. Hair salon. Tennis. Max. 2 dogs per pitch. No ball games. Off site: Private fishing and golf adjacent. Bicycle hire and riding 1 mile. Pitlochry with its famous salmon leap 6 miles. Bus or train from Blair Atholl.

Open: 17 March - 13 November.

Directions

From the A9 just north of Pitlochry, take B8079 into Blair Atholl and follow signs for River Tilt. O.S.GR: NN874655.

Charges 2007

Per unit incl. 2 persons	£ 10.00 - £ 16.00
incl. electricity	£ 12.00 - £ 18.00
extra person	£ 1.00
dog	£ 2.00

UK7300 Blair Castle Caravan Park

Blair Atholl, Pitlochry PH18 5SR (Perth and Kinross)

Tel: **01796 481263**. Email: **mail@blaircastlecaravanpark.co.uk**

This attractive, well kept park is set in the grounds of Blair Castle, the traditional home of the Dukes of Atholl. It has a wonderful feeling of spaciousness with a large central area left free for children's play or for general use. There is space for 280 touring units with 190 electricity connections (10/16A), 144 hardstandings and 60 fully serviced pitches with water and waste water facilities also. Caravan holiday homes, 78 privately owned and 27 for hire, are in separate areas. A quality park, quiet at night and well managed. The castle is open to the public, its 32 fully furnished rooms showing a picture of Scottish life from the 16th century to the present day, while the beautiful grounds and gardens are free to those staying on site. The castle grounds provide many walking trails and the village is within walking distance with hotels, shops, a water mill craft centre and folk museum.

Facilities

The five toilet blocks can be heated and are of excellent quality and very clean. Large hot showers, some incorporating WC and washbasin, and further cubicles with WC and washbasin. Facilities for disabled visitors with bath or shower, WCs and washbasins. Baby changing mats. Dishwashing. Motorcaravan service point. Reception, shop, games room, laundry and internet gallery. Gas supplies. American motorhomes are accepted (max. 30 ft. or 5 tons). Off site: Mountain bike hire, riding, golf and fishing within 1 mile.

Open: 1 March - 27 November.

Directions

From A9 just north of Pitlochry take B8079 into Blair Atholl. Park is in grounds of Blair Castle, well signed. O.S.GR: NN868659. GPS: N56:46.050 W03:50.644

Charges 2007

Per unit incl. 2 persons	£ 13.50 - £ 16.00
tent (no car)	£ 13.50 - £ 16.00
child (6-14 yrs)	£ 1.20 - £ 1.50
electricity	£ 3.00
dog (max. 2)	£ 1.00

UK7305 Tummel Valley Holiday Park

Tummel Bridge, Pitlochry PH16 5SA (Perth and Kinross)

Tel: **01882 634221**. Email: **enquiries@parkdeanholidays.co.uk**

Set in the Tay Forest Park on the banks of the River Tummel, this large family holiday park is part of the Parkdean Group. Divided into two areas by the roadway, the main emphasis is on chalets to let on the side that overlooks the river. Privately owned caravan holiday homes and touring pitches are on the other, quieter side. The 36 touring pitches, open plan with hardstanding, electricity hook-up and a shared water point, overlook a small fishing lake which is an added attraction for all the family. The leisure complex with indoor and outdoor activities is on the river side, as is the reception office. On arrival, you should turn right and park, then cross back to book in.

Facilities

The very clean toilet block has vanity style washbasins, preset showers and a bathroom in each section. Good facilities for disabled visitors. Well equipped laundry. Chemical disposal but no motorcaravan service point. Shop. Riverside entertainment complex with bar with terrace, restaurant and takeaway. Indoor heated pool and toddlers' splash pool. Solarium and sauna. Amusements. Separate area with pool tables. All weather sports court. Adventure play area. Crazy golf. Nature trails. Bicycle hire. Fishing. Note: all venues are non-smoking. Max. 2 dogs per unit. Off site: Golf and riding 10 miles. Buses leave near park entrance.

Open: 24 March - 1 November.

Directions

Travel through Pitlochry. After 2 miles turn left on B8019 to Tummel Bridge (10 miles). Park is on both the left and right. Tourers should turn right and park, then return to reception on the left. O.S.GR: NN764590.

Charges 2007

Per pitch	£ 12.50 - £ 29.50

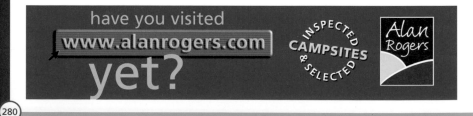

UK7310 Twenty Shilling Wood Caravan Park

Comrie PH6 2JY (Perth and Kinross)

Tel: **01764 670411**. Email: **alowe20@aol.com**

Everyone gets a warm welcome from the Lowe family when they arrive at Twenty Shilling Wood. Set amongst 10.5 acres of wooded hillside, this unusual park has a few touring pitches for caravans and motorcaravans (no tents), plus a number of owner occupied caravan holiday homes. However, with terracing and landscaping, not many of these are visible and flowering trees and shrubs help to hide them. There are just 16 level touring pitches on gravel with grass bays between them, all with electricity hook-ups (10A). Television reception is very poor.

Facilities

Clean and spacious toilet blocks have some washbasins in cubicles. Dishwashing area and laundry. No shop but rolls, milk and papers can be ordered at reception. Games room and lounge area with library. Fenced adventure playground. Entrance barrier (£10 deposit for card). Only two dogs per pitch. Off site: Buses pass the gate. Comrie is 1 mile. Golf or fishing within 1 mile. Riding or bicycle hire 6 miles. Crieff 7 miles. Watersports 11 miles.

Open: 23 March - 20 October.

Directions

Park is on north side of A85 Crieff - Lochearnhead road, about 0.75 miles west of B827 junction, 0.5 miles west of Comrie. O.S.GR: NN762222. GPS: N56:22.513 W04:00.390

Charges 2007

Per unit incl. 2 persons, electricity and TV hook-up	£ 15.50
extra person (over 2 yrs)	£ 1.75

UK7320 Witches Craig Caravan Park

Blairlogie, Stirling FK9 5PX (Stirling)

Tel: **01786 474947**. Email: **info@witchescraig.co.uk**

Witches Craig is a neat and tidy park, nestling under the Ochil Hills and the friendly Stephen family take each visitor to their pitch to make sure that they are happy. All 60 pitches have electrical hook-ups (10A) and 26 have hardstanding, 7 of these being large (taking American style motorhomes easily). Reasonably level, the park covers five well maintained acres with the grass beautifully manicured. Seven residential park homes are well kept and surrounded by flowering shrubs. Being by the A91, there is some daytime road noise but trees have been planted to try to minimise this.

Facilities

The modern, heated toilet block is well maintained, and includes one cubicle with washbasin and WC each for ladies and men. Free controllable showers. Baby bath and mat. Good unit for disabled campers. Dishwashing sinks. Laundry facilities. Bread, milk, drinks and papers are available daily (supermarket 2.5 miles). Large fenced play area. Field for games. Off site: Riding or bicycle hire 2 miles, fishing 3 miles, golf 1 mile. Buses stop at the park entrance. Castles, museums, cathedrals and parks.

Open: 1 April - 31 October.

Directions

Park is on the A91, 2 miles northeast of Stirling. O.S.GR: NS822968. GPS: N56:08.882 W03:53.920

Charges 2007

Per unit incl. 2 persons	£ 12.50 - £ 14.50
incl. electricity	£ 14.50 - £ 16.50
extra person	£ 2.00
child (2-13 yrs)	£ 1.00
awning (no groundsheet)	£ 2.00

£5 deposit for key to facilities. No credit cards.

UK7240 Lomond Woods Holiday Park

Tullichewan, Old Luss Road, Balloch G83 8QP (West Dunbartonshire)

Tel: **01389 755000**. Email: **lomondwoods@holiday-parks.co.uk**

A series of improvements over the last few years has made this one of the top parks in Scotland. Almost, but not quite, on the banks of Loch Lomond, this landscaped, well planned park is suitable for both transit or longer stays. Formerly known as Tullichewan Holiday Park, it takes 110 touring units on well spaced, numbered pitches on flat or gently sloping grass. Most have hardstanding, all have electrical connections (10A) and 27 have water and waste water too. This is a well run park, open all year, with very helpful wardens and reception staff.

Facilities

The single large heated, well kept toilet block includes some showers with WCs, baths for ladies, a shower room for disabled visitors and two baby baths. Covered dishwashing sinks. Launderette. Motorcaravan service points. Games room with TV. Playground. Caravan storage. American motorhomes accepted with prior notice. Off site: Restaurants in Balloch. Fishing and boat launching 400 yards. Riding 4 miles. Golf 5 miles.

Open: All year.

Directions

Turn off A82 road 17 miles northwest of Glasgow on A811 Stirling road. Site is in Balloch at southern end of Loch Lomond and is well signed. O.S.GR: NS389816. GPS: N56:00.093 W04:35.534

Charges 2007

Per unit incl. 2 persons and electricity	£ 15.00 - £ 20.00
incl. services and awning	£ 17.00 - £ 22.00
extra person	£ 2.00

281

UK7530 Aden Country Park Caravan Park

Station Road, Mintlaw AB42 8FQ (Aberdeenshire)

Tel: **01771 623460**

Aden Country Park is owned by the local authority and is open to the public. The caravan and camping site is on one side of the park. Beautifully landscaped and well laid out with trees, bushes and hedges, it is kept very neat and tidy. It provides 48 numbered pitches for touring units, with varying degrees of slope (some level) and all with electrical hook-ups (16A), plus an area for tents. There are also 12 caravan holiday homes. The park is in a most attractive area and one could spend plenty of time enjoying all it has to offer. Attractions for visitors include an Agricultural Heritage Centre, Wildlife Centre, Nature Trail and restaurant, as well as open and woodland areas with a lake, for walking and recreation.

Facilities

The modern toilet block is clean, with good facilities for disabled visitors. It can be heated and provides free, preset hot showers, hairdryer for ladies, and a baby bath, but no private cabins. Dishwashing and laundry facilities (metered). Motorcaravan service point. Gas supplies. Small shop in reception area. Restaurant in the Heritage Centre. Games areas. Play equipment (safety surfaces). Dog exercise area. Off site: Shops in Mintlaw 0.5 miles. Fishing 1 mile. Riding 2 miles.

Open: Easter - 25 October.

Directions

Approaching Mintlaw from west on A950 road, park is shortly after sign for Mintlaw station. From east, go to the western outskirts of village and entrance is on left – Aden Country Park and Farm Heritage Centre. O.S.GR: NJ985484.
GPS: N57:31.485 W02:01.567

Charges 2007

Per unit incl. 2 persons	
and electricity	£ 13.40 - £ 15.00
tent (2 persons)	£ 6.40 - £ 7.10
awning	£ 2.00

UK7550 Huntly Castle Caravan Park

The Meadow, Huntly AB54 4UJ (Aberdeenshire)

Tel: **01466 794999**. Email: **enquiries@huntlycastle.co.uk**

Huntly Caravan Park was opened in '95 and its hard-working owners, the Ballantynes, are justly proud of their neat, well landscaped 15 acre site that is managed under contract for the Caravan Club (non-members welcome). The 76 level grass and 41 hardstanding touring pitches are separated and numbered, with everyone shown to their pitch. Arranged in three bays with banks of heathers and flowering shrubs separating them, 66 pitches have electric hook-ups (16A) and 15 are fully serviced with water and waste water. Two bays have central play areas and all three have easy access to a toilet block, as has the camping area. Campers are provided with a covered cooking shelter (with work tops) should the weather turn inclement. The park also has 33 privately owned caravan holiday homes (3 to hire). An Activity Centre near the entrance contains two indoor safe play areas (one for up to 2 yrs old, the other up to height 1.37 metres). There are snooker and pool tables, table tennis, badminton and short tennis. The area abounds with things to do, from forest trails to walk or cycle, a falconry centre, malt whisky distilleries and an all year Nordic ski track. A member of the Best of British group.

Facilities

The three heated toilet blocks are well designed and maintained, with washbasins (in cubicles for ladies) and large showers. Each block also has a family shower room, dishwashing sinks and a room for disabled visitors. Laundry room. Milk and papers may be ordered at reception. Activity centre (charged and facilities are also open to the public; open weekends and all local school holidays). Off site: Huntly is 10 minutes walk. Fishing, golf or bicycle hire within 1 mile. Riding 5 miles.

Open: 31 March - 29 October.

Directions

Site is well signed from A96 Keith - Aberdeen road. O.S.GR: NJ526402. GPS: N57:27.123 W02:47.496

Charges 2008

Per unit incl. 2 persons	
and electricity	£ 14.50 - £ 18.00
extra person	£ 4.50
child (5-16 yrs)	£ 1.30 - £ 2.15
awning	£ 1.95

UK7540 Aberlour Gardens Caravan & Camping Park

Aberlour-on-Spey AB38 9LD (Moray)

Tel: **01340 871586**. Email: **Aberlourgardens@aol.com**

This pleasant park is within the large walled garden of the Aberlour Estate on Speyside. The owners have made many improvements to the sheltered, five acre, family run park which provides a very natural setting amidst spruce and Scots pine. Of the 73 level pitches, 35 are for touring units leaving the remainder for holiday homes (2 for rent) and seasonal units. All pitches have electrical connections (10A) and 9 are 'all-weather' pitches. This is an ideal area for walking, birdwatching, salmon fishing and pony trekking or for following the only 'Malt Whisky Trail' in the world, while Aberlour has a fascinating old village shop – a time capsule.

Facilities

The ladies toilet block has been refurbished. The mens is traditional in style (there are plans for refurbishment) with four large showers. Facilities for visitors with disabilities can also be used as family or baby changing room. Laundry facilities. Motorcaravan service point. Small licensed shop stocking basics and with an information area. Play area. Caravan storage. Off site: Riding 0.5 miles. Swimming and bicycle hire 1 mile. Fishing 1 or 5 miles. Golf 4 miles.

Open: 1 March - 28 December.

Directions

Turn off A95 midway between Aberlour and Craigellachie onto unclassified road. Site signed in 500 yds. Vehicles over 10' 6" high should use the A941 Dufftown road (site signed). O.S.GR: NJ282432. GPS: N57:28.491 W03:11.916

Charges 2007

Per caravan, large tent, trailer tent incl. 2 persons	£ 13.20 - £ 16.50
motorcaravan	£ 11.50 - £ 16.50
extra person (over 5 yrs)	£ 2.00
dog	free

Tel/Fax: 01340 871586

Open: 1st March - 28th December

Tourers, Motorhomes & Campers Always Welcome.
Holiday Homes For Sale

info@aberlourgardens.co.uk

Aberlour Gardens enjoys a beautiful setting within an historic walled garden in the magnificent valley of the river Spey, and is ideally situated in the heart of the Malt Whiskey Trail & for exploring the coast of the Moray Firth to the Mountains of the Cairngorms. So if you are looking just to relax with a stroll by the river or take your bike up a mountain, all is within easy reach.

See website for special offers: www.aberlourgardens.co.uk

UK7690 Torvean Caravan Park

Glenurquhart Road, Inverness IV3 6JL (Highland)

Tel: **01463 220582**

Torvean is a small and neat, select touring park for caravans and motorhomes only. It is situated on the outskirts of Inverness beside the Caledonian Canal and is within easy reach of the town's amenities which include an ice rink, theatre and leisure sports centre. Excursions to the coast and Highlands, including Loch Ness, are possible in several directions. The pitches on level grass are clearly marked with a tarmac access road and street lighting giving a very neat appearance. There are 47 touring pitches (27 with 10A electricity connections, 18 fully serviced with fresh water tap, waste water disposal and electricity).

Facilities

Two heated toilet blocks are of good quality – ladies have two cubicles with washbasin and toilet and a hair washing cubicle. Controllable hot showers on payment. Suite for disabled people with toilet and shower over a bath. Launderette. Motorcaravan service point. Gas supplies. Play area. Only one dog per unit is accepted. Off site: Golf adjacent, bicycle hire or fishing 3 miles.

Open: Easter - end October.

Directions

Park is off the main A82 road on the southwest outskirts of the town on the west side of the Tomnahurich Canal Bridge (looks like a railway crossing rather than a bridge). O.S.GR: NH638438. GPS: N57:27.924 W04:14.731

Charges guide

Per unit incl. 2 persons	£ 9.00 - £ 9.50
de-luxe pitch incl. electricity	£ 12.50 - £ 13.00
extra person	£ 2.00
child (under 16 yrs)	£ 1.00
No credit cards.	

283

UK7700 Pitgrudy Caravan Park

Poles Road, Dornoch IV25 3HY (Highland)

Tel: **01862 821253**

In a rural situation, Pitgrudy has superb views over the Dornoch Firth and the surrounding Ross-shire hills. There are 40 touring pitches for caravans, motorcaravans or tents, mostly on slightly sloping grass and with electrical connections (10A). A few have hardstanding (unfortunately still on a slope) and six are fully serviced (drinking water, waste water disposal point and electricity). Located at the top of the park are 35 caravan holiday homes, of which 25 are privately owned. The whole park is on immaculately tended grass with tarmac roads. The pleasant little town of Dornoch is less than a mile away with shops, restaurants, plus the cathedral.

Facilities

Sanitary facilities are in a modern, superior 'portacabin' style unit which is very clean and well equipped. Laundry with washing machine, dryer and iron. Dishwashing sinks. Gas supplies. Off site: Safe sandy beach 1 mile. The area is good for walking and golf (there are 7 courses within 15 miles of the park). Fishing 1 mile, bicycle hire or boat launching 3 miles, riding 5 miles.

Open: 25 April - 30 September.

Directions

At the war memorial in Dornoch, turn north (park signed) on the B9168. Park is 0.5 miles on the right (45 miles north of Inverness). O.S.GR: NH795911.

Charges guide

Per unit incl. 2 persons	£ 7.50 - £ 9.00
full service pitch	£ 11.00 - £ 12.00
extra person	£ 1.50

No credit cards.

UK7710 Ardmair Point Caravan Park

Ardmair Point, Ullapool IV26 2TN (Highland)

Tel: **01854 612054**. Email: **sales@ardmair.com**

This spectacularly situated park, overlooking the little Loch Kanaird, just round the corner from Loch Broom, has splendid views all round. The 68 touring pitches are arranged mainly on grass around the edge of the bay, in front of the shingle beach. Electrical hook-ups (10A) are available and some gravel hardstandings are on the other side of the access road. Tent pitches, together with cheaper pitches for some tourers are in a large field behind the other sanitary facilities. Scuba diving is popular at Loch Kanaird because the water is so clear. Seals and otters are regularly seen in the bay.

Facilities

Two toilet blocks, both with good facilities. One block has wonderful views from the large windows in the launderette and dishwashing rooms. Large en-suite rooms for disabled people. Motorcaravan service point. Shop. Play area. Fishing. Sailing and boating (with your own boat). Off site: Ullapool for shopping 3 miles. Golf and bicycle hire 3 miles.

Open: 1 April - late September (depends on the weather).

Directions

Park is off the A835 road, 3 miles north of Ullapool. O.S.GR: NH109983. GPS: N57:56.038 W05:11.821

Charges 2007

Per unit incl. 2 persons	£ 11.00 - £ 18.00
backpacker tent with 1 person	£ 7.00

Less for 7 or more nights pre-paid.

UK7720 Woodend Camping & Caravan Park

Achnairn, Lairg IV27 4DN (Highland)

Tel: **01549 402248**

Woodend is a delightful, small park overlooking Loch Shin and perfect for hill walkers and backpackers. Peaceful and simple, it is owned and run single-handedly by Mrs Cathie Ross, who provides a wonderfully warm Scottish welcome to visitors. On a hill with open, panoramic views across the Loch to the hills beyond and all around, the large camping field is undulating and gently sloping with some reasonably flat areas. The park is licensed to take 55 units and most of the 22 electrical hook-ups (16A) are in a line near the top of the field, close to the large, fenced play area which has several items of equipment on grass. There are opportunities for fishing and hill walking.

Facilities

The sanitary facilities are of old design but kept very clean and are quite satisfactory. Laundry with two machines and a dryer. Kitchen with dishwashing sinks and eating room for tent campers. Reception is at the house, Sunday papers, daily milk and bread may be ordered. Fishing licences for the Loch (your catch will be frozen for you). Off site: Mountain bikes can be hired in Lairg, 5 miles. Several scenic golf courses within 20-30 miles.

Open: 1 April - 30 September.

Directions

Achnairn is near the southern end of Loch Shin. Turn off the A838 single track road at signs for Woodend. From the A9 coming north take the A836 at Bonar Bridge, 11 miles northwest of Tain. O.S.GR: NC558127. GPS: N58:04.816 W04:26.823

Charges guide

Per unit incl. electricity	£ 7.00 - £ 8.00
tent	£ 6.00 - £ 7.00

No credit cards.

UK7670 Grantown-on-Spey Caravan Park

Seafield Avenue, Grantown-on-Spey PH26 3JQ (Highland)

Tel: **01479 872474**. Email: **warden@caravanscotland.com**

John Fleming takes care of this excellent park. Peacefully situated on the outskirts of the town, with views of the mountains in the distance, the park consists of well-tended gravel (raked so that it is perfect for each occupant) and grass pitches. Trees and flowers are a feature of this landscaped location. There are 136 pitches for caravans or motorcaravans, of which 14 offer fresh and waste water facilities and 16 have individual fresh water taps. A further 12 pitches are used for seasonal occupation, and there is space for 50 or more tents. More than 71 pitches have 10A electrical hook-ups, WiFi internet for small charge on every pitch. There are a furthur 53 super pitches with individual water and waste hook up, 16A electric and individual Sky TV box. The wardens escort visitors to their pitch and will help to site caravans if necessary. Caravan holiday homes are located in a separate area of the park.

Facilities

New toilet and shower block complete with laundry and drying room. A further block provides good, clean toilet facilities, with new wash-cabins for ladies. Facilities for disabled visitors. Dishwashing sinks. Laundry room. Motorcaravan service point. Gas cylinders, ice creams, cold drinks and camping accessories available at reception. Games room with table tennis and pool table. Touring and motorcaravan secure storage. Off site: Fishing, golf and mountain bike hire within 1 mile. Riding 3 miles.

Open: 15 December - 31 October.

Directions

Go into the town. Turn north at Bank of Scotland. Park straight ahead half a mile. O.S.GR: NJ028283. GPS: N57:20.088 W03:37.117

Charges 2007

Per pitch incl. 2 persons and 10A electricity	£ 14.50 - £ 18.50
small 2-man tent	£ 9.50 - £ 14.00
extra person	£ 1.50 - £ 3.00

UK7680 Forest Holidays Glenmore

Aviemore PH22 1QU (Highland)

Tel: **01479 861271**. Email: **info@forestholidays.co.uk**

Forest Holidays is a partnership between the Forestry Commission and The Camping and Caravanning Club. This site is attractively laid out in a fairly informal style in several adjoining areas connected by narrow part gravel, part tarmac roads, with access to the lochside. One of these areas, the Pinewood Area, is very popular and has 32 hardstandings (some distance from the toilet block). Of the 220 marked pitches on fairly level, firm grass, 122 have electricity (16A). This site with something for everyone would be great for family holidays. The Glenmore Forest Park lies close to the sandy shore of Loch Morlich amidst conifer woods and surrounded on three sides by the impressive Cairngorm mountains. It is conveniently situated for a range of activities, including skiing (extensive lift system), orienteering, hill and mountain walking (way-marked walks), fishing (trout and pike) and non-motorised watersports on the Loch.

Facilities

New toilet and shower blocks. Next to the site is a range of amenities including a well stocked shop (open all year), a café serving a variety of meals and snacks, and a Forestry Commission visitor centre and souvenir shop. Barbecues are not permitted in dry weather. Off site: The Aviemore centre with a wide range of indoor and outdoor recreations 7 miles. Golf within 15 miles. Fishing and boat trips.

Open: All year.

Directions

Immediately south of Aviemore on B9152 (not the A9 bypass) take B970 then follow sign for Cairngorm and Loch Morlich. Site entrance is on right past the loch. O.S.GR: NH976097. GPS: N57:10.022 W03:41.683

Charges 2007

Per unit incl. 2 persons (fee for 3 nights)	£ 33.40 - £ 49.90
premium pitch	£ 42.40 - £ 58.90
Less 20% all year for disabled guests and outside 7/7-28/8 for senior citizens.	

UK7730 Scourie Caravan & Camping Park

Harbour Road, Scourie IV27 4TG (Highland)

Tel: **01971 502060**

Mr Mackenzie has carefully nurtured this park over many years, developing a number of firm terraces with well drained grass and hardstanding pitches, some with 10A electric hook-ups. A few are on an area which is unfenced from the rocks (young children would need to be supervised here). Reception, alongside the modern toilet block, contains a wealth of tourist information and maps. There are very good facilities for disabled visitors on the park and at the restaurant, although the ramps leading to them are a little steep. Mr Mackenzie claims that this is the only caravan park in the world from where, depending on the season, you can see palm trees, Highland cattle and Great Northern divers from your pitch. Red throated divers have also been seen. Trips to Handa Island (a special protection area for seabird colonies) are available from here and Tarbet. The clear water makes this area ideal for diving.

Facilities

The toilet facilities can be heated. Showers have no divider or seat. Laundry. Dishwashing sinks. Motorcaravan service point. The 'Anchorage' restaurant at the entrance to the park (used as reception at quiet times) serves meals at reasonable prices - cooked to order (I/4-30/9). Boat launching. Fishing permits can be arranged. Off site: Village with shop and post office, gas is available from the petrol station and mobile banks visit regularly.

Open: Easter or April if Easter is in March - 30 September, but phone first to check.

Directions

Park is by Scourie village on A894 road in northwest Sutherland. O.S.GR: NC153446. GPS: N58:21.085 W05:09.406

Charges 2008

Per unit incl. 1-2 persons	£ 11.00 - £ 12.00
extra person	£ 2.50
child (3-16 yrs)	£ 1.50
electricity	£ 2.00
extra tent, vehicle or awning	£ 2.50
No credit cards.	

UK7735 Sango Sands Oasis Caravan & Camping Site

Durness via Lairg IV27 4QB (Highland)

Tel: **01971 511726**. Email: **keith.durness@btinternet.com**

Sango Sands Oasis is a quiet, ten acre site overlooking the beautiful Sango Bay, a Blue Flag beach. The site was established by the family in 1978 and they have worked hard improving the facilities over the years. There are 82 pitches for tents and touring caravans, 42 with electricity hook-ups. The land is well drained and fairly level. It is possible to see whales, porpoise, dolphins and seals from the site plus a variety of sea birds which nest nearby. An ideal area for walkers, including the less adventurous, there are numerous marked paths and there is an excellent variety of angling, from rivers to the sea. The nearby Durness golf course with its superb views welcomes visitors. Smoo Cave with the waterfall down into the dramatic tidal gorge is close by and worth seeing also it is possible to visit Cape Wrath. A good value café, bar and licensed restaurant serves home cooked meals and malt whiskies and Scottish beers. There are occasional dances or discos in the bar and a TV.

Facilities

Traditional toilet and shower blocks are lit at night but a torch may be useful. Free showers with curtains. Showers and toilets are separate. With the beach so close don't be surprised to find sand in the showers. En-suite facilities for disabled visitors. Laundry with sinks, washing machines, dryers, irons and boards. Campers kitchen with cooking rings. Café, bar and licensed restaurant. TV. Games room with pool and darts. Off site: Two grocery stores, post office, ATM, petrol, diesel and gas supplies in the village. Nearby Visitor Centre with extensive information on the area.

Open: All year.

Directions

From Thurso take the North Coast road (A836 as far as Tongue, where it continues on as the A838 to Durness). Site is on the right as you go through the village. From Ullapool follow A835 north to Ledmore Junction and turn left on the A837. After 8 miles turn right onto the A894 and continue to Laxford Bridge. Turn left on A838. Durness is 19 miles further on this road. Site is on the left going through the village. O.S.GR: NC420668.

Charges 2007

Per person	£ 5.00
child (5-15 yrs)	£ 2.50
electricity	£ 2.70
No credit cards.	

UK7830 Glen Nevis Caravan & Camping Park

Glen Nevis, Fort William PH33 6SX (Highland)

Tel: **01397 702191**. Email: **camping@glen-nevis.co.uk**

Just outside Fort William in a most attractive and quiet situation with views of Ben Nevis, this spacious park is used by those on active pursuits as well as sightseeing tourists. It comprises eight quite spacious fields, divided between caravans, motorcaravans and tents (steel pegs required). It is licensed for 250 touring caravans but with no specific tent limits. The large touring pitches, many with hardstanding, are marked with wooden fence dividers, 174 with electricity (13A) and 100 also have water and drainage. The park becomes full in the peak months but there are vacancies each day. If reception is closed (possible in low season) you site yourself. There are regular security patrols at night in busy periods. The park's own modern restaurant and bar with good value bar meals is a short stroll from the park, open to all. A well managed park with bustling, but pleasing ambience, watched over by Ben Nevis. Around 1,000 acres of the Glen Nevis estate are open to campers to see the wildlife and explore this lovely area.

Facilities

The four modern toilet blocks with showers (extra showers in two blocks); and units for visitors with disabilities. An excellent block in Nevis Park (one of the eight camping fields) has some washbasins in cubicles, showers, further facilities for disabled visitors, a second large laundry room and dishwashing sinks. Motorcaravan service point. Shop (Easter - mid Oct), barbecue area and snack bar (May - mid Sept). Play area on bark. Off site: Pony trekking, golf and fishing near.

Open: 15 March - 31 October.

Directions

Turn off A82 to east at roundabout just north of Fort William following camp sign. O.S.GR: NN124723. GPS: N56:48.271 W05:04.435

Charges 2007

Per person	£ 1.60 - £ 2.50
child (5-15 yrs)	£ 0.80 - £ 1.30
pitch incl. awning	£ 4.40 - £ 12.00
serviced pitch plus	£ 2.00 - £ 3.00

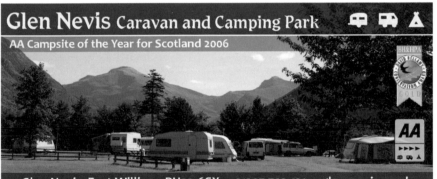

Glen Nevis Caravan and Camping Park

AA Campsite of the Year for Scotland 2006

Glen Nevis, Fort William, PH33 6SX - 01397 702 191 - glen-nevis.co.uk

UK7760 Reraig Caravan Site

Balmacara, Kyle of Lochalsh IV40 8DH (Highland)

Tel: **01599 566215**. Email: **warden@reraig.com**

This is a small, level park close to Loch Alsh with a wooded hillside behind (criss-crossed with woodland walks). Set mainly on well cut grass, it is sheltered from the prevailing winds by the hill and provides just 45 numbered pitches, 36 with electrical connections (10A) and 25 hardstandings. Large tents and trailer tents are not accepted at all. Small tents are permitted at the discretion of the owner, so it is advisable to telephone first. Awnings are not permitted during July and August in order to protect the grass. The ground can be stony so there could be a problem with tent pegs.

Facilities

The single sanitary block has been extensively refurbished and is kept immaculately clean. Children have their own low basins, controllable hot showers are on payment (10p for 2 minutes). Sinks for clothes and dishwashing. Use of a spin dryer is free. A slope replaces the small step into the ladies and sink rooms. Motorcaravan drainage point. Off site: Balmacara Hotel (with bar) adjacent, shop (selling gas), sub-post office and off licence.

Open: 1 May - 30 September.

Directions

Take A87 towards Kyle of Lochalsh. Park is signed very soon after sign for Balmacara, on the right just before Balmacara hotel. O.S.GR: NG815272. GPS: N57:16.988 W05:37.591

Charges 2007

Per unit incl. 2 persons	£ 11.00
extra person (13 yrs or over)	£ 2.00
awning (May, June, Sept only)	£ 3.00
electricity (10A)	£ 1.30

287

UK7800 Resipole Farm Caravan & Camping Park

Loch Sunart, Acharacle PH36 4HX (Highland)

Tel: **01967 431235**. Email: **info@resipole.co.uk**

This quiet, open park is marvellously set on the banks of Loch Sunart, 8 miles from Strontian, on the Ardnamurchan peninsula. It is a must for anyone seeking peace and tranquillity and really worth the journey. With views across the water and regularly visited by wild deer, Resipole Farm offers a good base for exploring the whole of this scenic area or, more locally, for fishing, boating (launching from the site's own slipway) and walking in the unspoilt countryside. There are 48 level and well drained touring pitches here, 40 with electric hook-ups (10/16A). Tents are sited by the hedges.

Facilities

The central, modern sanitary block can be heated and is kept very clean. Good dishwashing facilities. Excellent provision for visitors with disabilities. Laundry facilities. Motorcaravan service point. Caravan storage. Art gallery and studios. Off site: Riding 5 miles.

Open: Easter or 1 April - 31 October.

Directions

From A82 Fort William road, take Corran ferry (6 miles north of Ballachulish, 9 miles south of Fort William). Leaving ferry, turn south on A861. Park is on north bank of Loch Sunart, 8 miles west of Strontian. Single track for 8 miles to Resipole. O.S.GR: NM676740. GPS: N56:42.656 W05:43.213

Charges 2007

Per unit incl. 2 persons	£ 11.00 - £ 13.00
extra person	£ 3.00
serviced pitch incl. electricity	£ 13.00 - £ 15.00

UK7850 Linnhe Lochside Holidays

Corpach, Fort William PH33 7NL (Highland)

Tel: **01397 772376**. Email: **relax@linnhe-lochside-holidays.co.uk**

This quiet well run park has a very peaceful situation overlooking Loch Eil, and it is beautifully landscaped with wonderful views. There are individual pitches with hardstanding for 65 touring units (12 seasonal) on terraces leading down to the water's edge. They include 32 with electricity connection (16A), water and drainaway, plus 30 with electricity only (10A). A separate area on the lochside takes 15 small tents (no reservation). There are also 60 caravan holiday homes and 14 centrally heated pine chalets for hire. Fishing is free on Loch Eil and you are welcome to fish from the park's private beach or bring your own boat and use the slipway and dinghy park.

Facilities

Toilet facilities are excellent, heated in the cooler months and include baths (£1). Dishwashing room. First class laundry and outdoor drying room (charged per night). Self-service, licensed shop (end May - end Sept). Gas supplies. Barbecue area. Toddlers' play room and two well equipped play areas. Large motorhomes accepted but it is best to book first. Caravan storage. Max. two dogs per pitch. Off site: Bicycle hire 2.5 miles. Riding, golf 5 miles.

Open: 20 March - 31 October.

Directions

Park entrance is off A830 Fort William - Mallaig road, 1 mile west of Corpach. O.S.GR: NN072772. GPS: N56:50.869 W05:09.615

Charges 2007

Per person	£ 2.00
pitch	£ 11.00 - £ 14.50
tent	£ 7.50 - £ 10.50
dog (max. 2, not on tent pitches)	£ 1.00

UK7920 Laxdale Holiday Park

6 Laxdale Lane, Stornoway HS2 0DR (Isle of Lewis)

Tel: **01851 706966**. Email: **info@laxdaleholidaypark.com**

Whilst not in the most scenic of locations, this good park is well placed for touring. Surrounded by trees, it is on the edge of Stornaway (ferry port) and is well laid out with a tarmac road running through the centre. A level hardstanding area for touring caravans has 14 electricity hook-ups plus 2 for tents and a grassy area for the tents gently slopes away to the trees and boundary. There are 5 holiday caravans and a self catering holiday bungalow available for rent on the site, plus a bunkhouse. The site is centrally situated in an ideal spot for touring the Isle of Lewis.

Facilities

The well maintained and modern toilet block is heated. Good (but narrow) showers with dividing curtain (50p). Well equipped laundry. Indoor sink for dishwashing with hot water. Telephone. Off site: Bus stop 200 m. The busy fishing port of Stornoway has a comprehensive range of shops and restaurants. New sports centre with swimming pool. Library with free internet access.

Open: 1 April - 31 October.

Directions

From Stornoway take the A857 for 1 mile then take the second turning on the left past the hospital. O.S.GR: NB420348.

Charges 2007

Per person	£ 1.50 - £ 2.00
pitch	£ 5.00 - £ 8.00
electricity	£ 2.00
No credit cards.	

UK7950 Point of Ness Caravan & Camping Site

Well Park, Ness Road, Stromness KW16 3DN (Orkney)

Tel: **01856 873535**. Email: **recreation@orkney.gov.uk**

This quiet site is in an idyllic position bounded by the sea one side (an entrance to the harbour). It is sheltered by the land from the open sea and has views to the mountains and the island of Hoy. There is a rocky beach close by and walks from the site. It is a level, firm grassy site, protected from the small drop to the sea by a low fence. Access to the steps to the sea is gained by a gate in the fence. Whilst being located at one end of Orkney, it is still easy to visit the Churchill Barriers and the Italian Chapel as well as the closer Maes Howe and Skara Brae sites.

Facilities	Directions
The well maintained traditional style toilet block has good-sized showers (20p) with curtains separating the changing area. Well equipped laundry. Telephone and tourist information. Lounge for campers is at one end of the block.	Site is just west of Stromness. Campers can walk along the high street to the site on the edge of the town. Caravans and motorcaravans are advised to take the road at the back of town (2 miles), signed. O.S.GR: HY256079.

Open: 28 April - 30 September.

Charges 2007

Per pitch	£ 8.30
tent	£ 4.40 - £ 7.95
No credit cards.	

UK7980 Clickimin Caravan & Camp Site

Clickimin Leisure Complex, Lochside, Lerwick ZE1 0PJ (Shetlands)

Tel: **01595 741000**. Email: **clickimin.centre@srt.org.uk**

The caravan and camping site is in the grounds of the Clickimin leisure complex, but it is not dominated by the building with its swimming pool and restaurant, etc. The site is arranged in two tiers which are well laid out with a tarmac road in the centre of each tier. The lower grass tier is separated into areas by shrubs and provides a camping area for 30 tents. The upper tier has 20 touring pitches, each with a large gravel area and divided from its neighbour by a wide impressed concrete section for sitting out. A small lamppost with electricity, water and waste disposal points is provided at each pitch. From the pitches there is a view across a lake with its ruined 'broche' that is floodlit at night. The site is on the edge of Lerwick (ferry terminal), but with easy access to the town.

Facilities	Directions
The modern toilet block is clean and includes a toilet and shower cubicle for disabled visitors. Large, warm and well equipped laundry and drying room with an area for food preparation.	Site is on the west side of Lerwick. Take the A969 north or south. Just before leaving the town is the road North Lochside (turn south) or South Lochside (turn north). Clickimin Leisure Centre is on this road. O.S.GR: HU464413.

Open: May - September.

Charges 2007

Per pitch	£ 7.10 - £ 10.80
one-person tent	£ 5.10

UK7740 Loch Greshornish Camping Site

Arnisort, Edinbane IV51 9PS (Isle of Skye)

Tel: **01470 582230**. Email: **info@skyecamp.com**

Mr and Mrs Palmer took over this simple, spacious site with simple facilities in 1999. In a beautiful, peaceful setting with views over the loch to the low hills to the northwest of Skye, it is suitable for long or short stays. There are 30 level grass pitches for motorcaravans and caravans, 28 with 10A electric hook-ups. There are also places for up to 100 tents (but numbers never reach that level). A new building houses reception and a small, licensed shop selling basic essentials. A new launderette with washing machines, dryers and sinks will be completed this year.

Facilities	Directions
The refurbished toilet facilities are light, airy and spotlessly clean. The showers are a little cramped. Dishwashing sink in the ladies' and another in the men's. Launderette. Camper's shelter with seating, cooking and eating area. Small shop. Bicycle hire. Canoe hire. Off site: The local village has two hotels for drinks and meals; Portree, the nearest town, is 15 miles. Riding 2 miles. Golf 3 miles.	Site is 15 miles west of Portree on the A850 Dunvegan road by Edinbane. O.S.GR: NG343524. GPS: N57:29.113 W06:26.097

Open: Easter - 30 September.

Charges 2007

Per person	£ 3.50
child (5-15 yrs)	£ 1.25 - £ 2.25
pitch	£ 1.50 - £ 2.00
electricity	£ 2.00
No credit cards.	

UK7750 Staffin Caravan & Camping Site

Staffin IV51 9JX (Isle of Skye)

Tel: **01470 562 213**. Email: **staffincampsite@btinternet.com**

This simple camping site is on the side of a hill just outside Staffin, where the broad sweep of the bay is dotted with working crofts running down to the sea. A marked walk from the site leads to the seashore and slipway (good for walking dogs but too far to be taking a boat). With 50 pitches, the site is quite sloping but there are 18 reasonably level pitches with improved hardstanding for caravans and motorcaravans, all with electrical hook-ups (16A). Skye has many activities to offer and for the truly dedicated walker the Cuillins are the big attraction but the hills above Staffin look demanding! However, the first section of road from Portree should be treated with caution by those with caravans and large motorhomes. The entrance from the main road is via a single track.

Facilities

The sanitary block includes large, controllable showers. Dishwashing sinks are unfortunately not under cover and have only cold water. An older block only opens at very busy times. Large hardstanding area with motorcaravan service point. Gas available. Off site: Fishing or boat launching 1 mile. Bicycle hire 5 miles. Riding 9 miles. Staffin village is 400 yards and has a large shop (open six days a week), a restaurant and a launderette (useful as the site has no laundry). The Columbia centre in the village provides internet access.

Open: 1 April - 30 September.

Directions

Site is 15 miles north of Portree on A855 (2 miles of single track at the start), just before 40 mph signs on the right. O.S.GR: NG496668. GPS: N57:37.321 W06:11.760

Charges 2007

Per caravan or motorcaravan	
incl. 2 persons	£ 11.50
tent incl. 2 persons	£ 10.50
extra person	£ 1.50

No credit cards.

You might also like to consider...

MAP 8

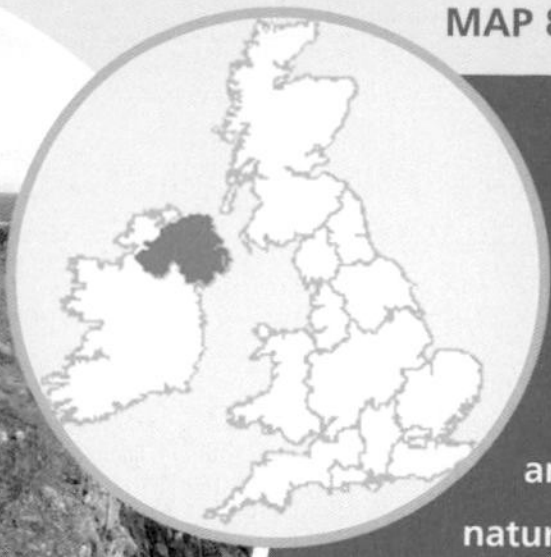

With a diversity of unspoilt landscapes, ranging from wild coastlines to green valleys, rugged mountains and shimmering lakes, to the natural phenomenon of the Giant's Causeway, Northern Ireland, though small, is crammed full of sights offering something for everyone.

NORTHERN IRELAND COMPRISES THE FOLLOWING COUNTIES: ANTRIM, ARMAGH, DOWN, FERMANAGH, LONDONDERRY AND TYRONE

The rugged coastline of the Causeway Coast and the nine Glens of Antrim, in the north, is an area of outstanding natural beauty, with white sandy shores and little bays, tranquil forests and romantic ruins and castles, full of tales of the ancient Irish Giants and other myths and legends. At over 60 million years old, with a mass of 4,000 tightly packed basalt columns, each a polygon shape, the Giant's Causeway is a popular attraction. One of the most beautiful regions is in the west around Londonderry, a delightful walled city set on a hill on the banks of the Foyle estuary. Further south is the beautiful region of Fermanagh, with glistening lakes and little islands all surrounded by lush green fields, hillsides and forests. The large lake of Lough Erne is to be found here: made up of two channels, the lower and upper Loughs, the meeting point of these channels is Enniskillen, a town steeped in history, boasting numerous preserved buildings including a castle. Across to the eastern shores lies the ancient Kingdom of Down, with its endless miles of spectacular coastline, little fishing villages, country parks and the Mountains of Mourne. And ringed by hills, sea lough and river valley is Belfast, a bustling city full of theatres, concert halls, art galleries and restaurants.

Places of interest

Antrim: Antrim Lough Shore Park; Rathlin Island; Giant's Causeway; Dunluce Castle near Portrush.

Belfast & environs: Belfast zoo and castle; Irish Linen Centre in Lisburn; Carrickfergus Castle.

Armagh: Gosford Forest Park near Markethill; Lough Neagh Discovery Centre on Oxford Island.

Down: County Museum and Downpatrick Cathedral; Mourne Mountains; Castlewellan forest park; Ballycopeland Windmill near Millisle.

Fermanagh: Enniskillen Castle and Castle Coole; village of Belleek; Marble Arch Caves, near Lough Macnean; Devenish Island on Lough Erne.

Londonderry: St Columb's Cathedral, Harbour Museum, Foyle Valley Railway Centre in Derry.

Tyrone: Omagh; Beaghmore stone circles near Cookstown; Dungannon; Sperrin Mountains.

Did you know?

Northern Ireland measures 85 miles from north to south and is about 110 miles wide.

The world's most famous ship the Titanic, was built in Belfast.

Legend has it that the rugged Giant's Causeway was built by Finn McCool, the legendary Irish Giant, when he travelled to Scotland to bring back his sweetheart.

At 2,240 yards an Irish Mile is 480 yards longer than a standard English mile.

Mountsandel near Coleraine is where Ireland's first known house was built 9,000 years ago.

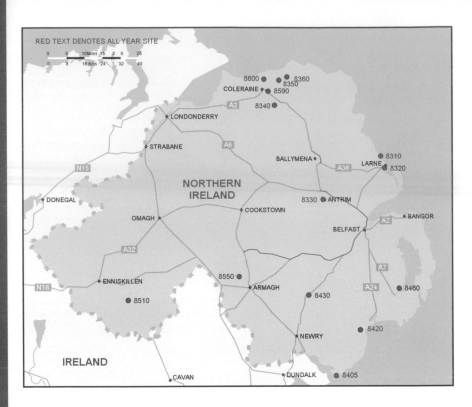

RED TEXT DENOTES ALL YEAR SITE

NORTHERN IRELAND

IRELAND

UK8340 Drumaheglis Caravan Park

36 Glenstall Road, Ballymoney BT53 7QN (Co. Antrim)
Tel: **028 2766 6466**. Email: **info@ballymoney.gov.uk**

A caravan park which continually maintains high standards, Drumaheglis is popular throughout the season. Situated on the banks of the lower River Bann, approximately 4 miles from the town of Ballymoney, it appeals to watersports enthusiasts or makes an ideal base for exploring this scenic corner of Northern Ireland. The marina offers superb facilities for boat launching, water-skiing, cruising, canoeing or fishing, whilst getting out and about can take you to the Giant's Causeway, seaside resorts such as Portrush or Portstewart, the sands of Whitepark Bay, the Glens of Antrim or the picturesque villages of the Antrim coast road. This attractive site is for touring units only and is well laid out with trees, shrubs, flower beds and tarmac roads. There are 55 serviced pitches with hardstanding, electricity (5/10A) and water points. Ballymoney is a popular shopping town and the Joey Dunlop Leisure Centre provides a high-tech fitness studio, sports hall, etc. There is much to see and do within this Borough and of interest is the Ballymoney museum in Townhead Street.

Facilities

Modern toilet blocks were very clean when we visited. Individual wash cubicles. Facilities for disabled visitors. Baby room and four family shower rooms. Dishwashing sinks. Washing machine and dryer. Play area. Volleyball and table tennis. Barbecue and picnic areas. Barrier with key system. Off site: Bus service from park entrance. Bicycle hire and golf 4 miles.

Open: 19 March - end October.

Directions

From A26/B62 Portrush - Ballymoney roundabout continue for approx. 1 mile on the A26 towards Coleraine. Site is clearly signed - follow International camping signs.

Charges 2007

Per unit incl. electricity	£ 15.00
tent	£ 11.00

UK8330 Six Mile Water Caravan & Camping Park

Lough Road, Antrim BT41 4DG (Co. Antrim)

Tel: **028 9446 4963**. Email: **sixmilewater@antrim.gov.uk**

Six Mile Water is located at the Lough Shore Park and is adjacent to the Antrim Forum leisure complex, a major amenity area that includes swimming pools, a bowling green, an adventure playground for children, fitness and health gyms and sports fields. Managed by Antrim Borough Council, the park is easily accessible when travelling to and from the ports of Belfast and Larne making it perfect for stop overs. It is also central for sightseeing in the area including the Antrim Castle Gardens and Clotworthy Arts Centre or for shopping in Antrim town. The Lough Shore Park offers visitors boating and water activities and boat launching on the beautiful Lough Neagh, as well as walking and cycling the Lough Shore Trail which takes in 25 places of interest along its 128 mile cycle route. The nearby golf club also offers a 20 bay driving range. Six Mile Water Caravan and Camping Park provides 20 pitches with electricity, arranged in a herringbone layout of hardstandings with grass for awnings. There are 24 pitches for tents to one side, plus picnic and barbecue areas. Advance booking is advisable.

Facilities

The small, modern toilet block provides bright facilities including toilets, washbasins and showers. Facilities for disabled campers. Baby changing unit. Laundry room. TV lounge and games room. Fishing and boat launching. Off site: The facilities of Lough Shore Park including a café open all year round. Antrim Forum leisure centre. Bus service 1 mile. Shops, pubs and restaurants within 1.5 miles. Golf 1.5 miles. Riding 6 miles.

Open: 14 March - 6 October.

Directions

Site is 1 mile south of the city centre. Follow signs for Antrim Forum and Lough Shore Park. On the Dublin road, turn off into Lough Road. Pass Antrim Forum and park is at the end of the road.

Charges 2008

Per pitch	£ 10.00 - £ 16.00
incl. electricity	£ 16.00

Six Mile Water Caravan and Camping Park

Lough Road, Antrim, Northern Ireland, BT41 4DG

Antrim borough council

Situated on the shores of Lough Neagh, an ideal base for Northern Ireland. On-site facilites include: TV lounge, games room, modern toilet and shower block, payphone, fully equipped laundry room, electric hook-up for 20 pitches and 24 camping sites. Maximum stay 7 nights. Open March - October.

Tel: 028 9446 4963   Email: sixmilewater@antrim.gov.uk
www.antrim.gov.uk/caravanpark

UK8320 Curran Court Caravan Park

131 Curran Road, Larne BT40 1XB (Co. Antrim)

Tel: **028 2827 3797**. Email: **curran.court-hotel@virgin.net**

Formerly run by the local borough council, this park is now managed by the Curran Court Hotel (opposite the park). Attractive garden areas add to the charm of this small, neat site which is very conveniently situated for the ferry terminal and only a few minutes walk from the sea. The 29 pitches, all with hardstanding and electricity connections (14A), give reasonable space off the tarmac road and there is a separate tent area of 1.5 acres. Larne market is on Wednesdays. You may consider using this site as a short term base for discovering the area as well as an ideal overnight stop. The warden can usually find room for tourists so reservations are not normally necessary.

Facilities

The toilet block is clean and adequate without being luxurious. Laundry room with dishwashing facilities. Play area with good equipment and safety surfaces. Bowls and putting. Late arrivals can call at the hotel. Off site: Train station and bus stop within a few minutes walk. Bicycle hire 0.5 miles. Golf 2 miles. Boat launching 500 yds. Many other amenities are very close including a shop (100 yds), the hotel for food and drink, tennis and a leisure centre with swimming pool (300 yds).

Open: Easter - 30 September.

Directions

Immediately after leaving the ferry terminal, turn right and follow camp signs. Site is 400 yards on the left.

Charges guide

Per caravan, motorcaravan or large tent	£ 11.00
tent	£ 5.00 - £ 10.00
electricity	£ 1.00

UK8310 Carnfunnock Country Park Caravan Park & Campsite

Coast Road, Drain's Bay, Larne BT40 2QG (Co. Antrim)

Tel: **028 2827 0541**. Email: **carnfunnock@larne.gov.uk**

In a magnificent parkland setting overlooking the sea, what makes this touring site popular is its scenic surroundings and convenient location. It is 3.5 miles north of the market town of Larne on the famed Antrim Coast Road and offers 28 level 'super' pitches, all with hardstanding, water, electricity (15A), drainage, individual pitch lighting and ample space for an awning. The site has a neat appearance with a tarmac road following through to the rear where a number of pitches are placed in a circular position with allocated space for tents. Run by the Borough Council and supervised by a manager, the surrounding Country Park is immaculately kept. The Visitor Centre includes a gift shop and information about local attractions and the restaurant/coffee shop is pleasant and looks towards the sea. Spending time around the parkland, you find a walled time garden with historic sundials, a maze, forest walk, children's adventure playground, putting green, 9-hole golf course, wildlife garden and miniature railway. There is also a summer events programme.

Facilities

A small building beside the entrance gates houses toilet facilities (entry by key) which are kept clean, but are now starting to show signs of wear. There are shower units, facilities for disabled people and dishwashing. Motorcaravan service point. Off site: Larne with bus services 3.5 miles. Fishing and boat launching 400 yds.

Open: Easter - 31 October.

Directions

From ferry terminal in Larne, follow signs for Coast Road and Carnfunnock Country Park; well signed 3.5 miles on A2 coast road.

Charges 2007

Per caravan or motorcaravan	£ 12.50 - £ 14.00
serviced hardstanding	£ 14.00 - £ 16.00
tent (2 persons)	£ 8.00 - £ 9.00
tent (3 or more persons)	£ 12.50 - £ 14.00

Carnfunnock Country Park

Carnfunnock Country Park offers 191 hectares of mixed woodland, colourful gardens, waymarked walking trails and stunning coastline. Seasonal attractions include: a 'Northern Ireland' maze, walled garden, miniature railway, 18 hole mini golf, bouncy castle, remote control boats, adventure playground, trampolines, 'mini silverstone' race track, putting 9 hole golf course and a gift and coffee shop.

Carnfunnock Country Park, Coast Road, Larne, Co.Antrim BT40 2QG
Tel: 028 2827 0541 (In season Easter - October) /
028 2826 0088 (Out of season)
Email: carnfunnock@larne.gov.uk
Website: www.larne.gov.uk/carnfunnock

UK8350 Bush Caravan Park

97 Priestland Road, Bushmills BT57 8UJ (Co. Antrim)

Tel: **028 2073 1678**

An ideal base for touring the North Antrim Coast, this family run, recently extended park is only minutes away from two renowned attractions, the Giant's Causeway and the Old Bushmills Distillery. This fact alone makes Bush a popular location, but its fast growing reputation for friendliness and top class facilities makes it equally appealing. Conveniently located just off the main Ballymoney - Portrush Road (B62), it is approached by a short drive. The site itself is partly surrounded by mature trees and hedging, but views across the countryside can still be appreciated. Tarmac roads around the site lead to 47 well laid out and spacious pitches, with hardstanding and electric hook-up (16A), or to a grass area for tents. Unique features on site are murals depicting the famed scenery, sights and legends of the Causeway Coast. The enthusiastic owners organise tours to the Distillery and coastal trips – a musical evening cannot be ruled out.

Facilities

The toilet block (opened by key-pad) is modern, clean and equipped to a high standard. Facilities include controllable showers with excellent provision for people with disabilities (can also be used by families). Washing machine, dryer and dishwashing sinks. Central play area. Recreation room for all ages. Off site: Riding 2 miles. Golf and fishing 3 miles. Bicycle hire and boat launching 4 miles. Beach 3 miles.

Open: Easter - 31 October.

Directions

From Ballymoney A26/B62 roundabout proceed north on B62 towards Portrush for 6.5 miles. Turn right onto B17 and site is 350 yds on the left.

Charges guide

Per unit incl. all persons and electricity	£ 12.50
tent	£ 5.00 - £ 10.00
awning	£ 1.50

UK8360 Ballyness Caravan Park

40 Castlecatt Road, Bushmills BT57 8TN (Co. Antrim)

Tel: **028 2073 2393**. Email: **info@ballynesscaravanpark.com**

Ballyness is immaculately cared for and is designed with conservation in mind. In keeping with the surrounding countryside, it is extensively planted with native trees and shrubs which attract local wildlife and birds and there are ponds with ducks and swans. The overall appearance of this site, with its entrance gate, white stone pillars and broad tarmac drive is attractive. The drive leads to 46 hardstanding pitches with electricity hook-ups, water and drainage. There is a dedicated area for tents and several caravan holiday homes, but these are placed away from the touring pitches. From the site you can enjoy a relaxing walk by way of the meadow ponds and winding pathway alongside the stream known as St Columb's Rill. The village of Bushmills, with its famous Whiskey Distillery, is within walking distance and the Causeway Coast a short drive.

Facilities	Directions
One spotlessly clean and well decorated, cottage style heated sanitary block (key coded) includes facilities for disabled visitors (toilet and shower), a bathroom and baby changing unit, laundry room and dishwashing area. Play area. Football field. Nature trail. Off site: Bus service 0.5 miles. Bicycle hire 0.5 miles. Beach and fishing 1 mile. Golf and boat launching 1.5 miles. Riding 5 miles.	From M2 follow A26 N. At Ballymoney turn right on B66 towards Dervock and turn left. Stay on B66 and site is 5.5 miles on right.

Open: 17 March - 31 October.

Charges 2007

Per unit incl. 2 persons, electricity, water and drainage	£ 17.00
extra person (over 5 yrs)	£ 1.00
awning or pup tent	£ 2.00

UK8405 Cranfield Caravan Park

123 Cranfield Road, Cranfield West, Kilkeel BT34 4LJ (Co. Down)

Tel: **028 417 62572**. Email: **jimchestnut@btconnect.com**

On the shores of Carlingford Lough with direct access to a blue flag beach, this friendly family run park immediately impresses with its well cared for flower beds, neat hedging, cordyline trees and the elegant building which incorporates the family home and reception. Situated at Northern Ireland's most southerly point, the surrounding scenery of the Mourne Mountains, the Lough and distant vistas is stunning. A focal point is the Haulbowline lighthouse, built in the 1800s, which sits in the middle of the sea. Despite the many privately owned caravan holiday homes on site, touring pitches are kept separate and situated towards the park entrance. Each pitch has a sea view, has hardstanding and all have tower units providing an electricity hook up (16A), water, waste water point and TV outlet; 19 have a main sewerage connection.

Facilities	Directions
A modern, heated toilet block (entrance by key) is well maintained with tiled walls/floors, preset showers (50p token) and open style washbasins. Excellent suite for disabled visitors doubles as a family room, also a night WC (by key). Dishwashing sinks and well equipped laundry in a separate building. Play area (outside park). Sea fishing, boat launching and beach (with lifeguard). Off site: Kilkeel town (3.5 miles). Golf, hill walking in the Mournes, Anglo Norman castle.	Travelling southeast on A2 Newry/Kilkeel Road turn right approx. 5.5 miles after passing through Rostrevor onto local road, signed Cranfield and Greencastle. Site signed at end of road. GPS: N54:01.796 W06:04.098

Open: 17 March - 31 October.

Charges 2007

Per unit incl. all persons and electricity	£ 15.00

UK8420 Tollymore Forest Caravan Park

178 Tullybrannigan Road, Newcastle BT33 6PW (Co. Down)

Tel: **028 4372 2428**

This popular park, for tourers only, is located within the parkland of Tollymore Forest. It is discreetly situated away from the public footpaths and is noted for its scenic surroundings. The forest park, which is approached by way of an ornate gateway and majestic avenue of Himalayan cedars, covers an area of almost 500 hectares. It is backed by the Mourne mountains and situated two miles from the beaches and resort of Newcastle. The site is attractively laid out with hardstanding pitches, 72 of which have electricity (6A). The Head Ranger at Tollymore is helpful and ensures that the caravan site is efficiently run and quiet, even when full.

Facilities

Toilet blocks, timbered in keeping with the setting, are clean and modern with wash cubicles, facilities for disabled people, dishwashing and laundry area. Off site: Confectionery shop and tea room nearby. Small grocery shop a few yards from the exit gate of the park with gas available.

Open: All year.

Directions

Approach Newcastle on the A24. Before entering the town, at roundabout, turn right on to A50 signed Castlewellan. Follow signs for Tollymore Forest Park.

Charges 2007

Per unit incl. car and occupants	£ 9.00 - £ 13.00
electricity	£ 1.50

Low season mid-week special rates.

UK8430 Banbridge Touring Caravan & Camping Park

200 Newry Road, Banbridge BT32 3NB (Co. Down)

Tel: **028 4062 3322**. Email: **tic@banbridge.gov.uk**

This conveniently situated little park on the main A1 Belfast - Newry road is an ideal place for a stop over if travelling between Southern and Northern Ireland. The local council have developed the area and the plan to fully reinstate the touring park should now be complete offering 16 hardstanding pitches. It is part of the Banbridge Gateway Tourist Information Centre complex. The restaurant and coffee shop within the complex (10.00-17.00 hrs daily) serves lunchtime specials, scones, cakes, etc. The town of Banbridge is 1 mile. The site is within easy towing distance of the main ports or would make an ideal base for discovering many tourist attractions.

Facilities

Excellent, ultra-modern toilet facilities, spotlessly clean and key operated, include two showers, good facilities for disabled people and an outside, covered dishwashing area. Extensive play area with safety base. Off site: Shops, restaurants, pubs and all services within 1 mile. Fishing, bicycle hire or golf within 3 miles.

Open: All year, but closed Sundays October - May incl.

Directions

Follow signs to Tourist Information Centre off the A1 Belfast - Newry dual carriageway, 1 mile south of Banbridge.

Charges 2007

Per unit incl. electricity	£ 10.00
tent	£ 5.00

Max. stay 5 consecutive nights. Refundable key deposit (gate, WCs and showers) £20.

UK8460 Delamont Country Park Camping & Caravanning Club Site

Delamont Country Park, Downpatrick Road, Killyleagh BT30 9TZ (Co. Down)

Tel: **028 4482 1833**

This is Northern Ireland's first Camping and Caravanning Club site and although not long in existence, it is proving to be one of the country's most popular sites. Within the boundaries of Delamont Country Park, it is an idyllic location for those seeking an away from it all feel, yet wanting to be within easy reach of major attractions. The country park is a designated area of outstanding natural beauty and commands from its highest point, breathtaking vistas of Strangford Lough and surrounding countryside. Facilities on the campsite itself are excellent and it has an orderly, neat and tidy appearance. The 64 all weather pitches on level terrain all have electricity, water and drainage.

Facilities

The single modern toilet block, with heating, has wash cubicles and a baby bath. En-suite facilities for disabled visitors. Laundry and dishwashing facilities. Small shop area selling basics. Adventure playground and miniature railway in country park. Free admittance to country park for campers. Off site: Tyrella beach 7 miles. Fishing and riding 1 mile. Golf 4 miles.

Open: March - October.

Directions

From Belfast follow A22 southeast to village of Killyleagh. Pass through village and site entrance is on left after 1 mile.

Charges 2007

Per person	£ 4.90 - £ 7.25
child	£ 2.15 - £ 2.25
non-member pitch fee	£ 5.65

UK8550 Dungannon Park

Moy Road, Dungannon BT71 6DY (Co. Tyrone)

Tel: **028 8772 8690**. Email: **dpreception@dungannon.gov.uk**

This small touring park nestles in the midst of a 70 acre park with a multitude of tree varieties, brightly coloured flower beds and a 12 acre fishing lake. The 12 pitches, which are discreetly sited, some with lake views, are on hardstanding with water, waste and 16A electricity connections. There is also an unmarked grass area for tents. Run by Dungannon Council the park, which also incorporates tennis courts, football and cricket pitches lies about one mile south of Dungannon town. Walkers can enjoy three miles of parkland walks which command from the high ground, views of the surrounding countryside and Lough Neagh. A modern Visitor Amenity Centre houses reception, sanitary facilities, a TV area and vending machines.

Facilities

Sanitary facilities which include showers (by token), washbasins, baby changing mat and spacious unit for disabled visitors are to the rear of the Amenity Centre. Laundry room with washing machine and dryer, dishwashing area and chemical disposal unit. Night watchman (until 6.00). Excellent play area. Tennis, fishing and walking. Off site: Bus stop and shop at main entrance to park. Restaurants, shops, leisure facilities in Dungannon. Tyrone Crystal (guided tours), walking and cycling in Clogher Valley, local markets.

Open: 1 March - 31 October.

Directions

Leave M1 motorway at junction 15 to join the A29 towards Dungannon. Turn left at second traffic lights signed Dungannon Park.
GPS: N54:23.413 W06:45.478

Charges 2007

Per pitch	£ 10.00 - £ 12.00

UK8510 Mullynascarthy Caravan Park

Lisnaskea BT92 0NZ (Co. Fermanagh)

Tel: **028 6772 1040**

This is a well kept touring site situated on the banks of the Colebrooke River. It has instant appeal, for the setting at Mullynascarthy is more like a mature garden. The pitches to the right of reception, which are grass on hardstanding, are mostly angled between the many tree varieties, also separated by low hedging and flowering shrubs. To the left of the facility block additional pitches are spread over meadow-like terrain and all have electric hook-ups. Sanitary facilities, although not ultra modern, are kept very clean and housed alongside reception, which doubles up as a sub-post office. The attention and care this site obviously receives is due to the warden who also extends a friendly warm welcome to her guests. Lisnaskea makes an ideal base for exploring this lakeland county which abounds in historic treasures, stately homes, and is excellent for watersports enthusiasts. The county town of Enniskillen is within a short drive and the Marble Arch caves are an experience not to be missed.

Facilities

The toilet block (key operated) has showers, open style washbasins, facilities for people with disabilities (washbasin/WC), laundry room and dishwashing sinks. Games and sports area. Play area. River fishing (licences and permits available). Off site: Bus service 1.5 miles. Golf and bicycle hire 10 miles.

Open: 17 March - 31 October.

Directions

From Enniskillen take A4 towards Dungannon for 8 miles, then turn right on A34 signed Lisnaskea. Continue on A34 for 2.5 miles and turn right onto B514 where site is signed Mullynascarthy.

Charges 2007

Per unit incl. 2 persons and electricity	£ 15.00
tent	£ 8.00 - £ 14.00

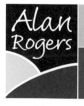

UK8590 Tullans Farm Caravan Park

46 Newmills Road, Coleraine BT52 2JB (Co. Londonderry)

Tel: **028 7034 2309**. Email: **tullansfarm@hotmail.com**

A high quality, well run family park convenient for the Causeway coast, Tullans Farm is one of the most popular in the area. It has a quiet, heart of the country feel, yet the University town of Coleraine is within a mile, the seaside resort Portrush and Portstewart five miles and a shopping centre a five minute drive. Tullans Farm has earned a reputation for its spotlessly clean toilet block, attractive flower displays and its well cared for appearance. In a central position, fronted by a parking space, stands a long white building housing the sanitary facilities and reception. Around the park roads are gravel and the 32 pitches are on hardstanding; all with electric hook-ups (10A). In season the owners organise barbecues, barn dances and line dancing (raising funds for charity).

Facilities

The toilet and shower rooms, including a family shower unit, are spacious, modern and include facilities for people with disabilities. Laundry and washing up room with sinks, washing machine, dryers and a large fridge. Play areas. TV lounge. Games room. Barn used for indoor recreation. Off site: Public transport in Coleraine 1 mile. Fishing and riding 1.5 miles. Golf and bicycle hire 5 miles. Beach 5 miles.

Open: March - 30 September.

Directions

From the Lodge Road roundabout (south end of Coleraine) turn east onto A29 Portrush ring road and proceed for 0.5 miles. Turn right at sign for park and Windy Hall. Park is clearly signed on left.

Charges 2007

Per unit incl. all persons, electricity and awning	£ 17.00
tent	£ 8.00 - £ 12.00

No credit cards.

UK8600 Bellemont Caravan Park

10 Islandtasserty Road, Coleraine BT52 2PN (Co. Londonderry)

Tel: **028 7082 3872**

Close to Coleraine and Portstewart, this well kept park makes an immediately favourable impression with its white concrete roads, its perfect grass areas and well laid out appearance. The gently sloping ground rises at the far right of the park to give views over Portstewart and towards the sea. To the left of the entrance and security gate are five privately owned caravan holiday homes. There are 30 touring pitches, all with hardstanding, electric hook-up and water. These are spacious and well distributed around this open, parkland style setting. In a central position stands a gleaming white building, with flower tubs decorating the forecourt, which houses reception and heated sanitary facilities. Bellemont makes a good base for visiting the university town of Coleraine, the resorts and beaches of Portstewart and Portrush, or famous sights such as Dunluce Castle, Carrick-a-Rede rope bridge and the Giant's Causeway.

Facilities

Toilet facilities with good sized showers (token operated). En-suite unit for disabled visitors. Laundry room with two washing machines, two dryers and iron (token operated), plus dishwashing sink and drainer to the outside. Play area with swings and slide on a bark surface. Dogs are not accepted. Off site: Bus service 0.5 miles. Fishing, bicycle hire, riding and golf 2 miles. Beach 2.5 miles.

Open: Easter - 30 September.

Directions

From Lodge Road roundabout on eastern outskirts of Coleraine follow A29 north to fourth roundabout. Continue towards Portrush and site is clearly signed on left after 400 yards.

Charges 2007

Per unit incl. all persons, electricity	£ 15.00
awning	£ 1.50

No credit cards.

MAP 8

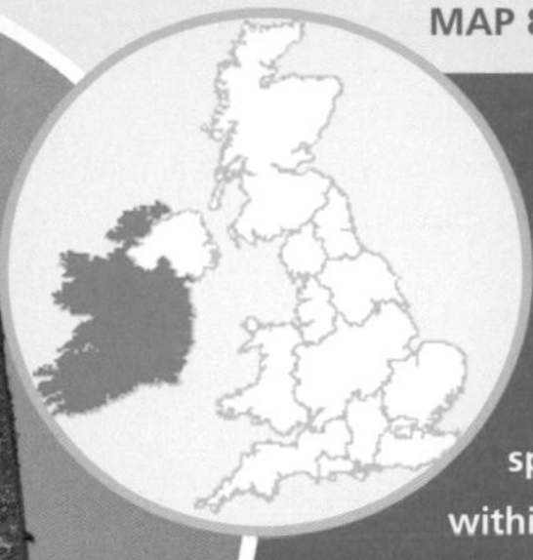

Famed for its folklore, traditional music, and friendly, hospitable people, the Republic of Ireland offers spectacular scenery contained within a relatively compact area. With plenty of beautiful areas to discover, and a decidedly relaxed pace of life, it is an idea place to unwind.

IRELAND IS MADE UP OF FOUR PROVINCES: CONNAUGHT, LEINSTER, MUNSTER AND ULSTER, COMPRISING 32 COUNTIES, 26 OF WHICH FALL IN THE REPUBLIC OF IRELAND

Ireland is the perfect place to indulge in a variety of outdoor pursuits while taking in the glorious scenery. There are plenty of way-marked footpaths, which lead through woodlands, across cliffs, past historical monuments and over rolling hills. The dramatic coastline, with its headlands, secluded coves and sandy beaches, is fantastic for watersports: from sailing to windsurfing, scuba diving and swimming; or for just simply relaxing and watching the variety of seabirds that nest on the shores. The Cliffs of Moher, in particular, is a prime location for birdwatching and Goat Island, just offshore, is where puffins make their nesting burrows. Fishing is another popular activity; the country is full of pretty streams, rivers, hidden lakes and canals, which can all be explored by hiring a boat. In the south the beautiful Ring of Kerry is one of the most visited regions. This 110-mile route encircles the Inveragh Peninsula, and is surrounded by mountains and lakes. Other sights include: the Aran Islands, home to some of the most ancient Christian and pre-Christian remains in Ireland, and the Rock of Cashel, with its spectacular group of medieval buildings; not to mention the bustling cities of Dublin, Galway and Cork.

Places of interest

Connaught: Boyle Abbey; Connemara National Park; Céide Fields at Ballycastle; Kylemore Abbey; Aran Islands; Galway city; Westport; Sligo Abbey; megalithic tombs of Carrowmore.

Leinster: Wicklow Mountains National Park; Rock of Cashel; Killkenny Castle; Guinness brewery, Trinity College and National Museum in Dublin; Dunmore Cave at Ballyfoyle; Wexford Wildfowl Reserve.

Munster: harbour towns of Kinsale and Clonakilty; Blarney Castle in Cork; historical city of Limerick with 13th century castle fortress and old town; Ring of Kerry; Bunratty Castle; Cliffs of Moher; Killarney National Park.

Ulster: Glenveagh National Park; Slieve League, the highest sea cliffs in Europe; Donegal Castle; Newmills Corn and Flax Mills in Letterkenny.

Did you know?

The official currency of the Republic of Ireland is the Euro.

The Blarney Stone, reputedly cast with a spell by a witch to reward a king who saved her from drowning, is said to bestow the gift of eloquence on all those who kiss it.

The harp is a symbol of the Irish people's love of music: since mediaeval times it has been the official emblem for Ireland.

Hurling is the oldest native sport.

Doctors once prescribed Guinness as a cure for debility, anaemia and to help patients through their convalescence, including nursing mothers.

On display in Trinity College, the Book of Kells is one of the oldest books in the world, written around the year 800 AD.

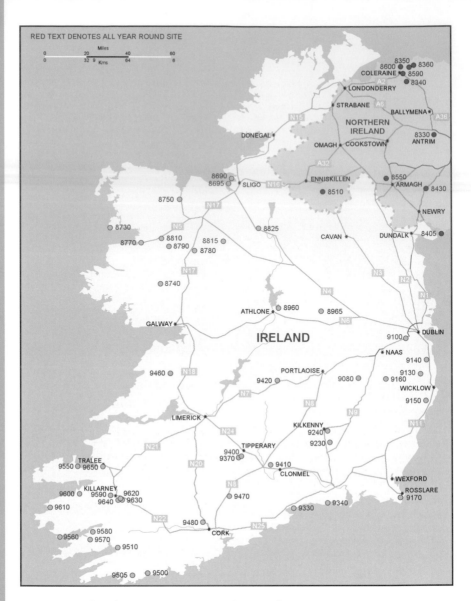

RED TEXT DENOTES ALL YEAR ROUND SITE

IRELAND

IR8690 Greenlands Caravan & Camping Park

Rosses Point (Co. Sligo)

Tel: **071 917 7113**. Email: **noelineha@eircom.net**

Just off the N15 road and 8 km. from Sligo town, this is a well run park at Rosses Point, in the sand hills adjoining a championship golf course. It is thoughtfully laid out on undulating ground which adds interest to the overall appearance. Your view depends on where you are pitched – look towards Coney Island and the Blackrock lighthouse which guards the bay, take in the sight of Benbulben Mountain or appreciate the seascape and the water lapping the resort's two bathing beaches.

Facilities

Modern toilet facilities, recently extended and refitted, are kept exceptionally clean, with hot showers (€ 1 token). Dishwashing and laundry facilities. Motorcaravan service point. New campers' kitchen. TV room. Play area. Night security. Dogs accepted only on leads.
Off site: Mini-market and restaurant in village. Fishing 100 m. Golf 50 m. Bicycle hire 8 km. Riding 14 km.

Open: 30 April - 14 September.

Directions

From Sligo city travel approx. 800 m. north on N15 road, turn left onto R291 signed Rosses Point. Continue for 6.5 km. and park is on right after village. GPS: N54:18.424 W08:34.161

Charges 2007

Per person	€ 1.00
pitch incl. electricity (10A)	€ 18.00 - € 21.00
hiker/cyclist incl. small tent	€ 11.00

IR8695 Strandhill Caravan & Camping Park

Strandhill (Co. Sligo)

Tel: **071 916 8111**. Email: **sxi@iol.ie**

This seaside park is located on 20 acres of undulating grass with a sandy base with natural protection from the onshore breezes of the famous Strandhill beach. There are 55 hardstanding pitches for caravans and motorcaravans, with electricity and ample water points, and two camping areas for tents, one with views of the sea and the second more sheltered. Throughout the site many hollows provide ideal pitches for tents. Strandhill, world recognised as a surfing Mecca, also provides activities for all the family. There are miles of sandy beach and dunes and the Knocknarea Mountain provides walkers with choice. The Megalithic Tombs at Carrowmore, older than the Pyramids at Giza, are 5 km. away and the flat beach at Culleenmore is 2 km. Strandhill provides an excellent touring base for the Benbulban, Yeat's Country and Lough Gill's 'Isle of Inisfree' combining nature, heritage, and fable. There are two flights daily into nearby Sligo airport.

Facilities

The toilet block (keys provided on deposit) is clean and fresh with hot showers (token € 1), electric hand dryers and hairdryer. Dishwashing area with hot water. Laundry including ironing facilities. TV and games room. Book swapping. Security on site all season. Off site: Public transport from village. Shops, restaurants, takeaway, pubs and ATM are just beyond the park's boundary in the village. Strandhill golf course 500 m. Riding 2 km. Swimming pool and sports centre in Sligo 8 km.

Open: Easter - 30 September.

Directions

Strandhill is 8 km. west of Sligo city on the N59. Site is on the airport road.

Charges 2007

Per person	€ 1.00
pitch	€ 14.00 - € 17.00
electricity (10A)	€ 4.00

IR8750 Belleek Caravan & Camping Park

Ballina (Co. Mayo)

Tel: **096 715 33**. Email: **lenahan@belleekpark.com**

Belleek has a quiet woodland setting, only minutes from Ballina, a famed salmon fishing centre. With excellent pitches and toilet block, the family owners are committed to ensuring that it is immaculate at all times. From the entrance gate, the park is approached by a drive that passes reception and leads to 58 well spaced pitches. With a very neat overall appearance, 32 pitches have hardstanding, 45 have electricity hook-ups, and you may choose your pitch. Sports facilities within a short distance of the park include a swimming pool, tennis and bicycle hire. Other local attractions are the Blue Flag beach at Ross, Ceide Fields (Neolithic farm), Down Patrick Head, Mayo North Heritage Centre or a seaweed bath at Kilcullen's Bath House, Enniscrone.

Facilities

Spotlessly clean, tastefully decorated toilet block providing showers (€ 1.00 token), baby sink and facilities for disabled people. Laundry sink, two washing machines and two dryers. TV room and games room with table tennis and football game. Campers' kitchen and emergency accommodation with beds provided. Play area, ball game area, basketball and tennis courts. Barbecue area. Reception includes a shop (June-Sept) and a tea room that also serves breakfasts. Off site: Fishing 1 km. Bicycle hire 3 km.

Open: 15 March - 1 November; by arrangement all year.

Directions

Take R314 Ballina - Killala road. Park is signed on right after approx. 3 km.

Charges 2007

Per unit incl. 2 persons	€ 18.00
extra person	€ 5.00
child	€ 2.50
electricity (10A)	€ 3.00
hiker/cyclist and tent	€ 8.00

Low season discounts for stays of 3 or more nights when pre-paid.

IR8730 Keel Sandybanks Caravan & Camping Park

Keel, Achill Island (Co. Mayo)

Tel: 098 432 11. Email: info@achillcamping.com

This is a park offering a taste of island life and the opportunity to relax in dramatic, scenic surroundings. Achill, Ireland's largest island, is 24 km. long and 19 km. wide and is connected to the mainland by a bridge. The site is situated beside Keel village and approached by the R319 from the swivel bridge at Achill Sound. Although there are static holiday mobile homes on this site, the 42 pitches for caravans and 42 for tents are kept separate. Some with hardstanding are located at the perimeter fence overlooking the beach. Although sand based, the ground is firm and level. Roads are tarmac and there is direct access to the beach which is supervised by lifeguards. Occasionally a traditional music evening is organised on the site. Whilst a treat in store is the natural beauty of Achill, worth seeing are Kildownet Castle, the Slievemore deserted village and the Seal Caves.

Facilities

Two modern toilet blocks serve the site, one at the entrance gate beside reception and the other in a central position. Heated facilities include WCs (one for disabled visitors), washbasins and hot showers (on payment). Hair and hand dryers. Dishwashing and laundry sinks. Chemical disposal facilities. Play area with safety base. TV room. Watersports enthusiasts can enjoy surfing, canoeing and board sailing on Keel Strand and Lough. Fishing trips can be arranged. Off site: Bicycle hire and golf 200 m. Riding 10 km. In the village there is a food shop, takeaway, restaurants and night music in the pubs.

Open: 27 May - 4 September.

Directions

From Achill Sound follow the R319 for 16 km. Site is on the left before Keel village.

Charges 2007

Per pitch	€ 12.00 - € 17.00
electricity (6A)	€ 3.00

No credit cards.

IR8740 Cong Caravan & Camping Park

Lisloughrey, Quay Road, Cong (Co. Mayo)

Tel: 094 954 6089. Email: info@quietman-cong.com

It would be difficult to find a more idyllic and famous spot for a caravan park than Cong. Situated close to the shores of Lough Corrib, Cong's scenic beauty was immortalised in the film 'The Quiet Man'. This well kept park is 1.6 km. from the village of Cong, near the grounds of the magnificent and renowned Ashford Castle. The owner's house that incorporates reception, shop and the hostel, stands to the fore of the site. Toilet facilities and the holiday hostel accommodation are entered from the courtyard area. The 40 grass pitches, 36 with electricity, are placed at a higher level to the rear, with the sheltered tent areas below and to the side. The park can be crowded and busy in high season. When not spending time around the village of Cong with its picturesque river setting and Monastic relics, there is much to keep the active camper happy. Watersports, cycling, walking, climbing, caving and scenic drives can all be pursued. Not least of the on-site attractions at this park is a mini cinema showing 'The Quiet Man' film nightly all season and associated museum guided tours can be arranged.

Facilities

Toilet facilities are tastefully decorated, kept clean and are heated when necessary. Hot showers with curtains (€ 1 charge), hairdryers, soap and hand towels. Dishwashing area (charge for hot water). Campers' kitchen. Launderette service. Central bin depot. Barbecue, games room and extensive play area. Shop. Catering is a feature - full Irish or continental breakfast, dinner or packed lunch may be ordered, or home baked bread and scones purchased in the shop. TV lounge. Bicycle hire. Off site: Riding and golf within 2 km. Fishing and boat slipway 500 m.

Open: All year.

Directions

Leave N84 road at Ballinrobe to join R334/345 signed Cong. Turn left at end of the R345 (opposite entrance to Ashford Castle), slow down take next road on right (approx. 300 m) and the park is on right (200 m). GPS: N53:32.357 W09:16.253

Charges 2007

Per unit with 2 persons	€ 21.00
exttra person	€ 3.00
child	€ 2.50
electricity	€ 5.00

IR8780 Knock Caravan & Camping Park

Claremorris Road, Knock (Co. Mayo)

Tel: 094 938 8100. Email: info@knock-shrine.ie

This park is immediately south of the world famous shrine that receives many visitors. Comfortable and clean, the square shaped campsite is kept very neat with tarmac roads and surrounded by clipped trees. The pitches are of a decent size accommodating 50 caravans or motorcaravans, 20 tents and 18 caravan holiday homes (for rent). All pitches have hardstanding (5 doubles) and there are 52 electrical connections (13A), with an adequate number of water points. There is also an overflow field. Because of the religious connections of the area, the site is very busy in August and indeed there are unlikely to be any vacancies at all for 14-16 August. Besides visiting the shrine and Knock Folk Museum, it is also a good centre for exploring scenic Co. Mayo.

Facilities

Two heated toilet blocks have good facilities for disabled visitors and a nice sized rest room attached, hot showers (on payment) and adequate washing and toilet facilities. Laundry and dishwashing room. Gas supplies. Playground. Dogs on leads are accepted. Off site: Fishing 4.5 km. Golf and riding 11 km.

Open: 1 March - 31 October.

Directions

Exit from the N17 at the Knock bypass and from the roundabout follow signs to the site which is just south of the village. GPS: N53:47.262 W08:55.165

Charges 2007

Per person	€ 2.00 - € 2.50
child	€ 1.00
pitch	€ 15.00 - € 16.00
electricity (13A)	€ 3.00
hiker or cyclist incl. tent	€ 9.50 - € 10.50

No credit cards.

IR8770 Parkland Caravan & Camping Park

Westport House Country Park, Westport (Co. Mayo)

Tel: 098 277 66. Email: camping@westporthouse.ie

Located in the grounds of an elegant country estate, this popular park offers the choice of a 'pitch only' booking, or a 'special deal' (min. stay three nights). This includes free admission to Westport House and children's animal and bird park, plus other activities, such as boating and fishing on the lake and river, pitch and putt, 'slippery dip', ball pond and 'supabounce', new play adventure world, hillside train rides and a flume ride. Stay one week or more and all the above are free, plus tennis, a par-3 golf course and 20% discount on bar food in the Horse and Wagon bar on the site. From Westport Quay, you enter the grounds of the estate by way of a tree lined road that crosses the river and leads to the site. In an attractive, sheltered area of the parkland, set in the trees, are 155 pitches. There are 65 with hardstanding and 76 electric hook-ups. The gate is closed 23.30 - 09.00 with good lighting around the site. If late, vehicles must be parked in the car park. Early in the season the site may not be fully prepared, and only minimal facilities may be available. Westport is an attractive town with splendid Georgian houses and traditional shop fronts.

Facilities

Toilet facilities are provided at various points on the site, plus a 'super-loo' located in the farmyard buildings. Facilities for disabled people. Dishwashing and laundry sinks, washing machines and dryers plus free ironing facilities. Fifties style function room and bar with food and musical entertainment (all 1/6-31/8). Dogs on leads are accepted. Off site: Within 5 km. of the estate are an 18-hole golf course and deep sea angling on Clew Bay.

Open: 14 May - 5 September.

Directions

Take R335 Westport - Louisburgh road and follow signs for Westport Quay, then turn in through gates of Westport House and continue through estate following signs for camping.
GPS: N53:48.320 W09:32.369

Charges 2007

Per unit incl. 2 persons and electricity	€ 28.00 - € 33.00
hiker or cyclist	€ 25.00 - € 27.50

Electricity incl. Family weekend rates in June.

303

IR8790 Carra Caravan & Camping Park

Belcarra, Castlebar (Co. Mayo)

Tel: 094 903 2054. Email: post@mayoholidays.com

This is an ideal location for those seeking a real Irish village experience in a 'value for money' park. Small, unpretentious and family run, it is located in Belcarra, a regular winner of the 'Tidiest Mayo Village' award. Nestling at the foot of a wooded drumlin, it is surrounded by rolling hills and quiet roads which offer an away from it all feeling, yet Castlebar the county's largest town is only an 8 km. drive. On the pleasant 1.5 acre park, the 20 unmarked touring pitches, 7 with electric hook-up (13A), are on flat ground enclosed by ranch fencing and shaded in parts by trees. An additional novel idea at Carra are eight horse-drawn caravans for hire. The owner and his daughter give talks on the area.

Facilities

The basic toilet block has adequate, well equipped showers (€ 0.50). Combined kitchen, dishwashing, laundry area with fridge/freezer, sink, table, chairs, washing machine and dryer. Lounge with TV, books and magazines. Off site: Village shops, a post office and 'Flukies' cosy bar which serves Irish breakfast and where Irish stew is a speciality. Leisure centre and tennis. Free fishing area and special walkway to the river. Golf 8 km.

Open: May - end September.

Directions

From Castlebar take N60 Claremorris road for 8.5 km. southeast and turn right at sign for Belcarra. Continue for 4.5 km. to village and site on left at end of village. GPS: N53:47.974 W09:12.989

Charges 2007

Per unit incl. all persons	€ 12.00
electricity	€ 2.00

No credit cards.

IR8810 Lough Lannagh Caravan Park

Castlebar (Co. Mayo)

Tel: 094 902 7111. Email: llv@eircom.net

Lough Lannagh is an attractive holiday village on the lake shore which comprises quality accommodation, self catering cottages and a caravan park. It is within walking distance of Castlebar with its many restaurants, pubs and shops. The caravan park has 20 touring pitches, well laid out in a separate dedicated corner of the village, all on hardstanding with electric connections. One reception area, to the right of the security barrier, serves all. The main attraction is the fitness suite, sauna and steam room, plus reflexology and therapies (over 18s only admitted to the gym).

Facilities

One modern heated sanitary block provides washbasins and well equipped, preset showers. En-suite unit for disabled people. Laundry room with sink, washing machines and dryers; dishwashing area. Café (serving breakfast). Fitness suite. Tennis. Table tennis. Bicycle hire.

Open: 15 March - 30 October.

Directions

To get to Castlebar take the N5, N60 or N84. At Castlebar ring road follow directions for Westport. Site is signed on all approach roads to the Westport roundabout. GPS: N53:50.950 W09:18.713

Charges 2007

Per unit incl. 2 persons, electricity and hardstanding	€ 20.00 - € 26.00
tent incl. 2 persons	€ 16.00 - € 18.00
child	€ 1.00

IR9080 Forest Farm Caravan & Camping Park

Dublin Road, Athy (Co. Kildare)

Tel: 059 863 1231. Email: forestfarm@eircom.net

This site makes an excellent stop over if travelling from Dublin to the southeast counties. It is also ideally placed to visit local places of interest including the Shackleton exhibition, the Japanese Gardens and the Irish National Stud. The park is signed on the N78 and approached by a 500 m. avenue of tall pines. Part of a working farm, the campsite spreads to the right of the modern farmhouse, which also provides B&B and holiday apartments. The owners have cleverly utilised their land to create a site which offers 64 unmarked touring pitches on level ground. Of these, 32 are for caravans, all with electricity and 10 with hardstanding, and 32 places are available for tents.

Facilities

The centrally located toilet block is heated and double glazed and includes a spacious shower unit for disabled visitors, a family room with shower and WC. Laundry room. Campers' kitchen (fridge/freezer, cooker, table and chairs and a lounge/games room; a TV can be provided). Basketball. Sand pit. Picnic tables. Off site: Shop, bar and restaurant 3 km. Golf. Fishing 4 km.

Open: All year.

Directions

Site is 4.8 km. northeast of Athy town off the main N78 Athy - Kilcullen road. GPS: N53:00.835 W06:55.534

Charges 2007

Per unit with electricity	€ 12.00
person	€ 4.00
child	€ 2.00
hiker, cyclist or motorcyclist incl. tent	€ 6.00

IR8815 Willowbrook Camping & Caravan Park

Kiltybranks, Ballaghaderreen. (Co. Roscommon)

Tel: **094 986 1307**. Email: **info@willowbrookpark.com**

This is a campsite with a difference. Willowbrook is a small family run caravan and camping park, which offers a unique holiday in an unspoiled part of Ireland. It has 8 hardstanding pitches with electricity and a central level grass area without power, all with ample water points. An additional tenting area is available in the adjoining field. The main difference is that meditation, Tai Chi and other relaxation techniques, all adding to the tranquillity of the setting, are organised by Dave and Lin Whitefield whose aim is to ensure their guests relax and unwind in this idyllic hideaway. Archery and guided walks on the Suck Valley Way and in the Ox and Curlieu mountains, and coarse fishing for more active relaxation are also provided. A bunkhouse (for up to twelve), a library and reading room with a TV in a renovated 100 year old cottage add to the ambiance of the park. The camper's kitchen is spotless and homely. This clean and well cared for park is located in an area rich with archaeology and heritage, about 20 minutes from Knock airport. It is ideal as a holiday base or as a stop over on the Dublin - Mayo route to the west of Ireland.

Facilities

The toilet block is immaculate and lit at night, with separate shower cubicles and facilities for disabled campers. Laundry room. Campers' kitchen with microwave, kettle and toaster. Library and reading room with TV. Fishing. Torches useful. Dogs on leads are accepted. Off site: Local sporting activities available include tennis, golf and fishing.

Open: All year.

Directions

Park is 6 km. from Ballaghaderreen. Take the R293 from Ballaghaderreen towards Castlerea and Ballyhaunis, then the R325 over the bridge. Bear left, still towards Castlerea and Ballyhaunis for 1.5 km. Turn right at sign to park in 500 m.

Charges 2007

Per unit incl. 2 persons	€ 16.00
family tent incl. 2 adults and 2 children	€ 20.00

No credit cards.

IR8825 Lough Key Caravan & Camping Park

Lough Key Forest Park, Boyle (Co. Roscommon)

Tel: **071 966 2212**

This caravan and camping park is set deep in the 320 hectares of the Lough Key Forest Park. Comprising mixed woodland including giant red cedar, beech, ash and oak trees, the forest is bounded by Lough Key and incorporates several of its islands. The history of the parkland goes back to 1184. A visit to the Lough offers views of islands inhabited by monks and hermits in days gone by, ring forts and tunnels, and natural and historical features like the Temple, the Wishing Chair, the Bog Gardens and Rockingham House and harbour. The rustic design of the main building on the park (which houses reception, a camper's kitchen, a TV room, and the sanitary and laundry facilities) blends well with the wooded environment. The well landscaped, five hectare site provides space for 52 touring units with electricity connections and ample water points. There is a separate area for tents. The location in Lough Key Forest Park offers a base for visiting Strokestown House, Boyle Abbey, Famine Museum and Garden, and the Elphin 18th century windmill. A fisherman's dream, there are pike, bream, roach and perch in Lough Key and brown trout at nearby Lough Arrow. Walks combine the historical and the legend with wildlife, flora and fauna. Boat tours of the lake and boat hire are also available. Coillte, the Irish Forestry Board, who manage the amenity, strictly enforces the forest code.

Facilities

The main toilet block includes metered hot showers. Facilities for disabled campers (key required). Campers' kitchen and sheltered eating area. Laundry. TV room. Play area in the centre of the park with adventure type play equipment in a hedged area, plus seating for parents. Forest walks and trails. Boat tours and boat hire. Security barrier closed at night. Off site: Restaurant at Rockingham harbour. Nearby town of Boyle for bars, restaurants and entertainment 3 km. Bicycle hire and golf 5 km.

Open: Easter - mid September.

Directions

Site is 4 km. east of Boyle on the A4 Carrick-on-Shannon road.

Charges 2007

Per unit incl. 2 persons	€ 16.00 - € 20.00
hiker/cyclist	€ 8.00 - € 10.00
electricity	€ 2.00
small tent	€ 8.00 - € 10.00

No credit cards.

IR8965 Lough Ennell Camping & Caravan Park

Tudenham Shore, Mullingar (Co. Westmeath)

Tel: **044 934 8101**. Email: **eamon@caravanparksireland.com**

Nature and rustic charm is the visitor's first reaction on arrival at Lough Ennell Caravan Park. Set in 18 acres of mature woodland beside a Blue Flag lake, Eamon and Geraldine O'Malley run this sheltered and tranquil park with their family. Just an hour from Dublin, it provides a good holiday base or a useful stop over en-route to the West of Ireland. The watersports permitted on the lake include canoeing, sailing, windsurfing, boating, fishing and safe swimming. The woodlands offer ample opportunities for walking and cycling. Numerous other lakes in the area provide fishing for all varieties especially wild trout. Other activities might include tennis, horse riding, golf, dog racing and of course forest walks. Belvedere House and Tullynally Castle are nearby and the large town of Mullingar is just 6 km. The O'Malley family, who live on the site, receive a complimentary blend of visitors – seasonal residents in camping holiday homes (private and to rent), caravanners and motorcaravanners and there are ample areas for tents. Pitches are varied, sheltered with trees and natural shrubbery, and spacious with gravel or gravel and grass combinations (ideal for those with awnings). Electricity is available on 44 hardstanding and grass pitches and there are water points on or near all the pitches.

Facilities

The toilet block provides toilets, washbasins and hot showers (€1 coin). Additional dishwashing areas are around the park. Laundry. Small shop. Café and coffee shop with takeaway. TV and games room. Play areas and area for ball games. Small lakeside beach. Fishing. Late arrivals area outside. Security including CCTV. Some breeds of dog are not accepted. Off site: Bus service 8 km. Golf 1.5 km. Riding 4 km. Bicycle hire 6 km.

Open: Easter/1 April - 30 September.

Directions

From N4 take the N52. Follow signs for Belvedere House and take turn 300 m. south of Belvedere House (signed for campsite). Continue to the shores of Lough Ennell and turn left.

Charges 2007

Per person	€ 5.00
child	€ 3.00
pitch	€ 10.00
electricity	€ 3.00
No credit cards.	

Lough Ennell Caravan & Camping Park

Tel: +353 - 44 - 9348101
Fax: +353 - 44 - 9342676

Tudenham Shore, Mullingar, County Westmeath. Republic of Ireland.

Beautiful family run park with 18 acres of of matured woodland. Facilities include service block, showers/toilets, kitchen, wash-up area, laundry room, TV room, games room, restaurant & coffee dock, take away and mini mart.

www.caravanparksireland.com

IR8960 Lough Ree (East) Caravan & Camping Park

Ballykeeran, Athlone (Co. Westmeath)

Tel: **090 647 8561**. Email: **athlonecamping@eircom.net**

This touring park is alongside the river, screened by trees but reaching the water's edge. Drive into the small village of Ballykeeran and the park is discreetly located behind the main street. The top half of the site is in a woodland situation and after the reception and sanitary block, Lough Ree comes into view and the remaining pitches run down to the shoreline. There are 60 pitches, 20 with hardstanding and 52 with electricity. With fishing right on the doorstep there are boats for hire and the site has its own private mooring buoys, plus a dinghy slip and harbour. A restaurant and 'singing' pub are close.

Facilities

The toilet block is clean without being luxurious. Hot showers (€ 1.00). Dishwashing sinks outside. Laundry room (wash and dry € 8.00). A wooden chalet houses a pool room with open fire and campers' kitchen (no cooking facilities). Off site: Riding 4 km. Golf 8 km.

Open: 1 April - 30 September.

Directions

From Athlone take N55 towards Longford for 4.8 km. Park is in the village of Ballykeeran, clearly signed. GPS: N53:26.915 W07:53.460

Charges 2007

Per unit incl. 2 persons	€ 18.00
extra person	€ 4.00
child (under 14 yrs)	€ 2.00
electricity (10A)	€ 3.00
No credit cards.	

IR9100 Camac Valley Tourist Caravan & Camping Park

Boot Road, Corkagh Park, Clondalkin, Dublin 22 (Co. Dublin)

Tel: **01 464 0644**. Email: **reservations@camacvalley.com**

Opened in 1996, this campsite is not only well placed for Dublin, but also offers a welcome stopover if travelling to the more southern counties from the north of the country, or vice versa. Despite its close proximity to the city, being located in the 300 acre Corkagh Park gives it a 'heart of the country' atmosphere. The site entrance and sign are distinctive and can be spotted in adequate time when approaching on the busy N7. Beyond the entrance gate and forecourt stands an attractive timber fronted building. Its design includes various roof levels and spacious interior layout, with large windows offering a view of the site. Housed here is reception, information, reading, TV and locker rooms plus shop and sanitary facilities. There are 163 pitches, 48 for tents placed to the fore and the hardstandings for caravans laid out in bays and avenues with electrical connections, drainage and water points. Maturing trees and shrubs separate pitches and roads are of tarmac. After a day of sightseeing in Dublin, which can be reached by bus from the site, Camac Valley offers an evening of relaxation with woodland and river walks in the park or some first class restaurants and pubs nearby.

Facilities

Heated sanitary facilities include good sized showers (token), facilities for disabled people, baby changing room, laundry and washing up. Playground with wooden play frames and safety base. Shop and coffee bar. Fishing. Electronic gate controlled from reception and 24 hour security. Dogs (not accepted in July/Aug) must be on leads at all times. Off site: Bicycle hire 1.5 km. Golf 6 km. Riding 9 km.

Open: All year.

Directions

From north follow signs for West Link and M50 motorway. Exit M50 at junction 9 onto N7 Cork road. Site is on right of dual carriageway (beside Green Isle Hotel) after 2 km. and is clearly signed. At City West business park, cross over bridge and return on dual carriageway following camp signs - site is on left after 800 m. GPS: N53:18.285 W06:24.931

Charges 2007

Per unit incl. 2 persons	€ 22.00 - € 24.00
incl. 2 persons and up to 4 children	€ 26.00
tent, car and 2 persons	€ 21.00
electricity (10A)	€ 10.00

Camac Valley Dublin
Tourist Caravan & Camping Park

DUBLIN'S PREMIER TOURIST CARAVAN & CAMPING PARK

- 113 hard stand, fully powered pitches & room for 70+ tents
- The only campsite close to Dublin city centre (Approx. 8km)
- Excellent facilities include showers, toilets, laundry rooms, baby changing room, wet weather room/campers kitchen, library, a fabulous childrens playground and a high speed broadband internet cafe.

+353 1464 0644   www.camacvalley.com AA

Camac Valley, Naas Road, Clondalkin, Dublin 22, Ireland

IR9130 Roundwood Caravan & Camping Park

Bray Roundwood (Co. Wicklow)

Tel: **01 281 8163**. Email: **info@dublinwicklowcamping.com**

In the heart of the Wicklow mountains, the hospitable owner of this park maintains high standards. It is neatly laid out with rows of trees dividing the different areas and giving an attractive appearance. There are 46 hardstanding pitches for caravans and motorcaravans, all with electricity (5A), plus 33 pitches for tents, arranged off tarmac access roads. There are excellent walks around the Varty Lakes and a daily bus service to Dublin city.

Facilities

The renovated sanitary block is kept clean, with adequate washing and toilet facilities, plus spacious showers on payment (€ 1). Good laundry facilities (ask at reception as machines are not self-service). Motorcaravan service point. Campers' kitchen and dining room. TV room. Adventure playground. Bicycle hire. Off site: Roundwood village has shops, pubs, restaurants, takeaway food, and a Sunday market. Fishing within 1 km. Riding, golf 3 km.

Open: 1 May - 31 August.

Directions

Turn off N11 Dublin - Wexford road at Kilmacanogue towards Glendalough and then 15 km. to Roundwood. Park is on the north side of the village. GPS: N53:04.149 W06:13.355

Charges 2007

Per unit incl. 2 persons and electricity	€ 30.00
extra person	€ 8.00
child (under 14 yrs)	€ 4.00
No credit cards.	

307

IR9140 Valley Stopover & Caravan Park

Killough, Kilmacanogue (Co. Wicklow)

Tel: 01 282 9565. Email: rowanbb@eircom.net

In a quiet, idyllic setting in the picturesque Rocky Valley, this small, neat, family run park is convenient for the Dublin ferries. Situated in the grounds of the family home, covering under an acre, it can be used either as a transit site or for a longer stay. It will appeal to those who prefer the more basic 'CL' type site. There are 15 grassy pitches, 11 with electric hook-ups, 8 hardstandings, 2 water points, night lighting and a security gate. Staying here you are only minutes from Enniskerry.

Facilities

Toilet facilities, clean when we visited, are housed in one unit and consist of two WCs with washbasins, mirrors, etc. and a shower. Dishwashing and laundry sink, a spin dryer and a campers' kitchen. Full cooked Irish breakfast is available in the family guest house. Off site: Riding 3 km. Golf 7 km. Fishing 16 km.

Open: Easter - 31 October.

Directions

Turn off N11 Dublin - Wexford road at Kilmacanogue, following signs for Glendalough. Continue for 1.6 km. and take right fork signed 'Waterfall'. Park is first opening on the left in approx. 200 m. GPS: N53:10.023 W06:09.803

Charges 2007

Per person	€ 2.50
pitch	€ 12.00 - € 15.00
awning	€ 1.50

IR9150 River Valley Caravan & Camping Park

Redcross Village (Co. Wicklow)

Tel: 040 441 647. Email: info@rivervalleypark.com

In the small country village of Redcross, in the heart of County Wicklow, you will find this popular, family run park. Based here you are within easy reach of many beauty spots and the safe beach of Brittas Bay. The 145 touring pitches at River Valley are mostly together in a dedicated area, all have electricity connections (6A) and offer a choice of hardstanding or grass – you select your pitch. Within this 16-acre site children can find day long amusement with the many facilities on offer.

Facilities

A luxurious new sanitary block has a modern, well designed appearance. Facilities for disabled visitors are excellent. Showers are on payment (€ 0.50). Laundry area. Campers' kitchen. Motorcaravan service points. Gas available. Wine/coffee bar and restaurant. TV and games room. Tennis. Par 3 golf course. Bowling. Sports complex with badminton and indoor football and basketball. Adventure and tiny tots playgrounds. Area for rallies. Caravan storage. Dogs must be on leads at all times and are only accepted in July/Aug. Off site: Riding 2 km.

Open: Mid March - end September.

Directions

From Dublin follow N11 Wexford road south, bypassing Ashford and Rathnew. After passing The Beehive pub look out for Doyle's pub on the right. Turn right at the pub and continue for 5km. to the park at the top of Redcross village. GPS: N52:53.351 W06:08.664

Charges 2007

Per caravan, motorcaravan incl. 2 persons	€ 22.00
extra person	€ 6.00
child (2-15 yrs)	€ 4.00
electricity	€ 2.00

IR9160 Moat Farm Caravan & Camping Park

Donard (Co. Wicklow)

Tel: 045 404 727. Email: moatfarm@ireland.com.

Providing a true feel of the countryside, this park is part of a working sheep farm. It offers incredible vistas across a scenic landscape, yet is within driving distance of Dublin and Rosslare. Driving into the village you little suspect that alongside the main street lies a well cared for and tranquil five acre campsite. There are 40 pitches for caravans and tents. Pitches are spacious with hardstanding and incorporate ample space for an awning and all have electricity and drainage. A large field takes tents and further caravans. Those with larger units are advised to contact the site to check accessibility.

Facilities

The toilet block is kept very clean and includes spacious showers, facilities for visitors with disabilities, and a well equipped laundry room. Good quality campers' kitchen and large recreation/entertainment room with an open fire. Three large barbecues and a patio area. Caravan storage. Off site: Mountain climbing or sites of archaeological interest nearby. Fishing 3 km. Bicycle hire 15 km. Golf 13 km.

Open: 15 March - 30 September.

Directions

Park is 16.5 km. south of Blessington. Leave M50 Dublin ring motorway at exit 10 to join N81 southwest for 19 km. to Blessington. Continue on N81 for a further 16.5 km. and turn left at Old Toll House pub onto local road. Follow signs to park in Donard (3.5 km). GPS: N53:01.262 W06:36.881

Charges 2007

Per unit incl. 2 persons and electricity	€ 22.00
extra person	€ 5.00
child	€ 4.00
No credit cards.	

IR9170 Saint Margaret's Beach Caravan & Camping Park

Lady's Island, Rosslare Harbour, Rosslare (Co. Wicklow)

Tel: **053 9131169**. Email: **stmarg@eircom.net**

'This park is loved' was how a Swedish visitor described this family run, environmentally friendly caravan and camping park, the first the visitor meets near the Rosslare ferry port. Landscaping with flowering containers and maze-like sheltered camping areas and a pretty sanitary block all demonstrate the Traynor family's attention to detail. Most pitches give shelter from the fresh sea breeze and ferries can be seen crossing the Irish sea. Just metres away, the safe, sandy beach (part of the Wexford coastal path) curves around in a horseshoe shape ending in a small pier and slipway. The immediate area boasts of thatched roof cottages and cottage gardens. The park is an ideal base from which to explore the sunny southeast or as an overnight stop to prepare for touring Ireland or for departure. Tourist information on the area is provided in the well stocked shop. Local lakes and the Saltee Islands, various locations of ornithological interest, deep sea and shore fishing, and award-winning pubs and restaurants provide something for everyone.

Facilities

The toilet block is spotless. Laundry room. Campers' kitchen including toaster, microwave and TV. Shop (June - Aug). Fresh milk and bread daily. Mobile homes for rent. Off site: Walking, beach and fishing. Boat slipway 2.5 km. Pitch and putt 2 km. Riding 6 km. Pubs and restaurants. The JFK Arboretum, Johnstown Castle and Gardens, the Irish National Heritage Park, Kilmore Quay and Marina, and Curracloe beach (featured in the film 'Saving Private Ryan').

Open: Mid March – October.

Directions

From the N25 south of Wexford town, outside village of Tagoat, follow signs for Lady's Island and Carne. After 3 km. pass Butlers Bar and take next left and continue for 2.5 km. Site is well signed.

Charges 2007

Per unit incl. 2 persons	€ 14.00 - € 22.00
extra person	€ 2.50
child (2-16 yrs)	€ 1.50
electricity	€ 2.00

IR9230 Nore Valley Park

Annamult, Bennettsbridge (Co. Kilkenny)

Tel: **0567 727 229**. Email: **norevalleypark@eircom.net**

This lovely site is set on a grassy hillock overlooking the valley and the river Nore, with a woodland setting behind. Situated on a working farm, it offers 70 touring pitches, 50 of which have 6A electricity. There is an additional area for tents and 4 mobile homes for rent. The owners, Samuel and Isabel, are proud of their park and Isabel's baking and jams must be sampled. An attractive courtyard houses several unusual facilities including a sand pit and a straw loft play area for wet weather. There is outdoor chess and tractor rides and go-karts in the fields. This is an ideal park for families, especially in school holidays, offering children and adults alike the opportunity to feed the animals (goats, lambs, ducks, chickens and donkey). It is a peaceful holiday base from which to explore the sunny southeast, including the historic city of Kilkenny, renowned for its history and craftwork, Kells Abbey and Dumoe Caves. The village of Bennettsbridge is 3 km. with shops and eating places. There is easy access to Waterford city, famous for its crystal.

Facilities

The modern toilet block is kept very clean and can be heated. Two units suitable for disabled visitors. Dishwashing sinks. Laundry room with washing machine and dryer. Motorcaravan services. The original block in the courtyard is used mainly in the low season. New reception, shop (basic items such as milk, bread and camping gaz) and café (June-Aug). Comfortable lounge. Games room with pool table. Fenced children's play area. Crazy golf. Bicycle hire. Off site: Bennettsbridge 3 km. Outdoor pursuits such as canoeing, walking or fishing 4 km. Riding 6 km. Golf 10 km.

Open: 1 March - 31 October.

Directions

From Kilkenny take R700 to Bennettsbridge. Just before the bridge turn right at sign for Stoneyford and after approx. 3 km. site is signed Nore Valley Park. GPS: N52:33.777 W07:11.698

Charges 2007

Per person (over 2 yrs)	€ 3.00
pitch	€ 6.00 - € 12.00
electricity (6A)	€ 3.00

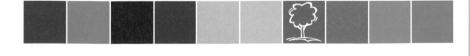

309

IR9240 Tree Grove Caravan & Camping Park

Danville House, Kilkenny (Co. Kilkenny)

Tel: 0567 770 302. Email: treecc@iol.ie

The entrance gate to this small family run site is easily spotted off the R700 road. Tree Grove is within walking distance of medieval Kilkenny, known for its elegance and famed for its beer and cats. An orderly, neat park, it appeals because its young owners are friendly and have designed a logical layout to suit both the terrain and campers needs. It is terraced with the lower terrace to the right of the wide sweeping driveway laid out with 11 hardstanding pitches for caravans. All 30 pitches have electrical hook-ups (10A) and plenty of water points are to be found. On a higher level, is a grass area for hikers and cyclists with further caravan and tent pitches sited near the elevated sanitary block. If needed more grass pitches face reception, which is housed in a modern wooden chalet. Whilst there are mature trees at the entrance and around the site perimeter, many shrubs have been effectively placed together with flower troughs. On the patio there are bench seats with tables and umbrellas. There is much to see and do around the ancient city of Kilkenny (1.5 km) with its cobbled streets and castle. County Touring Routes are worth following.

Facilities

House plants add decoration inside the toilet block giving a cared for look to this modern building which includes a family room with shower, WC and washbasin which can be used by disabled people. Laundry room. Open, covered kitchen for campers with fridge, worktop, sink and electric kettle adjoins a comfortable games/TV room with pool table, and easy chairs. Bicycle hire. Tents to rent on site. Off site: Fishing 500 m. Riding 1 km. Golf 2 or 15 km.

Open: 1 March - 15 November.

Directions

Travelling north on the N10 Waterford/Kilkenny Road turn right at roundabout on ring road. Continue to 2nd roundabout and turn right onto R700. Site is 150 m. on right. GPS: N52:38.400 W07:13.780

Charges 2007

Per unit incl. 2 persons	€ 18.00
tent (per person)	€ 7.50
electricity (10A)	€ 2.00

No credit cards.

IR9460 Corofin Village Camping & Caravan Park

Main Street, Corofin (Co. Clare)

Tel: 065 683 7683. Email: corohost@iol.ie

This compact green oasis in the centre of the village of Corofin occupies one acre and adjoins the family's hostel. The owners, Jude and Marie Neylon live on the site and have a policy of always having a family member on hand at all times. They are very environmentally aware and have excellent recycling facilities. The 20 pitches all have electricity and there are ample water points. A campers' kitchen, laundry room and the TV and games room are separate to the hostel facilities. This little site is neat and well maintained and makes an ideal base for sightseeing throughout Clare, especially for the world famous Burren and the Aillwee Caves, Craggaunown Megalithic Centre and Quinn and Knappogue Castles, as well as places of interest in Galway and Limerick. Public transport is available to the famous Lahinch beach and to the large town of Ennis. It is a peaceful location, yet central for the restaurants, takeaway, shops and pubs in the village. This area is renowned for its traditional music. There are several lakes in the immediate locality for boating and fishing enthusiasts.

Facilities

The sanitary block is bright and clean with free hot showers and separate facilities for disabled campers. Laundry room with washing machine and dryer. CCTV security. Torches useful. Site is not suitable for large units. Off site: Fishing and boat launching 2 km. Riding 8 km. Bicycle hire 10 km. Golf 20 km. Beach 20 km.

Open: 1 April - 30 September.

Directions

Corofin village is 12 km. from Ennis. Take the N85 to Ennistymon and after 2 km. (well signed) turn on R476. Site is in the centre of the village. GPS: N52:56.442 W09:03.536

Charges 2008

Per unit, all inclusive	€ 20.00

IR9330 Casey's Caravan & Camping Park

Clonea, Dungarvan (Co. Waterford)

Tel: **058 419 19**

Set on 20 acres of flat grass, edged by mature trees, this family run park is well managed and offers 284 pitches which include 154 touring pitches, 118 with electrical hook-ups and 30 with hardstanding. The remainder are occupied by caravan holiday homes. There is direct access from the park to a sandy, 'Blue Flag' beach with a resident lifeguard during July and August. A highly recommended leisure centre is adjacent should the weather be inclement. The park is 5.5 km. from Dungarvan, a popular town for deep sea angling, from which charter boats can be hired and three 18 hole golf courses are within easy distance. Suggested drives include the scenic Vee, the Comeragh Drive and the coast road to Tramore.

Facilities

The central toilet block (key system), has good facilities kept spotlessly clean, with showers on payment (€1), washing up sinks and small laundry with machine and dryer. A further luxurious and modern block provides an excellent campers' kitchen, laundry room and toilet for disabled visitors. Large adventure play area with bark surface in its own field (not supervised). Games room with pool table, table tennis and amusements. TV lounge. Crazy golf. Gas supplies. Full time security staff in high season. Off site: Two village stores near the beach. Golf.

Open: 26 April - 7 September.

Directions

From Dungarvan centre follow R675 east for 3.5 km. Look for signs on the right to Clonea Bay and site. Site is approx. 1.5 km.
GPS: N52:05.690 W07:32.766

Charges 2007

Per unit incl. 2 persons	€ 22.00 - € 24.00
extra person	€ 7.00
child	€ 2.00
electricity (10A)	€ 4.00

No credit cards.

CASEY'S CARAVAN & CAMPING PARK

Grade Category 4★ • Bord Failte Registered • Bord Failte / ICC Park Awards
Best 4★ 2004 • 2000 & 2002 Overall Winner Best Park
2001 & 2002 Personal Choice Awards • Merit Award 4★ 2003

Top class facilities including; playground, electric sites for tents & tourers (5A), crazy golf, games & TV rooms and also laundry & kitchen facilities. The park is situated next to EU Blue Flag beach. 2 shops with takeaway are also nearby.

Dungarvan town is 5.5km away and there's a choice of scenic views to visit. Adjacent hotel with 19 metre pool and leisure centre with bowling alley. Other activities can include deep sea and river angling and an 18 hole golf course which are all within easy reach.

Clonea, Dungarvan, Co Waterford   Tel: +353 (0)58 41919

IR9340 Newtown Cove Camping & Caravan Park

Newtown Road, Tramore (Co. Waterford)

Tel: **051 381 979**. Email: **info@newtowncove.com**

Well run and friendly, this very attractive small park is only five minutes walk from the beautiful Newton Cove. It offers views of the famous and historic Metal Man and is 2.5 km. from Tramore beach and 11 km. from Waterford. Neatly set out on gently sloping grass are 40 pitches, with the abundance of shrubs and bushes reflecting the efforts of the owners. All pitches have electrical connections (10A), some with hardstanding also, and access is by well lit, tarmac roads. There are around 50 privately owned caravan holiday homes. A modern building at the entrance houses reception, the amenities and additional sanitary facilities. The village of Tramore, with a wide range of shops and eating houses, is close and there is a choice of many delightful cliff walks.

Facilities

The main sanitary block at the bottom end of the site is not very modern but has been re-tiled and provides good, clean facilities including a bathroom. Showers on payment (token from reception). Facilities for disabled visitors. Also here are a campers' kitchen with cooking facilities, sheltered eating area, lounge, dishwashing room and small laundry. Small shop (1/7- 30/8). TV room. Games room. Small play area in centre of park. Off site: Golf 800 m. Fishing 400 m, riding 3 km.

Open: 7 April - 1 October.

Directions

From Tramore on R675 coast road to Dungarvan. Turn left 2 km. from town centre, following signs.
GPS: N52:08.877 W07:10.358

Charges 2008

Per person	€ 6.00
child (3-15 yrs)	€ 3.00
pitch	€ 8.00 - € 13.00
hiker, cyclist or motorcyclist	€ 8.00 - € 11.00
electricity (10A)	€ 4.00

No credit cards. No single sex groups.

311

IR9400 The Glen of Aherlow Caravan & Camping Park

Newtown, Glen of Aherlow (Co. Tipperary)

Tel: **062 565 55**. Email: **rdrew@eircom.net**

The owners of one of Ireland's newest parks, George and Rosalind Drew, are campers themselves and have set about creating an idyllic park in an idyllic location. This five acre park is set in one of Ireland's most picturesque valleys and is open all year. There are beautiful views of the wooded and hilly areas of Slievenamuck and the Galtee Mountains. This area is an outdoor paradise with a nature park and forest trails, with a six kilometre walk starting at the park entrance. With local pubs and a restaurant just 300 m. away, this is an ideal base from which to tour a variety of attractions such as the Rock of Cashel, Cahir Castle, Holycross Abbey and many more. There are 42 large and level pitches, with both hardstanding and grass places, each with a 10A electricity connection and water point. The Drew family is happy to welcome large groups and rallies and large units can be accommodated. The excellent facilities are located in a purpose built building.

Facilities

The modern toilet block includes free showers and facilities for disabled visitors. Motorcaravan service point. Laundry room with ironing. Campers' kitchen. Recreation and TV rooms. Off site: Holiday homes to rent 300 m. Restaurant 300 m. Outdoor activities. Fishing. Golf and riding 7 km.

Open: All year.

Directions

From Tipperary town take N24 via Bansha, then R663 to Newtown. Continue through village and pass Coach Road Inn to park in 300 m.

Charges guide

Per unit incl. 2 persons	€ 22.00
extra person	€ 4.00
child (2-14 yrs)	€ 2.00
electricity	€ 4.00

IR9410 The Apple Camping & Caravan Park

Moorstown, Cahir (Co. Tipperary)

Tel: **052 414 59**. Email: **con@theapplefarm.com**

This fruit farm and campsite combination offers an idyllic country holiday venue in one of the most delightful situations imaginable. For tourers only, it is located off the N24, midway between Clonmel and Cahir. Entrance is by way of a 300 m. drive which follows straight through the heart of the farm. Apple trees guard the route, as do various non-fruit tree species, which are named and of interest to guests who are free to spend time walking the paths around the farm. When we visited, strawberries were being gathered – the best we had tasted all season – and award winning apple juice, cordials, jams, etc. are also sold by Con and Noreen in the farm shop. Reception is housed with the other site facilities in a large farmyard barn. Although a rather unusual arrangement, it is central and effective. The park has 32 pitches in a secluded situation behind the barns and are mostly grass with a few hardstandings, with electricity connections to 25. The towns of Cahir and Clonmel are of historic interest and the countryside around boasts rivers, mountains, Celtic culture and scenic drives.

Facilities

Toilet facilities, kept very clean, quite modern in design and with heating, comprise showers, washbasins with mirrors, electric points, etc. in functional units occupying two corners of the large floor space. Facilities for disabled visitors. Also in the barn are dishwashing sinks, washing machine and a fridge/freezer for campers to use. Motorcaravan service point. Tennis court, basketball/football pitch and play area. Dogs are not accepted. Off site: Fishing, golf, bicycle hire and riding within 6 km.

Open: 1 May - 30 September.

Directions

Park is 300 m. off main N24, 9.6 km. west of Clonmel, 6.4 km. east of Cahir. GPS: N52:22.719 W07:50.509

Charges 2007

Per person	€ 6.00
child (0-12 yrs)	€ 4.00
electricity (13A)	€ 2.50
No charge per unit.	
Less 20% for groups of 4 or more.	

IR9370 Ballinacourty House Caravan & Camping Park

Glen of Aherlow, Tipperary (Co. Tipperary)

Tel: **062 565 59**. Email: **info@camping.ie**

Ballinacourty House and its cobble-stoned courtyard form the centrepiece of this south-facing park with views of the Galtee Mountains. Accessed by a tree-lined lane, the reception area is in part of the renovated 18th century building, as is the adjoining restaurant. The park is level with 26 touring pitches with 6A electricity and 25 grassy pitches for tents. Some areas are shaded areas and there are open spaces to accommodate rallies and larger groups. Self-catering cottages and B&B are also available. This tranquil site is an ideal base from which to tour the Rock of Cashel, the Mitchelstown Caves, Swiss Cottage and the towns of Tipperary, Cahir and Cashel. Activities in the area include horse riding and trekking, fishing for perch and brown trout, cycling, forest walks, three 18-hole golf courses, leisure centre with swimming pool,cinema theatre and pottery shop.

Facilities

Sanitary facilities provide free hot water and showers. Baby room. Facilities for disabled visitors are planned. Laundry with ironing facilities. Campers' kitchen. Ice pack freezing. Licensed restaurant (early booking advised). Motorcaravan services. Minigolf. TV and games rooms. Picnic benches. Tennis court. Play area. Gas supplies. Off site: Riding, fishing, golf.

Open: 1 May - 21 September.

Directions

From the N24 Tipperary - Cahir road, take Glen of Aherlow scenic route 6.5 km. from Cahir and follow signs. GPS: N52:24.590 W08:12.630

Charges 2008

Per unit incl. 2 persons	€ 8.00 - € 10.00
extra person	€ 5.00
child	€ 2.00
electricity	€ 3.00

IR9420 Streamstown Caravan & Camping Park

Streamstown, Roscrea (Co. Tipperary)

Tel: **050 521 519**. Email: **streamstowncaravanpark@eircom.net**

This family run site, set on a dairy farm in the centre of Ireland, has been open for over 30 years. It is conveniently situated off the N7 Dublin - Limerick road and makes a good overnight halt or for a longer stay if you are seeking a quiet, restful location with little to disturb the peace. This is a working farm and the owners, who are friendly and welcoming, are in the process of improving and developing their site. What impresses most here is the tidy overall appearance with neatly trimmed hedging, tables placed around the grass areas and with flower baskets a special feature. There are 27 touring pitches, 10 with hardstanding and separated by low hedges. The remainder are on grass and more suitable for units with awnings. Nearby pubs offer traditional music evenings and mountain walking and fishing can be enjoyed in the area.

Facilities

The sanitary facilities, very clean when we visited, are housed in a modern block. Showers (free), toilets and washbasins are older in style but a couple of washbasins are in cubicles. Facilities for disabled visitors in family shower room. Good laundry room with iron (free). Good campers' kitchen with fridge/freezer, electric cooker and TV. Play area with safety surface. TV and games room. Caravan storage. Off site: Fishing 1.8 km. Golf 5 km. Riding 8 km.

Open: 1 April - 9 October.

Directions

From Roscrea centre follow signs for R491 Shirone. Continue towards Shirone following camp signs for approx. 2.5 km. and site entrance is on left. GPS: N52:57.432 W07:50.362

Charges 2007

Per person	€ 4.50
child (under 14 yrs)	€ 2.00
pitch	€ 10.00
electricity (10A)	€ 3.00
5 nights for the price of 4.	

313

IR9470 Blackwater Valley Caravan & Camping Park

Mallow-Killarney Road, Fermoy (Co. Cork)

Tel: 025 321 47

The location of this park provides the best of both worlds, as it backs onto green fields adjacent to the Blackwater river, yet is within 200 metres of Fermoy town. Pat and Nora Ryan live overlooking the park which ensures supervision and attention to detail. Ideal for touring, there are 25 pitches with hardstanding and electricity connections (13A) and water supply nearby, and considerable additional space for tents towards the rear of the park. There are five caravan holiday homes to rent. Fermoy provides local amenities, such as a cinema and the town park with a leisure centre with pool and a play area. There are restaurants and pubs, many providing traditional music. The Mitchelstown Caves, Mount Mellary, Lismore Castle and many other attractions are within easy reach of the park.

Facilities

Modern, tiled toilet block provides the usual facilities including for disabled visitors. Laundry room with ironing facilities. Campers' kitchen with cooking facilities and good size dining area. TV and games room. Motorcaravan service point. Fishing adjacent to park. Off site: Bicycle hire 500 m. Golf 3.5 km. Beach 35 km. Internet access 100 m. Petrol station with gas across the road.

Open: 15 March - 31 October.

Directions

In Fermoy town take the N72 for Mallow. Park is 200 m. from the junction. GPS: N52:08.460 W08:16.700

Charges guide

Per unit incl. 2 persons	€ 17.00
extra person	€ 5.00
electricity	€ 3.50

No credit cards.

IR9480 Blarney Caravan & Camping Park

Stone View, Blarney (Co. Cork)

Tel: 021 451 6519. Email: con.quill@camping-ireland.ie

There is a heart of the country feel about this 'on the farm' site, yet the city of Cork is only an 8 km. drive. What makes this friendly, family run park so appealing is its secluded location and neatly laid out, open appearance. The terrain on the three acre park is elevated and gently sloping, commanding views towards Blarney Castle and the surrounding mountainous countryside. The 80 pitches, 39 of which have hardstanding and 10A electrical connections, are with caravans sited to the centre and left and tents pitched to the right. There are gravel roads, well tended young shrubs and a screen of mature trees and hedging marks the park's perimeter. In the Blarney area, apart from Blarney Castle, house and gardens, there are shops, restaurants, pubs with traditional music and an abundance of outdoor pursuits such as walking, riding and fishing, and easy access to sightseeing in Cork city.

Facilities

Excellent toilet areas, one new, are housed in converted farm buildings with reception and small shop. Facilities for disabled visitors. Laundry room with sinks, washing machine, dryer and ironing. Dishwashing area in the large campers' kitchen. Motorcaravan service point. Shop (1/6-31/8). TV lounge. 18-hole golf and pitch and putt course. Night lighting. Off site: Public bar and restaurant 100 m. serving food all day. Within easy reach of the ports of Cork and Rosslare.

Open: 1 April - 31 October.

Directions

Site is 8 km. northwest of Cork, just off the N20. Take N20 from Cork for approx. 6 km. and then left on R617 to Blarney. Site clearly signed at Top Filling station in village, in 2 km. GPS: N51:56.872 W08:32.776

Charges 2007

Per person	€ 6.00
child	€ 2.50
pitch	€ 6.50 - € 8.00
electricity (10A)	€ 4.00

IR9505 The Hideaway Camping & Caravan Park

Skibbereen (Co. Cork)

Tel: **028 222 54**. Email: **skibbereencamping@eircom.net**

A sister park to The Meadow at Glandore, the Hideaway is ideally situated as a touring base for the southwest of Ireland. It is a well run site under the constant supervision of the owners and although it enjoys tranquil surroundings, including preserved marshland, it is within a ten minute walk from the busy market town of Skibbereen. The Hideaway is a touring only park with 60 pitches, including 50 with hardstanding and 6A electric hook-up. The remainder for tents. Shrubs and low hedges divide the park giving an open feel overall and with commanding views across the fields and hills.

Facilities
The modern toilet block has non slip floors, well equipped showers (on payment), a baby room with bath and an en-suite unit for disabled visitors. Dishwashing sinks. Laundry machines. Campers' dining room. Motorcaravan service point. Night lighting. Adventure play area. Off site: Fishing 1.6 km. Golf 2 km. Riding 4 km. Bicycle hire 1 km.

Open: 14 - 24 March, 1 May - 15 September.

Directions
From Skibbereen town centre take R596 (signed Casteltownsend). Site is on the left after 1 km. GPS: N51:32.500 W09:15.605

Charges 2008
Per unit incl. 2 persons and electricity	€ 22.00
extra person	€ 8.00
child (under 16 yrs)	€ 3.00

No credit cards.

IR9510 Eagle Point Caravan & Camping Park

Ballylickey, Bantry (Co. Cork)

Tel: **027 506 30**. Email: **eaglepointcamping@eircom.net**

Midway between the towns of Bantry and Glengarriff, the spectacular peninsula of Eagle Point juts into Bantry Bay. The first impression is of a spacious country park rather than a campsite. As far as the eye can see this 20 acre, landscaped, part-terraced park, with its vast manicured grass areas separated by mature trees, shrubs and hedges, runs parallel with the shoreline providing lovely views. Suitable for all ages, this is a well run park devoted to tourers, with campers pitched mostly towards the shore. It provides 125 pitches (60 caravans, 65 tents), and electric hook-ups, thus avoiding overcrowding during peak periods. Eagle Point makes an excellent base for sightseeing .

Facilities
Three well maintained, well designed toilet blocks are above expected standards. Laundry and dishwashing. Motorcaravan services. Play area. Tennis courts. Football field to the far right, well away from the pitches. Fishing. Supermarket at park entrance. Dogs are not accepted. Off site: Bicycle hire 6 km. Riding 10 km. Golf 2 km.

Open: 21 April - 30 September.

Directions
Take N71 to Bandon, then R586 Bandon to Bantry. From Bantry take N71 to Glengarriif. 6.4 km. from Bantry; park entrance is opposite EMO petrol station. GPS: N51·43·207 W09:26.977

Charges 2007
Per unit incl. 2 persons	€ 23.00 - € 24.00
extra person	€ 3.00
motorcyclist, hiker or cyclist (per person)	€ 10.00
electricity (6A)	€ 3.00

IR9550 Anchor Caravan Park

Castlegregory (Co. Kerry)

Tel: **066 713 9157**. Email: **anchorcaravanpark@eircom.net**

Of County Kerry's three long, finger like peninsulas which jut into the sea, Dingle is the most northerly. Tralee is the main town and Anchor Caravan Park is 20 km. west of this famed town and under 4 km. south of Castlegregory on Tralee Bay. A secluded and mature, five acre park, it is enclosed by shrubs and trees that give excellent shelter. A gateway leads to a beautiful, sandy beach which is safe for bathing, boating and shore fishing. There are 30 pitches, all with electric hook-ups and some also with drainage and water points. Although there are holiday homes for hire, these are well apart from the touring pitches.

Facilities
Toilet facilities (entry by key) are kept very clean and provide showers on payment (€ 0,50), two private cabins, some low level basins and a toilet with handrail. Laundry facilities. Campers' kitchen with fridges, freezers and seating. Motorcaravan services at gate. Two play areas. Games and TV rooms. Night lighting. Off site: Beautiful sandy beach 2 minutes. Fishing 2 km. Riding or bicycle hire 3 km. Golf 4 km.

Open: Easter - 30 September.

Directions
From Tralee follow the Dingle coast road for 19 km. Park is signed from Camp junction. GPS: N52:14.646 W09:59.141

Charges 2007
Per unit incl. all persons	€ 16.00 - € 18.00
motorcyclist, hiker or cyclist incl. tent (per person)	€ 6.00 - € 7.00
electricity	€ 2.00

No credit cards.

IR9500 The Meadow Camping Park

Glandore (Co. Cork)

Tel: **028 332 80**. Email: **the_meadow@oceanfree.net**

The stretch of coast from Cork to Skibbereen reminds British visitors of Devon before the era of mass tourism. This is rich dairy country, the green of the meadows matching the emerald colours of the travel posters. Thanks to the warm and wet Gulf Stream climate, it is also a county of gardens and keen gardeners. The Meadows is best described not as a site, but as a one acre garden surrounded, appropriately, by lush meadows. It lies 1.5 km. east of the fishing village of Glandore, a haven in the summer for sailing. A further 5 km. west is the regional centre, Skibbereen, beyond which the landscape moves from unspoilt Devon to unspoilt Cornwall. West Cork has myriad small coastal villages and scenic routes. The owners, who live on the park, have cunningly arranged accommodation for 19 pitches among the flower beds and shrubberies of their extended garden. There are 10 hardstandings for motorcaravans with 6A electric hook-ups. Among the homely features are a sitting room and a well equipped kitchen.

Facilities

Facilities are limited but well designed and immaculately maintained. Showers on payment. Washing machine and dryer. Larger units may be accepted depending on length and available space; contact park before arrival. Off site: Riding 5 km. Fishing, swimming, boat launching and sailing at Glandore 2 km.

Open: 1 May - 15 September.

Directions

Park is 1.5 km. east of Glandore, off N71 road, on R597 midway between Leap and Rosscarbery (coast road). GPS: N51:34.009 W09:05.818

Charges 2008

Per unit incl. 2 persons	€ 19.00
extra person	€ 5.00
child (under 12 yrs)	€ 2.00
electricity (6A)	€ 3.00
No credit cards.	

IR9560 Wave Crest Caravan & Camping Park

Caherdaniel (Co. Kerry)

Tel: **066 947 5188**. Email: **wavecrest@eircom.net**

It would be difficult to imagine a more dramatic location than Wave Crest's on the Ring of Kerry coast. Huge boulders and rocky outcrops tumble from the park entrance on the N70 down to the seashore which forms the most southern promontory on the Ring of Kerry. There are spectacular southward views from the park across Kenmare Bay to the Beara peninsula. Sheltering on grass patches in small coves that nestle between the rocks and shrubbery, are 65 hardstanding pitches and 20 on grass offering seclusion. Electricity connections are available (13A). A unique feature is the TV room, an old stone farm building with a thatched roof. Its comfortable interior includes a stone fireplace heated by a converted cast iron marker buoy. Caherdaniel is known for its cheerful little pubs and distinguished restaurant. The Derrynane National Park Nature Reserve is only a few kilometres away, as is Derrynane Cove and Bay. This park would suit older people looking for a quiet, relaxed atmosphere.

Facilities

Two blocks house the sanitary facilities and include hot showers on payment (€ 1), toilet for disabled people and dishwashing sinks. Laundry service. Small shop and takeaway service (May - Sept). Play area. Fishing and boat launching. Off site: Riding 1 km. Bicycle hire and golf 10 km. Small beach near and Derrynane Hotel with bar and restaurant.

Open: 27 April - 30 September.

Directions

On the N70 (Ring of Kerry), 1.5 km. east of Caherdaniel.

Charges guide

Per person	€ 2.00
child	€ 1.00
pitch	€ 12.00 - € 13.00
electricity (13A)	€ 2.00

IR9570 Creveen Lodge Caravan & Camping Park

Healy Pass, Lauragh (Co. Kerry)

Tel: **064 831 31**. Email: **info@creveenlodge.com**

The address of this park is rather confusing, but Healy Pass is the well known scenic summit of the road (R574) crossing the Beara Peninsula, which lies between Kenmare Bay to the north and Bantry Bay to the south. Several kilometres inland from the north coast road (R571), the R574 starts to climb steeply southward towards the Healy Pass. Here, on the mountain foothills, is Creveen Lodge, a working hill farm with a quiet, homely atmosphere. Although not so famed as the Iveragh Peninsula, around which runs the Ring of Kerry, the northern Beara is a scenically striking area of County Kerry. Creveen Lodge, commanding views across Kenmare Bay, is divided among three gently sloping fields separated by trees. To allow easy access, the steep farm track is divided into a simple one-way system. There are 20 pitches, 16 for tents, 4 for caravans, with an area of hardstanding for motorcaravans, and electrical connections are available. The park is carefully tended with neat rubbish bins and rustic picnic tables informally placed. This is walking and climbing countryside or, of interest close by, is Derreen Gardens.

Facilities

Well appointed and immaculately maintained, the small toilet block provides showers on payment (€ 0.65), plus a communal room with very good cooking facilities, a fridge, freezer, TV, ironing board, fireplace, tables and chairs. Chemical disposal. Reception is in the farmhouse. Play area. Off site: Water sports, riding, 'Seafare' cruises, shops and a restaurant nearby. Fishing 2 km. Bicycle hire and boat launching 9 km.

Open: Easter - 31 October.

Directions

Park is on the Healy Pass road (R574) 1.5 km. southeast of Lauragh. GPS: N51:45.312 W09:45.615

Charges 2007

Per unit incl. 2 persons	€ 16.00
extra person	€ 3.00
child	€ 1.00
electricity (5A)	€ 4.00

No credit cards.

Creveen Lodge • Caravan & Camping Park

Set in the heart of beautiful scenery of the Ring of Beara

Ideal for walkers, cyclists, climbers and for those who want to relax. Cottage sleeping up to 6 also available. Dogs welcome.

Tel: +353 64 83 131 Web: www.creveenlodge.com

IR9580 Beara Camping The Peacock

Coornagillagh, Tuosist, Post Killarney (Co. Kerry)

Tel: **064 842 87**. Email: **campingthepeacock@eircom.net**

Five minutes from Kenmare Bay, The Peacock is a unique location for campers who would appreciate the natural surroundings of a campsite where disturbance to nature is kept to a minimum. This five acre site offers simple, clean and imaginative camping facilities. Located on the Ring of Beara, bordering the counties of Cork and Kerry, visitors will be treated with hospitality by a Dutch couple, almost more Irish than the Irish, who have made Ireland their home and run the site with their family and Kleintje, the pot-bellied Vietnamese pig. Bert and Klaske are only too anxious to share with visitors the unspoiled natural terrain, the local wildlife, the opportunity of a cosy sheltered campfire and advice on the walking and hiking routes in the area aided by maps provided on loan. The variety of accommodation at Beara Camping includes the hostel, caravan holiday homes, secluded hardstanding pitches with electricity and level grass areas for tenting. In addition, there are cabins sleeping two or four people and hiker huts sleeping two, ideal to avoid a damp night or to dry out. Breakfast, lunch and dinner plus 'good' coffee are available, plus fresh bread each morning.

Facilities

Three small blocks, plus facilities at the restaurant provide toilets, washbasins and free hot showers. Laundry service for a small fee. Campers' kitchens, dishwashing and sheltered eating area. Restaurant and takeaway (May - Oct). Small shop (May - Oct). Bicycle hire. Off site: Public transport from the gate in the summer. Pub 900 m. Riding 6 km. Golf 12 km. Boating, fishing and sea angling 200 m. Beach (pebble) 500 m.

Open: All year.

Directions

From the A22, 17 km. east of Killarney, take the R569 south to Kenmare. In Kenmare take R571, Castletownbere road and site is 12 km.

Charges 2007

Per unit incl. 2 persons	€ 12.50 - € 17.50
extra person	€ 3.00
child (4-10 yrs)	€ 1.75
electricity	€ 2.50

IR9590 Fossa Caravan & Camping Park

Fossa, Killarney (Co. Kerry)

Tel: **064 314 97**. Email: **fossaholidays@eircom.net**

This mature, well equipped park is in a scenic location, ten minutes drive from the town centre. Fossa Caravan Park is recognisable by its forecourt on which stands a distinctive building with reception area and shop. The well laid out park is divided in two – the touring area lies to the right, tucked behind the main building and to the left is an open grass area mainly for campers. Touring pitches, with electricity and drainage, have hardstanding and are angled between shrubs and trees in a tranquil, well cared for garden setting. To the rear at a higher level and discreetly placed are 30 caravan holiday homes. Sheltered by the thick foliage of the wooded slopes which climb high behind the park, these are unobtrusive. Not only is Fossa convenient for Killarney (5.5 km), it is also en-route for the famed 'Ring of Kerry', and makes an ideal base for walkers and golfers.

Facilities

Modern toilet facilities kept spotlessly clean include showers on payment. Laundry room, washing up area. Campers' kitchen. Shop (1/4-30/9). Takeaway (8/7-25/8). TV lounge. Tennis court. Play area. Picnic area. Games room. Night lighting and security patrol. Off site: Fishing and golf 2 km. Riding 3 km. Bicycle hire 5 km.

Open: 1 April - 30 September.

Directions

Approaching Killarney from all directions, follow signs for N72 Ring of Kerry/Killorglin. At last roundabout join R562/N72. Continue for 5.5 km. and Fossa is the second park to the right. GPS: N52:04.246 W09:35.147

Charges 2007

Per person	€ 5.50
child (under 14 yrs)	€ 2.00
pitch	€ 6.00 - € 8.00
electricity (10/15A)	€ 4.00

IR9620 Fleming's White Bridge

Ballycasheen Road, Killarney (Co. Kerry)

Tel: **064 315 90**. Email: **info@killarneycamping.com**

Once past the county border, the main road from Cork to Killarney (N22) runs down the valley of the Flesk river. On the final approach to Killarney off the N22 Cork road, the river veers away from the road to enter the Lower Lake. On this prime rural position, between the road and the river, and within comfortable walking distance of the town, is Fleming's White Bridge, a nine acre woodland park. The ground is flat, landscaped and generously adorned with flowers, shrubs and trees. There are now 92 pitches (46 caravans and 46 tents) that extend beyond a wooden bridge to an area surrounded by mature trees and where a new toilet block, one of three, is sited. This is obviously a park of which the owners are very proud, and the family personally supervise the reception and grounds, maintaining high standards of hygiene, cleanliness and tidiness. The park's location so close to Ireland's premier tourism centre makes this park an ideal base to explore Killarney and the southwest.

Facilities

Three toilet blocks are maintained to high standards. Dishwashing sinks. Motorcaravan service point. Campers' drying room and two laundries. Shop (1/6-1/9). Two TV rooms and a games room. Fishing (advice and permits provided). Canoeing (own canoes). Bicycle hire. Woodland walks. Off site: Riding 3 km. Golf 2 km.

Open: 13 April - 30 October (excl 16-25 October).

Directions

From Cork and Mallow: at N72/N22 junction continue towards Killarney and take first turn left (signed Ballycasheen Road). Proceed for 300 m. to archway entrance on left. From Limerick: follow N22 Cork road. After passing Super Valu and The Heights Hotel take first right (signed Ballycasheen Road) and continue as above. From Kenmare: On N71, pass Gleneagles Hotel and Flesk Bridge. Turn right at traffic lights into Woodlawn Road and Ballycasheen Road and continue 2 km. to archway. GPS: N52:03.372 W09:28.463

Charges 2007

Per unit incl. 2 persons	€ 14.00
child (under 14 yrs)	€ 2.50
hiker, cyclist	€ 8.50 - € 9.00
electricity (10A)	€ 4.00
No credit cards.	

IR9610 Mannix Point Camping & Caravan Park

Cahirciveen (Co. Kerry)

Tel: **066 947 2806**. Email: **mortimer@campinginkerry.com**

A tranquil, beautifully located seashore park, it is no exaggeration to describe Mannix Point as a nature lovers' paradise. Situated in one of the most spectacular parts of the Ring of Kerry, overlooking the bay and Valentia Island, the seven acre park commands splendid views in all directions. Laid out 20 years ago by keen gardener, Mortimer Moriarty, it his intention to cause as little disruption to nature as possible has succeeded. The site opens directly onto marshland which teems with wildlife (a two acre nature reserve) with direct access to the beach and seashore. The park road meanders through the level site and offers 42 pitches of various sizes and shape, many with shelter and seclusion. There are 36 electrical connections (13A) available. A charming, flower bedecked old fisherman's cottage has been converted to provide facilities including reception, a cosy sitting room with turf fire, and an 'emergency' dormitory for campers is a feature. There is no television, but compensation comes in the form of a knowledgeable, hospitable owner who is a Bord Fáilte registered local tour guide. This park retains a wonderful air of Irish charm aided by occasional impromptu musical evenings. A viewing platform allows observation of seals and birdlife and to consoder the secrets of the park sculpture, 'the pinicle'. This is also an ideal resting place for people walking the Kerry Way.

Facilities

Toilet and shower facilities were immaculate when we visited. Modern and well equipped campers' kitchen and dining area. Laundry facilities with washing machines and dryer. Motorcaravan service facilities. Picnic and barbecue facilities. Off site: Bicycle hire 800 m. Riding 3 km. Golf 14 km. Pubs, restaurants and shops 15 minutes walk. Watersports, bird watching, walking and photography. Local cruises to Skelligs Rock with free transport to and from the port for walkers and cyclists.

Open: 15 March - 1 October.

Directions

Park is 300 m. off the N70 Ring of Kerry road, 800 m. southwest of Cahirciveen (or Cahersiveen) on the road towards Waterville.
GPS: N51:56.571 W10:14.607

Charges 2007

Per person	€ 6.00
child (1 or 2 children)	€ 2.00

Reductions for activity groups and rallies if pre-paid. No credit cards.

IR9640 Killarney Flesk Caravan & Camping Park

Muckross Road, Killarney (Co. Kerry)

Tel: **064 317 04**. Email: **killarneylakes@eircom.net.**

At the gateway to the National Park and Lakes, near Killarney town, this family run, seven acre park has undergone extensive development and offers high quality standards. Pitches are well spaced and have electricity (10A), water, and drainage connections; 21 also have hardstanding with a grass area for awnings. The grounds have been well cultivated with further shrubs, plants and an attractive barbecue and patio area. This is to the left of the sanitary block and is paved and sunk beneath the level roadway. Surrounded by a garden border, it has tables and chairs, making a pleasant communal meeting place commanding excellent views of Killarney's mountains.

Facilities

Modern, clean toilet blocks are well designed and equipped. Baby bath/changing room. Laundry room. Campers' kitchen with dishwashing sinks. Comfortable games room. Night lighting and night time security checks. Winter caravan storage. Off site: Adjacent hotel (same ownership) with bar and restaurant. Fishing 300 m. Boat launching 2 km.

Open: 17 April - 30 September.

Directions

From Killarney town centre follow the N71 and signs for Killarney National Park. Site is 1.5 km. on the left beside the Gleneagle Hotel.
GPS: N52:02.594 W09:29.921

Charges 2007

Per person	€ 8.00
child (under 14 yrs)	€ 3.00
pitch	€ 8.00 - € 9.00
electricity (10A)	€ 5.00

IR9600 Glenross Caravan & Camping Park

Glenbeigh (Co. Kerry)

Tel: **066 976 8451**. Email: **glenross@eircom.net**

Its situation on the spectacular Ring of Kerry and the Kerry Way gives Glenross an immediate advantage, and scenic grandeur around every bend of the road is guaranteed as Glenbeigh is approached. Quietly located before entering the village, the park commands a stunning view of Rossbeigh Strand, which is within walking distance. On arrival, a good impression is created with the park well screened from the road and with new stone entrance and gates. There are 30 touring pitches including hardstanding pitches with electricity and, although there are six caravan holiday homes, the park is attractively laid out. There is no catering on site but the Glenbeigh Hotel next door is popular and village shops are near. Not least is the Kerry Bog Village where you can go back in time in this reconstructed pre-famine village.

Facilities

Well maintained modern toilet block includes facilities for laundry and dishwashing. Motorcaravan service point. Games room. Bicycle hire. Shelter for campers. Sun lounge and barbecue patio. Off site: Watersports and tennis near. Riding and fishing 200 m. Golf 500 m.

Open: 4 May - 26 September.

Directions

Park is on the N70 Killorglin - Glenbeigh road, on the right just before entering the village.
GPS: N52:03.524 W09:55.914

Charges 2007

Per person	€ 8.00
child (under 14 yrs)	€ 3.00
pitch	€ 6.00 - € 8.00
electricity (10A)	€ 5.00

No credit cards.

IR9630 Donoghues White Villa Farm Caravan & Camping Park

Killarney - Cork Road N22, Killarney (Co. Kerry)

Tel: **064 206 71**. Email: **killarneycamping@eircom.net**

This is a very pleasing small touring park in scenic surroundings on the N22 Killarney - Cork road. Set in the countryside surrounded by green fields, yet is only five minutes away from Killarney town. Trees and shrubs surround the park but dominant is a magnificent view of the MacGillicuddy's Reeks. There are 30 pitches for caravans and tents, 20 with hardstanding and a grass area for awnings, electricity (10A), water points and night lighting. One designated for disabled campers. An unusual novelty is old school desks placed around the site, plus an antique green telephone box. One can also enjoy walking through the oak wood, fishing on the Flesk or visiting the site's own National Farm Museum.

Facilities

The toilet block, a sandstone coloured building, is kept spotlessly clean and houses showers on payment, a good toilet/shower room for disabled visitors, laundry room and dishwashing sinks. Motorcaravan service area. Campers' kitchen with TV. Play area. Bicycle hire. Max. 2 dogs per pitch are accepted (not certain breeds). Daily coach tours from park. Off site: Riding, golf and boat launching 3 km. Pub/restaurant 1 km. Killarney town 5 minutes, the National Park is 10 minutes away.

Open: 18 April - 5 October (also 14 - 31 March).

Directions

Park is 3 km. east from Killarney town on N22 Cork road. Park entrance is 500 m. east of N22/N72 junction. From Killarney follow N22 Cork road signs and 'White Villa Farm' finger signs from Park Road roundabout. From Kenmare take R569 via Kilgarvan to the N22, or N71 to Killarney, then the N22 Cork road. GPS: N52:02.837 W09:27.224

Charges 2008

Per person	€ 6.00
child	€ 3.00
pitch	€ 5.00 - € 6.00
electricity	€ 4.00

No credit cards. Seven nights for the price of six.

IR9650 Woodlands Park Touring Caravan & Camping Park

Dan Spring Road, Tralee (Co. Kerry)

Tel: **066 712 1235**. Email: **wdlands@eircom.net**

Tralee is not only the Capital of County Kerry and gateway to the Dingle Peninsula, it is also Ireland's fastest growing visitor destination. Woodlands is is an ideal base, only ten minutes walk from the town centre. Located on a 16 acre elevated site approached by a short road and bridge that straddles the River Lee, once on site the town seems far removed, with a countryside environment taking over. Hedging, trees, grazing fields and the distant Slieve Mish Mountain create the setting. The owners of Woodlands have designed and equipped their park to a high standard. A distinctive feature is its impressive yellow coloured building which houses an 'on top' family dwelling and ground floor services. There are 135 pitches, 85 with hardstanding, electricity, water and drainage plus night light, to the left and centre behind the main building, and a grass area for 50 tents is to the right. Young shrubs, cordyline trees and flower beds have been planted around the park and a security barrier and CCTV are in operation. Interesting is the award winning 'Kerry the Kingdom' museum with its incredible time car trip through the Middle Ages. Evening entertainment in Tralee means a selection of singing pubs, restaurants and the National Folk Theatre.

Facilities

Excellent, heated sanitary facilities include sizeable showers (€1 token) and provision for disabled guests. Campers' kitchen, dishwashing sinks, fridge and freezer. Laundry room with washing machines and dryer. Motorcaravan service point and chemical disposal. Café/snack bar. Shop. Games room. TV and adult room. Internet access. Fenced adventure play area. Off site: The nearby Aqua Dome offers half price admission after 18.00. Golf 6 km. Riding 2 km. Blue Flag beaches on the Dingle Peninsula. Sailing 10 km.

Open: Easter - 30 September.

Directions

Site is 1 km. southwest of Tralee town centre. From N21/N69/N86 junction south of Tralee follow camp signs for 2.4 km. to park, 200 m. off the N86 Tralee - Dingle road. Site is 300 metres east of the Aqua Dome GPS: N52:15.673 W09:42.219

Charges 2007

Per unit incl. 2 persons	€ 15.50 - € 23.00
extra person	€ 6.00
child (under 16 yrs)	€ 2.00 - € 3.00
electricity (10A)	€ 4.00

MAP 9

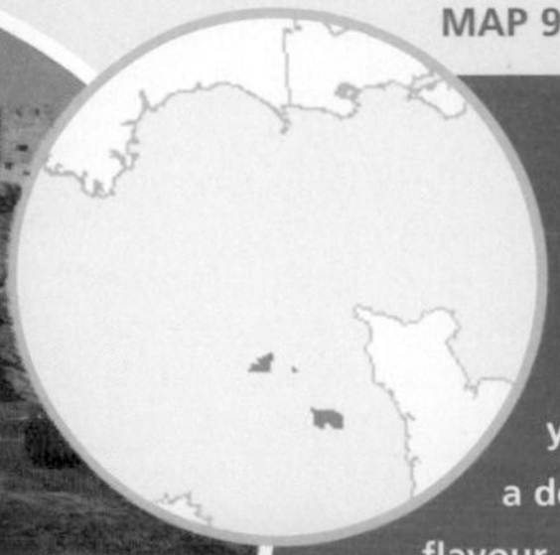

A visit to the Channel Islands offers a holiday in part of the British Isles, yet in an area which has a definite continental flavour. All the islands have beautiful beaches and coves, pretty scenery and fascinating histories.

THE CHANNEL ISLANDS ARE MADE UP OF THE ISLANDS OF: JERSEY, GUERNSEY, SARK, HERM AND ALDERNEY

The largest of the Channel Islands is Jersey, which is also the most commercial with more entertainment on offer. It has long stretches of safe beaches for swimming and water-based activities such as windsurfing and banana rides. Caravans and motor caravans are allowed on Jersey, but with a number of limitations (for example, length of stay, width and length of the unit). A permit is required which is obtained as part of the booking procedure with the campsite of your choice. You must book in advance but the campsite owner will advise you on all aspects of your visit.

Guernsey will suit those who prefer a quieter, more peaceful holiday. Caravans and motorcaravans are not allowed here. Guernsey too has wide, sandy beaches plus sheltered coves. The historic, harbour town of St Peter Port has steep and winding cobbled streets, with plenty of shops, cafes and restaurants.

For those who want total relaxation, one of the smaller islands – Sark or Herm, would be ideal. No cars are permitted on either of these islands. Explore on foot, by cycle or horse-drawn carriage.

Shopping on all the islands has the advantage of no VAT – particularly useful when buying cameras, watches or alcohol.

Places of interest

Jersey: St Helier; Jersey Zoo; Jersey War tunnels; Elizabeth Castle; German Underground Hospital in St Lawrence; Samarès Manor in St Clement; Shell Garden at St Aubin; Battle of Flowers Museum in St Ouen.

Guernsey: Castle Cornet at St Peter Port Harbour; Victor Hugo's House; Guernsey Folk Museum; German Occupation Museum; Fort Grey Shipwreck Museum; Saumarez Park.

Sark: La Coupée; La Seigneurie, with old dovecote and gardens; Gouliet and Boutique Caves; Le Pot on Little Sark; Venus Pool; Little Sark Village.

Herm: This tiny island has beautiful, quiet, golden beaches and a little harbour village and hotel. Arrive by ferry from Guernsey for a wonderful day out.

Did you know?

Jersey has been associated with knitting for nearly 400 years.

The Channel Islands were the only part of the British Isles to be occupied by the Germans during the Second World War.

The first road side letterboxes in the British Isles were erected in St Helier on 23rd November 1852.

Herm island is just one and a half miles long and only half a mile wide.

Le Jerriais is the native language of Jersey, a blend of Norse and Norman French.

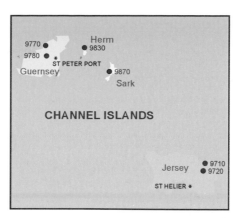

UK9720 Beuvelande Camp Site

Beuvelande, St Martin, Jersey JE3 6EZ (Channel Islands)

Tel: **01534 853 575**. Email: **info@campingjersey.com**

What a pleasant surprise we had when we called here – the outstanding sanitary building gives campers facilities often associated with top class hotels. A licensed restaurant with covered terrace area is also situated in this building, open morning and evening all season, but perhaps a few less hours at quiet times. There are 150 pitches, 60 with fully equipped tents for hire, but with plenty of space for those with their own. Cars may be parked next to your tent. 100 pitches have electric hook ups (5/10A). Torches would be useful. Car and bicycle hire can be arranged. This family run park prides itself on quality, cleanliness and hospitality.

Facilities

The toilet block is tiled top to bottom and spotlessly clean, with controllable showers, two fully equipped bathrooms for disabled people, and a baby room. Laundry. Games room. TV room. Well stocked shop. Licensed restaurant. Ice pack and battery charging services for a small charge. Outdoor heated swimming pool (41 x 17 ft) with sun terrace and small slide. Play area. Evening entertainment. Off site: Beach and sailing 1.5 miles. Fishing, golf or riding within 2 miles.

Open: 1 April - 30 September.

Directions

On leaving the harbour by Route du Port Elizabeth, take A1 east through the tunnel and the A17. At the fourth set of traffic lights turn left on A6. Continue to Five Oaks and on to St Martin's RC church, then right into La Longue Rue, right again Rue de L'Orme then left to site.

Charges 2007

Per person	£ 6.00 - £ 9.00
child (2-14 yrs)	£ 6.00
Single sex groups not accepted.	

UK9710 Rozel Camping Park

Rozel, St Martin, Jersey JE3 6AX (Channel Islands)

Tel: **01534 855 200**. Email: **rozelcampingpark@jerseymail.co.uk**

This family owned park is within walking distance of the famous Jersey Zoo and the pretty harbour and fishing village of Rozel, where the north coast cliff path commences. A car is probably necessary to reach the main island beaches, although a bus service does run to St Helier from close by. The park is quietly situated at the top of a valley and is surrounded by trees providing shelter. There are two main camping areas providing 130 pitches of which 120 have electricity and 16 are used for fully equipped tents to hire. Some pitches, mainly for smaller tents are arranged on terraced areas. The remainder are on a higher, flat field where pitches are arranged in bays with hedges growing to separate them into groups. In addition to package deals for tent hire, the site offers a good range of camping equipment for hire on a daily basis. Boats are accepted by prior arrangement.

Facilities

Two first rate, heated sanitary buildings include a bathroom for disabled people with a shower, toilet and washbasin. Family shower room. Laundry. Shop. Takeaway (peak season). Swimming pool (June-Sept). Play area. Crazy golf. Games and TV rooms. Torches useful. Bicycles for hire can be delivered. Off site: Fishing 1 mile. Beach 2 miles. Riding 3 miles. Golf 4 miles.

Open: 21 May - 9 September.

Directions

Leave harbour by Route du Port Elizabeth, take the A1 east and the A17. At fourth set of lights turn left on A6. Keep in the middle lane. Continue to Five Oaks and on to St Martin's church. Turn right, then left at the 'Royal' pub on B38 to Rozel, continue to end of road, turn right and park is on the right.

Charges 2007

Per person	£ 7.60 - £ 9.00
child (4-11 yrs)	£ 3.80 - £ 4.50
electricity	£ 1.80

323

UK9870 Pomme de Chien Campsite

Sark (Channel Islands)

Tel: **01481 832 316**

The island where 'time stands still' is an apt description of Sark, one of the smallest inhabited Channel Islands, some 45 minutes from Guernsey by boat. There is no airport, no cars or motorcycles and (apart from a tractor-drawn land-train up Harbour Hill) the only transport is by bicycle (which must be hired on the island) or horse-drawn carriage. However, all you are likely to need for a tranquil holiday is provided with several small shops, pubs, hotels, restaurants, a Tourist Office and even two banks! Situated five minutes from the shops and ten from the beach, the Pomme de Chien campsite is small with only 50 pitches, of which 8 are occupied by fully equipped tents for rent. The remainder are for campers with their own tents (no caravans, motorcaravans or trailer tents of course). The pitches are large, on fairly level ground, but none have electricity hook-ups. There is a warm welcome from the owners Chris and Jill Rang with the famous charm of Sark. Although you cannot take your car to the island, the Condor service via Guernsey means you can get there in a little over three hours either with your own small tent or of course you could hire one of the site's own (equipment includes everything you're likely to need except bedding and a torch).

Facilities

Modern sanitary block with free hot showers (large, with bench and hook), toilets and washbasins. Dishwashing sinks are outside. Outside washing line. Dogs are not accepted. Torches are necessary. Baggage can be transferred from the harbour to the site by tractor trailer, at a cost of £1 per item. Off site: Bicycle hire 5 minutes. Beach and fishing 10 minutes walk.

Open: All year - incl. for campers.
June - September for hire tents.

Directions

Take the tractor drawn 'train' up Harbour Hill (90p; you can walk but it is a ten minute hike). Once at the top take road leading off left, then second right, and follow the lane to the site entrance. Reception is at house with white gates.

Charges 2007

Per person	£ 6.00
child	£ 4.00

No credit cards.

UK9830 Seagull Campsite

The Administration Office, Herm Island GY1 3HR (Channel Islands)

Tel: **01481 722 377**. Email: **camping@herm-island.com**

This tiny site, and indeed the island of Herm, will appeal to those who are looking for complete tranquillity and calm. Reached by boat (20 minutes and approx. £8.50 return fare for adults, £4.25 for children) from Guernsey, the 300 acre island allows no cars only tractors on its narrow roads and paths (no bicycles either). One is free to stroll around the many paths, through farmland, heath and around the coast, where there are beautiful beaches. The campsite is a 20 minute uphill walk from the harbour, but your luggage will be transported for you by tractor. It consists of several terraced areas offering a total of 90 pitches, and 26 fully equipped tents for hire on flat grass areas. There are no electricity hook-ups. One may bring one's own tent and equipment or hire both (but not bedding, crockery and lighting) from the site. Herm is definitely not for those who like lively entertainment and plenty of facilities, but for total relaxation, with the absence of any bustle and noise it takes some beating! Due to the stony footpaths on Herm, sensible walking shoes are advised.

Facilities

Small, modern, but open, toilet block. Hot showers (£1 payment - there is a shortage of water on Herm). Laundry facility and small kitchen. Freezer for ice-packs. No dogs or pets are allowed. Torches useful. Off site: The harbour village is about ten minutes walk for small shop, gas, a post office, pub, restaurants and café. Fishing on the island.

Open: May - first w/end in September.

Directions

Reached by boat from St Peter Port - report to Administration Office on arrival. Do not take your car as it is unlikely you will be able to park long term in St Peter Port.

Charges 2007

Per person	£ 5.60
child (under 14 yrs)	£ 2.80
transportation of luggage	£ 7.00

Equipped tents for hire.
Groups of single people not accepted.

UK9770 Vaugrat Camping

Route de Vaugrat, St Sampson's, Guernsey GY2 4TA (Channel Islands)

Tel: **01481 257468**. Email: **enquiries@vaugratcampsite.com**

Vaugrat Camping is a neat, well tended site, close to the beach in the northwest of the island. Owned and run by the Laine family, it is centred around attractive and interesting old granite farm buildings dating back to the 15th century, with a gravel courtyard and attractive flower beds. It provides 150 pitches on flat grassy meadows, that are mostly surrounded by trees, banks and hedges to provide shelter. Tents are arranged around the edges of the fields, giving open space in the centre, and while pitches are not marked, there is sufficient room and cars may be parked next to tents. Only couples and families are accepted and the site is well run and welcoming. It also offers 30 fully equipped tents for hire. Housed in the old farmhouse, now a listed building, are the reception area, and shop where fresh croissants are baked every morning. Upstairs is the Coffee Barn/TV room, with views to the sea, where breakfast is served; one can also sit here in the evenings.

Facilities

Well kept sanitary facilities are in two buildings. The first block is in the courtyard, with hot showers on payment. Unit for disabled visitors with shower, basin and toilet (although there is a 6 inch step into the building). Laundry facilities. Second block near the camping fields provides toilets, washbasins and dishwashing facilities. Shop with ice pack hire and gas (open at certain times by arrangement). Café serving breakfast only. Dogs are not accepted. Torches may be useful. Off site: Bus service within easy reach. Car or bicycle hire can be arranged. Fishing, riding and golf within 1.5 miles. Hotel and bar nearby.

Open: July - August.

Directions

On leaving St Peter Port, turn right onto coast road for 1.5 miles. At filter turn left into Vale Road. Straight over at two sets of lights then first left turn by church. Follow to crossroads (garage opposite) turn right. Carry on past Peninsula Hotel, then second left, signed for site. Site on left after high stone wall (400 yds) with concealed entrance.

Charges 2007

Per person	£ 7.15
child (under 14 yrs)	£ 5.65
car or boat	£ 1.35

Families and couples only.
Fully equipped tents to hire (details from site).

UK9780 Fauxquets Valley Farm Campsite

Castel, Guernsey GY5 7QA (Channel Islands)

Tel: **01481 255 460**. Email: **info@fauxquets.co.uk**

Situated in the rural centre of the island, Fauxquets is in a pretty sheltered valley, hidden down narrow lanes away from busy roads and is run by the Guille family. A car would be useful here to reach the beaches, St Peter Port and other attractions, although there is a bus service each day (20 minutes walk). It was once a dairy farm, but the valley side has now been developed into an attractive campsite, with the old farm buildings as its centre. Plenty of trees, bushes and flowers have been planted to separate pitches and to provide shelter around the various fields which are well terraced. The 86 touring pitches are of a good size, most marked, numbered and with electricity, and there is lots of open space. There are also 15 smaller places for backpackers. The site has 23 fully equipped tents for hire, but there are no tour operators. The Haybarn licensed restaurant and bar provides breakfast, morning coffee and cake and evening meals. There is plenty of room to sit around the heated swimming pool, including a large grassy terrace with sunbeds provided.

Facilities

Good toilet facilities have controllable showers, some washbasins in private cabins with a shower, baby bath and changing unit. Dishwashing facilities under cover and a tap for free hot water. Laundry room with free irons, boards and hairdryers. Heated swimming pool (20 x 45 ft.) with paddling pool. Restaurant and bar (25/6-7/9). Small shop with ice-pack hire and gas. TV room. Table football and table tennis. Small play area and play field. Bicycle hire. Torches useful. Off site: Riding and golf 2 miles. Fishing, sailing and boat launching 3 miles.

Open: May - 15 September.

Directions

From harbour take second exit from roundabout. At top of hill, turn left at 'filter in turn' into Queens Road, then right at next filter. Follow straight through traffic lights and down hill past hospital, through pedestrian lights and straight on at next lights at top of hill. Continue for 0.75 miles, then turn right opposite sign for German Hospital. Fourth left is pedestrian entrance, cars carry on for 400 yds. to gravel entrance on left.

Charges 2007

Per person	£ 5.50 - £ 6.80
child (at school)	£ 2.75 - £ 3.40
electricity (6A)	£ 2.50

Fully equipped tents with fridge for hire.

Belle France

Walking & Cycling Holidays

Discover the easy going alternative

It's all on-line
www.**bellefrance.co.uk**

Belle France
Walking & Cycling Holidays in France

2008

Belle France offers leisurely holidays through the most beautiful and interesting parts of France.

On our walking and cycling holidays your luggage is moved for you whilst you find your own way, at your own pace with our detailed maps and notes.

Relax in the evening in charming family run hotels, offering a good standard of accommodation and a warm and friendly welcome.

Follow suggested routes, stopping where you choose and enjoy complete freedom.

Call now for a **FREE** brochure **01580 214010**

Insurance Expertise from The Caravan Club!

All our insurance policies are designed with caravanners and motor caravanners in mind so, whether you're at home or away touring, you can rely on The Club to be sure you are fully covered.

Caravan Insurance

Our competitive policies offer comprehensive and flexible cover, based on over 35 years' experience operating the UK's largest Caravan insurance scheme.
Call us on **01342 336610** or get a quote & buy online at **www.caravanclub.co.uk**

UK Breakdown & Recovery

The Club's Mayday UK vehicle rescue is provided in conjunction with Green Flag and offers fast and reliable rescue and recovery, whether you're towing or not.
Call us on **0800 731 0112** or get a quote & buy online at **www.caravanclub.co.uk**

Car Insurance

Competitive Car insurance from a name you can trust, with a guarantee of a lower premium than your current insurer*.
Call us on **0800 028 4809**

Home Insurance

Our Home insurance protects your buildings and/or contents against a wide range of risks and offers additional benefits.
Call us on **0800 028 4815**

Pet Insurance

Be sure your pets are protected at home or when away touring in the UK or abroad, no matter how many trips you take.
Call us on **0800 015 1396**

Motor Caravan Insurance

Another Club speciality, with wide cover at competitive rates and a guarantee to beat the renewal premium offered by your present insurer*.
Call us on **0800 028 4809**

Overseas Holiday Insurance

When you travel abroad, take The Club's Red Pennant Holiday Insurance with you. Our own 24-hour emergency team helps you relax, knowing you're in experienced hands.
Call us on **01342 336633** or get a quote & buy online at **www.caravanclub.co.uk**

Club Credit Card & Personal Loan

Financial services to meet your needs.
Call us on **0800 373 191** (Credit Card)
& **0800 032 5000** (Personal Loan)

To find out more, please call us stating reference AR07.
We look forward to hearing from you!

* Conditions apply

3 ISSUES FOR £1

Our practical titles are packed full of holiday tips, technical advice, reader reviews, superb photography…and much more! So subscribe to Practical Caravan or Practical Motorhome for just £1.

- **YOU** get your first 3 issues for £1
- **YOU** save 20% on the shop price after your trial ends
- **RISK-FREE** offer - you can cancel at any time
- **FREE** delivery, straight to your door!
- **EXCLUSIVE** subscriber offers and discounts

CALL 08456 777 812 NOW!

or visit **www.themagazineshop.com** quote code ALR08

☐ Please start my subscription to Practical Caravan. I will pay £1 for the first 3 issues and £8.40 every 3 issues thereafter, saving 20% on the shop price.

☐ Please start my subscription to Practical Motorhome. I will pay £1 for the first 3 issues and £7.90 every 3 issues thereafter, saving 20% on the shop price.

YOUR DETAILS BLOCK CAPITALS PLEASE (MUST BE COMPLETED)

Mr/Mrs/Ms _____ Name _____ Surname _____

Address _____

_____

_____ Postcode _____

Telephone _____

If you are happy to receive offers, news, product and service information from Haymarket Consumer Media and other carefully selected partners via email and SMS, please tick here ☐

E-mail _____

Mobile _____

This is an introductory offer open to UK residents only and is a Direct Debit only offer. Details of the Direct Debit guarantee are available on request. For international rates please call +44 (0) 1750 724703. Offer ends 31 December 2008. Direct Debit rates will remain the same for one year, after this time they are subject to change. Haymarket Consumer Media may contact you by post or phone from time to time, with special offers and product information. Please tick this box if you prefer not receive this information ☐. Occasionally we may pass your details to carefully selected partners whose products we think would be of interest to you. Please tick this box if you prefer not to receive this information ☐.

DIRECT DEBIT DETAILS
Instructions to your Bank or Building Society to pay by Direct Debit

To The Manager: Bank/Building Society _____

Address _____

Postcode _____

Name(s) of Account Holder(s) _____

Branch Sort Code ☐☐ ☐☐ ☐☐

Bank/Building Society account number ☐☐☐☐☐☐☐☐

DIRECT Debit
Originaton ID No. 850699

Reference Number (for office use only) _____

Signature(s) _____

Instruction to your Bank or Building Society
Please pay Haymarket Consumer Media Direct Debits from the account detailed in this instruction subject to the safeguards assured by the Direct Debit Guarantee. I understand that this instruction may stay with Haymarket Consumer Media and, if so, details will be passed electronically to my Bank/Building Society.

ALR08

Please return this form to:
Haymarket Consumer Media
FREEPOST SEA 14716 Haywards Heath RH16 3BR

A sign of excellence.

Just one of around 200 superb Caravan Club Sites to choose from

Caravan Club Sites are renowned for their excellence. With most of those graded achieving 4 or 5 stars from Visit Britain, you can be sure of consistently high standards. From lakes or mountains to city or sea, there are some 200 quality Club Sites throughout the British Isles to choose from.

With over 40 fabulous Club Sites open all year, why stay at home?

Whichever site you choose, you can be assured of excellent facilities and a friendly welcome from our Resident Wardens. Just look for the signs.

Broomfield Farm Caravan Club Site

Bunree Caravan Club Site

Burrs Country Park Caravan Club Site

Troutbeck Head Caravan Club Site

Our Site Collection

You don't have to be a member to stay on most Caravan Club Sites, but members save up to £7 per night on pitch fees!

Call today for your FREE Site Collection brochure
on 0800 521 161 quoting ARG08
or visit www.caravanclub.co.uk

THE CARAVAN CLUB

The Caravan Club, East Grinstead House, East Grinstead, West Sussex RH19 1UA

Great magazines for touring, holidays and inspirational ideas!

For buying information, top tips and technical help, **Caravan, Motor Caravan Magazine** and **Park Home & Holiday Caravan** are all you need — every month!

Subscribe today and save 30%

☎ 0845 676 7778

Lines are open seven days a week, 9am – 9pm. Closing date 31 December 2007
Quote code Caravan XCV 38E or Motor Caravan XMV 39A or
Park Home & Holiday Caravan XPH 35H when calling

30% discount is by quarterly direct debit only.

THE CARAVAN & MOTORHOME SHOWS

INTERNATIONAL
CARAVAN & MOTORHOME
2008 NEC BIRMINGHAM 14 - 19 OCTOBER

The UK's biggest selection of caravans, motohomes, trailer tents, holiday homes, awnings, folding campers and of course accessories! The NEC is the first place to see all the latest products, have a great day out and find exactly what you want for your 2008 holiday.

MANCHESTER CENTRAL
CARAVAN & MOTORHOME
SHOW 2008 MANCHESTER 17-20 JANUARY

Come and see the widest choice of caravans and a great selection of motorhomes from leading UK and overseas manufacturers. If it's a bargain you are looking for, many exhibitors are offering amazing deals that you won't find anywhere else!

FOR MORE INFORMATION VISIT
www.caravanshows.com

UnityPlus CARD

Unique Discounts for Campers and Caravanners

www.unity-plus.com

NEW

Whether you have a caravan, a motorhome or a tent, the UnityPlus Card is for you. It's not a club but it offers great benefits and it's free! Quite simply, it offers unique discounts for campers and caravanners on a range of products including cheap ferry deals, discounted holidays, camping accessories, specialist insurance and more.

Full details at www.unity-plus.com

Request your UnityPlus Card today!

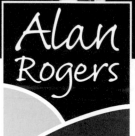

Discover a great deal more with a quote from Safeguard

We are passionate about caravans and motorhomes. They are unrivalled, in terms of the freedom they give you to explore and, of course, the people you meet are some of the nicest around. That's why we work hard to get you cover you can rely on, but it's at the right price too.

Motorhome insurance

- Annual European cover

- New-for-old replacement vehicle if your new motorhome is written off within 24 months of new purchase and has covered less than 15,000 miles

- AA breakdown cover in the UK and abroad, so you'll never be stuck in one place for longer than you want to be

- Cover for personal items up to £3000 in case they're stolen

Policy terms and conditions apply.

Caravan insurance

- European cover for up to 180 days

- New-for-old replacement vehicle if your caravan is written off within 5 years of first registration

- Up to £1000 alternative accommodation costs if your caravan becomes uninhabitable

- Liability cover of up to £2m

CALL SAFEGUARD FOR A QUOTE TODAY

for motorhomes call
0800 977 5048
Mon-Fri 9am-5.30pm, Sat 9am-1pm

for caravans call
0800 977 5047
Mon-Fri 9am-5.30pm, Sat 9am-1pm

or visit www.safeguarduk.co.uk

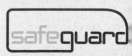

Reports by Readers

We always welcome reports from readers concerning sites which they have visited. Generally reports provide us with invaluable feedback on sites already included in the guides or, in the case of those not yet featured, they provide information which we can follow up with a view to adding them in future editions. However, if you have a complaint about a site, this should be addressed to the campsite owner, preferably in person before you leave.

Please make your comments either on this form or on plain paper. It would be appreciated if you would indicate the approximate dates when you visited the site and, in the case of potential new ones, provide the correct name and address and, if possible, include a site brochure. Send your reports to:

Alan Rogers Guides, Spelmonden Old Oast, Goudhurst, Kent TN17 1HE

Name and reference number of the campsite (or address for new recommendations):

_____

_____

Dates of visit: _____

Comments:

Reader's Name and Address: _____

_____

_____

_____

Name and reference number of the campsite (or address for new recommendations):

_____

_____

Dates of visit: _____

Comments:

Reader's Name and Address: _____

The following parks are understood to accept caravanners and campers all year round. It is always wise to phone the park to check as the facilities available, for example, may be reduced.

England

UK0030	Ayr
UK0165	Monkey Tree
UK0180	Carnon Downs
UK0310	Trekenning
UK0320	Polborder House
UK0430	Padstow
UK0440	Dolbeare
UK0690	Stowford Farm
UK0710	Hidden Valley
UK0790	Harford Bridge
UK0800	Higher Longford
UK0810	Riverside
UK0820	Moor View
UK1250	Woodland Springs
UK1340	Cornish Farm
UK1350	Quantock Orchard
UK1420	Southfork
UK1440	Baltic Wharf
UK1460	Newton Mill
UK1510	Chew Valley
UK1520	Waterrow
UK1630	Brokerswood
UK1655	Church Farm
UK1670	Alderbury
UK1700	Devizes
UK1820	Bagwell Farm
UK2030	Wareham Forest
UK2290	Sandy Balls
UK2590	Greenhill Farm
UK2600	Barnstones
UK2620	Wysdom
UK2800	Alderstead Heath
UK2810	Chertsey
UK2930	Sheepcote
UK2940	Honeybridge
UK2950	Washington
UK3030	Tanner Farm
UK3040	Broadhembury
UK3070	Canterbury
UK3090	Black Horse
UK3260	Abbey Wood
UK3270	Crystal Palace
UK3310	Low House
UK3340	Polstead
UK3345	The Dell
UK3382	Rose Farm
UK3385	Applewood
UK3455	Deer's Glade
UK3470	Breckland

UK3520	Searles
UK3575	Stroud Hill
UK3580	Ferry Meadows
UK3690	Bainland
UK3730	Skegness Sands
UK3765	Woodland Waters
UK3815	Lickpenny
UK3910	Shardaroba
UK3920	Riverside
UK3940	Smeaton's Lakes
UK4075	Hollyfast
UK4130	Moreton-in-Marsh
UK4170	Tudor
UK4210	Lickhill Manor
UK4300	Poston Mill
UK4400	Stanmore Hall
UK4410	Beaconsfield
UK4430	Oxon Hall
UK5280	Abbey Farm
UK5505	Stanwix Park
UK5560	Sykeside
UK5570	Wild Rose
UK5705	The Grange
UK5740	White Water
UK5755	South Meadows
UK5800	Ord House

Wales

UK5925	Cardiff
UK5955	Erwlon
UK6045	Gilestone
UK6310	Bacheldre
UK6330	Daisy Bank
UK6590	Beddgelert
UK6600	Bryn Gloch
UK6680	James'
UK6690	Bron-Y-Wendon

Scotland

UK6870	Glenearly
UK6930	Brandedleys
UK6950	Brighouse Bay
UK7020	Aird Donald
UK7030	Gibson Park
UK7050	Edinburgh
UK7240	Lomond Woods
UK7270	Auchterarder
UK7680	Glenmore
UK7735	Sango Sands
UK7790	Invercoe

Northern Ireland

UK8420	Tollymore

Republic of Ireland

IR8740	Cong
IR8815	Willowbrook
IR9080	Forest Farm
IR9100	Camac Valley
IR9400	Glen of Aherlow
IR9580	Beara The Peacock

Channel Islands

UK9870	Pomme de Chien

339

Dogs

For the benefit of those who want to take their dogs with them or for people who do not like dogs at the parks they visit, we list here the sites that have indicated to us that they do not accept dogs. If you are, however, planning to take your dog we do advise you to phone the park first to check – there my be limits on numbers, breeds, etc. or times of the year when they are excluded.

Never – these parks do not accept dogs at any time:

UK0250	Pentewan Sands	UK2130	Grove Farm	UK5982	Trefalun
UK0302	South Penquite	UK2300	Ashurst	UK6005	Brynawelon
UK0870	Beverley	UK3060	Yew Tree	UK7290	Craigtoun Meadows
UK1075	Golden Coast	UK3120	Gate House Wood	UK8600	Bellemont
UK1130	Hoburne Torbay	UK3335	Westwood Park	UK9770	Vaugrat
UK1150	Ruda	UK3675	Willow Holt	UK9830	Seagull
UK1355	Lowtrow Cross	UK4100	Hoburne Cotswold	UK9870	Pomme de Chien
UK1380	Blue Anchor	UK4160	Christchurch	IR9410	The Apple
UK1490	Greenacres	UK5550	Limefitt	IR9510	Eagle Point
UK2120	South Lytchett Manor	UK5945	River View		
		UK5980	Moreton Farm		

Sometimes – these parks do not accept dogs at certain times of the year:

UK0306 **Ruthern Valley**
no pets in high season - July and August

UK0720 **Easewell Farm**
not high season, max 1

UK0850 **Galmpton**
not mid July/August, max 2

UK0865 **Byslades**
no dogs from 14 July - 1 September

UK1550 **Bucklegrove**
not in high season

UK2080 **Merley Court**
outside 17 July - 3 September

UK2100 **Sandford**
not high season, max 1, advised to telephone

UK2110 **Pear Tree**
not July/Aug

UK6010 **Cenarth Falls**
not during main summer school holidays

UK6290 **Glan-y-Mor**
not from 14 July - 31 August

UK9710 **Rozel**
Up to 8 July and from 29 August

IR8810 **Lough Lanagh**
none July/August except guide dogs

IR9100 **Camac Valley**
not July/August

IR9150 **River Valley**
no pets in July or August

IR9580 **Beara The Peacock**
no dogs in July/August

We are pleased to include details of parks which provide facilities for fishing on the site. Many other parks, particularly in Scotland and Ireland, are in popular fishing areas and have facilities within easy reach. Where we have been given details, we have included this information in the site reports. It is always best to contact parks to check that they provide for your individual requirements.

England

UK0165	Monkey Tree
UK0170	Trevella
UK0220	Trevornick
UK0250	Pentewan Sands
UK0302	South Penquite
UK0380	Wooda Farm
UK0415	Trencreek
UK0530	Trethiggey
UK0725	Warcombe Farm
UK0750	Minnows
UK0810	Riverside
UK0950	River Dart
UK0970	Cofton
UK1060	Yeatheridge
UK1075	Golden Coast
UK1090	Peppermint Park
UK1150	Ruda
UK1390	Old Oaks
UK1460	Newton Mill
UK1480	Home Farm
UK1540	Batcombe Vale
UK1545	Cheddar Bridge
UK1570	Northam Farm
UK1575	Unity
UK1580	Warren Farm
UK1590	Exe Valley
UK1630	Brokerswood
UK1640	Greenhill Farm
UK1740	Golden Cap
UK1760	Wood Farm
UK1780	Freshwater Beach
UK2130	Grove Farm
UK2150	Woolsbridge
UK2290	Sandy Balls
UK2360	Hill Cottage
UK2450	The Orchards
UK2510	Whitecliff Bay
UK2515	Nodes Point
UK2610	Bo Peep
UK2700	Hurley
UK2810	Chertsey
UK2820	Horsley
UK2900	Horam Manor
UK2965	Brakes Coppice
UK3030	Tanner Farm
UK3210	Lee Valley CP
UK3290	Fen Farm
UK3300	Homestead Lake
UK3400	Old Brick Kilns
UK3430	Kelling Heath

UK3455	Deer's Glade
UK3480	Little Lakeland
UK3520	Searles
UK3680	Ashby Park
UK3750	Foreman's Bridge
UK3760	Tallington Lakes
UK3765	Woodland Waters
UK3940	Smeaton's Lakes
UK3970	Glencote
UK4080	Riverside
UK4090	Island Meadow
UK4100	Hoburne Cotswold
UK4140	Winchcombe
UK4150	Croft Farm
UK4170	Tudor
UK4185	Weir Meadow
UK4190	Kingsgreen
UK4210	Lickhill Manor
UK4300	Poston Mill
UK4310	Luck's All
UK4320	Broadmeadow
UK4345	Townsend
UK4380	Fernwood
UK4390	Westbrook
UK4410	Reaconsfield
UK4500	Burton Constable
UK4510	Thorpe Hall
UK4610	Moorside
UK4640	Goose Wood
UK4660	Woodhouse Farm
UK4715	Riverside
UK4720	Knight Stainforth
UK5280	Abbey Farm
UK5540	Fallbarrow
UK5555	White Cross Bay
UK5600	Pennine View
UK5615	Hill of Oaks
UK5625	Lowther
UK5710	Doe Park

Wales

UK5880	Springwater
UK6290	Glan-y-Mor
UK6040	Pencelli Castle
UK6045	Gilestone
UK6245	Morben Isaf
UK6250	Dolswydd
UK6305	Smithy Park
UK6345	Glanlynn
UK6590	Beddgelert
UK6600	Bryn Gloch
UK6670	The Plassey

Scotland

UK6890	Mossyard
UK6910	Hoddom Castle
UK6950	Brighouse Bay
UK7025	Seal Shore
UK7220	The Gart
UK7260	Ardgartan
UK7270	Auchterarder
UK7295	River Tilt
UK7305	Tummel Valley
UK7790	Invercoe
UK7840	North Ledaig
UK7860	Glendaruel
UK7710	Ardmair Point
UK7720	Woodend
UK7740	Loch Greshornish
UK7800	Resipole
UK7850	Linnhe Lochside

Northern Ireland

UK8330	Sixmilewater
UK8340	Drumaheglis
UK8405	Cranfield
UK8420	Tollymore
UK8550	Dungannon
UK8510	Mullynascarthy

Republic of Ireland

IR8815	Willowbrook
IR8825	Lough Key
IR8960	Lough Ree
IR8965	Lough Ennell
IR9100	Camac Valley
IR9230	Nore Valley
IR9470	Blackwater Valley
IR9510	Eagle Point
IR9560	Wave Crest
IR9620	Flemings
IR9630	White Villa

Bicycle Hire

We understand that the following parks have bicycles to hire on site or can arrange for bicycles to be delivered. However, we would recommend that you contact the park to check as the situation can change.

England

UK0145	Trewhiddle
UK0150	Sea View
UK0255	Sun Valley
UK0306	Ruthern Valley
UK0360	Lakefield
UK0690	Stowford Farm
UK0750	Minnows
UK0950	River Dart
UK1075	Golden Coast
UK1150	Ruda
UK1250	Woodland Springs
UK1350	Quantock Orchard
UK1390	Old Oaks
UK1490	Greenacres
UK1550	Bucklegrove
UK1575	Unity
UK1590	Exe Valley
UK2100	Sandford
UK2290	Sandy Balls
UK2315	Riverside (Hamble)
UK2350	Red Shoot
UK2450	The Orchards
UK2500	Heathfield Farm
UK3325	The Oaks
UK3330	Moat Barn
UK3370	Kessingland
UK3390	Dower House
UK3430	Kelling Heath
UK3485	Clippesby
UK3520	Searles
UK3660	Walesby Woodlands
UK3750	Foreman's Bridge
UK3904	Greendale Farm
UK4080	Riverside
UK4540	St Helens
UK4560	Golden Square
UK4620	Upper Carr
UK5330	Marton Mere
UK5505	Stanwix Park
UK5520	Skelwith Fold
UK5605	Woodclose

Wales

UK5925	Cardiff
UK5980	Moreton Farm
UK6040	Pencelli Castle
UK6045	Gilestone
UK6330	Daisy Bank
UK6340	Pen-y-Bont

Scotland

UK6950	Brighouse Bay
UK7000	Strathclyde
UK7230	Trossachs
UK7280	Nether Craig
UK7305	Tummel Valley
UK7740	Loch Greshornish

Republic of Ireland

IR8740	Cong
IR8790	Carra
IR9130	Roundwood
IR9400	Glen of Aherlow
IR9580	Beara The Peacock
IR9600	Glenross
IR9620	Flemings
IR9630	White Villa
IR9640	Killarney Flesk

Channel Islands

UK9780	Fauxquets Valley

Golf

We understand that the following parks have facilities for playing golf on site. Where facilities are within easy reach and we have been given details, we have included this information in the individual site reports. However, we recommend that you contact the park to check that they meet your requirements.

UK0220	Trevornick	UK3230	Lee Valley	UK6910	Hoddom Castle
UK0380	Wooda Farm	UK3520	Searles	UK6950	Brighouse Bay
UK0690	Stowford Farm	UK3690	Bainland	UK7060	Tantallon
UK0720	Easewell Farm	UK4070	Somers Wood	UK7690	Torvean
UK1010	Lady's Mile	UK4300	Poston Mill	UK8310	Carnfunnock
UK1070	Woolacombe Bay	UK4520	Flower of May	IR9150	River Valley
UK1575	Unity	UK4710	Rudding		
UK2250	Hoburne Bashley	UK6670	The Plassey		

Horse Riding

We understand that the following parks have horse riding stables on site. Where facilities are within easy reach and we have been given details, we have included this information in the individual site reports. However, we recommend that you contact the park to check that they meet your requirements.

UK0360	Lakefield	UK1575	Unity	UK2900	Horam Manor
UK0690	Stowford Farm	UK1780	Freshwater Beach	UK2950	Washington
UK0735	Woolacombe Sands	UK2100	Sandford	UK6950	Brighouse Bay
UK1060	Yeatheridge	UK2290	Sandy Balls	UK8510	Mullynascarthy
UK1370	Burrowhayes	UK2515	Nodes Point		

Boat Launching

We understand that the following parks have boat slipways on site. Where facilities are within easy reach and we have been given details, we have included this information in the individual site reports. However, we recommend that you contact the park to check that they meet your requirements.

UK0250	Pentewan Sands	UK4500	Burton Constable	UK7740	Loch Greshornish
UK0750	Minnows	UK5330	Marton Mere	UK7800	Resipole
UK1530	Slimeridge	UK5540	Fallbarrow	UK7850	Linnhe Lochside
UK1540	Batcombe Vale	UK5555	White Cross Bay	UK8330	Sixmilewater
UK2510	Whitecliff Bay	UK5615	Hill of Oaks	UK8340	Drumaheglis
UK2520	Thorness Bay	UK6345	Glanlynn	UK8405	Cranfield
UK2700	Hurley	UK6890	Mossyard	IR8825	Lough Key
UK3290	Fen Farm	UK6950	Brighouse Bay	IR8960	Lough Ree
UK3760	Tallington Lakes	UK7025	Seal Shore	IR8965	Lough Ennell
UK4080	Riverside	UK7260	Ardgartan	IR9510	Eagle Point
UK4150	Croft Farm	UK7410	Riverview	IR9560	Wave Crest
UK4210	Lickhill Manor	UK7840	North Ledaig	IR9610	Mannix Point
UK4310	Luck's All	UK7710	Ardmair Point		

mycamping.info

myexperience, myvoice

The Alan Rogers Guides have long been the authoritative voice when it comes to an independent assessment of a campsite's quality. But now is the chance to hear your voice – your opinions, your assessments, your tips...

A beta version of the website is now up and running – and it needs YOUR input before it goes fully live!

 Personal **reviews**    Inside **knowledge**

Real **holiday makers**   Honest **advice**

It's all about **YOU** and
YOUR experiences...

So get involved today!
Visit www.mycamping.info

Adults Only

We list here the parks that have indicated to us that they do not accept children at any time during the year, at certain times, or in certain areas of their park.

The following parks have made the decision not to accept children or young adults:

UK0010	Chacewater *(over 30 yrs only)*	UK3410	Sandy Gulls
UK0012	Killiwerris	UK3420	Two Mills
UK0065	Wayfarers	UK3450	Little Haven *(over 14 yrs only)*
UK0820	Moor View	UK3470	Breckland
UK1250	Woodland Springs	UK3575	Stroud Hill
UK1355	Lowtrow Cross	UK3650	Cherry Tree
UK1390	Old Oaks *(over 18 yrs only)*	UK3904	Greendale Farm
UK1500	Long Hazel	UK3980	Longnor Woods *(18 yrs and over)*
UK1510	Chew Valley	UK4070	Somers Wood
UK1520	Waterrow *(18 yrs and over)*	UK4410	Beaconsfield *(over 21 yrs only)*
UK1545	Cheddar Bridge	UK4534	Overbrook
UK1590	Exe Valley *(18 yrs and over)*	UK4580	Foxholme
UK1640	Greenhill Farm *(18 yrs and over)*	UK4610	Moorside *(over 16 yrs only)*
UK1680	Plough Lane *(21 yrs and over)*	UK5240	Lamb Cottage
UK1770	Binghams Farm	UK5510	The Larches
UK2620	Wysdom	UK5650	The Ashes *(over 18 yrs only)*
UK3325	The Oaks	UK6330	Daisy Bank
UK3340	Polstead		

The following parks also do not accept children at certain times or in certain areas of their park:

UK4380	Fernwood	UK4430	Oxon Hall
UK4400	Stanmore Hall		

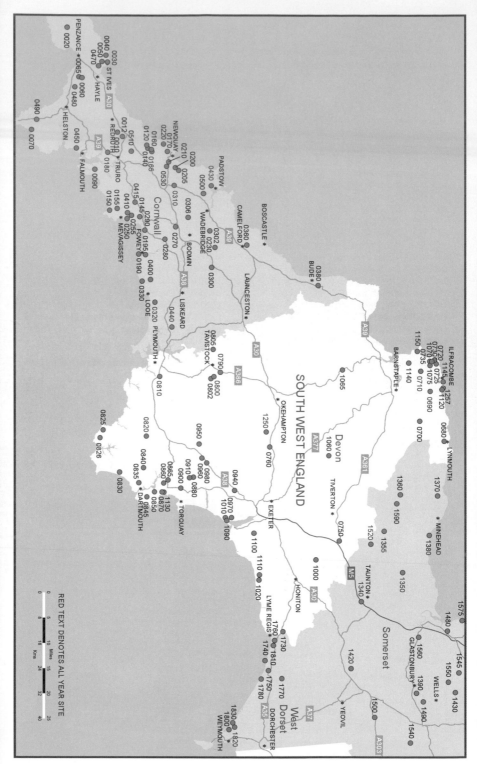

South West England

Cornwall

Devon

Somerset

West Dorset

RED TEXT DENOTES ALL YEAR SITE

0   5   10   15   20   25
Miles

0   8   16   24   32   40
Kms

Parks on this map are featured on pages 13-99 of the guide.
Please refer to the numerical index (page 357) for exact campsite page references.

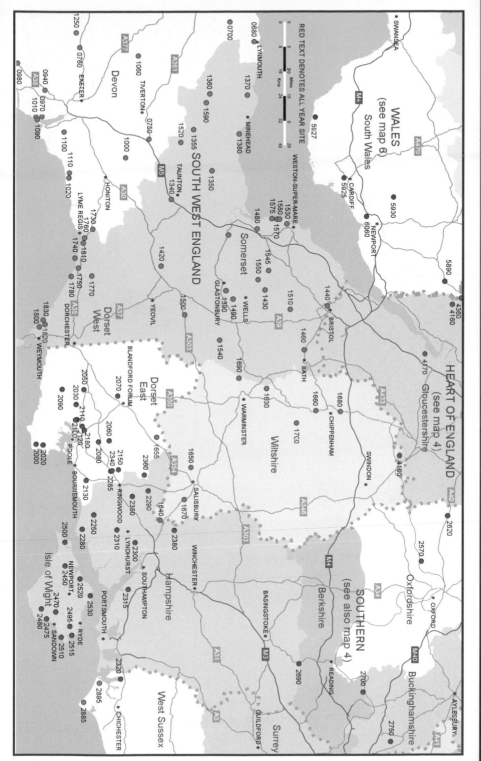

South West & Southern England

WALES
(see map 6)
South Wales

SOUTH WEST ENGLAND

Devon

Somerset

Dorset West

Dorset East

Wiltshire

HEART OF ENGLAND
(see map 4)
Gloucestershire

SOUTHERN
(see also map 4)

Hampshire

Berkshire

Isle of Wight

West Sussex

Surrey

Buckinghamshire

RED TEXT DENOTES ALL YEAR SITE

* SWANSEA
* CARDIFF
* NEWPORT
M4
A470
A465

WESTON-SUPER-MARE *
LYNMOUTH
MINEHEAD
TAUNTON *
WELLS *
GLASTONBURY *
YEOVIL *
BRISTOL
BATH *
CHIPPENHAM *
WARMINSTER *
SWINDON *
OXFORD *
AYLESBURY *
READING *
GUILDFORD *
BASINGSTOKE *
WINCHESTER *
SOUTHAMPTON *
PORTSMOUTH *
BOURNEMOUTH
POOLE
DORCHESTER *
WEYMOUTH *
LYME REGIS *
HONITON *
EXETER *
TIVERTON *
BLANDFORD FORUM *
SALISBURY
RINGWOOD *
LYNDHURST *
NEWPORT *
RYDE *
SANDOWN *
CHICHESTER *

Devon
A377
A361
A39
A30
A303
A350
A354
A36
A357
A35
A37
A338
A31
A3
A33
A34
A346
A433
A40
A41
A11
A361
M5
M4
M3
M40

0 5 20 Miles 15
0 8 16 Kms 24 32 40
0 25

0980
0940
0970
1010
1090
1250
0760
0700
0680
1060
1100
1110
1020
1000
1360
1370
1590
1520
1350
1355
1380
1340
1420
1730
1740
1810
1760
1770
1750
1780
1800
1830
1820
2090
2050
2030
2140
2120
2180
2060
2080
2070
2150
2340
2285
2130
2250
2280
2360
2290
2310
2300
2315
2500
2520
2450
2530
2470
2495
2475
2480
2510
2515
2320
2895
2885
5627
5925
5930
6060
5890
4360
4160
4470
4400
2570
2620
2700
2750
2690
1440
1460
1680
1660
1930
1700
1510
1545
1550
1430
1490
1390
1480
1575
1580
1530
1570
1590
1540
1500
655
1650
1670
1640
2360
2290
2380
1750
A303

EXETER *

2090

2020
2000

2320

2895

2885

Parks on this map are featured on pages 101-128 of the guide.
Please refer to the numerical index (page 357) for exact campsite page references.

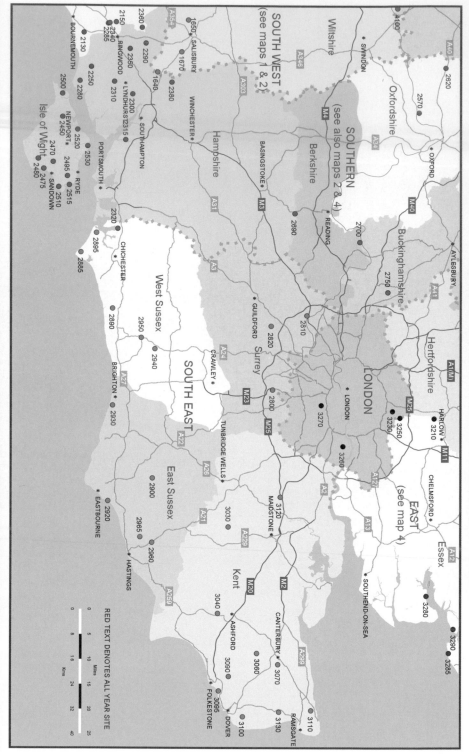

Parks on this map are featured on pages 129-146 of the guide.
Please refer to the numerical index (page 357) for exact campsite page references.

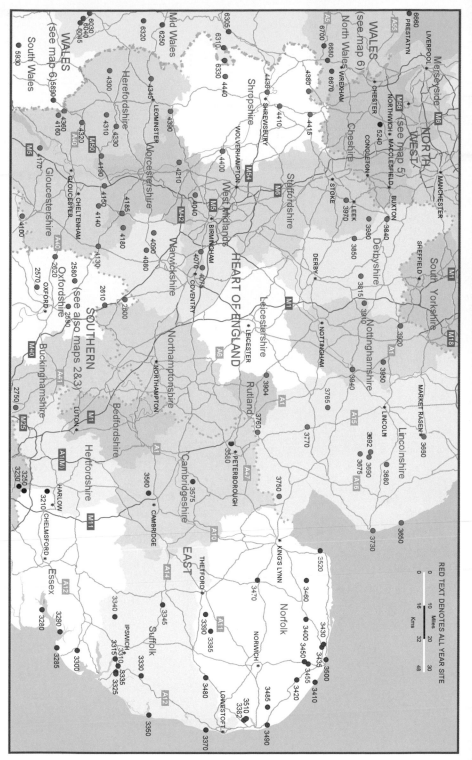

Parks on this map are featured on pages 147-189 of the guide.
Please refer to the numerical index (page 357) for exact campsite page references.

RED TEXT DENOTES ALL YEAR SITE

	Miles		
0	20	40	60
0	32	64	96
	Kms		

7270

7290

7060

7050   EDINBURGH   A1   7065

6980

6990

A72   6960

7030

SCOTLAND
(see map 7)   SELKIRK

BERWICK-UPON-TWEED
5800

Scottish Lowlands

* MOFFAT   A7

A68   A1

5755   5750

5770

Northumberland

* DUMFRIES
6910

NORTHUMBRIA

5810   NEWCASTLE
UPON TYNE

Tyne and Wear   SUNDERLAND

6875   5505   5640
5506   CARLISLE

A69   A1(M)

CUMBRIA   M6   DURHAM   5705
5700

PENRITH   Durham   BISHOP AUCKLAND
WORKINGTON   5670   5625
KESWICK   5620   5610   5710   5740   MIDDLESBROUGH
5660   5630   5720   DARLINGTON
A591   5560   5570   A66
A595   5590   5600   A1   4528

5520   5550   4532
5540   5555   4775   4770
5615   5545   KENDAL   HAWES   4690   North Yorkshire   4570   4590   SCARBOROUGH
5650   4534   4540   4550
5605   THIRSK   4580   4620   4740   4520
5350   5271   4560   4545   4780

4715   4720   4660   4760   BRIDLINGTON
SETTLE   4670   4638   4640   4610   4510
4750   4630
SKIPTON   4710   A166   DRIFFIELD
5272   4755   YORKSHIRE
5300   Lancashire   YORK
BLACKPOOL   East Riding of Yorkshire   4500
5330   PRESTON   BRADFORD   4645   HULL
5295   West Yorkshire   A15

NORTH   4700
WEST
5360   5280

Merseyside   MANCHESTER   South Yorkshire   M18   M180
LIVERPOOL   M6   M1

PRESTATYN   SHEFFIELD   3660
6660
6655   RUNCORN   Lincolnshire
A55   Cheshire   MACCLESFIELD   3920
NORTHWICH   3840   LINCOLN   3680
WALES   5240   BUXTON   A1   3950
(see map 6)   CHESTER   CONGLETON   3980   Derbyshire   3910   3692   3690
LEEK   3850   3815   Nottinghamshire   3675
WREXHAM   3970   3940
A5   6680   6670   STOKE   HEART   3765
6700   DERBY   (see map 4)   NOTTINGHAM
4380   4415   Staffordshire   3770
M6   M1
4410   A1

Parks on this map are featured on pages 190-235 of the guide.
Please refer to the numerical index (page 357) for exact campsite page references.

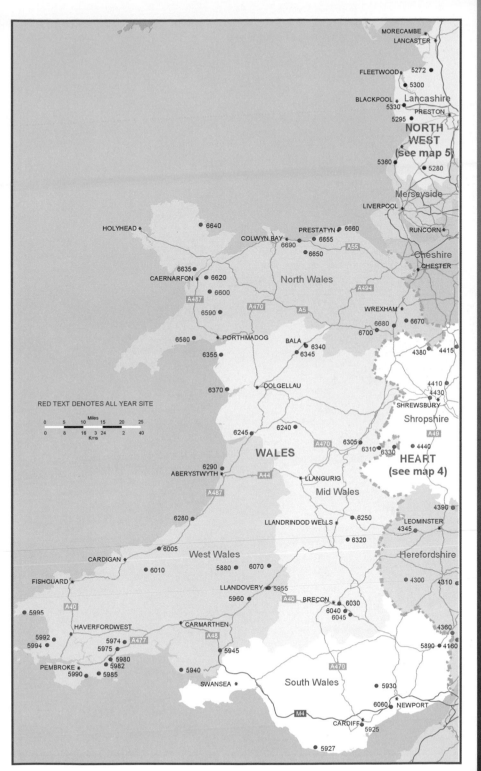

MORECAMBE
LANCASTER

FLEETWOOD ✳ 5272 ●
5300 ●
BLACKPOOL ✳ Lancashire
5330
PRESTON
5295 ●

NORTH
WEST
(see map 5)
5360 ●
5280 ●

Merseyside
LIVERPOOL ✳

HOLYHEAD ✳ 6640 ● PRESTATYN ✳ 6660 ● RUNCORN ✳
COLWYN BAY ✳ 6655 ●
6690 ● A55 Cheshire
6650 ● CHESTER

6635 ● North Wales
CAERNARFON ✳ 6620 ● A494
6600 ● WREXHAM ✳
A487 6680 ● 6670 ●
6590 ● A470 A5 6700 ●
4380 ● 4415 ●
6580 ● ✳ PORTHMADOG BALA
6355 ● 6340 ●
6345 ●
4410 ●
4430 ●
6370 ● ✳ DOLGELLAU SHREWSBURY

RED TEXT DENOTES ALL YEAR SITE Shropshire
A49
Miles
0 5 10 15 20 25 6240 ●
0 8 16 3 24 2 40 6245 ● 6305 ● 4440 ●
Kms 6310 ● 6330 ●
WALES HEART
6290 ● (see map 4)
ABERYSTWYTH ✳ A44 ✳ LLANGURIG
A487 Mid Wales
4390 ●
6280 ● LLANDRINDOD WELLS ✳ 6250 ● LEOMINSTER
4345 ● 4345 ●
6005 ● 6320 ●
CARDIGAN ✳ West Wales Herefordshire
6010 ● 5880 ● 6070 ●
FISHGUARD ✳ 4300 ● 4310 ●
LLANDOVERY ✳ 5955 ●
5995 ● 5960 ● A40 BRECON ✳ 6030 ●
A40 6040 ●
HAVERFORDWEST ✳ CARMARTHEN 6045 ●
5992 ● A48 4360 ●
5994 ● 5974 ● A477 5890 ● 4160 ●
5975 ● 5945 ●
5980 ●
PEMBROKE ✳ 5982 ● A470
5990 ● 5985 ● 5940 ● 5930 ●
SWANSEA ✳ South Wales 6060 ● NEWPORT
M4 CARDIFF ✳
5925 ●
5927 ●

*Parks on this map are featured on pages 236-261 of the guide.
Please refer to the numerical index (page 357) for exact campsite page references.*

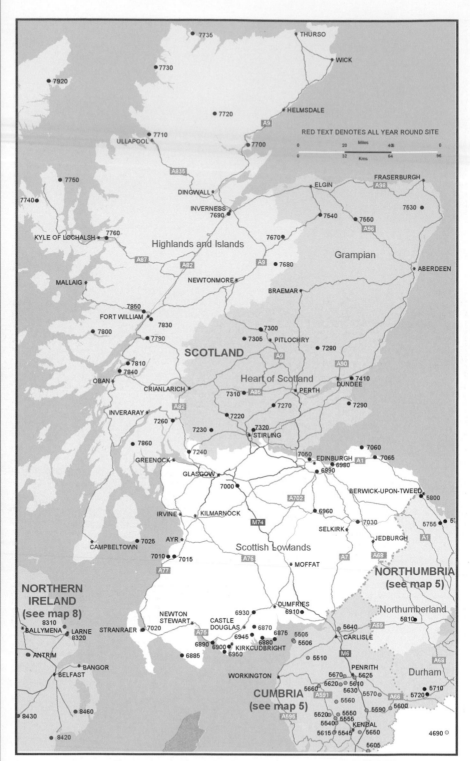

RED TEXT DENOTES ALL YEAR ROUND SITE

THURSO
WICK
7735
7730
7920
7720
HELMSDALE
A9
7710
ULLAPOOL
7700
A835
FRASERBURGH
A98
7750
DINGWALL
ELGIN
7530
7740
INVERNESS
7690
7540
7550
A96
KYLE OF LOCHALSH
7760
7670
Highlands and Islands
Grampian
A87
A82
A9
7680
ABERDEEN
MALLAIG
NEWTONMORE
BRAEMAR
7850
FORT WILLIAM
7830
7300
7800
7790
7305
PITLOCHRY
7810
SCOTLAND
7280
7840
A9
OBAN
CRIANLARICH
A90
7410
DUNDEE
Heart of Scotland
7310
A85
PERTH
7270
7290
INVERARAY
A82
7260
7220
7230
7320
STIRLING
7860
7240
7050
7060
GREENOCK
EDINBURGH
A1
7065
6980
GLASGOW
6990
7000
BERWICK-UPON-TWEED
5800
A702
IRVINE
KILMARNOCK
6960
5755
M74
7030
SELKIRK
JEDBURGH
A1
7025
AYR
CAMPBELTOWN
7010
7015
MOFFAT
NORTHUMBRIA
(see map 5)
A76
A7
A68
A77
NORTHERN
IRELAND
(see map 8)
8310
BALLYMENA
LARNE
8320
STRANRAER
7020
NEWTON
STEWART
CASTLE
DOUGLAS
6930
DUMFRIES
6910
Northumberland
5810
ANTRIM
A75
6870
6875
5640
A69
CARLISLE
6945
6890 6900
6880
5505
KIRKCUDBRIGHT
5506
M6
6885
6950
PENRITH
Durham
A68
BANGOR
5510
5670
5625
BELFAST
WORKINGTON
5620
5610
5710
5660
5630
5570
5720
A591
5560
A66
5600
CUMBRIA
(see map 5)
5520
5550
5590
5540
5555
8430
8460
KENDAL
5615
5545
5650
8420
5605
4690

Parks on this map are featured on pages 262-290 of the guide.
Please refer to the numerical index (page 357) for exact campsite page references.

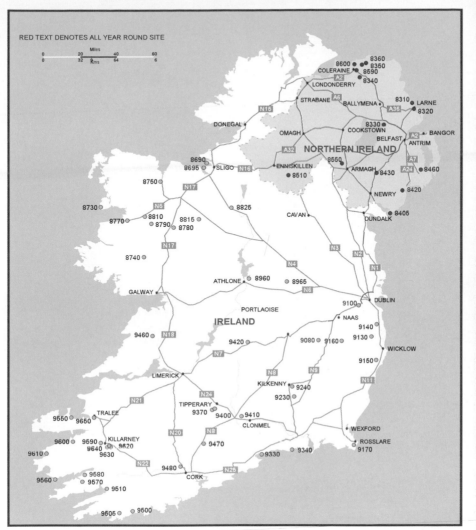

RED TEXT DENOTES ALL YEAR ROUND SITE

Parks on this map are featured on pages 291-321 of the guide.
Please refer to the numerical index (page 357) for exact campsite page references.

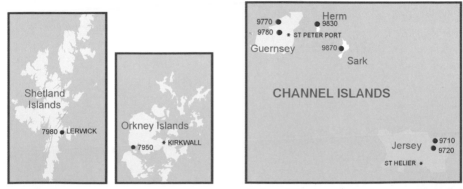

Parks on these maps are featured
on page 289 of the guide.

Parks on this map are featured
on pages 322-325 of the guide.

Index - town and village

England

South West England

Cornwall

Devon

Somerset

Index - campsite region, county and name

Channel Islands

Index of Advertisers

Images We would like to thank the following Tourist Boards for supplying images for this guide:

Somerset Tourist Board
South West Tourist Board
Southern Tourist Board
Southeast Tourist Board
East of England Tourist Board
Heart of England Tourist Board
Yorkshire Tourist Board
North West Tourist Board

Cumbria Tourist Board
Northumbria Tourist Board
Wales Tourist Board
Scotland Tourist Board
Fáilte Ireland
Jersey Tourism

Robin Hood's Tree © Photographer:
Sue Colvil/Agency: Dreamstime.com

Tell Us About the Alan Rogers Guides!

We're keen to constantly improve our service to you and the key to this is information. If we don't know what makes our readers 'tick' then it's difficult to offer you more of what you want.

About the Alan Rogers Guides

1 For how many years have you used the Alan Rogers Guides?

Never   1-2 yrs   3-6 yrs   7-10 yrs   Over 10 yrs

2 How frequently do you refer to it?

Never   Each year   Every 2 yrs   Every 3 yrs

3 How frequently do you buy a new copy?

Never   Each year   Every 2 yrs   Every 3 yrs

4 If you lend it to friends, how many others might refer to it?

1   2   3   4   Over 4

5 Please rate the Alan Rogers Guides on a scale of 1–10 where 10 is excellent and 1 is extremely poor

1   2   3   4   5   6   7   8   9   10

6 Do you have any comments about the Alan Rogers Guides?

7 What do you consider to be the best thing about the guides?

Independent reviews   Honest descriptions   Accurate information   Range of sites   Depth of information

Other

8 What do you consider to be the worst thing about the guides?

9 How many sites featured in the guides have you visited in the past? *(best estimate)*

10 Can you comment on any other campsite guides?

Title   Your opinion

About Your Holidays

11 a) Do you own any of the following?

Caravan   Motorhome   Trailer Tent   Tent

Other *(please specify)*

b) How many times a year do you use it?

1   2-3   4-6   7-10   More than 10

12 When on holiday, do you participate in any of the following?

Fishing   Golf   Cycling   Sailing/Boating   Walking   Bird Watching

Other *(please specify)*

13 How many years have you been camping / caravanning?

3 yrs or less   4 – 7 yrs   8 – 12 yrs   13 – 15 yrs   16 – 20 yrs   Over 20 yrs

About You

Mr/Mrs/Ms, etc.   Initial   Surname

Address

Post code

e-mail address   @   Telephone

14 **Your age**   30 and under   31-50   51-65   Over 65

15 **Do you have children – if so, how old is the youngest?**

6 and under   7-12   Over 12

16 **Do you work (full or part time)?**   Yes   No

17 **Are you retired?**   Yes   No

About Your Leisure Time

18 **Are you a member of any caravan/motorhome clubs?**
The Caravan Club   The Camping & Caravanning Club   The Motor Caravanners Club

Other (please specify)

19 **Are you a member of the following?**
National Trust   English Heritage   RSPB   CSMA   Ramblers

20 **Which (if any) camping/caravanning magazines do you read regularly?**
MMM   Practical   Practical   Caravan   Which   Motor-   Caravan
Motorhome   Caravan   Life   Motorcaravan   caravan

21 **Which other magazines do you read regularly?**

22 **Which newspapers do you read regularly?**
Express   Mail   Telegraph   Times   Guardian   Observer   Sun

Other (please specify)

23 **Do you enjoy any particular hobbies?** (please specify)

24 **Do you have regular access to the internet?**   Yes   No

If yes, which camping/caravanning websites do you visit regularly?

And Finally

25 **Do you have any useful camping/caravanning tips?**

26 **If you could change one thing about camping/caravanning holidays what would it be?**

We may wish to publish your comments, please tick this box if you would prefer us not to.

Might you be interested in becoming an Alan Rogers site inspector?
If so, please tick the box and we will send you further information

Camping Cheque and Alan Rogers may use this data to send you information and Special Offers.
Please tick here if you do not wish to receive such information

Thank you very much for your time and trouble in completing this questionnaire
Please return to: Alan Rogers Travel Service, FREEPOST NAT17734, Cranbrook, TN17 1BR